The Australian Year Book of International Law

The Australian Year Book of International Law

VOLUME 38 (2020)

Editor Emeritus

D W Greig

Editors

Donald R Rothwell | Imogen Saunders | Esmé Shirlow

Editorial Board

Vivienne Bath
Andrew Byrnes
Anthony Cassimatis
Natalie Klein
James Larsen

Amy Maguire
Sarah McCosker
Anne Sheehan
Dale Stephens
Tania Voon

Student Editors

Bridie Adams
Jessica Apolinar
Travis Ash
Samuel Bannister
Livija Berzins
Karla Brenner
Kate Butler
Callum Davis
Isabella Di Mattina-Beven
Vivian Duong
Alyssa Ellwood

Gabriela Freeman
Sarah Graham-Higgs
Georgia Grice
Penelope Han
Katharine Haywood
Emily I'Ons
Stefhan Meyer
Agata Nabaglo
Elizabeth Newman
Jason Nung
Sarah O'Connor

Huiruo Pang
Lily Pang
Lily Shen
Anna Stewart-Yates

Kevin Tanaya
Bede Thompson
Katarina Thompson

Assistant Editors

Sarah Graham-Higgs | Jacqueline Turner | Helen Whalan

Advisory Board

Philip Alston
Professor, New York University, USA

Christine Chinkin
Professor, London School of Economics, UK

Laurence Boisson de Chazournes
Professor, University of Geneva, Switzerland

Theodore Christakis
Professor, Grenoble Alpes University, France

Helen Brady
Senior Appeals Counsel, International Criminal Court

Katrina Cooper
Deputy Head of Mission, Australian Embassy, Washington, USA

Bill Campbell
Honorary Professor, ANU College of Law, Australian National University, Australia

James Crawford
Judge, International Court of Justice

Hilary Charlesworth
Professor, University of Melbourne, Australia

Karen Scott
Professor and Head of School, University of Canterbury, NZ

Simon Chesterman
Professor and Dean of Law, National University of Singapore, Singapore

Gerry Simpson
Professor, London School of Economics, UK

Typeface for the Latin, Greek, and Cyrillic scripts: "Brill". See and download: brill.com/brill-typeface.

ISSN 0084-7658
ISBN 978-90-04-44444-7 (hardback)
E-ISSN 2666-0229

Copyright 2021 by Koninklijke Brill NV, Leiden, The Netherlands except where stated otherwise.
Koninklijke Brill NV incorporates the imprints Brill, Brill Hes & De Graaf, Brill Nijhoff, Brill Rodopi, Brill Sense, Hotei Publishing, mentis Verlag, Verlag Ferdinand Schöningh and Wilhelm Fink Verlag.
Koninklijke Brill NV reserves the right to protect this publication against unauthorized use. Requests for re-use and/or translations must be addressed to Koninklijke Brill NV via brill.com or copyright.com.

This book is printed on acid-free paper and produced in a sustainable manner.

Contents

Lectures

The Sir Elihu Lauterpacht International Law Lecture 2019
The Crisis of Liberal Internationalism and the Future of International Law   3
   Anne Orford

Special Issue
The Backlash against International Law: Australian Perspectives

Introduction
The Backlash against International Law: Australian Perspectives   29
   Jeremy Farrall, Jolyon Ford and Imogen Saunders

Navigating the Backlash against Global Law and Institutions   33
   *Peter G Danchin, Jeremy Farrall, Jolyon Ford, Shruti Rana, Imogen
   Saunders and Daan Verhoeven*

Collective Security and the Prohibition on the Use of Force in Times of Global
Transition   78
   Christopher Michaelsen

The Status of Human Protection in International Law and Institutions:
The United Nations Prevention and Protection Architecture   110
   Cecilia Jacob

Navigating the Backlash: Re-Integrating WTO and Public International
Law?   134
   Imogen Saunders

Navigating the 'Backlash' against International Trade and Investment
Liberalisation: Economic Perspectives on the Future of Regional Trade
Agreements in Uncertain Times   157
   Martin Richardson

Backlash against a Rules-Based International Human Rights Order?
An Australian Perspective   175
   Jolyon Ford

Amidst Simmering Tensions: Improving the Effectiveness and Coherence of the International Human Rights System's Response to Mass Human Rights Violations   199
>   *Annemarie Devereux*

Backlashes against International Commitments and Organisations: Asylum as Restorative Justice   230
>   *Kate Ogg*

Articles

Transcending the Framing Contests over the Human Rights of Older Persons   253
>   *Annie Herro and Andrew Byrnes*

Notes

Revisiting *Lockerbie*: How a General Principle of Judicial Review Could Promote United Nations Security Council Reform   287
>   *Kate Renehan*

Book Reviews: Edited by Amy Maguire

The Greening of Antarctica: Assembling an International Environment   321
>   *Alessandro Antonello (Bruno Arpi and Jeffrey McGee)*

Solving the Internet Jurisdiction Puzzle   329
>   *Dan Jerker B Svantesson (Timothy Beale)*

The Oxford Handbook of International Law in Asia and the Pacific   335
>   *Simon Chesterman, Hisashi Owada and Ben Saul (eds) (Callista Harris)*

Maritime Legacies and the Law: Effective Legal Governance of WWI Wrecks   340
>   *Craig Forrest (Sarah Lothian)*

CONTENTS

VII

Oil under Troubled Water: Australia's Timor Sea Intrigue 344
Bernard Collaery (Donald R Rothwell)

Research Handbook on Feminist Engagement with International Law 349
Susan Harris Rimmer and Kate Ogg (eds) (Kate Slowey)

Regular Features

Cases before Australian Courts and Tribunals concerning Questions of Public International Law 2019 357
Mary Crock, Rowan Nicholson, Kailin Chen, Seric Han, Marcus Lee, Francis Manuel, John McCrorie, Edward Wu and Gordon Yen

Cases before International Courts and Tribunals concerning Questions of Public International Law Involving Australia 2019 415
Mary Crock, Rowan Nicholson, Corinne Lortie, Seric Han, Francis Manuel, Hae-Soo Park, Hannah Place and Gordon Yen

Australian Legislation concerning Matters of International Law 2019 472
Angad Keith, Malithi Karunaarachchi, Chiara Angeloni, Asha Belkin, Sarah Grant, Andrea Gronke, Kryssa Karavolas, Hayley Keen, Guy Kelleher, Fatima Malik, Pranamie Mandalawatta, Kate O'Connell, Caitlin O'Rourke, Amparo Santiago, Navina Vijaysegaran, Emma Wiggins and Phoebe Winch

Australian Practice in International Law 2019 491
Compiled and Edited by the Department of Foreign Affairs and Trade

Treaty Action 2019 723

Table of Cases 731
Table of Statutes 735
Table of International Instruments 739

Lectures

∵

The Sir Elihu Lauterpacht International Law Lecture 2019
The Crisis of Liberal Internationalism and the Future of International Law

Anne Orford*

1 Introduction

It is a great privilege and pleasure to be invited to present this annual lecture in honour of Sir Eli Lauterpacht. I am very grateful to the Department of Foreign Affairs and Trade for their warm invitation and for giving me this opportunity to discuss with you the crisis of liberal internationalism and the future of international law.

We are at a moment in which the future of the international order is on the table in many parts of the world. I first began teaching and researching international law in 1993, not long after the break up of the Soviet Union. For most of my career, international lawyers understood themselves to be dealing with a fairly stable object. At least in the West, international law was understood to be a profession and an academic discipline related, in some perhaps not clearly specified way, to the spread of liberalism. International law was understood to be on the right side of history, part of a progressive narrative in which we could witness across the past centuries a gradual shift towards sovereign equality, self-determination, protection of individual rights, economic integration, freedom of navigation, and—at least for some—freedom of movement, furthered through the emergence of regional and international institutions designed to oversee the project of liberalisation. Questions about the future of international order were somewhat more muted than they are today, and at the least we could anticipate the positions that different states and their leadership might be expected to take on particular issues. The situation today is more complex.

To illustrate this shift, I'd like to begin by comparing two quite different events separated in space and time at which issues relating to the future of liberal internationalism were discussed. The first was a seminar, available to

---

* Redmond Barry Distinguished Professor, Michael D Kirby Chair of International Law, and ARC Kathleen Fitzpatrick Australian Laureate Fellow, Melbourne Law School.

© KONINKLIJKE BRILL NV, LEIDEN, 2021 | DOI:10.1163/26660229_03801002

watch as part of the United Nations Audiovisual Library of International Law, that was held in 2011 to honour Sir Elihu Lauterpacht ('Sir Eli') and his sixty years in international legal practice.[1] The seminar was hosted by his Chambers, 20 Essex St, and by the British Institute of International and Comparative Law, and was chaired by Sir Daniel Bethlehem, who had just finished his term as principal Legal Advisor of the United Kingdom Foreign and Commonwealth Office. In his opening talk, Sir Eli focused on the expansion of international law over the sixty years of his engagement in the field. He noted that many of us 'tend to assume that the dimensions of the subject are firmly established by the time that we first come to it', but that often we 'do not realise that there have been changes in relatively recent times and that the process of change is continuous and far reaching'.

With that in mind, Sir Eli noted the significant changes that had occurred in the practice of international law over that sixty-year period. When he first came to international law, 'it was almost fully represented by the two volumes of Oppenheim—Peace in Volume 1; Disputes, War, and Neutrality in Volume 2'. Of the various waves of development that had emerged in the intervening decades, Sir Eli considered that the expansion and protection of individual rights stood at the forefront. In substantive terms, he pointed to the massive expansion in the articulation of individual rights to be protected. And in procedural terms, he noted the processes that had been established to enable individuals to pursue the recognition and enforcement of their rights under international and regional human rights regimes, together with the creation of international criminal courts and tribunals, and the growth of mechanisms allowing individuals and corporations to initiate claims relating to investment matters and expropriation. Sir Eli considered that all this amounted to 'a major advance in the international status of the individual and the far-reaching erosion of the sanctity of the concept of domestic jurisdiction'. And he gave what was then the very timely example of Security Council Resolution 1973 passed earlier that year relating to Libya.[2] The Security Council had there famously determined that the situation then prevailing internally in Libya constituted a threat to international peace and security, and acting under Chapter VII demanded that the Libyan authorities comply with their obligations under international law and take all measures to protect civilians and meet their basic

---

1 '60 Years in International Law: Seminar in Honour of Sir Elihu Lauterpacht CBE QC LLD' (20 Essex St and the British Institute of International and Comparative Law, 20 October 2011) <https://legal.un.org/avl/ls/lauterpachtseminar.html>.

2 SC Res 1973, 6498th mtg, UN Doc S/RES/1973 (19 March 2011).

THE SIR ELIHU LAUTERPACHT INTERNATIONAL LAW LECTURE 2019

needs, and authorised Member States to take all necessary measures to protect civilians and civilian populated areas under threat of attack in Libya.

Many members of the international legal establishment also gave presentations at the seminar that day, including Daniel Bethlehem, Judge Charles Brower, a US arbitrator and judge on the Iran-US Claims Tribunal, and the Canadian international trade lawyer Donald McRae. In the audience were Baroness Rosalyn Higgins, former President of the International Court of Justice ('ICJ'), Sir Christopher Greenwood, then the British judge on the ICJ, and many other legal luminaries. Watching the day's assured and slightly clubby proceedings from what is perhaps a colonial perspective, I was left with the feeling that this was how and from where the world (or, at least, the international law world) had been ruled for the past sixty years.

And yet the people gathered in that room in October 2011 could not have anticipated the changes that were coming—that the events in the Middle East and North Africa which were still being discussed optimistically as an 'Arab Spring' would lead to the unravelling of the region and the rise of a force like ISIS, that challenges to investor-state dispute settlement would become more concerted, that the United Kingdom would leave the European Union, that there would come a time when there was no British judge on the ICJ, or that the Appellate Body of the World Trade Organization might one day cease to function.

Let me then fast forward to a day in September 2019, when I was getting ready to take part in the Hongmen Forum on The Crisis of Liberal Internationalism and Future World Order, an event held at Peking University, at which I participated alongside European and Chinese professors of philosophy, international relations, and international law. On the morning of the Forum, the *New York Times* was reporting US President Donald Trump's speech at the 74th session of the UN General Assembly the day before. President Trump there declared:

> If you want freedom, take pride in your country. If you want democracy, hold on to your sovereignty. And if you want peace, love your nation.
>
> Wise leaders always put the good of their own people and their own country first. The future does not belong to globalists. The future belongs to patriots. The future belongs to sovereign and independent nations that protect their citizens, respect their neighbors, and honor the differences that make each country special and unique.[3]

---

3 *Address by Mr Donald Trump, President of the United States of America*, UN GAOR, 74th sess, 3rd plen mtg, Agenda Item 8, UN Doc A/74/PV.3 (24 September 2019) 11–16, 11 ('*Address by Donald Trump 2019*'). President Trump's addresses to the General Assembly in 2017 and 2018 had a

And speaking about the World Trade Organization ('WTO'), President Trump remarked: 'Globalism exerted a religious pull over past leaders, causing them to ignore their own national interests. But as far as America is concerned, those days are over'.[4]

On the other hand, the English-language newspaper available in the hotel dining room, the party-run *China Daily*, was focusing on a different speech that had also been presented that week in New York. This was the speech given by Foreign Minister Wang Yi at the UN Climate Action Summit. Wang Yi had stressed the importance of multilateralism and added:

> The withdrawal of certain parties [from the Paris Climate agreement] will not shake the collective will of the international community nor will it possibly reverse the historical trend of international cooperation ... To jointly tackle this challenge and to protect the planet we call home will be a journey critical to the future and destiny of mankind.[5]

And the paper reported that in a speech presented at the National Committee on US—China Relations the next day, Foreign Minister Wang Yi had declared China's commitment to the WTO: 'Economic globalization as the trend of the time cannot and should not be held back'.[6]

Those speeches reflected a historical moment in which China's leadership was speaking and thinking in terms of the role that China would play in promoting the liberal order and in the search for a sustainable future for humanity at large, while the great superpower that historically has been at the forefront of liberalisation retreated to a worldview based upon nationalism and the defence of sovereignty. And at the Hongmen Forum itself, participants reminded us that internationalism is not historically an alien concept beyond the North Atlantic, although the forms of internationalism developed in other parts of the world differ in kind from that promoted by the UK, the US, and their allies, and that the shaping the future of international order will involve a broad range of actors from many parts of the world.

---

similar tone. See further *Address by Mr Donald Trump, President of the United States of America*, UN GAOR, 72nd sess, 3rd plen mtg, Agenda Item 110, UN Doc A/72/PV.3 (19 September 2017) 10–15; *Address by Mr Donald Trump, President of the United States of America*, UN GAOR, 73th sess, 6rd plen mtg, Agenda Item 8, UN Doc A/73/PV.6 (25 September 2018) 14–19.

4   *Address by Donald Trump 2019*, 12.

5   Kong Wenzheng and Hong Xiao, 'Wang Yi: Cooperate on Climate' *China Daily* (Beijing, 25 September 2019).

6   Wang Yi (Speech, National Committee on US-China Relations, 24 September 2019) <https://www.ncuscr.org/event/wang-yi/transcript>.

What then should we make of this apparent reversal of roles and the related concern amongst internationalists that the rules-based order created over the course of the twentieth century is under challenge?

2 The Crisis in Context

In one sense, the idea that international law and international institutions are beleaguered is nothing new. International law is a system premised upon sovereign equality and state consent, and there is a long tradition of states choosing not to sign particular treaties, challenging the jurisdiction of international tribunals, or withdrawing from international institutions that are thought to have become unaccountable to their members.

Yet this moment of backlash seems to differ from other periods of criticism, contestation, or non-compliance with international law in the scale and intensity of challenges to existing treaties and institutions. The interrelated financial, climate, food security, and refugee crises of the early twenty-first century gave a new urgency to questions about the capacity of international law and institutions to respond to such crises, and indeed about their potential role in contributing to those crises. The sense that the existing international order was under challenge intensified with the political shifts evidenced by the rise of China and the resurgence of a more assertive Russia. Liberal internationalism also came under attack from within, with growing support in Europe and the US for populist movements attacking multilateralism, culminating in the Brexit vote and the return to a unilateralist foreign policy under the Trump administration. The practical result has been that over the past decade, and with surprising rapidity, the complex architecture of international treaties, tribunals and institutions consolidated since the end of the Cold War has begun to unravel. I could spend the rest of this lecture just setting out that process. Instead I will just give a few examples, which will be very familiar.

International investment law was the first field in which commentators began to express concerns about a backlash against liberal internationalism, in the context of mounting criticism of the perceived excesses of investor-state dispute settlement (or ISDS) awards.[7] This began with the withdrawal from the International Centre for the Settlement of Investment Disputes (ICSID) by a group of Latin American states (Bolivia, Ecuador, and Venezuela) starting in 2007, and since then numerous states in Latin America, Asia, Europe,

---

7   See Michael Waibel et al (eds), *The Backlash against Investment Arbitration: Perceptions and Reality* (Wolters Kluwer, 2010).

and Africa have announced their intention to terminate some or all of their bilateral investment treaties or BITs. Perhaps more strikingly, as Western states increasingly became respondents in investor-state proceedings, a growing political resistance to ISDS emerged within Canada, the EU, and now the US, as evidenced by the popular challenge to inclusion of ISDS provisions in the *Transatlantic Trade and Investment Partnership* ('TTIP') with the US (now shelved), the *EU—Canada Comprehensive Economic and Trade Agreement*, and in the renegotiated North American Free Trade Agreement ('NAFTA'). In March 2018, the Court of Justice of the EU held in the *Achmea* case that ISDS provisions in BITs between EU Member States were incompatible with EU law,[8] and all EU Member States subsequently declared their agreement to terminate their intra-EU BITs.[9] In addition, Italy and Russia have withdrawn from or unsigned the *Energy Charter Treaty*, one of the major multilateral agreements under which ISDS proceedings have been brought.[10]

A similar challenge is evident in the field of economic integration and regional trade agreements, with the United States initiating a renegotiation of NAFTA and 'unsigning' the *Trans-Pacific Partnership Agreement* ('TPP'),[11] and the UK withdrawing from the EU. In addition, many states have bridled at the limitations on freedom of action and regulation that expansive interpretations of WTO disciplines by the Appellate Body have imposed. In particular, both the Obama and Trump administrations have blocked appointments to the Appellate Body in protest at a series of primarily anti-dumping decisions about which the US disagreed, leading to a situation in which the Appellate Body ceased functioning. For trade lawyers, the challenge to *NAFTA* and the impasse at the WTO Appellate Body are symptoms of 'the curtailment of key

---

8   *Slovakia v Achmea BV (Judgment)* (Court of Justice of the European Union, Case No C-284/16, 6 March 2018).

9   European Commission, *Declaration of the Member States of 15 January 2019 on the Legal Consequences of the Achmea Judgment and on Investment Protection* <https://ec.europa .eu/info/publications/190117-bilateral-investment-treaties_en>.

10   For a discussion of the Russian withdrawal from participation, see Tania Voon and Andrew D Mitchell, 'Ending International Investment Agreements: Russia's Withdrawal from Participation in the Energy Charter Treaty' (2018) 111 *AJIL Unbound* 461.

11   The US 'unsigned' the TPP in a letter dated 30 January 2017 sent to New Zealand, as Depositary of the TPP, stating their intention not to become a Party to the TPP and that they have no legal obligations arising from their signature: 'Trans-Pacific Partnership Agreement (TPP)', *New Zealand Ministry of Foreign Affairs and Trade* (Web Page) <https://www.mfat .govt.nz/en/about-us/who-we-are/treaties/trans-pacific-partnership-agreement-tpp/>.

THE SIR ELIHU LAUTERPACHT INTERNATIONAL LAW LECTURE 2019

features of the liberal order, primarily international legal adjudication',[12] and signal 'the end of an era'.[13] I will come back to this a little later.

And the apparent backlash against multilateralism has extended beyond economic matters. In the field of international criminal law, Burundi and the Philippines have withdrawn from the International Criminal Court ('ICC'),[14] Russia and Malaysia joined the United States in withdrawing their signature from the *Rome Statute*,[15] and the African Union has adopted a coordinated 'Withdrawal Strategy' arguing that the court has become a political instrument targeting Africans.[16] The US threatened to retaliate against ICC judges and prosecutors with travel bans, funds seizures, and criminal prosecution if a potential investigation of war crimes and crimes against humanity in Afghanistan were initiated and extended to cover US nationals,[17] and in April 2019 revoked the US visa of the ICC Chief Prosecutor, Fatou Bensouda.[18]

In the field of human rights, numerous regional courts have experienced a backlash. In the European context, states including Russia and the UK have

12 Sergio Puig, 'The United States—Mexico—Canada Agreement: A Glimpse into the Geoeconomic World Order' (2019) 113 *AJIL Unbound* 56 (2019).

13 Gregory Shaffer, 'A Tragedy in the Making? The Decline of Law and the Return of Power in International Trade Relations' (2019) 44 *The Yale Journal of International Law Online* 1, 17.

14 'Burundi: Withdrawal', C.N.805.2016.TREATIES-XVIII.10 (28 October 2016); 'Philippines: Withdrawal', 138.2018.TREATIES-XVIII.10 (19 March 2018).

15 'Russian Federation: Communication' C.N.886.2016.TREATIES-XVIII.10 (30 November 2016); 'Malaysia: Withdrawal of the Instrument of Accession', C.N.185.2019.TREATIES-XVIII.10 (15 May 2019). For the earlier US notification of its intention not to become a party to the *Rome Statute*, see 'United States of America: Communication', C.N.434.2002. TREATIES-21 (6 May 2002).

16 African Union Assembly, *Decision on the International Criminal Court*, Doc EX.CL/1006(XXX), 28th ord sess, 30–31 January 2017.

17 In an address fiercely criticizing the ICC in September 2018, US National Security Advisor John Bolton declared: 'We will not cooperate with the ICC. We will provide no assistance to the ICC. We will not join the ICC. We will let the ICC die on its own. After all, for all intents and purposes, the ICC is already dead to us': John Bolton, 'Protecting American Constitutionalism and Sovereignty from International Threats' (Speech, The Federalist Society, 10 September 2018), <https://www.justsecurity.org/60674/national-security-adviser-john-bolton-remarks-international-criminal-court>.

18 Marlise Simons and Megan Specia, 'US Revokes Visa of ICC Prosecutor Pursuing Afghan War Crimes', *The New York Times* (online, 5 April 2019) <https://www.nytimes.com/2019/04/05/world/europe/us-icc-prosecutor-afghanistan.html>. See also Alex Whiting, 'The ICC's Afghanistan Decision: Bending to U.S. or Focusing Court on Successful Investigations?', *Just Security* (online, 12 April 2019) < https://www.justsecurity.org/63613/the-iccs-afghanistan-decision-bending-to-u-s-or-focusing-court-on-successful-investigations/> (discussing the relation of those US threats to the decision of the ICC Pre-Trial Chamber on 12 April 2019 to reject the Prosecutor's request to open investigation of war crimes and crimes against humanity in Afghanistan).

developed increasingly strained relations with the European Court of Human Rights.[19] The long history of resistance to judgments of the Inter-American Court of Human Rights has accelerated in recent years, with for example Venezuela denouncing the *American Convention on Human Rights* in 2012, constitutional court judgments in the Dominican Republic (in 2014) and Argentina (in 2017) challenging the authority of the Inter-American Court of Human Rights, and in April 2019 Argentina, Brazil, Chile, Colombia, and Paraguay sending a joint letter sent to the Inter-American Commission on Human Rights setting out their interpretation of the jurisdictional and procedural limits to the system's power.[20] In the African context, Gambia, Kenya, and Zimbabwe have each sought to restrict the jurisdiction of various sub-regional human rights courts in response to controversial rulings, and in 2018 the African Union Executive Council adopted a decision to curtail the activity of the African Commission on Human and Peoples' Rights.[21] At the international level, the US withdrew from the UN Human Rights Council in June 2018, claiming that the Council had become a 'protector of human rights abusers', a 'cesspool of political bias', and that it undermined the national interests and sovereignty of the US and its allies.[22]

In addition, the US has also signalled its intention to withdraw from the *Paris Agreement*,[23] the Optional Protocol to the 1961 *Vienna Convention on Diplomatic Relations*, the *Treaty of Amity, Economic Relations, and Consular Rights* with Iran, the *Intermediate-Range Nuclear Forces Treaty* with Russia and, for a time, the Universal Postal Union.[24] Other major powers have

---

19   Katja S Ziegler, Elizabeth Wicks and Loveday Hodson (eds), *The UK and European Human Rights: A Strained Relationship?* (Hart Publishing, 2015); Lauri Mälksoo and Wolfgang Benedek (eds), *Russia and the European Court of Human Rights: The Strasbourg Effect* (Cambridge University Press, 2018).

20   The Inter-American situation is discussed in Jorge Contesse, 'Conservative Governments and Latin America's Human Rights Landscape' (2019) 113 *AJIL Unbound* 375.

21   Karen J Alter, James T Gathii and Laurence R Helfer, 'Backlash against International Courts in West, East and Southern Africa: Causes and Consequences' (2016) 27(2) *European Journal of International Law* 293.

22   Mike Pompeo and Nikki Haley, 'Remarks on the UN Human Rights Council' (Press Conference, Treaty Room, Washington DC, 19 June 2018) <https://www.state.gov/remarks-on-the-un-human-rights-council/>.

23   United States Department of State, 'Communication Regarding Intent to Withdraw from Paris Agreement' (Media Note, 4 August 2017) <https://www.state.gov/communication-regarding-intent-to-withdraw-from-paris-agreement/>.

24   On 15 October 2018 the US Secretary of State Mike Pompeo announced the US withdrawal from the Universal Postal Union (UPU): CarrieLyn D Guymon (ed), *Digest of United States Practice in International Law 2018* (US State Department) 113–14 <https://www.state.gov/wp-content/uploads/2019/10/2018-Digest-Chapter-4.pdf>. In September 2019 the US

indicated limits to their acceptance of international adjudication under the UN *Convention on the Law of the Sea*, with the Russian Federation refusing to take part in the *Arctic Sunrise Arbitration* initiated by the Netherlands,[25] and China refusing to recognise the award in the *South China Sea Arbitration* initiated by the Philippines.[26]

In light of what appears to be a more widespread challenge to existing international institutions, treaties, and courts, many of the post-Cold War certainties about the nature of the international order, its desirability, and its longevity seem to be shifting. Much commentary in the field of international law interprets this situation as something more than a somewhat chaotic set of withdrawals from and criticisms of specific agreements, institutions, and processes. In particular, a growing body of literature interprets this situation as one in which the 'liberal international order' or 'the international rule of law' are being challenged by authoritarian leaders, while populist movements are 'rebelling against the globalized liberal world order' and the 'cosmopolitan elite'.[27] Certainly many authoritarian leaders and populist movements

---

rescinded its notice of withdrawal, following the decision of the UPU to adopt a proposal on terminal due rates for which the US had been pushing: 'United States Remains in the Universal Postal Union, Rescinding Its Notice of Withdrawal' (2020) 114(1) *American Journal of International Law* 128.

25   *Arctic Sunrise Arbitration (Netherlands v Russia) (Award on Merits)* (Permanent Court of Arbitration, Case No 2014-02, 14 August 2015). The Russian Federation indicated by a Note Verbale dated 27 February 2014 to the Permanent Court of Arbitration that it refused to take part in the arbitration.

26   *South China Sea Arbitration (Philippines v China) (Award)* (Permanent Court of Arbitration, Case No 2013-19, 12 July 2016). For the Chinese government position, see 'Statement of the Ministry of Foreign Affairs of the People's Republic of China on the Award of 12 July 2016 of the Arbitral Tribunal in the South China Sea Arbitration Established at the Request of the Republic of the Philippines' (12 July 2016) <https://www.fmprc.gov.cn/nanhai/eng/snhwtlcwj_1/t1379492.htm>.

27   See, from a broad literature, Craig Calhoun, 'Brexit is a Mutiny Against the Cosmopolitan Elite' (2016) 33(3) *New Perspectives Quarterly* 50; Philip Alston, 'The Populist Challenge to Human Rights' (2017) 9(1) *Journal of Human Rights Practice* 1; Eric A Posner, 'Liberal Internationalism and the Populist Backlash' (Public Law and Legal Theory Working Paper No 606, University of Chicago Law School, 11 January 2017); Francis Fukuyama and Robert Muggah, 'Populism is Poisoning the Global Liberal Order', *The Globe and Mail* (online, 29 January 2018) <https://www.theglobeandmail.com/opinion/populism-is-poisoning-the-global-liberal-order/article37777370/>; Select Committee on International Relations, House of Lords, *UK Foreign Policy in a Shifting World Order* (HL Paper No 250, 18 December 2018); Constance Duncombe and Tim Dunne, 'After Liberal World Order' (2018) 94(1) *International Affairs* 25; James Crawford, 'The Current Political Discourse Concerning International Law' (2018) 81(1) *Modern Law Review* 1; David Caron and Esmé Shirlow, 'Dissecting Backlash: The Unarticulated Causes of Backlash and its Unintended Consequences' in Andreas Follesdal and Geir Ulfstein (eds), *The Judicialization of*

appear enthusiastically committed to demolishing at least some of the institutions commonly associated with liberal internationalism, and have overtly championed nationalism over multilateralism, protectionism over free trade agreements, and tightened border controls over open migration.

Yet trying to make sense of the relations between populist politics and the excesses (or successes, depending on viewpoint) of liberal internationalism is not straightforward, for at least two reasons. First, international law and institutions do not represent a coherent project, and the 'liberal' international order means quite different things across the broad range of treaty regimes, institutions, and techniques to which it commonly refers. And second, it is difficult to diagnose what precisely has fuelled populist support for withdrawal from specific treaties or international institutions even within a particular country, let alone globally. This is particularly so when populist leaders are voted in as part of a general election in which international relations may only play a minor part in determining voting patterns, but it also seems to be the case where voters are directly called upon to address such questions, as in the referendum on Britain's withdrawal from the European Union. It is possible to attribute the causes of backlash to any one of numerous projects, institutions, events, or agreements.

As a result, the attempts to connect the dots between populism, the backlash against globalism, and decisions about specific treaties, agreements, and institutions often seem more like the conduct of a Rorschach test, in which each commentator reveals their perception of where the ambitions of international law went too far. For some, the problem was the signing of overly expansive trade and investment agreements, which lifted decisions relating to the balancing of private property and other interests out of the democratic process. For others, the mistake was the move to justify resort to force and military intervention in the name of liberal values, democratic regime-change, or humanitarian protection. For yet others, the over-ambitious expansion of human rights, leading to the break-up of national cultures and threats to social and religious norms, was the step too far that saw the emergence of the culture

---

International Law: A Mixed Blessing? (Oxford University Press, 2018), 159; Robert Jervis et al (eds), *Chaos in the Liberal Order: The Trump Presidency and International Politics in the Twenty-First Century* (Columbia University Press, 2018); Heike Krieger, 'Populist Governments and International Law' (2019) 30(3) *European Journal of International Law* 971; Harold Hongju Koh, *The Trump Administration and International Law* (Oxford University Press, 2019); Campbell McLachlan, 'The Assault on International Adjudication and the Limits of Withdrawal' (2019) 68(3) *International and Comparative Law Quarterly* 499.

wars that now threaten the institutions of global governance.[28] It has proved possible to attribute the causes of backlash to numerous projects, institutions, events, or missteps.

3 Split Roles and the Loyalty of International Lawyers

I would like to focus now on one further aspect of this backlash politics and the way it mirrors a particular set of claims made by international lawyers. This could best be characterised as a persistent concern by anti-globalists with issues of loyalty or representation—as captured in the claim made by Yves Dezalay and Bryant Garth that international lawyers and cosmopolitan elites function as 'double agents'.[29]

The double agent problem is presented by populist critics and by scholars in one of two ways. First, the populist backlash has been understood as a response to the failure of globalist elites to represent the national interest of their home states.[30] In this account, cosmopolitan elites and international lawyers have supported forms of international cooperation that furthered their interests at the expense of the people and the national interests that they should champion.[31] In that story, liberal internationalists were too committed to cosmopolitan agendas and insufficiently concerned with the national interests of their home states and the people they were supposed to be representing

---

28   For contrasting attempts to interpret the meaning of the perceived backlash against liberal internationalism, see Posner (n 27); Samuel Moyn, 'Beyond Liberal Internationalism' [2017] (Winter) *Dissent* 108; Martti Koskenniemi, *International Law and the Far Right: Reflections on Law and Cynicism* (Asser Press, 2019); Joseph HH Weiler, 'The European Circumstance and the Politics of Meaning: Not on Bread Alone Doth Man Liveth (Deut. 8:3; Mat 4:4)' (2020) 21 *German Law Journal* 96; Anne Orford, 'International Law and the Populist Moment' (2020) 35 *American University International Law Review* 427.

29   For the language of 'double agents', see Yves Dezalay and Bryant G Garth, *Dealing in Virtue: International Commercial Arbitration and the Construction of a Transnational Legal Order* (University of Chicago Press, 1996) ('*Dealing in Virtue*').

30   Michael Anton, 'The Trump Doctrine: An Insider Explains the President's Foreign Policy', *Foreign Policy* (online, 20 April 2019) <https://foreignpolicy.com/2019/04/20/the-trump-doctrine-big-think-america-first-nationalism/>.

31   Posner (n 27) 17 ('the problem was less that a hegemon like the United States seized an excessive share of the gains from international cooperation, than that elites in all countries supported forms of international cooperation that benefited them and harmed the masses or were perceived to harm the masses. This process was accompanied by a great deal of self-serving propaganda that the elites themselves may even have believed, with the members of the Invisible College [of international lawyers] participating as unwitting servants of power').

at international conferences. Alternatively, the double agent problem is presented in reverse mode—liberal internationalists weren't internationalist or cosmopolitan *enough*. Liberal internationalists were too intent on representing the interests of their own nation, and abandoned liberal principles when it came to international relations.[32] In that account, WTO decision-makers or international lawyers arguing in favour of humanitarian intervention or investment arbitrators were only masquerading as global cosmopolitans while in fact they systematically prioritised their own national—or perhaps broader Western—interests. In both accounts, the distrust of international law and institutions is presented as a distrust of the ambiguous loyalties of the people who represent the nation-state in the international world or who represent the international world in the nation-state.

It is perhaps not surprising to see that kind of scepticism about diplomats and international lawyers re-emerge in this populist moment, as a similar scepticism has been part of many earlier radical movements. In earlier eras, diplomats tasked with representing the interests of revolutionary states, for example, were seen as a necessary evil—necessary in that they work to advance the interests of their states globally, but evil in that they do so in ways that perpetuate the conventions that make possible ongoing relations between elites. So this could just be radical business as usual.

But it is also possible that something in the self-understanding, techniques, or style of governance adopted by liberal internationalists has made them, and the forms of international law they seek to develop, particularly vulnerable to the populist charge that international lawyers are double agents whose loyalty is in doubt. Before going any further, I should make clear that I see myself as a double agent, and indeed in a sense all lawyers have this dual loyalty to both a client and a system of law. But let me explain how a particular tradition of thinking about international law intensifies this sense of concern about the problem posed by double agents.

There is in fact a long tradition of international lawyers reflecting upon their role in ways that reproduce this idea of international lawyers as double agents, involved in 'role-splitting', invisible colleges, and transnational networks. We might think of the influential conception developed by the French international lawyer and member of the UN International Law Commission, Georges Scelle, who famously developed the concept of *dédoublement fonctionnel* (role

---

32   Moyn (n 28). See also the related argument by Anthea Roberts that international law is not sufficiently international: Anthea Roberts, *Is International Law International?* (Oxford University Press, 2017).

THE SIR ELIHU LAUTERPACHT INTERNATIONAL LAW LECTURE 2019

splitting) to address this phenomenon.[33] Scelle and his inter-war generation were trying to account for what they understood to be a system of international law that was beginning to take shape in the absence of any international institutions that could perform legislative, executive, and judicial functions on behalf of the whole community. Scelle developed an individualist theory of international law to explain that individuals could be understood to be acting either on behalf of the international community or as agents of international law.[34] He argued that while officials, lawyers, and agencies will always have a national status, to the extent that their actions deal with an international matter, they function as international agents.

Oscar Schachter further developed that conceptualization of the role played by internationalists. Schachter famously argued that the professional community of international lawyers dispersed throughout the world 'constitutes a kind of invisible college dedicated to a common intellectual enterprise'.[35] Whether engaged in the governmental, intergovernmental, nongovernmental, or scholarly worlds, the members of that college were part of a unified discipline and a shared endeavor aimed at developing 'global positions and actions'.[36] For Schachter, these positions should inform the 'legislative role' played by international lawyers.[37] He concluded that since the governments of the world were likely to be ambivalent about developing forms of international law that conformed with 'the requirements of *"la conscience juridique"*', the 'noblest function' that could be undertaken by the invisible college was to give meaning to that juridical conscience in the evolution of international law.[38]

Few if any international lawyers would today describe ourselves in the idealistic terms set out by Scelle or even Schachter. Yet the sense that international lawyers and institutions are capable of representing something more than

---

33   See, eg, Georges Scelle, *Précis de droit des gens: Principes et Systématique* (2 volumes) (Sirey, 1932, 1934); Georges Scelle, 'Règles générales du droit de la paix' (1933) 46 *Recueil des cours de l'Académie de La Haye* 327; Georges Scelle, 'Théorie et pratique de la function executive en droit international' (1936) 55 *Recueil des cours de l'Académie de La Haye* 87, 91; Georges Scelle, 'Quelques réflexions hétérodoxes sur la technique de l'ordre juridique interétatique' in Hildebraudo Accioly (ed), *Hommage d'une generation de juristes au Président Basdevant* (Pedone, 1960) 473.

34   Oliver Diggelmann, 'Georges Scelle (1878–1961)' in Bardo Fassbender and Anne Peters (eds), *The Oxford Handbook of the History of International Law* (Oxford University Press, 2012) 1162, 1164–5.

35   Oscar Schachter, 'The Invisible College of International Lawyers' (1977) 72 *Northwestern University Law Review* 217, 217.

36   Ibid 223.

37   Ibid.

38   Ibid 226.

mere national interest continues to shape the way that liberal internationalists explain the legitimacy of international judges or arbitrators, justify the use of force in the interests of collective security, or present the normative authority of major multilateral treaties. The sense that international lawyers or officials can remain neutral and independent when engaged in transnational legal processes has been central to legitimising the more ambitious roles claimed for international law since the ending of the Cold War.

For example, self-described liberal internationalists such as Anne-Marie Slaughter and Harold Koh have portrayed lawyers located within state bureaucracies as having the capacity also to be engaged in transnational legal processes or in embedded international networks. They argue that the actors involved in those processes and networks can no longer be understood as operating within the 'strict two-by-two matrix that divided all law into domestic and international', but are rather engaged in the work of uploading and downloading rules of transnational law from one system to the other, with a view to 'advancing an enlightened global system'.[39] They suggest that internationalism can be embedded in the heart of state bureaucracies and institutions, and that there is no need for a clear demarcation between international actors and state actors.

You may well have noticed that there is no conflict or struggle in any of those accounts, whether that be the struggles between policy makers within states seeking to strengthen their domestic policy choices by embedding them within international legal regimes, the potential conflicts that might play out between national interests and international obligations, or the broader questions about representation that such accounts raise. The idealized ways in which the role of international lawyers is conceptualized in these accounts underestimated the struggles that would result when those who benefit from and strategize within transnational alliances successfully began to implement or download the policies developed in their invisible colleges into enforceable domestic law.

A more politicized account of the doubled situation of transnational lawyers has been developed in the series of highly influential books published by Yves Dezalay and Bryant Garth.[40] In their view, when lawyers develop legal strategies transnationally, we 'serve as double agents', at once promoting our

---

39 Anne-Marie Slaughter, *A New World Order* (Princeton University Press, 2005); Harold Hongju Koh, 'Is There a "New" New Haven School of International Law?' (2007) 32(2) *Yale Journal of International Law* 559, 572.

40 Dezalay and Garth, *Dealing in Virtue* (n 29); Yves Dezalay and Bryant G Garth, *The Internationalization of Palace Wars: Lawyers, Economists, and the Contest to Transform Latin American States* (University of Chicago Press, 2002); Yves Dezalay and Bryant G

THE SIR ELIHU LAUTERPACHT INTERNATIONAL LAW LECTURE 2019

own place in domestic hierarchies and asserting the perceived universalism and autonomy of the transnational legal systems which we champion. International lawyers work in part by challenging the monopoly of domestic law and promoting the universals of international arbitration. International lawyers actively participate in constructing the sense of a 'requisite neutral place for arbitration—or at least a place that appears as such in the relations between different national powers'.[41] Such lawyers are valuable precisely because of 'their double agency on behalf of their local interests and the interests of international ... arbitration'.[42] In that account, transnationalizing the role of lawyers is not a way of lifting our work out of the messy business of politics and into a world of enlightened reason, but instead simply represents another way of engaging in political struggle.[43]

4   Politicizing the Role of International Lawyers

Current populist challenges raising questions about loyalty or representation go to the heart of those claims. The question of whether it was really possible for international lawyers, civil servants, or globalists to represent both national interests and international interests without betraying one or the other has become an increasingly pressing one in the age of backlash politics.

For some, the double agent problem arises when international lawyers take up the role of judges or adjudicators. We might think, for example, about the issues at stake in attacks on the legitimacy of the WTO Appellate Body. For most international lawyers, it seems self-evident that judges or arbitrators should and do function independently from their home country when they serve on international bodies. The question of whether that is fully possible has in large part been politely ignored, although the desire for states to have at least one member of the bench from their own country is reflected in the practice of appointing *ad hoc* judges in the ICJ and in the practice of parties

---

Garth, *Asian Legal Revivals: Lawyers in the Shadow of Empire* (University of Chicago Press, 2010).

41   Dezalay and Garth, *Dealing in Virtue* (n 29) 283. For the counter-argument that this double agency 'is intrinsic to the nature of law itself', and raises questions about 'the efficacy and implications of the alternatives to those so acting', see William Alford, 'Review of Asian Legal Revivals: Lawyers in the Shadow of Empire by Yves Dezalay and Byrant G Garth' (2013) 63(4) *The University of Toronto Law Journal* 671, 675.

42   Dezalay and Garth, *Dealing in Virtue* (n 29) 293.

43   David Kennedy, *A World of Struggle: How Power, Law, and Expertise Shape the Global Political Economy* (Princeton University Press, 2016).

having the power to choose arbitrators. Yet the idea that the resulting international decisions or awards represent something more than a reflection of the national interest of the judges or arbitrators involved is central to the symbolic capital upon which international courts and arbitral tribunals rely.

The creation in 1995 of the WTO complete with a compulsory dispute settlement system was seen by many as a high point in that process of judicialisation. For the trade regime, the creation of a new dispute settlement body, and in particular of a standing Appellate Body that would hear appeals from first instance Panels, was heralded as the moment in which the ethos of diplomats was replaced by the rule of law. Scholars argued that 'the importance of the mere existence of the Appellate Body to a shift in organizational legal culture could not be overestimated'.[44] The independence of its members was enshrined in the *Dispute Settlement Understanding* through the requirement that the Appellate Body shall 'comprise persons of recognized authority' who are 'unaffiliated with any government'. The Appellate Body was seen to represent a model of what might be possible in terms of international courts more generally. It was lauded as an approach to mandatory dispute settlement that 'surpasses' in 'effectiveness and sophistication' anything 'achieved by other international tribunals, such as the International Court of Justice'.[45] The overall ambition of the WTO agreements was to lift trade disputes out of the realm of domestic politics, lobbying, and special interests. The process of dispute settlement through which trade disciplines would be implemented relied upon the established traditions of international law, from the location of the WTO overlooking Lake Geneva to the role of distinguished professors and practitioners in its operations.

The contrast between the situation at the WTO today and the ambitions expressed by liberal internationalists at its creation are striking. Many states have since bridled at the limitations on freedom of action and regulation that subsequent interpretations of WTO disciplines imposed, but the US in particular has undertaken dramatic moves to restore the balance of rights and obligations to which it understood itself to have agreed when it joined the WTO. In particular, the US acted upon those concerns by taking steps to restrain the autonomy of the Appellate Body, in terms that open up questions

---

44   JHH Weiler, 'The Rule of Lawyers and the Ethos of Diplomats: Reflections on the Internal and External Legitimacy of WTO Dispute Settlement' (2001) 35(2) *Journal of World Trade* 191, 199.

45   See Robert Howse, 'Adjudicative Legitimacy and Treaty Interpretation in International Trade Law: The Early Years of WTO Jurisprudence' in Joseph HH Weiler (ed), *The EU, the WTO, and the NAFTA: Towards a Common Law of International Trade* (Oxford University Press, 2000) 35.

about the independence and competing loyalties of Appellate Body members. In 2011, the Obama administration blocked the reappointment of US member Jennifer Hillman for a second term on the Appellate Body, indicating that this was because she had not acted sufficiently forcefully to defend US interests and had not been willing to dissent in the trade remedy cases that concerned the US.[46] Critics of that step pointed to its implications for the concept of judicial independence. In 2013, the Obama administration blocked the appointment of James Gathii to a vacant chair on the Appellate Body, and in 2016 blocked the reappointment of the South Korean member Seung Wha Chang for a second term, on the basis that the US objected to his role in a series of decisions with which the US disagreed.[47]

Those simmering disagreements with and challenges to the Appellate Body were intensified after the election of President Trump. Opposition to the global economic order and to existing trade deals had been central to President Trump's worldview for decades.[48] During his campaigning and after his election, he continued to declare his opposition to the WTO and to many other trade deals negotiated during the previous decades, telling journalists that the WTO was 'set up for the benefit of everybody but us', that membership had been 'a disaster for this country', and that the agreement establishing the WTO 'was the single worst trade deal ever made'.[49] The concerns of the Trump

---

46 See the discussion in Jennifer Hillman, 'Independence at the Top of the Triangle: Best Resolution of the Judicial Trilemma?' (2017) 111 *AJIL Unbound* 364, 367.

47 *Statement by the United States at the Meeting of the WTO Dispute Settlement Body* (Geneva, 23 May 2016) <https://www.wto.org/english/news_e/news16_e/us_statment_dsbmay16_e.pdf>. See also Gregory Shaffer, 'Will the US Undermine the World Trade Organization?', *Huffington Post* (online, 23 May 2016) <https://www.huffpost.com/entry/will-the-us-undermine-the_b_10108970 >.

48 Charlie Laderman and Brendan Simms, *Donald Trump: The Making of a World View* (IB Tauris, 2017) 104–8.

49 Ian Schwartz, 'Full Lou Dobbs Interview: Trump Asks What Could Be More Fake Than CBS, NBC, ABC and CNN?', *RealClear Politics* (online, 25 October 2017) <https://www.realclearpolitics.com/video/2017/10/25/full_lou_dobbs_interview_trump_asks_what_could_be_more_fake_than_cbs_nbc_abc_and_cnn.html#!> ('The WTO, World Trade Organization, was set up for the benefit for everybody but us ... They have taken advantage of this country like you wouldn't believe. And I say to my people, you tell them, like as an example, we lose the lawsuits, almost all of the lawsuits in the WTO—within the WTO. Because we have fewer judges than other countries. It's set up as you can't win. In other words, the panels are set up so that we don't have majorities. It was set up for the benefit of taking advantage of the United States'); Chris Isidore, 'White House Lauded US Record with WTO, Which Trump Now Calls a "Disaster"', *CNN Money* (online, 2 March 2018) <https://money.cnn.com/2018/03/02/news/economy/trump-wto-white-house-economic-report/index.html>; John Micklethwait, Margaret Talev and Jennifer Jacobs, 'Trump Threatens to Pull US Out of WTO If It Doesn't "Shape Up"', *Bloomberg*

administration were subsequently set out in the US 2018 Trade Policy Agenda, which criticised specific decisions of the WTO adjudicative bodies, the interpretative approach taken by the Appellate Body, and procedural actions taken by the Appellate Body.[50] The Trump administration subsequently blocked the appointment of any new Appellate Body members, leading to the situation in which the Appellate Body ceased to be able to function after December 2019.[51]

For others, the problem with international lawyers as double agents arises when it comes to the processes of codification and legislation, which have played a central role in the creation of a liberal international order. With the 'move to institutions' in the twentieth century, international lawyers advocated for the development of legislative machinery that would enable international law-making to become more like domestic law-making, first at the League of Nations and then at the United Nations. In this account, domestic legislation was understood to be the result of a rational and technical process rather than simply an outcome of political bargaining. The establishment of the International Law Commission (ILC) in 1947, tasked with the codification and progressive development of international law, was one result of that desire for a more scientific approach to international law-making. Multilateral treaties began to be approached as potential law-making instruments that could be equated with domestic legislation rather than with private contracts—as potentially more than simply vehicles for recording bilateral agreements.

However already by the 1940s, scepticism about treating international law-making as a technical and consensual, rather than a political and contested, process was being expressed, perhaps most famously by Hans Morgenthau. In an article that effectively marked his farewell to international law as a discipline, Morgenthau argued that while international law could deal effectively with fairly stable interests such as those relating to diplomatic privileges or

---

(online, 30 August 2018) <https://www.bloomberg.com/news/articles/2018-08-30/trump-says-he-will-pull-u-s-out-of-wto-if-they-don-t-shape-up>, cited in Chad P Brown and Douglas A Irwin, 'What Might a Trump Withdrawal from the World Trade Organization Mean for US Tariffs?', (Policy Brief 18–23, *Peterson Institute for International Economics*, November 2018) 1.

50   Office of the United States Trade Representative, *2018 Trade Policy Agenda and 2017 Annual Report of the President of the United States on the Trade Agreements Program* (Report, March 2018) 132–82.

51   Gregory Shaffer, Manfred Elsig, and Mark Pollack, 'The Slow Killing of the World Trade Organization', *Huffington Post* (online, 17 November 2017) <https://www.huffpost.com/entry/the-slow-killing-of-the-world-trade-organization_b_5a0ccd1de4b03fe7403f82df>; Chad P Brown and Soumaya Keynes, 'Why Trump Shot the Sheriffs: The End of WTO Dispute Settlement 1.0' (Working Paper No 20-4, *Peterson Institute for International Economics*, March 2020) 2.

extradition, it could not adequately address more politically volatile and changeable interests concerned with security or economics.[52] In the following decades, the combined effect of the challenges posed to the existing order by decolonization and the Cold War suggested that faith in codification of international law as a purely technical process that could be managed by legal experts was misplaced. Few significant treaties or codes resulted from ILC processes, and many of the most important and influential multilateral treaties resulted from much more overtly political negotiating situations (think, for example, of the WTO agreements, Law of the Sea, or the *Rome Statute*), in which it was recognized that diplomats and policy elites negotiated primarily with national interests in mind.

The example of climate change illustrates the nature of current populist challenges to the idea that international law-making can somehow represent an idealised common humanity. Initially, as it became clear that negotiating universal law-making treaties on an issue such as climate change with serious distributional consequences would be extremely difficult, some international lawyers pushed for ways to dictate global solutions to problems such as climate change that could move beyond the need for state consent. For example, Frederic Kirgis argued in 1990:

> International lawmaking is a time-consuming business when traditional methods are used. The process is worse than time-consuming when it is applied to technological change and its effect on the human environment. In that arena, it has been recognized for quite a while that traditional methods—treaty making and state practice leading to custom—are simply inadequate by themselves.[53]

In 1993, Jonathan Charney published an article entitled 'Universal International Law', arguing that the international community needed 'to develop universal norms to address global concerns' such as environmental protection, and that to do so 'it may be necessary to establish new rules that are binding on all subjects of international law regardless of the attitude of any particular state'.[54] Similar arguments about the need to act unilaterally or develop 'nonconsensual

---

52 Hans Morgenthau, 'Positivism, Functionalism, and International Law' (1940) 34(2) *American Journal of International Law* 260.

53 Frederic L Kirgis, Jr, 'Standing to Challenge Human Endeavors That Could Change the Climate' (1990) 84 *American Journal of International Law* 525, 525.

54 Jonathan I Charney, 'Universal International Law' (1993) 87(4) *American Journal of International Law* 529, 529.

lawmaking mechanisms' in order to protect the environment have been made regularly in the intervening years.[55]

However as the political and ecological situation became more pressing and the problem of climate change more accepted, international lawyers have moved away from grand normative declarations or attempts to develop ambitious 'nonconsensual lawmaking mechanisms' and towards hard fought and complex negotiations aimed at achieving more modest but realistic outcomes. The resulting international instruments or mechanisms are only as strong as the domestic political support behind them, as the US withdrawal from the *Paris Agreement* makes clear. This is a field in which we see populist and counter-populist attempts to shape climate politics from the right and the left, illustrated by the *Gilets Jaunes* protests in France (and their call to focus on the end of the month rather than the end of the world), the Extinction Rebellion actions in London, and student climate strikes globally.[56] For that reason, I would argue that the more modest approaches taken in international negotiations and the comparative judicial passivism of international courts in relation to environmental disputes (in contrast to trade and investment disputes) are on the right track. The solution to the crisis of climate change cannot be found by trying to lift it out of politics—it will be necessary to embed global solutions to the big distributional questions raised by climate change within the domestic political processes of states. Solutions to the challenges posed by climate change require arrangements achieved through hard negotiations and political struggles, rather than through declaring norms for the world.

---

55   Daniel Bodansky, 'What's So Bad About Unilateral Actions to Protect the Environment?' (2000) 11(2) *European Journal of International Law* 339; Nico Krisch, 'The Decay of Consent: International Law in an Age of Global Public Goods' (2014) 108(1) *American Journal of International Law* 1, 1 (on the need for 'nonconsensual lawmaking mechanisms' to address global public goods such as preventing climate change).

56   For a range of analyses of the *Gilets Jaunes* movement that address its relation to and significance for broader political struggles of working people, see Cihan Askan and Jon Bailes (eds), 'One Question *Gilets Jaunes*', *State of Nature* (Blog Post, 6 June 2019) <https://stateofnatureblog.com/one-question-gilets-jaunes/>. For the interpretation of the *Gilets Jaunes* as inventing a form of 'counter-populism', see Étienne Balibar, "Gilets Jaunes": The Meaning of the Confrontation', *Open Democracy* (Webpage, 20 December 2018) <https://www.opendemocracy.net/en/can-europe-make-it/gilets-jaunes-meaning-of-confrontation/>. On the aims of the Extinction Rebellion movement, see Clare Farrell et al (eds), *This Is Not a Drill: An Extinction Rebellion Handbook* (Penguin Books, 2019). On the inspiration for the climate strikes, see Greta Thunberg, *No One is Too Small to Make a Difference* (Penguin Books, 2019).

5 Populism, Democracy, and International Law

To conclude, the populist challenge to international liberal legalism is another chapter in a longer story. The vision of international lawyers as neutral and independent agents of a universal international normative order has come under challenge in the era of backlash. Many international lawyers who saw themselves as part of a liberal internationalist project have responded strongly, treating the decision to critique or withdraw from international or regional regimes in the name of sovereignty as pathological while at the same time making the specifically liberal politics of transnational legal processes far more visible.[57] So what is to be done if we accept that transnationalizing the role of lawyers and policy makers is not a way of lifting our work out of the messy business of politics and into a world of enlightened reason or technical expertise, but instead simply represents another way of engaging in political struggle?

One response to the recognition that international lawyers and diplomats play a role in making decisions that have distributive effects is to insist upon a more transparent and open process of treaty-making internationally. As international law increasingly addresses more and more issues that were once the traditional business of national governments, those issues become part of 'a world that has always been characterised by secrecy, on the ground that relations with foreign powers are too subtle and delicate for publicity, and publicity would weaken a government's negotiating hand'.[58] This has serious implications for democratic accountability and governmental responsibility. We could think here of the heated political debates that accompanied attempts to negotiate the ambitious *TPP* and the *TTIP* agreements, and the criticism that those negotiations were conducted in secret, with the texts not made available to the public of contracting states until the very last minute, and with parliamentarians given limited opportunity to shape the negotiations or peruse the final texts, and then only after signing confidentiality agreements.[59] While

---

57   See, eg, Harold Hongju Koh, 'The Trump Administration and International Law' (2017) 56 *Washburn Law Journal* 413 (arguing that the liberal international order was set up to constrain governments (including US administrations with different policy agendas) that do not share the liberal internationalist view of where national interest lies).

58   Philip Allott, 'Britain and Europe: Managing Revolution' in Robert McCorquodale and Jean-Pierre Gauci (eds), *British Influences on International Law, 1915–2015* (Brill Nijhoff, 2016) 56, 63.

59   See, eg, Foreign Affairs, Defence and Trade References Committee, Parliament of Australia, *Blind Agreement: Reforming Australia's Treaty-Making Process* (Report, 25 June 2015) 29; Joseph Stiglitz, 'Tricks of the Trade Deal: Six Big Problems with the Trans-Pacific

the secretive nature of such treaty-making processes may increase the ability of negotiators to reach agreement in a timely fashion, it detracts from the legitimacy of the final outcomes.

A second and related response is to be more cautious about the scope of political matters that are lifted out of domestic politics and into the secretive world of international negotiations. While Brexit, the abandonment of *TTIP*, the US unsigning of the *TPP*, and the current stand-off at the WTO may have negative economic consequences, all involve responses to regimes that give international bodies and experts control over regulatory decision-making in sensitive areas such as public health and safety, labour standards, social rights, and environmental protection.[60] Those ambitious trade and regional economic integration agreements have been used to set in train a process of regulatory alignment that prioritises the creation of a frictionless world for commercial actors over state responsibilities for protecting human life, health, and the environment. Current challenges to international law and global governance offer an opportunity to reconsider the extent to which it is sustainable to lift such vital political decisions out of the democratic process.

A third response is to reconsider mechanisms for making it less onerous for states to withdraw from treaties, particularly in situations where judicial or arbitral interpretations of treaty terms are perceived to have expanded beyond the initial rights and obligations to which states and publics understood themselves to have committed. Extensive sunset clauses are particularly common in investment treaties, with some offering protection for third party property rights for up to twenty years after notification of withdrawal.[61] Where agreements have been negotiated in secret and have far-reaching effects on public interests, it is difficult to justify maintaining costly effects of revision or termination.

Overall, the recognition that there is a politics to international law is not the end of the story, but rather the beginning of a new chapter. A particular account of international legalism triumphed in the late twentieth century.

Partnership', *Roosevelt Institute* (Webpage, 28 March 2016) <http://rooseveltinstitute.org/tricks-trade-deal-six-big-problems-trans-pacific-partnership/>.

60   See further Anne Orford, 'Locating the International: Military and Monetary Interventions after the Cold War' (1997) 38(2) *Harvard International Law Journal* 443, 471–6; Anne Orford, 'Europe Reconstructed' (2012) 75(2) *Modern Law Review* 275; Anne Orford, 'Theorizing Free Trade' in Anne Orford and Florian Hoffmann (eds), *The Oxford Handbook of the Theory of International Law* (Oxford University Press, 2016) 701.

61   For a discussion of this issue in the context of the *Energy Charter Treaty*, see Tania Voon, 'Modernizing the *Energy Charter Treaty*: What about Termination?' (2019) 10(4) *International Treaty News* 4.

Its displacement poses both challenges and opportunities for contemporary thinking about the role of law in international politics. There are numerous ways in which this recognition could allow for a more conscious and overt re-embedding of international law-making, adjudication, and enforcement within political processes. Legal systems do not somehow exist in a world beyond politics but instead must be 'chosen and defended' politically.[62] The return of history into this story is valuable because it allows us to experience that sense of choice and responsibility anew.

---

62 Judith N Shklar, *Political Thought and Political Thinker,* ed Stanley Hoffmann (University of Chicago Press, 1998) 25.

Special Issue
The Backlash against International Law:
Australian Perspectives

∵

Introduction
The Backlash against International Law: Australian Perspectives

Jeremy Farrall, Jolyon Ford and Imogen Saunders

We write this introduction working from our homes in Canberra while the COVID-19 pandemic escalates around the globe. This is already a very different world to the one in which the contributions to this volume of the *Australian Year Book of International Law* first took shape. Indeed, the articles in this special edition of the *Year Book* all began as papers presented to a June 2019 workshop at the Australian National University (ANU) on the topic 'Navigating the Backlash against Global Law and Institutions: Australian Perspectives'.

The Canberra Backlash workshop launched a global research partnership project between scholars at ANU, Indiana University and the University of Maryland. It brought together a dynamic blend of international legal and interdisciplinary scholars from these three institutions, as well as Australian government practitioners, including from the Attorney General's Department, the Department of Environment and Energy, and the Department of Foreign Affairs and Trade. A series of engaging panel discussions examined the scope and ramifications of the backlash against International Law in relation to four thematic areas: peace and security, human rights, trade and finance, and the environment.

The articles published in this special edition provide thoughtful perspectives on the nature and impact of the backlash against International Law. Some of these perspectives are distinctly Australian. Others focus on international actors and themes. All were shaped by the workshop discussions in Australia and with Australian academics and practitioners. In the first article, 'Navigating the Backlash against Global Law and Institutions', Peter G Danchin, Jeremy Farrall, Jolyon Ford, Shruti Rana, Imogen Saunders and Daan Verhoeven set the stage by framing the contours and consequences of the backlash against international law and institutions. After interrogating the strengths and shortcomings of the backlash concept to describe the contemporary challenges facing international law and institutions, Danchin et al propose three different ways that Australia and other states are likely to respond to the backlash. These are to *reform and renew*, to *retreat and realign*, or to *reimagine and recreate*. The article then explores how these different responses might play out across

© KONINKLIJKE BRILL NV, LEIDEN, 2021 | DOI:10.1163/26660229_03801003

the thematic areas of peace and security, human rights, trade and finance, and the environment.

The second and third articles address the impact of the backlash on international peace and security. In 'Collective Security and the Prohibition on the Use of Force in Times of Global Transition', Christopher Michaelsen examines whether the current threats to the international legal order present a novel challenge to the normative framework regulating the use of force, or rather represent the latest manifestation of longstanding challenges. After surveying seven decades of threats to the prohibition on the use of force, Michaelsen suggests that the current backlash amounts to a new iteration of dynamics that have always been present. In 'The Status of Human Protection in International Law and Institutions: the United Nations Prevention and Protection Agenda', Cecilia Jacob examines whether international norms and institutions are facing a backlash in the specific area of human protection, including the prevention of violent conflict and mass atrocities. Drawing on her analysis of developments and dynamics in the core protection agendas of the protection of civilians in UN peacekeeping and the responsibility to protect, Jacob argues that while there is turbulence in the normative, institutional, and political contexts in which states engage with protection norms, this dynamic of contestation promotes the 'reconstituting', rather than the 'unravelling', of international order. Jacob views reform and renewal as the most pragmatic and productive of the three response scenarios to harness this reconstituting potential in relation to human protection. By contrast, she warns that the two alternative scenarios, of retreat and realign and reimagine and recreate, would lead to a lowest common denominator unravelling of such norms.

The fourth and fifth articles in the special edition concern trade and build upon one phenomenon identified in the first article—the fragmentation of international law. In 'Navigating the Backlash: Re-Integrating WTO and Public International Law?', Imogen Saunders argues that the siloisation of international trade law is *itself* a backlash against public international law: and that this backlash is causing states to withdraw from the multilateral trade system. States are retreating from World Trade Organisation negotiations and realigning by forming Regional Trade Agreements ('RTAS') which more easily meet their trade and non-trade objectives. By contrast, in 'Navigating the "Backlash" against International Trade and Investment Liberalisation: Economic Perspectives on the Future of Regional Trade Agreements in Uncertain Times', Martin Richardson argues that RTAS are themselves facing a decline in popularity. While this unpopularity may not rise to the level of a backlash, States are nonetheless showing less enthusiasm to enter into RTAS. As a consequence of this trade scepticism, States enter into RTAS with the possibility of exit in

INTRODUCTION   31

mind: and this itself necessarily decreases cooperation between them. Both Richardson and Saunders see problems with RTAS. Saunders highlights the increased fragmentation of international law and resulting complexity, while Richardson points to ambivalence of evidence of economic benefit from RTAS. While State scepticism of RTAS may be a recent phenomenon, that of economists is not. Ultimately, Saunders offers suggested solutions to allow a reform of international trade law to reintegrate public international law, while Richardson suggests States will still engage with RTAS: albeit with less cooperation and established exit strategies.

The final three articles comprise rather diverse reflections on the backlash theme in the context of the international system for the promotion and protection of human rights. In 'Backlash against a Rules-Based International Human Rights Order? An Australian Perspective', Jolyon Ford evaluates the merits of characterising recent Australian government postures towards that system as 'backlash' in the particular sense of system-threatening or anti-system behaviours. Ford zooms out to ask whether it is the very idea of the international rule of law, not compliance or engagement with particular elements of the overall system, that is at issue. On a broader global canvas, in 'Amidst Simmering Tensions: Improving the Effectiveness and Coherence of the International Human Rights System's Response to Mass Human Rights Violations', Annemarie Devereux argues that the backlash concept risks presenting mere continuity (of intra-system tensions) as change. Moreover, Devereux warns that framing contemporary dynamics as part of a backlash distracts attention from deeper structural challenges in the international human rights system. In 'Backlashes against International Commitments and Organisations: Asylum as Restorative Justice', Kate Ogg explores the backlash motif from a different perspective: vulnerable populations under the care of an international organisation and who may be more directly affected than most by the forces and consequences of politically-driven backlash against such organisations. In doing so, Ogg joins Devereux on common ground, by reflecting on the risk that in focussing on more dramatic moments of apparent flux (as backlash-thinking may lead us to do), we may not see the more subtle, systemic and entrenched ways in which states backpedal from their international commitments or responsibilities. Indeed, all three authors may be interpreted as concerned to explore, and ultimately question, whether there is anything particularly distinctive about recent instances of states 'pushing back' at the system that they have helped to build. In doing so, and if one accepts that backlash implies a noticeably new phenomenon, the authors raise a question apposite to the wider project as a whole: what if the structural continuities and state incentives for maintaining the approximate systemic status quo in fact outweigh the apparent shifts underway, including those attributable to domestic populist backlash? If so, how and when might we know whether developments that appear to represent crisis-driven *reform and renewal* in fact amount only to cosmetic changes to the global institutional map, missed opportunities to bolster the legitimacy, inclusivity and effectiveness of international law?

Taken as a collective, the eight articles in this special edition provide a series of rich reflections on the challenges facing international law and institutions as we move into the third decade of the 21st century. Each article sheds fresh light on the tensions that underpin and enliven both critical academic reflection on, as well as pragmatic policy responses to, the pronounced recent disengagement from international treaties and institutions by powerful states, such as the United States, which were traditionally active supporters and defenders of global cooperation. These tensions include whether the contemporary challenges facing international law and institutions represent something new, such as a populist backlash, or rather the latest manifestation of something old; and whether these challenges are caused by the external pressure of changing global dynamics or by the internal pressure of structural weakness. The manner in which contributors engage with these central tensions tends to shape their preferences in terms of which of the three response scenarios described by Danchin et al in the first article, namely *reform and renew*, *retreat and realign*, or *reimagine and recreate*, holds the greatest promise.

As a postscript, it is noteworthy that, although the articles in this special issue evolved prior to the outbreak of COVID-19, the critical analysis and pragmatic proposals they advance have become even more cogent in the COVID-19 era. If it has done nothing else, the rapid spread of the COVID-19 pandemic has graphically demonstrated the vital need for effective collective action to prevent and manage grave global threats. The constructive engagement of all states in improving the international law and institutions that support such action is as important now as it ever was.

Navigating the Backlash against Global Law and Institutions

Peter G Danchin,* Jeremy Farrall,** Jolyon Ford,*** Shruti Rana,+ Imogen Saunders++ and Daan Verhoeven+++

1 Introduction

This article considers the recent "backlash" against global norms and institutions fuelled by various contemporary political developments within and between states. Understanding the shape, significance and drivers of this phenomenon better is a pre-requisite to developing and analysing possible responses by Australia and other states. The current global legal order was established after World War II and is underpinned by the *Charter of the United Nations ('UN Charter')*,[1] international law in general, and the growing collection of multilateral international legal instruments by which states agree to conduct their international relations. The sweep of the global legal order is broad, encompassing norms and institutions that seek to foster international cooperation across a range of spheres, including development, the environment, finance, health, human rights, science, security, and trade. The United States ('US') has historically been considered the leader and guarantor of the post-1945 legal order, playing host to its most important institutions. The US has provided key economic, political, and diplomatic backing throughout its time as one of two superpowers during the Cold War, and as the hegemonic power for most of the period since. Australia has also been a strong supporter of the liberal rules-based order, commitment to which explicitly underpins

---

*   Peter G Danchin, Professor of Law; Director, International and Comparative Law Program, University of Maryland School of Law.

**   Jeremy Farrall, Associate Professor, ANU College of Law, Australian National University.

*** Jo Ford, Associate Professor, ANU College of Law, Australian National University.

+   Shruti Rana, Assistant Dean of Curricular and Undergraduate Affairs; Professor, International Law Practice and Director of the International Law and Institutions Program, Hamilton Lugar School of Global & International Studies, Indiana University Bloomington.

++   Imogen Saunders, Senior Lecturer, ANU College of Law, Australian National University.

+++ Daan Verhoeven, ANU College of Law, Australian National University.

1   *Charter of the United Nations ('UN Charter')*.

© KONINKLIJKE BRILL NV, LEIDEN, 2021 | DOI:10.1163/26660229_03801004

its current official foreign policy posture.[2] It was a founding member of the United Nations ('UN') and has traditionally been involved in the drafting of, and been swift to sign on to, new international covenants that clarify and crystalise the heretofore expanding reach of international law.

The recent rise of populism and illiberal democracy, especially within major Western democracies, has challenged the longstanding and widespread commitment of those states to the rules-based order.[3] These phenomena have also eroded the traditional global leadership, in multilateral forums, of key powers including UN permanent members the US and the United Kingdom ('UK'). The populations of these and other states have responded to perceptions of economic and political disempowerment by pressuring political representatives to focus their energies domestically. In order both to appeal and respond to domestic political forces, leaders in these states have sought to target or sometimes scapegoat the international institutions that have hitherto been so useful to their foreign policy agenda. Seen this way, backlash behaviours do not necessarily signal that a government is contesting the political utility *in foreign policy terms* of continuing to play by the global rulebook. These behaviours may show that the government has calculated that the domestic political gain from contesting international mechanisms and rules outweighs the damage done to those systems in terms of external influence and leverage. President Trump's initial rejection of any mention of the 'rules-based international order' during negotiations towards a December 2018 G20 joint communique provides a stark illustration of the sharp decline of the value and compliance-pull of global norms and institutions for a country that has long been their traditional cheerleader.[4] While the communiqué ultimately did contain the 'rules-based order' term, Trump only acquiesced to this once other G20 members agreed to include reference to the need for urgent reform of the World Trade Organisation.[5]

---

2 Australian Government, *2017 Foreign Policy White Paper* (White Paper, 23 November 2017) 3, 6–7, 79–97 ('*2017 White Paper*') <https://www.dfat.gov.au/sites/default/files/2017-foreign -policy-white-paper.pdf>. One of five objectives listed to be 'of fundamental importance to Australia's security and prosperity' is to 'promote and protect the international rules that support stability and prosperity and enable cooperation to tackle global challenges': at 3.

3 The *2017 White Paper* (n 2) provides one succinct and authoritative summary of some of these trends, noting a period of 'sharper challenge' to international rules and institutions: at 1, 6.

4 See Julian Borger, 'G20 Agreement Backs "Rules-Based" Order but Bows to Trump on Trade Reforms', *The Guardian* (Article, 1 December 2018) <https://www.theguardian.com/ world/2018/dec/01/g20-leaders-donald-trump-rules-based-order-wto-reform>.

5 For the text of the communique, see: G20 Leaders, 'G20 Leaders' Declaration: Building Consensus for Fair and Sustainable Development' (Joint Communique, 1 December 2018)

NAVIGATING THE BACKLASH AGAINST GLOBAL LAW AND INSTITUTIONS 35

One way of understanding the shift in the postures of leaders and governments, in the UK, US, Brazil, Italy and other states, is as part of a broader backlash against the Post-World War II framework of liberal norms and institutions. This article examines the utility and implications of such an understanding. It also explores how states and global institutions might respond to this backlash. The article's central argument is that while it is tempting to view the backlash as a new phenomenon that poses a clear and present existential threat to global law and institutions, we should not imagine that this is the first time that states have either disrupted international institutions or sought in more robust ways to shake up internationalist ideas. The challenge is to diagnose accurately what is distinct about this moment and to identify the ramifications for future efforts to build and promote peaceful and cooperative international relations. In addition, we should of course be conscious that factors other than populist backlash may account for changes in state behaviour towards international institutions.[6]

The article proceeds in five sections. Section 2 examines the consequences of understanding the current populist moment as part of a backlash against global law and institutions. Section 3 examines the ramifications of the backlash frame for international peace and security. Section 4 considers the implications of the backlash frame for the international human rights system. Section 5 explores the impact of the turn inward for global trade and finance. Section 6 discusses the backlash against environmental norms.

2   Framing the Backlash: Contours and Consequences

In this article, we explore the concept of a backlash as one way of understanding the sustained challenge that populist movements in countries around the world have posed to global norms and institutions. We seek to trace the causes, contours and consequences of this backlash, as well as what responses are being made in support of global law and institutions. According to a backlash narrative, the challenge to global law and institutions can be interpreted as a kneejerk reaction against and away from the global, and in particular globalisation, towards the local and the national. Many populists view globalisation,

---

<https://www.consilium.europa.eu/en/press/press-releases/2018/12/01/g20-leaders
-declaration/>.

6   The *2017 White Paper* (n 2) notes that along with anti-globalisation and protectionism other issues are challenging the international order, notably geopolitical competition and changes in the balance of global power: at 6.

global norms and institutions as having changed the world in a negative way, leaving them and their societies disempowered economically and politically.[7] These populists, whom we might call Trumpian, Dutertian or Bolsonaroan populists, tend to yearn for a bygone era when borders were watertight and events in faraway places had a much less direct effect on events in their own countries. They blame globalisation for a range of social and economic ills, such as slowing GDP, decreasing employment opportunities, and stagnating wages. They view globalisation, once welcomed as a 'rising tide that would lift all boats',[8] as decreasing, rather than increasing, national and personal prosperity.

2.1 *Contours*

The concept of backlash tends to beg as many questions as it answers. What action constitutes a backlash? What motivates such action and who participates in in it? Is the concept value-neutral or does it imply a positive or negative view of those taking backlash action and the forces that motivate them? What are the implications of the term for the actors, institutions or forces against which backlash action is taken? Does backlash connote (or is it confined to) a particular moment in time, or can it relate to or comprise a more long-term phenomenon?

Some scholars see backlash as an inevitability of the international system itself.[9] Others question its utility as a tool of analysis, describing it as 'a common language of recoil' rather than an analytical concept.[10] Yet others caution against rushing to the gloomy conclusion that this is the end of the internationalist era, arguing in Wildean terms that the reports of international law's demise are exaggerated.[11]

---

7   For thoughtful analysis of different motivations for, and manifestations of, populism, see Mark A Graber, 'Thick and Thin: Interdisciplinary Conversations on Populism, Law, Political Science, and Constitutional Change' (2001) 90 *Georgetown Law Journal* 233.

8   Gene Sperling, 'Rising-Tide Economics' [2007] (Fall) (6) *Democracy* <https://democracy journal.org/magazine/6/rising-tide-economics/>. The phrase 'a rising tide lifts all boats' was used by President John Fitzgerald Kennedy in a speech on 3 October 1963: John Fitzgerald Kennedy, 'Remarks in Heber Springs, Arkansas, at the Dedication of Greers Ferry Dam' (Speech, Greers Ferry Dam, 3 October 1963) <https://www.presidency.ucsb .edu/node/236260>.

9   See, eg, Eric A Posner, 'Liberal Internationalism and the Populist Backlash' (2017) 49 *Arizona State Law Journal* 795.

10   Mikael Rask Madsen, Pola Cebulak and Micha Wiebusch, 'Backlash against International Courts: Explaining the Forms and Patterns of Resistance to International Courts' (2018) 14(2) *International Journal in Context* 197.

11   See, eg, Philip Alston, 'The Populist Challenge to Human Rights' (2017) 9(1) *Journal of Human Rights Practice* 1.

Despite these different perspectives on the utility and ramifications of framing as a 'backlash' the current challenge posed by populism to globalism, it is clear that the notion of backlash resonates with twenty-first century international legal scholars. Some of these observe a rising number of national governments retreating from longstanding commitments to international norms and institutions in a variety of contexts, such as investment law,[12] human rights,[13] and the activities of international courts.[14]

These international legal scholars do not share a commonly agreed or accepted definition of backlash, and, indeed, acts described as a backlash can take many forms. Yet some commentators have identified central ingredients that tend to feature in most descriptions addressing backlash contexts. Here we take our lead from Caron and Shirlow, who draw on Sunstein to define backlash as 'intense and sustained public disapproval of a system accompanied by aggressive steps to resist the system and to remove its legal force'.[15] It is thus more than simple critique or discontent. It represents a fundamental resistance to and rejection of a system or institution of law.[16]

Our project centres on actions taken in opposition to the global legal system and the institutions within it: a backlash against the *international legal order* itself. In the initial stages of our project we have targeted four key areas where the phenomenon of backlash can be identified: peace and security, human rights, environmental concerns and international economic law. Madsen et al have suggested that backlash contains 'a reaction to a development with the goal of reversing that development'.[17] In one sense, the development that leads to resistance against the international legal order is shared across all these

---

12   See, eg, David Caron and Esmé Shirlow, 'Dissecting Backlash: The Unarticulated Causes of Backlash and Its Unintended Consequences' in Andreas Føllesdal and Geir Ulfstein (eds), *The Judicilization of International Law: A Mixed Blessing?* (Oxford University Press, 2018) 159; Malcolm Langford and Daniel Behn, 'Managing Backlash: The Evolving Investment Treaty Arbitrator?' (2018) 29(2) *European Journal of International Law* 551.

13   See, eg, Ian Siederman, 'The UN High Commissioner for Human Rights in the Age of Global Backlash' (2019) 37(1) *Netherlands Quarterly of Human Rights* 5; Laurence R Helfer, 'Overlegalizing Human Rights: International Relations Theory and the Commonwealth Caribbean Backlash against Human Rights Regimes' (2002) 102 *Columbia Law Review* 1832.

14   See, eg, Erik Voeten, 'Populism and backlashes against International Courts' (2019) *Perspectives on Politics* 1; Madsen, Cebulak and Wiebusch (n 10); Karen J Alter, James T Gathii and Laurence R Helfer, 'Backlash against International Courts in West, East and Southern Africa: Causes and Consequences' (2016) 27(2) *European Journal of International Law* 293.

15   Caron and Shirlow (n 12) 160; Cass R Sunstein, 'Backlash's Travels' (2007) 42 *Harvard Civil Rights—Civil Liberties Law Review* 435, 435.

16   Ibid.

17   Madsen, Cebulak and Wiebusch (n 10) 200.

areas: increasing globalism.[18] This resistance may take the form of political interdependence and fears of loss of identity—as seen in the Brexit debate; new treaty obligations leading to fears of loss of sovereignty—as seen in the US withdrawal from the *Paris Agreement*;[19] or more general concerns stemming from increased economic interdependence and the domestic consequences of movements of labour and industry as a consequence of free trade. However this resistance manifests, the central core is the same: a rebuff of integration and internationalisation, leading to acts of resistance against the system of international law and its institutions.

Taking backlash as these acts of resistance against the international global legal order, our project seeks to ascertain and identify *what* these actions are—do they represent something novel, or are they part of a more longstanding historical dynamic shaped by oppositional forces that pull the populations of nation-states inwards, towards national identity, or outwards, towards international community? Put another way, is this backlash a new tsunami threatening to overwhelm and sweep away international law: a rejection of the ideals of globalism and a retreat into national borders? Or is it more a case of the tide receding from the high water-mark of internationalisation in the 1990s, but still within bounds of the ebb and flow of the history of the evolving international legal order? It is to these questions we now turn.

2.2 *Roots and Causes of Backlash*

Since the birth and consolidation of the modern state system in the mid-seventeenth century, a particular understanding of the relationship between freedom and order has shaped international legal thought. The international legal imaginary is of a secular legal order of sovereign states possessing formal equality and equal freedom in the form of the rights, obligations and attributes of sovereignty. This vocabulary of state sovereignty and early modern natural law emerged at the moment of 'Crisis of European Conscience' following the Thirty Years War and European wars of religion. As Martti Koskenniemi has observed, at this moment, a clash of new and old vocabularies occurred:

> [O]n the one side, an anachronistic scholasticism, and an old elite clinging to its privileges; on the other side, complex technical words seeking to penetrate the tired surface of political life to give expression to the dynamic forces underneath. Modern international law was born from a

---

18 Caron and Shirlow (n 12) 160.

19 *Paris Agreement*, opened for signature 22 April 2016 [2016] ATS 24 (entered into force 4 November 2016).

defence of secular absolutism against theology and feudalism. The international world became an extension of sovereign rule.[20]

Today, we appear to be at another moment of great foment and turmoil as competing legal and moral vocabularies clash against each other and 'the inherited language of the modern states-system, and of international law, no longer seems able to give voice to important groups and interests'.[21] Today, however, it is political sovereignty itself that is challenged by the new idioms of globalisation and transnational governance:

> In both moments, the 'old' seems artificial and fragmented while the 'new' appears natural and universal. Now, as then, change is represented as a natural necessity.[22]

The current clash of vocabularies makes visible an ambiguity latent in the term 'liberal international order'. The backlash moment has presented no concentrated attack on the premises of national sovereignty itself, or indeed on the Westphalian foundations of the *UN Charter* legal order grounded in the twin principles of sovereign equality and national self-determination.[23] Rather, backlash political movements have targeted their ire on the post-Cold War vocabulary of globalisation and transnational governance and the implicit *critique* of national sovereignty internal to these discourses. Their target has thus been the rise, since the 1990s, of specialized governance regimes in functional areas such as trade, human rights, environment, security and migration, and the ensuing proliferation of complex managerial vocabularies that speak

---

20 Martii Koskenniemi, 'Miserable Comforters: International Relations as New Natural Law' (2009) 15(3) *European Journal of International Relations* 395, 396 ('Miserable Comforters').

21 Ibid.

22 Ibid.

23 Article 2(1) of the *UN Charter* (n 1) provides that that the United Nations 'is based on the principle of the sovereign equality of all its [Member States]'. The *Charter* thus begins from a presumption of initial State freedom. But once States are viewed as members of an international community, this initial State freedom is limited by the normative demands of the same 'equal' freedom of other States. Conversely, art 2(7) of the *UN Charter* (n 1) provides that '[n]othing contained in the present *Charter* shall authorize the United Nations to intervene in matters which are essentially within the domestic jurisdiction of any state'. While international law is normatively universal and binding on all States, it is thus limited by the national subjectivity and unique 'internal' identity of and need for consent of each State. This dialectic structure creates the distinctive double-bind of modern international legal argument.

'neither about sovereignty nor about rules but about the "objectives", "values" and "interests" behind them'.[24]

This global governance conception of liberal international legal order has become the mainstream or 'Establishment' narrative over the last thirty years. Consider the area of international trade. The dominant story told since the early 1990s is that everybody wins under an international trade regime because 'free trade' is a rising tide that lifts all boats,[25] or because it increases the overall size of the economic pie so that winners can compensate losers, leaving everyone better off. The result will be an increase in the prospects of both peace and prosperity: after all, as Friedman puts it, have two countries that have a McDonalds ever gone to war with each other?[26]

This thesis has been a key point of convergence for both neoliberal conservatives, who see no need to question relative gains or whether economic gains themselves are the right measure to be maximising, and social democrats, who see only a modest role for redistributing gains. The current populist moment has arisen in strong opposition to two interrelated faces of the global governance narrative of international law and institutions, in each case seeking a return to a more sovereignty-based model of international legal order.

As Michael Hardt and Antonio Negri argued in the mid-1990s, the first is the perception that these transformations in international law presage a project of empire.[27] On this account, empire is a form of sovereignty existing under the conditions of globalisation that is rescaled from the level of the nation-state to the level of the global. What is viewed as replacing discourses of state sovereignty and public international law is 'not a pluralistic, cooperative world political system under a new, impartial global *rule of law*, but rather a project of imperial world domination'.[28]

Beginning in the 1970s, the neoconservative project of employing American power and the use of force in the name of promoting democracy, human rights and the rule of law has deeply undermined the norms of sovereign

---

24   Koskenniemi, 'Miserable Comforters' (n 20) 406.

25   See Sperling (n 8).

26   The so-called 'Golden Arches' theory: Thomas Friedman, 'Foreign Affairs Big Mac I', *The New York Times* (Article, 8 December 1996) <https://www.nytimes.com/1996/12/08/opinion/foreign-affairs-big-mac-i.html>.

27   Michael Hardt and Antonio Negri, *Empire* (Harvard University Press, 2000).

28   Jean L Cohen, 'Whose Sovereignty? Empire Versus International Law' (2004) 18(3) *Ethics and International Affairs* 1, 2 (emphasis in original). As Cohen suggests, on this view 'governance, soft law, self-regulation, societal constitutionalism, trans-governmental networks, human rights talk, and the very concept of "humanitarian intervention" are simply discourses and deformalized mechanisms by which empire aims to rule (and to legitimate its rule) rather than ways to limit and orient power by law': at 2.

equality, nonintervention and the *UN Charter* system of collective security.[29] As many now recognise, this imperial project accelerated with the invasion of Afghanistan in 2001, and reached its apex with the 2003 intervention in Iraq. Exalting the pre-emptive attack, Michael Ignatieff argued that the '21st century imperium is a new invention in the annals of political science, an empire lite, a global hegemony whose grace notes are free markets, human rights and democracy, enforced by the most awesome military power the world has ever known'.[30]

It is possible to chart a direct line from this moment in 2003 to the rise of populist political movements on both the right and left in Western democracies now opposing neoconservative foreign policies as imperial overreach in the pursuit of unwise or costly 'liberal' American empire. In his 2019 speech to the 74th Session of the United Nations General Assembly (UNGA), President Donald Trump thus bellicosely proclaimed that the 'free world must [now] embrace its national foundations':

> If you want freedom, take pride in your country. If you want democracy, hold on to your sovereignty. And if you want peace, love your nation. Wise leaders always put the good of their own people and their own country first. The future does not belong to globalists. The future belongs to patriots. The future belongs to sovereign and independent nations who protect their citizens, respect their neighbors, and honor the differences that make each country special and unique.[31]

At the same time, the scope of American disengagement from traditional treaty and multilateral legal regimes has been staggering. From arms control,[32]

---

29   Of course, the use of force by Great Powers to transform the internal political identity of so-called 'rogue' or 'outlaw' states in the name of civilisation and progress has a long pedigree in the history of international law: see, eg, Gerry Simpson, *Great Powers and Outlaw States: Unequal Sovereigns in the International Legal Order* (Cambridge University Press, 2004).

30   Michael Ignatieff, 'The American Empire; the Burden,' *New York Times Magazine* (Article, 5 January 2003) <https://www.nytimes.com/2003/01/05/magazine/the-american-empire-the-burden.html>.

31   Donald J Trump, 'Remarks by President Donald J Trump to the 74th Session of the United Nations General Assembly (Speech, United Nations Headquarters, New York, 24 September 2019) <https://www.whitehouse.gov/briefings-statements/remarks-president-trump-74th-session-united-nations-general-assembly/>.

32   The US has refused to join the *Convention on the Prohibition of the Use, Stockpiling, Production and Transfer of Anti-Personnel Mines and on their Destruction*, opened for signature 3 December 1997, 2056 UNTS 211 (entered into force 1 March 1999) and the

to international criminal law,[33] to environmental regulation and the law of the sea,[34] to human rights treaties,[35] the US has either rejected or withdrawn from a vast number of contemporary treaties and their supervisory mechanisms.

The second, and arguably more complex face of backlash, however, has been visceral opposition to the project of *cosmopolitan law*, and in particular

---

Comprehensive Nuclear Test Ban Treaty, opened for signature 10 September 1996, 35 ILM (not yet in force), and has rejected the *Convention on the Prohibition of the Development, Production and Stockpiling of Bacteriological (Biological) and Toxin Weapons and on their Destruction*, opened for signature 10 April 1972, 1015 UNTS 163 (entered into force 26 March 1975) as well as the inspections regime of the *Convention on the Prohibition of the Development, Production, Stockpiling and Use of Chemical Weapons and on their Destruction*, opened for signature 13 January 1993, 1975 UNTS 45 (entered into force 29 April 1997). It replaced the *Treaty on the Limitation of Anti-Ballistic Missile Systems*, United States—Union of Soviet Socialist Republics, signed 26 May 1972 11 ILM 784 (entered into force 3 October 1972) with a bilateral negotiating framework, and recently announced US withdrawal from the *Treaty on the Elimination of their Intermediate-Range and Shorter-Range Missiles*, United States—Union of Soviet Socialist Republics, signed 8 December 1987, 27 ILM 84 (entered into force 1 June 1988).

33   The US failed to ratify and in fact 'unsigned' the *Rome Statute of the International Criminal Court*, opened for signature 17 July 1998, 2187 UNTS 90 (entered into force 1 July 2002). It is party to neither *Protocol Additional to the Geneva Conventions of 12 August 1949, and Relating to the Protection of Victims of International Armed Conflicts (Protocol I)*, opened for signature 8 June 1977, 1125 UNTS 3 (entered into force 7 December 1978) nor *Protocol Additional to the Geneva Convention of 12 August 1949, and Relating to the Protection of Victims of Non-International Armed Conflicts (Protocol II)*, opened for signature 8 June 1977, 1125 UTS 610 (entered into force 7 December 1978).

34   The US refused to sign the *Kyoto Protocol to the United Nations Framework Convention on Climate Change*, opened for signature 11 December 1997, 2303 UNTS 162 (entered into force 16 February 2005) or become a party to the *Convention on Biological Diversity*, opened for signature 5 June 1992, 1760 UNTS 79 (entered into force 29 December 1993). It has failed to ratify the *United Nations Convention on the Law of the Sea*, opened for signature 10 December 1982, 1833 UNTS 3 (entered into force 16 November 1994) and has recently announced US withdrawal from the *Paris Agreement* (n 19) on climate action.

35   The US has rejected most human rights treaties and their supervisory bodies, including the *International Covenant on Social, Economic and Cultural Rights*, opened for signature 19 December 1966, 993 UNTS 3 (entered into force 3 January 1976) (ie half of the International Bill of Rights), the *Convention on the Elimination of All Forms of Discrimination against Women*, opened for signature 1 March 1980, 1249 UNTS 13 (entered into force 3 September 1981) and the *Convention on the Rights of the Child*, opened for signature 20 November 1989, 1577 UNTS 3 (entered into force 2 September 1990). Those few treaties it has ratified, it has done so subject to extensive reservations, declarations and understandings (including declaring that such treaties are non-self-executing in US domestic law).

the perception of international human rights and individual freedom as a new hegemonic language of global morality.[36] As Jean Cohen makes the point:

> The emergence of human rights law based on consensus apparently implies that global cosmopolitan law trumps the will of states and their international treaties (consent). Today the very category 'international' appears outdated. The question thus becomes: What is to be the new 'nomos' of the earth and how should we understand globalized law?[37]

From the time of Immanuel Kant's 1784 essay *Idea for a Universal History with a Cosmopolitan Purpose*,[38] the general theoretical claim has been that the world is witnessing a move to cosmopolitan law and that 'sovereignty talk and the old forms of public international law based on the sovereignty paradigm have to go'.[39] As Louis Henkin argued in 1999, 'I don't like the "S word". Its birth is illegitimate, and it has not aged well. The meaning of "sovereignty" is confused and its uses are various, some of them unworthy, some even destructive of human values.'[40] On the basis of solely optimistic and progressive implications, Henkin thus suggested that 'suddenly, or perhaps slowly, the realization is sinking in that sovereignty has lost its nerve, and sovereign states have realized that they are losing their control, that the state system is losing control'.[41]

---

36 For an influential account of the rise of human rights since the early 1970s as the ultimate arbiter of international conduct, see Samuel Moyn, *The Last Utopia: Human Rights in History* (Harvard University Press, 2012).

37 Cohen (n 28) 1–2. The term 'nomos of the earth' is from Carl Schmitt, *The Nomos of the Earth in the International Law of the Jus Publicum Europaeum*, tr GL Ulmen (Telos Press, 2003). Cohen raises the question of Schmitt's *Nomos der Erde* in the context of the fact that the 'world's sole superpower has invaded and occupied Iraq': at 1.

38 Immanuel Kant and Allen Wood, 'Idea for a Universal History with a Cosmopolitan Aim', in Amélie Oksenberg Rorty and James Schmidt (eds), *Kant's Idea for a Universal History with a Cosmospolitan Aim* (Cambridge University Press, 2009) 9–23.

39 Cohen (n 28) 2.

40 Louis Henkin, 'The "S" Word: Sovereignty, and Globalization, and Human Rights, Et Cetera' (1999) 68(1) *Fordham Law Review* 1, 1. Henkin leaves no doubt as to his thesis: 'the sovereignty of states in international relations is essentially a mistake, an illegitimate offspring': at 2.

41 Ibid 7. For an early articulation of this view, see Hersch Lauterpacht, *The Function of Law in the International Community* (Clarendon Press, 1933) which celebrates international law against the arbitrariness of sovereignty. In the post-World War II period, see Wolfgang Friedmann, *The Changing Structure of International Law* (California University Press, Columbia University Press and Princeton University Press, 1964) which argues that the international law of coexistence was moving towards a world of cooperation as states were gradually being united by the emergence of specialised fields designed to manage

At the core of the cosmopolitan legal project is a radical transformation of 'domestic jurisdiction' in art 2(7) of the *UN Charter*, now viewed as an anachronism from an older time whose invocation is merely an attempt to shield leaders from legitimate and necessary international action. Koskenniemi suggests that under conditions of global law, 'sovereignty' has today lost its normative and descriptive meaning in the face of relentless moral, sociological and functional arguments made in the name of *international* or *global* approaches, now claimed to operate across artificial national boundaries free of territorial limitation.[42]

This shift to a cosmopolitan understanding of international law has paradoxically generated great anxiety in national political communities. Indeed, the question today arises: on what grounds, if at all, can the putative supremacy of the sovereign nation-state be justified?[43] This anxiety is evident in a palpable fear of loss of white male privilege as new cultural and political hierarchies emerge. There is a discernable sense that the key concerns are not whether the British economy retracts following Brexit, or whether the American heartland loses ground under the Trump administration. Rather, the sense is that 'we' are now at the bottom and need to 'take back control' not only at the domestic level in terms of political authority, but also at the international level in terms of national sovereignty.

If correct, this diagnosis of the roots of backlash helps to explain several of the 'nonliberal' and 'antiglobal' positions we see articulated today. It also debunks the deterministic arguments of realists like Mearsheimer and Walt. Nationalism is not an end in itself,[44] but a reaction to the current design and

---

global problems in areas such as law and technology, development and international trade.

42 From a *moral* perspective, sovereignty 'upholds egoistic interests of limited communities against the world at large, providing unlimited opportunities for oppression at home'; from a *sociological* perspective, it 'fails to articulate the economic, environmental, technological and ideological interdependencies that link humans all across the globe'; and from a *functional* perspective, it fails to 'deal with global threats such as climate change, criminality, or terrorism, while obstructing such beneficial projects such as furthering free trade and protecting human rights': Martti Koskenniemi, 'What Use for Sovereignty Today?' (2011) 1(1) *Asian Journal of International Law* 61, 61.

43 As Raz has argued, the striking function of human rights law today is precisely to disable or overcome arguments about sovereignty: Joseph Raz, 'Human Rights Without Foundations' (Oxford Legal Studies Research Paper Series, Working Paper No 14/2007, March 2007). More recently, see Joseph Raz, 'The Future of State Sovereignty' (Oxford Legal Studies Research Paper Series, Working Paper No 16/2017, 18 November 2007).

44 Stephen Walt, 'You Can't Defeat Nationalism, So Stop Trying', *Foreign Policy* (Article, 4 June 2019) <https://foreignpolicy.com/2019/06/04/you-cant-defeat-nationalism-so-stop-trying/>.

perceptions of the system. Spreading liberal democracy may have been a key policy of the hegemon, but it is not a necessary feature for the continuation of the core of the liberal legal order. Though some elements of the diagnosis are shared—that the turn to institutional and legal cosmopolitanism by intellectual elites has resulted in 'toxic political effects', and neoliberal economics have eroded the political foundations of the international system—the resulting prognosis diverges, from simply 'bound to fail'[45] to a normative understanding of the roots of, consequences resulting from and potential responses to this backlash moment.

Two primary developments, in particular, laid the ground for these developments. The first is the much-discussed fragmentation of international law as incommensurable trade, investment, environmental and human rights law regimes generated the rise of global governance by experts, while at the same time not providing any means by which to determine the jurisdiction of the competing regimes in particular cases.[46]

The second is the emergence of universal human rights as a purported global morality, often invoked by public lawyers as a response to the experience of deformalisation and as a means by which to override technocratic expert calculation.[47] But paradoxically this has had the effect of translating all preferences into the rights claims of a preference holder. As proliferating committees and tribunals have sought to balance conflicting rights claims, the result has been competing regimes of knowledge and clashing vocabularies of justice which stand in conflict with each other. In order to resolve such conflicts, international bodies and tribunals increasingly have:

---

45   John Mearsheimer, 'Bound to Fail: The Rise and Fall of the Liberal International Order' (2019) 43(4) *International Security* 7, 8.

46   Martti Koskenniemi, 'Global Governance and Public International Law' (2004) 37(3) *Kritische Justiz* 241, 243 (discussing the 'division of international regulation into specialized branches, deferring to special interests and managed by technical experts'). Koskenniemi notes that both Auguste Comte and Emile Durkheim prophesised a future of interdependence which would 'turn an ultimately pre-modern system of sovereignties into a single world society, governed by a single rationality, mastered by technical experts': at 242.

47   Paradoxically, human rights law arose to 'counteract the transfer of political power to "regulators" and managers, scientific and economic experts, and professional negotiators' and its emergence 'gives expression to the search for absolutes in a world whose complexity has created the danger of unfettered relativism and bureaucratic abuse': Martti Koskenniemi, 'Human Rights Mainstreaming as a Strategy for Institutional Power' (2010) 1(1) *Humanity* 47, 47–8.

developed complex balancing practices and rights-exceptions schemes that defer to general considerations of administrative policy, public interest, economic efficiency, and so on—precisely the kind of criteria that rights were once introduced to limit. From providing limits to administrative and bureaucratic discretion, rights became dependent on it.[48]

Together, these developments of regime fragmentation, deformalisation and norm conflict have led to increasing levels of cynicism regarding the chasm between expectation and experience. Expert knowledge is summarily rejected as mere elite privilege, while mainstream legal institutions are viewed as undemocratic and representative of nothing other than either illegitimate impersonal morality or an instrument for somebody else's purposes.

These trend lines reached crisis levels following the 2008 global financial crisis. In combination with the backlash against American neoconservative foreign policy, the devastating effects of decades of neoliberal economic policy became ever more starkly visible with the steady erosion of democratic norms and institutional forms of social justice at both the domestic and international levels. Forms of neoliberal legal order have always depended on and embedded powerful interests, while state sovereignty is always contingent on and reflects relative power among states. The rise of economic nationalism and Trump's America First policies towards liberal international order were simply saying out loud what everyone already knew: America would pursue her own interests, and would aggressively mobilise economic and military power to do so. In the words of Pankaj Mishra, the 'most objectionable thing about Trump may be his discarding of the veil that conceals the scramble for power and wealth among the traditional ruling classes.'[49]

2.3   *Consequences*

In addition to charting these contours and causes of the backlash, we also speculate as to what consequences are likely to follow. We thus ask *how* actors committed to the international rules-based order, such as nation-states, civil society and international organisations, are likely to respond to this backlash.

---

48   Ibid 49. The intractable difficulty is that since 'every significant rights claim involves the imposition of a burden on some other person, the latter may likewise invoke their preference to be free from such burden in rights terms' with the result that 'rights' end up supporting both sides: at 49. As technical expert bodies seek to resolve conflicting claims, some group interests will inevitably be better reflected in the exercise of discretion than others. Politically, this will trigger a backlash in the form of 'novel claims for absolute, nonnegotiable rules to limit bureaucratic discretion': at 48.

49   Pankaj Mishra, 'The Mask it Wears' (2018) 40(12) *London Review of Books*.

Moreover, what will the impact of such responses be for the international legal system and its global institutions?

When a dominant political, legal or social order is under assault, the members of the community within that order tend to have one or more of three instinctive responses. First, to strengthen, reinforce and renew the existing order. Second, to withdraw from the order and retreat to smaller, more proximate orders that are perceived to be less dysfunctional and more advantageous to one's own interests. Third, to imagine and pursue an altogether different type of order, with greater capacity to minimise the threats posed and maximise the opportunities presented by the current challenges to the existing order.

In this article we explore these three response scenarios across four focus areas, namely peace and security; human rights; trade and finance; and the environment. For each focus area we explore what steps Australia and other actors might take to strengthen, reinforce and renew the existing global legal order, norms and institutions. In the process, we examine what risks and opportunities these steps would create, as well as what strategies might be employed to minimise the risks and maximise the opportunities of taking such steps. We then explore across each area what steps Australia and other actors might take to retreat from the global order and engage in smaller, more proximate orders that better promote their core interests. Finally, we consider what measures Australia and other actors might take to reimagine and create a new, more effective and more resilient global order.

Here we set out how these three general response scenarios have unfolded in Western democracies following the interrelated failures of the neoconservative and neoliberal projects discussed above.

2.3.1 Reform and Renew

The first has been to seek to strengthen, reinforce and renew the existing global legal and political order. This impulse is especially evident in mainstream academic and policy responses to backlash. There is a tendency to explain the entirety of backlash phenomena solely in terms of economic factors and material well-being. This usually involves the invocation of Christoph Lakner and Branko Milanovic's 'elephant chart', first published in 2013, illustrating the changes in income distribution (so-called 'winners and losers of globalization') in the world between 1998 and 2008.[50]

---

50   Christoph Lakner and Branko Milanovic, 'Global Income Distribution: From the Fall of the Berlin Wall to the Great Recession' (Policy Research Working Paper No 6719, The World Bank Development Research Group, Poverty and Inequality Team, December 2013). See

The chart shows four groups of people, two of whom have prospered enormously and two of whom have stagnated. The first group is comprised of the middle classes in the emerging economies of China and India, while the second is comprised of the top 0.1%. The third, however, is the middle and lower-middle classes of the developed world which have seen income stagnate with zero growth, while the fourth is the poorest of the poor in developing states. As Koskenniemi has observed, the mainstream liberal understanding is to see the current backlash as a kind of sociological pathology, the solution to which is to double-down and seek to reform and renew existing international legal institutions.[51]

This renewal is said to focus on the need for more principled policy-making, the re-articulation of shared global values, and the reform of existing regimes and institutions to make them more effective and efficient. The analogy is to globalisation as a sort of train ride where both the destination and tracks are already preset and the only problem is that some passengers have been left behind, whether unintentionally or unjustly. The impulse to reform is thus to go back and ensure that everyone gets on the train.[52]

The underlying premise of this view is a recognition of the disastrous consequences over the last few decades of the conjoining of neoliberalism with unending economic austerity.[53] Beginning with the Reagan administration in the 1980s, and accelerating with the Blair and Clinton administrations in the 1990s, we have witnessed the steady collapse of Western social democracy. In the sphere of human rights, a notable feature of this post-Cold War era has been the framing of rights claims in terms solely of civil and political rights while at the same time uncritically accepting the vocabulary of privatisation, markets and austerity. Until recently, the language of economic, social and cultural rights had been almost completely marginalised in politics in the United States.[54] Human rights discourse has thus been relentlessly individualist,

---

 also Branko Milanovic, *Global Inequality: A New Approach for the Age of Globalization* (Belknap Press, 2016).

51 Martti Koskenniemi, *International Law and the Far Right: Reflections on Law and Cynicism* (TMC Asser Press, 2019) 23.

52 Ibid 43.

53 Ibid 22.

54 Thus, Aryeh Neier, founder of Human Rights Watch and former president of the Open Society Foundations, notoriously argued that, unlike civil and political rights, economic and social rights are not 'really' human, and 'the effort to achieve fairer distribution has to take place through the political process': Aryeh Neier, 'Social and Economic Rights: A Critique' (2006) 13(2) *Human Rights Brief* 1.

focused on self-realisation and measured in terms of prosperity, as opposed to advancing any substantive account of economic equality or fairness.[55]

2.3.2 Retreat and Realign

The impulse to reform and renew existing international arrangements is hoped to forestall current threats by states to retreat from global engagement and realign into smaller, more proximate orders or new bilateral relations. What this logic ignores, however, is the need for a *political* analysis of the roots and premises of these reactionary developments. Consider, for example, the following four narratives that have been advanced in the current backlash context.

The first is a recognition of the Janus-faced nature of populism.[56] Today, we are witnessing the rise of various forms of authoritarian populism in constitutional democracies around the world. But other forms of populism are possible, including democratic and antiestablishment populism. The idea that populism itself undermines the very substance of constitutional (liberal) democracy is not only historically inaccurate but also normatively flawed.[57] As Bojan Bugaric has argued, populist parties are the only ones to 'protest against the "consensus at the center" among the center-right and center-left around the idea that there is no alternative to neoliberal globalization.'[58]

This is related to a second narrative of protectionism and harsh anti-immigration policies. In his inaugural address as President, Donald Trump invoked images of shuttered factories strewn like tombstones across the American heartland and of millions of manufacturing and middle-class jobs lost to other countries leaving behind broken communities and families.[59] On this basis, Trump's 'nationalist, authoritarian populism, combined with either economic protectionism or almost left-wing-oriented social policy, promises to protect the ordinary people abandoned by the liberal elites ... "The populist surge is an illiberal democratic response to decades of undemocratic liberal policies."'[60]

---

55   Samuel Moyn, *Not Enough: Human Rights in an Unequal World* (Harvard University Press, 2018). Moyn observes that the rise of human rights has occurred alongside enduring and exploding inequality in today's neoliberal economic globalisation.

56   See Bojan Bugaric, 'Could Populism Be Good for Constitutional Democracy?' (2019) 15 *Annual Review of Law and Social Science* 41, 42.

57   Ibid.

58   Ibid 43. See also David Fontana, 'Unbundling Populism' (2018) 65(6) *UCLA Law Review* 1482. Fontuna discusses the relationship between authoritarian and antiestablishment populism.

59   Donald J Trump, 'The Inaugural Address' (Speech, Washington DC, 20 January 2017).

60   Bugaric (n 56) 43, quoting Cas Mudde, 'Europe's Populist Surge: a Long Time in the Making' (2016) 95(6) *Foreign Affairs* 25, 25.

Looking outward at the international level, we see parallel developments. The third narrative concerns geoeconomics and the return of great power competition, in particular between the United States and China. As Anthea Roberts observes, a striking reversal today defines the new geoeconomic order: on the one hand, there is an increasing *securitisation* of economic policy, ie a greater focus on relative economic gains in view of security implications; while on the other, there is an increasing *economisation* of strategic policy, ie heightened concern over the security risks posed by interdependence and connectivity.[61] This in turn relates to a fourth narrative of ever-increasing corporate power and the extractive role of multinational corporations in the global economy, reflecting again ongoing efforts to project Western power in the name of universal values and norms.[62]

The primary concern of all four narratives is the notion of distribution in relative terms. Each tells a different story regarding which actors have lost and which should be blamed as inequality grows within states and between states. Each of the narratives raises further critical questions and doubts regarding whether any attempt to reform and renew the existing liberal international order can succeed. This is because today's populist movements are not ultimately interested in the reform of institutions they view as illegitimate. As several international legal commentators have observed, these movements feel *defeated*: they have lost and someone else has won. On this view, the analogy of globalisation to a train ride with some passengers left behind is fatally flawed. These political movements hate the idea of the train itself and would not get onboard even if their ticket was prepaid.

All four of these narratives tend to have the effect of prompting states to retreat from the type of global collective action that is accused of creating an unfair distribution of the spoils of globalisation. Once globalisation loses its lustre and is perceived to carry risks that outweigh opportunities, the logical 'plan B' is to withdraw into more proximate, strategic arrangements that offer the promise of more profitable economic, trade and security alliances. But these arrangements might be piecemeal, opportunistic and low on longevity. Moreover, the more unequal the relations are between participants, the more they are themselves susceptible to the same uncomplimentary cost-benefit analysis that led to the unravelling of the great globalisation myth.

---

61 Anthea Roberts, Henrique Choer Moraes and Victor Ferguson, 'Toward a Geoeconomic Order' (2019) 22(4) *Journal of International Economic Law* 4. See also Anthea Roberts, 'Winners and Losers in an Age of Economic Globalization' (Public Lecture, ANU School of Law, 17 June 2019).

62 See Sundhya Pahuja, *Decolonising International Law: Development, Economic Growth and the Politics of Universality* (Cambridge University Press, 2011).

There is therefore something else driving resentment against the liberal international order and its core constitutional form of liberal democracy. For both Weiler and Koskenniemi, this resentment derives from an existential crisis of *values*.[63] Beyond the appealing and seductive idea that individuals have autonomy to choose the destiny of their own lives, values such as patriotism and a sense of identity grounded in nationalist discourses, and obligation and responsibility grounded in religious traditions, each provide sources of meaning beyond mere self-interest. Modern liberal regimes provide the conditions for individual and collective action in the procedural language of democracy, human rights and the rule of law, but they say little about their underlying meaning or content beyond the master value of individual choice. For Weiler therefore, our 'historical mistake was to fail to understand the importance of collective values and to adapt them to a modern progressive narrative'.[64]

2.3.3 Reimagine and Recreate

Faced with these two fraught alternatives, a third possibility is to seek to reimagine and develop an entirely new and different type of international order. The impulse to reform and renew faces the dilemma of how to secure freedom, security and happiness given the managerial critique of international law under conditions of globalisation. Conversely, backlash movements seek an apparently nostalgic return and retreat to a more sovereigntist conception of international legal order, one that is arguably no longer possible under these conditions. The enormous challenge then is how to reclaim international legal contestation as a conversation about global justice and as a non-instrumental standard of criticism of the projects of others.

Before turning to the question of new visions of international legal order, it is important to see how the current backlash moment both challenges and eludes the conceptual parameters of established theories of international law. In the post-Second World War *UN Charter* era, three main accounts of how and why nations obey international law have become dominant. Building on the ideas of the English school of international society and American school of liberal internationalists,[65] the New Haven 'Policy Science' school argued, in the 1970s, that international law has the goal of a world public order of human

---

63 Joseph HH Weiler, 'The European Culture Wars and the Decay of European Democracy' (Public Lecture, Graduate Institute of Geneva, 26 September 2019); Koskenniemi (n 51).

64 Weiler (n 63). While it is possible to 'respect love of society and country, and couple rights and duties, and have healthy respect for one's collective identity and culture', this has not been part of mainstream political discourse.

65 See, eg, Martin Wight, *Power Politics*, eds Hedley Bull and Carsten Holbread (Continuum, rev ed, 2002); Hedley Bull, *The Anarchical Society: A Study of Order in World Politics*

dignity and should be designed to serve particular ends and values by establishing regimes of effective control.[66] The Harvard 'International Legal Process' school sought to show the influence of law in the process of policy decisions in the international realm.[67] These developments laid the foundations for institutionalist accounts of why nations obey international law focusing on how states mutually gain through international cooperation and are unable to maximize preferences by pursuing narrow self-interest.[68] This in turn led to an increasing proliferation of institutional regimes and an era of transnationalism on the basis that legal rules do in fact foster compliance by allowing for the settlement of disputes and bringing order and stability to international relations.[69]

At the same time, there was a revival of Kantian accounts of normativity in international law. Scholars such as Thomas Franck explained rule compliance by states within the proliferating array of international regimes in terms of liberal notions of fairness and legitimacy.[70] In the immediate post-Cold War period with American power and influence at its apex, these institutionalist and liberal accounts combined to make multilateralism and international law seem both triumphant and inevitable. This moment of ascendant liberal internationalism in turn generated a third set of accounts of compliance in terms of a reconceinved understanding of international legal process with scholars such as Harold Koh emphasizing the tripartite dynamic effects of interaction of actors, interpretation and enunciation of international norms, and ultimately

---

(Columbia University Press, 1977); Hersch Lauterpacht, *International Law and Human Rights* (Archon Books, 1950).

66 Myres S McDougal, Harold D Lasswell and Lung-chu Chen, *Human Rights and World Public Order: The Basic Policies of an International Law of Human Dignity* (Oxford University Press, 2nd ed, 2018).

67 Abram Chayes, Thomas Ehrlich and Andreas F Lowenfeld, *International Legal Process: Materials for an Introductory Course* (Little Brown, 1968) vol 1 and 2; Abram Chayes and Antonia Handler Chayes, *The New Sovereignty: Compliance with International Regulatory Agreements* (Harvard University Press, 1995).

68 See, eg, William J Aceves, 'Institutionalist Theory and International Legal Scholarship' (1997) 12(2) *American University Journal of International Law and Policy* 227, 242–256.

69 Robert O Keohane, 'The Demand for International Regimes' (1992) 36(2) *International Organization* 325.

70 Thomas M Franck, *The Power of Legitimacy Among Nations* (Oxford University Press, 1990). Franck argues in favor of three fundamental rights in international relations: first, negative freedom from arbitrary authority; second, positive freedom to promote and protect the capacity for freedom: and third, a liberal right to democratic participation). See also Thomas M Franck, *Fairness in International Law and Institutions* (Clarendon Press, 1995).

internalization of norms into states' domestic legal orders.[71] Similarly, scholars working at the intersection of international law and international relations such as Anne-Marie Slaughter focused on the level of domestic structure and explained compliance with international norms in terms of whether a state can be characterized as 'liberal' in identity.[72]

What each of these institutionalist, cosmopolitan and legal process accounts share in common is an underlying set of assumptions regarding the modern role and function of international law. As Koh has noted, these asumptions are based on an 'epochal transformation of international law' and include the decline of national sovereignty; the increasing density and proliferation of international regimes, institutions and non-state actors; the collapse of the public/private distinction in favor of transnational and global views of norms and governance; the rapid development of international legal norms; and the increasing interpenetration of domestic and international systems.[73]

As argued in this article, each of these assumptions is challenged at a fundamental level by the politics of the current backlash. Populist movements and political parties advocate withdrawal from or severely curtailing the effectiveness of multilateral treaty regimes and institutions; they assail the fundamental normative premises of liberal accounts of democracy, human rights and the rule of law; and they have stridently rejected on national sovereigntist grounds the proposition that international norms should influence or bind decision-making at the domestic level.

In this respect, the current backlash exhibits many of the features traditionally associated with realism in international relations: the view of an anarchic international system navigable only by unitary states answerable to no higher power and taking action only to promote their own goals of survival or aggrandizement. On this realist view, international law and institutions are merely epiphenomena produced by the constant bargaining between states and dependent upon relative power and gain. The renewed emphasis on sovereignty, especially by the major Western powers such as the United States and United Kingdom, certainly may suggest an underlying rejection of the idea of international law as imposing rational constraints and limits on state action

---

71   Harold Hongju Koh, 'Why Do Nations Obey International Law?' (1997) 106(8) *Yale Law Journal* 2599, 2602.

72   Anne-Marie Slaughter, *A New World Order* (Princeton University Press, 2004). Slaughter argues to move beyond state-centric models of international law and focus on the formal and informal bundle of rules, roles and relationships that define and regulate the social practices of state and non-state actors alike in international affairs).

73   Koh (n 71) 2604.

and an embrace of a more broadly Nietszchean will to power view of international relations.

This is not, however, a complete picture. As discussed above, the same elements of power and interest of the major Western states are present and constantly projected within global governance conceptions of international law and institutions, as repeatedly observed by Third World Appoaches to International Law scholars and other critics.[74] Rather, as suggested by Weiler and Koskenniemi, a deeper reevaluation of the foundational values in contemporary global legal ordering is occurring.[75] The neoconservative idea of transformative occupation by force in order to change the internal identity of states to bring them within the community of liberal nation-states is today broadly discredited.[76] Similarly, the neoliberal idea of individual autonomy and choice disembedded from any deeper conceptions of community and tradition is rejected, as powerfully illustrated by the current resurgence of values of nationalism and religion, especially in the economic sphere.[77]

Consider the question of environmental sustainability. Even if GDP growth under the mainstream narrative is pursued relentlessly, everybody will ultimately lose, especially given the devastating and widespread effects of climate change. Instead of accepting that economic growth is the primary goal of the system while seeking to distribute economic gains more fairly, we need instead to rethink and reimagine the system's goals themselves. When transnational companies pollute the environment, powerful states engage in imperial wars or globalisation dislocates communities, we hear appeals to international law as the only public vocabulary connected with a horizon of transcendence. What can international legal history and the narratives embedded in the fabric of modern international law tell us about this puzzle? Do we need to move beyond linear liberal narratives of international law towards greater value pluralist ways of thinking about the relation of freedom and order?

This kind of imaginative work is being pursued today by political theorists and legal philosophers alike. Jean Cohen has thus proposed an approach

---

74 See, eg, BS Chimni, 'International Institutions Today: An Imperial Global States in the Making' (2004) 15(1) *European Journal of International Law* 1. For an exploration of Third World Approaches to International Law scholarship, see James Thuo Gathii, 'The Agenda of Third World Approaches to International Law (TWAIL)' in Jeffrey Dunoff and Mark Pollack (eds), *International Legal Theory: Foundations and Frontiers* (Cambridge University Press, forthcoming).

75 See generally Weiler (n 63); Koskenniemi (n 51).

76 Nehal Bhuta, 'The Antinomies of Transformative Occupation' (2005) 16(4) *European Journal of International Law* 721.

77 See Roberts, Moraes and Ferguson (n 61) who note the current *securitisation* of economic policy and the *economisation* of strategic policy.

NAVIGATING THE BACKLASH AGAINST GLOBAL LAW AND INSTITUTIONS

whereby legal cosmopolitanism can be linked to a project that is distinct from both empire and pure power politics, ie the democratisation of international relations and updating of international law:

> [This] project entails acknowledging the existence and value of a dualistic world order whose core remains the international society of states embedded within (suitably reformed) international institutions and international law, but that also has important cosmopolitan elements and cosmopolitan legal principles (human rights norms) upon which the discourse of transnationalism and governance relies, if inadequately.[78]

In a more philosophical register, Joseph Raz has similarly suggested that

> [t]he best we can hope for is ... [an] international regime of relatively sovereign states subject to extensive international organisations and laws. That requires a pluralistic jurisprudence of international organisations, allowing for great local diversity, of which we have so far seen only small beginnings.[79]

In order to address these questions, there is a need for disciplines of mind and practice that can forestall the premature push towards political closure and seek instead to hold open political judgement to different, even opposing, alternatives. At the same time, there is a need to develop a praxis of international law that is non-instrumentalist, but rather constitutionalist in its aspiration to universality. Critical to these two ideals of political freedom is the need for a deep engagement with comparative law and legal history and a self-critical willingness to engage with the conditions of modernity and modern legal rationality.

3   Peace and Security

3.1   *Key Global Norms and Institutions*
The *UN Charter* created an international peace and security system with unprecedented reach and ambition. At the San Francisco Conference on International Organisation in 1945, the founders of the United Nations were motivated by the need to secure active participation of the most powerful

---

78   Cohen (n 28) 3.
79   Raz, 'The Future of State Sovereignty' (n 43) 1.

states, thus creating an international organisation that 'would not stand idly by in the face of threats to international peace and security'.[80] While the *UN Charter* international peace and security system has never fulfilled its prefatory aspirational objective of ridding the world of the 'scourge of war',[81] it has proven remarkably resilient. It has not eradicated all war, but it has prevented another world war.

Unlike its predecessor, the League of Nations, which failed to attract all key players into its membership, then lost existing key members when international friction escalated through the 1930s, the UN system has attracted and retained great and small powers alike, achieving practically universal membership.[82] An important part of this resilience of the UN collective security system has been the way it has scaffolded global collective action on various regional organisations and arrangements envisaged by Chapter VIII of the *UN Charter*. Thus organisations such as the African Union, the Association of South-East Asian Nations, the European Union, the North Atlantic Treaty Organization (NATO), and the Organization of American States have promoted norms of behaviour and charters of rights that have the effect of promoting peace and security.

The *UN Charter* created the Security Council as not just one of the six principal UN organs, but the one tasked with taking action to maintain international peace and security. Chapter V of the *UN Charter* sets out the composition, functions and procedures of the Council. Article 23 lists the five permanent members of the United Nations, namely China, France, Russia, the United Kingdom and the United States, and notes that the UN General Assembly shall elect the ten remaining non-permanent members that round out the Council's current membership of fifteen.[83] Article 24 bestows upon the Council primary responsibility for the maintenance of international peace and security.[84] Article 25 then reinforces the power of the Security Council to take decisive and meaningful action by specifying that the Council's decisions are binding on all UN member states.[85] Chapter V is also significant for the way in which it shapes the Security Council's decision-making dynamics by granting

---

80   Jeremy Matam Farrall, *United Nations Sanctions and the Rule of Law* (Cambridge University Press, 2007) 58.

81   *UN Charter* (n 1) Preamble.

82   On the League of Nations and its shortcomings, see Paul Kennedy, *The Parliament of Man: The Past, Present, and Future of the United Nations* (Random House, 2006) 8–24.

83   *UN Charter* (n 1) art 23.

84   Ibid art 24(1).

85   Ibid art 25.

the permanent members under Article 27 the power to veto any prospective substantive decision.[86]

The Council's substantive powers are laid out in Chapters VI, VII & VIII of the *UN Charter*. Chapter VI sets out the Council's peaceful settlement powers, including the ability to call on member states to resolve their disputes peacefully through a range of dispute resolution mechanisms such as negotiation, enquiry, mediation, arbitration, conciliation and judicial settlement.[87] Chapter VII provides that the Council shall determine the existence of threats to the peace, breaches of the peace and acts of aggression,[88] and take action accordingly to maintain or restore international peace and security, including applying sanctions short of force,[89] or authorising the use of force itself.[90] Chapter VIII of the *UN Charter* encourages the Council to make use of regional arrangements or agencies in meeting its responsibilities and exercising its powers under Chapters VI and VII.[91]

3.2 *Examples of Backlash*

The dramatic Post-Cold War increase in the UN Security Council's capacity to meet its *UN Charter* responsibilities generated optimism that the Council and the UN system more broadly could finally deliver on the promise of effective global conflict management. But points of difference within the permanent five members have intensified following the divisive 2003 Iraq War and the problematic 2011 NATO intervention in Libya. At the same time, the growing confidence of China and Russia to pursue more aggressive foreign policies in the South China Sea and the Crimea, combined with the turn inward on the part of the US and the UK, has rendered Security Council relations perhaps more contentious than ever. Meanwhile, the value of the alliance system, which maintained stability during the Cold War and continues to play an important role today, is being fundamentally questioned by sceptics in the US and Europe.[92] In this context, some states are turning to alternative multilateral security constellations to pursue their security interests.

---

86   Ibid art 27(3).
87   Ibid art 33.
88   Ibid art 39.
89   Ibid art 41.
90   Ibid art 42.
91   Ibid arts 52–54.
92   See Uri Friedman, 'Trump vs. NATO: It's Not Just About the Money', *The Atlantic* (online, 12 July 2018) <https://www.theatlantic.com/international/archive/2018/07/trump-nato-allies/564881/>; Carol Morello, 'Skepticism Runs deep at NATO as Pompeo Meets with Allies', *The Washington Post* (online, 21 November 2019).

3.3 *Possible Responses*

3.3.1 Reform and Renew

Proposals to reform the Security Council have been on the UN General Assembly agenda since 1979.[93] Most of these efforts have focused on expanding membership to provide greater geographic representation of the full UN membership.[94] However, as Langmore and Thakur have noted, while most UN members can agree in the abstract that expansion should take place, they are not inclined to agree when it becomes clear precisely how concrete proposals will not benefit them.[95] For this reason, some reformist scholars and diplomats have advanced reform initiatives designed to improve the legitimacy, efficacy and credibility of the Security Council within the constraints of the Council's current composition and mandate. Some of these initiatives promote procedural modifications that would improve the Council's accountability to the general UN membership.[96] Others seek to advance recommendations to strengthen the extent to which Security Council decision-making promotes the rule of law,[97] or to increase the capacity of elected members to provide a check on the exercise of power by the permanent five.[98]

---

93 For helpful background, see Peter Nardin, *UN Security Council Reform* (Routledge, 2016).

94 Perhaps the most sophisticated Security Council reform proposal was made by UN Secretary-General Kofi Annan, who advocated expansion to 24 members, with 6 seats would be allocated to Africa, Asia/Pacific, Europe and the Americas. He further requested member states to choose between two models. Model A would create six new permanent seats without veto and three new two-year seats, divided among the major regions. Model B would add eight four-year renewable seats and one new two-year, non-renewable seat. Ultimately neither option was endorsed by the 2005 World Summit. For further details, see Kofi Annan, Secretary-General, *In Larger Freedom: Towards Development, Security and Human Rights for All*, UN Doc A/59/2005 (21 March 2005) 43 [170] .

95 John Langmore and Ramesh Thakur, 'The Elected but Neglected Security Council Members' (2016) 39(2) *The Washington Quarterly* 99, 103.

96 A prominent example is the agenda pursued by more than twenty states under the umbrella of the 'Accountability, Coherence and Transparency' (ACT) group. This agenda includes advocacy against the use of the veto power in cases of mass atrocities, and reforming the Security Council's role in conflict prevention and its relationship with regional organisations. See *Letter dated 14 December 2015 from the Permanent Representative of Liechtenstien to the United Nations addressed to the Secretary-General*, 70th sess, Agenda Item 122, UN Doc S/2015/978 (14 December 2015) annex 1 ('*Code of conduct regarding Security Council action against genocide, crimes against humanity or war crimes*'); Volker Lehmann, 'Reforming the Working Methods of the UN Security Council The Next ACT' (Paper, Friedrich Ebert Stiftung, Dialogue on Globalization, August 2013) <http://library .fes.de/pdf-files/iez/global/10180.pdf>.

97 See Jeremy Farrall and Hilary Charlesworth, *Strengthening the Rule of Law through the UN Security Council* (Routledge, 2016).

98 Jeremy Farrall et al, 'Elected Member Influence in the UN Security Council' (2020) 33(1) *Leiden Journal of International Law* 101.

3.3.2 Retreat and Realign

The second scenario would involve states responding to the backlash by disengaging from the Security Council and the *UN Charter* collective security framework it serves. According to this scenario, states might retreat and realign with like-minded and/or regional neighbour states to cooperate on, or at least reach a mutual understanding about the parameters of, more proximate frameworks of principles to manage the risk of future violent conflict within and between such states. There are a number of examples of regional or sub-regional security arrangements, including the Organization for Security and Cooperation in Europe, NATO, and the Association of South-East Asian Nations Regional Forum. These arrangements are traditionally viewed as falling within and complementing the *UN Charter* framework for security. But it is likely that these arrangements would form the first port of call for states who become disenchanted with the Security Council.

3.3.3 Reimagine and Recreate

This third scenario is both the most fascinating and the most challenging to flesh out. If the global community were to start from scratch with the mission of creating a new, fit-for-purpose framework of norms and institutions for maintaining global peace and security, what would they look like? Who would sit at the most important decision-making tables, for how long, and with what powers? What structures, mechanisms, norms and resources would be required to guarantee the responsiveness, credibility and resourcefulness of the new system? It is beyond the scope of this article to speculate in depth on the likely substance of such new peace and security norms and institutions. But in terms of process, a starting-point could be the lessons derived from UN efforts to facilitate peacemaking at the national level. For example, the *UN Guidance for Effective Mediation* identifies the concept of *inclusivity* as one of seven mediation fundamentals which increase the prospects of a sustainable peace agreement.[99] In a peacemaking context, *inclusivity* refers to the need to consider not just the views of the parties to recently concluded conflict, typically former government and rebel groups, but critically to take into account the perspectives of the many other stakeholders in post-conflict society.[100] These might be women's groups, religious communities, civil society organisations, or private sector corporations. Strategies to promote inclusivity include engaging different perspectives throughout the various phases of a

---

99   *Strengthening the Role of Mediation in the Peaceful Settlement of Disputes, Conflict Prevention and Resolution: Report of the Secretary-General*, UN Doc A/66/811 (25 June 2012) annex I ('*Guidance for Effective Mediation*') paras 16–52.

100   Ibid para 29.

peacemaking process, by using social media and opinion polls, to inform and engage a wide range of participants.[101] It should be possible in an increasingly interconnected world to devise a consultative process that provides an opportunity for not just 'all the Peoples of the United Nations', but *all people* in the world to feel included and therefore to hold a sense of ownership over and commitment to the new rules and institutions that emerge from the global constitution-making process.

4 Human Rights

4.1 *Key Global Norms and Institutions*

The universalisation after 1945 (and especially post-1989) of human rights discourses and frameworks is often seen as either a metaphor for or indicator of some wider globalisation processes.[102] On this account, if anything appears to have globalised during the late 20th to early 21st century era of globalisation it was norms (if not institutions) of human rights, and the human rights vernacular itself. One of the greatest achievements of the UN has been the creation, codification or adoption by states, acting largely together, of a new corpus of international norms and institutions dedicated to the promotion and protection of human rights. The progressive advancement of human rights norms, instrumentalities and institutions proceeded relatively smoothly throughout the second half of the 20th century. For better or worse—and perhaps partly due to their inherent susceptibility to appropriation by diverse sets of actors— human rights became a key feature and language of political discourse and engagement at local, national and international levels. After the 1948 *Universal Declaration of Human Rights*, the entry into force in the mid-1970s of the widely-ratified twin core international covenants has been followed by a whole array of subject-specific international instruments (and associated treaty mechanisms and other architectures) on issues ranging from racial discrimination to disability to the rights of children.[103] Moreover, coming into being alongside the UN human rights system have been certain regional charters, conventions, judicial and other mechanisms, notably the European, African and Inter-American regional systems.

---

101   Ibid para 34.

102   See, eg, André Siciliano, 'The Role of the Universalization of Human Rights and Migration in the Formation of a New Global Governance' (2012) 9(16) *SUR International Journal on Human Rights* 109.

103   See, eg, Thomas Buergenthal, 'The Evolving International Human Rights System' (2006) 100(4) *The American Journal of International Law* 783.

Of course, this trajectory of institutionalisation of human rights in politics and international relations has not necessarily yielded the substantive rights outcomes aspired to, or indeed even manifested in formal domestic implementation measures consequent upon international commitments on human rights.[104] Meanwhile, among other things many voices have consistently challenged the claimed cultural universality and non-relativity of the human rights agenda and normative scheme, or criticised its alleged use as a tool or justification for illegitimate and imperial external interference in other societies. There have also been—and remain—notable systemic weaknesses in the UN human rights system, including the underperformance of the Human Rights Commission leading to the creation of the Human Rights Council out of the 2005 round of UN reforms endorsed by the World Summit Outcome document.[105] The UN system's legitimacy and effectiveness can be subject to a range of other critiques, notably that their sometimes undemanding nature has helped promote shallow, ritualistic 'compliance' and engagement patterns by states whose substantive human rights record is at odds with their stated commitments to the scheme.[106] Nevertheless, even if one claims that human rights norms and systems do not constitute even a notional constraining and remediating factor on the exercise of raw power, the international human rights phenomenon and its forums indisputably provided a language and some channels by which to challenge power. Thus despite the enduring critiques sketched above (and many others), it is possible to describe in broad terms a narrative whereby human rights became a dialect and currency of politics in which it was possible to engage with injustice and contest (if not always constrain) power, and so became a key part of a rules-based international order.

104　See, eg, Douglass Cassel, 'Does International Human Rights Law Make a Difference?' (2001) 2(1) *Chicago Journal of International Law* 121; Oona A Hathaway, 'Do Human Rights Treaties Make a Difference?' (2002) 111(8) *Yale Law Journal* 1935; Eric Neumayer, 'Do International Human Rights Treaties Improve Respect for Human Rights?' (2005) 49(6) *Journal of Conflict Resolution* 925; Jack L Goldsmith and Eric A Posner, *The Limits of International Law* (Oxford University Press, 2005); Wade M Cole, 'Human Rights as Myth and Ceremony? Reevaluating the Effectiveness of Human Rights Treaties, 1981–2007' (2012) 117(4) *American Journal of Sociology* 1131.

105　*2005 World Summit Outcome*, GA Res 60/1, UN Doc A/Res/60/1 (24 October 2005, adopted 16 September 2005) paras 119–131.

106　Hilary Charlesworth and Emma Larking, 'Introduction: The Regulatory Power of the Universal Periodic Review' in Hilary Charlesworth and Emma Larking (eds), *Human Rights and the Universal Periodic Review: Rights and Ritualism* (Cambridge University Press, 2014) 1.

4.2 Examples of Backlash

The rise of populist and/or illiberal politics in Western democracies and the renewed confidence and brazen approaches of autocracies and 'cosmetic democracies' threatens to undermine and unravel the achievements represented by the multilateral human rights framework. That system was built—including during key periods first of decolonisation and later of post-Soviet democratisation—on the leadership and example of various countries, with the US at the forefront of championing human rights. It follows that perhaps the single most significant possible example of backlash against the global human rights system was the June 2018 US withdrawal from membership of the UN Human Rights Council.[107] Is this action best characterised as mere strong critique or discontent, or as evincing 'fundamental resistance to and rejection of' the multilateral law-based system and its institutions, of which the Human Rights Council is the peak body?[108] One question is whether the human rights context illustrates the rigidity of conceiving 'backlash' as rejection in an all-or-nothing sense of the rules-based system. This is because the Council is only one part of that system, and because the US will probably continue (even if just for calculated foreign policy strategy reasons) to frame values-based positions in international affairs by reference to universal human rights. It will simply do so outside of the Council.

Meanwhile, one important aspect of the pro-Brexit message in the UK has arguably been a severe reaction to the perceived legal imperialism of the Strasbourg courts on immigration-related issues, such as the UK's legal ability to extradite or deport individuals engaged in jihadist incitement and hate-speech.[109] Again, some Brexiteers' demand was not for reform of the European Convention system but for existentialist exit from it and from the 1988 *Human Rights Act* that implemented the Convention. More generally, state respect for and protection of civil and political rights in particular have been degraded by the rise of so-called 'illiberal democratic states' in Central

---

107 Michael Pompeo and Nikki Haley, 'Remarks on the UN Human Rights Council' (Joint Statement, United States Mission to the United Nations, 19 June 2018) <https://usun .usmission.gov/remarks-on-the-un-human-rights-council/>.

108 See Jolyon Ford, 'The Multilateral Human Rights System: Systemic Challenge or Healthy Contestation?' (2020) *Maryland Journal of International Law* (forthcoming).

109 See, eg, Katja Ziegler, *Elizabeth Wicks and* Loveday Hodson (*eds*) *The UK and European Human Rights: A Strained Relationship? (Hart Publishing, 2015).* For an example of contemporary UK media treatment of this issue that arguably fed into sentiment in the years leading up to the Brexit referendum, see Martin Beckford, 'ECHR Blocks More Deportations from the UK than Any Other Country', *Daily Telegraph* (online, 1 May 2012) <https://www.telegraph.co.uk/news/uknews/law-and-order/9239417/European-Court -of-Human-Rights-blocks-more-deportations-from-UK-than-any-other-country.html>.

Europe and the backslide of democracy more broadly. Not all of those settings necessarily represent systemic backlash, even if the permissive environment created by the US leadership vacuum has probably emboldened and enabled moves inimical to the 'progressive realisation' narrative described above. In Australia's case, it remains an open question whether government postures on the international human rights system can properly be characterised as evincing incipient or substantive elements of a rejection, as such, of that rules-based system. One plausible characterisation might be that if anything there is some degree of continuity in the sense of Australian selectivity around international human rights: fulsome engagement in general, but reactivity or non-engagement (but not necessarily rejection and exit) in relation to some particular human rights themes, notably in relation to treatment of irregular migrants.[110]

4.3   *Possible Responses*

For the purposes of exploring possible responses to the patterns outlined above, we might take the UN Human Rights Council as the most high-profile multilateral institution in the international human rights system.

4.3.1   Reform and Renew

One connotation of 'backlash' is the implied sense of desire by some constituencies for return to a previous equilibrium. Although the US was sceptical about the Human Rights Council from its creation (and well before Trumpism), one possible response is for states, including Australia, to revisit the governance of the Council and its mandate, agenda-setting and processes so as, in effect, to reform the Council such that the US feels comfortable engaging again and resuming its membership. In practical terms, any such re-engagement probably lies on the other side of a Trump presidency. However, such reform and renewal might alienate other members, depending on what changes in the Council's current practices are required to appease the US. This reminds us that backlash is not static, and may generate counter-acting forces.

4.3.2   Retreat and Realign

As noted above, it is not obvious that Australia itself is an exemplar of rejection-level backlash in the human rights context. Nevertheless, if the Council is perceived as ineffective, for example because of the US withdrawal, Australia might conceivably seek to realign its focus on institutional mechanisms by

---

110   See Jolyon Ford, 'Backlash against a Rules-Based International Human Rights Order? An Australian Perspective' (2020) 38 *Australian Year Book of International Law* 175.

expanding the emphasis on human rights within regional mechanisms (principally ASEAN, Pacific Islands Forum, the Commonwealth) or country-specific bilateral human rights dialogues (eg the one with China since the 2000s). This 'retreat' to more proximate, smaller-scale institutions is easier said than done, of course. Australia's membership or affiliation with regional groupings is relatively precarious. It may not seek to expend political capital on pushing human rights issues in these forums, for example in relation to the Philippines where an illiberal democratic government remains a key partner in countering violent extremism.

4.3.3 Reimagine and Recreate

There have long been political and cultural-doctrinal challenges to the claimed universality of the multilateral UN- and treaty-based global human rights system. The 'cultural relativity' and 'Asian values' debates in human rights illustrated tensions in a system that was sometimes portrayed as projecting Western culturally-specific values or privileging individual rights over communitarian concerns. Many of those tensions remain, and manipulation of these arguments remains an important tool for more autocratic states to delegitimise human rights mechanisms and norms. Nevertheless, the scale and embeddedness of the international human rights system makes it difficult to conceive of a wholesale reconstitution of that system. Various other factors also militate against wholesale change. Some relate to issues such as timing, given the prevailing global political climate for multilateral consensus, and the fact that (unlike the UN Security Council, for example) the UN human rights system underwent significant institutional reform comparatively recently, in the mid-2000s. Other factors are more confronting for those with a normative commitment to advancing human rights, such as the fact that while it has seen backlash from some key players, this may be due to domestic political reasons other than the utility of the current system itself. Seen this way, the human rights institutional status quo is useful for states seeking to leverage human rights to influence others, as well as for states seeking to avoid human rights criticism by engaging in the rituals of participation and performance in the Council and Universal Periodic Review in particular.[111] The existing system is unlikely to be recreated or reimagined partly because it can accommodate states with a poor human rights record: they can live with the system, and use their 'engagement' with it as insulation from criticism. In this context, the 'backlash' moment perhaps offers less of a challenge and more of an opportunity to refresh that status quo.

---

111   See Charlesworth and Larking (n 106).

The above analysis has the inherent limitation that the Council is merely one artefact (albeit a significant one) of the wider international human rights and treaty-body system. Yet this distinction puts at issue reactions, by reference to 'backlash' concepts, to the US withdrawal in 2018. This is because Washington framed its exit not in terms of a rejection of international human rights law, but as a principled position in the context of deep hypocrisy in the Council, a position calculated to engender reforms that would better advance the wider human rights project.[112] How, then, do we analyse a backlash that is seen as weakening (and that defunds) a key institution, yet is articulated in terms that reinforce, at least rhetorically, the validity and importance of the wider system?

5 Trade and Finance

5.1 *Key Global Norms and Institutions*
One of the perceived triumphs of the post-World War II global order was the creation and pursuit of an integrated global economy premised on an ideal of free trade. Trade liberalisation, managed internationally by multilateral institutions and domestically by states, was to provide a pathway to 'lift[ing] all boats' and growing the global pie.[113] It would also pay additional dividends in greater possibilities for peace, security, human rights, and global coordination to address challenges such as migration and climate change. Protectionism and economic or political fragmentation threatened all of these goals. If sometimes trade liberalisation led to harsh impacts on certain industries or regions, the environment, or human rights, these impacts would be transitory or localised and were to be tempered or smoothed by overall gains in economic welfare and living standards.[114]

The United States helped create and lead this postwar global economic order, leading other nations in constructing the foundations of this new liberal international economic system through multilateral institutions and agreements such as the International Monetary Fund ('IMF'),[115] the World

---

112 See Pompeo and Haley (n 107); Ford, 'The Multilateral Human Rights System: Systemic Challenge or Healthy Contestation?' (n 108).

113 See Sperling (n 8) describing the origins of the phrase 'a rising tide lifts all boats' in reference to globalisation.

114 Jeff D Colgan and Robert O Keohane, 'The Liberal Order is Rigged: Fix it Now or Watch It Wither', (May/Jun 2017) *Foreign Affairs* 36.

115 *Articles of Agreement of the International Monetary Fund*, opened for signature 27 December 1945, 2 UNTS 39 (entered into force 27 December 1945).

Bank, and the *General Agreement on Tariffs and Trade* ('GATT'),[116] and later the World Trade Organization ('WTO').[117] This system of 'embedded liberalism', spearheaded and dominated by a hegemonic United States, was intended to promote economic openness while providing governments with tools to regulate and manage domestic stability and policies.[118] This framework succeeded in creating a liberal hegemonic order that helped foster unprecedented levels of economic growth throughout the post-war period and much of the Cold War. Trade liberalisation and increased security and cooperation also appeared to foster shared norms and goals underpinning and sustaining the liberal international order, at least for those favourably positioned within this order.

While this system successfully expanded flows of capital and goods, it also suffered challenges and crises, exacerbated in part due to its successes in intertwining economies and liberalising trade across the globe. New political alignments, power dynamics and economic stagnation contributed to the collapse of the Bretton Woods system and a re-ordering of the international monetary order in the 1970s. While the collapse of the Cold War initially seemed to reinforce the spread of markets, liberal democracy, and greater interdependence among states, it also ultimately preceded the loosening of many of the foundations of this framework. The Asian Financial Crisis in the the late 1990s and the pain it rapidly inflicted further sparked critiques and conflicts about the framework, normative underpinnings, and uneven power distribution with the global economic framework.

The global financial crisis which began in 2007 struck a further devastating blow to the postwar global economic order. Public and elite support for a rules-based global economy across the globe has cratered in its wake, as globalisation appeared to unleash financial forces and spawn crises which seemed beyond the capacity of the actors and institutions of the international economic architecture to contain or address. In the US and other industrialised countries, it demonstrated a fact of the financially globalised system that was already long apparent to citizens of emerging economies: when finance flows unburdened across borders, relatively small economic ripples can quickly become tsunamis, ruining whole economies. Scepticism has grown towards the specific multilateral economic institutions and trade agreements established to promote the rules-based economy.

---

116   *General Agreement on Tariff and Trade*, opened for signature 1 January 1948, 55 UNTS 187 (provisionally entered into force 1 January 1948).

117   *Marrakesh Agreement Establishing the World Trade Organization*, opened for signature 15 April 1994, 1867 UNTS 3 (entered into force 1 January 1995).

118   G John Ikenberry, 'The End of Liberal International Order?' (2017) 94(1) *International Affairs* 7, 15–17.

Economists and policymakers have long warned that without mechanisms that soften the blow of trade agreements on specific groups of middle class workers and prevent the diversion of wealth to those who already have vast resources, popular discontent with open economic borders would multiply.[119] This has proven to be the case in many developed economies, most notably the United States and the United Kingdom. Millions of manufacturing jobs have been lost to countries with cheaper labour and, moreover, improved access to those markets through multilateral trade agreements in the past few decades.

The sting of these developments has been exacerbated as the pushes towards deregulation and trade liberalisation have been joined by the seemingly unstoppable advances of technology and financial innovation. Improved automation and other technological developments threaten to render jobs and industries just as obsolete as the prior technologies and processes they replace, in both developed and developing countries. They have also led to financial innovations that enhance capital mobility at the same time that these new instruments 'transfer risk of all kinds on a far larger scale'.[120] As virtual facilities replace physical ones, globalisation now also means that 'money can flow anywhere, instantly, regardless of national origin and boundaries, and once-exotic foreign markets have been able to dramatically increase their attractiveness as destinations for capital'.[121] Crucially, however, much of the wealth and benefits of these developments is flowing asymmetrically, crossing national borders but stratifying unevenly along divides such as class and urban/rural boundaries, while fueling populist and nativist demands.

5.2   *Examples of Backlash*
In the wake of these destabilising forces, the international economic order is facing serious challenges that can be viewed as a backlash to the institutions, agreements, and normative goals of globalisation, with key players in this framework seeking to retreat from international institutions and global governance mechanisms and rules. Shortly after his election, President Trump withdrew the United States from the Trans-Pacific Partnership ('TPP'),[122]

---

119   See generally Dani Rodrik, *Straight Talk on Trade: Ideas for a Sane World Economy* (Princeton University Press, 2018).

120   Chris Brummer, 'How International Financial Law Works (and How It Doesn't)' (2011) 99(2) *Georgetown Law Journal* 257, 266.

121   Ibid.

122   *Trans-Pacific Partnership Agreement*, signed 4 February 2016, [2016] ATNIF 2 (not yet in force).

sought to replace the North American Free Trade Agreement ('NAFTA'),[123] and thereafter continued to pursue protectionist trade policies and throw up trade barriers while rejecting multilateral institutions and approaches.[124] The United States, which once 'pressed harder than any nation' for the establishment of the WTO,[125] subsequently blocked appointments to a key WTO dispute settlement mechanism that brought 'certainty and predictability to the rules-based multilateral trading order', sending it into 'hibernation' and effectively paralysing it—flipping the previous political dynamic so completely that states that previously criticised the WTO's coercive pressures to liberalise their markets are now 'campaigning for its protection'.[126] Just weeks later, the United Kingdom began the formal withdrawal process from the European Union or 'Brexit', leaving a gaping hole in the bloc as it exits its single market and security and other governance arrangements.[127]

Underscoring these developments are the ways in which the anti-globalisation rhetoric and nationalism deployed by the leaders of the US and UK are being mirrored around the globe. Focusing on the claim that globalisation has been hijacked and 'rigged' by 'cosmopolitan elites', leaders in countries as diverse as the Philippines, Poland, Turkey, and Australia, among others, are combining 'a populist demand for a redistribution of gains' with 'a nationalist move to reclaim sovereignty from international arrangements',[128] while attempting to harden borders to migration as well as trade. These developments, challenging the core normative goals in addition to the frameworks of

---

123   *North Atlantic Free Trade Agreement*, United States–Canada–Mexico, signed 17 December 1992, (entered into force 1 January 1994).

124   Mark Copelovitch and Jon CW Pevehouse, 'International Organizations in a New Era of Populist Nationalism' (2019) 14 *The Review of International Organizations* 169, 170.

125   David E Sanger, 'Senate Approves Pact to Ease Trade Curbs; A Victory for Clinton', *The New York Times* (online, 2 December 1994) <https://www.nytimes.com/1994/12/02/us/senate -approves-pact-to-ease-trade-curbs-a-victory-for-clinton.html>.

126   See Prabhash Ranjan, 'WTO Appellate Body Going Into Slumber is a Serious Setback', *Financial Express* (online, 24 December 2019) <https://www.financialexpress.com/opin-ion/wto-appellate-body-going-into-slumber-is-a-serious-setback/1802397/>, noting that on 11 December 2019, the World Trade Organization's Appellate Body (AB) 'went into hibernation' as a result of US blocking new appointments, and describing this development as 'a serious setback for the rules-based multilateral trading order' and the rule of law as new appeals would now plunge into a 'void'.

127   Steven Erlanger, 'A Texas-Size Defeat for the E.U.: Brexit is Here', *The New York Times* (online, 29 January 2020) <https://www.nytimes.com/2020/01/29/world/europe/brexit -brussels-eu.html>.

128   Copelovitch and Pevehouse (n 124) 170.

economic liberalisation, are playing out in a variety of ways with significant implications for the future of the liberal global international economic order.

5.3   *Possible Responses*
As the ground shifts below the global economic order, it is important to examine how and where this order might be remade or replaced.

5.3.1   Reform and Renew
The commencement of Brexit has occurred with a finality that appears to mark the end of hopes that the UK and US-led retreat from global economic institutions can be undone at the ballot box in future elections. At the same time, however, the retreat of these key players has in many ways strengthened the institutions they have left or threatened, at least in terms of the commitment levels of their remaining members. In Europe, 'the shock of Brexit has produced a unity among the remaining 27 nations that is hard to find on any other issue' as the threat of other nations' withdrawal has at least momentarily dissipated.[129] As noted above, in the wake of the US attacks, nations who once questioned the WTO's methods and impact are now pushing to strengthen or preserve at least its presence. Without the hegemonic dominance of the US, global economic institutions and mechanisms might renew and reform along more globally inclusive and domestically protective (as opposed to protectionist) lines.

5.3.2   Retreat and Realign
Much of the fate of the global international order rests on whether the current retreat from global governance remains one largely limited to an Anglo-American development, or whether nationalism, strengthened by populism and nativism as discussed above, succeeds in not just fraying but severing the formal and informal ties that form the global economic architecture. This would open up possibilities for re-alignment where the unipolar moment is finally subsumed in a world of shifting, smaller alliances with more globally modest goals but potentially more locally sustainable impacts. Whatever the outcome, this possibility may be more fraught as states would be forced to re-align with others with whom they may share certain strategic goals but not, for example, even superficially similar approaches to human rights or environmental protection. Much also depends on whether nations experiencing a rise in populism can maintain responsiveness to their own domestic populations

---

129   Erlanger (n 127).

or whether they will seek to shore up their own constituencies by stamping out the conduits for dissent and democracy, thereby narrowing both domestic and international spaces for alignment. In a similar vein, as populist-led or more protectionist states seek to harden their national borders, they may attempt to address risk and contagion by retreating to ever narrower international spaces, where multilateral regimes give way to the bilateral or transactional relationships to which Anglo-American leaders appear to have pinned their hopes for shows of economic strength. However, the apparent safety of national sovereignty and self-interest may prove to be illusory. Retreat to a world of autonomous sovereign states may indeed protect against some types of risks and contagion, but may also render de-coupled states more fragile and with fewer resources and allies to address other risks, such as the cross-border challenges posed by climate change. States may be forced to realign in response to new threats, though these realignments will likely be more uneven, sporadic, and thinner than the multilateral regimes eroded by backlash.

5.3.3   Reimagine and Recreate

It is tempting to reimagine a future global economic order which addresses and escapes the failures of the past, perhaps supported and facilitated by technology and innovation. While it is unlikely that the previous order can simply be shored up and restored to its previous breadth with a few simple tweaks, the current moment could act as the crucible that leads to the creation of a new, more inclusive and socially and financially stable order.

Some current developments might prove to be glimmers of such a future. For example, after the US withdrawal from TPP, other nations continued to negotiate for trade liberalisation with the aim of creating a liberalised trade zone within the Asia-Pacific. Europe after Brexit might foster a new 'container' within which illiberal democracies could gain greater measures of security and protection to replace the one now fading, one that might sap the strength or forge greater resistance to excesses of the ideologues now in power. Even the US under Trump renegotiated rather than torpedoed NAFTA, now branded the 'USMCA', and updated it with changes drafted with bipartisan domestic support intended to protect workers, patients in need of cheaper medications, and intellectual property in the US. Moreover, as the existing order erodes, globalisation or some of its normative goals might grow more visible and thicker in informal ties or norms than formal, institutional arrangements that might otherwise stifle flexibility and diversity. The crucibles created by the crises and challenges ahead may yet contain the seeds of a more sustainable international economic order.

6 The Environment

6.1 Key Global Norms and Institutions

International environmental norms and institutions have developed more recently than some of the other international norms and institutions discussed in previous sections. Yet at the same time, global environmental challenges are stressing even these relatively new institutions and norms. We are living in the Anthropocene—the first era where human activity significantly and irrevocably impacts the global environment.[130] This impact brings significant challenges both for international environmental law and international law more generally. Rising sea levels will threaten the habitability of many low-lying States and island nations, polluting fresh water reserves and increasing salinity.[131] Some States risk losing their territory to sea level rise entirely. It is predicted that the impact of these changes will be disproportionally borne by the developing world.[132]

Although some earlier conventions and cases dealt with environmental issues,[133] it was not until 1972 that the foundations of modern environmental law were laid. The 1972 Stockholm Conference on the Human Environment was the first intergovernmental conference and provided a catalyst for the rapid expansion of environmental law.[134] In the almost 50 years since the Stockholm Conference, many fundamental international environmental treaties have been negotiated, drafted and entered into force—including the *UN Framework Convention on Climate Change* ('*UNFCC*').[135] The move toward a framework approach for environmental law allows States to progressively negotiate new binding commitments: but this approach is ultimately only as successful as States are willing to allow. This is illustrated by the failure of the second

---

130 See generally Jeremy Davies, *The Birth of the Anthropocene* (University of California Press, 2016).

131 Imogen Saunders, 'The Limits of the Natural State Doctrine: Rocks, Islands and Artificial Intervention in a Changing World' in Donald R Rothwell and David Letts (eds), *Law of the Sea in South East Asia: Environmental, Navigational and Security Challenges* (Routledge, 2019) 118, 127.

132 Intergovernmental Panel on Climate Change, *Climate Change 2014: Impacts, Adaptation and Vulnerability Part B: Regional Aspects*, C B Fields et al (eds) (Cambridge University Press, 2014) 1347.

133 See, eg, *Trail Smelter Case (United States v Canada)* (*Arbitral Awards*) (1935) 3 RIAA 1905.

134 Edith Brown Weiss, 'The Evolution of International Environmental Law' (2011) 54 *Japanese Yearbook of International Law* 1, 6.

135 *United Nations Framework Convention on Climate Change*, opened for signature 9 May 1992, 1771 UNTS 107 (entered into force 21 March 1994) ('*UNFCC*').

commitment phase of the *Kyoto Protocol*, as set out in the *Doha Amendment*:[136] the amendment has never entered into force, and only 7 of the 37 countries with binding emissions targets under the *Doha Amendment* have ratified it.[137]

Environmental concerns also bring challenges outside the field of international environmental law per se. Traditional and fundamental norms of international law may not be able to be easily reconciled with the realities of the impact of climate change. For example, conceptions of Statehood may struggle with a complete loss of territory: and traditional definitions of refugees would not cover those fleeing a land that has become uninhabitable through the impacts of climate change.[138] In addition to sea level rises, extreme weather events such as hurricanes, droughts and floods are set to intensify.[139] Such disasters could dramatically increase the number of internally and internationally displaced people, at a scale previously unseen.

Further, there are intersections with international environmental norms and other areas of international law. The link between trade and the environment has long been recognised: and the UNFCC contains a provision designed to protect domestic measures combatting climate change from falling foul of the chapeau of the exception provision of the *General Agreement on Tariffs and Trade*.[140] Yet the World Trade Organisation ('WTO') dispute settlement panels and Appellate Body have been reluctant to recognise the possibility of non-WTO treaties modifying WTO obligations[141]—it remains to be seen if, when such a measure is challenged, a WTO Panel or the Appellate Body would take the UNFCC into account.

---

136   *Doha Amendment to the Kyoto Protocol*, opened for signature 8 December 2012, [2016] ATNIF 24.

137   'The Doha Amendment', *United Nations Climate Change* (Web Page) <https://unfccc.int/process/the-kyoto-protocol/the-doha-amendment>; 'Status of the Doha Amendment to the Kyoto Protocol', *United Nations Treaty Collection* (Web Page) <https://treaties.un.org/Pages/ViewDetails.aspx?src=TREATY&mtdsg_no=XXVII-7-c&chapter=27&clang=_en>.

138   Angela Williams, 'Turning the Tide: Recognising Climate Change Refugees in International Law' (2008) 30(4) *Law and Policy* 502, 507–8.

139   Tim Stephens, 'Disasters, International Environmental Law and the Anthropocene' in Susan C Breau and Katja L H Samuel (eds) *Research Handbook on Disasters and International Law* (Edward Elgar, 2016) 153.

140   UNFCC (n 136) art 3(5); *Marrakesh Agreement Establishing the World Trade Organization*, opened for signature 15 April 1994, 1867 UNTS 3 (entered into force 1 January 1995) annex 1A ('*General Agreement on Tariffs and Trade 1994*') art XX.

141   See further discussion in Imogen Saunders, 'Navigating the Backlash: Re-Integrating WTO and Public International Law?' (2020) 38 *Australian Year Book of International Law* 134.

6.2 *Examples of Backlash*

Despite overwhelming international scientific evidence and consensus, contestation around the causes and consequences of the phenomenon of climate change has inhibited the development of effective global environmental regulatory mechanisms. International environmental law is facing a dual challenge. It aspires to prevent the worst impacts of climate change and its associated environmental catastrophes, or at least to mitigate their effects and impacts. At the same time, it is constrained by State behaviour that prioritises short term national interest over longer term global needs.

The domestic political capital that can be gained by such strategies is perhaps best illustrated by the US's withdrawal from the *Paris Agreement* in 2017. In his official statement, President Trump positioned the withdrawal as a triumph of domestic protectionism against non-American internationalism:

> The Paris Climate Accord is simply the latest example of Washington entering into an agreement that disadvantages the United States to the exclusive benefit of other countries, leaving American workers—who I love—and taxpayers to absorb the cost in terms of lost jobs, lower wages, shuttered factories, and vastly diminished economic production.[142]

This positioning did not result in popular support across party lines: but did achieve majority support from Republican voters.[143]

Recently, Brazil has responded to global concern over forest fires in the Amazon by characterising the matter as an issue of national sovereignty, while denying a 'climate change catastrophe'.[144] The positioning of national interest in inherent opposition to environmental protection poses a great risk to the success of international environmental cooperative efforts: particularly in the context of populism and rising nationalism.

---

142 Donald J Trump, 'Statement by President Trump on the Paris Climate Accord' (Remarks, President of the United States, 1 June 2017) <https://www.whitehouse.gov/briefings -statements/statement-president-trump-paris-climate-accord/>.

143 Scott Clement and Brady Dennis, 'Post-ABC poll: Nearly 6 in 10 oppose Trump Scrapping Paris Agreement', *The Washington Post* (online, 6 June 2017) <https://www.washington post.com/news/energy-environment/wp/2017/06/05/post-abc-poll-nearly-6-in-10 -oppose-trump-scrapping-paris-agreement/>.

144 '"There is No Climate Catastrophe": Brazil Hits Back as Amazon Continues to Burn', *SBS News* (online, 12 September 2019) <https://www.sbs.com.au/news/there-is-no-climate -catastrophe-brazil-hits-back-as-amazon-continues-to-burn>.

6.3 *Possible Responses*

6.3.1 Reform and Renew

There are positive signs that States are embracing international environmental challenges through the structures of the *Paris Agreement*. The very structures of the *Paris Agreement* themselves act to minimise the negative effects of the US withdrawal:[145] including allowing the US to easily re-join the *Paris Agreement* at a future date if there is a change of administration or US policy.[146] In this way, the *Paris Agreement* itself can be seen as *reform and renewal* of international environmental law following the problems that beset the *Kyoto Protocol*. There, US non-participation caused a cascade effect, with both Australia and Canada citing it as a reason for their decisions to not participate (in the case of Australia) or withdraw (in the case of Canada) from the Protocol.[147] In contrast, despite the US's withdrawal from the *Paris Agreement*, Australia, Canada and other major economies (and emitters) such as China, the EU and India have stood by their Paris commitments.

6.3.2 Retreat and Realign

The disproportionate impact of climate change has left smaller, more vulnerable States at risk of being marginalised. This was evident in the reporting following the 2019 Pacific Forum. Although the Forum released the 'Kainaki II Declaration' which set out emission reduction goals and statements of support for the UNFCC, the work of the Intergovernmental Panel on Climate Change and the commitments made under the *Paris Agreement*,[148] it also omitted any reference to coal, and watered down previously drafted language on zero-net emission and total global temperature warming goals[149]—at Australia's insistence.[150] This led to outcry from Pacific Island States, with the Fijian Prime Minster Frank Bainimarama describing the Australian approach as 'very

---

145 See Johnathan Pickering et al, 'The Impact of the US Retreat from the Paris Agreement: Kyoto Revisisted?' (2018) 18(7) *Climate Policy* 818, 819.

146 Ibid 822.

147 Ibid 823.

148 Pacific Islands Forum Secretariat, 'Kainaki II Declaration for Urgent Climate Change Action Now' (Forum Communiqué of the: Fiftieth Pacific Islands Forum, Tuvalu, PIF (19)14 13–16 August 2019) 12–15 <https://www.forumsec.org/wp-content/uploads/2019/08/50th-Pacific-Islands-Forum-Communique.pdf>.

149 Ibid para 19(i)–(ii).

150 Kate Lyons, 'Revealed: 'Fierce' Pacific Forum Meeting Almost Collapsed over Climate Crisis' *The Guardian* (online, 16 August 2019) <https://www.theguardian.com/environment/2019/aug/16/revealed-fierce-pacific-forum-meeting-almost-collapsed-over-climate-crisis>.

insulting and condescending',[151] and Tuvalu's prime minister, Enele Sopoaga, accusing Australia of being concerned with saving its own economy rather than the people of Pacific Island States.[152] It seems inevitable that specially affected States will realign with each other in the face of this common problem: however retreat from the international community is not a viable option. The only hope of mitigating catastrophic change for small island States is if the rest of the world acts in concert to limit global warming and reduce emissions drastically. Vulnerable nations cannot afford to take an insular approach, and must continue to try and engage with larger, more developed nations that are more able to weather the effects of climate change. This approach has been evident in the actions of such States: from the formation of a coalition of Pacific Island States which successfully pushed a 1.5°C temperature increase goal during Paris Agreement negotiations[153] to Fiji's successful bid to preside over the 2017 *UN Climate Change Conference COP 23*. As such, it is these States that are spearheading a push to embrace international environmental law: notwithstanding any backlash from other, larger States.

6.3.3 Recreate and Reimagine

Interestingly, another 'backlash' has been observed in international environmental law: an internal backlash *against* the US, carried out by people, communities and cities.[154] Following President Trump's withdrawal from the *Paris Agreement*, two initiatives were created. The United States Climate Alliance is an alliance of the Governors of 25 US States, committed to reaching *Paris Agreement* goals,[155] while the 'We Are Still In' initiative extends the same goal to commitments from local government as well as private institutions.[156] Such initiatives are anticipated by the *Paris Agreement*, which allows registration of support for the Agreement under the UNFCC's Non-State Actor Zone

---

151 Kate Lyons, 'Fiji PM Accuses Scott Morrison of 'Insulting' and Alienating Pacific Leaders', *The Guardian* (online, 17 August 2019) <https://www.theguardian.com/world/2019/aug/16/fiji-pm-frank-bainimarama-insulting-scott-morrison-rift-pacific-countries>.

152 Lyons, 'Revealed: 'Fierce' Pacific Forum Meeting Almost Collapsed over Climate Crisis' (n 151).

153 Ian Fry, 'The Paris Agreement: An Insider's Perspective—The Role of Small Developing Island States' (2016) 46(2) *Environmental Policy and Law* 105, 106–7.

154 Oliver Millman, 'Paris Deal: A Year After Trump Announced US Exit, a Coalition Fights to Fill the Gap', *The Guardian* (online, 1 June 2018) <https://www.theguardian.com/us-news/2018/may/31/paris-climate-deal-trump-exit-resistance>.

155 'Alliance Principles', *United States Climate Alliance* (Web Page) <https://www.usclimatealliance.org/alliance-principles>.

156 'Who's In', *We are Still In* (Web Page) <https://www.wearestillin.com/signatories>.

for Climate Action.[157] This is, in a way, a *reimagining and recreation* of international law, in that it pivots action away from States, and redistributes it to state and local levels of government as well as private companies and institutions. Such actors are not considered traditional subjects of international law: yet are acting in coordination to uphold it, despite the actions of their national State.

7   Conclusions

In this article we have sought to understand the implications and consider the possible responses of states and international institutions to the current backlash against the post-World War II international legal order in each of the four domains of peace and security, human rights, trade and finance and the environment. What emerges is a bewilderingly complex and quickly evolving normative and institutional picture. A central finding of our analysis is that the underlying root causes of the global backlash lie in the conjoined effects of neoconservativism and imperial overreach on the one hand, and neoliberalism and cosmopolitan global governance on the other, which are perceived to have deeply undermined the norms of state sovereignty and non-intervention that define the post-war international legal order. The interrelated nature of these phenomena was shown to be vividly illustrated first in the Iraq war of 2003 and second in the global financial crisis of 2008.

If correct, the current backlash should not be understood as a 'new tsunami threatening to overwhelm and sweep away international law', but instead as a decisive and foreseeable reaction to and retreat from the 'high water-mark of internationalisation in the 1990s'.[158] Much work remains to be done to understand the full implications and extent of this post-Cold War series of developments and political movements. We have sought in the article to map some initial lines of inquiry in terms of the three general scenarios of reform and renewal, retreat and realignment, and reimagination and recreation. Of course, such idealised responses are not mutually exclusive and there will always be a combination of actions, policies and strategies that state and non-state actors alike will take in each category.

---

157   'Data Partnerships for the Non-State Actor Zone for Climate Action (NAZCA)', *United Nations Climate Change* (Web Page) <https://unfccc.int/about-us/partnerships/current-calls-for-partnerships/data-partnerships-for-the-non-state-actor-zone-for-climate-action-nazca#eq-1>.

158   See above Section 1.

For a state such as Australia, each of these three scenarios poses significant and far-reaching consequences for its diplomatic, security, foreign policy and international legal interests. What, for example, would retreat by Australia from the UN Security Council, the WTO or the Human Rights Council and realignment towards more proximate regional mechanisms such as ASEAN, the Pacific Islands Forum and the Commonwealth mean in the long term for Australian foreign policy and Australia's role and participation in the global legal order? These are questions that international legal scholars and policy-makers are today only beginning to address. In order to do so, the article has argued that there is a need for deeper engagement with comparative legal analysis and legal history, as well as a greater self-critical willingness to examine the conditions and contradictions of modernity and modern forms of legal rationality.

As Pankaj Mishra has observed, the question of liberalism's relationship with imperialism has 'become particularly urgent as non-Western powers emerge and an endless economic and political crisis forces Western liberal democracies to expose their racial and inegalitarian structures, their leaders resorting to explicit appeals to white supremacism'.[159] The notion that the rules-based international order has *itself* been the incubator for authoritarian populism and illiberal democracy over the last thirty years will strike many as implausible and destabilising. But by adorning 'the Bush administration's pre-emptive assault on Iraq with the kind of humanitarian rhetoric about freedom, democracy, and progress that we originally heard from European imperialists in the 19th century', and by making 'human beings subordinate to the market, replacing social bonds with market relations and sanctifying greed',[160] the liberal international order can be seen to have laid the ground for the current backlash moment. In this paradox lie the seeds of its reimagination and recreation.

---

159 Pankaj Mishra, '"The Liberal Order is the Incubator for Authoritarianism": A Conversation with Pankaj Mishra', *Los Angeles Review of Books* (online, 15 November 2018) <https://lareviewofbooks.org/article/the-liberal-order-is-the-incubator-for-authoritarianism-a-conversation-with-pankaj-mishra/>.

160 Ibid.

Collective Security and the Prohibition on the Use of Force in Times of Global Transition

Christopher Michaelsen[*]

1 Introduction

The general prohibition on the use of force is enshrined in art 2(4) of the *Charter of the United Nations* ('*UN Charter*'), which requires United Nations ('UN') Member States to 'refrain in their international relations from the threat or use of force against the territorial integrity or political independence of any state, or in any other manner inconsistent with the Purposes of the United Nations'. This general prohibition—which the International Court of Justice has found to constitute a rule of contemporary customary international law— is generally only subject to the exception of self-defence as recognised in both art 51 of the UN Charter and customary international law.[1] Article 51 recognises the 'inherent right of individual or collective self-defence if an armed attack occurs against a Member of the United Nations, until the Security Council has taken measures necessary to maintain international peace and security'.

As is evident in art 51 itself, the rules on the unilateral use of force operate in conjunction with a system of collective security which bestows on the UN Security Council ('Security Council') the 'primary responsibility for the maintenance of international peace and security'.[2] If—pursuant to art 39 of the *UN Charter*—the Security Council finds that a situation amounts to a threat to the peace, breach of the peace or act of aggression, it can take enforcement measures under chapter VII of the *UN Charter* which may include measures short of force as well as military force. Established in 1945, this twin-track normative framework to regulate the use of force in international relations presented a novel and unprecedented attempt by the international community to 'save succeeding generations from the scourge of war'.[3] The historical innovation

---

[*] Associate Professor, UNSW Law, Sydney, and Adjunct Professor of International Law, LUISS 'Guido Carli', Rome.

[1] *Military and Paramilitary Activities in and Against Nicaragua (Nicaragua v United States of America) (Merits)* [1986] ICJ Rep 14, 93–7 [174]–[181] ('*Nicaragua*').

[2] *Charter of the United Nations* art 24(1) ('*UN Charter*').

[3] Ibid Preamble para 1. For a brief historical account of some of the key developments that led to the establishment of this twin-track *UN Charter* framework to regulate the use of force in international relations, see, eg, Shirley V Scott, Anthony John Billingsley and Christopher

---

© KONINKLIJKE BRILL NV, LEIDEN, 2021 | DOI:10.1163/26660229_03801005

COLLECTIVE SECURITY AND THE PROHIBITION ON THE USE OF FORCE 79

notwithstanding, the normative framework established by the *UN Charter* has been constantly challenged ever since its inception. These challenges often find their origin in the politics of international law itself or are related to the shifting nature of warfare as well as technological change.

This article focuses on collective security and the prohibition on the use force in times of global transition. It examines whether current threats to the so-called rules-based international order present a novel challenge to the normative framework of the use of force or whether they simply represent the latest manifestations of challenges that have existed in similar forms in the past. The article proceeds in four parts: first, it canvasses the scholarship that has critiqued the effectiveness and relevance of the general prohibition on the use of force with the aim of identifying certain themes in the relevant literature on the subject. It then sets this analysis in a historical context, suggesting that some of the benefits and shortcomings of the normative framework can be observed across the seven decades since the establishment of the United Nations. The third section of the article undertakes an assessment of whether the current period of global transition—characterised by key developments such as the rise of populism and climate change—presents unprecedented challenges for the legal order on the use of force. The final part offers some concluding observations.

2 The Scholarly Debate on Article 2(4) and Chapter VII of the *UN Charter*

2.1 *Doomsayers, Optimists and Micro-Analysts*
A cursory review of the literature on the *UN Charter* and the international law on the use of force suggests that commentators on the adequacy of the normative framework on the use of force and collective security generally fall into three camps: the 'doomsayers', the 'optimists' and the 'micro-analysts'. The doomsayers comprise those commentators who question the effectiveness or relevance of the general prohibition on the use of force and/or the collective security system of the *UN Charter*.[4] Often, their criticism is explicit in the article's title itself. A prominent case in point is Thomas Franck's seminal 1970

Michaelsen, *International Law and the Use of Force: A Documentary and Reference Guide* (Praeger Security International, 2009) xiii–xxii, 1–69.

4 See, eg, Robert J Delahunty and John C Yoo, 'Peace Through Law? The Failure of a Noble Experiment' (2008) 106 *Michigan Law Review* 923; James Larry Taulbee, 'Governing the Use of Force: Does the UN Charter Matter Anymore?' (2001) 4(2) *Civil Wars* 1.

piece published in the *American Journal of International Law* entitled 'Who Killed Article 2(4)?'[5] On the first two pages of his article Franck lays down his central argument and claims that 'the high-minded resolve of Article 2(4) mocks us from its grave', and further, that 'the [*UN Charter*] today bears little more resemblance to the modern world than does a Magellan map'.[6] A similar, more recent example is John Yoo and Will Trachman's 2005 article in the *Chicago Journal of International Law* entitled 'Less than Bargained for: The Use of Force and the Declining Relevance of the United Nations'.[7] In this article the authors bluntly find that 'the United Nations' rules on the use of force have become obsolete'.[8]

Opposing the doomsayers are the commentators in the optimists' camp.[9] A key proponent of this category is Louis Henkin. In what may well be one of the most entertaining rejoinders in the literature on the use of force, Henkin responded to Franck's above-cited article by arguing that the issuance of a 'death certificate' for art 2(4) and the collective security system in the *UN Charter* was 'premature'.[10] Henkin's principal criticism of Franck's article related to the fact that it judged 'the vitality of the law by looking only at its failures'.[11] He argued instead that '[d]espite common misimpressions', art 2(4) had 'indeed been a norm of behavior' and had 'deterred violations'.[12] Later publications by other 'optimists' contain a similar theme. Writing in the aftermath of the United States ('US') invasion of Iraq in 2003, former US Secretary of State Madeleine Albright, for instance, found that '[t]he United Nations may seem useless to the self-satisfied, narrow-minded, and micro-hearted minority, but to most of the world's population, it remains highly relevant indeed'.[13] Similarly, Shashi Tharoor, in a piece entitled 'Why America Still Needs the

---

5 Thomas M Franck, 'Who Killed Article 2(4)? Or: Changing Norms Governing the Use of Force by States' (1970) 64(5) *American Journal of International Law* 809.

6 Ibid 809, 810.

7 John C Yoo and Will Trachman, 'Less than Bargained for: The Use of Force and the Declining Relevance of the United Nations' (2005) 5(2) *Chicago Journal of International Law* 379.

8 Ibid 381.

9 See, eg, Richard A Falk, 'What Future for the UN Charter System of War Prevention?' (2003) 97(3) *American Journal of International Law* 590; Philippe Sands, 'Lawless World: International Law After September 11, 2001 and Iraq' (2005) 6(2) *Melbourne Journal of International Law* 437.

10 Louis Henkin, 'The Reports of the Death of Article 2(4) Are Greatly Exaggerated' (1971) 65(3) *American Journal of International Law* 544, 544.

11 Ibid.

12 Ibid.

13 Madeleine K Albright, 'United Nations' (2003) 138 *Foreign Policy* 16, 17.

COLLECTIVE SECURITY AND THE PROHIBITION ON THE USE OF FORCE

United Nations', argued that '[a] UN that provides a vital political and diplomatic framework for the actions of its most powerful member, while casting them in the context of international law and legitimacy (and bringing to bear on them the perspectives and concerns of its universal membership) is a UN that remains essential to the world in which we live'.[14]

The third camp consists of what might be referred to as 'micro-analysts': commentators who examine specific international crises or instances of the use of force with the aim of either measuring compliance with the international regulatory regime, or using a particular crisis as evidence to demonstrate why the rules on the use of force and collective security have either become toothless or remain relevant (hence ultimately joining one of the aforementioned camps). Olivier Corten's piece entitled 'The Russian Intervention in the Ukrainian Crisis: Was *Jus Contra Bellum* "Confirmed Rather than Weakened"?' is a good example.[15] In this article, Corten assesses the extent to which the Ukrainian crisis since 2014 has challenged traditional understandings of international law in general, and the scope of art 2(4) in particular. He concludes that international law was 'confirmed rather than weakened' by the events in the Ukraine, but, at the same time wonders whether the prohibition of the use of force 'was ever born'.[16] Recent literature on the failure of the international community to prevent, or adequately respond to uses of force in Syria is also illustrative of the 'micro-analytic' discourse. Some authors lament the Syrian tragedy as another example of the failure of the system of collective security.[17] Others, such as Carsten Stahn, question whether greater flexibility towards the use of force or an 'affirmative defense to Article 2(4)' offers 'a proper remedy' to deal with the dilemma of humanitarian protection.[18]

2.2 The Central Themes in the Literature on the Use of Force and Collective Security

What the literature across the three camps has in common is that it generally revolves around four major themes relating to the adequacy (or not) of

---

14 Shashi Tharoor, 'Why America Still Needs the United Nations' (2003) 82(5) *Foreign Affairs* 67, 78.

15 Olivier Corten, 'The Russian Intervention in the Ukrainian Crisis: Was *Jus Contra Bellum* "Confirmed Rather than Weakened"?' (2015) 2(1) *Journal on the Use of Force and International Law* 17.

16 Ibid 22, 41.

17 See, eg, Nigel D White, 'Peacemaking in Syria: Why the Security Council Fails' (2019) 28(1) *Nottingham Law Journal* 55.

18 Carsten Stahn, 'Between Law-Breaking and Law-Making: Syria, Humanitarian Intervention and "What the Law Ought to Be"' (2014) 19(1) *Journal of Conflict and Security Law* 25, 25.

the normative framework on the use of force and collective security. The *first* theme concerns what Franck referred to as the mistaken original assumption of great power unanimity. As he put it: '[a]lmost from the moment the San Francisco Charter was signed, this essential prerequisite for UN collective enforcement action—the unanimity of the great Powers—was seen to be an illusion'.[19] In many cases, the deadlock in the Security Council was facilitated by the creation of the veto power of the permanent five members ('P5')—implicit in art 27(3) of the *UN Charter*—which has been criticised as setting up a system of 'power over principle' and 'might makes right'.[20] Many scholars identify this power imbalance as a fundamental flaw that prevents the Security Council from meeting its responsibility to maintain international peace and causes it to act in an ad hoc and unprincipled manner.[21] The Security Council is pilloried for its inconsistency and for suffering a 'democratic deficit'.[22] Indeed, there exists now an extensive body of literature on Security Council reform.[23] Yet the ability of the P5 to veto any proposed reform means that there is little prospect of addressing what is seen to be the main problem—the veto itself. Moreover, the unwillingness of the most powerful non-permanent countries to set aside their own ambitions and agree on a broadly acceptable reform model has further thwarted reform efforts.[24]

The *second* major theme concerns the changing nature of warfare and the impact of technology. Franck's argument in this regard is twofold. First, he found the increasing occurrence of small-scale warfare as well as assistance

---

19   Franck (n 5) 810.

20   Bardo Fassbender, *UN Security Council Reform and The Right of Veto: A Constitutional Perspective* (Kluwer, 1998); Edward C Luck, *UN Security Council: Practice and Promise* (Routledge, 2006).

21   See, eg, Ian Johnstone, 'Security Council Deliberations: The Power of the Better Argument' (2003) 14(3) *European Journal of International Law* 437; Ian Hurd, *After Anarchy: Legitimacy and Power in the United Nations Security Council* (Princeton University Press, 2008); David L Bosco, *Five to Rule Them All: The UN Security Council and the Making of the Modern World* (Oxford University Press, 2009).

22   Erik Voeten, 'The Political Origins of the UN Security Council's Ability to Legitimize the Use of Force' (2005) 59 (Summer) *International Organization* 527; Jeremy Farrall, 'Does the UN Security Council Compound the Global Democratic Deficit?' (2009) 46(4) *Alberta Law Review* 913.

23   See, eg, Edward C Luck, 'How Not to Reform the United Nations' (2005) 11(4) *Global Governance* 407; Peter G Danchin and Horst Fischer (eds), *United Nations Reform and the New Collective Security* (Cambridge University Press, 2010); Spencer Zifcak, *United Nations Reform: Heading North or South?* (Routledge, 2009); Dominik Zaum (ed), *Legitimating International Organizations* (Oxford University Press, 2013).

24   Thomas G Weiss, 'The Illusion of UN Security Council Reform' (2003) 26(4) *Washington Quarterly* 147.

COLLECTIVE SECURITY AND THE PROHIBITION ON THE USE OF FORCE

to national liberation movements to have a catastrophic effect on art 2(4).[25] This 'growing fashion for mini-wars or quasi-wars', he argued, had 'made the rules devised at San Francisco hard to apply'.[26] Second, Franck claimed that the development of nuclear weapons had had a transforming impact on the *UN Charter* rules.[27] The effect of potential nuclear warfare on the normative framework on the use of force has since led to the development of an extensive body of literature.[28] As is well known, the issue has also busied the International Court of Justice. Handing down an Advisory Opinion in 1996, the Court found that it could not 'reach a definitive conclusion as to the legality or illegality of the use of nuclear weapons by a State in an extreme circumstance of self-defence, in which its very survival would be at stake'.[29] Recent literature on the impact of technology on the *UN Charter* rules has focused mainly on the question of whether, and to what extent, cyberwarfare fits within the framework of the international law on the use force.[30] While cyber-related challenges naturally differ from those associated with nuclear weapons, the essence of the debate has remained the same: can the normative framework cope with technological change?

The *third* theme concerns the adequacy of art 51 and the right of self-defence. In addition to doctrinal debates on the interpretation of art 51 and its relationship with any customary right of self-defence, much of the discourse has focused on the role and scope of self-defence in the face of the ever-changing nature of conflict. Whenever states and the international community are presented with a novel challenge or crisis the suitability of the rules of self-defence are called into question. The examples of small-scale warfare, nuclear weapons and cyberwarfare have already been mentioned. But perhaps one of the best examples to illustrate this point is the discourse on the availability of the right

---

25   Franck (n 5) 812–20.

26   Ibid 820.

27   Ibid 820–2.

28   See, eg, Istvan Pogany (ed), *Nuclear Weapons and International Law* (Gower, 1987); Jill M Sheldon, 'Nuclear Weapons and the Laws of War: Does Customary International Law Prohibit the Use of Nuclear Weapons in All Circumstances?' (1996) 20(1) *Fordham International Law Journal* 181; Ved P Nanda, 'Nuclear Weapons, Human Security, and International Law' (2009) 37(3) *Denver Journal of International Law and Policy* 331.

29   *Legality of the Threat or Use of Nuclear Weapons (Advisory Opinion)* [1996] ICJ Rep 226, 263 [97].

30   See, eg, Russell Buchan, 'Cyber Attacks: Unlawful Uses of Force or Prohibited Interventions?' (2012) 17(2) *Journal of Conflict and Security Law* 212; Michael N Schmitt (ed), *Tallinn Manual on the International Law Applicable to Cyber Warfare* (Cambridge University Press, 2013); Marco Roscini, *Cyber Operations and the Use of Force in International Law* (Oxford University Press, 2014).

to self-defence in response to non-state actor violence. In the aftermath of the 9/11 attacks and the so-called 'Global War on Terrorism' and, more recently, in the context of the fight against the 'Islamic State'/Daesh, commentators have extensively questioned whether the framework of art 51 allows for appropriate countermeasures.[31] As a consequence, commentators have argued in favour of extending self-defence to include pre-emptive measures beyond what has been commonly understood as anticipatory self-defence.[32] Indeed, the US National Security Strategy adopted in 2002 by the administration of George W Bush proclaimed that 'we must adapt the concept of imminent threat to the capabilities and objectives of today's adversaries'.[33] Others have advocated for embracing the so-called 'unable or unwilling test' which offers a justification for the unilateral use of force in self-defence on behalf of a victim state on the territory of a host state that is unwilling or unable to prevent a non-state actor located on its soil from carrying out attacks against the victim state.[34]

The *final* theme concerns the lack of impartial means to find and characterise facts as well as the difficulties of attributing conduct. These matters have been cited as evidence to suggest that the *UN Charter* rules on the use of force are ineffectual in practice.[35] Indeed, the International Court of Justice has dealt with these challenges in every major case involving the use of force.[36] In its first ever contentious case, the *Corfu Channel* case, the Court faced burden of proof issues involving secret evidence, lack of defensive evidence and

---

31 See, eg, Thomas M Franck, 'Terrorism and the Right of Self-Defense' (2001) 95(4) *American Journal of International Law* 839; Theresa Reinold, 'State Weakness, Irregular Warfare, and the Right to Self-Defense Post-9/11' (2011) 105(2) *American Journal of International Law* 244.

32 For discussion, see, eg, W Michael Reisman and Andrea Armstrong, 'The Past and Future of the Claim of Preemptive Self-Defense' (2006) 100(3) *American Journal of International Law* 525.

33 White House, *The National Security Strategy of the United States of America* (17 September 2002) 15 <http://nssarchive.us/wp-content/uploads/2020/04/2002.pdf>.

34 For discussion, see, eg, Olivier Corten, 'The "Unwilling or Unable" Test: Has It Been, and Could It Be, Accepted? (2016) 29(3) *Leiden Journal of International Law* 777; Mary Ellen O'Connell, Christian J Tams and Dire Tladi, *Self-Defence Against Non-State Actors* (Cambridge University Press, 2019).

35 Franck (n 5) 818.

36 For discussion, see, eg, Michael P Scharf and Margaux Day, 'The International Court of Justice's Treatment of Circumstantial Evidence and Adverse Inferences' (2012) 13(1) *Chicago Journal of International Law* 123.

circumstantial evidence.[37] In *Nicaragua*,[38] the Court struggled with how much weight should be accorded to circumstantial evidence. Similar challenges arose in *Oil Platforms*,[39] *Armed Activities on the Territory of the Congo*,[40] and *Crime of Genocide*,[41] each of which was accompanied by extensive academic commentary.[42] More recently, as Vladyslav Lanovoy has noted, the conflicts in Syria, Ukraine and Yemen have demonstrated the difficulty in applying the classical attribution framework of state responsibility to complex situations involving the use of force with multiple actors and varying degrees of state involvement.[43] Following the January 2020 downing of Ukraine International Airlines Flight 752 over Tehran, Marko Milanovic has posted a three-part series on *EJIL:Talk!* addressing the question of how international law deals with situations in which state agents use lethal force and do so under the influence of a

---

37   *Corfu Channel Case (United Kingdom v Albania) (Merits)* [1949] ICJ Rep 4. For commentary, see, eg, Karine Bannelier, Theodore Christakis and Sarah Heathcote (eds), *The ICJ and the Evolution of International Law: The Enduring Impact of the Corfu Channel Case* (Routledge, 2012).

38   *Nicaragua* (n 1). For commentary see, eg, Keith Highet, 'Evidence, the Court, and the Nicaragua Case' (1987) 81 *American Journal of International Law* 1; Edgardo Sobenes Obregon and Benjamin Samson (eds), *Nicaragua Before the International Court of Justice: Impacts on International Law* (Springer, 2018).

39   *Oil Platforms (Iran v United States of America) (Judgment)* [2003] ICJ Rep 161. For commentary, see, eg, Andreas Laursen, 'The Judgment by the International Court of Justice in the Oil Platforms Case' (2004) 73(1) *Nordic Journal of International Law* 135; Dominic Raab, '"Armed Attack" after the *Oil Platforms* Case' (2004) 17(4) *Leiden Journal of International Law* 719.

40   *Armed Activities on the Territory of the Congo (Democratic Republic of the Congo v Uganda) (Judgment)* [2005] ICJ Rep 168. For commentary, see, eg, Simone Halink, 'All Things Considered: How the International Court of Justice Delegated Its Fact-Assessment to the United Nations in the *Armed Activities* Case' (2008) 40 *New York University Journal of International Law and Politics* 13; Jörg Kammerhofer, The *Armed Activities* Case and Non-State Actors in Self-Defence Law (2007) 20(1) *Leiden Journal of International Law* 89.

41   *Application of the Convention on the Prevention and Punishment of the Crime of Genocide (Bosnia and Herzegovina v Serbia and Montenegro) (Judgment)* [2007] ICJ Rep 43. For commentary, see, eg, Claus Kreβ, 'The International Court of Justice and the Elements of the Crime of Genocide' (2007) 18(4) *European Journal of International Law* 619; Ademola Abass, 'Proving State Responsibility for Genocide: The ICJ in *Bosnia v Serbia* and the International Commission of Inquiry for Darfur' (2008) 31(4) *Fordham International Law Journal* 871.

42   Scharf and Day (n 36).

43   Vladyslav Lanovoy, 'The Use of Force by Non-State Actors and the Limits of Attribution of Conduct' (2017) 28(2) *European Journal of International Law* 563.

mistake or error of fact.[44] Evidentiary issues and attribution of conduct are not inherent or exclusive problems of the rules on the use of force, of course. But, as Henkin put it, they facilitate states taking the law 'into their own hands and distort[ing] and mangl[ing] it to their own purpose'.[45]

3 Six Decades of Promises and Pitfalls: Continual Backlash against or Natural Evolution of the Rules on Collective Security and the Use of Force?

The purpose of the previous section was to identify broad streams and themes in the literature examining the normative framework on the use of force and collective security. This section now takes a more historical approach. Its main purpose is to suggest that in each of the seven decades since the adoption of the *UN Charter* the international community faced key security challenges and crises that tested the legal framework and led to extensive debates about its relevance and adequacy. Rather than providing a detailed account of each individual crisis, the aim here is to identify key episodes of each decade that illustrate a continuum in the discourse on the use of force and collective security. What all episodes have in common is that they illustrate both the promises and pitfalls of collective security which, in turn, produced scholarship falling in either the 'doomsayer', the 'optimist' or the 'micro-analyst' camp. Furthermore, each of the cases under consideration highlight one or more of the themes identified in the previous section.

3.1 *The First Decade*

The defining challenges of the first decade of the United Nations were closely related to the evolving Cold War between the United States and the Soviet Union and their respective allies. As such, they were directly connected to the friction between the permanent members of the Security Council. The enforcement action in Korea in 1950 is a case in point. Although the Security Council was able to recommend to the Members of the United Nations to 'furnish such assistance to the Republic of Korea as may be necessary to repel the armed attack and to restore international peace and security in the area', resolution 83 (1950) could only be passed because the Soviet Union, at that time, boycotted

---

44   Marko Milanovic, 'Mistakes of Fact When Using Lethal Force in International Law: Part I', *EJIL:Talk!* (Blog Post, 14 January 2020) <https://www.ejiltalk.org/mistakes-of-fact -when-using-lethal-force-in-international-law-part-i/>.

45   Henkin (n 10) 544.

COLLECTIVE SECURITY AND THE PROHIBITION ON THE USE OF FORCE 87

the meetings of the Security Council.[46] This has led to commentators claiming that the resolution was illegal and invalid because of the absence of the Soviet Union from the Security Council chamber.[47] Others argued that art 28 of the *UN Charter* required the Security Council to 'function continuously' and that, therefore, the absence of a representative of a permanent member could not be construed to have the effect of preventing all substantive action by the Security Council.[48] Procedural aspects notwithstanding, the UN intervention in Korea was subject to extensive debate about the promises and pitfalls of the collective security system established by the *UN Charter.*[49] As Quincy Wright pointed out succinctly in 1951, '[t]he action of the United Nations in Korea has been interpreted on the one hand as the most significant and successful application of collective security in world history, and, on the other hand, as evidence that collective security cannot work and must be abandoned'.[50]

One of the consequences of the intervention in Korea and the early Cold War-related impasse in the Security Council led to institutional innovation within the United Nations itself. In August 1950, and after its boycott of Security Council meetings proved ineffective, the Soviet Union representative rejoined the Security Council to cast a veto on a United States draft resolution condemning the continued defiance of the United Nations by the North Korean authorities. In order to overcome potential future stalemates, the United States then succeeded in persuading the United Nations General Assembly ('General Assembly') that it should claim for itself a subsidiary responsibility with regard to international peace and security. The result of these efforts was the adoption, in November 1950, of the *'Uniting for Peace'* resolution 377 A (v).[51] This

---

46   SC Res 83, UN SCOR, 474th mtg, UN Doc S/RES/83 (27 June 1950).

47   For discussion, see Josef L Kunz, 'Legality of the Security Council Resolutions of June 25 and 27, 1950' (1951) 45(1) *American Journal of International Law* 137.

48   Ibid 141, citing 'Statement by the US Department of State' (30 June 1950), in US Department of State, *United States Policy in the Korean Crisis* (Publication 3922, Far Eastern Series 34, July 1950) 61–3.

49   See, eg, Kenneth W Thompson, 'Collective Security Reexamined' (1953) 47(3) *American Political Science Review* 753; Denis Stairs, 'The United Nations and the Politics of the Korean War' (1970) 25(2) *International Journal* 302; Samuel Pollack, 'Self Doubts on Approaching Forty: The United Nations' Oldest and Only Collective Security Enforcement Army, the United Nations Command in Korea' (1987) 6(1) *Dickinson Journal of International Law* 1; Dan Sarooshi, *The United Nations and the Development of Collective Security: The Delegation by the UN Security Council of its Chapter VII Powers* (Oxford University Press, 1999) 168–73.

50   Quincy Wright, 'Collective Security in the Light of the Korean Experience' (1951) 45 *American Society of International Law Proceedings* 165, 165.

51   *Uniting For Peace*, GA Res 377 A(v), 302nd plen mtg, UN Doc A/RES/377(V) (3 November 1950).

General Assembly resolution stated that in cases in which the Security Council, because of lack of unanimity of the permanent members, fails to exercise its primary responsibility for the maintenance of international peace and security, the General Assembly can seize itself of the matter.[52] This led to extensive debate about the constitutionality of the resolution and the collective security system more generally.[53] In 1962, the International Court of Justice, in its *Certain Expenses* Advisory Opinion, subsequently found the *Uniting for Peace* procedure compatible with the Charter.[54]

3.2 *The Second Decade*

The second decade of the United Nations saw the application of the *Uniting for Peace* mechanism in practice. When Egypt nationalised the Suez Canal in July 1956, the United Kingdom, France and Israel intervened militarily. The United States tabled a draft resolution in the Security Council for a ceasefire requesting Israel to withdraw behind the 1948 armistice lines—the de facto borders between Egypt and Israel. The resolution was vetoed by the United Kingdom and France, whereupon the United States introduced a resolution in the General Assembly under the *Uniting for Peace* provision. Resolution 997(ES-I) was carried overwhelmingly and, in the context of American political pressure, led to withdrawal of British, French and Israeli forces from Egypt.[55] A few days after the adoption of resolution 997, the General Assembly passed a companion resolution (1001 ES-I) to set up the United Nations Emergency Force ('UNEF').[56] Although a peacekeeping operation, the Secretary-General, U Thant, indicated that the Security Council could widen UNEF's mandate to meet chapter VII criteria.[57] Discussed as controversial in the literature, the General Assembly intervention in the Suez crisis has come to be regarded as an example of an effective exercise of collective security when the Security Council is unable or unwilling to exercise its primary responsibility for the maintenance of peace and security.[58]

---

52 See generally Dominik Zaum, 'The Security Council, the General Assembly and War: The Uniting for Peace Resolution' in Vaughan Lowe et al (eds), *The United Nations Security Council and War: The Evolution of Thought and Practice Since 1945* (Oxford University Press, 2008) 154.

53 Juraj Andrassy, 'Uniting for Peace' (1956) 50(3) *American Journal of International Law* 563.

54 *Certain Expenses of the United Nations (Advisory Opinion)* [1962] ICJ Rep 151.

55 GA Res 997 (ES-I), 563rd plen mtg, UN Doc A/RES/997 (ES-I) (4 November 1956).

56 GA Res 1001 (ES-I), 567th plen mtg, UN Doc A/RES/1001 (ES-I) (7 November 1956).

57 Scott, Billingsley and Michaelsen(n 3) 199.

58 See, eg, David B Price, 'The Charter of the United Nations and the Suez War' (1958) 1(10) *International Relations* 494; Herbert Nicholas, 'UN Peace Forces and the Changing Globe: The Lessons of Suez and Congo' (1963) 17(2) *International Organization* 320.

The 'Goa Incident' in late 1961, a rather obvious violation of the prohibition on the use of force, did not trigger any similar response. On 18 December 1961 Portugal requested the Security Council to intervene after India launched military operations against what was then Portuguese colonial territory. France, Turkey, the United Kingdom and the United States subsequently tabled a draft resolution 'deploring' the use force by India and calling for an 'immediate cessation of hostilities' as well as an immediate Indian withdrawal 'to positions prevailing before 17 December 1961'.[59] The draft resolution, however, was defeated by the Soviet veto. International reactions were divided. The United States Permanent Representative to the UN, Adlai Stevenson, expressed the US sentiment eloquently. Speaking in the Security Council, he stated:

> Let us be perfectly clear what is at stake here, gentlemen. It is the question of the use of armed force by one state against another and against its will, an act clearly forbidden by the [*UN Charter*]. We have opposed such action in the past by our closest friends as well as by others. We opposed it in Korea in 1950, in Suez and Hungary in 1956, in the Congo in 1960, and we do so again in Goa in 1961 ... If it is to survive, if the United Nations is not to die as ignoble a death as the League of Nations, we cannot condone the use of force in this instance and thus pave the way for forceful solutions of other disputes which exist in Latin America, Africa, Asia, and Europe. In a world as interdependent as ours, the possible results of such a trend are too grievous to contemplate.[60]

3.3   *The Third Decade*

The various international crises referred to in Stevenson's statement as well as other developments, such as the 1962 Cuban Missile Crisis and the emerging US involvement in Vietnam, provided the background for challenges to the prohibition on the use of force and the collective security system in the third decade of the United Nations. In the 1960s and early 1970s, most violations of the prohibition on the use for force were connected to either Cold War dynamics or violent struggles for self-determination, or both. The Indonesian invasion of Timor is a case in point.

---

59   Draft Resolution, UN Doc S/5033 (18 December 1961).

60   'United States Views on the Invasion of Goa by India; Statement Made by the US Representative (Stevenson) in the UN Security Council, December 18, 1961', in Department of State Publication 7808 (ed) *American Foreign Policy, Current Documents 1961* (June 1965) 956, 957–8.

After Indonesia had launched military action against Timor on 7 December 1975, it took the Security Council until 22 December to adopt resolution 384 which called on Indonesia 'to withdraw without delay all its forces from the Territory' of Portuguese Timor.[61] However, the Security Council did not characterise Indonesia's conduct in chapter VII terms or otherwise engage chapter VII directly or indirectly by the effect of the wording of its decision—despite the fact that reports unequivocally placed Indonesian military units in Timor's main city of Dili. Indonesia made no case for purporting to act in self-defence under art 51, and was not a competing claimant to the territory of Portuguese Timor. Indeed, as Carolyn Evans has noted, the Security Council made active decisions but Indonesia failed to comply.[62] The Security Council retained this situation on its agenda but did not invest further in persuading or compelling Indonesia to meet its obligations. The General Assembly wanted further Security Council attention, as demonstrated in resolutions adopted in December 1976,[63] November 1977,[64] and December 1978.[65] However, other than listing them in the annual report, the Security Council did not acknowledge this correspondence or reply to it. Rather, it practically disengaged and only reconsidered the situation in Timor in May 1999, some two decades later.

Another illustrative example of the dynamics of the third decade of the United Nations is the conflict in the Western Sahara, a conflict continuing to this day. Much of its origin related to Spain abandoning its colonies in North Africa. In the case of the Western Sahara, Morocco stepped in to claim sovereignty invoking ancestral cultural and political ties. After the International Court of Justice, in its *Western Sahara* Advisory Opinion of 16 October 1975,[66] held that neither Morocco nor Mauritania had any valid claim to the Sahara based on historic title—but that, even if they did, contemporary international law accorded priority to the Sahrawis' right of self-determination—the Moroccan Government announced that there would be a 'massive march of 350,000 "unarmed civilians" from Morocco into the Sahara "to gain recognition

---

61 SC Res 384, UN Doc S/RES/384 (22 December 1975) para 2.

62 Carolyn M Evans, *Being Accountable: Why, to Whom and for What should the United Nations Security Council owe, and own, Accountability under International Law?* PhD Thesis, UNSW 2018, 217–20, on file with author.

63 *Question of Timor*, GA Res 31/53, 85th plen mtg, UN Doc A/Res/31/53 (1 December 1976).

64 *Question of East Timor*, GA Res 32/34, 83rd plen mtg, UN Doc A/Res/32/34 (28 November 1977).

65 *Question of East Timor*, GA Res 33/39, 81st plen mtg, UN Doc A/Res/33/39 (13 December 1978).

66 *Western Sahara (Advisory Opinion)* [1975] ICJ Rep 12.

COLLECTIVE SECURITY AND THE PROHIBITION ON THE USE OF FORCE

of [Morocco's] right to national unity and territorial integrity'".[67] Morocco's claim was vehemently opposed by the Polisario, a politico-military organisation first created to fight off Spain, which subsequently proclaimed the Sahrawi Arab Democratic Republic in 1976. Years of military conflict between Morocco and the Polisario followed, leading to Morocco controlling 80 per cent of the territory, with little, if any, intervention by the Security Council. This led Franck to argue that the conflict had been 'monumentally mishandled' by the United Nations which, in turn, had significant adverse implications for 'numerous other irredentist territorial claims such as those of Guatemala on Belize, Somalia on Djibouti, and Argentina on the Falkland Islands'.[68]

3.4   *The Fourth Decade*

Some of the defining conflicts involving the use of force in the fourth decade concerned American interventionism in Latin America and the Caribbean, as well as the Iran—Iraq war of 1980–88. In October 1983, following a formal appeal for help from the Organization of Eastern Caribbean States, the United States invaded Grenada to oust the (communist) People's Revolutionary Government. A few days after the successful US military operation, the General Assembly passed resolution 38/7 by a vote of 108 to 9 'deeply deploring' the armed intervention and condemning it as a 'a flagrant violation of international law'.[69] The Security Council did not intervene. A draft resolution condemning the US intervention was supported by China, France, Guyana, Jordan, Malta, the Netherlands, Nicaragua, Pakistan, Poland, the Soviet Union and Zimbabwe, but vetoed by the United States (with the United Kingdom abstaining). The sentiment of the majority of the Security Council was expressed by the representative of Guyana. Speaking after the vote, he stated:

> The American veto notwithstanding, or perhaps the veto does underscore, there is a compelling need for us to be very emphatic that we shall never condone intervention and interference; we shall never condone the violation of the sovereignty and territorial integrity of a State. We shall never forsake the [*UN Charter*].

---

67   Thomas M Franck, 'The Stealing of the Sahara' (1976) 70(4) *American Journal of International Law* 694, 711–12, citing Letter from the Permanent Representative of Morocco to the President of the United Nations Security Council, 18 October 1975.

68   Ibid 694.

69   *The Situation in Grenada*, UN Res 38/7, 43rd plen mtg, UN Doc A/RES/38/7 (2 November 1983). See also L Doswald-Beck, 'The Legality of the United States Intervention in Grenada' (1984) 31(3) *Netherlands International Law Review* 355.

The events in Grenada this week and the outcome of the debate this evening show the clear need for that great majority of States which still see value in the [*UN Charter*] and in international relations based on the rule of law to redouble our efforts to ensure that respect for independence, sovereignty and territorial integrity shall never perish from the face of the earth.[70]

Perceiving the governing, leftist Sandinistas as a threat to the economic interests of American corporations in Nicaragua, the administration of US President Ronald Reagan supported the Contra Rebels in their efforts to overthrow the government. In addition to significant financial aid, the United States provided extensive military training of the Contras throughout the early 1980s. This support also extended to Central Intelligence Agency operatives mining Nicaraguan ports. The US intervention was subsequently brought before the International Court Justice which handed down its decision on 27 June 1986.[71] The *Nicaragua* case remains one of the most extensive judicial treatments of the nature and scope of the prohibition on the use of force as well as its exception of individual and collective self-defence. In its decision, the Court found that the United States' support of the Contras constituted a violation of the principle of non-intervention as well as the prohibition on the use of force. It did not accept the United States' claim to be acting in collective self-defence of El Salvador, Honduras or Costa Rica, as those states had never requested the assistance of the United States on the grounds of self-defence.

International and judicial condemnation in the wake of the interventions in Grenada and Nicaragua did not prevent the United States from deploying military forces to Panama in December 1989. Announcing the decision to use force on national television, President George H W Bush referred to the Panamanian General Manuel Noriega's 'reckless threats and attacks' as creating an 'eminent [sic] danger to the 35,000 American citizens in Panama'.[72] He outlined the US objectives in Panama as safeguarding 'the lives of Americans', defending the democracy in Panama, combatting drug trafficking and protecting the integrity of the Panama Canal Treaty.[73] The official justifications offered by the United States were narrower. Speaking in the Security Council, the US Permanent Representative to the UN, Thomas Pickering, clarified the

---

70   *The Situation in Grenada*, UN SCOR, 2491st mtg, UN Doc S/PV.2491(OR) (27 October 1983) 41 [447]–[448].

71   *Nicaragua* (n 1).

72   'Fighting in Panama: A Transcript of Bush's Address on the Decision to Use Force in Panama, *New York Times* (New York, 21 December 1989) A19.

73   Ibid.

COLLECTIVE SECURITY AND THE PROHIBITION ON THE USE OF FORCE 93

US argument in a statement which had been delivered verbatim by Luigi Einaudi, the US Permanent Representative to the Organization of American States (OAS) in Washington DC the day before:

> I am not here today to claim a right on behalf of the United States to enforce the will of history by intervening in favour of democracy where we are not welcomed. We are supporters of democracy but not the *gendarme* of democracy, not in this hemisphere nor anywhere else ... The United States acted in Panama in self-defence and in defence of the Panama Canal Treaties.[74]

The intervention attracted widespread condemnation in the Security Council.[75] It was also the subject of extensive scholarly debate, including an *American Journal of International Law* symposium entitled 'US Forces in Panama: Defenders, Aggressors or Human Rights Activists?'. While Tom Farer and Ved Nanda were critical of the intervention, Anthony D'Amato regarded it as a 'lawful response to tyranny'.[76] Writing in the *Columbia Journal of Transnational Law*, Henkin, on the other hand, saw the intervention as a 'gross violation' of international law.[77] Hence, the Panama invasion, much like the US interventions in Grenada and Nicaragua triggered extensive academic debate with commentators representing the 'doomsayer' and 'optimist' camps.

This decade also saw a bitter, eight years' war between Iran and Iraq that featured extensive mistreatment of prisoners of war, attacks on neutral shipping in the Persian Gulf, the use of chemical weapons, and so-called 'human wave' attacks.[78] Until a ceasefire agreement took effect on 20 August 1988, repeated efforts by the United Nations and regional organisations had failed to halt the fighting. These efforts had included several Security Council resolutions such as 479 (1980) and 514 (1982) which had called on the parties 'to

---

74   *Provisional Verbatim Record of the Two Thousand Nine Hundred and Second Meeting*, UN Doc S/PV.2902 (23 December 1989) 8, 9–10 ('*Record of the 2902nd meeting*'); *Panama: A Just Cause* (United States Department of State, 1990) 3.

75   *Record of the 2902nd meeting*, UN Doc S/PV.2902 (n 76).

76   Ved P Nanda, 'The Validity of United States Intervention in Panama under International Law' (1990) 84(2) *American Journal of International Law* 494; Tom J Farer, 'Panama: Beyond the Charter Paradigm' (1990) 84(2) *American Journal of International Law* 503; Anthony D'Amato, 'The Invasion of Panama Was A Lawful Response to Tyranny' (1990) 84(2) *American Journal of International Law* 516.

77   Louis Henkin, 'The Invasion of Panama under International Law: A Gross Violation' (1991) 29(2) *Columbia Journal of Transnational Law* 293.

78   Mike Gallagher, 'The "Beauty" and the Horror of the Iran—Iraq War', *BBC News* (online, 26 September 2015) <https://www.bbc.com/news/magazine-34353349>.

refrain immediately from any further use of force' and 'to settle their dispute by peaceful means'.[79] However, early resolutions by the Security Council did not name Iraq as the aggressor, a failure which would be cited repeatedly by Iran as evidence of the Security Council's bias against Iran.[80] The Secretaries-General Kurt Waldheim and Javier Pérez de Cuéllar also undertook several good offices initiatives which eventually led to peace talks in Geneva.[81] As Matthew Ferretti has noted, an evaluation of attempts by the United Nations to intervene in the Iran—Iraq war 'necessarily hinges upon the standard by which those attempts are measured'.[82] On the one hand, the United Nations 'demonstrated again that it cannot operate effectively in the manner envisaged by the drafters of the [UN Charter]'.[83] On the other hand, the achievement of a ceasefire after nearly eight years of war appears 'more like a success than a failure' and thus, 'the temptation to make the United Nations a scapegoat for the length and bitterness of the war must be avoided'.[84]

3.5 The Fifth Decade

The defining geopolitical event of the fifth decade was, of course, the fall of the 'iron curtain' and the end of the Cold War. The general international optimism of the time was well-reflected in the contemporary literature as well as in actual practice.[85] From 1990 onwards, the Security Council passed resolutions under its chapter VII powers that were unprecedented both in number and in scope. During 1990–93 alone, the Security Council passed 245 resolutions, an average of more than sixty per year. As Oscar Schachter has documented, citing UN Secretariat data, 58 of those resolutions were adopted under chapter VII compared to 14 resolutions that had been adopted in the pre-1990 era.[86] Iraq's invasion of Kuwait triggered an unparalleled global response and led

---

79   SC Res 479 (1980), 2248th mtg, UN Doc S/RES/479(1980) (28 September 1980); SC Res 514 (1982), 2383rd mtg, UN Doc S/RES/514(1982) (12 July 1982).

80   *Letter from the Permanent Representative of Iran to the United Nations Secretary-General*, UN Doc S/15292 (14 July 1982).

81   Matthew J Ferretti, 'The Iran—Iraq War: United Nations Resolution of Armed Conflict' (1990) 35(1) *Villanova Law Review* 197, 242.

82   Ibid 234.

83   Ibid 236.

84   Ibid 241.

85   See, eg, Andrew Bennett and Joseph Lepgold, 'Reinventing Collective Security after the Cold War and Gulf Conflict' (1993) 108(2) *Political Science Quarterly* 213; Sean D Murphy, 'The Security Council, Legitimacy, and the Concept of Collective Security after the Cold War' (1994) 32(2) *Columbia Journal of Transnational Law* 201.

86   Oscar Schachter, 'United Nations Law' (1994) 88(1) *American Journal of International Law* 1, 12; n 30.

COLLECTIVE SECURITY AND THE PROHIBITION ON THE USE OF FORCE 95

to the Security Council, in resolution 678 (1990), authorising 'Member States co-operating with the Government of Kuwait' to 'use all necessary means to uphold and implement resolution 660 (1990) and all subsequent relevant resolutions and to restore international peace and security in the area'.[87]

Speaking to a joint session of Congress on 11 September 1990, US President George H W Bush summed up the positive atmosphere at the time when he stated:

> A new partnership of nations has begun.
>
> We stand today at a unique and extraordinary moment. The crisis in the Persian Gulf, as grave as it is, also offers a rare opportunity to move toward a historic period of cooperation. Out of these troubled times, our fifth objective—a new world order—can emerge: a new era—freer from the threat of terror, stronger in the pursuit of justice and more secure in the quest for peace. An era in which the nations of the world, East and West, North and South, can prosper and live in harmony.[88]

The successful exercise of collective security in the 1990/91 Gulf crisis notwithstanding, the international community was soon confronted with a range of new challenges which, in many cases, were a direct result of the end of the Cold War and the disintegration of the Soviet Union. Although longstanding conflicts such as in Afghanistan, Namibia, Angola and Mozambique were settled, new conflicts emerged, including those in Yugoslavia, Georgia/Abkhazia, Tajikistan, the Central African Republic, Somalia, Ethiopia and Eritrea, and Sierra Leone. What many of these conflicts had in common was the increasing role of irregular forces, civilian victims, humanitarian emergencies and refugees—challenges that had already been identified in Secretary-General Boutros Boutros-Ghali's 1992 report *Agenda for Peace*.[89] Furthermore, disagreements among the permanent members led to inaction or renewed deadlock in the Security Council with catastrophic consequences for the conflicts in Rwanda (1994), Bosnia (1995) and Kosovo (1998–99). The failure of the Security Council to prevent genocide and large-scale humanitarian tragedies in these cases triggered initiatives such as the development of the 'Responsibility to

---

87 SC Res 678 (1990), 2963rd mtg, UN Doc S/RES/678(1990) (29 November 1990).
88 'Ultimate Objective in the Crisis: "A New World Order"', Address by President Bush before a Joint Session of Congress, 11 September 1990 (Extract)' in US Department of State (ed), *American Foreign Policy Current Documents* (1991) 505.
89 *An Agenda for Peace: Preventive Diplomacy, Peacemaking and Peace-Keeping—Report of the Secretary-General Pursuant to the Statement Adopted by the Summit Meeting of the Security Council on 31 January 1992*, 47th sess, UN Doc A/47/277 (17 June 1992).

Protect' doctrine which was first articulated in a 2001 report by the International Commission on Intervention and State Sovereignty.[90] It also led to extensive scholarly debate on whether the collective security architecture of the United Nations was fit for purpose in the post-Cold War era.[91] For Max Boot, writing in *Foreign Affairs* in 2000, at the end of the 1990s the United Nations remained what it had always been: 'a debating society, a humanitarian relief organization, and an occasionally useful adjunct to great-power diplomacy—but not an effective independent force'.[92]

3.6   *The Sixth Decade*

The 9/11 attacks on the United States set the scene for the sixth decade. Although the Security Council had previously classified 'terrorism' as a 'threat to the peace' in terms of art 39 of the *UN Charter*, resolutions 1368 (2001) and 1373 (2001) broke novel ground in expressly recognising, for the first time in Security Council history, that terrorist attacks perpetrated by non-state actors had triggered a right of self-defence.[93] As Christian Tams has noted, this recognition amounted to a multilateral endorsement of a claim to use force unilaterally, rather than multilateral enforcement action in the sense of art 42 of the *UN Charter*.[94] In fact, the Security Council has since been careful in reaffirming the right of self-defence in the context of terrorism attacks by non-state actors and has refrained from doing so in the context of other major terrorism-related incidents. Nonetheless, commentators subsequently engaged in seemingly endless discussions about the nature and scope of the right of self-defence in the post-9/11 era.[95] These debates ranged from doctrinal analyses of art 51 and the customary right of self-defence—most prominently

---

90   International Commission on Intervention and State Sovereignty, *The Responsibility to Protect* (Report, December 2001). For discussion, see, eg, Jeremy I Levitt, 'The Responsibility to Protect: A Beaver Without a Dam?', (2003) 25(1) *Michigan Journal of International Law* 153; Carlo Focarelli, 'The Responsibility to Protect Doctrine and Humanitarian Intervention: Too Many Ambiguities for a Working Doctrine' (2008) 13(2) *Journal of Conflict and Security Law* 191.

91   See, eg, Karen A Mingst and Margaret P Karns, *The United Nations In the Post-Cold War Era* (Westview Press, 1995); Anthony Parsons, 'The United Nations in the Post-Cold War Era' (1992) 11(3) *International Relations* 189.

92   Max Boot, 'Paving the Road to Hell: The Failure of UN Peacekeeping' (2000) 79(2) *Foreign Affairs* 143, 145.

93   SC Res 1368 (2001), 4370th mtg, UN Doc S/RES/1368(2001) (12 September 2001); SC Res 1373 (2001), 4385th mtg, UN Doc S/RES/1373(2001) (28 September 2001).

94   Christian J Tams, 'The Use of Force against Terrorists' (2009) 20(2) *European Journal of International Law* 359, 377.

95   See, eg, Thomas M Franck, 'Terrorism and the Right of Self-Defense' (2001) 95(4) *American Journal of International Law* 839; Michael J Glennon, 'The Fog of Law: Self-Defence,

COLLECTIVE SECURITY AND THE PROHIBITION ON THE USE OF FORCE 97

the question whether 'pre-emptive' rather than 'anticipatory' self-defence was now permissible—to discussions on the actual application of self-defence to military operations conducted in the name of the so-called War on Terror.[96] The latter included the US military intervention in Afghanistan (Operation Enduring Freedom) as well the invasion of Iraq in 2003.[97]

Indeed, it was the US invasion of Iraq and the role of the Security Council in authorising or failing to authorise the use of force that prompted (again) extensive debate about the relevance of the *UN Charter* system of collective security.[98] In resolution 1441 (2002) the Security Council had found Iraq in 'material breach' of prior resolutions and had warned of 'serious consequences' if Iraq again failed to disarm.[99] The Security Council, however, had not used its 'all necessary means' language which led most commentators to consider the US military intervention illegal.[100] But, leaving specific legal questions aside, many saw the Iraq episode as evidence of a broader crisis of legitimacy for the United Nations more generally.[101] For Michael Glennon, the 'dramatic rupture' of the Security Council made 'clear that the grand attempt to subject the use of force to the rule of law had failed'.[102] Others, such as Jutta Brunnée and Stephen Toope, continued to regard the collective security regime within the *UN Charter* as 'vital in addressing threats to international peace and security' and argued that the Security Council, 'disturbing failures notwithstanding', remained the 'only plausible source of legitimation for the collective use of force'.[103] What made the Iraq 2003 episode stand out from previous crises was that both 'doomsayers' and 'optimists' experienced a crisis of confidence in the

---

Inherence and Incoherence in Article 51 of the United Nations Charter' (2002) 25 *Harvard Journal of Law and Public Policy* 539.

96   See, eg, Sean D Murphy, 'The Doctrine of Preemptive Self-Defense' (2005) 50(3) *Villanova Law Review* 699.

97   Nico Schrijver, 'Responding to International Terrorism: Moving the Frontiers of International Law for "Enduring Freedom"?' (2001) 48(3) *Netherlands International Law Review* 271.

98   See, eg, Tom J Farer, 'The Prospect for International Law and Order in the Wake of Iraq' (2003) 97(3) *American Journal of International Law* 621.

99   SC Res 1441 (2002), 4644th mtg, UN Doc S/RES/1441 (8 November 2002).

100   Christian Enemark and Christopher Michaelsen, 'Just War Doctrine and the Invasion of Iraq' (2005) 51(4) *Australian Journal of Politics and History* 545; George Williams and Devika Hovell, 'Advice to Hon Simon Crean MP on the Use of Force Against Iraq' (2003) 4(1) *Melbourne Journal of International Law* 183.

101   For discussion see, eg, Erik Suy, 'Is the United Nations Security Council Still Relevant? And Was It Ever?' (2004) 12 *Tulane Journal of International & Comparative Law* 7.

102   Michael J Glennon, 'Why the Security Council Failed' (2003) 82(3) *Foreign Affairs* 16, 16.

103   Jutta Brunnée and Stephen J Toope, 'The Use of Force: International Law after Iraq' (2004) 53(4) *International & Comparative Law Quarterly* 785, 804.

United Nations. As Deputy Secretary-General Louise Fréchette put it, 'many who supported the war saw the Security Council's failure to authorize action as symptomatic of the UN's inability to provide a muscular response to today's threats. Many who opposed the war were disillusioned that the United Nations appeared helpless to prevent what they saw as a premature and dangerous war, fought on uncertain grounds'.[104]

3.7 *Continual Backlash or Natural Evolution?*

A historical review of some of the key security challenges and crises that the international community faced in the first sixty years since the establishment of the UN demonstrates that in each decade the normative framework on the use of force and collective security was challenged by dynamics connected to one of the four central themes identified earlier (under II (b)) or indeed a combination thereof. Cold War-related tensions between the United States and the Soviet Union as well as divisions between the P5 more generally shaped the way in which the Security Council responded to crisis and was able to exercise its functions under the *UN Charter*. Technological change and the changing nature of warfare triggered extensive academic discourse on the relevance, scope and interpretation of arts 2(4), 51 and chapter VII of the *UN Charter* as well as on actual state compliance with these rules. These debates were accompanied by challenges related to the application of the rules on the use of force and collective security in practice, chief among which where the lack of impartial means to determine facts and difficulties of attributing conduct.

Stepping back, and viewing these challenges in unison, may lead one to observe that the normative framework on the use of force and collective security had to endure some form of continual backlash ever since its inception. This backlash manifested itself in states challenging the conventional interpretation of existing rules, superficial engagement with those rules, or, at times, displaying total disregard for them altogether. Yet, it would be misplaced to conclude that this continual backlash amounted to a rejection of the normative framework altogether. Even in extreme cases of (perceived) backlash, such as the 2003 invasion of Iraq, states (in this case, the United States, the United Kingdom and Australia) justified their actions by way of reference to the relevant international rules. One may thus argue that moments of significant backlash against the rules of on the use of force may have even strengthened the overall normative framework in the long term. After all, as the International Court of Justice famously found in *Nicaragua*, 'if a State acts in a way prima

---

104 United Nations, 'Bold, Far-Reaching UN Reform Urgent, Necessary, says Deputy Secretary-General in Ontario Address' (Press Release DSG/SM/250, 4 April 2005).

facie incompatible with a recognized rule, but defends its conduct by appealing to exceptions or justifications contained within the rule itself, then whether or not the State's conduct is in fact justifiable on that basis, the significance of that attitude is to confirm rather than to weaken the rule'.[105]

Indeed, the instances of backlash against the rules on the use of force and collective security over the period of six decades seem more suggestive of a natural evolution of the normative framework, or to quote Peter Danchin et al, 'within bounds of the ebb and flow of the history of the evolving international legal order'.[106] Contraction and expansion often occurred concurrently, too. The Uniting for Peace example is a case in point. Early Cold War-related deadlock in the Security Council triggered by US—Soviet antagonism (the backlash) led to institutional innovation (natural evolution) which was then first applied in practice in Suez crisis when the Security Council was paralysed due to British and French opposition. The example of US interventionism in Latin America and the Caribbean is equally illustrative of the relationship between backlash and natural evolution. On the one hand, US actions pushed the doctrinal and practical boundaries of the normative framework on the use of force (backlash *and* natural evolution?), in particular on issues of self-defence, protection of nationals or pro-democratic intervention. On the other hand, the response of the international community to the US interventions in Granada, Nicaragua and Panama was generally unsympathetic, both politically (for instance, in the Security Council) and legally (for instance, by the International Court of Justice), and may itself amount to a backlash against an expansive or permissive application of the rules on the use or force (in this case by the United States).

Even at the 'high water-mark of internationalisation in the 1990s',[107] the framework on the use of force and collective security experienced moments of backlash and evolution concurrently. While this decade featured a successful exercise of traditional collective security in response to the 1990 Iraqi invasion of Kuwait, the examples of the international community's failure to prevent mass-atrocities in Rwanda, Bosnia and Kosovo are illustrative of key member states disengaging from the Security Council on various occasions and with disastrous consequences. Yet, these failures, caused by (P5) states retreating from the collective security framework also prompted doctrinal evolution, in particular as far as the use of force for humanitarian protection purposes is

---

105   *Nicaragua* (n 1) [186].
106   Peter G Danchin et al, 'Navigating the Backlash against Global Law and Institutions' (2020) 38 *Australian Year Book of International Law* 33, 38.
107   Ibid.

concerned. A comparable dynamic can be observed in the 2000s. On the one hand, the Security Council, itself contributed to the evolution of the normative framework on the use of force by recognising that the right to self-defence extended to instances of armed attack by non-state actors. On the other, the majority of Security Council members opposed claims that pre-emptive self-defence provided a valid justification for the 2003 US invasion of Iraq, or that the Security Council had authorised military intervention in resolution 1441. The adoption of that resolution is also illustrative of the fact that engagement with, and disengagement from the collective security framework can occur simultaneously. The United States and the United Kingdom sought Security Council authorisation for the use of force against Iraq, but ultimately went ahead without an explicit UN mandate. Russia, France and Germany, on the other hand, employed Security Council diplomacy in an attempt to prevent what they considered to be a premature resort to military enforcement measures.

4 The Current Decade and Recent Challenges to the Rules-Based International Order

The previous section considered the promises and pitfalls of the *UN Charter* rules on the use of force and collective security in the first six decades of the United Nations. This section now focuses on the past decade and considers key crises and developments which have been commonly invoked in the discourse on the continued relevance of the collective security system: the crises in Libya, Syria and the Ukraine; climate change; and general challenges to the so-called rules-based international order and the rise of populism in particular.

4.1 *The Conflicts in Libya, Syria and Ukraine*

Adopting resolution 1973 (2011), the Security Council, acting under chapter VII of the *UN Charter*, authorised UN Member States, acting nationally or through regional organisations, 'to take all necessary measures ... to protect civilians and civilian populated areas under threat of attack in the Libyan Arab Jamahiriya'.[108] Two days after the adoption of the resolution, on 19 March 2011, a multi-state coalition began the military intervention. The effort was initially largely led by France and the United Kingdom, with command shared with the United States until the North Atlantic Treaty Organization (NATO) took control of the arms embargo and the no-fly zone in late March. Mistakenly hailed as the first successful test-case of the 'Responsibility to Protect', the Libya

---

108   SC Res 1973 (2011), 6498th mtg, UN Doc S/RES/1973 (17 March 2011).

COLLECTIVE SECURITY AND THE PROHIBITION ON THE USE OF FORCE 101

intervention rather was a classic exercise of collective security as envisaged by the *UN Charter*, adapted to the realities of the 21st century.[109] However, NATO's air campaign also led to severe criticism, including from regional leaders who were initially supportive of the military intervention. South African President Jacob Zuma, for example, lamented that NATO's campaign had left 'a scar on the continent' that would take long to heal.[110]

Furthermore, the expansive interpretation of the mandate included in resolution 1973 by key NATO States has had a chilling effect on the ability of the Security Council to respond to other crises. In particular, it resulted in Security Council paralysis in the emerging crisis in Syria which continues to this day. For years, the Russian Federation and China blocked any draft resolution that threatened chapter VII measures, even those falling significantly short of collective security measures involving the use of force. Those resolutions that avoided Russian and Chinese vetoes contained attempts to stop the fighting, end the use of chemical weapons, and to facilitate humanitarian assistance to civilians.[111] As Nigel White has noted, the split between the permanent members into those that support the Assad regime (Russia and China), and those who want its removal (France, United Kingdom and United States), signified that 'substantial peacemaking had little chance of gaining traction in the period 2011–15'.[112] Even when the Security Council, more recently, adopted resolution 2401 (2018) demanding a cease-fire, Russia continued to provide military support to the Assad regime while the United States and allies were continuing airstrikes.[113] On the other hand, as Saira Mohamed has pointed out, the Security Council continues to provide a forum for negotiations over how to respond to developments in Syria as well as governments' declarations of their

---

109 Gareth Evans, 'Interview: The "RtoP" Balance Sheet After Libya', 2 September 2011, available at: <http://www.gevans.org/speeches/speech448%20interview%20RtoP.html>; Ramesh Thakur, 'Libya and the Responsibility to Protect: Between Opportunistic Humanitarianism and Value-Free Pragmatism' (2011) 7(4) *Security Challenges* 13; For detailed critique, see David Berman and Christopher Michaelsen, 'Intervention in Libya: Another Nail in the Coffin for the Responsibility-to-Protect?' (2012) 14(4) *International Community Law Review* 337.

110 'Zuma Blasts Nato's Campaign in Libya for "Lasting Scar"', *Mail & Guardian* (online, 10 December 2011), <https://mg.co.za/article/2011-12-10-zuma-blasts-natos-campaign-in-libya-for-lasting-scar/>.

111 For summary and analysis, see, eg, Martin Hartberg, Dominic Bowen and Daniel Gorevan, *Failing Syria: Assessing the Impact of UN Security Council Resolutions in Protecting and Assisting Civilians in Syria* (Oxfam International Briefing Paper, March 2015).

112 White (n 17) 65.

113 SC Res 2401 (2018), 8188th mtg, UN Doc S/RES/2401 (24 February 2018).

attitudes toward the protection of civilians, the proper role of the Security Council, and the limits of international cooperation.[114]

The Security Council has been similarly impaired in the Ukraine crisis which, inter alia, led to the Russian annexation of Crimea. As Thomas Grant has noted, outside the context of decolonisation, the annexation of Crimea represented the first time in the United Nations era that a permanent member of the Security Council employed force to appropriate territory of another UN Member State.[115] For Peter Hilpold, the Ukrainian crisis thus posed a 'new challenge of an extraordinary dimension to traditional international law'.[116] For other commentators like William W Burke-White, the annexation of the Crimea simply amounted to Russian exploitation of the tension between the principles of non-intervention and self-determination which he considered in the 'tradition of great-power interaction with international law'.[117] Most international lawyers, however, denounced the use of force by Russia as being in violation of the *UN Charter*, or even an aggression.[118]

At the Security Council itself, 42 UN Member States tabled a draft resolution on 15 March 2014 which 'reaffirmed' that 'no territorial acquisition resulting from the threat or use of force shall be recognized as legal'.[119] This draft resolution further urged all parties to the conflict in Ukraine 'to pursue immediately the peaceful resolution of this dispute through direct political dialogue, to exercise restraint, to refrain from unilateral actions and inflammatory rhetoric that may increase tensions, and to engage fully with international

---

114 Saira Mohamed, 'The UN Security Council and the Crisis in Syria' (2012) 16(11) *A SIL Insights*, <https://www.asil.org/insights/volume/16/issue/11/un-security-council-and-crisis-syria>.

115 Thomas D Grant, 'Annexation of Crimea' (2015) 109(1) *American Journal of International Law* 68.

116 Peter Hilpold, 'Ukraine, Crimea and New International Law: Balancing International Law with Arguments Drawn from History' (2015) 14(2) *Chinese Journal of International Law* 237, 237.

117 William W Burke-White, 'Crimea and the International Legal Order' (2014) 56(4) *Survival* 65, 73.

118 Daniel Wisehart, 'The Crisis in Ukraine and the Prohibition of the Use of Force: A Legal Basis for Russia's Intervention?' *EJIL:Talk!* (Blog Post, 4 March 2014) <https://www.ejiltalk.org/the-crisis-in-ukraine-and-the-prohibition-of-the-use-of-force-a-legal-basis-for-russias-intervention/>; Mary Ellen O'Connell, 'Ukraine Insta-Symposium: Ukraine Under International Law' *Opinio Juris* (Blog Post, 7 March 2014) <http://opinio juris.org/2014/03/07/ukraine-insta-symposium-ukraine-international-law/>; Antonello Tancredi, 'The Russian Annexation of the Crimea: Questions Relating to the Use of Force' (2014) 1 *Questions of International Law* 5, <http://www.qil-qdi.org/wp-content/uploads/2014/05/CRIMEA_Tancredi_FINAL-1.pdf>; Corten (n 15).

119 *Draft Resolution*, UN Doc S/2014/189 (15 March 2014).

COLLECTIVE SECURITY AND THE PROHIBITION ON THE USE OF FORCE 103

mediation efforts'.[120] Two weeks later, after Russia had vetoed a draft Security Council resolution, the General Assembly adopted, by 100 votes against 11 and 58 abstentions, resolution 68/262 which called 'upon all States, international organizations and specialized agencies not to recognize any alteration of the status of the Autonomous Republic of Crimea and the city of Sevastopol on the basis of the above-mentioned referendum and to refrain from any action or dealing that might be interpreted as recognizing any such altered status'.[121] The dynamics in the Ukraine crisis thus resembled those in Syria. While deep divisions between the permanent members prevented the Security Council from exercising its collective security functions envisaged by the *UN Charter*, the Security Council nonetheless continued to serve as a forum for dialogue and diplomacy. In the case of the Ukraine crisis, this led to regular Arria-formula meetings, briefings on the implementation of the Minsk Peace Agreements as well as reports by representatives of the Organization for Security and Cooperation in Europe.

4.2 Climate Change as a Threat to Peace and Security

Another defining international challenge of the past decade with potential implications for the normative framework on the use of force and collective security concerns climate change. The Security Council held its first ever debate on the topic on 17 April 2007.[122] The debate was initiated by the United Kingdom and focused on the linkages between climate change and international security. A second debate was organised by the German presidency of the Security Council on 20 July 2011 and scheduled under the agenda item 'Maintenance of international peace and security'.[123] Both meetings highlighted divisions in the international community which are also reflected in the scholarly literature on climate change and security.[124] On the one hand there are those states and commentators who argue that climate change is a

---

120 Ibid.

121 GA Res 68/262, 68th sess, Agenda Item 33(b), UN Doc A/RES/68/262 (1 April 2014).

122 United Nations, 'Security Council holds First-Ever Debate on Impact of Climate Change on Peace, Security, Hearing Over 50 Speakers', (Press Release SC/9000, 17 April 2007).

123 *Verbatim Record of the 6587th Meeting*, UN SCOR, 6587th mtg, UN Doc S/PV.6587 (20 July 2011) ('*Verbatim Record of the 6587th Meeting*').

124 Francesco Sindico, 'Climate Change: A Security (Council) Issue?' (2007) 1 *Carbon & Climate Law Review* 29; Stephanie Cousins, 'UN Security Council: Playing a Role in the International Climate Change Regime?' (2013) 25(2) *Global Change, Peace & Security* 190; Shirley V Scott, 'Implications of Climate Change for the UN Security Council: Mapping the Range of Potential Policy Responses' (2015) 91(6) *International Affairs* 1317; Shirley V Scott and Charlotte Ku (eds), *Climate Change and the UN Security Council* (Edward Elgar, 2018).

security challenge and that it is, therefore, a legitimate issue to bring before the Security Council. On the other hand, there are those who believe that climate change is rather a matter of sustainable development.[125] China and Russia, for instance, saw qualifying climate change as a threat to the peace as neither 'right' nor beneficial.[126] For them, the Security Council was not the venue to consider these questions as it 'lacked expertise' as well as the 'necessary means and resources'.[127]

The divisions in the Security Council notwithstanding the issue of climate change remained on its agenda. In March 2017, the Security Council adopted resolution 2349 (2017), addressing the conflict in the Lake Chad Basin in March 2017. This resolution recognised the 'adverse effects of climate change and ecological changes among other factors on the stability of the Region, including through water scarcity, drought, desertification, land degradation, and food insecurity' and emphasised 'the need for adequate risk assessments and risk management strategies by governments and the United Nations relating to these factors'.[128] A further open debate in the Security Council was organised by the Dominican Republic on 25 January 2019 and scheduled under the agenda item 'Maintenance of international peace and security: addressing the impacts of climate-related disasters on international peace and security'.[129] In this debate climate change was referred to as either 'risk multiplier' or 'threat multiplier' on 23 occasions. Commentators have welcomed this new qualification as a 'step forward' and have argued—perhaps too optimistically—that the Security Council has 'understood its importance and is carefully assessing ways to opening the door to coercive measures'.[130] On the other hand, Member States have increasingly made climate change a

---

125   See, eg, Christopher K Penny, 'Greening the Security Council: Climate Change as an Emerging "Threat to International Peace and Security"' (2007) 7(1) *International Environmental Agreements: Politics, Law and Economics* 35; Nicole Detraz and Michele M Betsil, 'Climate Change and Environmental Security: For Whom the Discourse Shifts' (2009) 10(3) *International Studies Perspectives* 303.

126   *Verbatim Record of the 6587th Meeting*, UN Doc S/PV.6587 (n 126) 13. The Russian representative stated that 'involving the Security Council in a regular review of the issue of climate change would bring no added value whatsoever and would merely lead to a further politicization of the issue and increased disagreements among countries, which would be an extremely undesirable outcome ...'.

127   Ibid 9.

128   SC Res 2349, UN SCOR, UN Doc S/RES/2349 (31 March 2017) 26.

129   *Verbatim Record of the 8451st Meeting*, UN SCOR, 8451st mtg, UN Doc S/PV.8451 (25 January 2019).

130   Valentine Bourghelle, 'Climate Change in the Security Council: On the Road to Qualifying Climate Change as "Threat Multiplier"', *Völkerrechtsblog*, (Blog Post, 9 December 2019) <https://voelkerrechtsblog.org/climate-change-in-the-security-council/>.

core part of their campaign for election to the Security Council. Standing for election to the Security Council in June 2020, Kenya, for instance, made seeing 'lasting solutions to security challenges caused by erratic climatic conditions' one of its ten campaign pledges.[131]

4.1 The Rise of Populism and the Implications of the Trump Presidency

The past decade has also seen a rise of populism across the globe which, in turn, has been considered to have significant implications for what is commonly termed the 'rules-based international order'.[132] As the 2017 Foreign Policy White Paper of the Australian Government put it, the 'system of international institutions and rules designed to help support economic growth, global security and human development' is now 'under significant challenge' and tested for 'its effectiveness and cohesion'.[133] A 2015 Chatham House background paper for a conference on 'Challenges to the Rules-Based International Order' struck a similar tone. It argued that key challenges to this order have come 'from rising or revanchist states; from unhappy and distrustful electorates; from rapid and widespread technological change; and indeed from the economic and fiscal turmoil generated by the liberal international economic order itself'.[134] It went on to identify three main problems associated with these challenges:

> The first is the problem of legitimacy. For a system based on rules to have effect, these rules must be visibly observed by their principal and most powerful advocates. The second problem, which is tied to the question of legitimacy, is one of equity, in that a rules-based order must work to the advantage of the majority and not a minority. The third problem is one of self-confidence. The longevity of the current international system may have led to the assumption that it was in some way the natural order of things, requiring only occasional repair and defence against particular challengers. This has bred complacency.[135]

---

131 'Kenya's 10-point pledge for Africa at UN Security Council', *Daily Nation* (online, 17 September 2019) <https://www.nation.co.ke/news/Kenya-10-point-pledge-Africa-UN -Security-Council/>.

132 Danchin et al (n 106) Section II.

133 Australian Government, *2017 Foreign Policy White Paper*, 79.

134 Chatham House, 'Challenges to the Rules-Based International Order' (London Conference, Background Paper, Session One, 2015), <https://www.chathamhouse.org/ london-conference-2015/background-papers/challenges-to-rules-based-international -order>.

135 Ibid.

It is clear that the above-mentioned challenges and problems have implications for the rules on the use of force and collective security as well. Indeed, as Matthew LeRiche and Friedrich Opitz have pointed out, the contemporary political environment has seen a 'paradoxical hijacking of key liberal peace and security concepts which helped to secure the post-Cold War era', including 'collective security, a pillar of post WW2 liberal order.[136] Much of this order had been underpinned by US power and global leadership. It is thus unsurprising that commentators have been particularly worried about the repercussions the domestic political developments in the United States have for the international community. As Kirsten Boon has noted, the Trump presidency 'has demonstrated a disinterest in the institutions and instruments that normally act as a forum for international cooperation' which may lead to 'withdrawing from its leadership role in international law and institutions'.[137] She further pointed to an 'additional concern' is the multiplier effect: the United States' retreat towards nationalism must be seen in light of other recent events, including: the 'Brexit' referendum, the move to the right in other European nations, and Russia's call for a 'post-West' world order.[138] Bruce Jentleson expressed similar concerns, but also identified possible opportunities for the United Nations.[139] As he put it, 'one potentially helpful element is that Trump's antagonism can be an incentive and opportunity for other major and emerging powers to take the lead in being pro-UN'.[140]

5   Concluding Observations

Considering the key crises and developments of the past decade, and setting them against the background of those experienced in the first six decades of the United Nations, begs the question of whether the challenges the international community has been facing in recent times are indeed novel, or whether they are essentially a continuum of what has troubled the *UN Charter*-based

---

136 Matthew LeRiche and Friedrich W Opitz, 'Right-Wing Populism and the Attack on Cooperative International Security', *E-International Relations*, (Web Page, 23 August 2019) <https://www.e-ir.info/2019/08/23/right-wing-populism-and-the-attack-on-cooperative-international-security/>.

137 Kristen Boon, 'President Trump and the Future of Multilateralism' (2017) 31 *Emory International Law Review* 1075.

138 Ibid.

139 Bruce W Jentleson, 'Global Governance, the United Nations, and the Challenge of Trumping Trump' (2017) 23(2) *Global Governance* 143.

140 Ibid 146.

system of collective security ever since its inception. Leaving the actual implementation of the Security Council mandate aside, the Libyan intervention of 2011 constituted a successful episode of collective security in the sense that it demonstrated that the Security Council is still able to exercise the functions envisaged by the *UN Charter*. The conflicts in Syria and Ukraine, on the other hand, are reminiscent of several tragic collective security failures of the past, including those in Goa, Timor, Grenada, Rwanda, Bosnia and Kosovo. Akin to these earlier crises, the conflicts in Syria and Ukraine have brought the practical limits of the *UN Charter* rules on the use of force and collective security into stark relief. Wherever and whenever major geopolitical interests of one of the permanent members of the Security Council are at stake, realpolitik takes precedence over averting humanitarian catastrophes and complying with international law. As a consequence, the Security Council is prevented from playing the role envisaged by the *UN Charter*. However, these dynamics are not new. They have plagued the *UN Charter* since its adoption in 1945.

Climate change may well constitute the ultimate security issue of our times as it potentially threatens the very survival of humanity. But is it qualitatively much different from the risk of nuclear holocaust? The point here is that any regulatory (legal) system has its inherent limits in the context of coping with existential threats. One may thus argue that the simple fact that the collective security framework is being considered to apply to shaping the international community's response to climate change demonstrates it continued relevance, political impediments in the Security Council notwithstanding. The rise of populism, on the other hand, may not harbour any existential threats for the *UN Charter* rules on collective security and the use of force. Indeed, reflecting about the three fundamental problems that populism is considered to pose for the international order—legitimacy, equity, self-confidence—it is difficult to see what is really novel about them. The legitimacy of the Security Council and its role in maintaining international peace and security has been questioned in every decade since the adoption of the *UN Charter*. The problem of equity has persisted over seven decades, too. Indeed, while the United Nations (and the international legal system at large) is based on the principle of the sovereign equality of all its Members, as recognised by art 2(1) of the *UN Charter*, the Security Council was created unequal from the beginning. Similarly, problems of self-confidence have also undermined the *UN Charter* system since its establishment. But, as the responses to crises in Korea, Suez and, more recently, Libya, have shown, this did not prevent states from resorting to diplomacy within the United Nations in efforts to maintain peace and security in general. Indeed, crises in confidence have, at times, led to institutional innovation itself.

It is, of course, conceivable that the general populist and nationalist uprisings will deepen or sharpen long-term threats to the prohibition on the use of force and the collective security system. The US government's current approach to its conflict with Iran may be indicative of such a trend. As Melinda Rankin has noted, the Trump administration's 'America First' policy provides Iran and other countries little incentive to continue to engage with the international legal framework.[141] Indeed, the assassination of Iranian General Qasem Soleimani in Iraq in early January 2020 demonstrated disregard for the principles of international (and domestic) law.[142] On the other hand, the Pentagon characterised the operation as 'defensive action' to prevent imminent attacks, a category of action which, if in fact true, is arguably permissible under the *UN Charter*. Irrespective of the merits of such a claim, the invocation of international law may be regarded as evidence that the United States continues to engage with the international legal framework on the use of force. A similar argument can be made in relation to the Russian justifications for its actions throughout the crisis in Ukraine. More generally, the international rules on the use of force may be an area of international law which is withstanding the populist trend of retreating from the institutions and instruments that have shaped international cooperation in the UN era. After all, the principle of non-intervention and the prohibition on the use of force may be seen as rules that can fundamentally reinforce the populist narrative of exclusive nationalism identity politics. It is too early to tell with any degree of certainty whether the past decade saw the beginnings of a more fundamental backlash against the normative framework on the use of force and collective security or whether it just featured new iterations of dynamics which had been present in the first six decades of the United Nations. Much points to the latter alternative and suggests that the rules in this area of international law are robust enough to withstand challenge in times of global transition. Delivering an honorary address at Tulane University in the wake of the 2003 invasion of Iraq, Erik Suy, a former Under-Secretary-General of the United Nations and seasoned Belgian diplomat, cited an old French proverb to respond to criticisms about the

---

141 Melinda Rankin, 'The Looming International Law Paradox between the US and Iran', *The Interpreter*, (Web Page, 19 May 2019) <https://www.lowyinstitute.org/the-interpreter/looming-international-law-paradox-between-us-and-iran>.

142 John B Bellinger III, 'Does the US Strike on Soleimani Break Legal Norms?' *Council on Foreign Relations*, (Web Page, 6 January 2020), <https://www.cfr.org/in-brief/does-us-strike-soleimani-break-legal-norms>; Mary Ellen O'Connell, 'The Killing of Soleimani and International Law', *EJIL:Talk!*, (Blog Post, 6 January 2020) <https://www.ejiltalk.org/the-killing-of-soleimani-and-international-law/>.

continued relevance of the United Nations in moments of great uncertainty: 'Les chiens aboient, mais la caravane passe' [dogs bark, but the caravan passes by].[143] There is, perhaps, no better way to characterise the contemporary discourse on the adequacy and continued relevance of the *UN Charter* rules on collective security and the use of force today.

---

143   Suy (n 105) 25.

The Status of Human Protection in International Law and Institutions: The United Nations Prevention and Protection Architecture

*Cecilia Jacob**

1 Introduction[1]

The United Nations (UN) peace and security architecture, established through the UN Charter and the authority of the Security Council created in 1945, has played a central role in promoting global cooperation and mitigating interstate conflict. As the character of armed conflict has evolved over the past 75 years, the UN peace and security architecture has become increasingly complex and far-reaching. For example, the creation and evolution of peacekeeping brings the presence of the UN deeper into local contexts of instability and violent conflict, and today the tasks of peacekeepers range from forceful intervention through to the promotion of the rule of law and human rights.[2] The development of international legal and normative frameworks for human protection have become more precise in terms of regulating actor behaviour,[3] and addressing an ever-growing array of thematic issues deemed to fall within the remit of international peace and security.[4] Nonetheless, the UN remains

---

*   Senior Lecturer and ARC Discovery Early Career Research Fellow in the Department of International Relations at The Australian National University.

1   The author's work focuses on civilian protection, mass atrocity prevention, and the implementation of international human protection norms.

2   See, eg, Hanne Fjelde, Lisa Hultman and Desirée Nilsson, 'Protection Through Presence: UN Peacekeeping and the Costs of Targeting Civilians' (2019) 73(1) *International Organization* 103; Andrea Ruggeri, Han Dorussen and Theoride-Ismane Gizelis, 'Winning the Peace Locally: UN Peacekeeping and Local Conflict' (2017) 71(1) *International Organization* 163; Emily Paddon Rhoads, 'Putting Human Rights up Front: Implications for Impartiality and the Politics of UN Peacekeeping' (2019) 26(3) *International Peacekeeping* 281.

3   Bellamy identifies 'eight streams' of the international human protection regime, an overview is found in: Alex Bellamy, 'The Humanisation of Security? Towards an International Human Protection Regime' (2016) 1(1) *European Journal of International Security* 112, 119.

4   These include: Justice, Rule of Law and Impunity; Human Rights; Protection of Civilians; Women, Peace and Security; Youth, Peace and Security; Children and Armed Conflict; Terrorism; Small Arms; Arms Control and Disarmament, including small arms; Drug Trafficking and Security; Energy, Climate and Natural Resources; Piracy; Health Crises; Non-Proliferation.

© KONINKLIJKE BRILL NV, LEIDEN, 2021 | DOI:10.1163/26660229_03801006

mired in conflict management[5] as we witness the increasing fragmentation of conflicts within states.[6] This trend persists at a time when shifting geopolitical trends thwart collective action by the international community in response to major conflicts and human protection crises.

Much of the recent literature on the status and future of the international liberal order conveys a sense of crisis in multilateralism. Systemic-level shifts in power due to the rise of emerging powers, particularly the BRICS (Brazil, Russia, India, China, and South Africa) grouping, and their increasing assertiveness in contesting Western leadership of the global order, generates anxiety among observers that core international laws, norms, and institutions constructed in the wake of the Second World War are gradually being eroded.[7] Others argue that the international liberal order is undergoing a fundamental transformation, but challenge the assumption that the current order will be overturned anytime soon.[8] This article inserts itself in these debates by asking whether international norms and institutions are indeed facing a backlash in the specific area of human protection, including the prevention of violent conflict and mass atrocities. This article understands the term "backlash" in this context to assume that actors in the international system are resisting, dissenting, seeking to undermine, or at the most extreme end, to unravel the foundational values of international order. The area of human protection is illuminating in this regard, as the endeavour to avert mass human tragedy is one that states approve in principle.[9] Yet the contours of contestation by member states around the human protection agenda reveal deeper rifts in regard to how this agenda should be implemented, conveying a sense of erosion or weakening of international protection norms.[10]

---

5 Security Council Report, *Can the Security Council Prevent Conflict?* (Research Report No 1, 9 February 2017) 2.

6 Therése Pettersson, Stina Högbladh and Magnus Öberg, 'Organized Violence, 1989–2018' (2019) 53(5) *Journal of Peace Research* 589, 5.

7 Philip Alston, 'The Populist Challenge to Human Rights' (2017) 9(1) *Journal of Human Rights Practice* 1, 2.

8 G John Ikenberry, 'The End of Liberal International Order?' (2018) 94(1) *International Affairs* 7, 8.

9 Over 170 member states present at the 2005 UN World Summit voted unanimously for the inclusion of the two paragraphs on the responsibility to protect (R2P) in the Outcome document. See *2005 World Summit Outcome*, GA Res 60/1, UN Doc A/RES/60/1 (24 October 2005, adopted 16 September 2005), [138]–[139]. Member states that have persistently objected to R2P have done so on the premise that the doctrine is used as a foil for major powers to intervene unjustly into the internal affairs of member states rather than on the core principle of protecting populations from mass atrocities per se.

10 See generally, Nicole Deitelhoff and Lisbeth Zimmermann, 'Norms Under Challenge: Unpacking the Dynamics of Norm Robustness' (2019) 4(1) *Journal of Global Security Studies* 2.

The argument developed in the article is that international norms of human protection have developed significantly over the past three decades, pointing to robust interpretation of the individual protection provisions found in international humanitarian, human rights, and international criminal legal frameworks. Concurrent with these normative trends, there have been significant institutional reform and institution-building efforts at the multilateral level to improve the implementation of human protection norms within the context of increasingly localised and fragmented conflicts within and across state borders.

States have, on the whole, demonstrated a strong commitment to the core objective of international human protection norms—to prevent or halt human suffering on a large-scale due to violent conflict. This article tells a story largely about progress and an expanding presence of human protection in international law and institutions. That said, a number of states have demonstrated strong resistance to the human rights foundations of human protection norms as advocates, such as successive UN secretaries-general, certain member states, and civil society organisations, have sought to integrate human rights deeper within existing protection frameworks. The contours of this resistance are familiar—including the insistence of the primacy of sovereignty, non-interference, and the pursuit of a more equitable distribution of power among states to define the normative grounding of global order.[11] There has also been a concerted campaign to undermine the human rights foundations of primarily Western-led prevention and protection agendas at the UN in both public debate and state practice. While these areas of dissent—and the countries expressing dissent—at the UN are familiar, I argue that the normative, institutional, and political context in which states are contesting the expansion and application of human protection norms has changed in recent years. States, such as those belonging to the Like-Minded Group and the G77 member states that routinely oppose perceived Western bias at the UN, are not unravelling the emergent international human protection regime as the

---

11   See, eg, Courtney J Fung, 'Rhetorical Adaptation, Normative Resistance and International Order-Making: China's Advancement of the Responsibility to Protect' [2019] *Cooperation and Conflict* 1; Katrin Kinzelbach, 'Will China's Rise Lead to a New Normative Order? An Analysis of China's Statements on Human Rights at the United Nations (2000–2010)' (2012) 30(3) *Netherlands Quarterly of Human Rights* 299; Suraj Jacob, John A Scherpereel and Melinda Adams, 'Will Rising Powers Undermine Global Norms? The Case of Gender-Balanced Decision-Making' (2017) 23(4) *European Journal of International Relations* 780.

THE UNITED NATIONS PREVENTION AND PROTECTION ARCHITECTURE   113

backlash narrative suggests.[12] Rather, they are contesting and recreating the fabric of this regime in a way that simultaneously permits experimentation with innovative protection approaches, yet arguably is eroding its core human rights foundations in the process, in exchange for a more pragmatic response to protection crises.

Given the enormous progress made in the area of strengthening human protection norms over the past few decades, this article seeks to make sense of these changing trends and patterns by focusing on the normative and institutional development of human protection within the UN. It focuses on core protection agendas: the protection of civilians (PoC) in UN peacekeeping, the responsibility to protect (R2P), and looks briefly at the pushback on the relationship between human rights and prevention at the UN. For each of these agendas the article explains, first, the development of the normative and institutional architecture through which they are implemented. Second, it examines the current reform process aimed at strengthening the UN's prevention and protection capacity in each of these three areas, to show the direction in which the human protection regime is heading. Third, the article demonstrates the contours of member-state engagement with the latest series of UN peace and security reforms to determine whether this engagement does indeed constitute a backlash or something else. The concluding section of the article sets out characteristics of the altered international context that has generated paralysis in international cooperation over more assertive efforts to prevent violent conflict and protect populations. It considers avenues through which countries, such as Australia, that are committed to the values of human rights and the international rule of law, can promote the strengthening of these important human protection norms.

2   The Evolution of the International Human Protection Regime in International Law and Institutions

One of the most radical shifts that has defined the peace and security agenda of the UN since the end of the Cold War has been the elevation of human rights, and individual rights protection, in the development of global

---

12   These states are comprised primarily from the African Group, the Organisation of Islamic Cooperation, the Arab Group, and the Non-Aligned Movement that constitutes a significant majority in the United Nations Human Rights Council. See Amr Essam, 'The Like Minded Group (LMG): Speaking Truth to Power', *Universal Rights Group* (Web Page, 10 May 2016) <www.universal-rights.org/blog/like-minded-group-lmg-speaking-truth-power>.

human protection norms and their implementation. The UN Charter was foundational in repurposing the use of military force in international relations from a tool of statecraft, towards individual and collective security of states. The Charter, however, is ambiguous on the applicability of the collective security provisions in Chapter VII to permit the use of force for human protection purposes.[13] It was not until the 1990s that human rights and protection came to the fore as a justification for the use of force, as the concept of humanitarian intervention became widely debated.

Today, human protection frameworks have expanded significantly—both in number, and in conceptual clarity and substance. Any discussion of a backlash on the current regime needs to first take account of the extent to which international norms and institutions have been fundamentally reoriented in the past three decades. Human protection has become a core mandate of peace and security interventions, and while normative principles within this regime are continually being contested,[14] the overarching protection objectives are not.

During the Cold War, the international community, divided by ideological conflict, failed to agree on collective responses to aid civilian populations suffering from major atrocity events and genocides of this period, such as those in Indonesia, East Pakistan, Biafra, and Cambodia.[15] Given its foucs on interstate conflict, the scholarly literature on armed conflict during this period did not associate the systematic study of causality of interstate conflict with the study of local dynamics of violent conflict, to understand when and where civilians became strategic targets.[16] The political science and international relations research on the causality, dynamics, and decline of situations of internal

---

13   Ian Hurd, 'Is Humanitarian Intervention Legal? The Rule of Law in an Incoherent World' (2011) 25(3) *Ethics & International Affairs* 293, 310.

14   Emily Paddon Rhoads and Jennifer Welsh, 'Close Cousins in Protection: The Evolution of Two Norms' (2019) 95(3) *International Affairs* 597, 605–615.

15   Although scholars have pointed to the actions of Vietnam in Cambodia, India in East Pakistan, and Tanzania in Uganda as precursors to the notion of humanitarian intervention. Gareth Evans, *The Responsibility to Protect: Ending Mass Atrocity Crimes Once and For All* (Brookings Institution Press, 2008) 23–25.

16   Benjamin A Valentino, 'Why We Kill: The Political Science of Political Violence against Civilians' (2014) 17 *Annual Review of Political Science* 89, 94; Barbara Harff, 'Genocide and Political Mass Murder: Definitions, Theories, Analyses' in Michael Stohl, Mark I Lichbach and Peter Nils Grabosky (eds), *States and Peoples in Conflict: Transformations of Conflict Studies* (Routledge, 2017) 208.

THE UNITED NATIONS PREVENTION AND PROTECTION ARCHITECTURE   115

conflict and mass atrocities is therefore a relatively new addition to both scholarly literature and policy frameworks.[17]

Debates around humanitarian intervention—the use of military force for protecting populations within the jurisdiction of another state—came to prominence in the 1990s, following the end of the Cold War. In the early years of the decade, the new geopolitical dynamics precipitated an initial surge in cooperation within the Security Council,[18] including early success in ending the Iraqi invasion of Kuwait in 1991. However, the end of the Cold War also precipitated a spike in the number of civil conflicts that tragically unravelled in mass atrocity situations throughout the decade.[19] From Somalia, to Rwanda, and Bosnia, the UN failed to protect civilians from genocide and ethnic cleansing. Despite the presence of UN peacekeepers in these locations, these operations had no mandate to protect the civilian populations, nor appropriate doctrinal guidance or operational procedures in place to deal with such scenarios.[20]

The tragic events of the 1990s propelled a rapid development of human protection norms, alongside robust debate around the ethics and legality of humanitarian intervention.[21] The influence of human rights in the post-Second World War era has, as argued by Theodor Meron,[22] 'humanized' the laws of war and facilitated a reinterpretation of international humanitarian law to prioritise individual human rights protection. This context served as a precursor to the emergence of a human-rights centred protection doctrine in situations of armed conflict, reorienting the international legal order from

---

17   Scott Straus, *Fundamentals of Genocide and Mass Atrocity Prevention* (United States Holocaust Memorial Museum, 2016) 54.

18   The Security Council established nearly twice as many peace operations from 1988 to 1994 than in the 40 years prior. See Conor Foley, *UN Peacekeeping Operations and the Protection of Civilians: Saving Succeeding Generations* (Cambridge University Press, 2017) 78.

19   The Uppsala Conflict Database Program uses 1989 as a reference point for measuring state-based violence, the resurgence in the number of state-based conflicts underway have matched immediate post-Cold War numbers. See Pettersson, Högbladh and Öberg (n 6) 590.

20   Foley (n 18) 59–105.

21   See generally, Anne Orford, *International Authority and the Responsibility to Protect* (Cambridge University Press, 2011); Simon Chesterman, *Just War or Just Peace? Humanitarian Intervention and International Law* (Oxford University Press, 2002); Nicholas J Wheeler, *Saving Strangers: Humanitarian Intervention in International Society* (Oxford University Press, 2000).

22   See generally, Theodor Meron, 'The Humanization of Humanitarian Law' (2000) 94(2) *American Journal of International Law* 239; Ruti G Teitel, *Humanity's Law* (Oxford University Press, 2011).

the protection of state security towards the individual human rights protection (and accountability), or the 'individualisation' of war.[23]

International humanitarian law is the touchstone for this new protection paradigm. Distinguishing between combatants and non-combatants has been instrumental in shaping the modern understanding of civilians,[24] affording special protections to civilian populations, and urging restraint on behalf of belligerent parties. However, as contemporary armed conflicts are predominantly internal and generate significant costs for civilians in terms of fatalities, casualties, displacement, and livelihoods lost, the international human protection regime incorporates human rights as a more comprehensive legal framework to protect individuals from atrocities in situations of armed conflict and peacetime. The consolidation of international criminal law through the *Rome Statute of the International Criminal Court* (1998) further expanded the basis for individual prosecution and accountability for crimes against humanity.

Core protection doctrines at the UN are grounded in international law, yet are not legally binding on members of the international community— state and non-state. Rather, they serve to guide UN operations and regulate member-state behaviour in response to situations of violent conflict. Among these international protection doctrines are children and armed conflict,[25] protection of civilians,[26] women, peace, and security,[27] R2P,[28] Human Rights up Front,[29] and youth, peace, and security.[30] A combination of the above international legal standards and these protection doctrines has generated a comprehensive regime for advancing the protection of civilian populations during periods of armed violence. The remit of this regime includes a variety

---

23   Jennifer M Welsh, 'The Individualisation of War: Defining a Research Programme' (2019) 53(1) *Annals of the Fondazione Luigi Einaudi: An Interdisciplinary Journal of Economics, History and Political Science* 9, 9–28; Gabriella Blum, 'The Individualization of War: From War to Policing in the Regulations of Armed Conflicts' in Austin Sarat, Lawrence Douglas and Martha Merrill Umphrey (eds), *Law and War* (Stanford University Press, 2014) 48, 52.

24   See generally, Helen M Kinsella, *The Image before the Weapon: A Critical History of the Distinction between Combatant and Civilian* (Cornell University Press, 2011).

25   SC Res 1261, UN Doc S/RES/1261 (25 August 1999).

26   SC Res 1296, UN Doc S/RES/1296 (19 April 2000).

27   SC Res 1325, UN Doc S/RES/1325 (31 October 2000).

28   International Commission on Intervention and State Sovereignty, *The Responsibility to Protect: Report of the International Commission on Intervention and State Sovereignty* (International Development Research Centre, 2001).

29   United Nations, *Rights up Front: A Plan of Action to Strengthen the UN's Role in Protecting People in Crises: Follow-up to the Report of the Secretary-General's Internal Review Panel on UN Action in Sri Lanka* (2013).

30   SC Res 2419, UN Doc S/RES/2419 (6 June 2018).

THE UNITED NATIONS PREVENTION AND PROTECTION ARCHITECTURE   117

of interventions by UN member states to prevent or halt the targeting of civilians through armed violence. These range from capacity building and human rights promotion, through to tools of preventive mediation and diplomacy, sanctions, including asset freezes and travel bans, no-fly zones, targeted aerial strikes, and the full spectrum of peace operations from peacekeeping through to peace enforcement and stabilisation missions.

As this brief survey has illustrated, current doctrinal and institutional developments on the protection of populations affected by violent conflict are unprecedented, and extensive. Implementing human protection in today's difficult geopolitical environment and complex armed conflicts remains a daunting challenge, however. The next sections considers the core civilian protection frameworks, PoC and R2P, and look at the relationship between human rights and prevention, to suggest that states have demonstrated a surprising willingness to support expansion of the human protection agenda into new and unprecedented areas of institutionalisation and operationalisation. However, there has been a parallel campaign to undermine human rights across the UN, and this campaign has influenced both the way that member states contest the human rights foundations of human protection norms, and the way that states have interpreted and negotiated on the UN peace and security reform process. While many of the reforms being implemented are much needed and rectify many of the inefficiencies and lack of coordination that has hampered effective UN prevention and protection, these dynamics of contestation have weakened other aspects of the human protection agenda, most importantly in the area of consensus on its normative foundations.

3   Protection of Civilians

UN peacekeeping was never anticipated or included in the UN Charter; rather it was an 'invention of the United Nations',[31] with UN troops first deployed to monitor the Arab-Israeli ceasefire in 1948. The legitimacy of UN peacekeeping is based on Chapter VI of the UN Charter that calls for the peaceful resolution of disputes, and Chapter VII that allows the Security Council to take forceful and non-forceful measures to maintain international peace and security.[32]

---

31   *An Agenda for Peace: Preventive Diplomacy, Peacemaking and Peace-keeping: Report of the Secretary-General*, UN Doc A/47/277–S/24111 (17 June 1992) [46].

32   United Nations Department of Peacekeeping Operations, *United Nations Peacekeeping Operations: Principles and Guideines* (United Nations, 2008) 13 <https://peacekeeping .un.org/sites/default/files/capstone_eng_0.pdf>.

Traditional peacekeeping operations were deployed with mandates to monitor ceasefires and assist with the implementation of peace accords. Operating on principles of neutrality, impartiality, consent, and non-use of force except for self-defence, the ability of UN peacekeepers to fulfil their mandates was compromised in situations where they were stationed in volatile conflicts, and there was no peace to keep.[33] The PoC doctrine developed during the 1990s alongside a transformation in the function of peacekeeping at the end of the Cold War into complex stabilising missions, and in recognition of the increasing need to adapt to the types of conflict environments in which they were deployed.[34] Peacekeepers were not only witnesses to mass atrocities in countries like Angola, Somalia, Rwanda, and Bosnia, but were complicit in committing atrocities themselves, as has been documented by peacekeepers in Somalia.[35]

New applications of international law were used in the context of peacekeeping during this era, for example, the Security Council first mandated a Chapter VII forceful intervention in an internal conflict in the United Nations Operation in Somalia in 1992.[36] Throughout the 1990s, the UN developed doctrine to provide guidance on when it would be appropriate to use force to protect civilians within the jurisdiction of a host state, leading to the first Security Council resolution on PoC in 1999.[37] In 2000, the *Report of the Panel on United Nations Peace Operations* to the Security Council (referred to as the 'Brahimi report' after the Algerian panel chair, diplomat Lakhdar Brahimi) proposed a series of reforms to strengthen UN peacekeeping, that included better resourcing and clearer mandates with sufficient support from UN member states.[38] The Brahimi report questioned the relevance of traditional

---

33   Literature exploring the challenges facing traditional peacekeeping principles include: Emily Paddon Rhoads, *Taking Sides in Peacekeeping: Impartiality and the Future of the United Nations* (Oxford University Press, 2016); John Karlsrud, 'The UN at War: Examining the Consequences of Peace-enforcement Mandates for the UN Peacekeeping Operations in the CAR, the DRC and Mali' (2015) 36(1) *Third World Quarterly* 40; Mats Berdal and David H Uck, 'The Use of Force in UN Peacekeeping Operations' (2015) 160(1) *The RUSI Journal* 6.

34   These complex missions deployed primarily in situations of internal conflict have been labelled as 'second generation' peacekeeping missions, starting in the late 1980s. See Michael W Doyle and Rosalyn Higgins, 'Second Generation Peacekeeping' (1995) 89 *Proceedings of the Annual Meeting (American Society of International Law)* 275.

35   Foley (n 18) 85–87.

36   SC Res 794, UN Doc S/RES/794 (3 December 1992).

37   SC Res 1265, UN Doc S/RES/1265 (17 September 1999).

38   *Identical Letters Dated 21 August 2000 from the Secretary-General to the President of the General Assembly and the President of the Security Council: Report of the Panel on United Nations Peace Operations*, UN Doc A/55/305–S/2000/809 (21 August 2000).

THE UNITED NATIONS PREVENTION AND PROTECTION ARCHITECTURE   119

peacekeeping principles of state consent, neutrality, and impartiality, arguing that the contemporary context of armed conflict required mandates that were more 'robust'. It stated: 'when the United Nations does send its forces to uphold the peace, they must be prepared to confront the lingering forces of war and violence, with the ability and determination to defeat them'.[39]

Today, over 95% of UN peacekeepers operate under a PoC mandate,[40] including a Chapter VII mandate for the use of force in every multi-dimensional peacekeeping mission since 1999.[41] In the past 20 years, the UN has developed a PoC doctrine and operational guidelines, and provided training to UN peacekeepers in an effort to bring coherence to international standards and practices around PoC.[42]

The catalyst for a new round of major reforms came in 2015 with the release of the *Report of the High-Level Independent Panel on United Nations Peace Operations*.[43] The report put forward a series of recommendations that included the need to prioritise the prevention and resolution of violent conflicts through political processes and mediation,[44] and to empower actors in the field, including a wider range of local and regional stakeholders.[45] The report called for a better realignment of peacekeeping mandates with the actual capacity and resourcing of peacekeeping forces on the ground.[46] One of the greatest challenges for UN peacekeeping has been the growing number of tasks that are being included in mission mandates (often referred to as 'Christmas Tree' operations) at a time when major state funders are cutting their financial contributions.[47]

---

39   Ibid viii.

40   'United Nations Peacekeeping', *United Nations Department of Peacekeeping Operations* (Web Document, 2018) <https://peacekeeping.un.org/sites/default/files/dpko-brochure -2018v17.pdf>.

41   The use of force in peacekeeping missions is a last resort option for the sole purpose of self-defence (including defence of the peacekeeping mandate): see Lise Morjé Howard and Anjali Kaushlesh Dayal, 'The Use of Force in UN Peacekeeping' (2018) 72(1) *International Organization* 74.

42   Victoria Holt, Glyn Taylor and Max Kelly, *Protecting Civilians in the Context of UN Peace Operations: Successes, Setbacks and Remaining Challenges* (United Nations, 2009); *Protection of Civilians: Implementing Guidelines for Military Components of United Nations Peacekeeping Missions*, UN Doc PK/G/2015.02 (13 February 2015).

43   High-Level Independent Panel on United Nations Peace Operations, *Uniting our Strengths for Peace: Politics, Partnership and People* (Report to Secretary-General, 16 June 2015).

44   Ibid 11–12.

45   Ibid xi–xiv.

46   Ibid ix.

47   Security Council Report, 'Is Christmas Really Over? Improving the Mandating of Peace Operations' (Research Report No 1, 22 February 2019).

The report also called on the UN to deploy the 'full spectrum'[48] of peace operations through a 'continuum'[49] of responses to sequence the transition between phases of operations in a more coherent and responsive way. In response, UN Secretary-General Ban Ki-moon set out his priorities for reforming peacekeeping, which included the pursuit of political settlements, protecting civilians, creating more flexible and tailored mandates, increasing accountability, strengthening global-regional partnerships, and renewing a focus on prevention and mediation.[50] Ban's tenure was ending, and he chose to leave the details and implementation of the reform to his successor.

António Guterres commenced his tenure as UN Secretary-General in January 2017 based on his promise to embark on an ambitious reform process that prioritised the organisation's capacity for prevention of major humanitarian crises.[51] Guterres moved swiftly to implement reforms in the areas of peace and security, development, management, and peacekeeping. As a result of the peace and security reforms, in 2018, the Department of Peacekeeping Operations and the Department of Political Affairs were restructured into the new Department of Peace Operations, and Department of Political and Peacebuilding Affairs in an effort to remove overlap and competition between the two departments that had been undermining effective operational capacity in the field.[52]

In addition to the restructuring, Guterres launched a major peacekeeping reform initiative, 'Action for Peacekeeping' (A4P), at the Security Council on 28 March 2018.[53] The Declaration of Shared Commitments on A4P was opened on 16 August 2018 for endorsement, and at the time of writing has been affirmed by 152 member states and four regional organisations.[54] A4P

---

48   High-Level Independent Panel on United Nations Peace Operations (n 43) 12.

49   Ibid viii.

50   *The Future of United Nations Peace Operations: Implementation of the Recommendations of the High-Level Independent Panel on Peace Operations: Report of the Secretary-General,* UN Doc A/70/357–S/2015/682 (2 September 2015) 3–8.

51   António Guterres, 'Challenges and Opportunities for the United Nations' (Vision Statement, 4 April 2016), 3.

52   *Restructuring of the United Nations Peace and Security Pillar: Report of the Secretary-General,* UN Doc A/72/525 (13 October 2017).

53   *United Nations Peacekeeping Operations,* UN Doc S/PV.8218 (28 March 2018), 3.

54   'Action for Peacekeeping: Declaration of Shared Commitments on UN Peacekeeping Operations', *United Nations Peacekeeping* (Web Document, 16 August 2018) <https://peacekeeping.un.org/sites/default/files/a4p-declaration-en.pdf>. The regional organisations were the European Union, the Organisation internationale de la Francophonie, the African Union Commission, and the North Atlantic Treaty Organization (NATO). For the full list of endorsing states and organisations see 'Action for Peacekeeping',

THE UNITED NATIONS PREVENTION AND PROTECTION ARCHITECTURE 121

addresses key challenges facing contemporary UN peacekeeping missions that were highlighted in the *Report of the High-Level Independent Panel on United Nations Peace Operations* mentioned above. It did so by, among other commitments, affirming the primacy of politics in conflict resolution, including the role of UN peacekeeping, and committing to 'pursue clear, focused, sequenced, prioritized and achievable mandates by the Security Council matched by appropriate resources'.[55] The declaration also brings peacekeeping reform in line with the visions of sustaining peace, and the peace and security architecture reforms, by encouraging stronger local engagement, and better coherence between the security, development, and human rights pillars of the UN. However, despite the political commitments to the declaration by member states, A4P has yet to translate into specific policy or any notable changes in Security Council mandating practices or the mandates of existing missions, political strategies, or resourcing.[56]

Further, although political commitment has been achieved on the aspirational goals of the declaration to improve the effectiveness and coherence of peace operations, the Security Council has objected to the directives on mandating processes, with the five permanent member states particularly concerned that the text imposes unwarranted restraint on its authority to craft mandates.[57] In 2018, the Security Council refused to pass a resolution drafted by the Netherlands and Côte d'Ivoire endorsing the A4P proposals to reform mandating processes.[58] There has also been resistance to efforts by the Secretary-General to integrate human rights more deeply within peace operations. Notably, Russia has been vocal in clarifying that its support for the peacekeeping reforms does not extend to the provisions for strengthening human rights protections:

> [W]e do not support equating the tasks of monitoring human rights and protecting civilians, since the latter could involve the use of force by peacekeepers ... During strategic reviews of missions their mandates

---

United Nations Peacekeeping (Web Page, 12 July 2019) <https://peacekeeping.un.org/en/action-for-peacekeeping-a4p>.

55 'Action for Peacekeeping: Declaration of Shared Commitments on UN Peacekeeping Operations' (n 54) [5].

56 Jake Sherman, 'Action for Peacekeeping: One Year into the Implementation of the Declaration of Shared Commitments' (Issue Brief, International Peace Institute, September 2019) 1–2.

57 Security Council Report (n 47) 10.

58 Richard Gowan, 'The Security Council and the Protection of Civilians' in Lisa Sharland (ed), *Special Report: Evolution of the Protection of Civilians in UN Peacekeeping* (Australian Strategic Policy Institute, 2019) 7, 7–9.

should be systematically purged and their peripheral human rights, humanitarian and social tasks handed over to their host Governments.[59]

The discursive contestation of the human rights dimension of peacekeeping in Security Council dialogues has been matched by behavioural contestation through efforts by Russia and China to cut funding for human rights posts in peacekeeping budgets.[60] China has been a strong supporter of PoC through its major role in providing peacekeeping financing and troops, and both Russia and China have approved innovative PoC mandates in recent years.[61] Yet their insistence on marginalising the human rights dimensions of peacekeeping illustrates how rising powers are being more assertive in contesting the normative structure of international order, or 'global order norms',[62] with the increased support of member states in the Like-Minded Group.[63] As argued in the introduction, while the contours of their resistance to human rights norms are familiar in global politics, the current geopolitical context has strengthened their influence in the UN to reshape the global protection agenda in alignment with their broader values and interests.

4   The Responsibility to Protect

The R2P doctrine made a transformative entry into the debates on humanitarian intervention, articulating the legal, political, and moral obligations for protecting civilian populations that extend to the international community.

---

59   *United Nations Peacekeeping Operations*, 8349th mtg, UN Doc S/PV.8349 (12 September 2018) 11.

60   Rick Gladstone, 'China and Russia Move To Cut Human Rights Jobs in UN Peacekeeping', *New York Times* (online, 27 June 2018) <https://www.nytimes.com/2018/06/27/world/africa/china-russia-un-human-rights-cuts.html>; Colum Lynch, 'Russia and China see in Trump Era a Chance to Roll Back Human Rights Promotion at U.N.', *Foreign Policy* (online, 26 June 2018) <https://foreignpolicy.com/2018/06/26/russia-and-china-see-in-trump-era -a-chance-to-roll-back-human-rights-promotion-at-u-n/>.

61   See, eg, SC Res 2165, UN Doc S/RES/2165 (14 July 2014) on humanitarian access into Syria; this was the first resolution of its kind to authorise humanitarian access inside a state without consent. See also SC Res 2098, UN Doc S/RES/2098 (28 March 2013) which mandated a forceful intervention through the Force Intervention Brigade in the Democratic Republic of Congo to 'neutralize and disarm' Congolese Rebels (M23) and foreign armed groups.

62   Rosemary Foot and Andrew Walter, *China, the United States, and Global Order* (Cambridge University Press, 2011).

63   Ted Piccone, 'China's Long Game On Human Rights at the United Nations' (Report, The Brookings Institute, September 2018).

THE UNITED NATIONS PREVENTION AND PROTECTION ARCHITECTURE 123

The origins of the principle began in the same context of the 1990s in which the PoC doctrine was established, yet pertained to a much broader question than what capacity UN peacekeepers had to deploy force to protect civilian populations in missions where they were already present. Rather, the Canadian government commissioned the International Commission on Intervention and State Sovereignty to consider to what extent the international community at large held a political, moral, and legal duty to use military force to protect civilians during major humanitarian crises.[64] The purpose of the Commission was to grapple with the indeterminate status of humanitarian intervention in international law, and to recommend guidance to the international community in responding to situations like the genocide in Rwanda. Of particular consequence were the experiences of the North Atlantic Treaty Organization (NATO)-led military intervention in Kovoso—without Security Council backing—that was credited with halting large-scale human suffering yet failing to prevent ethnic cleansing.[65]

In response to the request by the Canadian government, the Commission produced the report *The Responsibility to Protect* in 2001, seeking to recalibrate the language of humanitarian intervention that implied the international community had a right to intervene in the internal affairs of states. Instead, it emphasised the responsibility of states to prevent large-scale humanitarian crises, and the legal, moral, and political prerogative of the international community to protect the human rights of populations where states failed to do so themselves.[66] A condensed articulation of the R2P principle was included in the *2005 World Summit Outcome* document.[67] The references to R2P state that the primary responsibility of member states is to uphold their responsibility to prevent and protect populations from mass atrocities, which it clarified as constituting genocide, war crimes, ethnic cleansing, and crimes against humanity.[68] It charges the international community with a responsibility to assist states in fulfilling this responsibility.

---

64   International Commission on Intervention and State Sovereignty (n 28) vii, 2.
65   Independent International Commission on Kosovo, *The Kosovo Report: Conflict, International Response, Lessons Learned* (Oxford University Press, 2000) 5.
66   International Commission on Intervention and State Sovereignty (n 28) 19–28.
67   *2005 World Summit Outcome*, UN Doc A/RES/60/1 (n 9) paras 138–140.
68   The scope of R2P is limited to these four international crimes—distinguishing it from PoC that concerns itself with the protection of civilians in situations of armed conflict. Operationally, there are overlaps in these two doctrines. See Charles T Hunt and Lisa Sharland, 'Implementing R2P through United Nations Peacekeeping Operations: Opportunities and Challenges' in Cecilia Jacob and Martin Mennecke (eds), *Implementing the Responsibility to Protect: A Future Agenda* (Routledge, 2020) 215.

124 AUSTRALIAN YEAR BOOK OF INTERNATIONAL LAW VOLUME 38

According to the text, when states are unwilling or manifestly fail to do so, the international community '[h]as the responsibility to use appropriate diplomatic, humanitarian and other peaceful means, in accordance with Chapters VI and VIII of the Charter, to help protect populations from genocide, war crimes, ethnic cleansing and crimes against humanity'.[69] The document further clarified the conditions and right authority under which the use of military force may be warranted for the purpose of protection:

> In this context, we are prepared to take collective action, in a timely and decisive manner, through the Security Council, in accordance with the Charter, including Chapter VII, on a case-by-case basis and in cooperation with relevant regional organizations as appropriate, should peaceful means be inadequate and national authorities are manifestly failing to protect their populations from genocide, war crimes, ethnic cleansing and crimes against humanity.[70]

R2P is a guiding principle that was endorsed by member states at the UN, and draws its authority from existing legal provisions in the UN Charter, alongside other sources such as international criminal and human rights law, and the *Convention on the Prevention and Punishment of the Crime of Genocide* (1948).[71] Yet from the outset, the doctrine lacked an institutional 'home' with commensurate resourcing, implementation requirements or compliance mechanism. Since 2009, there has been a Special Advisor to the UN Secretary-General (SASG) on the R2P, based in the Joint Office on the Prevention of Genocide and the Responsibility to Protect in the Secretariat, to promote the implementation of R2P across the UN, although this role does not have an implementation or compliance mandate, nor a regular UN budget.

The SASGs have, over successive terms, been instrumental in developing the conceptual understanding of R2P within the UN and among member states.[72] Publication of annual reports on R2P by the Secretary-General, as with annual

---

69 *2005 World Summit Outcome*, UN Doc A/RES/60/1 (n 9) para 139.

70 Ibid.

71 For analysis on the legal foundations of R2P, see generally, Ekkehard Strauss, 'A Bird in the Hand is Worth Two in the Bush–On the Assumed Legal Nature of the Responsibility to Protect' (2009) 1(3) *Global Responsibility to Protect* 291; Jennifer Welsh and Maria Banda, 'International Law and the Responsibility to Protect: Clarifying or Expanding States' Responsibilities?' (2010) 2(3) *Global Responsibility to Protect* 213.

72 For more details, see Cecilia Jacob, 'From Norm Contestation to Norm Implementation: Recursivity and the Responsibility to Protect' (2018) 24(3) *Global Governance: A Review of Multilateralism and International Organizations* 391.

THE UNITED NATIONS PREVENTION AND PROTECTION ARCHITECTURE 125

reports on PoC, has fostered a deepened engagement on the substance of the norm and scope of activities related to its implementation. Other networks have been developed to promote and implement R2P, such as the diplomatic Group of Friends on R2P based both at UN headquarters in New York, and the Human Rights Council in Geneva. The non-governmental organisation Global Centre for the Responsibility to Protect serves as a secretariat for a global network of R2P focal points—nominated officials from 61 countries and two regional organisations—committed to deepening the domestic implementation of R2P.[73]

As this brief survey suggests, R2P has been implemented in a very ad hoc and differentiated manner both across UN agencies, and by national and regional actors.[74] R2P has been cited in over 80 Security Council resolutions and presidential statements,[75] and many more times in the General Assembly and Human Rights Council. Yet, R2P has rarely been invoked to mandate meaningful interventions in situations of severe atrocities and civilian suffering, as witnessed by the international paralysis in situations such as Syria, Yemen, and more recently in Myanmar. The R2P–inspired intervention in Libya in 2011 was the significant exception to this reluctance due to intense diplomatic negotiations at the Security Council led by France and the United Kingdom.[76] Following the imposition of a no-fly zone and NATO-led airstrikes that enabled rebel groups to depose Muammar Gaddafi, fallout from the Libyan intervention included charges of over-reach of mandate and regime change that significantly affected the willingness of the UNSC, particularly China and Russia, to mandate the use of force for protection, notably in the Syrian crisis that emerged in 2012.[77] The devastating fallout from this intervention marked a watershed moment in global politics. Not only was R2P discredited as a viable doctrine for mass atrocity prevention in the Security Council, but the internal dynamics of the Security Council evidenced a serious downturn in relations

---

73 See 'Global Network of R2P Focal Points', *Global Centre for the Responsibility to Protect* (Web Page) <https://www.globalr2p.org/the-global-network-of-r2p-focal-points/>.

74 For a detailed study of this phenomenon, see Cecilia Jacob and Martin Mennecke (eds), *Implementing the Responsibility to Protect: A Future Agenda* (Routledge, 2020).

75 'UN Security Council Resolutions and Presidential Statements Referencing R2P', *Global Centre for the Responsibility to Protect* (Web Page, 8 October 2019) < https://www.globalr2p .org/resources/un-security-council-resolutions-and-presidential-statements-referencing -r2p/>.

76 Jason Ralph and Jess Gifkins, 'The Purpose of United Nations Security Council Practice: Contesting Competence Claims in the Normative Context Created by the Responsibility to Protect' (2017) 23(3) *European Journal of International Relations* 630, 637.

77 Justin Morris, 'Libya and Syria: R2P and the Spectre of the Swinging Pendulum' (2013) 89(5) *International Affairs* 1265, 1274.

between Council members, and an unwillingness to act assertively on protection mandates across the many conflict zones in which peace operations are engaged.[78]

The 'toxic' nature of 'R2P talk' post-Libya within the UN[79] has had a bearing not only on efforts by R2P advocate states, civil society, and UN officials to preserve the norm, but also on the nature of the reform process currently underway, which places prevention at the heart of institutional reform.[80] On the first, R2P advocates have sought to recalibrate the language and framing of R2P through the Secretary-General's annual reports and annual General Assembly dialogues to emphasise the atrocity prevention dimension of R2P, and to demonstrate areas of intersection with other UN agendas where it could be fruitfully advanced. These include agendas such as human rights, transitional justice, international accountability, and peacebuilding. To this end, R2P has evolved from its cosmopolitan underpinnings towards an increasingly pragmatic agenda focused on strengthening state-capacity and early prevention. While these objectives are useful in moving forward practical prevention efforts in localised contexts, the overall result has been that R2P as a doctrine has lost much of its relevance for application in the most severe cases of humanitarian crisis for which it was initially conceived.

On the reform process, the most recent reforms proposed by the Secretary-General to UN member states in 2017 foregrounded prevention as the over-riding priority for the UN.[81] However, the Secretary-General did not directly promote R2P within his prevention agenda given, first, the broad conceptualisation of prevention he advanced that encompasses armed conflict, climate-induced disasters, and other major humanitarian crises, in which atrocities crimes are part of this broader picture. Second, he chose not to use language that would generate controversy among member states as part of his pragmatic approach to gaining consent by member states needed to

---

78   For an analysis on the parallel resistance to mandating assertive protection measures in the field under both both PoC and R2P after the 2011 Libyan intervention, see Paddon Rhoads and Welsh (n 14) 613–615.

79   Paddon Rhoads and Welsh (n 14) 615.

80   For a detailed account of the rationale and design of the reform process built on prevention, see Cecilia Jacob, 'Institutionalising Prevention at the UN: International Organisation Reform as a site of norm Contestation' *Global Governance: A Review of Multilateralism and International Organizations* (forthcoming).

81   António Guterres, 'Remarks to the Security Council Open Debate on "Maintenance of International Peace and Security: Conflict Prevention and Sustaining Peace"', *United Nations Secretary-General* (Web Page, 10 January 2017) <https://www.un.org/sg/en/content/sg/speeches/2017-01-10/secretary-generals-remarks-maintenance-international-peace-and>.

endorse the proposed reform package.[82] Internally, the Secretary-General has remained committed to strengthening the remit of the SASG role and the Joint Office on Genocide Prevention and the Responsibility to Protect.[83] The Joint Office plays a substantive role in the core prevention mechanisms of the Secretariat[84] described further below. Yet the Secretary-General's commitment to R2P was not communicated with clarity to UN member states at the outset of his tenure, creating a level of ambiguity around the status of R2P in the overall push for prevention across the UN.[85] The inclusion of R2P on the formal agenda of the UN General Assembly in 2018–2019 has signalled the ongoing commitment by member states to the principle, even though concern over the lack of implementation remains disquieting.[86] The overall trajectory of the R2P doctrine therefore suggests that rather than being rolled back or dismantled, key international actors have contested and reshaped the R2P norm to accommodate the interests of a growing number of assertive states, and to preserve the core function of R2P as a preventive doctrine at the UN. While this strategic reframing has facilitated a more diverse discussion around the implementation of R2P in a range of institutional sites, from the Human Rights Council, to peacekeeping and development cooperation,[87] it also illustrates the lack of appetite at the international level among UN states to endorse intervention (with military force reserved as a last resort) into humanitarian situations where the interests of powerful states are at stake. It is for this reason that a number of proposals to reform Security Council working methods and accountability have been forwarded, without which norms such as R2P remain political commitments and aspirational norms, with limited potential to effect change on the ground.

---

82   Interviews with 37 UN officials, experts, and diplomats closely engaged with the reform process (Cecilia Jacob, New York and Washington, DC, April–May 2018, April 2019).

83   Interviews with Executive Office of the Secretary-General officials (Cecilia Jacob, New York, 19 April 2018, 30 April 2018).

84   Interviews with Joint Office on Genocide Prevention and the Responsibility to Protect officials (Cecilia Jacob, New York, 11 April 2018, 4 April 2019).

85   Interview with Group of Friends on R2P diplomat (Cecilia Jacob, New York, 2 May 2018).

86   'Summary of the UN General Assembly Plenary Meeting on the Responsibility to Protect', *Global Centre for the Responsibility to Protect* (Web Page, 30 July 2019) <https://www .globalr2p.org/publications/summary-of-the-2019-un-general-assembly-plenary-meeting -on-the-responsibility-to-protect/>.

87   Further discussion of these proposals is found in Jacob (n 72) 399–401.

5   Implications (for Prevention) of UN Contestation over Human Rights

Because of the current global pushback on human rights within the UN, a number of practical challenges have arisen that restrain the preventive capacity of the organisation. The former United Nations Human Rights Commissioner was repeatedly prevented from addressing the Security Council on systematic human rights violations in major conflict situations,[88] reinforcing the selectivity of the UN's protection agenda, and undermining its legitimacy to put prevention at the heart of its operations. Both UN officials and diplomats who were engaged in closed-door negotiations cite a concerted campaign by Russia to break the link between prevention and human rights as the guiding normative structure for the prevention agenda.[89] Likewise, China has supported prevention as the guiding principle for reform, but has simultaneously pursued an agenda to weaken human rights within the UN system—often partnering with Russia in forums such as the Human Rights Council and the Security Council.[90] This competition often puts major players such as China, Russia, the G77 group of 134 developing country member states, and the Like-Minded Group of 52 member states in direct ideological opposition[91] to member states such as the United States, the United Kingdom, European member states, and like-minded partners such as Australia.

Examples of such competitive posturing are found in open debates on themes such as R2P and the protection of civilians.[92] The British representative to the 2018 ministerial-level open debate on the protection of civilians at the Security Council opposed ongoing efforts by member states to undermine the human rights dimension of peacekeeping through budgetary processes:

---

88   Rodrigo Campos, 'Russia Blocks UN Security Council Meeting on Human Rights in Syria', *Reuters* (online, 20 March 2018) <https://www.reuters.com/article/us-mideast -crisis-syria-un/russia-blocks-u-n-security-council-meeting-on-human-rights-in-syria -idUSKBN1GV2TQ>.

89   Colum Lynch, 'At UN, Russia and US Wage Quiet War over Appointments to Advance Broader Agendas', *Foreign Policy* (online, 12 June 2018) <https://foreignpolicy.com/2018/ 06/12/at-u-n-russia-and-u-s-wage-quiet-war-over-appointments-to-advance-broader -agendas/>; Interview with Department of Political Affairs' official (Cecilia Jacob, New York, 20 April 2018).

90   Piccone (n 63) 4; Human Rights Watch, *The Costs of International Advocacy: China's Interference in United Nations Human Rights Mechanisms* (Report, 5 September 2017) 53, 85.

91   Human Rights Watch (n 90) 9.

92   Jennifer M Welsh, 'Norm Robustness and the Responsibility to Protect' (2019) 4(1) *Journal of Global Security Studies* 53, 59–66.

THE UNITED NATIONS PREVENTION AND PROTECTION ARCHITECTURE   129

'Worryingly, we see at times the General Assembly seeking to weaken mandates agreed by the Council and the Fifth Committee by defunding human rights posts. This must stop'.[93]

Countering the sustained call by European and British delegates to integrate human rights and stronger accountability for human rights violations into reforms on UN peacekeeping in the same open debate, the Russian delegate claimed:

> [T]wo of the fundamental principles at issue are respect for the sovereignty of States and non-interference in their internal affairs. We continue to be seriously concerned about attempts to freely interpret the norms of international humanitarian law with regard to the protection of civilians in armed conflict, as well as their association with all kinds of concepts. Just recently, one delegation on the Security Council pulled the concept of so-called humanitarian intervention out of thin air.[94]

Such statements illustrate the ongoing effort by member states to contest the human rights foundation of related human protection norms, such as PoC and R2P as implemented in new structural reforms of the UN by emphasising alternative framings of protection of state sovereignty and non-interference, a strict interpretation of the UN Charter and international law, and a preference, as China stated, for 'pragmatic and effective measures'[95] over principled approaches to protection. Agreement over the centrality of prevention and the need for structural reform of the system is accepted, yet the normative foundations and principles that should guide a reformed institutional design remain a site of ongoing applicatory contestation.

UN bodies such as the Department of Political and Peacebuilding Affairs, the Department of Peace Operations, and the OHCHR, operate with a concept of prevention that maintains human rights at the core, both in terms of identifying early warning signs of mass atrocities, and strengthening national human rights systems as a mechanism of prevention. Officials within each of these departments express deep concerns over the rift emerging between member states, and the misalignment between stated reform priorities and the compromises being made by the Secretariat to have them passed.[96]

---

93   *Protection of Civilians in Armed Conflict: Ministerial-Level Open Debate on the Protection of Civilians*, UN SCOR, 8264th mtg, UN Doc S/PV.8264 (22 May 2018) 12.
94   Ibid 26.
95   Ibid 16.
96   Interview with Department of Political Affairs' official (Cecilia Jacob, New York, 20 April 2018); Interview with Department of Peacekeeping Operations' official (Cecilia

An independent inquiry into the actions of the UN in Rakhine state, published in May 2019, reiterated the fundamental structural weakness of the UN in preventing atrocities. It identified ongoing division between the UN agencies over the centrality of human rights, and the absence of an empowered resident coordinator, backed appropriately at the headquarters level, to lead on decisive early action in the context of situations with a high level of atrocity risk, including evidence of systematic human rights abuses.[97] The reform package introduced by Guterres in 2017 targets these shortcomings directly. Therefore the interaction between states and UN officials in contesting, reshaping, and designing new institutional configurations for the implementation of prevention and protection is an ongoing endeavour. The non-binding nature of UN human protection doctrines opens the door to reconstitution of the underlying norms in practice, which is both a weakness in terms of selectivity and inconsistency in application, but also a strength in terms of the way that protection agendas and mandates have, in a number of cases, been both pragmatic and responsive.

6   Conclusion

The emergence and expansion of the international human protection regime described in this article attests to the ability of the international community to respond to its failures through the development of law, norms, and institutions. This regime includes a robust interpretation of the human rights foundations of international law to develop doctrine and mechanisms for its implementation. The rationale of the current reform agenda is to institutionalise further the UN capacity to prevent situations of violent conflict and large-scale human rights violations. Member states have supported the prevention agenda by approving key aspects of the proposals set out by the Secretary-General in 2017.

Despite these efforts, contestation persists in a number of key areas that continue to undermine effective prevention and protection in many of the world's most volatile situations of violent conflict. As argued in the preceding sections, the contours of contestation by member states in relation to human protection norms are familiar terrain. This includes a persistent effort

---

Jacob, New York, 23 April 2018); Interviews with OHCHR officials (Cecilia Jacob, New York, 30 April, 3 May 2018, 7 May 2018, 3 April 2019).

97   Gert Rosenthal, 'A Brief and Independent Inquiry into the Involvement of the United Nations in Myanmar from 2010 to 2018' (Independent Report, United Nations, 29 May 2019) <https://www.un.org/sg/sites/www.un.org.sg/files/atoms/files/Myanmar%20Report%20 -%20May%202019.pdf>.

to undermine the human rights foundations of the prevention and protection agenda, and an emphasis on the primacy of sovereignty and non-intervention. Despite consistency in the nature of contestation from dissenting states, this contestation is occurring in an altered international political context that has rendered ineffective many of the efforts by the international community to protect civilians in today's most pressing conflicts, feeding into the belief that the regime is becoming redundant.

First, geopolitical tensions—notably between the United States, China, and Russia—escalated after the 2011 intervention in Libya and have prompted a paralysis in the ability of the Security Council to cooperate on the world's most significant humanitarian crises. Conflicts in Syria, Yemen, and Ukraine have enhanced these geopolitical tensions, and are exacerbated by the involvement of states such as Iran, Russia, Saudi Arabia, and Turkey in these regional conflicts. These high-stake conflicts have global ramifications, yet the complex internal dynamics and fragmentation within inflict the greatest toll on the civilians impacted by the fighting.

Second, we are witnessing a growing lack of unity across Western states that have traditionally championed international human rights and protection norms. The politics of Donald Trump, Brexit, and tensions between NATO members and Russia are key dynamics that have enhanced the perception of declining power in the West,[98] and encouraged increasing assertiveness by emerging powers to contest and redefine elements of the international order in line with their interests. The current drive to reform the UN creates opportunity for improved effectiveness and accountability within the organisations. However, it also exposes key peace and security departments and management processes to contestation and potential compromise over the positioning of human rights in field operations.

Given the context described above, backlash is understood in this article as the function of contestation by UN member states to reconfigure normative underpinnings of the international order. The status of human protection indicates that states are not reneging on established commitment to human protection as a core international peace and security objective. Notably in the area of peacekeeping, states have been willing to prioritise civilian protection in the formation of mandates and, perhaps worryingly, in increasingly coercive and robust interventions. The politics of R2P and the pushback on human rights as a feature of contemporary international politics, however, is demonstrative of the assertiveness of rising powers that are increasingly willing to

---

98   See generally Jess Gifkins, Samuel Jarvis and Jason Ralph, 'Brexit and the UN Security Council: Declining British Influence?' (2019) 95(6) *International Affairs* 1349.

challenge the prevailing liberal values underpinning the international system. States are reconstituting rather than unravelling international order, including the institutions that structure and maintain this order.

This article has also described aspects of the current reform process under-way, and I argue here that from a pragmatic standpoint, reform and renewal of the international peace and security legal and institutional order are currently the best of three potential scenarios presented by the editors of this special issue.[99] These three scenarios are reform and renew; retreat and realign; and reimagine and recreate. Were the current protection system, and norms, to be unravelled, there are no alternative institutional arrangements that could provide the comprehensive system of norm-building, decision-making, and coordination to address peace and security threats comparable to the UN. To retreat and realign would mean relying on regional organisations, alliances, and bilateral arrangements to respond in a piecemeal fashion to violent conflicts. The UN Charter provides for regional solutions to crises,[100] and organisations such as the African Union, European Union, the Organisation for Security and Cooperation in Europe, and NATO do have conflict prevention and peacekeeping functions. However, authorisation and legitimacy for interventions within the domestic jurisdiction of states come from the Security Council, which is necessary to prevent overreach and unwarranted interventionism within states.

For this reason it is crucial that the rules and institutional safeguards that do exist to preserve the sovereign integrity of states and hence the stability of international order are strengthened and renewed, rather than abandoned through retreat into unstable and fragmented arrangements. The final scenario, reimagine and recreate, presents an ideal view of the world—believing that the necessary vision, leadership and global consensus around the recreation of world order through the design of its core institutions—would offer a solution to the current deficiencies in the present day multilateral and international legal system. The UN was created in a very different era than today, with clear US leadership, depth of resolve and shared normative values among its key architects, years of strategic planning, and diplomacy.[101] The current international political context lacks clear leadership and ever-widening distribution of power among states with competing priorities and interests. This would mean that any effort to recreate core international legal and institutional structures

---

99   Peter G Danchin et al, 'Navigating the Backlash against Global Law and Institutions' (2020) 38 *Australian Year Book of International Law* 33, 47–49.

100   *Charter of the United Nations* ch VIII.

101   For a detailed account of this period, see Stephen C Schlesinger, *Act of Creation: The Founding of the United Nations* (Westview Press, 2003).

would move towards the lowest common denominator in terms of consensus outcomes and compromise. Rather than promising the most optimal outcome, this approach would result in much weaker alternatives to the current system, and therefore, reimagine and recreate represents the least desirable alternative at this point in history.

What then are the implications of these trends for actors such as Australia, Canada, the European Union, the United Kingdom, the United States, and those actively committed to promoting a strong normative foundation for the transforming global order? With the move towards a 'multiplex'[102] international order(s) with multiple centres of power, states need to identify partners with whom they can cooperate to articulate and advocate principled strategies in key international threats and challenges. With many competing and overlapping agendas, there is a need for states to identify core objectives that they seek to achieve through these agendas, and formulate coherent strategies to build into their diplomacy and advocacy at the international level.

Finally, these states need to support efforts to reform the UN and multilateral organisations, particularly in the area of prevention, with a strong commitment to preserving and strengthening human rights protection and accountability. Much of the perceived crisis in legitimacy of multilateralism stems from a very real inability of the UN and other regional organisations to act early on emerging crises or to transcend political difference to bring about meaningful resolution of ongoing conflicts. With the UN mired in conflict management, and unable to demonstrate success in preventing and resolving conflicts, or in reversing trends in forced migration flows, this failure feeds into a lack of faith in multilateralism and international cooperation to resolve these key issues, and a retreat away from global cooperation. Areas for strengthening the UN's prevention capacity have been identified and are well-known; investment in early warning systems, improving channels of communication from local level to international decision-makers, preventive diplomacy, and utilising the prevention 'toolbox' along a spectrum of increasingly assertive actions[103] to nudge difficult situations towards preventive outcomes. It is important that states such as Australia reaffirm their commitment to international cooperation through genuine and sustained support if they are to remain relevant and influential in shaping the laws, norms, and institutions of global order in the years to come.

102　See generally Amitav Acharya, 'After Liberal Hegemony: The Advent of a Multiplex World Order' (2017) 31(3) *Ethics & International Affairs* 271.

103　Ruben Reike, Serena K Sharma and Jennifer M Welsh, 'Conceptualizing the Responsibility to Prevent' in Serena K Sharma and Jennifer M Welsh (eds), *The Responsibility to Prevent: Overcoming the Challenges of Atrocity Prevention* (Oxford University Press, 2015) 21.

Navigating the Backlash: Re-Integrating WTO and Public International Law?

*Imogen Saunders**

1 Introduction

The World Trade Organisation ('WTO') is a relative youngster on the international scene: born in 1995 in the heights of internationalism, it is a Generation Z institution flanked by its mostly Boomer[1] and Generation X[2] companions. Yet at the tender age of 25, the WTO is being challenged like never before. Shifting geopolitical power and the ongoing trade war between the United States ('US') and China present new challenges to the way that trade rules are viewed and enforced. The blocking of Appellate Body ('AB') appointments by the US—a policy which began in earnest in 2017—threatens to leave the WTO dispute settlement system unable to function.[3] Yet although this tactic is new, it is only possible because of an overhang from the pre-WTO, ad-hoc *General Agreement on Tariffs and Trade ('GATT')*[4] years of international trade law—which enshrines primacy of consensus in decision making in the WTO.[5]

Viewing "backlash" as 'intense and sustained public disapproval of a system accompanied by aggressive steps to resist the system and to remove its legal force',[6] the US actions fit the bill. However, for this article, my focus is not on

---

* Dr Imogen Saunders is a senior lecturer in international law and international trade law at the ANU College of Law.

1 Such as the United Nations, the International Monetary Fund, the World Bank, the North American Treaty Organisation, the International Atomic Energy Agency and the World Health Organisation.

2 Such as the World Intellectual Property Organisation, the Association of South East Asian Nations, the Organisation for Islamic Cooperation and the World Economic Forum.

3 Bernard Hoekman and Petros Mavroidis, 'Party Like It's 1995: Necessary but Not Sufficient to Resolve WTO Appellate Body Crisis', *VOX* (Web Page, 26 August 2019) <https://voxeu.org/article/party-it-s-1995-resolving-wto-appellate-body-crisis>.

4 *General Agreement on Tariffs and Trade,* signed 30 October 1947, 64 UNTS 187 (entered into force 1 January 1948) ('*GATT*'); *Marrakesh Agreement Establishing the World Trade Organization,* opened for signature 15 April 1994, 1867 UNTS 3 (entered into force 1 January 1995) annex 1A ('*Marrakesh Agreement*').

5 See Wenwei Guan, 'Consensus Yet Not Consented: A Critique of the WTO Decision-Making by Consensus' (2014) 17(1) *Journal of International Economic Law* 77, 79–82.

6 David Caron and Esmé Shirlow, 'Dissecting Backlash: The Unarticulated Causes of Backlash and its Unintended Consequences' in Andreas Follesdal and Geir Ulfstein (eds), *The Judicialization of International Law: A Mixed Blessing?* (Oxford University Press, 2018) 159, 160.

these US acts but rather on two systemic issues in the WTO itself that have been present since its conception. This article will analyse these issues through the lens of backlash and the responses to it developed in our project.[7] Although both issues have been well-explored, the backlash analysis allows a different understanding of these issues, and potential responses to the problems caused by them. This article takes into account developments up to February 2020.

The first issue is the self-imposed siloisation of international trade law from general international law by the WTO panels and AB. This has seen international trade law *itself* retreat and realign, creating a sui generis space which at best does not fit with and at worst actively threatens the broader project of international law.

The second issue, which I argue is partly a consequence of the first, is the choice of States to disengage with the WTO system in favour of negotiating regional trade agreements ('RTAs')[8] that are more ably suited to meet their international trade *and* non-trade goals and obligations alike. The backlash here is not active resistance, but passive non-engagement. This is best illustrated in the ongoing failure of the Doha Development Round: a failure that has occurred at the same time participation in RTAs has grown dramatically.[9]

The issue of causation is no less vexed here than elsewhere in international law: States' use of free trade agreements and the lack of success of the Doha Round are attributed to each other, in an ongoing chicken and egg cycle.[10] Nonetheless, as will be argued, the use of free trade agreements to enshrine non-trade goals within a trade context shows the desire of States to reconcile trade with broader interests and the current siloisation of trade law by the WTO dispute settlement bodies ensures States must go outside the WTO system to achieve these goals.

Part 2 and Part 3 of this article will examine these dual retreats—in Part 2 the retreat from international law by the trade law system and in Part 3 the retreat from the trade law system by States. Using the responses developed in our project, Part 4 will then suggest that embracing the response of *reform and*

---

7   See Peter G Danchin et al, 'Navigating the Backlash against Global Law and Institutions' (2020) 38 *Australian Year Book of International Law* 33.

8   These are variously called 'free trade agreements', 'preferential trade agreements' and 'regional trade agreements'. This article uses the term regional trade agreements as it is the term used by the WTO.

9   See Xiaohua Bao and Xiaozhuo Wang, 'The Evolution and Reshaping of Globalization: A Perspective Based on the Development of Regional Trade Agreements' (2019) 27(1) *China and World Economy* 51, 53.

10   See on this point Martin Richardson, 'Navigating the "Backlash" against International Trade and Investment Liberalisation: Economic Perspectives on the Future of Regional Trade Agreements in Uncertain Times' (2020) 38 *Australian Year Book of International Law* 157.

136   AUSTRALIAN YEAR BOOK OF INTERNATIONAL LAW VOLUME 38

renew in two key facets of the dispute resolution system could help alleviate both of these problems.

As will be explored, these responses concern fundamental questions as to the identity and function of the WTO—is it a forum for diplomacy and politically expedient trade solutions, or is it a body of international law that fits within and operates in congruence with the greater international rules based order? This article suggests that in order to maintain the WTO's relevance and functioning as an ongoing international institution, it must be the latter.

2   Retreat from International Law: The Siloisation of International Trade Law

The phenomenon of the fragmentation of international law is hardly new: it has been the subject of academic discussion since at least 1953,[11] and was put on the program of the International Law Commission ('ILC') in 2000, culminating in a 256-page report finalised by Martti Koskenniemi in 2006.[12] Similarly the WTO, and the *GATT* system before it, have long been described as 'special fields'[13] or 'self-contained regimes'[14] of international law.

Although the phenomenon is not new, two features of the WTO system make it particularly pertinent: first, the sheer number of treaties in the WTO framework, and second, the requirement that all WTO members become a party to the great majority of these treaties. Of the 29 treaties contained in the annexes to the *Marrakesh Agreement*, WTO members must be party to 25 of these.[15] Many of these treaties contain overlapping obligations. As such, much of the WTO dispute settlement process that deals with conflicting treaties and/or conflicting obligations of law has been taken up with determining how the WTO treaties interact with each other.[16]

---

11   C Wilfried Jenks, 'The Conflict of Law-Making Treaties' (1953) 30 *British Yearbook of International Law* 401, 403.

12   International Law Commission, *Fragmentation of International Law: Difficulties Arising from the Diversification and Expansion of International Law*, 58th sess, UN Doc A/CN.4/L.682 (13 April 2006).

13   See, eg, Pieter Jan Kuyper, 'The Law of GATT as a Special Field of International Law' (1994) 25 *Netherlands Yearbook of International Law* 227.

14   See, eg, Bruno Simma, 'Self-Contained Regimes' (1985) 16 *Netherlands Yearbook of International Law* 111.

15   With some very limited exceptions: see *Marrakesh Agreement* (n 4) art XIII.

16   See Claude Chase, 'Norm Conflict Between WTO Covered Agreements: Real, Apparent or Avoided?' (2012) 61(4) *International and Comparative Law Quarterly* 791.

The question remains how the WTO treaties interact with wider general international law. Unlike other 'special regime' treaties,[17] the WTO treaties are almost silent in terms of their interaction with general international law—save for a confirmation that the 'customary rules of interpretation of public international law' apply.[18] It has been suggested that the negotiators of the WTO 'did not *think* of public international law' when drafting the treaties.[19]

Yet the overlaps between WTO law and general international law are many, and States that regulate trade to achieve environmental,[20] public health,[21] animal welfare[22] or human rights[23] goals may be in breach of WTO rules. This can be the case even if those States are under another competing international law obligation to make such regulations.[24]

There have been suggestions that the idea of the WTO as a 'self-contained regime' in practice is an overstretch.[25] This is supported by early WTO

---

17   See, eg, *United Nations Convention on the Law of the Sea,* opened for signature 10 December 1982, 1833 UNTS 3 (entered into force 16 November 1994) arts 2(3), 19, 21, 31, 34(2), 58, 87, 138 and 235.

18   *Marrakesh Agreement* (n 4) annex 2 (*'Understanding on Rules and Procedures Governing the Settlement of Disputes'*) art 3(2) (*'DSU'*).

19   Joost Pauwelyn, 'The Role of Public International Law in the WTO: How Far Can We Go?' (2001) 95(3) *American Journal of International Law* 535, 538 (emphasis in original).

20   Such as US laws on gasoline pollutants: see Appellate Body Report, *United States— Standards for Reformulated and Conventional Gasoline,* WTO Doc WT/DS2/AB/R (29 April 1996) (*'US—Reformulated Gasoline'*). See also Gerhard Hafner, *Risks Ensuing From Fragmentation Of International Law,* UN GAOR 55th sess, Supp No 10, UN Doc A/55/10 (1 May–9 June and 10 July–18 August 2000) 145.

21   Such as Australia's tobacco plain packaging legislation: see Panel Report, *Australia— Certain Measures Concerning Trademarks, Geographical Indications and Other Plain Packaging Requirements Applicable to Tobacco Products and Packaging,* WTO Doc WT/DS435/R, WT/DS441/R, WT/DS458/R, WT/DS467/R (28 June 2018).

22   See, eg, Appellate Body Report, *European Communities—Measures Prohibiting the Importation and Marketing of Seal Products,* WTO Doc WT/DS400/AB/R; WT/DS401/AB/R (22 May 2014).

23   Although no country has yet claimed an exception on the basis of human rights, it is suggested that Article XX could nevertheless cover such measures. See, eg, Misha Boutilier, 'From Seal Welfare to Human Rights: Can Unilateral Sanctions in Response to Mass Atrocity Crimes Be Justified under the Article XX(a) Public Morals Exception Clause?' (2017) 75 *University of Toronto Faculty Law Review* 101; Rachel Harris and Gillian Moon, *'GATT* Article XX and Human Rights: What Do We Know from the First 20 Years?' (2015) 16(2) *Melbourne Journal of International Law* 1.

24   See, eg, Appellate Body Report, *Brazil—Measures Affecting Imports of Retreaded Tyres,* WTO Doc WT/DS332/AB/R (3 December 2007) (*'Brazil—Retreaded Tyres'*).

25   See generally Anja Lindroos and Michael Mehling, 'Dispelling the Chimera of 'Self-Contained Regimes' International Law and the WTO' (2006) 16(5) *European Journal of International Law* 857.

jurisprudence where the AB confirmed that the WTO treaties are 'not to be read in clinical isolation from public international law'.[26] This directive has been followed, as seen in Graham Cook's digest which comprehensively sets out the instances the WTO tribunals have looked to general international law concepts and principles.[27] An examination of these instances, however, reveals that they are *overwhelmingly* either concerned with matters of treaty interpretation and application, or with procedural principles of international law.[28]

In terms of treaty interpretation and application, the dispute panels have considered issues such as state responsibility,[29] good faith,[30] non-retroactivity,[31] ordinary meaning,[32] reasonableness[33] and the meaning of specific words and phrases.[34] However, for almost all instances, the use of these concepts has been to apply and interpret the WTO treaties themselves. That is, general international law concepts *are* used, but they are used *in the context* of the substantive law of the self-contained regime.

The same can be said for the procedural matters: dispute panels have looked at issues such as indispensable third parties,[35] due process,[36] representation, the competence of the court and burden of proof[37]—all factors which determine how the WTO treaties *themselves* are applied. This application imports

---

26   *US—Reformulated Gasoline* (n 20) 17.

27   Graham Cook, *A Digest of WTO Jurisprudence on Public International Law Concepts and Principles* (Cambridge University Press, 2015).

28   Lindroos and Mehling, (n 25) 876.

29   See, eg, Appellate Body Report, *United States—Definitive Anti-Dumping and Countervailing Duties on Certain Products from China*, WTO Doc WT/DS379/AB/R (11 March 2011) paras 310–11; Cook (n 27) 31–47.

30   See generally Cook (n 27) 153–71.

31   See, eg, Appellate Body Report, *Canada—Term of Patent Protection*, WTO Doc WT/DS170/AB/R (18 September 2000) paras 70–4; Cook (n 27) 207–16.

32   See, eg, Panel Report, *China—Measures Affecting Trading Rights and Distribution Services for Certain Publications and Audiovisual Entertainment Products*, WTO Doc WT/DS363/R (12 August 2009) para 348; Cook (n 27) 276–7.

33   Although many other terms than 'reasonable' have been used by GATT and WTO adjudicators: see Cook (n 27) 230.

34   See generally Cook (n 27) 325–60.

35   Panel Report, *Turkey—Restrictions on Imports of Textiles and Clothing Products*, WTO Doc WT/DS34/R (31 May 1999); Cook (n 27) 14–16.

36   See, eg, Appellate Body Report, *Canada—Continued Suspension of Obligations in the EC—Hormones Dispute*, WTO Doc WT/DS321/AB/R (16 October 2008) paras 433–5; Cook (n 27) 107–19.

37   See, eg, Appellate Body Report, *United States—Measures Affecting Imports of Woven Wool Shirts and Blouses from India*, WTO Doc WT/DS33/AB/R (25 April 1997) 14; Cook (n 27) 122–31.

general international law in terms of applying WTO law, but does not step outside the regime in any substantive sense.

What happens, then, when the question becomes one of substantive law? There is much written on conflicts of norms within international law, including within the context of international trade law.[38] It is outside the scope of this article to engage comprehensively with the wider debates on this point: rather this section presents three cases as illustrations of the interaction between general international law and international trade law on substantive matters. These three cases are *US—Shrimp*,[39] *EC—Biotech*[40] and *Brazil—Retreaded Tyres*.[41] All three examples show a marked reluctance of the WTO dispute settlement bodies to allow a non-trade obligation to modify or override a WTO obligation.

2.1 United States—Import Prohibition of Certain Shrimp and Shrimp Products[42]

This case is illustrative of two points: first, how the WTO *will* use international treaties—that is, as evidence of facts. Second, how it generally *will not*—as a competing obligation that could potentially conflict with and even override WTO obligations.

This case involved an environmental policy enacted by the US Government to protect sea turtles by requiring the use of a turtle excluder device ('TED') while fishing for shrimp. This requirement was enforced on US shrimp fishers and non-US shrimp fishers and was found to be a breach of Article XI of the GATT.[43]

The US had attached to its appeal amicus curiae briefs from various environmental non-governmental organisations.[44] Despite objections from India,

---

38   See, eg, Joost Pauwelyn, *Conflict of Norms in Public International Law: How WTO Law Relates to Other Rules of International Law* (Cambridge University Press, 2003) 25–88; Isabelle Van Damme, *Treaty Interpretation by the WTO Appellate Body* (Oxford University Press, 2009) 355–74.

39   Appellate Body Report, *United States—Import Prohibition of Certain Shrimp and Shrimp Products*, WTO Doc WT/DS58/AB/R (12 October 1998) ('*US—Shrimp*').

40   Panel Report, *European Communities—Measures Affecting the Approval and Marketing of Biotech Products*, WTO Doc WT/DS291/R; WT/DS292/R; WT/DS293/R (29 September 2006) ('*EC—Biotech*').

41   *Brazil—Retreaded Tyres* (n 24).

42   *US—Shrimp* (n 39).

43   Ibid para 7.

44   Ibid para 79.

Pakistan, Thailand and Malaysia (the appellees),[45] the AB agreed to accept the briefs as 'part of' the US's submission.[46]

The amicus briefs explicitly asked the AB to clarify the relationship between various multilateral environmental agreements ('MEAs'), general international law and the WTO treaties.[47] Although the US was only party to one of the MEAs in question,[48] the briefs used other MEAs to argue customary obligations requiring States to protect endangered species,[49] as well as a customary international law principle of sustainable development.[50] The briefs argued that these customary law norms should allow the US to take the actions it did in requiring the use of TEDs. Ultimately, although the AB accepted it could consider the arguments made in the briefs, it did not—seemingly because of the US's expressed view that its main legal arguments were in its primary submission.[51]

Thus, this case represents a missed opportunity where the AB could have considered a potential substantial conflict between international environmental law obligations and the *GATT* obligations, but chose not to do so.

The AB did however accept the treaties as *evidence*. The US argued its actions were justified under Article XX(g) of the *GATT* which allows for measures relating to the conservation of 'exhaustible natural resources'. The appellees argued that sea turtles—being naturally renewable—could not fall into the meaning of this term.[52] The AB disagreed—first on a textual analysis of the *GATT* provision, with reference to the preamble of the *WTO Agreement*.[53] Second, after analysing the WTO treaty framework, the AB looked to external treaties to show the term 'natural resources' can encompass both living and non-living resources.[54] The AB stated:

---

45 Ibid paras 29, 46.

46 Ibid para 91.

47 See Centre of International Environmental Law, Amicus Brief to the Appellate Body, *United States—Import Prohibition Of Certain Shrimp and Shrimp Products* (1999) <http://www.ciel.org/Publications/shrimpturtlebrief.pdf>) ('CIEL Brief'); World Wildlife Fund, Amicus Brief to the Appellate Body, *United States—Import Prohibition Of Certain Shrimp and Shrimp Products* (1997) <https://www.peacepalacelibrary.nl/ebooks/files/WTO_WWF_Cameron_WWF-Amicus-Brief-to-WTO.pdf> ('WWF Brief').

48 *Convention on International Trade in Endangered Species of Wild Fauna and Flora*, opened for signature 9 March 1973, 993 UNTS 243 (entered into force 1 July 1975).

49 WWF Brief (n 47) 3.1.6–3.1.9.

50 CIEL Brief (n 47) 3.41–3.47.

51 *US—Shrimp* (n 39) para 90.

52 Ibid para 127.

53 Ibid paras 128–9.

54 Ibid para 130.

RE-INTEGRATING WTO AND PUBLIC INTERNATIONAL LAW? 141

Given the recent acknowledgement by the international community of the importance of concerted bilateral or multilateral action to protect living natural resources, and recalling the explicit recognition by WTO Members of the objective of sustainable development in the preamble of the *WTO Agreement*, we believe it is too late in the day to suppose that Article XX(g) of the GATT 1994 may be read as referring only to the conservation of exhaustible mineral or other non-living natural resources.[55]

This use of external treaties as evidence of facts, or meaning of phrases, has continued in WTO jurisprudence.[56]

2.2 EC—Measures Affecting the Approval and Marketing of Biotech Products[57]

This case is also illustrative of WTO institutional resistance to general international law, as seen through the WTO panel's interpretation of Article 31(3)(c) of the *Vienna Convention on the Law of Treaties* ('VCLT'). Article 31(3)(c) states that for the purpose of treaty interpretation, 'relevant rules of international law applicable in the relations between the parties' should be taken into account.

The meaning of 'parties', here, is debated in commentary—a broad interpretation would allow any rules of international law applicable to the parties *to the dispute* to be considered, while a narrow interpretation would require all parties to the original treaty being interpreted to also be bound by the relevant rule of international law.[58]

The case involved challenges to European Communities ('EC') measures over approval and marketing of various biotech products by the US, Canada and Argentina.[59] In response, the EC relied upon various rules of international

---

55   Ibid para 131.
56   See, eg, Panel Report, *United States—Measures Affecting the Production and Sale of Clove Cigarettes*, WTO Doc WT/DS406/R (2 September 2011), [7.427]; Chang-fa Lo 'The Difference between Treaty Interpretation and Treaty Application and the Possibility to account for Non-WTO Treaties During WTO Treaty Interpretation' (2012) 22(1) *Indiana Comparative and International Law Review* 1, 12–13.
57   *EC—Biotech* (n 40).
58   See, eg, Benn McGrady, 'Fragmentation of International Law or "Systemic Integration" of Treaty Regimes: *EC—Biotech Products* and the Proper Interpretation of Article 31(3)(c) of the Vienna Convention on the Law of Treaties' (2008) 42(4) *Journal of World Trade* 589, 591–2.
59   See Margaret A Young, 'The WTO's Use of Relevant Rules of International Law: An Analysis of the *Biotech* Case' (2007) 56(4) *The International and Comparative Law Quarterly* 907, 909.

law, including the *Convention on Biological Diversity*,[60] to which itself, Argentina and Canada were parties, but the US was not, and the *Cartagena Protocol on Biosafety to the Convention on Biological Diversity*[61]—which the EC had ratified, Argentina and Canada had signed but not ratified and the US had neither signed nor ratified.[62]

Thus neither the broad nor narrow interpretation of 'parties' pursuant to Article 31(3)(c) of the *VCLT* would have allowed the WTO Panel to take these instruments into account, as for both at least one of the parties to the dispute was not a party to the instrument in question. However, the panel in its comments made a more general pronouncement about the meaning of the term 'parties':

> It may be inferred from these elements that the rules of international law applicable in the relations between 'the parties' are the rules of international law applicable in the relations between the States which have consented to be bound by the treaty which is being interpreted, and for which that treaty is in force. This understanding of the term 'the parties' leads logically to the view that the rules of international law to be taken into account in interpreting the WTO agreements at issue in this dispute are those which are applicable in the relations between the WTO Members.[63]

The panel would only allow an international rule to be considered if it binds all WTO members. This may be relatively easily satisfied for customary rules—barring the existence of persistent objectors who are also WTO members—but a near impossibility when considering treaties. The US is not party to many of the major human rights and environmental treaties that have developed post 1995.[64] Further, there are some WTO members—such as the Customs Territory

---

60   *Convention on Biological Diversity,* opened for signature 5 June 1992, 1760 UNTS 79 (entered into force 29 December 1993).

61   *Cartegena Protocol on Biosafety to the Convention on Biological Diversity*, opened for signature 29 January 2000, 2226 UNTS 208 (entered into force 11 September 2003).

62   Young, 'The WTO's Use of Relevant Rules of International Law: An Analysis of the *Biotech Case*' (n 59) 910.

63   *EC—Biotech* (n 57) [7.68].

64   See, eg, *Convention on the Rights of the Child,* signed 20 November 1989, 1577 UNTS 3 (entered into force 2 September 1990); *Convention Against Torture and Other Cruel, Inhuman or Degrading Treatment or Punishment,* signed 10 December 1984, 1465 UNTS 85 (entered into force 26 June 1987); *Convention on the Elimination of All Forms of Discrimination against Women,* signed 18 December 1979, 1249 UNTS 13 (entered into force 3 September 1981).

RE-INTEGRATING WTO AND PUBLIC INTERNATIONAL LAW?

of Taiwan—which due to their disputed status as States cannot be members of other international treaties or regimes.[65]

Some commentary has suggested that the restrictive interpretation of Article 31(1)(c) is overstated, pointing to a later paragraph from the WTO Panel:[66]

> [I]t is important to note that the present case is not one in which relevant rules of international law are applicable in the relations between all parties to the dispute, but not between all WTO Members, and in which all parties to the dispute argue that a multilateral WTO agreement should be interpreted in the light of these other rules of international law.[67]

The meaning of this paragraph is far from clear.[68] However, even if it can be taken as suggesting an instrument could be taken into account where not all WTO Members are parties, this is only in the context where *all* parties to the dispute agree it *should* be. This is an additional restriction on the requirements of the *VCLT*.

Subsequent jurisprudence of the WTO has also suggested a relaxation from the very strict *EC—Biotech* approach: but not to the extent of an enthusiastic embrace of non-WTO instruments. For example, in 2011, the AB talked of maintaining a 'delicate balance' between taking 'due account of an individual WTO Member's international obligations' and 'ensuring a consistent and harmonious approach to the interpretation of WTO law among all WTO members'.[69] This is at odds with the broad approach favoured by the ILC, which expressly recognises different interpretation of a regime's laws for different combinations of its members as reflecting 'the need to represent (inherently divergent) party will as elucidated by reference to those other treaties'.[70]

---

65   Margaret A Young, 'Fragmentation or Interaction: The WTO, Fisheries Subsidies, and International Law' (2009) 8(4) *World Trade Review* 477, 491.

66   See Panos Merkouris, *Article 31(3)(c) VCLT and the Principle of Systemic Integration: Normative Shadows in Plato's Cave* (Brill Nihjoff, 2015) 46–7.

67   *EC—Biotech* (n 57) [7.72].

68   Young, 'The WTO's Use of Relevant Rules of International Law: An Analysis of the Biotech Case' (n 59) 910, 913.

69   Appellate Body Report, *European Communities and Certain Member States—Measures Affecting Trade in Large Civil Aircraft*, WTO Doc WT/DS13/AB/R (18 May 2011) [845] (emphasis added).

70   International Law Commission (n 12) [472].

2.3 *Brazil—Measures Affecting Imports of Retreaded Tyres*[71]

This final illustrative case is one where the respondent State was under a binding obligation from another international tribunal. In an attempt to reduce the number of waste tyres which caused environmental and health problems, Brazil enacted various measures affecting imports of re-treaded tyres.[72] This was challenged by Uruguay before a MERCOSUR arbitral tribunal.[73] That challenge was successful and as a consequence of the ruling, Brazil introduced an exemption into the measure for MERCOSUR members.[74]

Brazil's measures were also challenged by the EC before the WTO. Brazil argued the measure was justified pursuant to article XX of the GATT. The measure failed the article XX chapeau standard of 'arbitrary or unjustifiable discrimination' because of the MERCOSUR exemption.[75] Brazil conceded the discrimination but argued it was justified, as it was done pursuant to Brazil's international obligations. The AB said:

> Brazil could have sought to justify the challenged Import Ban on the grounds of human, animal and plant health under Article 50(d) of the Treaty of Montevideo. Brazil, however, decided not to do so. It is not appropriate for us to second-guess Brazil's decision not to invoke Article 50(d) ... However, [its existence] as well as the fact that Brazil *might* have raised this defence in the MERCOSUR arbitral proceedings, show, in our view, that the discrimination associated with the MERCOSUR exemption does not necessarily result from a conflict between provisions under MERCOSUR and the GATT ...[76]

The AB essentially rejected Brazil's argument as to a competing legal obligation because, in its view, Brazil would not have incurred that obligation if it had argued its case before the MERCOSUR tribunal in a different way. This is a clear interference with Brazil's sovereign right to argue its international law interests as it sees fit.[77] Further, the reasoning is troubling when extended to non-trade international obligations more generally. Let us take, for example, a treaty

---

71   *Brazil—Retreaded Tyres* (n 24).

72   Nikolaos Lavranos and Nicolas Vielliard, 'Competing Jurisdictions between MERCOSUR and WTO' (2008) 7 *The Law and Practice of International Courts and Tribunals* 205, 208.

73   *Import Prohibition of Remoulded Tyres from Uruguay (Uruguay v Brazil) (Award)* (MERCOSUR Ad Hoc Arbitral Tribunal, 9 January 2002).

74   Lavranos and Vielliard (n 72) 208–9.

75   This standard is further discussed in Part 4, below.

76   *Brazil—Retreaded Tyres* (n 24) [234].

77   Lavranos and Vielliard (n 72) 229.

whose substantive obligations require countries to restrict trade in some way that is inconsistent with *GATT*, but where the obligation provision is capable of reservations. In the case of conflict between that treaty and the *GATT*, would the WTO AB find there was in fact no conflict because the country *could* have made reservation to the provision in question, even though in fact they did not do so? The reality is Brazil *was* under a competing international obligation and the AB refused to take this as justification for the discrimination.

2.4   *Institutional Isolationism*

Much of the discussion of backlash in the context of States has centred on ideas of isolationism. From President Trump[78] to Brexit,[79] State isolationism and withdrawal is characterised as a rejection of the international system itself.[80] The WTO's approach to general international law can be seen through a similar lens. The three cases discussed above illustrate an overall reluctance from the WTO AB to engage with general international law in cases of substantive conflict with WTO treaties. Instead, the WTO retreats to its own treaty regime and isolates legal analysis to international trade law rather than international law more generally. Further, as seen in *Brazil—Retreaded Tyres*, it appoints itself as supreme arbitrator of international trade issues, regardless of findings of other international dispute resolution bodies.[81]

The problem with such institutional isolationism is it ignores the realities that States *are* under overlapping and sometimes competing international obligations. It is, as Joost Pauwelyn states, 'normatively undesirable: it denies the sovereign rights of countries to consent to other treaties or waive their WTO rights in fulfilment of their own, diverse preferences, albeit subject to respect for acquired third party rights'.[82] States who wish to have their trade *and* non-trade obligations considered together must look outside the WTO: and they do

---

78   See, eg, Meghnad Desai, 'The Revival of US Isolationism', *The Japan Times* (online, 29 October 2019) <https://www.japantimes.co.jp/opinion/2019/10/29/commentary/world -commentary/revival-u-s-isolationism>.

79   See, eg, Edward Luce, 'Britain's Voyage to Inglorious Isolation', *The New York Times* (online, 6 June 2017) <https://www.nytimes.com/2017/06/06/opinion/britains-voyage-to -inglorious-isolation.html>.

80   Deborah Barros Leal Farias, 'Trade, Conflict, and Opportunity: Taking Advantage of Others' Protectionism and Isolationism—the Case of MERCOSUL' [2019] *Canadian Foreign Policy Journal* 1, 3–4.

81   Lavranos and Vielliard (n 72) 229.

82   Joost Pauwelyn, 'Interplay between the WTO Treaty and Other International Legal Instruments and Tribunals: Evolution after 20 years of WTO Jurisprudence', SSRN (Paper, 10 February 2017) 7 <http://dx.doi.org/10.2139/ssrn.2731144>.

so in the form of RTAS. This is an inevitable consequence of the siloisation of WTO law from general international law.

3 Refuge in Regional Trade Agreements

The WTO system, unlike other self-contained or specialised regimes, explicitly allows States to go outside the system in the form of RTAS. RTAS effectively operate as an exception to the WTO rules. There is debate both between States and in academic commentary[83] about the limits of the exception, but in reality, RTAS are only very rarely challenged under the WTO system.[84]

As of 2018, every WTO member had become a member of at least one RTA.[85] There are almost 700 RTAS in existence, 302 of which are in force and have been notified to the WTO.[86] RTAS have long included what are referred to as WTO plus ('WTO+') provisions—trade obligations that go beyond the provisions of the WTO agreements. Increasingly, RTAS are also including what have been termed 'WTO-extra' ('WTO-X')[87] provisions: non-trade obligations that go *outside* the WTO treaties.[88] Such WTO-X provisions are commonly environmental obligations and human rights obligations (usually relating to labour rights and standards).

The link between trade and non-trade obligations is seen very strongly in the case of the European Union ('EU'). The EU's own legal framework requires it to 'uphold and promote its values' in its external dealings,[89] which includes

---

83   See Nicolas JS Lockhart and Andrew Mitchell, 'Regional Trade Agreements under GATT 1994: An Exception and Its Limits' in Andrew Mitchell (ed), *Challenges and Prospects for the WTO* (Cameron May, 2005) 217.

84   Only 11 requests for consultations to the WTO have cited Article XXIV of GATT or its sub-provisions: see 'Disputes by Agreement', *World Trade Organisation* (Web Page) <https://www.wto.org/english/tratop_e/dispu_e/dispu_agreements_index_e.htm>.

85   Devin McDaniels, Ana Cristina Molina and Erik Wijkström, 'How Does the Regular Work of WTO Influence Regional Trade Agreements?' (WTO Staff Working Paper, 23 March 2018) 1 <https://www.wto.org/english/res_e/reser_e/ersd201806_e.pdf>.

86   'Regional Trade Agreements: Facts and Figures', *World Trade Organisation* (Web Page) <https://www.wto.org/english/tratop_e/region_e/region_e.htm#facts>.

87   Henrik Horn, Petros C Mavroidis and André Sapir, 'Beyond the WTO? An Anatomy of EU and US Preferential Trade Agreements' (2010) 33(11) *The World Economy* 1565, 1567.

88   Karolina Milewicz et al, 'Beyond Trade: The Expanding Scope of the Non-Trade Agenda in Trade Agreements' (2016) 62(4) *Journal of Conflict Resolution* 743, 751.

89   *Consolidated Version of the Treaty on European Union* [2016] OJ C 202/13, art 3(5).

negotiation of RTAs.[90] This has seen a 'new generation' of EU RTAs,[91] starting with the 2010 EU—Korea Free Trade Agreement, all of which contain a binding sustainable development chapter encompassing labour rights and environmental protections.[92] For the EU, trade is inherently linked with non-trade values: 'EU trade policy is not just about interests but also about values'.[93]

This phenomenon is not limited to the EU. All but one of the US's RTAs contain enforceable environmental obligations.[94] The *Comprehensive and Progressive Agreement for Trans-Pacific Partnership* between Australia, Brunei Darussalam, Canada, Chile, Japan, Malaysia, Mexico, New Zealand, Singapore and Vietnam has enforceable environmental and labour chapters,[95] and China's RTAs with Korea[96] and Switzerland[97] contain environmental chapters.

There are many theories as to *why* States include WTO-X provisions in their RTAs,[98] exploration of which is beyond the scope of this article. What is, however, clear is that States—Western and non-Western, developing and developed—*do* include such provisions. There is a desire to have trade obligations linked to and modified by other substantive international law obligations.

As was seen in Part 2 above, the isolationist approach taken by the WTO to general international law means such concerns cannot be resolved within the framework of the institution: instead States are achieving this aim through RTAs. This encourages a disengagement from the system: resources and political will that could be directed towards WTO issues are instead concentrated on negotiating and concluding RTAs. The existence of so many RTAs in itself

---

90 Ibid art 3(3).

91 Sikina Jinnah and Elisa Morgera, 'Environmental Provisions in American and EU Free Trade Agreements: A Preliminary Comparison and Research Agenda' (2013) 22(3) *Review of European, Comparative & International Environmental Law* 324, 325.

92 Lisa Lechner, 'The Domestic Battle over the Design of Non-Trade Issues in Preferential Trade Agreements' (2016) 23(5) *Review of International Political Economy* 840, 845.

93 Cecilia Malmström, European Commission, *Trade for All: Towards a More Responsible Trade and Investment Policy* (14 October 2015) 5.

94 Horn, Mavroidis and Sapir (n 87) 1578.

95 *Comprehensive and Progressive Agreement for Trans-Pacific Partnership*, signed 8 March 2018, [2018] ATS 23 (entered into force 30 December 2018), incorporating the *Trans-Pacific Partnership Agreement*, signed 4 April 2016, [2016] ATNIF 2 (not yet in force) chs 19 and 20.

96 *Free Trade Agreement between the People's Republic of China and the Government of the Republic of South Korea*, signed 1 June 2015, (entered into force 20 December 2015) <http://fta.mofcom.gov.cn/korea/annex/xdzw_en.pdf>.

97 *Free Trade Agreement between the People's Republic of China and the Swiss Confederation*, signed 6 July 2013, (entered into force 1 July 2014) <http://fta.mofcom.gov.cn/ruishi/xieyi/xieyizw_en.pdf>.

98 See generally Lechner (n 92); Milewicz et al (n 88).

148 AUSTRALIAN YEAR BOOK OF INTERNATIONAL LAW VOLUME 38

is also of institutional concern for the WTO.[99] This is not a backlash in terms of sustained critique of a system, but it does show a disengagement with the institution, and a shift away from global multilateralism to bilateralism and regional plurilateralism.

4   Through the Lens of Backlash: Responses

These twin withdrawals—those of the WTO from international law, and States from the WTO—are further fragmenting international law. This is seen in those cases that concern both trade and non-trade issues that have been simultaneously brought before the WTO and other international tribunals.[100] It is also evident in the increasing number of RTAs with their own dispute settlement systems, which can lead to incoherence and inconsistency in international trade law.[101] Although these actions are not an explicit critique of the international trading system, they nonetheless threaten the relevance and legitimacy of the WTO, as well as impacting the coherence and unity of international law more generally.

Given the impasse in the current negotiation round at the WTO, it is highly unlikely WTO members would agree to any amendment of WTO treaties to promote increased interaction between WTO law and general international law. This article instead identifies two ways that this interaction could be enhanced without needing to amend any of the WTO treaties themselves. The first way is a cultural shift around the appointment of Appellate Body members, and the second is through the interpretation of 'unjustifiable or arbitrary discrimination' in the chapeau of Article XX of the *GATT*.

4.1   *Appointment of Appellate Body Members*
There have been some AB members with considerable public international law backgrounds, such as Florentino Feliciano and Georges Abi Saab.[102] This is not

---

99   Horn, Mavroidis and Sapir (n 87) 1566.

100   Such as the swordfish dispute between Chile and the EU: see Marcos Orellana 'The EU and Chile Suspend the Swordfish Case Proceedings at the WTO and the International Tribunal of the Law of the Sea' (2001) 6(1) *ASIL Insights* <https://www.asil.org/insights/volume/6/issue/1/eu-and-chile-suspend-swordfish-case-proceedings-wto-and-international>.

101   Although it is suggested that States show a preference for the WTO dispute settlement system over RTA dispute settlement systems: Valerie Hughes, 'Working in WTO dispute settlement: pride without prejudice' in Gabrielle Marceau (ed), *A History of Law and Lawyers in the GATT/WTO: The Development of the Rule of Law in the Multilateral Trading System* (Cambridge University Press, 2015) 400, 416–18.

102   Donald McRae, 'International Economic Law and Public International Law: The Past and The Future' (2014) 17(3) *Journal of International Economic Law* 627, 629–30.

the norm. Indeed, WTO Panellists are not even required to be lawyers, let alone international lawyers.[103] WTO AB members are required to be 'a person of recognized authority, with demonstrated expertise in law, international trade and the subject-matter of the covered agreements generally'.[104] Thus, they must have a background in law, but not necessarily *international* law. In practice, AB members are mostly former government officials, with both practitioners and academics a 'minority across all appointments'.[105] Joost Pauwelyn has pointed out that even in the AB, members are appointed without law degrees, and only a very small minority have any experience as a judge.[106] This means that

> WTO Members increasingly select candidates with extensive trade policy experience and who have a familiarity with the WTO system and its peculiarities ... to the disadvantage of other key characteristics (eg public international law background, court experience).[107]

This has led to a disparity in views of the role and function of the WTO and its treaties. To public international lawyers, WTO treaties are '"just" a branch of public international law'[108] but, as Pauwelyn observes, 'to many negotiators and other WTO experts in Geneva [this fact] comes as a surprise'.[109] It is hardly surprising then that the trend to restrict appointments to a pool of these negotiators and experts may lead to a lack of consideration of general international law in WTO jurisprudence. In contrast, if new appointments focus on people who have not only a trade background but also one in public international law more generally, a more comprehensive settling of WTO law in the context of general international law may follow. This idea of letting international law flow from and be influenced by a judge's experience or background is not new: the link between nationality of judges and creation of law was raised as

---

103   *DSU* (n 18) art 8.1.

104   Ibid art 17.3.

105   Louise Johannesson and Petros C Mavroidis, 'Black Cat, White Cat: The Identity of the WTO Judges' (2015) 49(4) *Journal of World Trade* 685, 692.

106   Joost Pauwelyn, 'Who Decides Matters: The Legitimacy Capital of WTO Adjudicators versus ICSID Arbitrators' in Nienke Grossman et al (eds), *Legitimacy and International Courts* (Cambridge University Press, 2018) 216, 221–2 ('Who Decides Matters').

107   Manfred Elsig and Mark A Pollack, 'Agents, Trustees and International Courts: The Politics of Judicial Appointment at the World Trade Organisation' (2014) 20(2) *European Journal of International Law* 391, 402.

108   Pauwelyn, *Conflict of Norms in Public International Law: How WTO Law Relates to Other Rules of International Law* (n 37) 26.

109   Ibid.

early the 1907 Court of Arbitral Justice Convention,[110] and is enshrined in the Statute of the International Court of Justice.[111]

The problem with this proposal, is of course the *reason* why WTO AB members are overwhelmingly from government backgrounds: they are appointed by diplomats, following a 'diplomatic/insider' ethos.[112] This ethos isn't (just) a global diplomatic cronyism, but rather, as Pauwelyn points out, reveals fundamental conceptions of the WTO dispute settlement system itself:

> It is not an adjudicator-driven, carefully designed 'constitutional' legal system with sophisticated, long-term, economics-based, but easy to read rulings that compel rule compliance following a logic of appropriateness ... Instead, it is a relatively ad hoc, party-driven mechanism to settle disputes under the cautious control of government members, based on lengthy, often impenetrable rulings that only insiders can understand and where politically sensitive cases against big players result in diplomatic, give-and-take settlements with trade or cash compensations rather than rule compliance.[113]

This conception does not sit easily with the idea presented in this article: that WTO dispute resolution should move *towards* general international law and *away* from an insiders-only, siloisation of WTO rules. This conception also explains the US justifications for the recent blocking of AB reappointments. That is, the protests that the AB has engaged in discussion of obiter dicta,[114] considered arguments not brought up by the parties to the dispute,[115] treated

---

110 James Brown Scott, 'Report to the Conference from the First Commission Recommending the Creation of a Court of Arbitral Justice' in James Brown Scott (ed) *The Reports to the Hague Conference of 1899 and 1907* (Clarendon Press, 1917) 242.

111 *Statute of the International Court of Justice* art 9. See also Michel Virally, 'The Sources of International Law' in Max Sørensen (ed), *Manual of Public International Law* (St Martin's Press, 1968) 116, 146.

112 Pauwelyn, 'Who Decides Matters' (n 106) 226.

113 Ibid 226–7.

114 Office of the United States Trade Representative, *Report on the Appellate Body of the World Trade Organisation* (February 2020) 52, <https://ustr.gov/sites/default/files/Report_on _the_Appellate_Body_of_the_World_Trade_Organization.pdf>.

115 *Dispute Settlement Body: Minutes of Meetings Held in Centre William Rappard on 23 May 2016*, WT/DSB/M/379 (29 August 2016) (Meeting Minutes of 23 May 2016) [6.5] *Statement by the United States at the Meeting of the WTO Dispute Settlement Body* (Geneva, May 23 2016) <https://www.wto.org/english/news_e/news16_e/us_statment_dsbmay16_e .pdf>, 4.

RE-INTEGRATING WTO AND PUBLIC INTERNATIONAL LAW? 151

prior reports as precedent,[116] and interpreted 'deliberate ambiguities' of the WTO Agreements best left to States to interpret for themselves,[117] can be seen as a protest that the AB is shifting from the second type of dispute resolution body described by Pauwelyn to the first.

Ironically, however, it may be these precise actions that could allow the shift this article suggests. Pauwelyn argues that the sociological legitimacy of the AB is an internal legitimacy, derived from mandate providers (the DSB members appointing AB members), and thus WTO adjudicators are 'careful not to exceed the explicit mandate given to them'.[118] Yet criticism of the US actions have come from many WTO member States,[119] and past AB members:[120] and these criticisms reveal the view that it is the US actions that are robbing the AB—and the WTO itself by extension—of institutional legitimacy. To bow down to US demands and further restrict the mandate of AB members would, at this point, seem to neither serve sociological or normative legitimacy goals. Instead, supporting appointments of AB members that bring general international law experience to their role could restore the perceived rigour of the

---

116 Office of the United States Trade Representative, 'Statement on WTO Appellate Report on China Countervailing Duties' (Press Release, 16 July 2019) <https://ustr.gov/about-us/policy-offices/press-office/press-releases/2019/july/statement-wto-appellate-report-china>.

117 *Negotiations on Improvements and Clarifications of the Dispute Settlement Understanding: Further Contribution of the United States on Improving Flexibility and Member Control in WTO Dispute Settlement (Addendum)*, WTO Doc TN/DS/W/82/Add.1 (25 October 2005) 2.

118 Pauweyln, 'Who Decides Matters' (n 106) 227.

119 See, eg, *Dispute Settlement Body: Minutes of Meeting Held in the Centre William Rappard on 15 August 2019*, WTO Doc WT/DSB/M/433 (29 October 2019) (Meeting Minutes of 15 August 2019) [10.3], [10.14], [10.30]. See also *Appellate Body Appointments: Proposal by Afghanistan; Angola; Argentina; Australia; Benin; Plurinational State Of Bolivia; Botswana; Brazil; Burkina Faso; Burundi; Cabo Verde; Cameroon; Canada; Central African Republic; Chad; Chile; China; Colombia; Congo; Costa Rica; Côte D'ivoire; Cuba; Democratic Republic Of Congo; Djibouti; Dominican Republic; Ecuador; Egypt; El Salvador; Eswatini; The European Union; Gabon; The Gambia; Ghana; Guatemala; Guinea; Guinea-Bissau; Honduras; Hong Kong, China; Iceland; India; Indonesia; Israel; Kazakhstan; Kenya; Republic Of Korea; Lesotho; Liechtenstein; Madagascar; Malawi; Malaysia; Maldives; Mali; Mauritania; Mauritius; Mexico; Morocco; Mozambique; Namibia; New Zealand; Nicaragua; Niger; Nigeria; North Macedonia; Norway; Pakistan; Panama; Paraguay; Peru; Qatar; Russian Federation; Rwanda; Senegal; Seychelles; Sierra Leone; Singapore; South Africa; Switzerland; The Separate Customs Territory Of Taiwan, Penghu, Kinmen And Matsu; Tanzania; Thailand; Togo; Tunisia; Turkey; Uganda; Ukraine; Uruguay; The Bolivarian Republic Of Venezuela; Viet Nam; Zambia And Zimbabwe*, WTO Doc WT/DSB/W/609/Rev.15 (6 December 2019).

120 See, eg, Peter Van den Bossche 'Farewell Speech of Appellate Body Member Peter Van den Bossche', (Speech, WTO Dispute Settlement Body, 28 May 2019) <https://www.wto.org/english/tratop_e/dispu_e/farwellspeech_peter_van_den_bossche_e.htm>.

WTO dispute settlement process while also increasing the likelihood that WTO obligations will be considered in the context of members' other international legal obligations.

4.2   Arbitrary or Unjustifiable Discrimination

The second shift towards general international law could come through a reconsideration of how WTO dispute bodies interpret the phrase 'arbitrary or unjustifiable discrimination'. Many of the GATT cases that deal with competing international legal obligations will ultimately come down to an article XX exception argument—because article XX explicitly allows for those instances where Governments are regulating trade to achieve some non-trade priority. States seeking to rely on article XX must first show that their GATT breaching measure falls within one of the enumerated paragraphs within article XX,[121] and then show that the measure does not breach the chapeau of article XX.[122] Most article XX cases fail at the chapeau, particularly with a finding that the measure in question is 'arbitrary or unjustified' discrimination.[123] The following analysis proceeds on the assumption that a WTO member has taken a measure pursuant to some non-trade international obligation which affects trade in a way that breaches the GATT. The member has then argued an article XX exception successfully up until the chapeau stage.

It is here that a new understanding of the meaning of 'arbitrary or unjustified' could allow a WTO dispute body to evaluate a member's measures in light of their other (non-trade) obligations. Specifically, the interpretation of the phrase 'arbitrary or unjustifiable' could include a recognition that a measure will not be arbitrary or unjustified if it is taken pursuant to an international obligation undertaken in good faith.

This is particularly relevant where an initial trade restricting measure is imposed for one purpose but an exception is granted based on another international obligation: thus rendering the measure discriminatory and at risk of being in breach of the chapeau of article XX. This was the situation faced by the EU in *EC—Seals*.[124] The EU restricted the sale of products from seal hunts which breached Article I of the GATT.[125] It then argued an exception under

---

121   Consisting of XX(a) to XX(j).

122   *US—Reformulated Gasoline* (n 20).

123   See, eg, Appellate Body Report, *European Communities—Measures Prohibiting the Importation and Marketing of Seals Product*, WTO Doc WT/DS400/AB/R and WT/DS401/AB/R (22 May 2014) ('*EC—Seals*'); *US—Reformulated Gasoline* (n 20); *Brazil—Retreaded Tyres* (n 24).

124   *EC—Seals* (n 123).

125   Ibid [5.96], [5.130].

article xx(a), the public morals exception, on the basis of animal welfare. While the characterisation of the measure as one to protect public morals[126] and the argument it was necessary were successful,[127] the measure failed at the chapeau stage of analysis.

An exception had been included in the seal products ban to allow products from seals hunted by Inuit groups in traditional hunts to be sold.[128] This exception was included to protect the 'fundamental economic and social interest of Inuit people' in line with *United Nations Declaration on the Rights of Indigenous People*.[129] In considering this exception in light of the chapeau, the AB stated:

> We therefore turn to examine whether such discrimination is 'arbitrary or unjustifiable' within the meaning of the chapeau. As noted above, one of the most important factors in the assessment of arbitrary or unjustifiable discrimination is the question of whether the discrimination can be reconciled with, or is rationally related to, the policy objective with respect to which the measure has been provisionally justified under one of the subparagraphs of Article xx.[130]

The answer was, of course, no—because the hunts by the Inuit groups caused 'the very pain and suffering for seals that the EU public is concerned about'.[131] As long as the most important factor for 'arbitrary and unjustifiable' discrimination is related to the *primary* goal of the measure, and does not take into account adjustments made to fulfil other international legal obligations, any State that is under several non-trade obligations will find it hard to justify a trade-impacting measure pursuant to article xx of the *GATT*.

If, instead, 'arbitrary and unjustifiable discrimination' expressly assessed whether a State was acting under an international obligation in good faith, a State could legitimately discriminate to fulfil non-trade obligations. This would include obligations that are unrelated to the actual goal of the measure. This reflects the reality that States' behaviours cannot be neatly segregated into various parcels: a State pursuing, for example, a public health measure may need to apply the measure differently to different States to ensure it does not breach other international obligations. The additional requirement of good

---

126   Ibid [5.201].

127   Ibid [5.290].

128   Ibid [1.4].

129   *Regulation (EC) No 1007/2009 of the European Parliament and of the Council of 16 September 2009 on trade in seal products* [2009] OJ L 286/36, recital 14.

130   *EC—Seals* (n 123) [5.318].

131   Ibid [5.320].

faith would ensure that States could not enter into international obligations solely for the purpose of defeating their WTO obligations.

In truth, this solution is not so bold. The WTO already explicitly allows for reference to external legal instruments to modify WTO obligations through its reference to international standard setting bodies in the *Agreement on the Application of Sanitary and Phytosanitary Measures*[132] and the *Agreement on Technical Barriers to Trade*.[133] Indeed, the approach outlined above would avoid much of the controversy with reference to such standards[134] as reference would not be made to non-binding standards which the State in question did not necessarily participate in the drafting of, but to obligations of international law which the State had consented to be bound by. At the same time, the approach does not go as far as other (failed) proposals for shared adjudication between the WTO and other non-trade international groups.[135] Rather, the adjudicative process is kept within the existing WTO framework and limited to WTO panels and the AB: but the interpretation of 'arbitrary or unjustifiable' is done in light of a State's wider international law obligations.

This solution would also not breach the requirement that WTO dispute bodies not take action to diminish the rights of WTO members,[136] as article XX is an inherent part of the GATT. Thus it is not a case that the WTO dispute body would conclude that the WTO treaty has to be 'set aside'.[137] Rather, it would entail an 'evolutionary' approach to the meaning of 'arbitrary or unjustifiable': an approach that is not without precedence in WTO jurisprudence.[138] This approach essentially finds there *is* no conflict between the trade and non-trade treaties, as article XX expressly allows members to take such measures, provided the criteria of article XX are met. It is a normatively desirable solution, as it allows the WTO treaty and the non-trade treaty to be 'read as coherent'[139]

---

132 *Agreement on the Application of Sanitary and Phytosanitary Measures*, opened for signature 15 April 1994, 1867 UNTS 493 (entered into force 1 January 1995) art 3.2.

133 *Agreement on Technical Barriers to Trade*, opened for signature 12 April 1979, 1186 UNTS 276 (entered into force 1 January 1980) art 2.

134 See Young, 'Fragmentation or Interaction: The WTO, Fisheries Subsidies, and International Law' (n 65) 499–500.

135 Ibid 507.

136 For the meaning of conflict in the context of WTO treaties, see Gabrielle Marceau, 'Conflicts of Norms and Conflicts of Jurisdictions: The Relationship between the WTO Agreement and MEAs and other Treaties' (2001) 35(6) *Journal of World Trade* 1081, 1084–6.

137 See Martti Koskenniemi and Päivi Leino, 'Fragmentation of International Law? Postmodern Anxieties' (2002) 15(3) *Leiden Journal of International Law* 553, 572.

138 See *US—Shrimp* (n 39) 130.

139 Koskenniemi and Leino (n 137) 573.

with each other, fulfilling the principle of harmonisation.[140] Further, it is a practically desirable solution as it allows WTO members to balance their WTO obligations and their non-trade obligations without diminishing either.

5 Conclusion

The WTO is facing many challenges, not least a seeming shift from rule-based trade policy to a power based trade policy by the US, and the ongoing issue with AB appointments. However, potentially the most fundamental challenge is that posed by the WTO's own siloisation from general international law, twinned with the increasing desire from States to combine trade and non-trade obligations.

As States look outside the WTO system to achieve this goal, they disengage with the WTO as an institution, preferring instead to govern their trade by bilateral and/or multilateral RTAs. In this space, there seems to be a trend to embrace multiple smaller bilateral treaties rather than larger regional treaties. Even recent success stories such as the *Comprehensive and Progressive Agreement for Trans-Pacific Partnership* only came about after the US withdrew from the original *Trans-Pacific Partnership*.[141] Negotiations for the US—EU *Transatlantic Trade and Investment Partnership* have failed,[142] and the United Kingdom's ('UK') withdrawal from the EU will inevitably lead to a number of a new, smaller trade treaties between the UK and other States. This retreat from multilateralism—from the WTO and larger RTAs—and realignment to bilateral treaties increases complexity in international trade rules as any transfer of goods and services across borders may be subject to a number of overlapping and potentially inconsistent treaties. This is antithetical to the idea of mutual and reciprocal trade obligations for all members that underpins the WTO as an institution. The growing complexity runs the risk of increasing costs associated with trade and, ironically, decreasing any economic gains that are perceived to flow from such RTAs. States recognised that clarity and coherence in trade law best served their interest when establishing the WTO. This is

---

140   Van Damme (n 38) 357–8.

141   Donald J Trump, 'Presidential Memorandum Regarding Withdrawal of the United States from the Trans-Pacific Partnership Negotiations and Agreement', *WhiteHouse .gov* (Presidential Memoranda, 23 January 2017) <https://www.whitehouse.gov/presiden tial-actions/presidential-memorandum-regarding-withdrawal-united-states-trans -pacific-partnership-negotiations-agreement/>.

142   *Council Decision Authorising the Opening of Negotiations with the United States of America for an Agreement on the Elimination of Tariffs for Industrial Goods* [2019] OJ L 282 6052/19.

seen in the declaration made by Ministers at the end of the Uruguay Round which welcomed the 'stronger and clearer legal framework' established by the WTO as well as expressing their resolution to 'strive for greater global coherence of policies in the fields of trade, money and finance'.[143] The WTO was lauded as heralding a 'new era of global economic cooperation'.[144]

Yet as States disengage from the WTO to negotiate their own RTAs, they may still be seeking clarity and coherence: not in trade law in isolation, but in their international obligations more widely. The desire to couple trade and non-trade obligations cannot be fulfilled currently by staying within the WTO system. The WTO's own institutional isolationism risks rendering it at best incoherent with a State's non-trade obligations and at worst irrelevant. This leads to the worst outcome for all States—increased complexity in trade rules coupled with a stagnating institution that is unable (or unwilling) to balance the multiple international obligations that any State is under. States are consequently more vulnerable to challenge in multiple international fora for the same policy, leading to increased burdens of costs of defence. Governments also face greater uncertainty and complexity as they attempt to legislate, needing to juggle multiple RTAs and trade and non-trade obligations.

To bridge this growing chasm, this article suggests that the WTO and its members move to integrate substantive international law into WTO obligations. This could be done by refreshing and renewing the institution in two ways: first in the qualifications considered desirable for AB members and second in the interpretation of the term 'arbitrary or unjustifiable discrimination'. This suggestion may seem improbable in light of the trend in State disengagement from the WTO system. Yet it is in the best interest of those very States who are disengaging. A greater clarity around trade rules as well as how these rules interact with States' non-trade obligations will provide certainty for States and those who wish to invest in them alike.

---

143 *Marrakesh Agreement Establishing the World Trade Organization,* opened for signature 15 April 1994, 1867 UNTS 3 (entered into force 1 January 1995) (*'Marrakesh Declaration of 15 April 1994'*) para 16, 18.

144 Ibid para 17.

Navigating the 'Backlash' against International Trade and Investment Liberalisation: Economic Perspectives on the Future of Regional Trade Agreements in Uncertain Times

Martin Richardson *

1 Introduction

Elizabeth Warren, in criticising aspects of the proposed Trans-Pacific Partnership (TPP) in 2015, suggested that dissatisfaction with the trade agreement

> isn't a partisan issue. Conservatives who believe in US sovereignty should be outraged that ... [it] would shift power from American courts, whose authority is derived from our Constitution, to un-accountable international tribunals.[1]

She was certainly correct that this was not a partisan issue: one of Donald Trump's first executive orders as President was to withdraw the US from the TPP negotiations.[2] Dissatisfaction with this proposed agreement was not confined to the US. Similar concerns that these provisions represented a loss of economic sovereignty were expressed in Australia.[3]

---

* Professor Martin Richardson, Research School of Economics, The Australian National University.

1 Elizabeth Warren, 'The Trans-Pacific Partnership Clause Everyone Should Oppose', *The Washington Post* (online, 25 February 2015) <https://www.washingtonpost. com/opinions/kill-the-dispute-settlement-language-in-the-trans-pacific-partnership/2015/02/25/ec7705a2 -bd1e-11e4-b274-e5209a3bc9a9_story.html?utm_term=.192c1abcc1b7>.

2 Donald J Trump, 'Presidential Memorandum Regarding Withdrawal of the United States from the Trans-Pacific Partnership Negotiations and Agreement' (Presidential Memorandum, 23 January 2017).

3 See Peter Martin, 'Trans-Pacific Partnership: We're Selling Economic Sovereignty for Little Return', *Sydney Morning Herald* (online, 13 October 2015) <http://www.smh.com .au/comment/transpacific-partnership-were-selling-our-sovereignty-for-little-return -20151011-gk6fhw.html>. These concerns were given short shrift, however, by the Trade Minister at the time, Andrew Robb, who applied a remarkably low threshold to policy evaluation in noting that Australia had such provisions in a number of other trade agreements but, 'the sun has still come up' each morning: Peter Martin, 'Australia Faces $50m Legal Bill in Cigarette Plain Packaging Fight with Philip Morris', *Sydney Morning Herald* (online,

President Trump has also balked at a number of other trade agreements,[4] describing the North Atlantic Free Trade Agreement (NAFTA) as 'the worst trade deal ever made by any country ... in the world'[5] and issuing critical commentary on the European Union and its relationship with the United Kingdom.[6] To the extent that Mr Trump represents a populist backlash against the 'metropolitan liberal elite', does his scepticism about the value of trade deals reflect a more general "backlash" against trade liberalisation?

In this paper I argue that concerns about the merits of regional trading agreements (RTAs) are very old and, indeed, are very mainstream in neoclassical economics. The questioning of gains from such agreements does not necessarily represent a new mindset or *zeitgeist* but rather, a broader realisation that RTAs are not unambiguously welfare improving arrangements. Nevertheless, these concerns have been joined by other concerns about RTAs and the prospects for further trade liberalisation are significantly impacted by this. I cite recent work in economics that suggests that trade agreements in an era of enhanced scepticism are very likely to be far less ambitious in scope and more likely to end in exit.

The paper first outlines the massive increase in popularity of RTAs over recent decades and highlights the success of multilateral trade liberalisation as a motivation for this increased focus on bilateral and regional deals. It then discusses the economic case against these arrangements and some recent economic literature on international agreements in an uncertain world environment, particularly when the possibility of unilateral exit from an agreement is taken seriously. A final section concludes that, although countries may be engaging less ambitiously with RTAs, to describe this as a backlash is an overstatement.

2 Regional Trading Arrangements

First, some terminology. I shall use the term regional trading agreement/ arrangement (RTA) as a catch-all phrase to cover so-called free trade areas,

---

28 July 2015) <https://www.smh.com.au/politics/federal/australia-faces-50m-legal-bill-in
-cigarette-plain-packaging-fight-with-philip-morris-20150728-gim4xo.html>.

4 Henceforth 'trade agreements' is used as a shorthand for agreements covering trade in goods and services as well as other trade-related matters, such as international investment flows.

5 Fox Business, 'Trump: NAFTA is the Worst Trade Deal Made by any Country' (YouTube, 31 March 2017, 0:09–0:15) <https://www.youtube.com/watch?v=s5hIBNwoqjo>.

6 Katie Rogers, 'Trump Calls on Britain to 'Walk Away' if E.U. Does Not Concede to its Demands', *New York Times* (online, 1 June 2019) <https://www.nytimes.com/2019/06/01/us/politics/trump-brexit-britain.html>.

customs unions and any other bilateral or regional, primarily trade-based, agreements. Under the terms of the *General Agreement on Tariffs and Trade* ('GATT'),[7] notably Article XXIV, any exemption from the general presumption of non-discriminatory tariffs would be granted only for internal liberalisation of 'substantially all trade'[8] between the relevant partner countries. Subject to some administrative caveats, since 1948, RTAS have tended to be either free trade areas (FTAS) in which the member countries are free to select their own trade policy against non-members, or customs unions (CUS) wherein members also have a common external tariff against the rest of the world.[9] In both of these structures, however, the presumption is that trade amongst members is effectively unrestricted.[10]

The popularity of RTAS has exploded in the last 25 years. Figure 1 illustrates the accumulation of regional trade agreement notifications to the World Trade Organisation ('WTO') since its inception.

There are a number of reasons behind this increased popularity of RTAS, in contrast to multilateralism as embodied in the GATT/WTO. One of these is, perversely, the very success of multilateralism.[11] Figure 2, adapted from Bown and Irwin and their careful exercise in reconstructing tariffs immediately post WWII, illustrates a significant decline in average tariffs across the major participants in GATT from around 22% to less than 5% by the turn of the millennium.[12]

---

7   *General Agreement on Tariffs and Trade,* signed 30 October 1947, 64 UNTS 187 (entered into force 1 January 1948) ('GATT'); *Marrakesh Agreement Establishing the World Trade Organization,* opened for signature 15 April 1994, 1867 UNTS 3 (entered into force 1 January 1995) annex 1A ('*General Agreement on Tariffs and Trade 1994*').

8   *GATT* (n 7) art XXIV(8).

9   Ibid.

10   Although there is some debate about the quantum of 'substantially all trade', most approaches suggest this should correlate to 95% of trade between members: see Nicolas JS Lockhart and Andrew D Mitchell, 'Regional Trade Agreements Under GATT 1994: An Exception and its Limits' in Andrew D Mitchell (ed) *Challenges and Prospects for the WTO* (Cameron May, 2005) 217, 232–4.

11   See Friedrich Hayek, *The Road to Serfdom* (Dymock's Book Arcade Ltd, 1944) 25. This echoes Hayek's concerns for classic liberalism expressed in 1944:

> [L]iberalism ... came to be regarded as a 'negative' creed because it could offer to particular individuals little more than a share in the common progress—a progress which came to be taken more and more for granted and was no longer recognized as the result of the policy of freedom. It might even be said that the very success of liberalism became the cause of its decline ... Because of the growing impatience with the slow advancement of liberal policy, [and] the just irritation with those who used liberal phraseology in defence of anti-social privileges ... it came to pass that ... belief in the basic tenets of liberalism was more and more relinquished.

12   Chad P Bown and Douglas A Irwin, 'The GATT's Starting Point: Tariff Levels Circa 1947' (Working Paper No 21782, National Bureau of Economic Research, December 2015) 28.

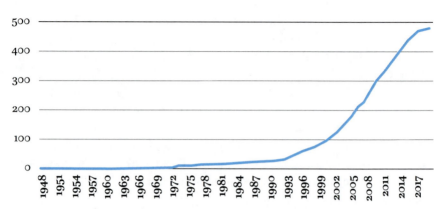

FIGURE 1   Cumulative notifications to WTO of RTAs in force, 1948–2018
Note: World Trade Organisation, 'RTAs Currently in Force (By Year of Entry into Force), 1948–2020', *Regional Trade Agreements Database* (Chart, 2020) <https://rtais.wto.org/UI/charts.aspx#>.

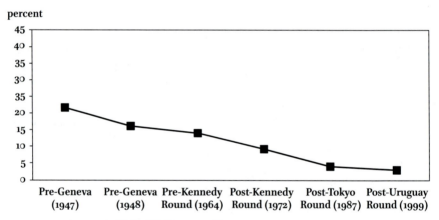

FIGURE 2   Average tariffs for US, Europe and Japan, 1947–1999
Note: Adapted from Bown and Irwin (n 13).

For individual countries the declines have been even greater. Lloyd suggests that the average duty on dutiable imports into Australia in 1946–47 was over 41% and that this had fallen to less than 10% by 2004–05.[13] Similarly, certain goods have experienced far greater reductions in protection—tariffs on

---

13   Peter Lloyd, '100 Years of Tariff Protection in Australia' (Research Paper No 1023, Department of Economics, University of Melbourne, December 2007) table 5.

passenger motor vehicles in Australia fell from over 46% to around 10% over this period, for example.[14]

2.1 Some Economic Attractions of RTAS

Some significant barriers to continued progress on tariff liberalisation in the GATT/WTO stem from its success over its first 50 years. First, there is the obvious fact that its success means there is less room for further progress to be made on industrial tariff reduction. Second, its success is also reflected in its growing membership: there were 23 GATT signatories in 1947 while the WTO reports 164 members as of July 2016.[15] Consequently, consensus agreement—a cornerstone of the WTO—is significantly more challenging to achieve.

The relative success of the GATT in reducing industrial tariffs led to countries with protectionist urges deviating into other areas of import controls such as nontariff barriers and arguably led countries with liberalising interests to turn their attention to other areas of policy coordination. The heterogeneity of interests across such a vast membership meant that the GATT/WTO features many specific agreements beyond just tariffs, as well as some plurilateral (voluntary) arrangements.[16] While the institution provides a ready-made forum and dispute settlement mechanism, for many countries it seems too unwieldy for the handling of certain issues. By contrast, a bilateral RTA, for example, is negotiated between two countries only and, if they are both WTO members, is only constrained by the WTO largely to the extent that it is compliant with Article XXIV. Larger regional groupings are less flexible, of course, but even the sixteen member Regional Comprehensive Economic Partnership (RCEP) expected to be concluded in 2020, was only commenced in 2012.

Perhaps unsurprisingly then, recent RTAs tend to cover significantly more than just border tax reductions. In this way, the RCEP is something of an exception in confining itself to tariffs and some service and investment market access issues, in contrast to the TPP which featured a number of clauses related to labour conditions, the environment, intellectual property and more.[17] Horn,

---

14   Ibid table 1.

15   World Trade Organisation, 'Members and Observers', *Understanding the WTO: The Organisation* (Web Page) <https://www.wto.org/english/thewto_e/whatis_e/tif_e/org6_e .htm>.

16   See, eg, *Agreement on Trade in Civil Aircraft*, signed 12 April 1979, BISD 26S/162 (entered into force 1 January 1980).

17   See *Comprehensive and Progressive Agreement for Trans-Pacific Partnership*, signed 8 March 2018 (entered into force 30 December 2018) incorporating the *Trans-Pacific Partnership Agreement*, signed 4 February 2016 (not in force).

Mavroidis and Sapir consider all US and EC agreements with other WTO members as of late 2008.[18] They look at provisions that cover issues within the ambit of the WTO but in which the parties go beyond their multilateral commitments (so-called WTO+ issues such as tariff reductions) and provisions that lie outside the extant mandate of the WTO (WTO-X issues such as labour standards). WTO-X issues that are covered in many of these agreements range from competition policy issues through data protection, cultural cooperation, health matters, money laundering, nuclear safety and political dialogue to terrorism and visa and asylum issues.[19]

On reflection, it is perhaps obvious that some matters would be more efficiently dealt with on a bilateral basis than a multilateral one. Consider the harmonisation of competition policy. For two countries to be willing to take such a step, they must have similar legal systems and practices and similar objectives in such policy. In a multilateral institution of 164 members, the only possibility of such harmonisation would be through plurilateral side deals and, even then, it is not clear that mediating the necessary negotiations through that institution would be efficient compared to direct bilateral discussions. A good example of the latter is found in the abolition of anti-dumping (AD) complaints across the Tasman, as embodied in 1990 amendments to the Closer Economic Relations (CER) FTA between Australia and New Zealand.[20]

Whilst I argue that the relative attractions of RTAs have, at least in part, been heightened by the *success* of multilateralism, one might also argue that they have been heightened by the more recent *failures* of multilateralism, most specifically in the Doha Round of the WTO.[21] However, the timing of events works against this to some extent: the initial take-off of RTAs shown in Figure 1 pre-dates the initiation of the Doha Round in 2001 by a few years and significantly pre-dates the general realisation and acceptance of that Round's failures

---

18   Henrik Horn, Petros C Mavroidis and André Sapir, 'Beyond the WTO? An Anatomy of EU and US Preferential Trade Agreements' (2010) 33(11) *The World Economy* 1565.

19   Of some interest to a legal audience, perhaps, but beyond the scope of the present paper, the authors suggest that while the EC tends to include a greater number 'of areas where exhortatory language has been agreed' than does the US, it tends to have a smaller number of areas with enforceable obligations, a phenomenon the authors refer to as 'legal inflation': See ibid 1580.

20   See Kerrin M Vautier and Peter Lloyd, *International Trade and Competition Policy: CER, APEC and the WTO* (Institute of Policy Studies, 1997). The discussion here should not be taken to suggest that there is no role for the WTO in harmonising aspects of competition policy—indeed, its agreement on Trade-Related Aspects of Intellectual Property Rights (TRIPS) and the General Agreement on Trade in Services (GATS) both have important competition policy dimensions.

21   I am very grateful to a referee for making this point.

NAVIGATING THE 'BACKLASH' AGAINST INTERNATIONAL TRADE

by 2008 or so. Furthermore, one could also make a strong case that the failure of the Doha Round itself sheets home to the earlier successes of multilateralism, for the reasons exposited above. By reducing tariffs (particularly industrial tariffs) so successfully, the GATT/WTO left only the high-hanging fruit for Doha to address—agriculture, services, intellectual property and trade and development.

2.2 Some Economic Downsides to RTAS

Given the enthusiasm of mainstream economics for free trade, dating back over 200 years to David Ricardo's initial exposition of the principle of comparative advantage,[22] it might seem that, as RTAs represent a move towards freer trade, they should meet with the profession's approbation. But, in the presence of trade restrictions that are not being removed—namely, those against non-members—the analysis of a preferential tariff reduction occurs in what economists refer to as a second-best environment. In such a world the removal of a single given 'distortion' may not be beneficial.

A simple numerical example illustrates the point. Consider three WTO member countries and suppose that small home country A imports a thousand widgets from overseas. It can buy these from country B at $15 a piece or buy the identical product from country C at $10 a piece. Suppose that, for whatever domestic political reasons, country A levies a $10 per unit tax on widget imports (a specific tariff). If this tax is applied in an MFN non-discriminatory fashion to all import sources, then clearly A will source all of its widget imports from country C: consumers in A will pay $20 per widget (and any domestic widget produces in country A will be able to charge $20 for their own product in A) and for each imported widget $10 will go to the producer in C and $10 to A's government. Were a consumer to import a widget from country B, they would pay $25 so, on the maintained assumption that widgets from B and C are identical, they are better off importing solely from C. Importing 1000 units means that consumers are paying $20,000 for imports, of which $10,000 goes to C's suppliers and the rest into the coffers of the government in A.

Now suppose that countries A and B form a RTA; specifically, a free trade area in which they do not coordinate their external tariffs against non-members. Under this RTA, A agrees to abolish its tariff against country B. As C is not a member of the RTA, A need not change the tariff against country C. Widget imports from C now still cost a consumer $20, given the maintained tariff, but imports from partner country B are only $15; clearly all of A's imports are

---

22   Piero Sraffa and MH Dobb (eds), *The Works and Correspondence of David Ricardo* (Cambridge University Press, 1951) vol 1.

now sourced from B rather than C. For expositional simplicity we unrealistically suppose that imports are still 1000 units so now consumers pay only $15,000 for their widget imports, but all of this now goes to the supplying country. While A's consumers have $5,000 more in their pockets, A's government has $10,000 less. As a first approximation, country A is $5,000 worse off.

The phenomenon described here is known as trade diversion and the second-best context is clear: were A to abolish its tariff against country C as well, then its consumers would continue to buy only from country C and country A would *not* be worse off.[23] The problem here is that the preferential tariff reduction has led to a diverting of supply away from an efficient but unfavoured supplier towards the less efficient partner supplier. This downside to RTAs was first exposited by Jacob Viner in 1950[24] and is widely known and understood; indeed, it is generally the first thing that economics students learn about RTAs.

A second downside of RTAs is, potentially, their consequences for multilateral liberalisation. The debate on whether RTAs constitute, in Jagdish Bhagwati's memorable phrase, building blocks or stumbling blocks to multilateral liberalisation remains unsettled, but there are a number of ways in which the proliferation of RTAs might harm multilateralism. For example,

- To the extent that countries devote limited resources to the negotiation of international agreements, engagement with RTAs must come at the expense of engagement with the WTO.[25]
- The explosion of RTAs can also cause third countries to pursue them, where they otherwise might not, for 'fear of missing out'.[26]
- Levy notes that RTAs can create domestic interest groups that oppose multilateral liberalisation.[27]

There are also many ways in which RTAs might lead to more liberal trade more generally; as noted, the jury, at least in economics, is still out in this matter.

---

23   In the more realistic setting where demand for widgets increases as their price falls, country A would be strictly better off in this 'trade creation' context, but in the simple setting of this example consumers would gain $10,000 while the government would lose that same sum for approximately no net effect.

24   Jacob Viner, *The Customs Union Issue* (Carnegie Endowment for International Peace, 1950).

25   See, eg, Daniel A Sumner, 'Domestic Support and the WTO Negotiations' (2000) 44(3) *Australian Journal of Agricultural and Resource Economics* 457.

26   This can also lead to the opposite result whereby the costs of being excluded rise as RTAs form so countries all join up: a global RTA is, of course, just global free trade. See Kamal Saggi and Halis M Yildiz, 'Bilateralism, Multilateralism, and the Quest for Global Free Trade' (2010) 81(1) *Journal of International Economics* 26.

27   Philip Levy, 'A Political-Economic Analysis of Free-Trade Agreements' (1997) 87(4) *American Economic Review* 506, 507.

NAVIGATING THE 'BACKLASH' AGAINST INTERNATIONAL TRADE

The essential point here, though, is that RTAs are not necessarily viewed as benign arrangements within mainstream economics. This stands in contrast to a general acceptance of the gains from freer trade, a proposition that, 'is so very manifest that it seems ridiculous to take any pains to prove it; nor could it ever have been called in question had not the interested sophistry of domestic merchants and manufacturers confounded the common sense of mankind'.[28] As a crude characterisation, economists tend to agree on the desirability of freer trade but disagree over what to do about the income distributional consequences of that: those at the *laissez-faire* end of the spectrum are inclined to let losses lie where they fall, while those at the more interventionist end would argue for more efficient, directly targeted policies to deal with such effects.[29]

Even when RTAs are desirable with respect to the *status quo*, multilateral liberalisation will often be preferable: the case for RTAs, in this view, is a second best case rooted in *realpolitik*.[30] The WTO has made little measurable progress since the end of the Uruguay Round; in particular, the Doha Round has been a disappointment to those hoping for a competitive alternative to RTAs. But while it can consequently be tempting to dismiss the WTO as being irrelevant because of this lack of significant change, that is to overlook the extremely important role it plays in monitoring the world trading system. That is, focusing on the 'flows' of incremental change risks overlooking the 'stocks' of accumulated progress. The WTO continues to play a vital role in the settlement of trade disputes—modulo Sino-American wars current as this paper is being written—and maintains, for the most part, the dominance of rules-based trade over power-based trade.[31] The exception to this is current US behaviour. It is particularly odd, as Mattoo and Staiger note, that the US seems to be initiating a shift from 'rules-based' to 'power-based' tariff negotiations in defiance

---

28   Adam Smith, *An Inquiry into the Nature and Causes of the Wealth of Nations* (W Strahan and T Cadell, 1776) bk 4 ch 3 pt 2.

29   See, eg, the cogent discussion in Alan S Blinder, *Hard Heads, Soft Hearts: Tough-minded Economics for a Just Society* (Addison-Wesley Publishing, 1987) ch 4.

30   See Paul Krugman, 'Is Bilateralism Bad?' in Elhanan Helpman and Assaf Razin (eds), *International Trade and Trade Policy* (MIT Press, 1991) 9. In Krugman's model of bilateralism, for example, world welfare is maximised when there is but a single trading bloc—global free trade—but is non-monotonic in the number of trading blocs. So more blocs can be better than fewer.

31   See Kyle Bagwell, Chad P Bown and Robert W Staiger, 'Is the WTO Passé?' (Working Paper No 21303, National Bureau of Economic Research, June 2015) for an excellent survey of many of the issues touched upon here from the perspective of more formal economic analysis.

of what must surely be its longer-term interests.[32] There is accumulating evidence, too, that purely 'political' explanations are inadequate: Blanchard *et al* find empirical evidence that, 'Republican candidates lost support in the 2018 congressional election in counties more exposed to trade retaliation, but saw no commensurate electoral gains from US tariff protection'.[33]

2.3 *'Civil Society' and RTAS*

As noted above, opposition in the US to the proposed TPP trade agreement was bipartisan (and it is fairly clear that it was based on objections other than trade diversion!). Having said that, however, the mainstream economic evidence concerning the effects of RTAS on participating countries is often far from convincing, in line with the discussion above. In 2016, the office of the US International Trade Commission released an 812-page report on a computable general equilibrium (CGE) analysis of the likely effects of the TPP on the US economy, projecting forward over its fifteen year implementation period. It concluded that, 'by 2032, U.S. real GDP would be ... [0.15%] higher than a baseline scenario that reflects expected global economic conditions without TPP.... [and] [e]mployment would be 0.07% higher, or close to 128,000 full-time equivalents'.[34] To put this into some context, in the month of November 2016 alone, 5.219 million jobs were created in the United States, and 5.028 million jobs were destroyed for net growth of 191,000.[35] It takes the US economy about 20 days, then, to create 128,000 jobs and it seems a small increment over 15 years. And a recent paper, using a rather different method, suggests that the Australia-US bilateral trade agreement reduced the volume of trade between the two countries by a significant margin.[36]

---

32   Aaditya Mattoo and Robert W Staiger, 'Trade Wars: What do They Mean? Why are They Happening Now? What are the Costs?' (Working Paper No 25762, National Bureau of Economic Research, April 2019) 1.

33   Emily Blanchard, Chad P Bown and David Chor, 'Did Trump's Trade War Impact the 2018 Election?' (Working Paper No 26434, National Bureau of Economic Research, December 2019) 1.

34   United States International Trade Commission, *Trans-Pacific Partnership Agreement: Likely Impact on the U.S. Economy and on Specific Industry Sectors* (Report No 4607, May 2016) 22–3.

35   U.S. Bureau of Labor Statistics, 'Job Openings Labor Turnover Survey News Release', *Economic News Release* (Web Page, 10 January 2017) <https://www.bls.gov/news.release/archives/jolts_01102017.htm>.

36   Scott L Baier, Yoto V Yotov and Thomas Zylkin, 'On the Widely Differing Effects of Free Trade Agreements: Lessons from Twenty Years of Trade Integration' (2019) 116 *Journal of International Economics* 206, 214 tb 1.

NAVIGATING THE 'BACKLASH' AGAINST INTERNATIONAL TRADE 167

On the other side of the Atlantic, Brexit was nominally driven by a desire to 'repatriate' trade policy rather than a general opposition to openness and, indeed, the Conservative Party has been quite vocal about the possibility of signing a raft of RTAs post-Brexit.[37] But the same issue that plagues the economic case for TPP also affects this objective: the British government's own modelling of the effects of '[h]igh ambition rest of world trade deals' suggests an increase in GDP of 0.2 percentage points.[38]

Economically, then, the benefits of RTAs seem modest at best. But what of the view of the lay person? Some evidence comes from recent US surveys undertaken by the Monmouth University Polling Institute in New Jersey. In 2015, in response to the question, 'In general, do you think that free trade agreements with different countries are good or bad for the United States, or are you not sure?', 26% of respondents said 'bad' (for registered voters this was 33% for Republicans and 24% for Democrats).[39] By 2019, only 14% responded 'bad' (17% of Republicans and only 8% of Democrats.[40] By self-declared political ideology, a category not recorded in 2015, only 8% of liberals but 19% of conservatives answered 'bad' in 2019.). When asked specifically in 2019 about whether President Trump's recent decision to impose tariffs on a range

---

37   See Conservative and Unionist Party, 'Get Brexit Done: Unleash Britain's Potential' (Conservative and Unionist Party Manifesto, 2019) 57 <https://assets-global.website -files.com/5da42e2cae7ebd3f8bde353c/5dda924905da587992a064ba_Conservative%20 2019%20Manifesto.pdf>:

  We aim to have 80 per cent of UK trade covered by free trade agreements within the next three years, starting with the USA, Australia, New Zealand and Japan. These will be negotiated in parallel with our EU deal. We will also forge stronger links with the Commonwealth, which boasts some of the world's most dynamic economies such as India, with which we already share deep historical and cultural connections.

38   Prime Minister of the United Kingdom, *EU Exit: Long-term Economic Analysis* (Parliamentary Paper No 9742, November 2018) 76. This stems from analysis at 22 [48]–[49] assuming:

  that all EU trade agreements with third countries are transitioned in their current states to UK-specific arrangements ... [and that] in the long run, the UK secures new trade agreements with international partners. These agreements are assumed to cover a broad range of potential trading partners, including ... the United States, Australia, New Zealand, Malaysia, Brunei, China, India, Mercosur (Brazil, Argentina, Paraguay and Uruguay) and the Gulf-Cooperation Council (UAE, Saudi Arabia, Oman, Qatar, Kuwait and Bahrain).

39   Monmouth University Polling Institute, 'National: No Opinion on Free Trade Pact: Obama Rating Ticks Up Slightly' (Poll Report, 5 November 2015) 1 <https://www.monmouth.edu/ polling-institute/documents/monmouthpoll_us_110515.pdf/>.

40   Monmouth University Polling Institute, 'National: American Consumers Expect To Bear Cost of China Tariffs 2019' (Poll Report, 28 May 2019) 1 <https://www.monmouth.edu/ polling-institute/documents/monmouthpoll_us_052819.pdf/>.

of imported products would help or hurt the US economy, 47% of respondents said it would hurt.[41] The apparent fall in trade sceptics from 2015 to 2019 suggested by these polls certainly does not seem to indicate a backlash against trade liberalisation and, if anything, the low overall opposition to RTAs seems to suggest that non-economists are perhaps less divided on this matter than are economists.

The Trump administration is another matter altogether. Their opposition to trade liberalisation seems an equal opportunity opposition, levelled as it is both at preferential agreements and at the multilateral system itself. As a declared fan of tariffs ('I am a tariff man')[42] and trade wars ('good, and easy to win'),[43] President Trump has had no reservations about taxing the US' trade and in criticising the 'broken' WTO and its alleged bias against the US.[44] Amiti, Redding and Weinstein show that in 2018 alone, the cumulative effect of the series of tariffs imposed by the US, principally on China but also on other trading partners, raised the average import-weighted tariff rate in the US from around 1.5% to almost 3.5%, an enormous increase in the space of less than a year.[45] As the Monmouth University polls cited above suggest, however, it is not at all clear that this anti-trade sentiment extends much beyond the White House.

Nevertheless, whilst there are good grounds for scepticism about the economic benefits of recent RTAs, the focus of organised opposition to these agreements has been more on the fact, noted above, that these agreements are not simply trade-related but, rather, are seen as Trojan horses for agreements on other matters.[46] Governments too frequently seem to regard RTAs

---

41   Ibid 2. Interestingly, 62% of respondents thought that American consumers would bear more of the costs of these tariffs than Chinese producers, in stark contrast to President Trump's (mis)understanding of the mechanics of tariffs. Even amongst Republicans, 40% felt that implications of the tariffs' incidence would be primarily on US consumers.

42   @realDonaldTrump (Donald Trump) (Twitter, 5 December 2018, 2:03am EST) <https://twitter.com/realdonaldtrump/status/1069970500535902208?lang=en>.

43   @realDonaldTrump (Donald Trump) (Twitter, 2 March 2018, 9:50pm EST) <https://twitter.com/realdonaldtrump/status/969525362580484098?lang=en>.

44   'The WTO is BROKEN when the world's RICHEST countries claim to be developing countries to avoid WTO rules and get special treatment. NO more!!! Today I directed the U.S. Trade Representative to take action so that countries stop CHEATING the system at the expense of the USA!': @realDonaldTrump (Donald Trump) (Twitter, 26 July 2019, 11:29am EST) <https://twitter.com/realdonaldtrump/status/1154821023197474817?lang=en>.

45   Mary Amiti, Stephen J Redding and David E Weinstein, 'The Impact of the 2018 Tariffs on Prices and Welfare' (2019) 33(4) *Journal of Economic Perspectives* 187, 193, figure 3.

46   This is not to suggest, of course, that the directly trade related aspects of international negotiations are universally accepted. The extensive protests in Seattle at the WTO's

as trophies to be gathered and displayed, almost regardless of content, and many elements of civil society have expressed concern at what is being agreed to simply to get a deal completed. In particular, much opposition in Australia to the original TPP was focused on the Investor-State Dispute Settlement (ISDS) clauses and on intellectual property concerns.[47] While an economic case can be made for ISDS (in providing incentives for domestic governments to consider a wider range of consequences of domestic policy initiatives),[48] it was seen by many as a vehicle to advance the interests of large corporates— Smith's sophist merchants and manufacturers—over those of the public.[49] Similarly, to foster increased trade in services, greater harmonisation of standards would be required across countries and the TPP was widely (and fairly accurately, in my view) perceived to harmonise to US standards.[50] It is perhaps no coincidence, then, that the RCEP, centred on the ASEAN countries, is far more modest in terms of the non-trade issues it purports to cover than have been more US-centric agreements.

Regarding intellectual property, this was controversial in the TPP from the start. A series of leaked drafts of the US' position caused a great deal of concern amongst many commentators[51] and, even though that position shifted somewhat through the negotiations, it always remained controversial.[52]

---

meetings in 1999 certainly included opponents of trade liberalisation in and of itself, for example. See Gillian H Murphy, 'The Seattle WTO Protests: Building a Global Movement' in Rupert Taylor (ed), *Creating a Better World: Interpreting Global Civil Society* (Kumarian Press, 2004) 27, 29. Murphy notes that, while the key issues to be discussed in Seattle were 'the Forest Products Agreement, the Multilateral Agreement on Investments (banking and finance), biotechnology, and intellectual property rights ... an even more serious issue overall was that the social and environmental consequences of trade policies were *not* to be discussed'.

47   Kimberlee G Weatherall, 'Intellectual Property in the TPP: Not 'The New TRIPS' (2016) 17(2) *Melbourne Journal of International Law* 257, 257 n 4.

48   See generally Wilhelm Kohler and Frank Stähler, 'The Economics of Investor Protection: ISDS Versus National Treatment' (2019) 121 *Journal of International Economics* 103254: 206.

49   Martin, 'Trans-Pacific Partnership: We're Selling Economic Sovereignty for Little Return' (n 3).

50   Ibid.

51   See, eg, Sean M Flynn et al, 'The US Proposal for an Intellectual Property Chapter in the Trans-Pacific Partnership Agreement' (2012) 28(1) *American University International Law Review* 105.

52   Kimberlee G Weatherall, 'Intellectual Property in the TPP: Not 'The New TRIPS' (2016) 17(2) *Melbourne Journal of International Law* 257, 257.

3 Trade Policy in a Time of Scepticism

In the 'Navigating the Backlash against Global Law and Institutions' contribution to this issue, a definition of "backlash" is given as 'intense and sustained public disapproval of a system accompanied by aggressive steps to resist the system and to remove its legal force'.[53] It 'represents a fundamental resistance to and rejection of a system or institution of law'.[54] The discussion so far suggests that describing recent concerns about trade liberalisation, and a general cooling of past enthusiasm for increased openness in trade, as a backlash might not be entirely warranted. From the perspective of mainstream economics, I have suggested that the political shift towards RTAs in preference to multilateralism as the vehicle for liberalisation would inevitably lead to some (non-violent) lessening of enthusiasm for it, and I have also suggested that the concerns of lay people about recent trends in globalisation are frequently driven more by concerns about the Greeks inside the horse, rather than the horse itself.

Nevertheless, whether it is labelled a backlash or not, it seems clear that the appetite for trade liberalisation has lessened in many countries in recent years. What, then, does this imply for the conduct of trade policy—how do we negotiate this shift in sentiment?

3.1 *International Agreements, Economic Sovereignty and Exit*

Some recent work considers the design of international agreements between sovereign nations in a world of political uncertainty.[55] One consequence of sovereignty is that countries are free to withdraw from their prior agreements, if they so wish. The interest of Richardson and Stähler is in the consequences, if any, of this possibility of exit for the initial design of an agreement.[56]

The broad set-up of their model is as follows. Suppose two countries are considering an agreement to cooperate over policy settings in some context. Whilst the model is fairly general and could apply to agreements over trade, migration, emissions, competition policy and so on, for concreteness let us consider the example of trade policy. Each government has some particular objective function and, importantly, this need not be the economist's standard definition of economic welfare but may reflect the political interests of the decision-maker. There is a relationship between policy choices and the

---

53 Peter G Danchin et al, 'Navigating the Backlash against Global Law and Institutions' (2020) 38 *Australian Year Book of International Law* 33, 37.

54 Ibid.

55 See Martin Richardson and Frank Stähler, 'International Agreements, Economic Sovereignty and Exit' (2019) 120 *European Economic Review* 103326: 1.

56 Ibid.

NAVIGATING THE 'BACKLASH' AGAINST INTERNATIONAL TRADE 171

outcome for the government and this is *ex ante* uncertain. As a consequence, a given policy choice can lead to quite different outcomes for the government, depending on the realisation of this relationship. For instance, a low tariff on imported steel might be very attractive to a government when the electorate is sympathetic to globalisation, but very unattractive if there is a populist shift and voter sentiment moves towards protectionism. The link between a policy choice and a political outcome for the policy-maker is captured by a parameter denoted ϑ and it is assumed to be drawn from a distribution over some range of possible values. While the distributions are the same for both countries the actual realisations are assumed to be independent and uncorrelated.

For international agreements to hold any interest for a government, it must be the case that the government's political outcomes also depend on the policy choices made in the partner country. That is, foreign tariff choices affect outcomes for domestic politicians.[57] If a policy-maker acts in isolation, then, while they can choose their own policies unconstrained by considerations of their partner's objectives, they also get no consideration in their partner's decisions. The attraction of an international agreement here is that the parties can cooperate, at least to some extent, on the joint setting of policy choices. The paper considers a simple but very general set up in which a country in an international agreement will choose its policy actions to maximise the sum of its own objectives and its partner's objective functions, the weight on the latter being given by some parameter denoted $\lambda \leq 1$. This parameter is common to both countries and is a key choice variable in the design of the agreement. If $\lambda = 0$ then the countries are not cooperating at all: each sets its policy completely independently to maximise its own objectives with no concern for their partner. But, at the other extreme, if $\lambda = 1$ then the two countries cooperate fully: both policy choices are made to maximise the joint objectives of the coalition. Fractional values of λ indicate partial cooperation.

A central innovation in this analysis is the introduction of the possibility of exit. Should a sufficiently small realisation of ϑ occur for one of the parties and a large one for the other,[58] then the first country will simply leave the agreement. Essentially, this supposes that renegotiation of the agreement after an otherwise exit-inducing shock is prohibitively costly.[59] The reason for this is to take the possibility of exit seriously: under the informational structure of the

---

57 Cf Blanchard, Bown and Chor (n 35).
58 Essentially, a low ϑ_1 for country 1 means that its government wants a small policy action for its own constituency, but a high ϑ_2 in country 2 means a larger policy action is best there, and, in the context of the agreement, country 1 would then be required to act for country 2's benefit at its own expense.
59 Richardson and Stähler (n 57) 5.

model, absent this assumption it would always be profitable for the two countries to renegotiate their arrangement. This prohibition of renegotiation is not as restrictive as it might seem. In the context of Brexit, for example, one of our two 'countries' represents the European Union and the assumption of costly renegotiation can be thought of as representing the Union's concern that renegotiating a deal with the United Kingdom could encourage other members to pursue the same strategy of threatened exit—a significant cost to such renegotiation. If exit by one party occurs then both parties are effectively out of the agreement, clearly, and so both revert to acting independently.

In this model, if there were no possibility of exit then the parties would both agree on full cooperation. This provides a useful benchmark for comparison with the case where exit might occur. When exit is possible—that is, when the range of possible shocks is sufficiently great that it includes some which would induce a party to exit—then, for a given range of potential shocks, the analysis shows that greater cooperation between the countries makes exit more likely, all other things being equal.[60] The reason for this is that, as cooperation increases, each country is required to make policy choices that are, in a sense, further from those they would choose if left to their own devices. Consequently, the relative attraction of defaulting to unilateral action becomes greater.

The two central findings of the paper are that, while (1) full cooperation will never be optimal so long as there is some chance of exit by one or other of the countries, (2) the degree of cooperation chosen by the two countries will never be so low as to completely rule out the very possibility of exit.[61] The first result establishes the intuitive proposition that, when default is a possibility in the agreement (and that default is more likely the greater is the degree of cooperation between the parties) then the parties will cooperate less *ex ante* in anticipation of this problem. The second result, however, suggests that cooperation will never fall so low that there will be no possibility of the agreement breaking apart. What this implies for trade policy in an era of uncertainty is that it is likely to be less cooperative, and so to have less value to the parties, in a sense, than would otherwise be the case and that, nevertheless, an optimally designed agreement could still be one on which a country might renege in sufficiently extreme circumstances.

In this analysis, exit can occur as an equilibrium phenomenon, its likelihood fully anticipated by the agreement's parties, but it can also be triggered by unexpected political shocks. For example, an increase in the variability of the ϑ parameter will generally increase the probability of exit; that is, in an

---

60   Ibid 7.
61   Ibid 8.

NAVIGATING THE 'BACKLASH' AGAINST INTERNATIONAL TRADE   173

environment where the political rewards of policy interventions are more uncertain, the probability of international agreements breaking down is greater.[62]

All in all, the bottom line conclusion of this analysis is perhaps best characterised as one of tempered pessimism: in a more uncertain world, international agreements themselves become less cooperative by design, but cooperation is still *ex ante* optimal, even as its degree is reduced. How does this tie into our concept of backlash? Exit, in this model, occurs either because of extreme realisations of the underlying links between policy choices and political outcomes (captured by the ϑ parameter), even though the underlying distributions are unaltered, or because the whole distribution is subject to an unexpected disturbance. The 'sustained challenge that populist movements in countries around the world have posed to global norms and institutions'[63] is certainly consistent with the latter idea that the political payoffs from policy choices have changed discretely and significantly. The analysis nevertheless would still apply in this new world and the conclusions still follow: international agreements are likely to be less cooperative in the future and, even then, are still likely to be fragile.

4   Conclusion

Writing in 1999, Bhagwati commented on, 'the dangerous drift to [RTAs] that has been aided by the unfortunate conversion of the United States to the thesis that any trade liberalization is as good as any other. Perhaps, as often happens in economic policy, what presently looks like a politically irreversible trend will yield to economic wisdom'[64]. We will see twenty years on, if one understood the United States to refer to the Trump administration, then one might change the 'good' to 'bad' in this remark, and it would still seem to apply: the resurrection of multilateralism as the prime vehicle for liberalisation still seems an unlikely prospect. This paper has suggested that current dissatisfaction with

---

62   Interestingly, though, as the world becomes more uncertain, in the sense discussed here, while the optimal degree of cooperation is always lower than when exit is not possible, it varies non-monotonically with uncertainty and it is possible that countries will become more cooperative as uncertainty rises. The reason lies in the fact that there are still gains from cooperation to be had and, while increased uncertainty raises the probability of exit, it does so at a decreasing rate.

63   Danchin et al (n 55) 33, 35.

64   Jagdish Bhagwati and Arvind Panagariya, 'Preferential Trading Areas and Multilateralism— Strangers, Friends, or Foes?' in Jagdish Bhagwati, Pavin Krishna and Arvind Panagariya (eds), *Trading Blocs: Alternative Approaches to Analyzing Preferential Trade Agreements* (MIT Press, 1999) 33, 79.

trade liberalisation stems from a number of features of the recent forms of liberalisation and that characterising it as a backlash may not be entirely accurate. In particular, I have stressed the long agnosticism of economists with respect to the merits of preferential trading arrangements and highlighted the role of such arrangements as vehicles for non-trade related issues. One can be sceptical about RTAs in their purely trade related dimensions but also suspicious of them because of this secondary feature in which intellectual property regimes, investor rights and other such matters are bundled together into them.

The question then arises of 'negotiating' these concerns. Beyond what I would consider to be fairly self-evident considerations—much greater openness and clarity about the terms in, and consequences and potential benefits and costs of, trade agreements—I have argued that greater scepticism about the value of international agreements leads naturally to a situation in which such agreements become less cooperative, by design. Furthermore, I have suggested that agreements should never be immune to parties 'changing their minds' and exiting, even though it is anticipation of that very possibility that leads to decreased cooperation in the establishment of the agreement in the first place. Thus, although States may not be *rejecting* trade liberalisation and RTAs in the sense of a true backlash, they are nonetheless unlikely to cooperate to the same extent as in the past.

Backlash against a Rules-Based International Human Rights Order? An Australian Perspective

Jolyon Ford*

1   Introduction

This article engages—from an Australian perspective—with the question of whether we can identify a recent populist political "backlash" within some Western democracies against the institutions, instruments and even the ideas of the multilateral (United Nations ('UN') and treaty-based) human rights system. An associated question concerns what the implications of any such phenomenon might be for the universalist human rights system (or at least Australia's participation therein), and perhaps the implications for the wider global legal order of which the human rights project has, for decades now, been such an important part.

Much depends, of course, on how one defines or marks a threshold for what constitutes backlash, and whether it describes an action, event, driver or other phenomenon (which may or may not have certain effects), or rather describes an outcome, effects, or impacts. A definition that was influential in the workshops to which this Special Issue relates would distinguish mere discontent with an institution or status quo and instead cast backlash as involving 'fundamental resistance to and rejection of a system or institution of law' including 'aggressive steps to resist the system and to remove its legal force'.[1] Central to how the backlash concept was erected in those workshops, in a somewhat stylised way so as to stimulate debate, was that it involved in some way the domestic political cultivation of or response to "populism" (howsoever defined).[2]

In the global human rights area one recent event, in particular, stands out as potentially significant enough in systemic terms that this definition of backlash (including a populist context) might be though apt. This was the

---

*   Associate Professor, Australian National University School of Law.

1   See David Caron and Esmé Shirlow, 'Dissecting Backlash: The Unarticulated Causes of Backlash and its Unintended Consequences' in Andreas Follesdal and Geir Ulfstein (ed), *The Judicilization of International Law: A Mixed Blessing?* (Oxford University Press, 2018) 159, 160, quoting Cass R Sunstein, 'Backlash's Travels' (2007) 42 *Harvard Civil Rights—Civil Liberties Law Review* 435, 435; Peter G Danchin et al, 'Navigating the Backlash against Global Law and Institutions' (2020) 38 *Australian Year Book of International Law* 33.

2   Danchin et al (n 1) 35–6.

Trump administration's announcement in June 2018 that it would withdraw the United States' ('US') membership and funding from the UN Human Rights Council ('the Council').[3] While foreshadowed at least a year beforehand, the announcement came the day after the UN High Commissioner for Human Rights, speaking in the Council in Geneva, criticised US immigration detention policy.[4] The recent Australian context offers nothing with quite the same "shock factor" in terms of stark embrace or rejection of the international human rights system (or, perhaps more precisely, of parts or artefacts thereof). Still, in October 2019 Australia's Prime Minister announced that he had commissioned a 'comprehensive audit of global institutions and rule-making processes where [Australia has] the greatest stake'.[5] The Prime Minister indicated that while attracted to a general posture of 'pragmatic international engagement', Australia would look in future to play a *more* active role in global standard setting.[6] Yet an interpretation was certainly open that the audit process (and the speech itself) amounted to flagging a *less* active and committed role (potential systematic Australian disengagement from some global institutions and regimes). This is because the announcement was in the context of a speech in which the Prime Minister criticised the 'negative globalism' of supposedly coercive, conformity-imposing international institutions staffed by 'unaccountable internationalist bureaucracy'.[7]

Couched as it was amid rhetoric about the sovereignty of the Australian citizenry, one can envisage an argument being raised that such language can be viewed as having some of the hallmarks of putative "populist backlash" against the global legal order and its institutions.[8] Together with Australia's reactions

---

3 Michael Pompeo and Nikki Haley, 'Remarks on the UN Human Rights Council' Joint Statement, (Speech, US Mission to the UN in Washington DC, 19 June 2018). For one overview, see American Society of International Law, 'United States Withdraws from the UN Human Rights Council, Shortly After Receiving Criticism About its Border Policy' (2018) 112(4) *American Journal of International Law* 745. For recent analysis of this event in the US context (including whether it should be characterised at all as a system-rejecting or system-threatening backlash on the definition discussed here), see Jolyon Ford, 'The Multilateral Human Rights System: Systemic Challenge or Healthy Contestation?' [2020] *Maryland Journal of International Law* (forthcoming).

4 Zeid Ra'ad al Hussein, 'Opening Statement and Global Update of Human Rights Concerns' (Speech, 38th session of the UN Human Rights Council, 18 June 2018).

5 Scott Morrison, 'In Our Interests' (Speech, Lowy Lecture Sydney, 3 October 2019).

6 Ibid.

7 Ibid.

8 For examples of claims that such a backlash has occurred or is underway in respect of the international human rights system in particular, see Ian Siederman, 'The UN High Commissioner for Human Rights in the Age of Global Backlash' (2019) 37(1) *Netherlands Quarterly of Human Rights* 5; Philip Alston, 'The Populist Challenge to Human Rights'

AN AUSTRALIAN PERSPECTIVE

to criticism from UN-system entities of its handling of irregular migrants, the Prime Minister's statements constitute the principal context chosen in this article for the undertaking outlined in its first sentence above: whether there is or has been some kind or degree of Australian backlash against global norms and institutions.

It is useful to reflect briefly on this article's attempted focus on the international legal order on human rights and associated institutions. One topic for another time is the extent to which it is viable to analyse particular international subject-matter regimes in isolation (trade, human rights, peace and security, etc) in terms of a backlash or set of backlashes. We might also ask whether any discernible backlash behaviours are specific to states' particular issues with human rights regimes and institutions, or (as this Special Issue implies) part of a pattern observable across the wider rules-based international order.[9] Finally, one might ask whether a backlash directed against or confined to the human rights system might have consequences for that wider international order. Exploring this last question inescapably raises profound questions about the nature of international law. Is it a single regulatory idea, or merely a severable bundle of possible obligations, one legal system or a set of systems? Thus this article will come to ask how tenable it might be over time—for a coherent and credible idea of the rule of law at an international level—for Australia to "back" some or most parts of the rules-based order but "lash" out against other parts.

As the most striking example in the human rights context of a possible backlash-driven shock to the international human rights system, the US exit from the Council raises at least three conceivable questions of interest from an Australian perspective:

1. First, whether US backlash against (rejection of/withdrawal from) the Council as a particular event might—given the disproportionate significance of the US as the post-1945 champion and bank-roller of the global human rights project—constitute or be part of a broader

---

(2017) 9(1) *Journal of Human Rights Practice* 1. See also Kenneth Roth, 'Pushback Against the Populist Challenge to Human Rights' in Human Rights Watch, *World Report 2018: Events of 2017* (Annual Report, New York, 2018).

9   Thus James Crawford's 2017 LSE Chorley Lecture, engaging with statements antagonistic to international law by some world leaders, noted that one key question is whether there is indeed 'a pattern to all this'. Crawford noted a need to look for 'underlying tendencies' potentially lying behind the 'foreground noise': James Crawford, 'The Current Political Discourse Concerning International Law' (2018) 81(1) *The Modern Law Review* 1, 1–2. My article does not attempt to engage with Crawford's follow-on to the pattern question ('how should we respond?').

system-threatening development of real consequence for Australia (as a hitherto largely committed member of that wider system). That question has been addressed elsewhere in detail,[10] with at least three reasons why the answer to this question is not necessarily "yes". We can put the question to one side.

2. A second question-bundle is whether some broader global backlash trend now pertains of states exiting from and/or de-legitimising international institutions,[11] whether we can discern signs recently (such as the Lowy address)[12] that Australia may be one of those backlash states, and what systemic implications this may have for Australia's oft-repeated fidelity to, and reliance upon, the international rules-based order.

3. Sitting above or behind these two questions is the broader third question of whether the concept of backlash (at least as defined above) is useful at all in explaining or analysing recent developments, and/or what modifications or qualifiers it might need.

This article attempts to address questions two and three above. It does so in reverse order. It focusses first on question three, exploring ways to approach, unpack refine or reframe the backlash concept. It then takes the resulting frame(s) to address question two: a general overview of recent Australian practice and rhetoric. This is so as to advance a useful characterisation of Australia's conduct, even if it does not in a "yes/no sense" meet Sunstein's definition of systemic-level backlash intended to reject a legal order and remove its legal force.[13]

2   Framing the Backlash Concept

2.1   *Exploring the Utility of the Backlash Motif*
Before one can ask what is to be done about it,[14] one needs to know what backlash might refer to. This section first advances seven observations on the backlash concept. First, it is useful to erect the Sunstein definition as a

---

10   See Ford (n 3). That article does not engage with an Australian perspective or consequences for Australia itself.

11   See Ford (n 3), discussing Catherine M. Brölmann et al, 'Exiting International Organizations' (2018) 15(2) *International Organizations Law Review* 243; Inken von Borzyskowski and Felicity Vabulas, 'Hello, Goodbye: When Do States Withdraw from International Organizations?' (2019) 14 *The Review of International Organizations* 335.

12   See Morrison (n 5).

13   See Caron and Shirlow (n 1).

14   See Crawford (n 9); Danchin et al (n 1) 46–55.

AN AUSTRALIAN PERSPECTIVE

starting point not because it is some inviolable one but because it provides a foil for fleshing out the backlash idea. That is, we might experience backlash or backlashes that are non-negligible (in terms of impact on the coherence, legitimacy or effectiveness of the international legal order or a part thereof)[15] even if they do not amount to Sunsteinian fundamental rejection of that order. Second, and related, the Sunstein formula perhaps does not sufficiently distinguish 'intention' from 'effect' or impact. A state may attempt fundamental resistance to and rejection of an institution or system or regime,[16] and this might have domestic effects, but the conduct may have no particularly significant or enduring effect or impact on the system's viability (coherence, authority, legitimacy, effectiveness). We might call this intended or attempted backlash.[17] This would be a posture which, while regrettable in the eyes of some or even counter-productive for the state concerned, may have no *systemic* or system-threatening consequences unless certain conditions exist (eg, the conduct is mimicked at scale by a critical mass of states).[18] Third, and again related, deployment of the backlash notion comes with an imperative to be clear whether one is making a set of empirical findings (either about patterns of backlash, or the posited drivers of them), or rather making projections and claims about the possible impact of discerned behaviours. Inescapably, research on the global backlash involves a commitment to empiricism, which may be easier in relation to 'intended or attempted backlash' than in relation to 'the effects or impacts of backlash'. Precision may not be possible because although ideally when using backlash we specify things like "against whom, by whom and in what degree of concerted or deliberate way, why and to achieve what, through what ways?", the motivations and objectives (etc) of such phenomena may be unclear even to those supposedly driving them.

Fourth, perspective and context matter because the term backlash—heard in isolation—can equally connote either something negative and threatening, or a legitimate push-back, as discussed below. The question "what should we do to respond to backlash" depends obviously on whether one considers it a positive, negative or "mixed blessings" development. Elsewhere at least three

---

15   On legitimacy, effectiveness and coherence as core attributes of any regulatory endeavour, see Christine Parker et al (eds) *Regulating Law* (Oxford University Press, 2004).

16   See Caron and Shirlow (n 1).

17   Ford (n 3).

18   Meanwhile, one would want to consider the *timeframe* over which systemic effects are to be assessed if one is to attempt any empirical exercise. Backlash conduct may not register "in the system" at once, or depend on later mimicry or other factors beyond the particular state or set of actions or statements said to exhibit backlash.

180 AUSTRALIAN YEAR BOOK OF INTERNATIONAL LAW VOLUME 38

possible ways to interpret events such as the US withdrawal from the Council have been described:[19]

(i) *Crisis*: a new, systemic and system-threatening—and potentially irreversible—wave of actions and impacts involving a possible existential disengagement crisis for human rights or for the international legal order;

(ii) *Business-as-usual*: a somewhat unusually robust and notable but ultimately neither wholly novel nor systemically-significant development in a rules-based order that has seen waves like this before and continues to muddle through (and evolve, where backlash and counter-backlash is part of that evolution);

(iii) *Opportunity*: a significant but potentially ultimately healthy or necessary period of shocks, contestation, resistance and engagement, through which the global system (here, of human rights) emerges the better, in terms objectively of the coherence, legitimacy and effectiveness of the system.

The "opportunity" framing raises an important fifth point about the backlash concept, one evident enough if we adopt an everyday (not Sunstein) understanding of that term. A backlash arguably connotes a reaction that is not just a foreseeable, predictable or explicable reaction (for example, to overreach of authority or over-exertion of pressure) but one in which it is implicit that there is something understandable, legitimate or justified about the response.[20] Otherwise, we would speak in terms of an *attack on* something rather than a *backlash against* that thing. Indeed in decrying world leaders' attacks on international law and withdrawal from international regimes and commitments, James Crawford has observed that sometimes backlash can be an appropriate response, for example to institutional mandate overreach or to 'norm fatigue' from proliferating instruments and measures.[21]

Sixth, again related to "opportunity", the backlash device may tend to force us unnaturally into an "all or nothing" (and especially a wholly negative) approach.[22] This would be neither useful nor accurate, since both motives and effects may be mixed. Within the global human rights system, an impactful backlash that we might agree undermined or crippled one institution might be paralleled by "progress" in the human rights project elsewhere or in other

---

19   See Ford (n 3).

20   See especially Ford (n 3).

21   Crawford (n 9) 6. Later he observes that international law is (must be) flexible and that withdrawal from institutions or instrument regimes 'is not always to be condemned': Crawford (n 9) 22.

22   Ford (n 3).

AN AUSTRALIAN PERSPECTIVE

respects. Indeed, backlash behaviours by one state might stimulate pro-institution counter-balancing actions by other states.[23] Again, the "perspective" point above matters because what one diplomat committed to promoting human rights might decry as a regrettable backlash decision, another equally rights-committed diplomat might see as an important stance on a matter of high principle, or a necessary stimulus for reform.[24] Moreover, backlash events or effects may only seem alarming if one starts from the position that international law and institutions (here, the human rights system) were hitherto legitimate, flourishing and indeed "international".[25] It is true that international communal achievements in areas ranging from nuclear non-proliferation to the law of the sea are certainly not 'illusory or trivial'.[26] Yet it would be naïve—at least after Iraq 2003—to base ones dismay at backlash behaviour on the premise that the international legal system was just fine before Trump and others came along.

Finally, the Sunstein formula makes us conflate "resistance" to a regime with "rejection" thereof, or requires both to be present. Yet resistance is arguably a form of engagement (however reluctant and robust) and distinct from the dis-engagement that rejection connotes. If it mattered whether something met the Sunstein backlash threshold, one would have to show resistance *and* rejection. As noted in the first comment above, such a categorical definition might not be particularly useful: one can envisage many acts and statements by states that are not negligible and that seriously undermine international law and institutions yet do not necessarily involve rejection of those things. This brings us to whether we ought replace or at least supplement the backlash idea with some framing that offers more precision or insight, at least into the question here of recent Australian approaches.

2.2   *Typological Insights from Regulatory Theory?*

International law "regulates" state conduct in the sense that states accept it (or in some limited cases must accept it) as the authoritative normative framework governing their relations with other states and entities.[27] Of course, a

---

23   See also Ford (n 3). This discusses the idea of a 'pushback': Roth (n 8). Crawford notes that as some states retreat from their international obligations and relationships, 'we can expect others to step forward': Crawford (n 9) 22.

24   See, eg, Ford (n 3). The discussion explains US representatives' formal 'good faith' and 'reform' rationale for the June 2018 decision to exit the Council.

25   Anthea Roberts, *Is International Law International?* (Oxford University Press, 2018).

26   Crawford (n 9) 5.

27   Hilary Charlesworth, 'Regulatory Frameworks in International Law' in Christine Parker et al (eds) *Regulating Law* (Oxford University Press, 2004).

hallmark of the international legal system is its flat, horizontal nature, lacking as it does the singular ultimate sovereign characteristic of domestic legal orders.[28] In this sense, there is a limit to the utility to conceiving of states as regulated entities (regulatory subjects) of international law. Nevertheless, for present purposes—testing the backlash thesis while seeking an accurate characterisation of Australia's posture—it is useful to adopt from regulatory scholarship some ideas about the differing ways in which states might respond to adverse or unpalatable developments in international law. Oliver's typology of possible 'strategic responses to institutional processes' posited five possible postures: 'acquiescence', 'compromise', 'avoidance', 'defiance' and 'manipulation'.[29] This offers somewhat more promise, than the categorical Sunstein backlash concept, in describing some of the obvious nuances that exist in relation to state behaviour. The Oliver typology's deficiency is that a position such as "defiance" does not necessarily cater for the more extreme possibility of "rejection", "exit" or "disengagement". One can engage defiantly. Nor does it really capture the opposite extreme: fulsome committed engagement with and investment in the regulatory scheme, a position that goes well beyond Oliver's mere 'acquiescence'.[30]

A preferable typology is Valerie Braithwaite's categorisation of the differing motivational postures of entities subject to regulation:[31]

A. *'Game-playing'* (subject's engagement is contingent and highly strategic, perhaps similar to Oliver's 'manipulation');

B. *'Disengagement'* (subject is unresponsive to regulatory interventions or overtures);

C. *'Resistance'* (subject is engaged with the regulator or scheme, but defiantly so);

---

28   James Crawford, *Brownlie's Principles of Public International Law* (Oxford University Press, 9th ed, 2019), Part I.

29   Christine Oliver, 'Strategic Responses to Institutional Processes' (1991) 16(1) *Academy of Management Review* 145, 152.

30   Ibid.

31   VA Braithwaite, as developed in John Braithwaite, Toni Makkai and VA Braithwaite, *Regulating Aged Care: Ritualism and the New Pyramid* (Edward Elgar, 2007), 295. For one not unrelated and authoritative attempt to distinguish among four relationships between stated norms and observed conduct, see Koh's distinction between 'coincidence' as an explanation for state adherence to international law relative to 'conformity', 'compliance' and a posture of 'obedience' (internalised acceptance rather than conformity to law when convenient: Harold Hongju Koh, 'Why Do Nations Obey International Law?' (1997) 106(8) *Yale Law Journal* 2599, 2603).

AN AUSTRALIAN PERSPECTIVE

D. *'Capitulation'* (subject is responsive but without internalisation or commitment); and

E. *'Commitment'* (subject embraces and pursues the regulatory goal and process).

Assessing Australia's recent approach to the multilateral human rights system by reference to these postures has inherent limits because Braithwaite's typology was in the context of imperative non-optional regulatory schemes dealing with a confined issue. In international life a state may have more options in terms of what counts as 'compliance'.[32] Moreover, a state may be exhibiting more than one of these postures in different parts of the system. And it may be exhibiting one of these behaviours merely as a tactic for its actual motivation (in the sense that A: "game-playing" might easily be seen as accounting for at least B, C, and D).[33]

We turn now to consider Australia's actions and rhetoric around the UN-related human rights architecture, alive already to the possibility that the story of Australia's posture(s) may be more complex and variegated than the Sunstein backlash formula[34] allows for. At very least, even conduct to leave or fundamentally destabilise or delegitimise an international order or institution could be characterised (depending on its motivation, eg to shock a system into desired reform) as 'manipulation'[35] or 'game-playing'[36] and so as a form, if somewhat perversely, of engagement overall. Yet the point above about multiple postures raises the most difficult question going, ultimately, to the nature of international law as a single-system entity. At what point does it become untenable for a state to be selective about which parts of an international legal system it is rejecting and which parts it is engaging with? Can a state be said credibly to be 'committed' (Braithwaite posture E) to the rules-based international order overall yet in practice adopt a range of other postures (A–D, including backlash-style systemic rejection) in relation to particular parts of that order?

---

32 The extensive literature on the enduring 'compliance question' in international law discussed in Koh (n 29) 2600 is beyond the scope of this exercise.

33 This *Article's* ambition does not extend to traversing the ostensibly related issue of how International Relations scholarship has engaged with theories of how states may attempt to "game" international institutions and regimes.

34 See Caron and Shirlow (n 1).

35 Oliver (n 29) 152.

36 Braithwaite (n 31) 295.

3 Australia's Engagement in the International Human Rights System

A full history of Australian engagement with the UN human rights system lies beyond this *Article's* scope,[37] as does the place of human rights in Australian regional diplomacy,[38] and shifts towards using bilateral over multilateral platforms of human rights dialogue.[39] It is sufficient to note that since about 2000, Australia has adopted a more robust and critical approach to the UN human rights system. This coincided with, or related to, greater international scrutiny of Australia's human rights performance (especially in relation to indigenous peoples and, increasingly over time, immigration detention and offshore processing of irregular migrants).[40] A key early marker was a joint ministerial statement of 29 August 2000 on the need to reform UN human rights treaty bodies.[41] The government's treaty body campaign was not necessarily a Sunstein-style backlash to reject those mechanisms, but a sustained

---

37   See, eg, Jon Piccini, *Human Rights in Twentieth-Century Australia* (Cambridge University Press, 2019); Katharine Gelber, 'The Universal Declaration of Human Rights at 70: Protection of Human Rights in Australia' (2019) 73(4) *Australian Journal of International Affairs* 313; Phil Lynch, 'Australia at the Human Rights Council' (2018) 43(1) *Alternative Law Journal* 3; Philip Lynch, 'Australia, Human Rights and Foreign Policy' (2009) 34(4) *Alternative Law Journal* 218; Michael Kirby, 'Herbert Vere Evatt, the United Nations and the Universal Declaration of Human Rights After 60 Years' (2009) 34(2) *University of Western Australia Law Review* 238; Annemarie Devereux, *Australia and the Birth of the International Bill of Human Rights: 1946–1966* (Federation Press, 2005); Devika Hovell, 'The Sovereignty Stratagem: Australia's Response to UN Human Rights Treaty Bodies' (2003) 28(6) *Alternative Law Journal* 297; Elizabeth Evatt, 'How Australia "Supports" the United Nations Human Rights Treaty System' (2001) 12(1) *Public Law Review* 3; Peter Bailey, *Human Rights: Australia in an International Context* (Butterworths, 1990).

38   For one overview (1945–2011), see Ben Saul 'Throwing Stones at Streetlights or Cuckolding Dictators? Australian Foreign Policy and Human Rights in the Developing World' (2011) 100(415) *The Round Table: Australia and the Developing World* 423. See, eg, Andrew Byrnes, 'The Asian Development Bank and the Role of Human Rights in the Pursuit of Just and Sustainable Development in the Asia-Pacific Region: An Advocacy Role for Australia?' (2011) 18(18) *Australian International Law Journal* 1.

39   This is especially in relation to China since the 2000s: Caroline Fleay, 'Engaging in Human Rights Diplomacy: The Australia-China Bilateral Dialogue Approach' (2008) 12(2) *The International Journal of Human Rights* 233.

40   For a comprehensive analysis of the treaty reform process 2000–03 and its domestic political context, see Spencer Zifcak, 'The New Anti-Internationalism: Australia and the United Nations Human Rights Treaty System' (Discussion Paper, No 54, Australia Institute, 2003).

41   Minister for Foreign Affairs, Attorney-General, Minister for Immigration and Multicultural Affairs, 'Improving the Effectiveness of UN Committees' (Joint Media Release FA97, 29 August 2000) <https://webarchive.nla.gov.au/awa/20030815234818/http://www.dfat .gov.au/media/releases/foreign/2000/fa097_2000.html>.

AN AUSTRALIAN PERSPECTIVE

effort to reform their effectiveness (as perceived by Australia). The motivations were almost certainly a mix of commitment to more effective, credible global human rights protection (on one hand), and concern about the scope for treaty bodies' criticism of Australia's domestic human rights performance (on the other hand). Such motivational factors are more interesting than, but not really captured by, a "backlash as rejection" framing.

Soon after 2000 something of a pattern emerged. Special Rapporteurs and other mechanisms would submit adverse reports especially (and increasingly) in relation to immigration policies, and the Australian government would variously disregard, dismiss, deny, deflect, disagree with or discredit these reports. For example, the UN Special Rapporteur in relation to Racial Discrimination at first struggled to arrange the visit that led to one critical 2002 report.[42] The government's response was a joint ministerial press release dismissing the report as having 'no credibility'.[43] Scholars around this time described the government's posture as 'dismissive or hostile',[44] or as 'denial' exhibiting 'dismissive disregard' for UN mechanisms' reports.[45]

This 2000–07 period pattern was replicated after 2013. In 2014 the Minister for Immigration's response to reported opinions from a UN official at a regional conference that Australia's boat 'turn-back' policy was inconsistent with Australia's international refugee law obligations was to 'completely disagree' with that opinion.[46] In 2015 the response of Prime Minister Tony Abbott to a Special Rapporteur report[47] asserting that Australia's immigration detention policies amounted to systematic violations of the *Convention against Torture*

---

42 Maurice Glèlè-Ahanhanzo, *Racism, Racial Discrimination, Xenophobia and All Forms of Discrimination*, UN Doc E/CN.4//2002/24/Add.1 (26 February 2002).

43 Minister for Foreign Affairs and Minister for Immigration and Multicultural Affairs, 'UN Report Has No Credibility' (Joint Media Release, 22 March 2002) <https://webarchive.nla.gov.au/awa/20030822194607/http://www.foreignminister.gov.au/releases/2002/fa033l_02.html>.

44 Zifcak (n 40) 55.

45 David Kinley and Penny Martin 'International Human Rights Law at Home: Addressing the Politics of Denial' (2002) 26(2) *Melbourne University Law Review* 466, 471.

46 Sarah Whyte, 'Scott Morrison Dismisses UN Criticism of Boat Turn-Backs', *Sydney Morning Herald* (online, 23 April 2014) <https://www.smh.com.au/politics/federal/scott-morrison-dismisses-un-criticism-of-boat-turnbacks-20140423-zqy3c.html>; Michael Bachelard and Sarah Whyte, 'UN Representatives Criticise Abbott Government's Boat Tow-Back Policy', *Sydney Morning Herald* (online, 23 April 2014) <https://www.smh.com.au/politics/federal/un-representatives-criticise-abbott-governments-boat-towback-policy-20140423-zqxz1.html>.

47 Human Rights Council, *Report of the Special Rapporteur on Torture and Other Cruel, Inhuman or Degrading Treatment or Punishment*, 28th Session, A/HRC/28/68/Add.1 (6 March 2015).

('CAT') was to state publicly that Australians were 'sick of being lectured to' by the UN.[48] The critical reports, statements or calls from UN agencies or treaty system entities, and corresponding dismissive governmental responses, continued through the ensuing years (2015–18)[49] as Australia prepared to run for and then take up an elected seat at the Council.[50]

Domestic critics of the 2015–17 Council campaign pointed to Australia's domestic human rights record and trajectory in the years immediately before, one arguing that the bid was 'conceived in a parallel universe' given the disjuncture between anti-human rights trends domestically and pro-human rights diplomacy internationally.[51] Some organisations questioned in 2015 whether Australia was 'ready for a leadership role' in the Council, partly because of its domestic record and partly because of its record as an ordinary member in the Council, where Australia was said to too often have been 'passive' and 'at times acted in an inconsistent and unprincipled manner'.[52] Australia's domestic

---

48   Ben Doherty and Daniel Hurst, 'UN Accuses Australia of Systematically Violating Torture Convention', *The Guardian* (online, 10 March 2015) <https://www.theguardian .com/australia-news/2015/mar/09/un-reports-australias-immigration-detention -breaches-torture-convention>.

49   In 2017, see, eg, UN High Commissioner for Refugees, 'UNHCR Chief Filippo Grandi Calls on Australia to End Harmful Practice of Offshore Processing' *UNHCR* (Web Page, 24 July 2017) <https://www.unhcr.org/en-au/news/press/2017/7/597217484/unhcr-chief -filippo-grandi-calls-australia-end-harmful-practice-offshore.html>; in 2018, see, eg, Stefan Armbruster, 'Australia Again Deflects UN Criticism Over Off-Shore Detention Policy', *SBS News* (online, 19 September 2018) <www.sbs.com.au/news/australia-again -deflects-un-criticism-over-off-shore-detention-policy>. Analysis of the extensive scholarly and other criticism of Australia's immigration (offshore detention) policy is beyond this *Article's* scope.

50   Minister for Foreign Affairs, 'United Nations Security Council & Human Rights Council' (Media Release, 29 September 2015) <https://www.foreignminister.gov.au/ minister/julie-bishop/media-release/united-nations-security-council-human-rights -council>; Ben Doherty, 'Australia Up for Human Rights Council Seat Despite UN Official's Criticism of Asylum Secrecy', *The Guardian* (online, 26 September 2015) <https://www.theguardian.com/law/2015/sep/26/australia-up-for-human-rights-council -seat-despite-senior-un-officials-criticism>.

51   Richard Ackland, 'Australia's Bid for the UN Human Rights Council Was Conceived in a Parallel Universe', *The Guardian* (online, 30 October 2015) <https://www .theguardian.com/commentisfree/2015/oct/30/australias-bid-for-the-un-human -rights-council-was-conceived-in-a-parallel-universe>.

52   'Australia at the Human Rights Council: Ready for a Leadership Role?' *Human Rights Watch* (Web Page, 22 September 2015) <https://www.hrw.org/report/2015/09/22/ australia-human-rights-council/ready-leadership-role>. Australia was eventually elected unopposed after Spain and then France withdrew their bids: Ben Doherty, 'Australia to be Elected to Powerful UN Human Rights Council', *The Guardian* (online, 14 October 2017) <https://www.theguardian.com/world/2017/oct/14/australia-to-be

record on human rights promotion and protection has recently worsened. This is especially so in relation to new legislative restrictions on media freedom, whistleblowing and freedom of expression,[53] and in relation to sustained public criticism by the government in 2014–15 of Professor Gillian Triggs, Australian Human Rights Commission head, that arguably undermined that institution's independence. On the international stage, it is difficult to deny that Australia's advocacy has been somewhat selective. That is, its relationship with or reliance for cooperation on source countries of irregular migrants or asylum seekers (or host countries for those detained by Australia) has resulted in a noticeable reluctance by Australia to criticise those partner countries' human rights records.[54]

Nevertheless, passivity or inconsistency in the Council and selective non-criticism of human rights issues abroad or backsliding on human rights at home are not necessarily relevant to this *Article's* question. That is, whether we can discern, in the Australian context and possibly as part of a wider trend in Western democracies, a backlash against the norms, institutions and mechanisms of the international human rights system. For the reasons that follow, the answer is no if the Sunstein system-rejection definition of backlash is applied.[55] If we ditch that definition and just ask whether the Australian government has pushed back strongly against the international system, the answer is yes, but that does not necessarily lead to a "finding" of post-2015 populist-era backlash. This is because there is nothing particularly new about Australia's strong reactions to criticism from UN-system mechanisms, and because it is impossible to diagnose a general uniform system-rejecting backlash against the international human rights system in a period when Australia was so obviously engaging with that system, in particular via the Council. A far more useful exercise than to wrestle with a backlash diagnosis is to attempt

---

-elected-to-powerful-un-human-rights-council>; 'Australia Wins Seat on UN Human Rights Council Despite Criticism', *SBS News* (online, 17 October 2017) <https://www.sbs.com.au/news/australia-wins-seat-on-un-human-rights-council-despite-criticism>.

53 Notably in relation to communications relating to border protection or the intelligence services, see, eg, Australian Law Reform Commission, *Traditional Rights and Freedoms—Encroachments by Commonwealth Laws* (Report No 129, 2 March 2016); George Williams, 'The Legal Assault on Australian Democracy' (2016) 16(2) *Queensland University of Technology Law Review* 19. Many of the restrictive provisions widely criticised as unnecessarily constraining human rights in the context of reporting and whistleblowing have been more recent.

54 See, eg, Asher Hirsch, 'The Borders beyond the Border: Australia's Extraterritorial Migration Controls' (2017) 36 *Refugee Studies Quarterly* 48.

55 Caron and Shirlow (n 1).

(for example by reference the Braithwaite's typology)[56] to properly characterise the various contours and features of Australia's practice.

What are some reasons Australia 2015–20 does not necessarily illustrate the backlash phenomenon on the Sunstein definition? Australia's response has not amounted to rejection of the UN treaty system or its emanations, and there is some pattern of engagement. For example, in 2015–16 around Special Rapporteur assertions of violations of the CAT, Australia engaged formally with the UN mechanism. The Rapporteur's reports acknowledge those government responses, even while critical of the fulsomeness and swiftness of Australia's responses.[57] Australia the ratified the Optional Protocol to the Convention against Torture in 2017, as undertaken in its Council campaign.[58] This response is hardly anti-system or system-undermining backlash behaviour. Unless we require a new framing of backlash to encompass supposedly disingenuous ratification and reporting efforts, on its face such moves cannot be described as rejection or de-legitimisation of the UN treaty system. It may be "gameplaying" (eg, election campaigning) in the Braithwaite sense, but is certainly not backlash (as rejection or exit or de-legitimisation) in the Sunstein sense. At the time Banham labelled Australia's response to the 2015 torture 'finding' as 'indignation, not engagement'.[59] Yet a more accurate description might be "indignant engagement" even the engagement involves "resistance" and is not

---

56   Oliver (n 29).

57   Human Rights Council, *Report of the Special Rapporteur on Torture and Other Cruel, Inhuman or Degrading Treatment or Punishment*, UN Doc A/HRC/31/57/Add.1 (24 February 2016), 8; see too above n 44. The government has responded within domestic mechanisms too: Australian Government, Parliament of Australia, *Australian Government Response to the Report of the Select Committee on the Recent Allegations Relating to Conditions and Circumstances at the Regional Processing Centre in Nauru: Taking Responsibility: Conditions and Circumstances at Australia's Regional Processing Centre in Nauru* (Government Response, 4 August 2016). This was a response to the report Senate Select Committee on the Recent Allegations Relating to Conditions and Circumstances at the Regional processing Centre in Nauru: Parliament of Australia, *Taking Responsibility: Conditions and Circumstances at Australia's Regional Processing Centre in Nauru* (Report, 31 August 2015) <https://www.aph.gov.au/Parliamentary_Business/Committees/Senate/Regional_processing_Nauru/Regional_processing_Nauru/Final_Report >.

58   Minister for Foreign Affairs, 'Ratification of OPCAT Caps Year of Significant Human Rights Achievements for Turnbull Government' (Media Release, 15 December 2017) <https://www.foreignminister.gov.au/minister/julie-bishop/media-release/ratification-opcat-caps-year-significant-human-rights-achievements-turnbull-government >.

59   Cynthia Banham, 'Indignation, Not Engagement: Australia's Response to International Criticism of Asylum Seeker Detention', *ANU Centre for International Governance and Justice* (Web Page, 18 March 2015) <http://regnet.anu.edu.au/news-events/news/619/regarding-rights-blog-australia%E2%80%99s–response-international-criticism-asylum>.

AN AUSTRALIAN PERSPECTIVE 189

fulsome "commitment" (in a Braithwaite sense) to this particular mechanism or issue.

Completely disagreeing with an opinion or recommendation, or publicly being "sick of" such interventions, is not the same as denying the authority or legitimacy of the institution that made those interventions. It may be a long way from an ideal posture of 'commitment' and mature fulsome responsiveness but is not necessarily backlash of the sort that the Sunstein definition proposes. Some scope may exist for suggesting that repeated discrediting, dismissal or disregard of institutional overtures is conduct that (in the final words of the Sunstein formula) seeks to deprive the mechanism of legal effect.[60] Yet it would be very difficult to characterise merely disagreeing with a Rapporteur's opinion, which is not a legal ruling, in that way. It is one thing to describe Australia's responses, especially in 2000–07 and after 2013, as 'severely critical, legally indefensible and highly nationalistic'.[61] It is more difficult, in light of the engagement patterns (such as OPCAT ratification and the Council election) and lack of systematic moves to disable or disengage from the institutions themselves, to agree with Zifcak's 2003 assertion that the government's positions amounted to 'disengagement from international human rights law'.[62] Meanwhile misconceptions in some criticism of Australia's response to UN mechanisms may provide some context for what critics see as the defensiveness of Australian officials and politicians, perhaps feeding in some way into backlash-style resistance behaviours.[63]

In February 2015 UN Special Rapporteur on Human Rights Defenders Michel Forst reportedly wrote to the Australian mission to the UN in Geneva expressing grave concern about its senior members' verbal statements attacking Gillian Triggs and urging the government to put an end to these.[64] Subsequent to this,

---

60   See above n 1.

61   Zifcak (n 40) 57 (writing in 2003, but about a pattern that, as noted, continued thereafter).

62   Ibid 54.

63   For example, Juss writes of Australia ignoring "decisions" of UN treaty bodies, attributing these opinions, findings or recommendations with an inaccurate quasi-judicial nature: Satvinder S Juss, 'Detention and Delusion in Australia's Kafkaesque Refugee Law' (2017) 36(1) *Refugee Survey Quarterly* 146. Crawford notes that backlash against international institutions can be expected where officials over-reach their mandate with respect to member governments: Crawford (n 9) 6. In the May 2019 ANU "Backlash Project" workshop, a number of Australian government international lawyers, not speaking officially, opined that perceived overreach (exceeding an institution's mandate) was, in their experience, undeniably a source of push-back from within the government in areas of human rights and migration (author notes).

64   Michael Gordon, 'Revealed: how the UN told Abbott government to back off on Gillian Triggs' *Sydney Morning Herald*, 9 June 2015. The letter also reportedly questioned whether

in June 2015, then Immigration Minister Peter Dutton called Triggs 'a complete disgrace' and questioned her continuation in the role.[65] Yet while regrettable conduct that undermines a domestic institution, this was not necessarily conduct signaling a backlash-style rejection of the UN system that Forst represents. Perhaps the highest it could be put is that by rejecting particular reports of or acting inconsistently with overtures from special rapporteurs, Australia constructively rejected a part of the UN human rights system. In principle, enough rejection or de-legitimisation of individual reports (etc) of institutions might become tantamount to rejection of the institutions themselves. For Braithwaite, this might be "resistance" to the point of "disengagement". This scenario—of rejection or disregard of particular reports without necessarily proactively attacking or undermining the mechanism itself—raises an issue discussed further below. How we should approach backlash against particular *parts* of a system in the context of fulsome engagement with the system *overall*? What might be the effect of a government's behaviour on erosion, over time, of its audiences' respect for the standing of UN mechanisms that it criticises, dismisses, or ignores?

Still, in the Forst (Triggs) example the "constructive rejection" argument is not a straightforward one. While disregarding Forst's request, no minister attacked Forst or his office as such, or questioned its mandate or legitimacy. Indeed Australia *was* engaging with the mechanism in Geneva in recognisable institution-affirming ways within that system, by a formal written reply on 24 April 2015 to Forst's letter.[66] This response stated that the government respected the Commission's independence, the fact that it will sometimes be critical of the government (and that the government will not always agree with its recommendations), and welcoming a 'vigorous and diverse debate' on human rights in Australia.[67] No doubt much can be said about whether domestic practice resonates with official responses or rhetoric in international forums, but that is true and constant across the world in the human rights sphere. For present purposes, the response to Forst as a UN-system entity hardly smacks of backlash and may not even amount to "resistance" (in Braithwaite terms) to this "regulatory" overture by a Special Rapporteur.

Noting again the conundrum of "words versus deeds", a backlash diagnosis is ultimately made difficult because of Australia's strong and frequent stated

---

then-recent budget cuts to the Commission were related to the Triggs decisions that appeared to have generated the government's reaction, such as to institute a Commission inquiry into children in immigration detention.

65   Ibid.

66   Ibid.

67   Ibid.

commitments to a strong multilateral human rights system. This has not been a case of Australia delegitimising or withdrawing from that system or seeking to deprive it of legal force. The 2017 Foreign Policy White Paper, unless one dismisses it as pre-dating populist anti-globalism in the West and Australia, makes that commitment very explicit: 'We continue to support the independent mandate of the Office of the High Commissioner for Human Rights. We promote efforts to strengthen the Human Rights Council and the wider human rights system.'[68]

A full review of Australia's engagement at the Council since 2017 is beyond this article's scope. Yet Australia's reaction to the June 2018 US withdrawal from the Council hardly smacks of a state in the throes of backlash against the wider human rights system. Foreign Minister Julie Bishop expressed disappointment with the US withdrawal decision.[69] While stating that Canberra shared many of Washington's concerns, Bishop stated that Australia's strong preference was for the US to remain, and counselled Trump officials against withdrawal.[70] Bishop re-stated Australia's commitment to 'work constructively on human rights issues with other countries' and 'progress effective and meaningful reform' to the Council to enable it 'more effectively [to] carry out its role'.[71] In 2018, Australia and allies abstained from a rare China-sponsored Council resolution on *Mutually Beneficial Cooperation in the Field of Human*

---

68   Australian Government, Parliament of Australia, *2017 Foreign Policy White Paper* (White Paper, November 2017) 89. This provides that as a Council member 2018–20, Australia will:
- 'advance the rights of women and girls,
- promote good governance, democratic institutions and freedoms of expression, association, religion and belief,
- promote the rights of people with disabilities,
- advance human rights for indigenous peoples around the globe,
- promote national human rights institutions and capacity building, and
- advocate the global abolition of the death penalty'.

69   Minister for Foreign Affairs, 'The United States withdraws from the UN Human Rights Council' (Media Release, 20 June 2018) <https://www.foreignminister.gov.au/minister/julie-bishop/media-release/united-states-resigns-un-human-rights-council>. See Stephen Dziedzec, 'The US withdrawal from the UN Human Rights Council leaves ally Australia in an awkward, lonely position' *ABC News* (online, 20 June 2018) <https://www.abc.net.au/news/2018–06–20/analysis-what-does-us-united-nations-move-mean-for-australia/9889216>; James Elton-Pym, '"Cesspool of Bias": US withdraws from UN Human Rights Council', *SBS News* (online, 20 June 2018) <https://www.sbs.com.au/news/cesspool-of-bias-us-withdraws-from-un-human-rights-council>.

70   Minister for Foreign Affairs (n 69). See eg, Dziedzec (n 69), Elton-Pym (n 69).

71   Minister for Foreign Affairs (n 69).

Rights.[72] Yet abstentions of this sort, or indeed votes against resolutions, hardly signify backlash. They are not even necessarily "resistance" in the Braithwaite model or "defiance" in the Oliver typology since they are not reactions to *the system* but routine acts of contestation within the system. Such robust debate and conduct should be entirely unsurprising in any inter-state forum dealing with such a highly politicised topic.

Maguire and others recently argued that Australia's 2018–20 Council membership has been categorised by "performativity" rather than performance, that is, a tokenistic approach to compliance and implementation rather than a substantive one.[73] That argument has some echoes of the extensive work by Charlesworth and others on formalistic, ceremonial and reiterative but largely superficial state compliance, or 'regulatory ritualism', in relation to the Council's Universal Periodic Review process.[74] Of course, while engaging and nominally complying with reporting and review procedures in multilateral forums, a state may in fact be incapable of, indifferent to, or highly resistant to, promoting substantive human rights.[75] For our purposes here, such critiques are of less relevance. State engagement in multilateral forums may be poor, perfunctory or "performative" yet not amount to a backlash rejection or de-legitimisation. Whatever the quality of Australia's participation in the Council there is no question that its bid for election and subsequent engagement there is at odds with any sense of a Sunstein backlash (either in intent or effect) against the global human rights architecture with the connotations of rejection

---

72   Human Rights Council, *Resolution Adopted by the Human Rights Council on 23 March 2018 Promoting Mutually Beneficial Cooperation in the Field of Human Rights*, HRC Res 37/23, UN Doc A/HRC/RES/37/23 (6 April 2018, adopted 23 March 2018). The Resolution passed 28:1 (US) with seven abstainers including Australia. See discussion of this Resolution in Annemarie Devereux, 'Amidst Simmering Tensions: Improving the Effectiveness and Coherence of the International Human Rights System's Response to Mass Human Rights Violations' (2020) 38 *Australian Year Book of International Law* 199.

73   Amy Maguire, Fiona McGaughey and Georgia Monaghan, 'Performance or Performativity? Australia's Membership of the United Nations Human Rights Council' (2019) 25(2) *Australian Journal of Human Rights* 317.

74   Hilary Charlesworth and Emma Larking, 'Introduction: The Regulatory Power of the Universal Periodic Review' in Hilary Charlesworth and Emma Larking (eds), *Human Rights and the Universal Periodic Review: Rights and Ritualism* (Cambridge University Press, 2014) ('Regulatory Power'). See also Benjamin Authers, Hilary Charlesworth, Marie-Bénédicte Dembour and Emma Larking 'Introduction: The Rituals of Human Rights' (2018) 9(1) Humanity 63.

75   Charlesworth and Larking, 'Regulatory Power' (n 74) 10–12, 16, 18. See generally Jolyon Ford and Claire Methven O'Brien, 'Empty Rituals or Workable Models? Towards and Business and Human Rights Treaty' (2017) 40(3) *UNSW Law Journal* 1223, 1228–32, discussing scholarship on the UN system as largely 'ceremonial' and performative.

AN AUSTRALIAN PERSPECTIVE

and de-legitimisation. It could be a very passive or highly obstructive member. It could pursue a radical reform agenda. Moreover, any such approach could be driven by a motivation to respond or nurture "populism" at home. Yet we would perhaps still not be able to call this an example of anti-globalism back-lash (in the Sunstein sense) so long as Australia was engaged and not seeking to exit from, dismantle, or disable ("deprive of legal effect") the Council.[76] A Braithwaite-style set of frames is far more useful, and accurate, in seeking to understand what Australia may have been seeking to do and why.

Australia's approach in the last five years to the UN human rights archi-tecture (including the treaty system) is not new. Back in 2003 an Australia Institute paper on this topic was entitled 'The New Anti-Internationalism'.[77] Inherent in the concept of a backlash that this is a notable event departing from the trend hitherto. But here we have a pattern of continuity. There is little that is new since 2000 in the tone of Australia's response to UN reports and rapporteurs on the particular topic of immigration detention. In any event, it is not obvious that Australia's reaction or response to UN mechanisms can be called 'anti-internationalism' (2003) or 'anti-globalism' (2019). It has been limited to processes emanating from one part of the human rights order, which is itself only one part of the overall international rules-based order. Also, the sometimes "indignant" response even on the immigration issues has involved at least as much engagement (disagreement or pushback) as non-engagement (ignoring recommendations and requests). It has not involved dis-engagement in the sense of withdrawal from the process or institution. Nor has Australia directly attacked particular mechanisms in an effort to dismantle them, choosing instead a more broadly-framed UN human rights and Council reform agenda.

We can characterise Australia's posture as pushing back strongly against reports (etc) from parts of the UN human rights system, and to some extent undermining, by disregard or dismissal, the authority of those entities.[78] The point here is that this probably does not meet the threshold, if it matters, of

---

76 In any event, supposed unilateral withdrawal from the 'core' of international human rights obligations might prove very difficult: see above Crawford n 9. It might also be rather unlikely in political terms that a state would go this far precisely because of the legitimacy costs from denouncing the entire human rights system when that system can accommodate (as "compliance") a level of engagement and implementation that is not particularly demanding or, as above, tolerates high levels of 'ritualistic' engagement.

77 Zifcak (n 40).

78 As below, I refrain from calling that backlash in the general (non-Sunstein) way because, as below, it is a long-standing pattern, not a distinct phenomenon of the post-2015/16 'populist' era in Western liberal democracies.

Sunstein's anti-system or exit-system backlash formula. No such backlash has occurred; or it has been very piecemeal and in parallel with engagement; or the engagement *was* the manifestation of the backlash sentiment: 'we must reform these institutions whose rapporteurs (etc) trouble and critique us, and it will be popular at home to do so'. It is difficult to describe the latter two possibilities as a notable backlash against the rules-based international human rights order *as a system*, even if Australia has not acted as the most faultless exemplar proponent of international citizenry. There does not appear to be any empirical basis for characterising Australia's rhetorical positions and actions in recent years as "fundamental resistance to and rejection of"[79] the multilateral human rights system and its normative underpinnings, much less of the rules-based international order more generally. At most, on the basis that Australia has taken some (not particularly "aggressive") "steps to resist the system",[80] one might describe a pattern of *resistance* to institutional aspects of the human rights system without necessarily a *rejection* of those aspects or of that system.

Australia's posture towards the vast majority of the international human rights institutional and instrumentation architecture is one of "commitment". Its criticism of the treaty bodies or other mechanisms can be described as "resistance" but could equally be portrayed as an example of highly engaged commitment in the sense that it involves constructive criticism intended to reform an international arena so that is more effective, legitimate and coherent. In any event, deep indignation and discontent may manifest as a perceived backlash but do not necessarily represent disengagement and exit (unless, perhaps, ignored or patronised). They may be inevitable and endemic features of a values-based normative system that tests the parameters of what sovereignty states concede to joint mechanisms. Australia's particular acute reaction to some mechanisms is not well captured by a backlash motif, especially not a Sunstein one. It has varied between resistance and reaction (including calls for reform) and non-engagement (simply ignoring unwanted inputs). While it has resulted in rejection of particular inputs or mandate interpretations, there is little evidence of "disengagement" in the sense of a systematic attempt to de-legitimise and de-couple from the international human rights system. Seeking an elected Council seat is not the behaviour of a state surfing a backlash wave away from international engagement, even if it might represent backlash-type political forces seeking greater influence on how international mechanisms do their work.

---

79   Sunstein (n 1).

80   Ibid.

AN AUSTRALIAN PERSPECTIVE   195

In his 2019 Lowy speech while signalling a very contingent commitment to the international institutional order, the Prime Minister nevertheless clearly stated Australia's commitment in net terms to a 'positive and practical globalism' and an intention to play a more active role in global standard-setting and governance.[81] Even if it is driven by discontent with the status quo in global governance, this is manifestly a posture overall of engagement. It is difficult to reconcile it with a characterisation of backlash as rejection of a system and efforts to deprive it of legal force. Yet perhaps the key term in the above is *"overall"* or *"in net terms"*. We need to accept that a domestically-driven backlash can (a) be partial, selective and nuanced in the sense of confined to some particular international regimes or indeed parts thereof (rather than against the rules-based international order overall), and (b) can be something short of fulsome rejection of a system (abandoning an all-or-nothing conception of backlash). If so, then a basis arguably does exist to portray some Australian approaches to the international human rights system as exhibiting characteristics of backlash. However, at least two problems arise.

First, the backlash enquiry as framed in the workshops relating to this Special Issue posits that something has changed about Western support for international law and institutions in the post-2015 (Trump, Brexit, etc) world.[82] Yet in this article's context (human rights), and as noted above, very little indeed is new about Australia's often indignant reaction to criticism from UN platforms and mechanisms on issues at the nexus of "human rights" and "migration". Putting the 'anti-globalism' of the 2019 Lowy speech in the context of some recent Australian, US and other behaviours ought not, of itself, lead necessarily to the conclusion that a distinctive backlash phenomenon has been underway. This is mostly because Australia has long attempted both (i) a strong and apparently genuine commitment (in both state practice and *opinio iuris* terms) to human rights governance at the international level, alongside (ii) selective and shifting robust reformism, resistance or non-engagement (cf. disengagement) on confined subjects of particular sensitivity (viz, treatment of irregular migrants).[83] Second, even if one can, as above, characterise recent Australian approaches as showing some attributes of backlash, that label does

---

81   See Morrison (n 5).
82   Danchin et al (n 1). It may be that the Sunstein concept of system-threatening backlash (see above n 1), developed as it was for a US federal constitutional context, is simply not apposite to analysing states' complex relationships with international law and international institutions.
83   In this regard, Ford (n 3) sought to put the US Council withdrawal in June 2018 in the context of fairly long-standing ambivalence by Washington towards engaging with or joining the Council and its predecessor.

not seem to be a particularly useful one in analytical, empirical or typological terms. At very least, a typology of postures such as Braithwaite's would appear to offer more in terms of advancing our understanding of how best to characterise state conduct at different points in time on different issues. Backlash might then better describe the political forces at work, but leave us with a need for framings that enable us to delineate in a more nuanced way how that phenomenon is manifesting or not in terms of state behaviour. The institutional impacts of those behaviours is then another distinct and mostly empirical question.

4 Conclusion

There is a third issue with making the above "finding" of partial, highly selective or subject-specific but somewhat endemic Australian backlash against parts of the international legal order on human rights. It relates to deploying, as I have above, terms such as engagement "*overall*" or "*in net terms*", or (on the other hand) resistance, non-engagement or disengagement (as signs of some backlash) that is "*confined to*" certain institutions or regimes or issues. One can reach a finding, as offered here, that any Australian backlash against *some aspects of* the international human rights system is hardly system-threatening and does not amount to "fundamental ... rejection of"[84] that system. Yet that is not necessarily the end of the question. Instead, a more profound question arises, perhaps even going to the very nature of international law. This is about how viable it is, in terms of damage to the idea of a universal community under the rule of law at the international level, to maintain that one is committed overall to a rules-based international order, and yet to seek to strongly resist, ignore or discredit (to the point of rejection) select "confined" aspects or parts of that order. Some might argue that this opt-in, opt-out approach is inherent to international law's horizontal nature and that flexibility is critical to international law's enduring success. One might argue that the Council is merely one institution for the global promotion of human rights, and embrace of or exit from it cannot be given wider systemic significance.

Yet Crawford has warned—in the context of post-2015 negative populist discourse in the West about international law and institutions—that the rules-based international order might be eroded over time, layer by layer.[85] Thus backlash forces and phenomena may not necessarily result in a distinct "either

---

84   Sunstein (n 1).
85   Crawford (n 9).

AN AUSTRALIAN PERSPECTIVE

survive or die" systemic shock, but may cumulatively (for instance, through various "confined" reactions or rejections) result in the weakening of the fabric of the legal order. Viewed this way, the more important question may not be "is any backlash against the international order exhibited by Australia (a) merely discontent or, given the US position in particular, does it (b) represent more permanent systemic threat to the order?". There is arguably no real empirical basis, at least yet, for beginning to arrive at finding (b). Instead, the more important question may be "how long can an international legal system flourish, or perhaps survive, if a state (or, enough important states) are so obviously highly selective about which parts of the system they commit to or dismiss?" The opt-in/out spirit of much international law is its hallmark and strength, but it is more difficult to conceive of selective fidelity to the rule of law as that system's organising principle.

Crawford's argument is that the international legal system is a sort of "layer cake" or a "sedimentary formation" some of which, with scale over time and if not eroded, may turn to rock.[86] Crawford distinguishes the core 'necessary' law of nations from the 'voluntary' 'top layers',[87] non-compliance (and presumably backlash) against which constitutes no threat to the overall system and society that orders itself thereon. Yet Crawford's distinction perhaps assumes very particular types of threat that either affect only top layers, or that may be aimed at the rocky core but which have no prospect (he argues) of shaking or splitting this solid base. The stratification metaphor does not account for the possibility that due to leading states undermining of or attacks on particular parts of the system, doubts grow over the utility or importance or authority of the whole. Multiple and repeated statements and actions as part of a backlash that appear only to erode the top layer (as Crawford diagnoses) might come to affect the idea that ultimately gives the edifice normative significance at all. Backlash behaviours might de-legitimise the common substance ('sand') of which the overall edifice is made (whether soft or hard, necessary or voluntary, core or top-layer). "But one cannot ignore or exit this regime, this is core rock!!?" is then met with the riposte "state rejection of the top layer shows that this is *all* made of sand". Neither Crawford's somewhat convenient 'layers' metaphor nor the oft-repeated Henkin 'most states mostly comply' maxim[88] really answer

---

86   Crawford (n 9) 2, 7, 21: 'a core of institutions and associated rules ... at its base ... a solid set of principles, norms and institutions: the fundamentals of the post-War global legal structure'.

87   Crawford (n 9) 2, 7.

88   That is, that almost all states observe almost all international law principles and obligations almost all of the time: Louis Henkin, *How Nations Behave* (Columbia University Press, 2nd ed, 1979) 47.

the question here. This is whether an international legal system can flourish or survive where states' backlash-style rhetoric and actions suggest that definitions of untouchable "rock" or "core" are in fact written in sand, often by the state concerned.

Might a state exhibit backlash ("disengagement") behaviour in some respects—conduct that explicitly casts doubt on the idea of a consensus-based but not entirely voluntaristic international legal order—yet in other areas declare its deep commitment to the international rule of law? At issue is the idea of the rule of law, not compliance or engagement with particular elements of the overall system. Perhaps the proof is in the pudding (here, the layer cake). If states accept this selectivity, and presumably if there is some implicit consensus on what the "core", rock-solid fundamentals are, then perhaps the system can survive it (indeed, that flexibility may be vital to the system's survival and traction or compliance-pull with states).[89] The possibility that we cannot rule out is that backlash behaviours are not undermining some given, eternal system, but (like the constant if cyclical natural forces that mostly create sedimentation or erosion) shaping a different or at least altered system. Human intervention can reduce or amplify natural processes of erosion and cohesion: backlash can, by concerted and deliberate interventions and responses, yield outcomes that we might mostly agree are "positive" defined by reference to anything from the UN Charter to the 2017 White Paper. Thus to the Crawford question—unanswered in this article—of 'what is to be done',[90] the response must be that we must first understand the phenomenon better and typologise better its supposed manifestations. Above all we must certainly not simply dismiss or decry it as "populist".

---

89   Crawford concludes that in an age of populist scepticism of international law, it is flexible enough to accommodate dissent and will only survive 'if it has the capacity to change and develop over time' and accommodate 'adjustments ... to respond to perceived inequalities or injustices': Crawford (n 9) 22.

90   See Crawford (n 9).

Amidst Simmering Tensions: Improving the Effectiveness and Coherence of the International Human Rights System's Response to Mass Human Rights Violations

Annemarie Devereux*

1 Introduction

Rather than signalling an unprecedented backlash against global norms and institutions, recent developments in the international human rights field, such as the United States' withdrawal from the Human Rights Council, can be viewed as manifesting resurgent tensions with a much longer history.[1] A dual reality continues to exist within the international human rights system. Strong support for international human rights principles coexists with divergent views as to the desirable system of international oversight and response. Despite its effectiveness in establishing norms and both expert and peer review mechanisms, the international human rights system has been less successful in building consensus around issues of international enforcement. Abiding questions have included: what is the role of the international community vis-a-vis an individual state in relation to that state's human rights record? What constitutes legitimate intervention versus a breach of sovereignty? What is the "fit" between the specialised international human rights machinery and other United Nations ('UN') bodies? Adopting a historical perspective provides a useful antidote to perceiving some form of contemporary crisis, a characterisation which risks underestimating the ongoing work of the system and framing issues requiring attention in very narrow terms.

In contrast to the backlash paradigm which focuses attention on recent debates, this article argues that one of the most pressing challenges for the international human rights system, at least in relation to addressing mass violations, is to build support for a more fully integrated system. A sharper focus on prevention and early intervention by relevant bodies, together with a

---

* BA(Hons)/LLB(Hons) (ANU), LLM (Columbia), PhD (ANU), international lawyer and Adjunct Professor, Griffith Law School.

1 The author wishes to thank the organisers and participants of the Navigating the Backlash Workshop and the anonymous peer reviewers for their helpful comments.

© KONINKLIJKE BRILL NV, LEIDEN, 2021 | DOI:10.1163/26660229_03801010

fine-tuning of the operation of the international human rights response system, is vital. Attempts to limit the discussion of reform to the Geneva-based specialised bodies should be resisted. Renewed efforts are required to ensure human rights perspectives are incorporated into all relevant inter-governmental debates, including those of the Security Council. Any proposals for reform will have to navigate pre-existing divisions between states. Yet, remembering that key elements of the current system were forged during the Cold War, such a task should not be considered impossible. Ultimately, the effectiveness of the system will be judged according to the extent to which it contributes to the better promotion and protection of human rights "on the ground".

In order to critique the backlash analysis, Part 2 of this article examines two events that attracted significant attention in the international human rights system in 2018, namely the United States' withdrawal from the Human Rights Council and China's sponsorship of the 'mutually beneficial cooperation' resolution in the Human Rights Council. These developments are considered from a historical perspective to show how such events might be viewed as rumblings of existing tensions, rather than unprecedented challenges. Rather than focusing exclusively on such recent high-profile events, this article argues it is preferable to explore deeper issues within the international architecture. Part 3 thus moves to an examination of how the system currently responds to situations of mass violations, using a case-study of responses to Libya and Syria. On the basis of the challenges identified in this case-study, Part 4 makes some reform proposals, suggesting steps that might be undertaken to increase the coherence and effectiveness of the overall human rights protection system.

2 Placing Current Developments concerning the International Human Rights System within Their Historical Context

In the framing article for this issue of the Year Book, entitled 'Navigating the Backlash against Global Law and Institutions', reference is made to a rising number of national governments 'retreating from longstanding commitments to international norms and institutions'.[2] The postures of leaders in recent years are seen as 'part of a broader backlash against the Post-World War II framework of liberal norms and institutions'.[3] Backlash, in its common usage, refers to a sudden recoil, a strong negative reaction to developments. In the

---

2   Peter G Danchin et al, 'Navigating the Backlash against Global Law and Institutions' (2020) 38 *Australian Year Book of International Law* 33, 37.

3   Ibid 35.

AMIDST SIMMERING TENSIONS

framing article, particular use is made of the work of Madsen, Cebulak and Wiebusch (in their study of responses to international courts and tribunals) in considering backlash as 'a reaction to a development with the goal of reversing that development'.[4] The contemporary challenge is presented as 'a kneejerk reaction against and away from the global, and in particular globalisation, towards the local and the national'.[5] Whilst acknowledging that hostility towards internationalist ideas is not itself new, the authors nonetheless ask whether there is something distinct about the current environment. The task is framed as identifying the ramifications of this distinct moment for future efforts to build and promote peaceful and cooperative international relations.

With specific reference to the international human rights field, the argument appears to be that states are increasingly pushing back against international norms and an international system of enforcement. While some states are undoubtedly questioning elements of the international human rights system, this development should not be regarded as an existential threat. Throughout the history of the international human rights system, there have been vigorous debates, particularly about what is considered to be ideal and/or effective forms of international oversight. The system itself has weathered such debates, and even at times been strengthened as a result of open debate on controversial issues. The abiding challenge is to remain open to critiques, without being provoked into undue defensiveness or a siege-like mentality. Instead, it is vital to continue to identify and address weaknesses that represent a longer-term threat to the operation of the system.

In order to explore the significance of current challenges, this article focuses on the international human rights system in its institutional sense, that is the framework for international oversight and intervention—rather than exploring attitudes towards substantive human rights and/or any increase in breaches of human rights.[6] The rationale for prioritising the international architecture is two-fold: firstly, it reflects the focus of the most high-profile debates about the

---

4   Mikael Rask Madsen, Pola Cebulak and Micha Wiebusch, 'Backlash against International Courts: Explaining the Forms and Patterns of Resistance to International Courts' (2018) 14(2) *International Journal of Law in Context* 197, 200.

5   Danchin et al (n 2) 35.

6   In relation to particular areas of human rights, for instance, the use of the language of backlash to describe regression in the area of women's rights: see, eg, comments of UN Assistant Secretary-General for Human Rights, Andrew Gilmour, in *Violence Against Women in Politics: Expert Group Meeting Report and Recommendations* (Report, 8–9 March 2018) 4. The language of a 'pushback' has also been used to describe the escalation of violations, including by authoritarian nationalist governments: see Andrew Gilmour, 'Celebrating Human Rights Day: Youth Standing Up for Human Rights' (Speech, UN Headquarters New York, 10 December 2019).

international system in recent years and secondly, it allows for examining what is distinct about the international system.[7] Examining two of the most high-profile events of 2018—the United States' withdrawal from the Human Rights Council and the controversy surrounding the 'mutually beneficial cooperation' resolution—illustrates the point that recent events are less a sudden backlash than manifestations of simmering tensions.

2.1   *The United States' Withdrawal from the Human Rights Council*

In June 2018, the United States announced that it was withdrawing from the Human Rights Council: not as a retreat from human rights, but because its commitment to human rights did 'not allow us to remain a part of a hypocritical and self-serving organization that makes a mockery of human rights'.[8] The withdrawal took place the week after the UN High Commissioner for Human Rights criticised United States' policies separating children from their parents in immigration processing,[9] a fact that some commentators saw as causally linked with the announcement.[10] However, clear notice had been given a year earlier that the United States might reconsider its membership of the Council if steps were not taken to address what it identified as the major shortcomings of the system. In particular, the United States was dissatisfied with the alleged selectivity of the Human Rights Council in unfairly singling out Israel for condemnation, and the fact that its members included states failing to uphold the 'highest standards' of human rights such as Venezuela, China and Saudi Arabia.[11] US Secretary of State Mike Pompeo and Ambassador Nikki Haley lambasted the Human Rights Council, stating:

> [T]he Human Rights Council has become an exercise in shameless hypocrisy—with many of the world's worst human rights abuses going

---

7   Given that most national systems incorporate understandings of human rights (either in law or in broader discourse), debates about the content of human rights are not necessarily international, or exclusively international, in nature.

8   Secretary of State Mike Pompeo and Ambassador Nikki Haley, 'Remarks on the UN Human Rights Council' (Speech, Washington DC, 19 June 2018).

9   UN High Commissioner for Human Rights, Zeid Ra'ad Al Hussein, 'Opening Statement and Global Update of Human Rights Concerns', Statement to the 38th Session of the Human Rights Council (18 June 2018).

10   See 'United States Withdraws from the UN Human Rights Council, Shortly After Receiving Criticism About Its Border Policy' in Jean Galbraith (ed), 'Contemporary Practice of the United States' (2018) 112(4) *American Journal of International Law* 735, 745–751.

11   Ambassador Nikki Haley, 'Remarks at the Graduate Institute of Geneva' (Speech, Geneva, 6 June 2017).

AMIDST SIMMERING TENSIONS

ignored, and some of the world's most serious offenders sitting on the council itself.

The only thing worse than a council that does almost nothing to protect human rights is a council that covers for human rights abuses and is therefore an obstacle to progress and an impediment to change.[12]

Despite the forcefulness of this language, the significance of the United States' withdrawal from the Human Rights Council should not be overstated. Firstly, its stance towards the Council has been one of longstanding ambivalence. In 2006, the United States voted against the General Assembly resolution creating the Council and indicated it would not seek membership of the body, citing similar concerns to those expressed in 2018.[13] It was only after a change of administration in 2009 that the United States reversed its position, declaring that it would work for change of the Council 'from within'.[14] Secondly, although some commentators viewed the withdrawal as setting a 'dangerous and worrying precedent',[15] the United States' example has not been followed by other states, nor has its withdrawal stymied ongoing efforts at reform within the Human Rights Council.

At the heart of the United States discontent with the Human Rights Council is the perception that it is a hypocritical body whose members include states with poor human rights records. It levelled the same complaints against the Council's predecessor body, the Commission on Human Rights. In 2004, for instance, in prosecuting the case for reform, the United States argued that the Commission 'should not be allowed to become a protected sanctuary for human rights violators who aim to pervert and distort its work'.[16] In 2005, US Ambassador Rudy Boschwitz memorably argued that members of

---

12 Pompeo and Haley (n 8).

13 As to the history of the US engagement with the Council: see Luisa Blanchfield, *The United Nations Human Rights Council: Background and Policy Issues* (United States Congressional Research Service Reports, No RL33608, 26 February 2019) 6–7.

14 Ibid 6.

15 Rosa Freedman, 'Why the US Left the Human Rights Council—and Why It Matters', *The Conversation* (online, 20 June 2018) <http://theconversation.com/why-the-us-left -the-un-human-rights-council-and-why-it-matters-98644>.

16 Ambassador Richard S Williamson, Statement to the 60th Session of the Commission on Human Rights (19 March 2004) quoted in Philip Alston, 'Richard Lillich Memorial Lecture: Promoting the Accountability of Members of the New UN Human Rights Council' (2005) 15(1) *Journal of Transnational Law and Policy* 49, 59 ('Promoting the Accountability of Members of the New UNHRC').

the Commission 'must be the firefighters of the world, not the arsonists'.[17] Sensitivities around membership of the Commission were particularly acute when, after failing to be elected in 2001, the United States succeeded in its bid in 2003 alongside states such as Sudan and Libya.[18] More broadly, the Commission on Human Rights was seen as having little credibility, with some states using their membership to shield themselves and allies from critical comments and/or as a launching pad for political attacks on their enemies. In 2005, UN Secretary-General Kofi Annan described the Commission as 'undermined by its declining credibility and professionalism ... states have sought membership of the Commission not to strengthen human rights but to protect themselves against criticism or to criticize others'.[19]

When the Human Rights Council was created in 2006, some reforms were introduced to address membership-related concerns. Firstly, the number of states represented in the Council (compared with the Commission on Human Rights) was reduced slightly. The Council was to be composed of 47 members, compared with the Commission on Human Rights' 53 members. Secondly, the General Assembly resolution establishing the Human Rights Council stipulated that members were to be committed 'to the highest standards of human rights'.[20] When casting votes to select members, states were directed to take into account a nominee's 'contribution ... to the promotion and protection of human rights' and any pledges made.[21] Proposals for more rigorous membership criteria faced and continue to face a number of challenges. Firstly, some states adhere to a universalist perspective: that all states should retain the right to be elected to all bodies. Secondly, for those who support preconditions for membership, the difficulty lies in finding objective criteria that are sufficiently rigorous to exclude the worst violators, whilst not excluding major powers, since the latter would cripple political support for reform.[22] Consistent with the approach they took to the Commission on Human Rights, the United States argued that membership of the Human Rights Council should be limited to 'democratic' states.[23] A majority of states, however, considered this category

---

17   Ambassador Rudy Boschwitz, 'UN Democracy Caucus at the UN Commission on Human Rights' (Speech, Freedom House, 31 March 2005).

18   Henry J Steiner, Philip Alston and Ryan Goodman, *International Human Rights in Context: Law, Politics, Morals* (Oxford University Press, 3rd ed, 2008) 793.

19   *In Larger Freedom: Towards Development, Security and Human Rights for All—Report of the Secretary-General*, UN Doc A/59/2005 (21 March 2005) para 182 ('*In Larger Freedom*').

20   See GA Res 60/251, UN Doc A/RES/60/251 (3 April 2006, adopted 15 March 2006) para 9.

21   Ibid para 8.

22   Alston, 'Promoting the Accountability of Members of the New UNHRC' (n 16) 57.

23   See Philip Alston, 'Reconceiving the UN Human Rights Regime: Challenges Confronting the New UN Human Rights Council' (2006) 7(1) *Melbourne Journal of International Law* 185, 193–4, 196 ('Reconceiving the UN Human Rights Regime').

AMIDST SIMMERING TENSIONS

too amorphous. As Philip Alston has highlighted, more objective criteria have been seen as either overly broad (for example, a requirement that states have ratified core international human rights treaties would exclude the United States and China) or unduly narrow (for example, excluding countries condemned by a Human Rights Council resolution would not cover all egregious human rights violators).[24] The continuing dominance of regional bloc nominations ("clean slate" voting) further limits the competitive nature of elections. Given these factors, what might be termed the human rights diversity in the Council's membership is unlikely to change considerably and may continue to provoke discontent.

The United States' other major complaint about the Council in 2018 related to its perceived selectivity in unfairly targeting Israel and focusing disproportionate attention on the human rights situation in the Occupied Palestinian Territory. The United States had been agitating to have the Council remove standing Agenda Item 7 ('Human rights situation in Palestine and other occupied Arab territories') from its program of work. To the evident chagrin of the United States, removal of the agenda item proved virtually impossible given the impact of regional voting blocs. The efficiency-related reform proposals advanced in February 2018 by the President of the Human Rights Council, Ambassador Šuc of Slovenia—which included staggering debates on agenda items across the three annual Human Rights Council meetings instead of dealing with each agenda item at each meeting—would have had the side effect of reducing the frequency of Item 7 debates.[25] When these proposals failed to garner sufficient support for immediate adoption, the United States reverted to its former position of seeking the immediate deletion of Item 7 (together with changes to the Council's membership rules). Further, the United States strategy shifted to pursuing this change through a General Assembly resolution,

---

24 Alston, 'Promoting the Accountability of Members of the New UNHRC' (n 16) 57. For an excellent overview of the range of criteria suggested in the lead up to the creation of the Council, see also Alston, 'Reconceiving the UN Human Rights Regime' (n 23) 193–9.

25 See Human Rights Council Bureau, 'Proposal of the Bureau: Clustering and staggering of general debates throughout the Annual Programme of Work and restructuring the panel discussions', available at *Universal Rights Group* (Web Page, February 2018) <https://www.universal-rights.org/wp-content/uploads/2018/01/HRC37-Bureau-proposals.pdf>. Opposition to this proposal came from within the European Union (Belgium, France and Portugal, against a background of significant non-governmental organisation ('NGO') protests) and from Organisation of Islamic Cooperation countries: see Marc Limon, 'US Departure from the Human Rights Council: What Really Happened and What Will Happen Next?', *Universal Rights Group: Geneva* (Blog Post, 27 June 2018) <https://www.universal-rights.org/blog/us-departure-from-the-human-rights-council-what-really-happened-and-what-will-happen-next/> ('US Departure from the HRC').

rather than the internal reform process of the Council.[26] Even European allies warned that if the United States persisted with its efforts, there was a significant risk of damaging amendments being added into any reform resolution, such as amendments limiting the annual reviews of country situations or the operation of international commissions of inquiry ('ICOIs').[27]

Tensions over selectivity in relation to human rights scrutiny are not new. Similar charges were directed against the Commission on Human Rights.[28] Nor has the United States been alone in its concern that a focus on this Middle East situation prevents attention being given to other situations. In 2006, mindful of the situation evolving in Darfur, Secretary-General Kofi Annan urged the Council to handle issues associated with the Arab-Israeli conflict 'in an impartial way, and not allow it to monopolize attention at the expense of others where there are equally grave or even graver violations'.[29] Yet, as Connors and Schmidt have noted, whether the Council will address a country situation depends on the willingness of its membership, which in turn is heavily influenced by the operation of regional groupings and alliances.[30] Between 2006 and 2017, the Council convened 23 special sessions on country situations. Of these, six related to the situation in the Occupied Palestinian Territory, one to Israeli military operations, five to the Syrian Arab Republic, with other sessions focused on Burundi, the Central African Republic, Cote d'Ivoire, Darfur, Democratic Republic of Congo, Haiti, Iraq, Libya, Myanmar, Sri Lanka and South Sudan.[31] Whether or not the United States seeks membership of the Council again in the future, it seems likely that the Council will continue to address a range of critical human rights situations.

Rather than leading to a cascading loss of confidence in the Council, the United States' withdrawal from membership in 2018 has not been followed by similar action by other states, nor an emboldening of critics of the Council. Expressions of regret have been voiced by some of the United States' closest allies. The then United Kingdom Foreign Minister Boris Johnson characterised

---

26 Limon, 'US Departure from the HRC' (n 25).

27 See Colum Lynch, 'US Thwarted in Bid to Change UN Rights' Council's Approach to Israel', *Foreign Policy* (online, 30 May 2018) <https://foreignpolicy.com/2018/05/30/u-s-thwarted-in-bid-to-change-u-n-rights-councils-approach-to-israel/>.

28 See, eg, *In Larger Freedom* (n 19) para 2.

29 UN Secretary General, 'Secretary-General, in Message to Human Rights Council, Cautions Against Focusing on Middle East at Expense of Darfur, Other Grave Crises'(Press Release SG/SM/10769-HR/4907, 29 November 2006).

30 Jane Connors and Markus Schmidt, 'United Nations' in Daniel Moeckli, Sangeeta Shah, Sandesh Sivakumaran (eds), *International Human Rights Law* (Oxford University Press, 3rd ed, 2018) 369, 376.

31 Ibid 375.

the United States' withdrawal as 'regrettable'[32] and then Australian Foreign Minister Julie Bishop counselled the United States against withdrawal.[33] Rather than completely severing its ties, the United States has remained active in the proceedings of the Council as an observer state—for example, participating in the Universal Periodic Review ('UPR') of other states.[34] Further, the United States has not closed the door to future membership, with President Trump in his 2018 speech to the General Assembly allowing for the possibility of return should 'real reform' of the Council take place.[35] Whilst the international human rights system remains vulnerable to removal of funding by the United States,[36] there is little evidence that the United States action has stymied the work of the Council. The reform agenda is continuing to be carried forward through successive Presidents of the Council, albeit at a slow pace. In 2015, the then President of the Human Rights Council advanced an "efficiency drive" agenda,[37] which has been taken up by successive Presidents. Proposals include forward planning of the Council's programme of work, clustering of debates and amendments to the UPR process.[38] As noted above, the United States' attempt to short-circuit this process through development of a draft General Assembly resolution was resisted by states opposed to the content of suggested reforms, those opposed on procedural grounds to the manner in which the United States was pursuing reform, and key non-governmental organisations ('NGOs') that were fearful of embarking upon a broader reform process at this

---

32 Nada Tawfik, 'US Quits "Biased" UN Human Rights Council', *BBC News* (online, 20 June 2018) <https://www.bbc.com/news/44537372>.

33 Stephen Dziedzic, 'The US Withdrawal from the UN Human Rights Council Leaves Ally Australia in an Awkward, Lonely Position', *ABC News* (online, 20 June 2018) <https://www.abc.net.au/news/2018-06-20/analysis-what-does-us-united-nations-move-mean-for-australia/9889216>.

34 See, eg, *Report of the Working Group on the Universal Periodic Review: Viet Nam*, UN Doc A/HRC/41/7 (28 March 2019) paras 4, 21, 38.145, 38.204 and 38.205.

35 President Donald Trump, Statement to the 73rd Session of the General Assembly, UN Doc A/73/PV.6 (25 September 2018) 17.

36 The United States withheld $7.67 million from its contributions to the UN in Financial Year 2017 and 2018. Similar action was taken by the Bush Administration in 2008, withholding a proportionate sum of its UN funding equivalent to its expected contribution to the Human Rights Council: see Blanchfield (n 13) 9.

37 See, eg, *Statement by the President: Enhancing the Efficiency of the Human Rights Council*, UN Doc A/HRC/PRST/29/1 (23 July 2015).

38 For a useful history of the debates about efficiency-related reform of the Human Rights Council, see the reports of the Universal Rights Group: eg Marc Limon, 'Crunch Time for Human Rights Council Efficiency Reforms', *Universal Rights Group* (Blog Post, 14 November 2018) <https://www.universal-rights.org/blog/crunch-time-for-human-rights-council-efficiency-reforms/>.

time.[39] NGO reluctance was in large part due to their bruising experiences of the *Mutually Beneficial Cooperation Resolution* ('MBC resolution')[40] of 2018, discussed below.

2.2 Debates over the 'Mutually Beneficial Cooperation' Resolution of the Human Rights Council

In March 2018, the Human Rights Council passed the MBC resolution. The resolution calls upon states to uphold multilateralism and work together to promote mutually beneficial cooperation.[41] Other stakeholders such as international and regional organisations, NGOs, and human rights mechanisms and procedures are encouraged to focus on mutually beneficial cooperation. The resolution champions the UPR process and emphasises the utility of technical assistance and capacity building at the request of, and in accordance with, the priorities of the state concerned. Representing only the second resolution that China has sponsored in the Human Rights Council, the resolution uses language—such as references to 'mutually beneficial cooperation' and pursuing a 'community of shared future'[42]—that resonates strongly with the approach to international relations and international law being promoted by the Chinese government. This approach emphasises principles of cooperation, inclusivity, equality and a 'win-win' approach.[43] The MBC resolution attracted criticism both for what it contained (the emphasis on inter-state discussions) and what it left out (the centrality of individual rights holders, civil society, and the importance of monitoring, accountability and transparency). Former

---

39 The United States developed a draft General Assembly resolution which would have deleted Agenda Item 7 and brought about immediate changes to the Human Rights Council's membership rules. 18 International NGOs authored a joint letter to states requesting that support not be given to the resolution given the unfavourable political climate, the risk of hostile amendments and having contestation rather than consensus around reforms. The text of the NGO letter can be found via the website of the International Service for Human Rights: <https://www.ishr.ch/sites/default/files/documents/17052018 -gares-hrc-letter_final_0.pdf>. See also Limon (n 25). Subsequent to its withdrawal from the Human Rights Council, Ambassador Nikki Haley said that the NGO action, seen as thwarting reform, had been a 'contributing factor' in the US decision to withdraw from the Council: the text of Haley's letter can be found at <https://www.amnesty.org/down load/Documents/AMR5186502018ENGLISH.PDF>.

40 *Promoting Mutually Beneficial Cooperation in the Field of Human Rights*, HRC Res 37/23, UN Doc A/HRC/RES/37/23 (6 April 2018, adopted 23 March 2018).

41 Ibid para 1.

42 Ibid Preamble and paras 1, 2, 4 and 5.

43 Chatham House, *Exploring Public International Law Issues with Chinese Scholars—Part 4* (International Law Programme Roundtable Meeting Summary, 2–3 June 2018) 4.

Special Rapporteur Miloon Koothari labelled the resolution a 'trojan horse', voicing specific concerns about the invisibility of the "accountability agenda":

> [The resolution] seeks to downplay and even discredit a vital pillar of the human rights framework and the Council's mandate: accountability for violations and justice for victims.
>
> The 'cooperation' which the resolution presents can become an escape route for governments who prefer an absence of scrutiny for their questionable practices and go to great lengths at home and abroad to avoid it. For civil society and affected populations, however, the move away from scrutiny is a move to entrench impunity for human rights violations.[44]

During the debate on the resolution, China argued that the resolution was in line with previous documents, including the *Vienna Declaration and Programme of Action*,[45] which called for strong cooperation and dialogue among states. At the same time, it referred to a 'new type of international relations, which reflected the times'.[46] Several states speaking in favour of the resolution also stressed the importance of international cooperation in the area of human rights.[47] The US accused China of attempting to 'weaken the United Nations human rights system and the norms underpinning it', arguing that '[t]he "feel-good" language about "mutually beneficial cooperation" was intended to benefit autocratic states at the expense of people whose human rights and fundamental freedoms all were obligated, as states, to respect'.[48] Australia regarded the draft resolution as lacking balance and focusing overly on the relations between states instead of the rights of individuals. It also considered the use of phrases such as 'mutually beneficial cooperation' and a 'community of shared values'

---

44   Miloon Koothari, 'China's Trojan Horse Human Rights Resolution', *The Diplomat* (online, 22 March 2018) <https://thediplomat.com/2018/03/chinas-trojan-horse-human-rights-resolution/>. See also Ryan Mitchell, 'Was the UN Human Rights Council Wrong to Back China's "Shared Future" Resolution?', EJIL: Talk! (Blog Post, 10 April 2018) <https://www.ejiltalk.org/was-the-un-human-rights-council-wrong-to-back-chinas-shared-future-resolution/>.

45   *Vienna Declaration and Programme of Action*, adopted by the World Conference on Human Rights, UN Doc A/CONF 157/23 (12 July 1993, adopted 25 June 1993).

46   Quoted in UN Human Rights Council, 'Human Rights Council Adopts 10 Texts, Requests a High-Level Panel Discussion on Genocide and a Study on the Role of Capacity Building in the Promotion of Human Rights' (Press Release, 23 March 2018) <https://www.ohchr.org/EN/HRBodies/HRC/Pages/NewsDetail.aspx?NewsID=22893&LangID=E>.

47   Ibid. See, eg, statements by Egypt and Pakistan.

48   Ibid.

210   AUSTRALIAN YEAR BOOK OF INTERNATIONAL LAW VOLUME 38

vague and ambiguous.[49] Whilst supporting technical assistance and capacity building, Australia noted the need for transparency and monitoring, and to recognise the role of national human rights institutions. The final resolution passed with 28 votes in favour, 17 abstentions (including Australia, Japan, Germany and the UK), and one vote against (the US).[50]

The stress by China and like-minded states on the supremacy of inter-state dialogue and the need for a cooperative approach has significant precedents. In 1997 in the Commission on Human Rights, for instance, the Head of the Chinese Delegation suggested that the Commission 'should encourage cooperation and reject confrontation', declaring that '[o]nly when the principle of sovereign equality and mutual respect is sincerely adhered to and dialogue and cooperation encouraged, can the Commission make great achievements in promoting the human rights cause'.[51] When the resolution establishing the Human Rights Council was formulated, a strong push by China led to the inclusion of language supporting 'constructive international dialogue and cooperation' as a foundational principle, and for the Council to pursue 'genuine dialogue'.[52] It is an approach that accepts human rights principles, but favours more confined discussions between states, conciliatory dialogue and technical assistance, rather than public "naming and shaming".[53]

Although the 2018 MBC resolution mentions other mechanisms of the Human Rights Council, it downplays the role of independent bodies in monitoring and evaluating performance. In this there are some resonances with the cautious approach to international oversight seen in the late 1960s. Periodic reporting under the *International Covenant on Civil and Political Rights* ('*ICCPR*'), for example, was designed as a relatively soft means of oversight whereby states would record their progress without being subject to specific adverse comments by the Human Rights Committee that would make only 'general comments'.[54] Over time, the practice of the treaty bodies has expanded

---

49   Ibid.

50   Details of the vote can be found at the end of the MBC resolution: HRC Res 37/23 (n 40).

51   Ambassador Wu Jianmin, Statement to the 53rd Session of the Commission on Human Rights (8 April 1997), quoted in Steiner, Alston and Goodman (n 18) 791.

52   GA Res 60/251 (n 20) Preamble para 4.

53   As to a similar divisions at a senior level of the UN on strategies on engaging with countries on human rights issues: Gert Rosenthal, *A Brief and Independent Inquiry into the Involvement of the United Nations in Myanmar from 2010 to 2018* (Report, 29 May 2019).

54   *International Covenant on Civil and Political Rights*, opened for signature 16 December 1966, 999 UNTS 171 (entered into force 23 March 1976). Art 40(4) states that the Human Rights Committee, after studying the periodic reports, shall 'transmit its reports, and such general comments as it may consider appropriate, to the States parties'. As Caporti noted in 1968, the Human Rights Committee as an expert committee was probably not regarded

AMIDST SIMMERING TENSIONS

to include more rigorous examination of states' records and greater space for NGO participation. Not all states have been equally enamoured with these developments. For many states, the UPR is the preferable forum for engagement precisely because it is perceived as a state-driven process.

In so far as the MBC resolution sought to advance a more conciliatory form of international dialogue on human rights issues than that associated with robust accountability-oriented discussions, it reflects an emphasis on national sovereignty and a wariness of international intervention that has been a feature of debates in the human rights realm since the early years of the UN. In its foundational period, there was significant debate as to whether the General Assembly even had the power to discuss human rights records in individual states, or whether that represented an illegitimate intervention in matters of 'domestic jurisdiction' under art 2(7) of the *UN Charter* ('the *Charter*').[55] The debate over the General's Assembly's powers played out in discussions of draft resolutions on particular human rights situations: whether dealing with discrete topics such as the trials of Christian Church leaders in Bulgaria and Hungary in the late 1940s or in ongoing discussions such as those relating to apartheid in the 1950s and 1960s. It was the latter subject which led to many previously opposed states (including the United Kingdom and Australia) to accept the desirability of General Assembly action and desist with 'domestic jurisdiction' arguments.[56] Ultimately, the view which prevailed was that the General Assembly had the requisite power by virtue of arts 10, 55 and 56 of the *Charter*.

A similar debate took place in the Commission on Human Rights regarding the handling of individual human rights complaints. Despite the political divides of the Cold War, support to scrutinise human rights performances grew, fostered in particular by the determination of newly decolonised states to take effective action against apartheid and racism. Thus, in 1967, the Economic and Social Council approved the Commission on Human Rights examining

---

as having the political authority to address recommendations to government: Francesco Caporti, 'The International Measures of implementation included in the Covenants on Human Rights' in Asbjorn Eide and August Schou (eds), *International Protection of Human Rights* (Interscience Publishers, 1968) 131, 138.

55 As to the early art 2(7) debates, see JES Fawcett, 'Human Rights and Domestic Jurisdiction' in Evan Luard (ed), *The International Protection of Human Rights* (Camelot Press, 1967) ch 11.

56 For coverage of debates during the 1946–1966 period, including Australia's stance, see, eg, Annemarie Devereux, *Australia and the Birth of the International Bill of Human Rights: 1946–1966* (Federation Press, 2005), 215–225.

information in the communications received by the Commission.[57] In the case of the Human Rights Council, there can be no real debate as to the legitimacy of discussions of individual country situations given its specific powers with respect to the UPR or in responding to human rights emergencies. However, the support which the MBC resolution garnered demonstrates that a number of states are hesitant about robust approaches to compliance and accountability. Divisions within the international community on the best strategy of engagement or intervention complicates not only the operation of the Human Rights Council, but also other organs of the United Nations, including the Security Council (as will be seen further in Part 3).

2.3 Conclusion

Events such as the United States' withdrawal from the Human Rights Council and the MBC resolution debate are undoubtedly significant and unsettling. However, viewing these events in their broader historical context should be both reassuring and unnerving: reassuring in so far as the system is not facing an unprecedented crisis; but unnerving as a reminder of the longstanding tensions simmering away beneath the surface of the international human rights system. Notwithstanding a wide degree of acceptance of international human rights standards, ideal approaches to oversight and accountability remain contested. To characterise recent events as a unique backlash underestimates the longevity of these debates and the way in which the system has, nevertheless, continued to function and evolve. At a minimum, it should indicate that contemporary developments are within the 'ebb and flow of the history of the evolving international legal order',[58] to use the words of the project organisers, rather than representing any cataclysmic event.

In the author's view, it is preferable to avoid use of the backlash analysis in this context given its significant limitations. Such an approach unduly narrows our critical gaze by funneling attention to the immediate source of controversy (for example, recent developments at the Human Rights Council) at the expense of a broader examination of the international human rights system's operation. Re-conceptualising contemporary challenges as manifestations of

---

57   ECOSOC Resolution 1235 (XLII) UN Doc E/4393 (6 June 1967). See Marc Limon, *Reform of the UN Human Rights Petitions System: An Assessment of the UN Human Rights Communications Procedures and Proposals for a Single Integrated System* (Universal Rights Group, 2018) 7–13. This development was preceded by the development of the first 'individual communication' systems in the *International Convention on the Elimination of All Forms of Racial Discrimination*, opened for signature 21 December 1965, 660 UNTS 195 (entered into force 4 January 1969) ('*CERD*') in 1965 and the *ICCPR* (in 1966).

58   Danchin et al (n 2) 38.

simmering tensions rather than a backlash (with its connotations of a more wholescale rejection of the system) opens up the space to ask: what are the gravest threats to the operation of the international human rights system? How might those threats be addressed? What are the prospects for reform? This analysis can then be informed by (rather than constrained by) an acknowledgement of ongoing tensions.

In an effort to elucidate some of the deeper issues confronting the international human rights system, Part 3 of this article examines the current operation of the system in responding to situations of mass violations. Given the gravity of the violations occurring and the high-profile nature of many such situations, it is an area in which the strengths and fault lines of the international human rights system may be particularly apparent. As a result, concrete actions that might be taken to improve the coherence and effectiveness of the system can be identified. These measures might also be considered measures of 'reform and renewal' to use the language of the framing article, offering states the opportunity to renew their commitment to the UN human rights system and to reform its functioning in a substantive fashion.

3 Operation of the International Human Rights System in Responding to Mass Violations: Libya and Syria

Exploring the way in which the international human rights system responds to situations of mass violations highlights the extent of unresolved debates within the international human rights field—in particular the divides between states preferring more conciliatory, less interventionist approaches to issues of enforcement and those states supporting more accountability driven agendas. In this, it is similar to the contestation seen in Part 2. However, undertaking this analysis also highlights structural difficulties associated with ensuring a coherent approach across multiple UN fora and targeting effective action to respond to mass violations. It is possible to identify a range of options to increase the impact of the system, together with the likely flash-points in pursuing such reform. In this part, two situations, Libya and Syria, are used as vehicles to examine the current operation of the international human rights system. For the purposes of clarity, this part considers not only the action of specialised human rights machinery, but what might be termed the broader international human rights response system. This includes the Geneva-based bodies, as well as other parts of the UN system involved in addressing human rights-related issues—such as the Security Council, the General Assembly, thematic Special Representatives, and relevant international courts and tribunals. In general, this part is focused on international responses in the 2011–2012 time-period. However, recognising that the situations which arose in Libya and Syria in 2011 did not occur in a human rights vacuum, this part begins with an analysis of Libya and Syria's interactions with the human rights system in the years leading up to 2011.

3.1   Pre-2011: Engagement with the International Human Rights System

Examining Libya and Syria's engagement with the international human rights system in the years prior to 2011 highlights specific limitations in the specialised human rights system relating to the treaty body system, the Special Procedures and the UPR. It also reveals weaknesses in "early warning" capacities, and ensuring accurate portrayals of situations of endemic human rights violations. Both Libya and Syria were active in ratifying international human rights treaties.[59] Both states were also overdue with most of their reports to treaty bodies,[60] limiting the opportunities for detailed international scrutiny. Libya and Syria accepted a limited number of individual communication procedures,[61] and Libya, in particular, was the subject of a number of individual complaints under the ICCPR.[62] Neither Libya nor Syria had issued Standing Invitations to the Special Procedures of the Human Rights Council,

---

59   By 2011, Libya had ratified the ICCPR (n 54); *International Covenant on Economic, Social and Cultural Rights* ('ICESCR'), opened for signature 16 December 1966, 993 UNTS 3 (entered into force 3 January 1976); CERD (n 57); *Convention on the Elimination of all Forms of Discrimination Against Women* ('CEDAW'), opened for signature 18 December 1979, 1249 UNTS 13 (entered into force 3 September 1981); *Convention on the Rights of the Child* ('CRC'), opened for signature 20 November 1989, 1577 UNTS 3, (entered into force 2 September 1990) and its protocols; *Convention against Torture and Other Cruel, Inhuman or Degrading Treatment or Punishment* ('CAT'), opened for signature 10 December 1984, 1465 UNTS 85 (entered into force 26 June 1987), and the *International Convention on the Protection of the Rights of All Migrant Workers and Members of their Families* ('CMW'), opened for signature 18 December 1990, 2220 UNTS 3, (entered into force 1 July 2003). Syria's record was similarly impressive: having ratified all these treaties, plus the *Convention on the Rights of Persons with Disabilities* ('CRPD'), opened for signature 13 December 2006, 2515 UNTS 3, (entered into force 3 May 2008).

60   Prior to 2011, Libya last submitted reports under the ICCPR and ICESCR, for example, in 2005 and 2004 respectively (albeit with some engagement in the follow-up process of the HRC in 2010), and Syria last submitted reports in 2004 and 1999.

61   Prior to 2011, Libya had accepted the individual communications procedures related to the ICCPR and CEDAW, and Syria had accepted the individual communications procedure related to the CRPD.

62   According to the OHCHR treaty body jurisprudence database, there were 21 communications lodged and 8 views adopted by the Human Rights Committee involving Libya between its accession to the *Optional Protocol to the ICCPR* ('OP-ICCPR'), opened for signature 16 December 1966, 999 UNTS 171, (entered into force 23 March 1976) and 2011.

but Syria in 2010 accepted visits from Special Rapporteurs focused on the right to the highest attainable standard of health[63] and the right to adequate food.[64] Neither of these Special Rapporteurs predicted any imminent deterioration in the human rights situation, though the Special Rapporteur on the right to health recommended that the Syrian Government reconsider the state of emergency declaration that had been in effect since the 1960s.[65] It is perhaps more revealing that Libya was the subject of a number of complaints received by Special Rapporteurs: in 2010 alone, six Special Rapporteurs were involved in such communications, together with the Working Group on Enforced or Involuntary Disappearances.[66] The figures for Syria are similar with communications to/from six Special Rapporteurs in 2010.[67] In each country, many of the complaints concerned alleged violations against human rights defenders.

Both states engaged with the UPR process at a time proximate to the deterioration in the human rights situation: with Libya undertaking its first UPR cycle in November 2010 and Syria in October 2011. In the case of Libya, the political nature of the UPR process is highlighted in the number of positive endorsements Libya received from friendly nations,[68] though recommendations also included pointed references to the incidence of torture, arbitrary detention and enforced disappearance, amongst other violations.[69] Syria's first UPR in October 2011 (after the armed insurgency had developed) shows more open and widespread concern with the deteriorating human rights situation.[70]

---

63   Anand Grover, *Report of the Special Rapporteur on the Right of Everyone to the Enjoyment of the Highest Attainable Standard of Physical and Mental Health: Addendum: Mission to the Syrian Arab Republic*, UN Doc A/HRC/17/25/Add.3 (21 March 2011).

64   Olivier De Schutter, *Report of the Special Rapporteur on the Right to Food: Addendum: Mission to the Syrian Arab Republic*, UN Doc A/HRC/16/49/Add.2 (27 January 2011).

65   Grover (n 63) 19.

66   In the *Charter*-based body database maintained by OHCHR, there are references to communications sent or received in 2010 in reports of the Special Rapporteurs dealing with extra-judicial executions, freedom of opinion and expression, contemporary forms of racism, torture, human rights defenders, and migrants (short titles used here). In some cases, several Special Rapporteurs were involved in issuing a joint communiqué.

67   In the *Charter*-based body database maintained by OHCHR, there are references in 2010 to communications sent or received in reports of Special Rapporteurs dealing with human rights and terrorism, adequate housing, human rights defenders, torture, freedom of opinion and expression and the independence of judges (short titles used here).

68   *Report of the Working Group on the Universal Periodic Review: Libyan Arab Jamahiriya*, UN Doc A/HRC/16/15 (4 January 2011). See, eg, the statements made by countries such as Algeria, Qatar, and Syria.

69   See, eg, statements and recommendations by the United Kingdom, Japan, Switzerland, Australia and the United States: Ibid.

70   *Report of the Working Group on the Universal Periodic Review: Syrian Arab Republic*, UN Doc A/HRC/19/11 (24 January 2012).

To be fair, perhaps no review could have been expected to predict the rapid deterioration of the human rights situation in either Libya or Syria in 2011. Many situations of endemic human rights violations do not spiral downwards in such a dramatic fashion. In the specific context of developments in 2011, other countries that experienced the Arab Spring and the removal of authoritarian leaders did not necessarily witness prolonged conflict and the associated commission of international crimes. Nor is it realistic to expect the international human rights system by itself to be able to prevent the outbreak of conflict and the associated spike of human rights violations. However, given the number of conflicts in which the outbreak of violence is integrally related to demands for improvements in the enjoyment of rights, and the deterioration of human rights that usually accompanies conflict, situations of endemic human rights violations deserve higher visibility in the system. From the existing information on Libya and Syria, Special Procedure mechanisms seem to offer particular potential in providing early warning of critical human rights situations. Yet, there remains no clear institutional avenue for either Special Procedure mechanisms or other UN bodies or officials to classify situations as "at risk".

Looking through UN reports prior to 2011, one is left with the impression that perhaps in the desire to encourage engagement with the international human rights system or simply through the use of familiar diplomatic language, softer language was used to express assessments of the human rights situation in Libya and Syria than the situations warranted. In both Libya and Syria, for instance, reports of ICOIs written after the outbreak of conflict made reference to years of repressive rule in which human rights were routinely infringed,[71] using franker language than is apparent in many earlier UN reports. In the case of Libya, for instance, the Committee against Torture in 1999, merely expressed concern that the government had not addressed issues raised with it previously and reiterated the fact that allegations of torture continued to be received by the Committee.[72] The Committee on Economic, Social and Cultural Rights' Concluding Observations were similarly largely written in the form of regretting insufficient information being provided on particular topics, rather than

---

71   See, eg, *Report of the International Commission of Inquiry to Investigate All Alleged Violations of International Human Rights Law in the Libyan Arab Jamahiriya*, UN Doc A/HRC/17/44 (12 January 2012) 9–11 ('ICOI-Libya Initial Report'); *Report of the Independent International Commission of Inquiry on the Syrian Arab Republic*, UN Doc A/HRC/S-17/2/Add.1 (23 November 2011) 6.

72   *Report of the Committee Against Torture*, UN Doc A/54/44 (26 April–14 May 1999) para 182.

AMIDST SIMMERING TENSIONS

reaching conclusions on the basis of publicly available information.[73] The most forthright treaty body was the Human Rights Committee.[74] Yet, even if pre-2011 assessments had been harsher, the question remains: would this have triggered deliberations of how the international community could and should respond?

3.2   Responses in 2011–2012

Once the scale of the violations taking place became clear in 2011 in the case of both Libya and Syria, the international human rights system sprang into action. Special sessions of the Human Rights Council were convened on both country situations.[75] The Human Rights Council established ICOIs to examine alleged international human rights and international humanitarian law violations and abuses and identify perpetrators (with the ICOI-Syria continuing to operate to the present day).[76] In relation to Libya, a range of Special Procedures of the Human Rights Council and thematic Advisers/Representatives of the Secretary-General focused attention on violations within their remit. Statements of concern were issued for instance by the Secretary-General, the High Commissioner for Human Rights, the Chair of the Working Group on Mercenaries (on behalf of all the Special Procedure mandate holders), the Special Representative of the Secretary General for Children and Armed Conflict, the Working Group on Enforced or Involuntary

---

73   *Concluding Observations of the Committee on Economic, Social and Cultural Rights on the Libyan Arab Jamahiriya*, UN Doc E/C.12/LYB/CO/2 (25 January 2006).

74   The Human Rights Committee in issuing concluding observations in relation to Libya, highlighted a wide range of concerns (with respect to topics such as enforced disappearances, arbitrary detention, over-usage of the death penalty, the use of Special Courts not providing appropriate guarantees, gender based discrimination and restrictions on freedom of expression and assembly): *Concluding Observations of the Human Rights Committee on the Libyan Arab Jamahiriya*, UN Doc CCPR/C/LBY/CO/4 (15 November 2007). Taken in aggregate, the comments reflected a critical level of non-compliance, even if the overall situation was not labelled in this fashion.

75   The special session in relation to the situation in Libya (then called the Libyan Arab Jamahiriya) was the 15th special session of the Human Rights Council, held on 25 February 2011. The 16th to the 19th special sessions were all focused on the situation in Syria (Syrian Arab Republic): on 29 April 2011, 22 August 2011, 2 December 2011 and 1 June 2012. A further special session was convened in 2016 (ie outside the time period for this Article).

76   The Libya ICOI was mandated in February 2011: HRC Res S-15/1, UN Doc A/HRC/RES/S-15/1 (3 March 2011, adopted 25 February 2011). In the case of Syria, the HRC first mandated an OHCHR investigation: HRC Res S-16/1, UN Doc A/HRC/RES/S-16/1 (4 May 2011, adopted 29 April 2011), followed by an ICOI in August 2011: HRC Res S-17/1, UN Doc A/HRC/RES/S-17/1 (22 August 2011).

Disappearances, the Special Representative of the Secretary-General on Sexual Violence in Conflict as well as several treaty bodies.[77] Alarm was also expressed by the Secretary-General's Special Advisers on the Prevention of Genocide and on the Responsibility to Protect.[78] A similar grouping of officials and Special Procedure mandate holders issued statements indicating concern at the deteriorating human rights situation in Syria.[79] The General Assembly suspended Libya's membership of the Human Rights Council for a period in 2011,[80] being the first and only country to have its membership so suspended. Syria was intending to stand for election as a member of the Human Rights Council in 2011 at the time of the 16th special session on Syria, but in the light of significant criticism, Syria did not pursue its candidature.[81]

Stark differences emerge in relation to the treatment of Libya and Syria by the Security Council. In the case of Libya, the Security Council imposed targeted sanctions under Resolution 1970 (2011). Individuals who were involved or complicit in human rights abuses were liable to be listed and subject to a travel ban and assets freeze.[82] The Libyan situation was referred to the International Criminal Court ('ICC'),[83] with arrest warrants issued for three individuals in June 2011 (though the ICC is yet to gain custody of the individuals against whom arrest warrants remain current). Military intervention by the North Atlantic Treaty Organisation ('NATO') was authorised by the Security Council in order to protect civilians, though the scope of subsequent military action undertaken proved controversial.[84] In the case of Libya, a peace mission, United Nations Support Mission in Libya ('UNSMIL'), was established in September 2011 with the inclusion of a significant Human Rights, Rule of Law and Transitional Justice Section. UNSMIL, together with the Office of the High

---

77 ICOI-Libya Initial Report (n 71) 13–14.

78 See UN Secretary-General Special Adviser on the Prevention of Genocide, Francis Deng, and Special Adviser on the Responsibility to Protect, Edward Luck, 'On the Situation in Libya' (Press Release, 22 February 2011) <https://www.un.org/en/genocidepreven tion/documents/media/statements/2011/English/2011-02-22-OSAPG,%20Special%20 Advisers%20Statement%20on%20Libya,%2022%20February%202011.pdf>.

79 See for instance, statements referred to in the preamble of HRC Res S-17/1 (n 76).

80 GA Res 65/265, UN Doc A/RES/65/265 (3 March 2011, adopted 1 March 2011).

81 Marty Harris, 'International Responses to the Syrian uprising: March 2011–June 2012' (Background Note, Parliamentary Library, Parliament of Australia, 13 July 2012) 6.

82 SC Res 1970, UN Doc S/RES/1970 (2011) (26 February 2011) para 22(a).

83 Ibid para 4.

84 The arguments concerning the legitimacy of the military action concerned the extent it went beyond the SC mandate to protect civilians through enforcing a no-fly zone to include actions to force regime change: see Andrew Garwood-Gowers, 'The Responsibility to Protect and the Arab Spring: Libya as the Exception, Syria as the Norm?' (2013) 36(2) *University of New South Wales Law Journal* 594.

Commissioner for Human Rights ('OHCHR'), continued to issue regular reports on human rights violations occurring in Libya. Sadly, the emergence of dual civilian authorities, and the proliferation of armed groups (not under state control), and the outbreak of further conflict(s) has meant that Libya has had little respite from ongoing serious violations.

In the case of Syria, a political impasse stymied Security Council action under Chapter VII of the *Charter*. In the face of opposition from China and Russia in particular, the Security Council could not agree to express concern at the spiraling human rights situation until months after other UN mechanisms.[85] It was not until 3 August 2011 that a Presidential statement was released condemning the 'widespread violations of human rights and the use of force against civilians by the Syrian authorities'.[86] The statement also declared that those responsible for violations should be held to account.[87] Human rights groups, such as Amnesty International, voiced severe disappointment that the Security Council could not reach agreement on a resolution, and had instead passed a 'limp statement that is not legally binding and does not refer the situation to the International Criminal Court'.[88] A number of draft resolutions were circulated during subsequent months, some of which would have imposed sanctions, but even resolutions not including such enforcement measures failed to pass.[89] The Russian Federation expressed concern that the West was aiming to ultimately achieve regime change through military intervention.[90] Other arguments in opposition to action focused on the need to create an environment conducive to a political solution.[91] The High Commissioner

---

85   See, eg, the reports of Russia and Lebanon's opposition to the release of a press statement: Security Council Report, 'Insights on Syria', What's in Blue series (28 April 2011) <https://www.whatsinblue.org/2011/04/insights-on-syria-2.php>. Russia saw Council action on Syria as constituting interference in a domestic matter.

86   UN Doc S/PRST/2011/16 (3 August 2011).

87   Ibid.

88   Amnesty International, 'UN Security Council statement 'Completely Inadequate'' (Press Release, 4 August 2011) <https://www.amnesty.org/en/press-releases/2011/08/un-security-council-syria-statement-e28098completely-inadequatee28099/>.

89   See, eg, the draft resolutions of 2011 and 2012: UN Doc S/2011/612 (4 October 2011); UN Doc S/2012/77 (4 February 2012).

90   See, eg, the statements of Russian Ambassador Vitaly Churkin at Security Council proceedings on 4 October 2011: UN Doc S/PV.6627 (4 October 2011) 3–5. Similar comments were made by some of the abstaining states eg South Africa who feared any moves towards authorising military intervention to achieve regime change: at 11.

91   See, eg, the statements made by the Russian Ambassador Vitaly Churkin and Chinese Ambassador Li Baodong in the Security Council: ibid 3–5. China's statement made repeated references to the need of the international community to engage in a constructive fashion and ensure respect for Syria's sovereignty: at 5.

for Human Rights addressed the Security Council during its consultations on Syria,[92] and the Chair of the ICOI-Syria was also invited to address at least one informal Arria-formula meeting during 2012.[93] Yet such briefings were not sufficient to prompt the Security Council to act. The then High Commissioner for Human Rights, Navi Pillay, expressed frustration at the continuing failure of the Security Council to agree on firm collective action, suggesting that its inaction had emboldened the Syrian regime and led to an escalation of violence.[94]

Meanwhile the ICOI-Syria continued to report on gross human rights violations occurring in Syria.[95] The General Assembly passed a number of resolutions condemning the widespread and systematic violations occurring in Syria.[96] Despite the High Commissioner for Human Rights and the ICOI-Syria's conclusion that war crimes and crimes against humanity were occurring, and vigorous calls for the Syrian situation to be referred to the ICC, no referral was formally considered by the Security Council in 2011–2012. It was not until 2014 that a resolution concerning referral was put before the Security Council, at

---

92   This briefing was referred to in a subsequent document of the Security Council and prospectively in the press briefing of 18 August 2011: Security Council, UN Doc S/PV.6602 (25 August 2011); 'Daily Press Briefing by the Office of the Spokesperson for the Secretary-General (Press Briefing, United Nations, 18 August 2011) < https://www.un.org/press/en/2011/db110818.doc.htm>. There are no minutes of the consultations. Note that the High Commissioner does not have an automatic right to appear before the Security Council. Reflecting the sensitivity of the Syria issue, in March 2018, a briefing by the High Commissioner requested by 7 Security Council members was blocked through the calling of a procedural vote, with states including China and Russia arguing that human rights was the competence of the Human Rights Council and not the Security Council: see Security Council, UN Doc S/PV.8209 (19 March 2018). By way of contrast, the High Commissioner has been welcomed to other meetings of the Security Council to discuss the human rights situation in individual countries: see eg in discussions of Haiti: Security Council, UN Doc S/PV.8502 (3 April 2019).

93   According to the listing of Arria-formula meetings collated by Security Council Report, the Chair of the ICOI-Syria addressed an Arria-formula meeting on 22 March 2012: Security Council Report, 'Arria Formula Meetings, 1992–2019' (Web Page, 2 July 2019) <https://www.securitycouncilreport.org/atf/cf/%7B65BFCF9B-6D27-4E9C-8CD3-CF6E4FF96FF9%7D/working_methods_arria_formula-16.pdf>.

94   'Top UN Human Rights Official Says Member States "Must Act Now" to Protect Syrian People, as Violent Crackdown Continues, in Briefing to General Assembly' (Press Release, GA/11206, 13 February 2012) <https://www.un.org/press/en/2012/ga11206.doc.htm>.

95   *Report of the Independent International Commission of Inquiry on the Syrian Arab Republic*, UN Doc A/HRC/19/69 (22 February 2012) 1.

96   See for instance, GA Res 66/176, UN Doc A/RES/66/176 (23 February 2012, adopted 19 December 2011); GA Res 66/253, UN Doc A/RES/66/253 (21 February 2012, adopted 16 February 2012); GA Res 66/253 B, UN Doc A/RES/66/253 B (7 August 2012, adopted 3 August 2012); GA Res 67/183, UN Doc A/RES/67/183 (12 February 2013, adopted 20 December 2012).

AMIDST SIMMERING TENSIONS

which time it was vetoed by China and Russia.[97] In time, this failure led the General Assembly to establish the International, Impartial and Independent Mechanism for Syria ('IIIM-Syria') to conduct criminal-justice focused investigations.[98] The Security Council did however agree to the deployment of unarmed military observers through the United Nations Supervision Mission in Syria ('UNSMIS').[99] This initiative had to be disbanded within months, however, due to the escalating violence. Human rights monitoring of both sides of the conflict continued through the auspices of the ICOI-Syria as well as OHCHR. With the conflict now having entered its eighth year, the sheer magnitude and brutality of the ongoing violations continues to shock the community.

3.3   Key Lessons from Libya and Syria

These two examples are helpful in reflecting firstly, the breadth of the international human rights response system. It encompasses not only Geneva-based treaty and Charter bodies, but the General Assembly and the Security Council, the ICC, the High Commissioner for Human Rights, the Secretary-General, and a range of thematic Special Representatives of the Secretary-General ('SRSGs')/ Special Advisers (for example, SRSGs on Sexual Violence in Conflict, Children in Armed Conflict, Special Advisers on the Prevention of Genocide and the Responsibility to Protect), other UN agencies, UN Country Teams, peace missions and other field presences. This is not to suggest that the international human rights response system is the only actor—given the important contribution of national actors, regional actors, and national and international civil society. It is rather to note that the international human rights response system is more extensive than the Geneva-based bodies. The number of actors and institutions brings with it opportunities, but also challenges. Key amongst them, is how best to ensure coordination and coherence in responses to a given situation. In particular, how does one ensure that the specialised human rights perspective is heard within political decision-making processes in New York, including in the Security Council?

Secondly, the deterioration of the human rights situation, and the outbreak of conflict in contexts such as Libya and Syria, highlights the need for the system to be able to better target responses to situations before they reach a breaking point. Might the specialist human rights system be able to do more

---

97   UN Doc S/2014/348 (22 May 2014).

98   See Annemarie Devereux, 'Accountability for Violations in Syria: Reasons for Hope' (2019) 25 (3) *Australian Journal of Human Rights* 391.

99   SC Res 2043, UN Doc S/RES/2043 (2012) (21 April 2012). This resolution was introduced into the Security Council by the Russian Federation.

in relation to deteriorating human rights situations? How can human rights be more effectively integrated into conflict de-escalation activities of the UN given both the significance of human rights for predicting the outbreak of conflict, and the impact of conflict on human rights? What are the implications for the already stretched funding for human rights related activities and interventions?

Thirdly, despite both situations involving the ongoing commission of egregious violations of human rights, it was only in the case of Libya that the Security Council was prepared to act expeditiously, condemn the violations, refer the situation to the ICC and take enforcement action under Chapter VII of the *Charter*. In the case of Syria, a political impasse blocked effective action. Certainly, the experience of NATO's intervention in Libya in 2011 caused some states to be hesitant about any decision that might move the Security Council closer to military intervention in Syria.[100] The level of intervention in Libya thus seems exceptional rather than the norm, used only where the regime in question has become isolated from all major powers and there is regional support for intervention. A level of unpredictability may be expected in the Security Council given the ability of the five permanent members ('P5') to use the veto to defeat substantive motions. This still begs the question whether there might be procedural reforms that would force a greater discipline or transparency in relation to key Security Council decisions.

Particularly in the case of Syria, there was a vast gap between the attitude of the UN's specialised human rights bodies and the Security Council. This is evident when contrasting calls by the ICOI-Syria, the Human Rights Council and the High Commissioner for Human Rights, with the relative silence of the Security Council. Whilst political factors may have been the predominant reason for this gap, it is relevant to ask whether the institutional separation of human rights from the peace and security machinery may also have played a contributory role. Are there ways of bringing the institutions closer together with a view to more closely integrating human rights perspectives into Security Council deliberations? Despite human rights being the 'third pillar' of the UN,[101] and the multitude of statements concerning the centrality of human rights to both peace and security and development, ensuring the human rights voice(s) is heard and integrated in key decision-making processes remains a challenge. The stumbling blocks might be conceptual, with resistance to consideration of human rights topics outside the specialist machinery in

---

100   Garwood-Gowers (n 84).

101   Peace and security, development, and human rights are commonly referred to as the 3 pillars of the United Nations.

Geneva. They might also include practical impediments, including the impact of the geographic divide between bodies focused on human rights (which are largely Geneva-based) and those focused on peace and security (which are largely New York-based). Specific outcomes in the Security Council are likely to remain somewhat unpredictable given its inherently political nature, and the ability of P5 states to exercise their veto to prevent action, even action otherwise supported by a majority of states. Yet, might there be additional means of harnessing political energies for better human rights outcomes? How might a more principled approach to action (such as referrals to the ICC or imposition of sanctions) be encouraged? How could there be more follow-up in relation to recommendations of relevant bodies including maximising the contribution of ICOIs?

4   Some Suggestions for Reform and Renewal

Fears of a generalised backlash against global law and institutions may tend to prompt a siege-like defensive mentality, curbing enthusiasm for openly critiquing current operations and sapping energy for pursuing longer-term reform. However, once current debates are placed in their historical perspective (as Part 2 has attempted), the threat level associated with current debates can be lowered. Attention can then be given to more profound challenges facing the system.

Part 3 of this article highlighted some key limitations in the international human rights system's ability to prevent and respond to mass violations of rights. Responding to such underlying weaknesses is critical for the system to maintain (and in some quarters, restore) credibility. Many of the weaknesses identified are structural in nature. The international human rights system remains somewhat quarantined from other parts of the international legal system. Compounding the situation has been a tendency to consider issues of reform in a siloed fashion (for example, tackling treaty body reform, Human Rights Council reform, and Security Council reform discretely) rather than taking a systems-wide approach. Reform proposals must look at both the operation of the component parts of the specialised international human rights system *and* the overall human rights protection system. In particular, it is necessary to examine how the differing parts of the protection system interact and influence each other. Any reforms need to be considered not purely as ends in themselves (in terms of increasing the efficiency of the system), but as a means of increasing effectiveness and coherence. Ultimately, the aim must be to maximise the prospects of the international system improving the human rights situation on the ground. Given longstanding simmering tensions around issues of oversight and accountability noted in Part 2, pursuing reform is not an easy task. It is likely that debates over conciliatory versus accountability-driven approaches will continue to feature prominently in any discussion of holistic human rights reform (as occurred in relation to the MBC resolution discussed above). However, seeking reform is neither impossible nor unprecedented.

As noted in Part 2, significant advances have been made by the international human rights system amidst periods of acute international tensions. The broader role for the Commission on Human Rights to consider individual country situations and indeed the adoption of the twin Covenants (the *ICCPR* and the *International Covenant on Economic, Social and Cultural Rights* ('*ICESCR*')), occurred during the Cold War. Opportunities can also arise out of periods of tension. There has been some discussion of the United States, for example, expanding its engagement on human rights matters with other UN bodies including the Security Council, as a result of its withdrawal from the Human Rights Council.[102] Rather than bunkering down into a defensive position, it is important to recognise the resilience of the existing system and persist with efforts to strengthen its coherence and effectiveness.

To be successful, reform proposals will require the backing of a strong alliance of states and leading human rights NGOs. Historically, incremental change, rather than wholescale change, has tended to be the norm. Procedural reforms are likely to have a greater chance of success than substantive alteration of organs' functions or any perceived diminution in the power or discretion afforded to political bodies such as the Security Council. In the belief that advances can and have been made by the system notwithstanding tensions, this article concludes by selecting four areas that warrant particular attention in any substantive review of the human rights response system.[103] In undertaking any reform, it will, of course, be important for the chronic under-funding of UN human rights activities to be addressed,[104] and for any new initiatives to be properly resourced.

---

102 See Blanchfield (n 13) 10.

103 UN human rights system reform has been the subject of much academic and practitioner reflection, going back decades: see, eg, Philip Alston (ed), *The United Nations and Human Rights: A Critical Appraisal* (Clarendon, 1992); Anne F Bayefsky (ed), *The Human Rights System in the 21st Century* (Kluwer, 2000). In more recent years, much of the reform literature has focused on specific aspects of the system: eg the treaty monitoring bodies, or the Human Rights Council. Given space constraints in this article, the decision has been made to identify four areas of reform that might warrant particular attention, giving particular priority to reforms that may have an institutional intersectional effect.

104 As to the underfunding of UN human rights activities: see, eg, OHCHR, *United Nations Human Rights Report 2018* (Report, 2018). This Report highlights that of the 51.7% of total

4.1 Increasing the Preventive Function of the Human Rights System

Additional ways could be explored for specialised human rights mechanisms to engage more rapidly and effectively to emerging situations of mass violations. This entails having accurate information about such emerging situations (including situations of serious endemic violations) and ensuring that the response is timely and constructive. There are of course a range of existing mechanisms designed to respond to critical human rights situations (such as ICOIs and responses by field missions), but the case study presented in Part 3 suggests that these mechanisms need to be bolstered. Some innovations in this field that might be considered include:

– Having the Human Rights Council establish a Special Rapporteur on Critical Human Rights Situations, and/or having the High Commissioner for Human Rights maintain a list of countries experiencing critical human rights situations. Linked to this might be specific additional funding that might be made available for a range of purposes such as rapid deployment visits by the Special Rapporteur (with other mechanisms as relevant and OHCHR), and/or rapid technical assistance/capacity building projects that could be deployed.
– Expanding the functions of the High Commissioner for Human Rights and/ or the President of the Human Rights Council in relation to critical country situations.

4.2 Increasing the Follow-Up in Relation to Specialised Investigations of Mass Violations

In order to develop appropriate responses (at both the national and international levels), it is necessary for actors to understand the scope of violations that have occurred and the contributory factors. It is also vital to identify what steps need to be taken to bring an end to the violations, prevent their recurrence, and provide remedies to affected victims. Specialised investigations such as ICOIs have come to play an important role in providing further clarity on these issues (as in the case of the ICOIs for Libya and Syria discussed above).[105]

---

regular budget funding directed to the 3 pillars of the UN, only 7.7% is allocated to the human rights pillar: at 73.

105   For an overview of the various roles of ICOIs, see Patrick Butchard and Christian Henderson, 'A Functional Typology of Commissions of Inquiry' in Christian Henderson (ed), *Commissions of Inquiry: Problems and Prospects* (Hart Publishing, Oxford, 2017) 11, 11–34. As to the limited empirical research, though, on the impact of ICOIs, see Michael Becker and Sarah Nouwen, 'International Commissions of Inquiry: What Difference Do They Make? Taking an Empirical Approach' (2019) 30(3) *European Journal of International Law* 819.

Yet, despite the impressive work being undertaken by ICOIs and other fact-finding bodies, getting actors to focus on the findings of such investigations and commit to implementing recommendations within their respective fields of operation remains a major challenge. At the international level, some additional steps that might be taken to encourage such follow-up include:

- For bodies mandating ICOIs[106] to routinely establish specific follow-up procedures to monitor implementation of ICOIs. This might include, for instance, requesting states and other actors involved (including international bodies) to report back within a set period on their response to recommendations and progress in implementing ICOI recommendations.
- Encouraging the Security Council to routinely offer the heads of ICOIs/FFMs the opportunity to formally address it when that country situation is being considered.

4.3 Further Integrating the Specialised International Human Rights Machinery with Other UN Institutions/Organs Involved in Human Rights-Related Responses

Despite the strong level of rhetorical support for the integration of human rights into all activities of the UN and the oft-repeated relevance of human rights to the other two pillars of the UN (peace and security and development), too frequently attempts are made to confine human rights discussions to the specialised machinery in Geneva.[107] The geographical divide between the human rights machinery in Geneva and the broader protection systems (primarily in New York) compound the separation of issues and hinder

---

106   ICOIs and other fact-finding procedures have been established by a variety of bodies including the General Assembly, Security Council, Human Rights Council, Secretary-General and High Commissioner for Human Rights. See Annemarie Devereux, 'Investigating Violations of International Human Rights Law and International Humanitarian Law through an International Commission of Inquiry: Libya and Beyond' in David W Lovell (ed), *Investigating Operational Incidents in a Military Context: Law, Justice, Politics* (Brill, 2015) 99, 101.

107   See Garwood-Gowers (n 84). As to expressions of differing views as to whether human rights issues are appropriately discussed in the Security Council, see the Security Council's first thematic discussion on the topic of human rights and the prevention of armed conflict: UN Doc S/PV.7926 (18 April 2017). Note the contrasting views, for instance, of the US who encouraged the Security Council to be prepared to engage 'early and often' in relation to widespread violations, and the Russian Federation who cautioned that the Security Council could not be transformed into a forum for discussing human rights. Several delegations expressed concern that human rights might be used as a means to exert power over other countries (Russian Federation) or as a 'back door' to interfere in sovereign state affairs (eg Egypt). For a good analysis of the Security Council's 'evolving' relationship with human rights, see Security Council Report, *Human Rights in the Security Council: An Evolving Role* (Research Report, 25 January 2016).

having effective and coherent responses to mass violations. Some potential reforms in this area to encourage greater integration include:

- Encouraging the Security Council to give a standing invitation to the High Commissioner for Human Rights to address the Security Council.[108]
- Making the Human Rights Council an organ of the UN (rather than a subsidiary body of the General Assembly) to boost its status within the system.[109]
- Having the Security Council establish a Human Rights and Peace and Security Working Group to consider the intersection of human rights and threats to international peace and security. Such a Working Group could then be tasked with, for example, developing further modalities with regards to human rights-related sanctions regimes, or develop criteria for referrals to the ICC (see further under (4.4) below) or undertake other relevant policy work.[110]
- Supporting a more explicit human rights response element of conflict de-escalation activities carried out by the UN and increasing the visibility of human rights concerns in such activities (for example, increasing human rights expertise amongst UN Mediators).

4.4 Undertaking Procedural Reform at the Security Council Level to Encourage Greater Transparency and Disciplined Analysis

Given the Security Council's dismal record in embracing substantive reform,[111] a more productive route may be to identify relatively modest procedural changes. In the key area of Security Council referrals to the ICC, for instance,

---

108 Whilst the High Commissioner has been invited to address the Security Council on many occasions, there is no right of address for the High Commissioner (see n 92 for variable practice in this regard) nor for other mandate holders such as Special Rapporteurs of the Human Rights Council: see Bardo Fassbender, 'The Role for Human Rights in the Decision-Making Process of the Security Council', in Bardo Fassbender (ed), *Securing Human Rights? Achievements and Challenges of the UN Security Council* (Oxford University Press, 2011) 74, 95–6.

109 The status of the Human Rights Council was considered in the context of the review of the Council in 2011. The decision taken was to maintain the Human Rights Council as a subsidiary body of the GA for the present time, with the question of the status of the body to be revisited at some point between 2021–2026: see GA Res 65/281, UN Doc A/RES/65/281 (20 July 2011, adopted 17 June 2011) para 3. Bardo Fassbender has noted how 'status' issues also impact on who is invited to address the Security Council: Fassbender (n 108) 95–6.

110 An example of the type of policy work that might be taken by such a group is how the topic of reparations for victims of human rights violations might be further integrated into the work of the Security Council.

111 An example is the the failure of previous reform efforts aimed at increasing the membership of the Security Council: see for instance, Alischa Kugel, 'Reform of the Security Council—A New Agenda' (FES Briefing Paper, 2009).

introducing more defined systems of analysis preceding decision-making offers the potential to encourage more consistent decision-making. By making the process more transparent, there would also be greater pressure on states (including the P5) to make more consistent, reasoned decisions in line with human rights principles, including the importance of accountability. There can, of course, be no certainty of outcomes. The Security Council will remain a political body. However, one can hope for a more detailed discussion of the relevant factors, and thus greater integration of human rights consider-ations into the decision-making process.[112] Particular reforms that might be pursued include:

- Having the Security Council, either through a Human Rights and Peace and Security Working Group or a more narrowly focused ICC group, develop cri-teria to be considered in relation to requests to refer a country situation to the ICC.
- Having the specialised Working Group also be empowered to undertake a preliminary analysis of requests made and provide a report to the Security Council.

5   Conclusion

This article has argued that, rather than facing an unprecedented backlash, the international human rights system continues to operate and evolve not-withstanding simmering tensions around issues of international oversight and accountability. Events such as the United States' withdrawal from the Human Rights Council and China's advocacy for greater recognition of 'mutu-ally beneficial cooperation', have created sharp debates in and around the Human Rights Council. However, to focus solely on such recent events under-estimates the overall operation of the system globally, and the way in which reform has occurred notwithstanding significant tensions. It also risks divert-ing attention away from broader challenges. One of these key challenges is to reform and renew the international human rights system to ensure a holistic response to mass human rights violations. Through its case-study of responses

---

112   For a similar argument in relation to achieving greater respect for rule of law principles in the Security Council, see Marie-Eve Loiselle, 'The Penholder System and the Rule of Law in the Security Council Decision Making: Setback or Improvement?' (2020) 33(1) *Leiden Journal of International Law* 139, 141; Joanna Harrington, 'Use of Force, Rule-of-Law Restraints and Process: Unfinished Business for the Responsibility to Protect Concept' in Jeremy Farrall and Hilary Charlesworth (eds), *Strengthening the Rule of Law through the UN Security Council* (Routledge, 2016) 224.

to Libya and Syria, this article has highlighted the desirability of strengthening the preventive function of the UN human rights machinery and increasing the integration of the broader international human rights response system. Whilst divergent attitudes of states on issues of enforcement are likely to bedevil discussions, creative procedural reforms offer particular potential for improving the effectiveness and coherence of the current system.

Backlashes against International Commitments and Organisations: Asylum as Restorative Justice

Kate Ogg *

1 Introduction[1]

After the 1948 Arab-Israeli conflict, the international community, through two United Nations General Assembly ('UNGA') resolutions, pledged to provide protection and assistance to displaced Palestinians.[2] That commitment is a continuing one as evidenced by the UNGA repeatedly renewing and expanding the mandate of the organisation that today provides this care: the United Nations Relief and Works Agency for Palestinian Refugees in the Near East ('UNRWA').[3] However, since 2015 UNRWA has been facing significant financial difficulties.[4] This was exacerbated by the United States' ('US') July 2018 decision to cut $300 million in funding to UNRWA (the largest reduction in funding

---

* Senior Lecturer, ANU College of Law.

1 Kate would like to thank Sam Rutherford for his invaluable research assistance. Thank you also to Associate Professor Jolyon Ford and the anonymous reviewer for feedback on earlier versions of this article.

2 *Palestine—Progress Report of the United Nations Mediator*, GA Res 194(III), UN Doc A/RES/194(III) (11 December 1948) ('GA Res 194(III)'); *Assistance to Palestine Refugees*, GA Res 302(IV), UN Doc A/RES/302(IV) (8 December 1949) ('GA Res 302(IV)'). These two resolutions established the United Nations Conciliation Commission for Palestine ('UNCCP') and the United Nations Relief and Works Agency for Palestinian Refugees in the Near East ('UNRWA') respectively. Part 2 of this article outlines their protection and assistance mandates.

3 UNRWA's mandate is renewed every three years: UNRWA, 'Immense Support for the Renewal of the UNRWA Mandate at the UN General Assembly' (Press Release, 16 December 2019) <https://www.unrwa.org/newsroom/press-releases/immense-support-renewal-unrwa-mandate-un-general-assembly>.

4 See, eg, Nisreen El-Shamayleh, 'UNRWA Funds Crisis Worries Palestinian Refugees', *Al Jazeera* (online, 6 August 2015) <http://www.aljazeera.com/blogs/middleeast/2015/08/unrwa-funds-crisis-worries-palestinian-refugees-150805155300792.html>; UNRWA, 'Lack of Funds Forces UNRWA to Suspend Cash Assistance for Housing for Palestinian Refugees from Syria in Lebanon' (Press Release, 22 May 2015) <https://www.unrwa.org/newsroom/press-releases/lack-funds-forces-unrwa-suspend-cash-assistance-housing-palestine-refugees>. See also *AD (Palestine)* [2015] NZIPT 800693–695 [168]–[172] ('*AD (Palestine)*'), a case in which the New Zealand and Immigration Protection Tribunal reviewed evidence of UNRWA's financial stress.

UNRWA has faced).[5] As a result of these funding cuts, UNRWA was forced to discontinue food assistance programs, community mental health programs and mobile health clinics.[6] In August 2018, the US announced that it would no longer fund UNRWA at all.[7] UNRWA's Commissioner-General described the decision as a 'radical departure from almost 7 decades of genuine—if at times critical—US support to our Agency'.[8] The US had traditionally been UNRWA's largest donor, supplying approximately one third of UNRWA's budget.[9]

In this article, I examine this backlash from the perspectives of those most affected: the people living under the care of an international organisation struggling to carry out its protection and assistance mandate where key support has been withdrawn altogether. In particular, I use Palestinian refugees as a case study to explore the normative grounds on which a person can seek asylum in circumstances where the international community has broken a promise to provide for his or her protection in situ. This question opens unexplored issues in debates on forced migration. Existing discussions of who should have a special claim to international protection do not encompass circumstances where the international community has committed to protect a community but resiled from these promises. While my focus is on Palestinian refugees, other protection and displacement situations share similar dynamics.

In the first section of this article, I discuss the protection and assistance regime created by the UNGA for displaced Palestinians. I then explain why UNRWA's current financial stress and some Palestinians' choice to leave an UNRWA region can be considered within a backlash framework. Next, I highlight that existing normative theories of forced migration do not accommodate the legal and moral complexities inherent in the decision some Palestinians make to leave an UNRWA area of operation and seek protection elsewhere. I propose that restorative justice theories, and specifically feminist restorative justice theories, provide a more appropriate normative base to conceptualise

---

5   UNRWA, 'Statement by UNRWA Spokesperson Sami Mshasha on Implications of Funding Shortfall on Emergency Services in the OPT' (Official Statement, 26 July 2018) <https://www.unrwa.org/newsroom/official-statements/statement-unrwa-spokesperson-sami-mshasha-implications-funding>.

6   Ibid.

7   UNRWA, 'Open Letter from UNRWA Commissioner-General to Palestine Refugees and UNRWA staff' (Official Statement, 1 September 2018) <https://www.unrwa.org/newsroom/official-statements/open-letter-unrwa-commissioner-general-palestine-refugees-and-unrwa>.

8   Ibid.

9   Christian Saunders, 'Acting UNRWA Commissioner-General Saunders Outlines 2020 Plans to Support Palestinian Refugees' (Speech, Geneva, 31 January 2020) <https://www.un.org/unispal/document/in-annual-speech-in-geneva-acting-unrwa-commissioner-general-saunders-outlines-2020-plans-to-support-palestine-refugees/>.

international journeys made in the wake of these backlashes. While the application of this analysis beyond Palestinian refugees is outside this article's scope, I conclude by briefly considering the extent to which these ideas could be applied to other persons and communities in need of protection.

2   United Nations Protection and Assistance for Palestinian Refugees

Palestinian refugees were specifically excluded from the *Convention Relating to the Status of Refugees* ('*Refugee Convention*'),[10] *Convention Relating to the Status of Stateless Persons*,[11] and the *Statute of the Office of the United Nations High Commissioner for Refugees* ('*UNHCR Statute*')[12] when these instruments were drafted. There are divided opinions as to why this occurred. Akram argues that Palestinians 'were excluded from the various instruments because their case was deemed unique and of such particular concern that the UN established a separate and special protection regime for them'.[13] One reason why the 'international community decided that this particular refugee crisis warranted special measures' was that 'the UN body itself bore heavy responsibility for their plight'.[14] Hathaway and Foster instead argue that Western states were motivated more by the fact that they did not want to open their doors to a large group of Arab refugees, and Arab states, while prepared to temporarily host Palestinian refugees, ultimately wanted them to be repatriated.[15] There is also disagreement as to whether Palestinian refugees remain excluded from the *Refugee Convention*.[16]

---

10   *Convention Relating to the Status of Refugees*, opened for signature 28 July 1951, 189 UNTS 150 (entered into force 22 April 1954) art 1D, as amended by *Protocol Relating to the Status of Refugees*, opened for signature 31 January 1967, 606 UNTS 267 (entered into force 4 October 1967) ('*Refugee Convention*').

11   *Convention Relating to the Status of Stateless Persons*, opened for signature 28 September 1954, 360 UNTS 117 (entered into force 6 June 1960) art 2(i) ('*1954 Statelessness Convention*').

12   *Statute of the Office of the United Nations High Commissioner for Refugees*, GA Res 428(V), UN Doc A/RES/428(V) (adopted 14 December 1950) art 7(c).

13   Susan Akram, 'Palestinian Refugees and their Legal Status: Rights, Politics, and Implications for a Just Solution' (2002) 31(3) *Journal of Palestine Studies* 36, 40.

14   Ibid. See also Guy Goodwin-Gill and Susan Akram, 'Brief *Amicus Curiae* on the Status of Palestinian Refugees under International Law' (2000) 11 *Palestine Yearbook of International Law* 187, 250–1.

15   James Hathaway and Michelle Foster, *The Law of Refugee Status* (Cambridge University Press, 2nd ed, 2014) 512.

16   See, eg, Guy Goodwin-Gill and Jane McAdam, *The Refugee in International Law* (Oxford University Press, 3rd ed, 2007) 156–61; Hathaway and Foster (n 15) 513–21; Mutaz Qafisheh and Valentina Azarova, 'Article 1 D' in Andreas Zimmermann, Felix Machts and Jonas

While these debates continue, what is relevant for this article is that the international community has always treated Palestinian refugees as a distinct refugee group in need of different protection arrangements. In 1948, the UNGA established the United Nations Conciliation Commission for Palestine ('UNCCP').[17] Its mandate included assisting the relevant governments and authorities in achieving a final settlement in relation to Palestinian refugees,[18] as well as assisting the refugees themselves to return to their homes or seek compensation for property loss or damage.[19] The UNCCP still exists and reports annually to the UNGA but has been inactive since the mid-1960s.[20] The UNGA established UNRWA in 1949 with a mandate to carry out direct relief and works programs for Palestinian refugees.[21] The UNGA renews UNRWA's mandate every three years.

At the time the UNCCP and UNRWA were created, it was understood that the UNCCP had a protection mandate and UNRWA's mandate was limited to humanitarian assistance.[22] There is disagreement as to whether UNRWA's mandate has subsequently developed and now extends to protection activities. Akram argues that UNRWA's 'protection function is virtually non-existent'.[23] This has created a protection gap whereby displaced Palestinians and their descendants are left without 'even the minimal protections afforded all other refugees under the international burden-sharing system'.[24] However, other scholars argue that this view is not tenable in light of the UNCCP becoming inactive and UNRWA's mandate expanding to include individualised protection activity.[25]

Dörschner (eds), *The 1951 Convention Relating to the Status of Refugees and its 1967 Protocol: A Commentary* (Oxford University Press, 2011); United Nations High Commissioner for Refugees ('UNHCR'), *Guidelines on International Protection No 13: Applicability of Article 1D of the 1951 Convention Relating to the Status of Refugees to Palestinian Refugees*, UN Doc HCR/GIP/17/13 (December 2017).

17   GA Res 194(III), UN Doc A/RES/194(III) (n 2).

18   Ibid para 6.

19   Ibid para 11.

20   Terry Rempel, 'From Beneficiary to Stakeholder: An Overview of UNRWA's approach to Refugee Participation' in Sari Hanafi, Leila Hilal and Lex Takkenberg (eds), *UNRWA and Palestinian Refugees: From Relief Works to Human Development* (Routledge, 2014) 145.

21   GA Res 302(IV), UN Doc A/RES/302(IV) (n 2) para 7.

22   Akram (n 13) 38–9.

23   Ibid 43. See also Goodwin-Gill and Akram (n 14) 192–201 for arguments as to why 'UNRWA's mandate never envisioned a protection role'.

24   Akram (n 13) 42.

25   Lance Bartholomeusz, 'The Mandate of UNRWA at Sixty' (2009) 28(2–3) *Refugee Survey Quarterly* 452, 466; Scott Custer, 'United Nations Relief and Works Agency for Palestine Refugees in the Near East (UNRWA): Protection and Assistance to Palestine Refugees' in Susan Akram et al (eds) *International Law and the Israeli—Palestinian Conflict: A*

The Chief of UNRWA's Department of Legal Affairs insists that UNRWA 'has a very clear mandate for protection'.[26] The first UNGA resolution to specifically use the word 'protection' was Resolution 37/120 of 1982, which urges UNRWA to both protect and provide assistance to Palestinian refugees.[27] The UNGA has resolved that UNRWA should 'undertake effective measures to guarantee the safety and security and the legal and human rights of the Palestine refugees in the occupied territories'.[28] UNRWA also provides primary and secondary education to Palestinian refugees.[29] UNRWA's mandate also extends to addressing the needs and rights of children, women and people with disabilities,[30] in accordance with the *Convention on the Rights of the Child*,[31] the *Convention on the Elimination of All Forms of Discrimination against Women*,[32] and the *Convention on the Rights of Persons with Disabilities*.[33] Further, UNRWA also has

---

Rights-Based Approach to Middle East Peace (Routledge, 2011) 45; Hathaway and Foster (n 15) 520; Michael Kagan, 'Is there Really a Protection Gap? UNRWA's Role Vis-à-Vis Palestinian Refugees' (2009) 28(2–3) *Refugee Survey Quarterly* 511, 518; Qafisheh and Azarova (n 16) [13]; Lex Takkenberg, *The Status of Palestinian Refugees in International Law* (Oxford University Press, 1998) 301.

26   Bartholomeusz (n 25) 466.

27   GA Res A/37/120, UN Doc A/RES/37/120 (adopted 16 December 1982) ss J–K ('GA Res A/37/120'); Qafisheh and Azarova (n 16) [13].

28   GA Res A/37/120, UN Doc A/RES/37/120 (n 27) s J para 1.

29   UNRWA, *What We Do: Education* (Web Page) <https://www.unrwa.org/what-we-do/education>.

30   *Operations of the United Nations Relief and Works Agency for Palestine Refugees in the Near East*, GA Res 59/119, UN GAOR, 59th sess, 71st plen mtg, Agenda Item 75, UN Doc A/RES/59/119 (15 December 2004, adopted 10 December 2004) para 7; *Operations of the United Nations Relief and Works Agency for Palestine Refugees in the Near East*, GA Res 62/104, GAOR, 62nd sess, 75th plen mtg, Agenda Item 32, UN Doc A/RES/62/104 (10 January 2008, adopted 17 December 2007) para 8; *Operations of the United Nations Relief and Works Agency for Palestine Refugees in the Near East*, GA Res 63/93, GAOR, 63rd sess, 64th plen mtg, Agenda Item 29, UN Doc A/RES/63/93 (18 December 2008, adopted 5 December 2008) para 9; *Operations of the United Nations Relief and Works Agency for Palestine Refugees in the Near East*, GA Res 69/88, GAOR, 69th sess, 64th plen mtg, Agenda Item 50, UN Doc A/RES/69/88 (16 December 2014, adopted 5 December 2014) para 14. For discussion of this aspect of UNRWA's mandate see Bartholomeusz (n 25) 466–7.

31   *Convention on the Rights of the Child*, opened for signature 20 November 1989, 1577 UNTS 3 (entered into force 2 September 1990).

32   *Convention on the Elimination of All Forms of Discrimination against Women*, opened for signature 18 December 1979, 1249 UNTS 13 (entered into force 3 September 1981).

33   *Convention on the Rights of Persons with Disabilities*, opened for signature 13 December 2006, 2515 UNTS 3 (entered into force 3 May 2008).

a human development mandate that includes the 'provision of services for the well-being and human development of the Palestine refugees'.[34]

Reflecting on this expanded mandate, Kagan and Morris suggest that UNRWA's role is analogous to a domestic government's responsibilities with respect to access to education, health care and social welfare.[35] Concerning UNRWA's responsibility for individualised human rights protection, Kagan suggests that it extends to, for example, ensuring victims of domestic violence have access to shelters and providing special assistance to unaccompanied or orphaned children, or children who have experienced abuse or neglect.[36] That these types of rights protections are included in the mandate of an international organisation disrupts one of the foundational principles of international human rights law—that it is nation-states that are responsible for human rights protections. Kagan describes it as a 'state-to-UN responsibility shift'.[37] This does not mean that the states in which Palestinian refugees reside are not responsible for human rights protection. Palestinian refugees are still entitled to the human rights protection of the state in whose territory they are in or whose jurisdiction they are subject to. The extent of this rights protection will depend upon the treaties that state has ratified, any reservations made and the development of customary human rights law. What the 'state-to-UN responsibility shift' indicates is that the international community recognises that displaced Palestinians need a special and additional form of protection and that UNRWA is the international organisation best placed to carry this out.

UNRWA is funded by the United Nations ('UN') and UN member states. For many years, UNRWA has been facing a financial crisis that has hampered its ability to carry out its protection and assistance mandate. One-third of Palestinian refugees in Gaza live in extreme poverty.[38] Many Palestinian refugee camps

---

34 *Assistance to Palestine Refugees*, GA Res 63/91, GAOR, 63rd sess, 64th plen mtg, Agenda Item 29, UN Doc A/RES/63/91 (18 December 2008, adopted 5 December 2008) para 3; *Assistance to Palestine Refugees*, GA Res 62/102, GAOR, 62nd sess, 75th plen mtg, Agenda Item 32, UN Doc A/Res/62/102 (10 January 2008, adopted 17 December 2007) para 3. For discussion of this aspect of UNRWA's mandate see Bartholomeusz (n 25) 464–5.

35 Kagan (n 25) 524; Nicholas Morris, 'What Protection Means for UNRWA in Concept and Practice' (Report, UNRWA, 31 March 2018) [4.6] <https://www.unrwa.org/user files/20100118155412.pdf>.

36 Kagan (n 25) 524.

37 Ibid.

38 United Nations Children's Fund ('UNICEF'), *The Situation of Palestinian Children in the Occupied Palestinian Territory, Jordan, Syria and Lebanon: An Assessment Based on the Convention on the Rights of the Child* (Report, 2010) <https://www.unicef.org/oPt/ PALESTINIAN_SITAN-final.pdf>.

resemble slum conditions,[39] are overcrowded and lack adequate infrastructure and sanitation,[40] and residents experience high levels of violence,[41] including domestic violence.[42] Many Palestinian refugees do not have access to adequate healthcare.[43] Availability of work and education vary,[44] but many Palestinian refugees feel that they have no future because of a dearth of study and employment opportunities.[45] In 2015, UNRWA faced its 'most serious financial crisis ever' and was 'expected to run out of funding by September 2015'.[46] At the time, it had to consider whether it could continue to run schools for Palestinian children.[47] The US decision in 2018 to significantly reduce and then withdraw funding exacerbated UNRWA's existing financial difficulties. In response to the US funding cuts, the European Union, Germany, Ireland and Jordan promised to increase funding to UNRWA.[48] However, this additional funding eventually waned and in 2019, UNRWA had a USD55 million shortfall and reported that it was facing the 'worst financial crisis in its history'.[49] Complicating this picture is that in 2019 some states suspended funding in reaction to an UNRWA corruption scandal.[50]

---

39   JE Zabaneh, GC Watt and CA O'Donnell, 'Living and Health Conditions of Palestinian Refugees in an Unofficial Camp in the Lebanon: A Cross-Sectional Survey' (2008) 62(2) *Journal of Epidemiology & Community Health* 91, 95.

40   Henri Rueff and Alain Viaro, 'Palestinian Refugee Camps: From Shelter to Habitat' (2009) 28(2–3) *Refugee Survey Quarterly* 339, 359.

41   UNRWA, *Jenin Camp* (Web Page) <https://www.unrwa.org/where-we-work/west-bank/jenin-camp>.

42   UNICEF (n 38).

43   Ibid; UNHCR, *The Situation of Palestinian Refugees in Lebanon* (Report, February 2016) <http://www.refworld.org/pdfid/56cc95484.pdf>.

44   Akram (n 13) 44–5.

45   Clancy Chassay and Duncan Campbell, 'We Have No Rights and No Future', *The Guardian* (online, 30 May 2007) <https://www.theguardian.com/world/2007/may/29/syria.israel andthepalestinians>; UNHCR (n 43); UNICEF (n 38).

46   *AD (Palestine)* (n 4) [223].

47   El-Shamayleh (n 4).

48   'Donors to Increase UNRWA Support and Funding Despite US Cuts', *Al Jazeera* (online, 2 September 2018), <https://www.aljazeera.com/news/2018/09/donors-increase-palestine -refugee-agency-funding-cuts-180902085540064.html>.

49   Lisa Schlein, 'UN Warns Stability and Protection of Palestinian Refugees Threatened by Trump Peace Plan', *Voice of America* (online, 31 January 2020) <https://www.voanews .com/middle-east/un-warns-stability-and-protection-palestinian-refugees-threatened -trump-peace-plan>.

50   UN Watch, *UNRWA Corruption Scandal Fact Sheet* (Web Page, 11 September 2019) <https://unwatch.org/unrwa-ethics-scandal-fact-sheet/>.

3   Backlashes, Actors and Consequences

Many scholars opine that the term "backlash" is being used too liberally to encompass ordinary forms of dissent or protest.[51] To limit the boundaries of what can be classified as a backlash, some adopt Sunstein's definition originally developed in his analysis of opposition to judgments of the US Supreme Court: an '[i]ntense and sustained public disapproval of a ... [system], accompanied by aggressive steps to resist that ... [system] and to remove its legal force'.[52] UNRWA's financial situation is complex but the US decisions to significantly reduce and then cease all funding to UNRWA comes within this narrow and extreme understanding of a backlash. However, as noted above, the US's actions heightened an existing financial crisis and mismatch between what UN member states expect UNRWA to do and the funding they provide. This exposes some of the dangers of focusing on dramatic moments of backlash and ignoring the more subtle and incremental ways states backslide from international commitments. More generally, Charlesworth highlights the tendency of international law practitioners and scholars to fixate on moments of crisis and how this draws attention away from every day and ongoing violations of international law.[53] Rather than proposing a broader definition of the term backlash, the analysis in this article insists that instances of 'aggressive' resistance to the international order, such as US decisions to defund UNRWA, be analysed in conjunction with less sensational tactics states employ to undermine particular international law obligations.

The reason for adopting this larger viewpoint is that in this article I consider the consequences of pushbacks against international law on natural persons and how the choices they make in response have the capacity to transform aspects of the international legal order. Scholarship addresses the consequences of a backlash against international law for states, institutions and

---

51   David Caron and Esmé Shirlow, 'Dissecting Backlash: The Unarticulated Causes of Backlash and its Unintended Consequences' in Andreas Follesdal and Geir Ulfstein (eds), *The Judicilization of International Law: A Mixed Blessing?* (Oxford University Press, 2018) 159, 160; Mikael Rask Madsen, Pola Cebulak and Micha Wiebusch, 'Backlash against International Courts: Explaining the Forms and Patterns of Resistance to International Courts' (2018) 14(2) *International Journal of Law in Context* 197, 198.

52   Cass R Sunstein, 'Backlash's Travels' (2007) 42(2) *Harvard Civil Rights—Civil Liberties Law Review* 435, 435. This definition is the one adopted by Peter G Danchin et al, 'Navigating the Backlash against Global Law and Institutions' (2020) 38 *Australian Year Book of International Law* 33, 37 and by Caron and Shirlow (n 51) 160.

53   Hilary Charlesworth, 'International Law: A Discipline of Crisis' (2002) 65(3) *Modern Law Review* 377.

advocates[54]—but there is no examination of the repercussions for the ordinary people most affected. When writing on backlashes against international law and institutions, it is important to focus not just on how international actors do and should react but also on the decisions natural persons make in response. In doing so, it is often impossible to divorce the effects of dramatic moments of pushback from more subtle ones. In addition, the remedy available to natural persons may not be one that directly responds to the perpetrator of the 'aggressive' backlash. This is evident in the positions faced by many Palestinian refugees. Most will choose to stay in the UNRWA region (Gaza, Jordan, Lebanon, Syria, the Gaza strip, East Jerusalem or the West Bank) despite the difficulties imposed by UNRWA's continuing financial stress. However, some will make the difficult choice to leave their homes and communities to seek the basic protection and assistance they are being denied. Cross-border travel is particularly difficult for Palestinian refugees, many of whom are stateless,[55] but some have travelled to and sought protection in states such as Australia, New Zealand, the United Kingdom, Hungary and Belgium.[56]

There is already scholarship on how international law, and in particular the *Refugee Convention*, responds to Palestinians seeking protection elsewhere.[57] An unexplored issue is the normative grounds on which a state must open its borders to those the international community has promised but failed to

---

54 See, eg, Philip Alston, 'The Populist Challenge to Human Rights' (2017) 9(1) *Journal of Human Rights* 1; Karen J Alter, James T Gathii and Laurence R Helfer, 'Backlash against International Courts in West, East and Southern Africa: Causes and Consequences' (2016) 27(2) *European Journal of International Law* 293; Caron and Shirlow (n 51).

55 Omer Karasapan, 'The State of Statelessness in the Middle East', *Brookings Institute* (Blog Post, 15 May 2015) <https://www.brookings.edu/blog/future-development/2015/05/15/the-state-of-statelessness-in-the-middle-east/>; Abbas Shiblak, 'Stateless Palestinians' 26 *Forced Migration Review* 8, 8; Lex Takkenberg, *The Status of Palestinian Refugees in International Law* (Oxford University Press, 1998) ch 5. Statelessness is defined as 'a person who is not considered as a national by any State under the operation of its law': *1954 Statelessness Convention* (n 11) art 1(1). Many Palestinian refugees fit within this definition—Jordan is the only country in which UNRWA operates to have granted collective citizenship to Palestinian refugees: Akram (n 13) 51. However, art 1(2)(i) of the *1954 Statelessness Convention* (n 11) contains an exclusion clause similar to art 1D of the *Refugee Convention* (n 10).

56 See discussion of case law in Kate Ogg, 'New Directions in Article 1D Jurisprudence: Greater Barriers for Palestinian Refugees Seeking the Benefits of the Refugee Convention' in Satvinder Singh Juss (ed), *Research Handbook on International Refugee Law* (Edward Elgar, 2019) 358.

57 This is governed by art 1D of the *Refugee Convention* (n 10). There is division amongst courts and refugee law scholars with respect to how art 1D should be interpreted. For a discussion see Goodwin-Gill and McAdam (n 16) 151–61; Hathaway and Foster (n 15) 509–23; Qafisheh and Azarov (n 16); Ogg (n 56).

protect. If we are, as some assert, seeing increased backlashes against international law and institutions,[58] asking people in need of protection to remain where they are until the international community reacts or responds in an appropriate fashion is akin to asking them to wait for Godot. The actions ordinary people take to place their destiny into their own hands demand serious and sympathetic attention. Below, I highlight that normative theories justifying why some people have a special claim to international protection overlook some of the most salient factors in the UNRWA backlash scenario.

4 Normative Theories on Who Should be Entitled to International Protection

There are many studies of who comes within existing legal frameworks for refugee and complementary protection.[59] More specifically, there are also examinations of when Palestinians are entitled to protection under the *Refugee Convention.*[60] In this article, I instead focus on normative discussions of who *should* be entitled to international protection. Many scholars argue that the circumstances that necessitate international protection are much broader than what is captured by legal refugee and complementary protection definitions. However, Achiume observes that most of the arguments for broadening

---

58 Andrew Gilmour, United Nations Assistant Secretary-General for Human Rights, 'The Global Backlash Against Human Rights' (Edited text of lecture, 12–13 March 2018) <https://www.ohchr.org/EN/NewsEvents/Pages/DisplayNews.aspx?NewsID=23202&LangID=E>; Martti Koskenniemi, 'Conclusion: After Globalisation: Engaging the Backlash' in Robert Schütze (ed), *Globalisation and Governance: International Problems, European Solutions* (Cambridge University Press, 2018) 453; Madsen, Cebulak and Wiebusch (n 51); Eric A Posner, 'Liberal Internationalism and the Populist Backlash' (2017) 49 *Arizona State Law Journal* 795.

59 See, eg, Michelle Foster, *International Refugee Law and Socio-Economic Rights: Refuge from Deprivation* (Cambridge University Press, 2007); Satvinder S Juss, 'Problematizing the Protection of "War Refugees": A Rejoinder to Hugo Storey and Jean-François Durieux' (2013) 32(1) *Refugee Survey Quarterly* 122; Constance MacIntosh, 'When "Feminist Beliefs" Became Credible as "Political Opinions": Returning to a Key Moment in Canadian Refugee Law' (2005) 17(1) *Canadian Journal of Women and the Law* 135; Audrey Macklin, 'Opening the Door to Women Refugees: A First Crack' in Wenona Giles, Helene Moussa and Penny Van Esterik (eds), *Development and Diaspora: Gender and the Refugee Experience* (Artemis Enterprises, 1996); Penelope Mathew, 'First Do No Harm: Refugee Law as a Response to Armed Conflict' in David W Lovell and Igor Primoratz (eds), *Protecting Civilians During Violent Conflict: Theoretical and Practical Issues for the 21st Century* (Ashgate, 2012) 159; Jason M Pobjoy, *The Child in International Refugee Law* (Cambridge University Press, 2017).

60 See above n 57.

the categories of people entitled to international protection continue the 'political stranger exceptionalism' inherent in refugee law.[61] Achiume explains that international and regional human rights and refugee law position refugees as political strangers.[62] This is because they are grounded on the premise that states have the sovereign right to exclude people from their territories but nonetheless provide 'limited exceptions' for those 'otherwise at risk of persecution or extreme human rights violations'.[63] This precludes consideration of the connections that may exist between the host state (or potential host state) and those seeking asylum.[64] Drawing on Achiume's ideas, I suggest that political outsider exceptionalism is a poor fit for Palestinian refugees because, as highlighted by Goodwin-Gill and Akram, 'the international community has continually recognized' them 'as a problem demanding special attention'.[65]

An example of conceptualising those in need of protection as political outsiders can be found in Shacknove's well-known critique of the definition of a refugee in the *Refugee Convention*.[66] He argues that this definition should be broadened to include not only those who face a well-founded fear of persecution, but also those whose countries of origin cannot provide for their basic needs due to, for example, natural disasters or economic or political collapse. Shacknove grounds his argument in a person's lack of state protection, which places them in a situation where they have 'no remaining recourse other than to seek international restitution of their needs ...'[67] While this argument provides normative grounds for enlarging our understanding of who is entitled to international protection, it still frames refugees as political outsiders who should be welcomed by host countries due to the exceptionality of their circumstances. There is no consideration of whether the international community or a prospective host state may have some form of connection to the person seeking protection. For example, Shacknove does not contemplate whether the potential host state is a former colonial power in the asylum seeker's country of origin or contributed to their harm through, for instance, economic policy or military intervention.

Another example is Betts' position that the international protection regime should respond to what he calls 'survival migrants'—persons 'outside their

---

61   E Tendayi Achiume, 'Migration as Decolonization' (2019) 71(6) *Stanford Law Review* 1509, 1516.

62   Ibid.

63   Ibid.

64   Ibid 1520–1.

65   Goodwin-Gill and Akram (n 14) 201.

66   Andrew E Shacknove, 'Who is a Refugee?' (1985) 95(2) *Ethics* 274.

67   Ibid 277.

country of origin because of an existential threat for which they have no access to a domestic remedy or resolution'.[68] Betts defines an 'existential threat' as a situation in which a person's basic rights are being violated.[69] He argues that a person is a survival migrant and entitled to international protection if they are denied basic liberty, basic security or basic subsistence.[70] Thus, Betts' normative basis for international protection is the exceptionality of survival migrants' circumstances rather than any pre-existing relationship between them and the prospective host state.

Breaking away from the political outsider approach to normative debates of transnational migration, Achiume argues that discussions on transnational migration require a 'reconceptualization of sovereignty as interconnection'.[71] Taking migration from the Global South to the Global North as her case study, she asserts that citizens of many Global South states are 'part of a shared demos' of former Global North colonisers.[72] Achiume explains that '[r]ather than being political strangers to First World nation-states, Third World persons are, in effect, political insiders, and for this reason, the First World nation-states have no right to exclude Third World persons'.[73] Drawing on theories of distributive and corrective justice, Achiume positions this type of migration as a form of decolonisation.[74] Achiume does not define distributive corrective justice but it is well-accepted that corrective justice seeks to address a wrong and distributive justice speaks to how things such as goods, wealth or status should be apportioned.[75] She explains that the current power and economic imbalances between the Global North and Global South can be traced back to colonial powers' exploitation of their former colonies.[76] Those who endure

---

68   Alexander Betts, *Survival Migration: Failed Governance and the Crisis of Displacement* (Cornell University Press, 2013) 4–5.

69   Ibid 5.

70   Ibid.

71   Achiume (n 61) 1520. For a discussion of sovereignty as interconnection see Abram Chayes and Antonia Handler Chayes, *The New Sovereignty: Compliance with International Regulatory Agreements* (Harvard University Press, 1998); Anne-Marie Slaughter, 'Disaggregated Sovereignty: Towards the Public Accountability of Global Government Networks' (2004) 39(2) *Government and Opposition* 159, 186; Chantal Thomas, 'What Does the Emerging International Law of Migration Mean for Sovereignty?' (2013) 14 *Melbourne Journal of International Law* 392, 447–50.

72   Achiume (n 61) 1549.

73   Ibid.

74   Ibid 1551.

75   See Fanny Thornton, *Climate Change and People on the Move: International Law and Justice* (Oxford University Press, 2018) 51–2 for a discussion of the 'Aristotelian roots' of distributive and corrective justice.

76   Achiume (n 61) 1533–47.

the legacy of this exploitation should be able to migrate to former colonisers to enjoy better prospects as a form of corrective distributive justice.[77] The novelty in Achiume's contribution to debates on international migration is that it 'supplants the extant international legal logic of formally independent, autonomous nation-states, each with a right to exclude nonnationals as a matter of existential priority, with the logic and ethics of imperial interconnection (specifically neocolonial interconnection)'.[78]

There are other voices in normative debates on forced migration that, like Achiume, consider the relationship or connection between the person seeking protection and the host state, or potential host state. For example, Souter argues that states should provide asylum to refugees for 'whose lack of state protection they are responsible'.[79] States may be responsible for refugees because of 'their military interventions, support for oppressive regimes or imposition of damaging economic policies'.[80] Souter acknowledges that causality is difficult to discern in many of these situations.[81] Nevertheless, he argues that theories of reparation grounded in rectifying historical injustices provide a strong normative basis for asylum in these situations.[82]

Other examples of normative approaches to forced migration that recognise connections between the host state and migrant can be found in climate change scholarship. Docherty and Giannini, in arguing for a climate change refugee treaty, state that because 'the nature of climate change is global and humans play a contributory role, the international community should accept responsibility for mitigating climate-induced displacement'.[83] They define climate change as 'an anthropogenic phenomenon for which humans should be held morally and legally responsible'[84] but do not explore any theoretical grounds on which to assert such responsibility. Thornton argues that theories of corrective and distributive justice may respond to situations in which those more vulnerable to climate change migrate to countries that are the greatest greenhouse gas emitters.[85] Notions of corrective and distributive justice

---

77   Ibid 1551–6.

78   Ibid 1567.

79   James Souter, 'Towards a Theory of Asylum as Reparation for Past Injustice' (2014) 62(2) *Political Studies* 326, 326.

80   Ibid.

81   Ibid 339–40.

82   Ibid.

83   Bonnie Docherty and Tyler Giannini, 'Confronting a Rising Tide: A Proposal for a Convention on Climate Change Refugees' (2009) 33(2) *Harvard Environmental Law Review* 349, 349.

84   Ibid 361.

85   Thornton (n 75).

underline that those most affected by climate change rarely reside in states that are the largest polluters and that everyone is entitled to live in a safe environment where their basic needs can be met.

The above studies push the normative grounds for a state granting asylum beyond political outsider exceptionalism by recognising interconnections between nation-states and asylum-seekers and speak to some aspects of Palestinian refugeehood. Achiume's and Souter's theories could be applied to Palestinian refugees: Palestine has a long history of colonisation and Palestinians' displacement can be partly attributed to states' support for the creation of Israel. Palestinians who travel across borders looking for a better life could also be classified as people whose basic needs are not met, which would bring them into the normative frameworks created by Betts and Shacknove respectively.

However, these theories overlook three of the most important factors in displaced Palestinians' situation—factors that come to the fore when the situation is viewed using a backlash framework. First, the international community has pledged to provide a special form of protection and assistance to Palestinian refugees. Second, this protection and assistance is provided by an international organisation funded by the UN and member states. Third, withdrawal of funding from UNRWA and persistent underfunding have hampered this international organisation's ability to carry out its protection and assistance mandate. In sum, these theories do not contemplate situations where the international community has made but resiled from a promise to provide protection to a specific community in situ.

Further, the theories of justice employed in the above studies do not encapsulate the nuances of backlashes against international commitments and organisations exemplified in the Palestinian situation. These theories of justice speak to some aspects of the Palestinian experience. Corrective justice and notions of reparations underscore the harms and suffering endured by Palestinians following the creation of Israel. Distributive justice can inform ideas on the rights and protections they should be afforded. However, what these theories overlook is the commitments made by the international community to the Palestinian people and the relational dynamics created by backlashes against and backsliding from these promises. Corrective and reparative justice can be used to address any form of harm—they do not specifically respond to refusals to honour an obligation or harm done in the context of an existing relationship of care. Distributive justice takes account of equitable division of goods but does not focus on the continuing relationship between a victim and wrongdoer. Below, I suggest that principles of restorative justice provide a more appropriate normative framework for conceptualising the international community's broken promises to the Palestinian people and how they should respond to Palestinians seeking asylum at their borders.

5   Backlashes: Acknowledging the Wrong, Repairing the Harm and Restoring the Relationship

Restorative justice is most well known in domestic criminal justice settings.[86] The foundational idea is that a person who has committed a crime should meet with the victim and the community and work towards repairing the harm caused and restoring broken relationships.[87] This can be instead of or in addition to criminal prosecution. While this is the most common understanding of restorative justice, it has broader meanings and uses. Burford, Braithwaite and Braithwaite explain that 'restorative justice is not simply a way of reforming the criminal justice system; it is a way of transforming the entire legal system ... [i]ts vision is of a holistic change in the way we do justice in the world'.[88] They define restorative justice as a 'relational form of justice'[89] that 'heals the harms that derive from injustice' and a form of 'regulation as what we do when obligations are not being honored'.[90] Burford, Braithwaite and Braithwaite also stress that restorative justice can apply in all spheres of human activity and in domestic as well as international contexts.[91]

Feminist theories of restorative justice critically interrogate who should be considered victim and wrongdoer and accentuate the relational aspects of restorative justice. For example, in Roberts' study of African American mothers whose actions bring them into contact with the criminal justice and foster care systems, she asks: 'I want to think more broadly and critically about the meaning of restorative justice. Who are the victims and who needs to make amends? Who needs to be reconciled and who should be held accountable? To whom should justice be restored?'.[92] Roberts discusses the ways in which

---

86   John Braithwaite, 'Principles of Restorative Justice' in Andrew von Hirsch, Julian V Roberts and Anthony Bottoms (eds), *Restorative Justice and Criminal Justice: Competing or Reconcilable Paradigms* (Hart Publishing, 2003) 1, 1.

87   Ibid.

88   Gale Burford, John Braithwaite and Valerie Braithwaite, 'Introduction: Restorative and Responsive Human Services' in Gale Burford, John Braithwaite and Valerie Braithwaite (eds), *Restorative and Responsive Human Services* (Routledge, 2019) 1, 4.

89   Ibid 1.

90   Ibid.

91   Ibid 5.

92   Dorothy Roberts, 'Black Mothers, Prison, and Foster Care: Rethinking Restorative Justice' in Gale Burford, John Braithwaite and Valerie Braithwaite (eds), *Restorative and Responsive Human Services* (Routledge, 2019) 116, 116.

the US political and economic systems discriminate against black women. She argues that '[r]ather than treat these women as offenders who need to make amends to their families and communities, restorative justice should hold the state accountable for harming all of them'.[93] The relational aspect of restorative justice theory has strong links with feminist ideas of relational autonomy.[94] Relational autonomy critiques the liberal conceptualisation of society being comprised of lone individuals and calls for a reconceptualisation of legal, political and moral life from an individualistic to a relational perspective.[95] This necessitates an understanding and acknowledgement of interconnectedness and interdependence.[96]

Feminist approaches to restorative justice, when applied to a backlash scenario, focus attention beyond singular, dramatic acts of backlash, require a more contextual approach to questions of wrongdoing, and prompt consideration of repercussions and creative ways in which harms can be repaired and relationships transformed. Applying feminist restorative justice theory to Palestinian refugees who choose to cross international borders in search of protection upends ingrained narratives about asylum seeking and calls attention to the international community's backsliding from promises to Palestinian refugees. People who arrive uninvited at a state's borders are often criminalised and depicted as violating state sovereignty.[97] Restorative justice theory, and in particular feminist approaches, urges us to instead see these transnational journeys as inherently connected to the international community's unheeded commitments to Palestinian refugees. UN member states pledged to provide protection and assistance to Palestinian refugees when initially displaced and have continued that promise through three yearly renewals of UNRWA's mandate. However, backlashes against and backsliding from these commitments has resulted in UNRWA being unable to deliver the protection and assistance it is mandated to provide. Palestinian refugees' journeys in search of protection elsewhere, while motivated and enabled by myriad factors,[98] cannot be understood without reference to these broken promises.

---

93   Ibid 123.

94   Jennifer Llewellyn, 'Responding Restoratively to Student Misconduct and Professional Regulation: The Case of Dalhousie Dentistry' in Gale Burford, John Braithwaite and Valerie Braithwaite (eds), *Restorative and Responsive Human Services* (Routledge, 2019) 127, 140.

95   See Jennifer Nedelsky, *Law's Relations: A Relational Theory of Self, Autonomy, and Law* (Oxford University Press, 2011).

96   Ibid 3.

97   See, eg, Sharon Pickering, *Refugees and State Crime* (Federation Press, 2005).

98   Turton explains that a person's decision to cross a border is motivated by a number of different factors: David Turton, 'Conceptualising Forced Migration' (Working Paper 12/2003, Refugee Studies Centre Working Paper Series, October 2003).

With respect to how the relationship between the international community and displaced Palestinians can be restored and transformed, when a Palestinian refugee arrives in a foreign state's territory, this is an opportunity for that state to provide the care the international community promised but failed to deliver. Restorative justice is more focussed on healing relationships than identifying a specific wrongdoer. While the US decision to cease funding UNRWA was the gravest single breach of the international community's commitment to protect and assist Palestinian refugees, these obligations are shared ones. A Palestinian refugee can seek restorative justice at the borders of any UN member state.

6   Restorative Justice in Other Displacement and Protection Contexts

Can these restorative justice ideas apply to other asylum seeking contexts or is this another case of Palestinian exceptionalism?[99] Within the confines of this article, I cannot explore all scenarios in which transnational journeys can be analysed from a restorative justice lens. Nevertheless, it is important to highlight that some factors crucial to the arguments made in this article may not be unique to Palestinian refugees. Kagan highlights that the 'state-to-UN responsibility shift' also occurs with respect to the United Nations High Commissioner for Refugees ('UNHCR').[100] The UNHCR Statute states that the organisation 'shall assume the function of providing international protection, under the auspices of the United Nations, to refugees ...'.[101] This mandate has expanded to include stateless persons.[102] The UNHCR describes its mandate as the provision of 'international protection and humanitarian assistance' to

---

99   Kagan explains that Palestinians are often treated as an anomalous group of refugees: Michael Kagan, 'The (Relative) Decline of Palestinian Exceptionalism and its Consequences for Refugee Studies in the Middle East' (2009) 22(4) *Journal of Refugee Studies* 417, 417.

100   Kagan (n 25) 524.

101   *Statute of the Office of the United Nations High Commissioner for Refugees*, GA Res 428(V), UN Doc A/Res/428(V) (14 December 1950) annex art 1.

102   *Question of the Establishment, in Accordance With the Convention on the Reduction of Statelessness, of a Body to Which Persons Claiming the Benefit of the Convention May Apply*, GA Res 3274 (XXIX), UN GAOR, 3rd comm, 29th sess, 2311th plen mtg, Agenda Item 99, Supp No 31, UN Doc A/Res/3274(XXIX) (10 December 1974); *Question of the Establishment, in Accordance With the Convention on the Reduction of Statelessness, of a Body to Which Persons Claiming the Benefit of the Convention May Apply*, GA Res 31/36, UN GAOR, 3rd comm, 31st sess, 83rd plen mtg, Agenda Item 78, Supp No 39, UN Doc A/Res/31/36 (30 November 1976).

these populations.[103] States remain responsible for protecting refugees but in many situations states deflect these responsibilities to the UNHCR.[104] UNHCR only receives 2% of its funding from the UN general budget. UNHCR sources the remainder predominately from states but also private donors. There is usually significant discrepancy between UNHCR's budget needs and the funds it raises. For example, in 2018 the UN approved a budget of USD 8,220.5 million but UNHCR only raised USD 4,710.3 million—a gap of USD 3,510.2 million or 43%.[105] Because of lack of funds, UNHCR in the past has had to cut back on, for example, provision of shelter, clothing and education.[106] While the international community has not made specific commitments to particular refugee populations similar to those undertaken in the Palestinian context, it has brought into creation an international organisation charged with protecting refugees but has not provided sufficient funding for it to properly carry out its mandate. If a refugee has not received adequate protection in their first country of asylum, feminist approaches to restorative justice would suggest that when they seek entry to another host country they should not be viewed as an outsider but as a person the international community has failed to protect. A way of repairing the harm would be for that host state to provide the protection the refugee did not receive in her first country of asylum.

UN peacekeeping operations may also be understood as a commitment to particular populations that they will be protected if they remain in their community. Since 1999, protection of civilians has formed a key part of UN peacekeeping mandates.[107] While there is a lack of clarity with respect to the scope of protection to be provided,[108] there is agreement that one of the 'most immediate and pressing needs' is protection from attacks and physical violence.[109] There are many example of failures of UN peacekeeping

---

103   'Mandate of the High Commissioner for Refugees and His Office: Executive Summary', UNHCR <https://www.unhcr.org/publications/legal/5a1b53607/executive-summary-of-the-mandate-of-the-high-commissioner-for-refugees.html>.

104   Michael Kagan, 'A Beleaguered Gatekeeper: Protection Challenges Posed by UNHCR Status Determination' (2006) 18(1) *International Journal of Refugee Law* 1, 14–17.

105   Executive Committee of the High Commissioner's Programme, *Updates on Budgets and Funding for 2019 and Reporting on 2018*, standing comm, 74th mtg, EC/70/SC/CRP.15 (29 May 2019).

106   Beth Elise Whitaker, 'Funding the International Refugee Regime: Implications for Protection' (2008) 14(2) *Global Governance* 241, 246–7.

107   Haidi Willmot and Scott Sheeran, 'The Protection of Civilians Mandate in UN Peacekeeping Operations: Reconciling Protection Concepts and Practices' (2013) 95 *International Review of the Red Cross* 517, 521.

108   Ibid 518.

109   Ibid 538.

forces to achieve this core aspect of their protection mandate.[110] The reasons behind these failures are myriad and complex but states have highlighted lack of funding as one leading cause.[111] In addition, far from protecting civilians from violence, there have been many instances of UN peacekeepers perpetrating violence, including sexual violence, against the civilian population.[112] The UN response has been criticised as inadequate, leading to a situation of impunity for these crimes.[113] The UN has failed to care for the victims of this violence or to assist children fathered by UN peacekeepers[114] many of whom are abandoned, ostracised and have little social support.[115] There may be situations where victims of violence perpetrated by UN peacekeepers seek safety across borders or abandoned children of UN peacekeepers make transnational journeys in search of necessities of life. These journeys can be understood with reference to existing normative approaches of forced migration such as survival migration. However, the theory I have outlined in this article would not frame these protection seekers merely as people who do not have enough to survive or who are escaping threats to life or physical security. Rather, feminist ideas of restorative justice would depict these individuals as people who were promised protection but denied it due to individual actions and institutional failure. The act of seeking asylum would be viewed as an opportunity for the host state, on behalf of the international community, to make amends for those wrongs.

---

110 For discussion see Lise Morjé Howard, *UN Peacekeeping in Civil Wars* (Cambridge University Press, 2007); Sarah-Myriam Martin-Brûlé, *Evaluating Peacekeeping Missions: A Typology of Success and Failure in International Interventions* (Routledge, 2017).

111 United Nations, 'Overburdened, Underfunded, Overstretched Peacekeeping Operations Create "Yawning Gap" between Expectations, Performance, Fourth Committee Told at Close of Debate' (Press Release, GA/SPD/465, 27 October 2010).

112 Elizabeth F Defeis, 'UN Peacekeepers and Sexual Abuse and Exploitation: An End to Impunity' (2008) 7(2) *Washington University Global Studies Law Review* 185; Muna Ndulo, 'The United Nations Responses to the Sexual Abuse and Exploitation of Women and Girls by Peacekeepers During Peacekeeping Missions' (2009) 27(1) *Berkeley Journal of International Law* 127; Olivera Simić, 'Policing the Peacekeepers: Disrupting UN Responses to "Crises" Over Sexual Offence Allegations' (2016) 20(1–2) *Journal of International Peacekeeping* 69.

113 Defeis (n 112) 192; Ndulo (n 112); Simic (n 112) 72.

114 Olivera Simić and Melanie O'Brien, '"Peacekeeper Babies": An Unintended Legacy of United Nations Peace Support Operations' (2014) 21(3) *International Peacekeeping* 345, 346.

115 Ibid 349; Ndulo (n 112) 130.

7 Conclusion

Backlashes against international organisations and longstanding international commitments can have significant and often devastating effects on people's everyday lives. These consequences, what people choose to do in response and how this can transform aspects of the international order need to be part of any research endeavour examining the backlash phenomenon in international law. To this end, this article offers a new way of conceptualising the cross-border journeys some Palestinian refugees choose to make in the context of backlashes against UNRWA. Existing normative theories of who should be entitled to international protection obscure some of the salient aspects of the Palestinian experience: that the international community promised protection and assistance in situ but backslid from these commitments. Feminist restorative justice theory provides a more holistic approach to analysing these backlashes because it draws attention to the interconnections between UN member states and Palestinian refugees and focuses on redressing the harm these nations have caused and restoring the relationship of care. The relational aspect of feminist restorative justice theory is particularly significant for analysing backlashes against international law and institutions. It encourages consideration of how these instances of backlash alter existing structures and relationships but also provide opportunities for restoration and transformation. While I have shown that feminist approaches to restorative justice bring to the fore aspects of the Palestinian refugee experience that other normative theories of forced migration disregard, I have also suggested that feminist restorative justice theory can be applied to other protection and displacement contexts. I leave the application of the normative framework developed in this article to these and other case studies as issues to be explored in future research.

Articles

∵

Transcending the Framing Contests over the Human Rights of Older Persons

Annie Herro* and Andrew Byrnes**

1 Introduction[1]

Population ageing is one of the biggest demographic transformations of this century. By 2050, humankind will reach a point where there are fewer children than older persons in the world, and the very old (those over 80) will constitute a significant group of adults. The fastest increase will take place in developing countries, while Europe will continue to have the oldest population in the world.[2] While the experience of old age can be quite different depending on a person's gender, race, class and other identities,[3] older persons share common experiences of ageism, discrimination, denial of rights and deprivation of their dignity regardless of any geographic, political, social, or economic differences and even in societies where respect for elders has traditionally been the norm.[4] As far back as 2007, reports made by countries around the world in accordance with their commitment under the Madrid International Plan of Action on

---

* Visiting Adjunct Lecturer and former Vice-Chancellor's Postdoctoral Fellow at UNSW (2016–2019).

** Professor of Law, UNSW; Research Associate, Australian Human Rights Institute, UNSW, and associate investigator, Ageing Futures Institute, UNSW.

1 We gratefully acknowledge the helpful comments made by Gerard Quinn, Justine Nolan, Lucas Lixinski, Bridget Sleap and members of the Oxford Human Rights Hub reading group on a draft of this paper. Some of the research on which the paper is based was carried out while Andrew Byrnes was a Visiting Research Fellow at the Bonavero Institute for Human Rights at the University of Oxford in 2019.

2 Rosa Kornfeld-Matte, *Report of the Independent Expert on the Enjoyment of All Human Rights by Older Persons*, UN Doc A/HRC/33/44 (8 July 2016).

3 Eleanor Palo Stoller and Rose Campbell Gibson, *Worlds of Difference: Inequality in the Aging Experience* (Sage, 1999); David F Warner and Tyson H Brown, 'Understanding How Race/ Ethnicity and Gender Define Age-Trajectories of Disability: An Intersectionality Approach' (2011) 72(8) *Social Science & Medicine* 1236. See also Sian Moore, '"No Matter What I Did I Would Still End Up in The Same Position" Age As A Factor Defining Older Women's Experience Of Labour Market Participation' (2009) 23(4) *Work, Employment and Society* 655.

4 See Global Alliance for the Rights of Older People, *In Our Own Words: What Older People Say About Discrimination and Human Rights in Older Age* (2015) <http://www.rightso folderpeople.org/in-our-own-words/>; Bridget Sleap, *Entitled To The Same Rights: What Older Women Say about Their Rights to Non-Discrimination and Equality, and to Freedom From Violence, Abuse and Neglect* (HelpAge International, 2017) <https://www.helpage.org/silo/ files/entitled-to-the-same-rights.pdf>.

© KONINKLIJKE BRILL NV, LEIDEN, 2021 | DOI:10.1163/26660229_03801012

Ageing ('MIPAA') adopted by the Second World Assembly on Ageing,[5] demonstrated how discrimination, abuse, and neglect are almost universal issues facing older persons around the globe.[6]

While the United Nations ('UN') has adopted human rights conventions that specifically protect the rights of groups such as women and persons with disabilities, there is no similar treaty at the universal level that explicitly and comprehensively addresses the human rights of older persons.[7] This has left important human rights issues unaddressed or inadequately dealt with under the international human rights system. These include the lack of an explicit right to autonomy and full and active participation and inclusion in all areas of social life, access to palliative and long-term care, and protection against and freedom from physical, psychological and financial abuse. There is sufficient persuasive evidence based on studies on the effects of existing group-specific or issue-specific treaties[8] to suggest that the establishment of a convention on the rights of older persons could empower older persons to claim their rights, and to participate in international and national affairs on an equal basis with others whose rights are enshrined in specific treaties. Specifically, a new human rights convention for older persons would demonstrate that the abrogation of these human rights is unacceptable and stipulate the positive obligations on states to realise equality and the enjoyment of rights by older people. To achieve these goals, national governments would be required to ensure that the rights set forth in the convention were reflected in their national legislation. Advocates argue that a convention on the rights of older persons, like other, similar conventions, would be a powerful advocacy, education and

---

5   *Report of the Second World Assembly on Ageing—Madrid, 8–12 April 2002*, UN Doc A/CONF.197/9 (23 May 2002) annex II.

6   *Report of the Secretary-General: First Review and Appraisal of the Madrid International Plan of Action on Ageing: Preliminary Assessment*, UN Doc E/CN.5/2008/7 (23 November 2007).

7   See generally on the current state of international and regional protection of the human rights of older persons: Claudia Martin, Diego Rodríguez-Pinzón and Bethany Brown, *Human Rights of Older People: Universal and Regional Legal Perspectives* (Springer, 2015).

8   See, eg, Beth A Simmons, *Mobilizing for Human Rights: International Law in Domestic Politics* (Cambridge University Press, 2009); Susanne Zwingel, *Translating International Women's Rights: The CEDAW Convention in Context* (Palgrave Macmillan, 2016); Neil A Englehart and Melissa K Miller, 'The CEDAW Effect: International Law's Impact on Women's Rights' (2014) 13(1) *Journal of Human Rights* 22. Another way of viewing the issue that might lead to a different convention, would be to guarantee human rights to all persons without discrimination based on older age. This approach would eschew defining and reifying a group that is contingent and socially constructed. It would focus on guaranteeing human rights to everyone in 'older age' without discrimination based on age. This notion is potentially more flexible and reflective of the socially constructed meanings of age and ageing than a definition of 'older persons' might be. See, eg, Jarlath Clifford, 'The UN Disability Convention and its Impact on European Equality Law' (2011) 6 *The Equal Rights Review* 11–25.

THE HUMAN RIGHTS OF OLDER PERSONS   255

empowerment tool as well as a helpful tool for policy development at the national level, and for litigation in domestic and international tribunals.[9]

The absence of a convention on the rights of older persons is not for want of trying. In 1948, in an effort to embody the rights of older persons in an international instrument, Argentina presented a draft declaration of old age rights to the UN General Assembly,[10] but its proposal did not garner enough support among member states to be adopted. The draft was referred to the UN Economic and Social Council for further study and reporting back to the General Assembly (1948), but nothing came of this. In the 1990s an international non-government organisation ('INGO'), the International Federation on Ageing ('IFA'), teamed up with the Mission of the Dominican Republic to the UN to try to advocate the adoption of a legally binding instrument on the rights of older persons,[11] but they too were unsuccessful.[12]

The long-term lack of interest in the explicit legally binding protection of the human rights of older persons at the international level shifted in 2010 when once again Argentina, this time with support from other countries in Latin America and the Caribbean, made yet another attempt to spearhead an effort to put the issue of the development of a convention on the rights of older persons on the UN's agenda. This push resulted in the General Assembly voting in late 2010 to establish the UN Open-Ended Working Group on Ageing ('Working Group on Ageing') to review the 'existing international framework of the human rights of older persons' and to identify 'possible gaps and how best to address them'.[13] In 2012 the General Assembly expanded the mandate of the Working Group on Ageing, requesting it to consider 'proposals for an international legal instrument to promote and protect the rights and dignity of older persons'.[14] While many are hopeful that a convention will eventually

---

9   Israel Doron and Itai Apter, 'The Debate Around the Need for a New Convention on the Rights of Older Persons' (2010) 50(5) *The Gerontologist* 586.

10   Israel Doron and Kate Mewhinney (eds), *The Rights of Older Persons: Collection of International Documents* (Association for the Planning and Development of Services for the Aged in Israel, 2007) <https://ifa.ngo/publication/rights-of-older-people/the-rights -of-older-persons-a-collection-of-international-documents/>.

11   Ibid 15–18.

12   Jennifer Dabbs Sciubba, 'Explaining Campaign Timing and Support for a UN Convention on the Rights of Older People' (2014) 18(4–5) *International Journal of Human Rights* 462, 468.

13   *Follow-Up to the Second World Assembly on Ageing, Report of the Secretary-General*, 64th sess, Item 62(c), UN Doc A/64/127 (6 July 2009) [28] (*'Follow-Up Report to the Second World Assembly on Ageing'*).

14   *Towards a Comprehensive and Integral International Legal Instrument to Promote and Protect the Rights and Dignity of Older Persons*, GA Res 67/139, UN Doc A/RES/67/139 (13 February 2013, adopted 20 December 2013) para 1.

be adopted, the process of generating political support for formal negotiations has been slow.[15]

There is a range of reasons why states have not supported the proposed convention. These include the institutional and technocratic concerns that the current UN treaty body system is overstretched and does not need the addition of yet another treaty committee that will require significant resources; and that government officials are already overloaded in reporting to existing human rights treaty monitoring bodies.[16] Some commentators have also suggested material explanations for the sluggish pace at which the international process to establish a convention has unfolded. These include austerity measures adopted by many states after the 2008 Global Financial Crisis and the concomitant concerns of many developed countries, which are the most aged in the world, about the high cost of implementing any proposed treaty.[17] The perceptions of some countries, following their ratification of the 2006 UN *Convention on the Rights of Persons with Disabilities* (the 'CRPD'),[18] that implementation of that treaty has involved significant unanticipated financial expenditure might also have reinforced states' concerns about the financial costs of adopting a similarly ambitious treaty relating to older persons. Many states make these arguments in good faith, though some of them are based on inaccurate factual assumptions, for example about the net cost-benefit result of introducing rights guarantees. Other explanations include the weakness and the lack of coordination of the transnational advocacy network working on these issues when compared to similar alliances that had helped to drive forward the negotiations of the CRPD.[19]

---

15   Annie Herro, 'The Human Rights of Older Persons: The Politics and Substance of the UN Open-Ended Working Group on Ageing' (2017) 23(1) *Australian Journal of Human Rights* 90.

16   Australian Human Rights Centre, *Workshop on Advancing the Campaign to Elaborate a United Nations Convention on the Rights of Older Persons: Outcome Report* (Report, 2016) <http://archive.ahrcentre.org/news/2017/02/20/881>; See also Doron and Apter (n 9); Marthe Freevang and Simon Biggs, *The Rights of Older Persons: Protection and Gaps Under Human Rights Law* (Social Policy Working Paper No 16, Centre for Public Policy and Brotherhood of St Laurence, 13–14 August 2012); Bridget Sleap, *Why it's Time for a Convention on the Rights of Older People* (Position Paper, HelpAge International, 2009 <www.helpage.org/download/4c3cfa0869630/>.

17   Sciubba (n 12); Jennifer Dabbs Sciubba, 'Securing Rights in the Twenty-First Century: A Comparison of the Disability and Older Persons' Rights Conventions' (2016) 15(4) *Journal of Human Rights* 533; Herro (n 15).

18   *Convention on the Rights of Persons with Disabilities*, opened for signature 30 March 2007, 2515 UNTS 3 (entered into force 3 May 2008) ('CRPD').

19   Sciubba, 'Securing Rights in the Twenty-First Century: A Comparison of the Disability and Older Persons' Rights Conventions' (n 17).

In this article, we examine the norms and other ideational constructs which have influenced political support for a convention, a subject that has received little attention. Frames are normative and sometimes causal ideas that are located in the foreground of policy and legal debates.[20] The framing of issues by both activists and their opponents has been used to explain the success or failure of international campaigns for legal and policy adoption or reform.[21] Scholars of social movements, public policy and international relations have found that the framing of issues is especially powerful in the agenda-setting and pre-negotiation phases of the development of new international law norms, this being the time when problems and solutions are identified.[22] This is precisely the stage which the international community has reached in the process towards establishment of a convention on the rights of older persons.

This article makes two principal contributions. First, we map different, competing frames on the problems, the cause of these problems and their solutions as they relate to older persons and the creation of a new international human rights treaty. Specifically, we highlight the tension between the human rights and social development frames to explain the *problems* faced by older persons in an era of unprecedented demographic transformation and argue that the human rights frame has won this particular framing contest. Next, we identify an additional tension between the *diagnosis* of the widely-accepted human rights violations experienced by older persons around the world—whether it is due in whole or part to a 'normative gap' in international law or rather due to significant practical failures to implement applicable international human rights standards through existing procedures, and a lack of information on the rights of older persons. We show how this framing contest has not yet been

---

20   Margaret E Keck and Kathryn Sikkink, *Activists Beyond Borders: Advocacy Networks in International Politics* (Cornell University Press, 1998); John L Campbell, 'Ideas, Politics, and Public Policy' (2002) 28 *Annual Review of Sociology* 21.

21   Richard Price, 'Reversing the Gun Sights: Transnational Civil Society Targets Land Mines' (1998) 52(3) *International Organization* 613; Rodger A Payne, 'Persuasion, Frames and Norm Construction' (2001) 7(1) *European Journal of International Relation* 37; Jutta Joachim, 'Framing Issues and Seizing Opportunities: The UN, NGOs, and Women's Rights' (2003) 47(2) *International Studies Quarterly* 247; Joshua William Busby, 'Bono Made Jesse Helms Cry: Jubilee 2000, Debt Relief, and Moral Action in International Politics' (2007) 51(2) *International Studies Quarterly* 247; Clifford Bob, *The Global Right Wing and the Clash of World Politics* (Cambridge University Press, 2012).

22   I William Zartman and Maureen R Berman, *The Practical Negotiator* (Yale University Press, 1982) 70–82; Thomas Risse, '"Let's Argue!": Communicative Action in World Politics' (2000) 54(1) *International Organization* 1; Campbell (n 20); Joachim (n 21); Michael Lipson, 'A "Garbage Can Model" of UN Peacekeeping' (2007) 13(1) *Global Governance: A Review of Multilateralism and International Organizations* 79.

resolved and, consequently, how each frame leads to different, competing *solutions*: the normative gap analysis to the promotion of a new treaty, the implementation and information gap analysis to rejection of this option and, instead, to strengthening the current system of international human rights law as it pertains to older persons. We therefore conclude that it is this framing contest at the diagnostic level that is creating a challenge for advocates seeking to advance the process of establishing a convention on the rights of older persons. While we present the emergence of new frames in tension with one other, we also show that frames often overlap.

The second contribution this article makes in an attempt to break the current deadlock is to offer a new diagnostic frame that draws on the precedent set by the negotiations on the CRPD. We are prompted to apply this novel framing perspective because the pre-negotiation process is entering its eleventh year and foregrounding what might potentially be a more convincing frame of the limitations of international human rights law to address the widespread rights violations of older persons around the world—a 'relative invisibility' frame—might help to overcome a key objection posed by state opponents to establishing a treaty. That is, we suggest significantly de-emphasising the 'normative gap' frame, which is based on the idea that there are gaps in the current system of international human rights law that justify the establishment of a treaty, given the contested and malleable definition of a 'normative gap'. Instead, we make a case for the utility of emphasising a 'relative invisibility' frame, which holds that, while older persons are conceptually within the confines of existing rights laws, they are practically invisible.

We argue that, notwithstanding a significant number of general references, some substantial, to the human rights of older persons as part of the protection that other international human rights instruments provide in a formal or theoretical sense, these guarantees are not translated sufficiently into a substantive and systematic engagement with the human rights of older persons at the international level; this neglect flows through to the implementation of human rights at the national level. For example, there are relatively few references or recommendations relating substantively to the human rights of older persons in the concluding observations of the human rights treaty bodies supervising the implementation of the existing UN human rights treaties, and limited references by states parties themselves in their reports to those bodies. Similarly, there are relatively few references to older persons' issues in the many recommendations made by states in the Universal Periodic Review process.[23] Following in the footsteps of some of the architects of the CRPD, we

---

23   In a 2019 report the OHCHR stated that 'among more than 13,000 recommendations related to discrimination classified under the Universal Human Rights Index, less than

THE HUMAN RIGHTS OF OLDER PERSONS

argue that a central way to make older persons visible within UN and domestic laws is through the creation of a UN convention on the rights of older persons.

The article starts with a discussion of framing theories, their relevance to our case study and the use of such frames by principal stakeholders in the debate. We next map different, competing frames on the problems faced by older persons today, the cause of these problems and solutions to them. The final section explores ways to reconcile and move beyond current frames based largely on the precedent set by the CRPD.

2   A Framing Approach

Framing is a concept originally coined by the sociologist Erving Goffman;[24] it was popularised by David Snow and his co-authors, who used it as a heuristic tool to understand the nature and function of social movements.[25] It refers to the strategic use of speech acts, such as public statements or written material, to assign meaning to an issue in a way that helps to 'organise experience and guide action'.[26] The underlying assumption of framing is that social phenomena emerge as social problems or issues through a process of definition rather than objectively existing outside our collective understandings. As sociologist Herbert Blumer puts it, 'a social problem does not exist for a society unless it is recognized by that society to exist'.[27]

---

1 percent concern age discrimination against older persons': *Activities of the Office of the United Nations High Commissioner for Human Rights, the United Nations System and Regional Organizations to Support States' Efforts to Promote and Protect the Human Rights of Older Persons: Report of the Office of the United Nations High Commissioner for Human Rights*, UN Doc A/HRC/41/32 (21 June 2019) [42] ('*Activities to Support States' Efforts to Promote and Protect the Human Rights of Older Persons*'). The Universal Human Rights Index is a UN database containing country-specific human rights information from UN human rights mechanisms: the Treaty Bodies, the Special Procedures and the Universal Periodic Review.

24   Erving Goffman, *Frame Analysis: An Essay on the Organization of Experience* (Harvard University Press, 1974).

25   Daniel M Cress and David A Snow, 'The Outcomes of Homeless Mobilization: The influence of Organization, Disruption, Political Mediation, and Framing' (2000) 105(4) *American Journal of Sociology* 1063; Robert D Benford and David A Snow, 'Framing Processes and Social Movements: An Overview and Assessment' (2016) 26 *Annual Review of Sociology* 611.

26   David A Snow et al, 'Frame Alignment Processes, Micromobilization, and Movement Participation' (1986) 51 *American Sociological Review* 464, 464.

27   Herbert Blumer, 'Social Problems as Collective Behaviour' (1971) 18(3) *Social Problems* 298, 301–02. To similar effect, Autesserre points out that 'one of the most important insights of the extensive literature on frames is that problems are not given, they have to be constructed and frames shape peoples' views on what counts as a problem and

The concept of framing articulated by Snow and his colleagues is one of the most often-cited models to understand the characteristics of frames that have an impact on the achievement by social movements of their goals.[28] Their model identifies three types of frames. The first is a 'diagnostic' frame that specifies a problem that needs to be addressed and then identifies the causes of the problem and responsibility for it.[29] For example, Shawki reveals how activists' ability to effectively demonstrate the cause of a problem can contribute to the success or demise of a campaign. Based on her analysis of Jubilee 2000, which sought to alleviate the burden of foreign debt on developing countries, she argues that its relative success was partly because advocates effectively identified the problem as being one of poverty and portrayed 'the heavy burden of debt as one of the *causes* of poverty and one of the impediments to development.'[30] In this sense, she is illustrating the close link between the characteristics of the problem-naming or construction frame and the frame that identifies the cause of the problem.

The second type of frame is the 'prognostic' (or solutions) frame that proposes a solution to the diagnosed problem. As Benford and Snow put it, prognostic framing 'involves the articulation of a proposed solution to the problem, or at least a plan of attack, and the strategies for carrying out the plan'.[31] In doing so, framing can make one set of policies seem appropriate and another seem inappropriate:[32] 'prognostic framing is important because it stipulates specific remedies or goals ... to work toward and the means or tactics for achieving these objectives'.[33] There is also the 'motivational' frame which is a call to arms or rationale for engaging in ameliorative or corrective action but the diagnosis and prognosis frames are the most important of the three[34] and these will be the focus of this paper. Benford and Snow tell us that the more

---

what does not': Séverine Autesserre, 'Hobbes and the Congo: Frames, Local Violence, and International Intervention' (2009) 63(2) *International Organization* 249, 254.

28   Cress and Snow (n 25) 1071.

29   'Diagnostic framing is important because it problematizes and focuses attention on an issue, helps shape how the issue is perceived, and identifies who or what is culpable, thereby identifying the targets or sources of the outcomes sought ...' Cress and Snow (n 25) 1071. One might also see this as two related frames: the first identifying a particular situation as a social problem, followed by a further frame that diagnoses the causes of that problem, which then will point to possible responses.

30   Noha Shawki, 'Issue Frames and the Political Outcomes of Transnational Campaigns: A Comparison of the Jubilee 2000 Movement and the Currency Transaction Tax Campaign' (2010) 24(2) *Global Society* 203, 226.

31   Benford and Snow (n 25) 616.

32   Autesserre (n 27); Campbell (n 20).

33   Cress and Snow (n 25) 1071.

34   Ibid; Shawki (n 30) 205.

richly developed and interconnected the frames are, the more successful the mobilisation effort is likely to be.[35]

Another prominent framing theorist, Robert Entman, presents a similar framing schema. He says that frames define problems, diagnose causes of the problem, make moral judgments (which evaluate causal agents and their effects), and suggest remedies.[36] Combining the work of these theorists, we employ an approach which involves three stages of framing: problem identification or definition of the problem, diagnosis frames identifying the cause of the problem, and frames that identify solutions (and there are competing frames within each of these framing stages). Applying this perspective to the study of the emergence of a human rights norm assumes rights are socially constructed and that their 'meanings are subjectively defined, contestable, and continually negotiated'.[37] We use this approach to locate different frames that have emerged in the debates surrounding the establishment of a convention relating to defining the problem of population ageing, the diagnosis of the problem(s) and the solution.

As Figure 1 shows and as we will discuss further below, the frames used to discuss the rights of older persons in international law map onto this schema in the following way:

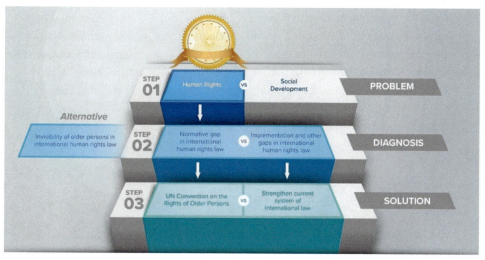

FIGURE 1

---

35 Benford and Snow (n 25).
36 Robert M Entman, 'Framing: Toward Clarification of a Fractured Paradigm' (1993) 43(4) *Journal of Communication* 51, 52.
37 Lisa Vanhala, 'The Diffusion of Disability Rights in Europe' (2015) 37 *Human Rights Quarterly* 831, 839.

Step 1, representing the problem frame, shows the tension between human rights and the social development frames, with the human rights frame winning the framing contest. The dominance of the human rights frame led to the establishment of the Open-ended Working Group on Ageing by the UN General Assembly where a new contest emerged at the diagnostic level, which is represented by Step 2. Here, some claim that the human rights violations that older persons experience are due to 'normative gaps' in international human rights law.[38] This approach maintains that general human rights guarantees do not apply as a matter of legal interpretation to the common rights violations suffered by older persons or that such guarantees do not adequately specify such wrongs—and are therefore not applied to them. Others argue that there are no normative gaps but rather implementation and other gaps (eg information and monitoring gaps).[39]

Each of these frames leads to different solutions, as represented by the two different arrows pointing from Step 2 to Step 3. The 'normative gap' frame leads proponents to call for the adoption of a UN convention on the rights of older persons (alongside improved implementation of existing protections as well), while the 'other gaps' frame leads opponents to insist that, because there are no normative gaps relating to older persons in the international human rights regime, the question is simply one of strengthening the current system, rather than the creation of new or more specific legal norms. As is now clear, the major obstacle in this framing schema is Step 2, since neither frame has come to dominate the discussions, and thus there is no consensus on the solution. We therefore propose an alternative frame—the 'relative invisibility' of older persons in international human rights law—which we argue might circumvent the current deadlock at diagnostic level. Before we explain this schema, we first discuss the protagonists in the debate surrounding older persons and a proposed UN treaty.

3   The Use of Frames by Stakeholders in the Debate

Frames are commonly used by transnational advocacy networks, which according to Keck and Sikkink's classic definition, can comprise states,

---

38   See, eg, United Nations Office of the High Commissioner for Human Rights, *Human Rights of Older Persons: International Human Rights Principles And Standards* (Working Paper, Open-Ended Working Group on Ageing, 18–21 April 2011) 3.

39   See, eg, Matthias Dettling, 'Statement by Matthias Dettling, Second Secretary' (Switzerland, 21 August 2012) (emphasis added) <https://social.un.org/ageing-working -group/documents/Switzerland.pdf>.

THE HUMAN RIGHTS OF OLDER PERSONS 263

inter-governmental organisations and non-governmental organisations and others with similar principled goals, to effect legal or policy change.[40] The frames that emerged from civil society, which were subsequently adopted by some states during the process of elaborating the CRPD, are a case in point.[41]

Frames may also be used by states to resist an advocacy network's effort to effect political and legal change. These opposing forces might favour the status quo or articulate an alternative definition of a problem and its solution compared to those promoted by activists.[42] Andrew Payne, for example, has explored how the failure of those seeking to generate new global labour norms to improve the plight of vulnerable workers in the developing world was largely due to the strength of the counter-frames. The opponents characterised the activists' rights claims as the attempts by the global North to coerce the global South and as a new form of protectionism.[43] Similarly, Bob, in his study of the efforts of the Western evangelical Christian groups and the American gun lobby to oppose liberal norms of toleration of homosexuality and gun control, describes opponents' counter-frames in stark terms: 'Does a ... frame bring opponents to their knees? No. They pull out the hammer and smash it to smithereens....'[44] While Bob's description of the battle between liberal advocates and their detractors is perhaps too strong for our purposes, it illustrates the ongoing contest for meaning and ideas surrounding campaigns for legal and normative change.

The older persons' rights network we examine in this article comprises UN agencies, certain states, and domestic and international civil society organisations. States from Latin America and the Caribbean have been the principal proponents of a convention, with Argentina leading the charge.[45] Slovenia has been the other key advocate and, as of mid-2019, the only country in the EU to openly support a convention. Apart from these strong advocates, support from many other states has been haphazard and inconsistent. Opponents of a

---

40 Keck and Sikkink (n 20). See, eg, Jennifer Hadden, *Networks in Contention* (Cambridge University Press, 2015); Richard Price, 'Reversing the Gun Sights: Transnational Civil Society Targets Land Mines' (1998) 52(3) *International Organization* 613.

41 Most important of these was the 'paradigm shift' from viewing persons with disabilities as objects of charity and recipients of welfare to recognising them as the holders of rights and full participants in society. See generally Maya Sabatello, 'A Short History of the International Disability Rights Movement' in Maya Sabatello and Marianne Schulze (eds), *Human Rights and Disability Advocacy* (University of Pennsylvania, 2014) 1.

42 Bob (n 21); Alan Bloomfield, 'Norm Antipreneurs and Theorising Resistance to Normative Change' (2016) 42(2) *Review of International Studies* 310.

43 Payne (n 21).

44 Bob (n 21) 29.

45 Sciubba (n 12).

convention include the US, Russia, China, Israel and a few others. States from Africa and Asia have, with few exceptions, not been extensively engaged in the discussions.

The reasons why countries from Latin America are championing the convention include a reaction to a common history of dictatorship; a commitment of newer regimes, such as that of former Brazilian President Luiz Inácio Lula da Silva, to systematically strengthening the rights of vulnerable populations; and an opportunity for progressive governments to ensconce new rights in law in case a less progressive regime comes into power again.[46] Slovenia has supported a convention because of a mix of pressure from a powerful pensioners' interest groups and an attempt to realise the aspirational identity of Slovenia as a regional and international human rights leader.[47]

In the next three sections, we examine how the different types of frames— definitional, diagnostic and prognostic—have been developed and deployed in the Working Group on Ageing discussions around the need for a new convention. We explore how civil society organisations engage with or even adopt frames formulated by states and UN actors, but also promote their own frames in an effort to expedite the process of adopting a convention. We also demonstrate how some states use counter-frames to obstruct efforts to commence drafting a convention. We do this because an analysis of such frames sheds light on the public arguments states and others are making to justify their support for a convention or their rejection of it. Mapping these frames helps us to identify if and where there are competing arguments and provides the opportunity to propose alternatives to overcome the impasse.

4   Defining the Problem

This section explores two separate but inter-connecting frames that have been used to convey the challenges older persons face in society. While they were conceived before the commencement of the Working Group on Ageing, they continue to be used throughout it. The frames relate to older persons and ageing populations as a development challenge requiring a social and economic policy response[48] versus the position of older persons posing a challenge that

---

46   Ibid.

47   Annie Herro, 'Domestic Interest Groups and Rights Mobilization: Explaining the Case of Slovenia's Support for the Proposed Convention on the Rights of Older Persons' (2018) 18(4) *Global Networks* 625.

48   Within this broad frame there are a number of competing frames, eg the provision of care for older persons being the responsibility of the state as opposed to being the responsibility of their family.

THE HUMAN RIGHTS OF OLDER PERSONS   265

requires a human rights-based approach. While it would be easy to say that the former is broadly supported by countries from the global South and the latter finds support among countries from the global North, these divisions are not so clear cut. Much of the discussion in developed countries is also about the need to address the social and economic dimensions of the ageing population as a collective problem rather than exclusively starting from human rights. This tension has its parallels in the evolution of thinking about disability issues: preceding the adoption of the CRPD, there was a move from seeing persons with disability as the passive beneficiaries of welfare to rights-holders, active agents and participants in the community. We discuss each of these frames in turn.

4.1 Social Development versus Human Rights: The Dominance of the Human Rights Frame

The challenges facing older persons have been framed in a number of ways, including as welfare and biomedical issues,[49] but perhaps the most striking framing contest that appears in international policies on ageing is whether the situation of older persons should be viewed from and addressed through a social development perspective or a human rights perspective.[50] The former primarily sees older persons as a social group made up of individuals with particular needs, which the state should endeavour to satisfy as a matter of social policy so far as it is able to do so. From this vantage point, older persons are the beneficiaries of social policies, especially in the areas of social welfare, health and other forms of support. The latter takes as its starting point older persons as right-holders, with claims on society to enjoy rights to health, an adequate standard of living and the full range of other civil, political, economic, social and cultural rights. A central difference between the two is that the latter is substantively deeper and wider than the former in that it covers more issues that affect the lives of older persons and in different circumstances, and is based on the premise that states are *legally obliged* to respect, protect and fulfil these rights. We argue that the human rights frame has prevailed in the framing contest, even though there are still a few states in the Working Group on Ageing that characterise the challenges facing older persons as one of social development, as well as some that merge these two frames.

---

49   Sandra Huenchuan and Luis Rodríguez-Piñero, 'Ageing and the Protection of Human Rights: Current Situation and Outlook' (Project Document LC/W.353, Economic Commission for Latin America and the Caribbean, March 2011) 13–20.

50   For an excellent account of the various narratives that have been put forward in relation to ageing and older persons and their implications for the policy approaches to be adopted in response, see Alison Kesby, 'Narratives of Aging and the Human Rights of Older Persons' (2017) 18(4) *Human Rights Review* 371.

The progression in thinking has been seen in the series of international documents on ageing issues adopted since the early 1980s. The first major international intergovernmental declaration on older persons was the Vienna International Plan of Action on Ageing in 1982. It focused on areas such as the family, social welfare, health and income security. The document makes general references to human rights, by reaffirming the application of the Universal Declaration of Human Rights to older people. Kendig et al note that '[w]hile it [the Vienna Plan] recognised a need for active participation of older people in society, the overwhelming focus was on service provision'.[51]

Almost a decade after the adoption of the Vienna Plan, the UN General Assembly (1991) adopted the non-binding UN Principles for Older Persons,[52] which 'reaffirm faith in fundamental human rights', and in its 1992 *Proclamation on Ageing* declared 1999 the International Year of Older Persons (thereby establishing 1 October each year as the International Day of Older Persons).[53] However, the Principles, in contrast to the proposed Declaration put forward at the same time by the IFA and Dominican Republic mentioned in the introduction, do not themselves use the language of rights: they articulate aspirations which consequently limit their scope and potential impact.[54] For example, they provide that '[o]lder persons *should* have access to adequate food ...' rather than using the language of rights ['everyone has the right to ...'].[55] This means that while the provisions in the UN Principles are important, as they are contained in a General Assembly resolution, they do not as such set out binding obligations for governments (though they may to some extent reflect obligations contained in human rights treaties or in customary international law). Consequently, governments are under no obligation to implement them. There are striking parallels with the development of international norms on

---

51 Hal Kendig, Nina Lucas and Kaarin J Anstey, 'Thirty Years of the United Nations and Global Ageing: An Australian Perspective' (2013) 32(2) *Australasian Journal on Ageing* 28, 29.

52 *Implementation of the International Plan of Action on Ageing and Related Activities*, GA Res 46/91, UN GAOR, 46th sess, 74th plen mtg, UN Doc A/RES/46/91 (16 December 1991), annex.

53 *Proclamation on Ageing*, GA Res 47/5, UN GAOR, 47th sess, 42nd plen mtg, UN Doc A/RES/47/5 (16 October 1992), annex.

54 Luis Rodríguez-Piñero and Sandra Huenchuan, 'Los Derechos de las Personas Mayores en el Ámbito Internacional: Materiales de Estudio y Divulgación' [The Rights of Older Persons at the International Level: Study and Dissemination Materials] (Latin American and Caribbean Demographic and Population Division of the United Nations Economic Commission for Latin America and the Caribbean, June 2011).

55 *Implementation of the International Plan of Action on Ageing and Related Activities*, UN Doc A/RES/46/91 (n 52) annex, principle 1 (emphasis added).

THE HUMAN RIGHTS OF OLDER PERSONS   267

disability. In that context a plethora of soft law instruments were adopted preceding the Disability Convention: these, at first, framed persons with disabilities as a social issue, slowly morphing into a human rights frame, but ultimately failed to address the invisibility of persons with disabilities in international human rights law.

MIPAA, which was adopted by the Second World Assembly on Ageing[56] to replace the 1982 Vienna International Plan of Action on Ageing, set the context for global policies on ageing for the twenty-first century. MIPAA framed ageing and older persons as a social development issue and called for the inclusion of ageing into the international development agenda. MIPAA's 239 recommendations for action are organised in three priority directions: older persons and development; advancing health and wellbeing into old age; and ensuring enabling and supportive environments.

While the MIPAA 'is not a human rights document, it contains a number of references relevant to human rights and adopts a conceptual approach that is in accordance with human rights principles.'[57] The introductory section of the MIPAA states that 'the full realization of all human rights and fundamental freedoms of all older persons' is one of the 'central themes' running through the MIPAA, as are ensuring the full enjoyment of economic, social and cultural rights, a commitment to gender equality, and the elimination of discrimination against older people.[58] It has the ultimate goal of bringing about 'an inclusive society for all ages in which older persons participate fully and without discrimination and on the basis of equality'.[59] For each of its three 'priority directions for action'[60] MIPAA sets out recommendations under each of the issues and objectives relevant to each priority. Human rights goals are referred to among the large number of recommendations.

In 2012 the Office of the United Nations High Commissioner for Human Rights, in 'an analysis of the human rights situation of older persons in the light

---

56   *Report of the Second World Assembly on Ageing—Madrid, 8–12 April 2002*, UN Doc A/ CONF.197/9 (n 5).

57   Kornfeld-Matte (n 2) [96]. Kornfeld-Matte also notes at [123]: 'Moreover, while the Madrid International Plan of Action contains a number of references to human rights, it is not a human rights instrument and it addresses ageing issues mainly from a developmental perspective. It has not been designed to comprehensively address existing protection gaps and is therefore not sufficient to ensure the full enjoyment of their human rights by older persons'.

58   *Report of the Second World Assembly on Ageing—Madrid, 8–12 April 2002*, UN Doc A/ CONF.197/9 (n 5) [12].

59   Ibid [13].

60   These were 'Older Persons and Development', 'Advancing Health and Well-Being into Old Age', and 'Ensuring Enabling and Supportive Environments'.

of the indivisible, interdependent and interrelated nature of all human rights', noted that even though human rights were a foundational theme throughout MIPAA, its implementation 'does not systematically consider linkages to the obligations of State parties under international human rights instruments'.[61]

Similarly, the Independent Expert on the enjoyment of all human rights by older persons of the UN Human Rights Council, Rosa Kornfeld-Matte, noted in her 2016 report that the implementation of MIPAA 'may have positive implications for the enjoyment of some human rights by older persons' and 'contains a number of references to human rights', but that 'it has not been designed to comprehensively address existing protection gaps and is therefore not sufficient to ensure the full enjoyment of their human rights by older persons'.[62]

Therefore, even though MIPAA is broadly aligned with human rights objectives and some commitments in MIPAA might reinforce human rights, it does not provide a comprehensive human rights framework, nor does it address key human rights issues for older people, such as equality before the law and non-discrimination.[63] The most recent review of MIPAA has underlined its uneven and limited implementation in many countries.[64]

The shift from a social policy/development/social welfare approach to a human rights approach has gathered critical momentum over the last five to ten years to bring about the emergence of a new and competing frame or paradigm. The Human Rights Council's Independent Expert on the human rights of older persons described the change as a:

> paradigm shift from a predominant economic and development perspective [on] ageing to the imperative of a human rights-based approach that views older persons as subjects of law, rather than simply beneficiaries, with specific rights, the enjoyment of which has to be guaranteed by States.[65]

---

61 *Report of the United Nations High Commissioner for Human Rights*, UN ESCOR, UN Doc E/2012/51, (23–27 July 2012), [1], [11].

62 Kornfeld-Matte (n 2) [123].

63 To similar effect see the assessment in 2010 by a member of the UN Human Rights Council's Advisory Committee: Chinsung Chung, *The Necessity of a Human Rights Approach and Effective United Nations Mechanism for the Human Rights of the Older Person: Working Paper Prepared by Ms Chinsung Chung, Member of the Human Rights Council Advisory Committee*, UN GAOR, 4th sess, UN Doc A/HRC/AC/4/CRP.1 (25–29 January 2010) [59].

64 See *Third Review and Appraisal of the Madrid International Plan of Action on Ageing, 2002*, UN ESCOR, 56th sess, UN Doc E/CN.5/2018/4 (29 January–7 February 2018) [60].

65 Kornfeld-Matte (n 2) [126].

THE HUMAN RIGHTS OF OLDER PERSONS   269

Despite the previous international statements acknowledging the importance of the rights of older persons, this sentiment had not been translated into an international treaty explicitly and comprehensively guaranteeing those rights. An increasing number of states and civil society organisations came to the view that the rights of older persons should be enshrined in specific, legally binding norms, in the form of a treaty, rather than as social policy objectives or as non-binding standards in non-binding instruments. However, the human rights frame began to be promoted in earnest when the member states of the United Nations Economic Commission for Latin America and the Caribbean adopted a Regional Strategy to implement MIPAA,[66] which aimed to promote the human rights of older persons, and recommended specific legislation to define and protect those rights.[67] Latin American states continued their push for the rights of older persons to be recognised in the following years, for example, by adopting the 2007 Brasilia Declaration,[68] which explicitly called on the UN Human Rights Council to consider appointing a Special Rapporteur on the human rights of older people as well as pledging to 'promote the drafting of a convention on the rights of older persons within the framework of the United Nations'.[69] Civil society actively lobbied for a convention as well,[70] and at the regional level the Organisation of American States adopted the *Inter-American Convention on Protecting the Human Rights of Older Persons* in 2015.[71] In the meantime, the establishment of the Working Group on Ageing by the UN General Assembly in 2010 had provided a new forum to debate these questions and push forward the project of a convention. This largely represents an acceptance that consideration of a human rights frame is an essential part of addressing the rights of older persons, though it did not completely displace social development frames.

Most states therefore now agree that the issue of older persons should be viewed through a human rights lens—indeed, the mandate of the Working

---

66   Economic Commission for Latin America and the Caribbean, 'Regional Strategy for the Implementation in Latin America and the Caribbean of the Madrid International Plan of Action on Ageing' (Conference Paper, Regional Intergovernmental Conference on Ageing, 19–21 November 2003).

67   Huenchuan and Rodríguez-Piñero (n 49) 37–8.

68   Economic Commission for Latin America and the Caribbean, 'Brasilia Declaration: Second Regional Intergovernmental Conference on Ageing in Latin America and the Caribbean' (Conference Paper, Regional Intergovernmental Conference on Ageing, January 2008).

69   Ibid [25]–[26].

70   Sciubba (n 12); Huenchuan and Rodríguez-Piñero (n 49).

71   *Inter-American Convention on Protecting the Human Rights of Older Persons*, opened for signature 15 June 2015, 55 ILM 985 (entered into force 11 January 2017).

Group on Ageing is based on a human rights framework.[72] However, there is still a minority that principally support a social development frame—seeing older persons as beneficiaries of welfare rather than claimants as rights holders—and as a broader development issue. This means that the state's discretion to adopt policies and measures to address the challenges posed by an ageing population is central rather than its obligations to individual citizens or groups of citizens.

China's position at the Working Group on Ageing is a good example of a state prioritising the social development frame over the human rights frame. China, which has consistently opposed a convention, insisted at the first Working Group on Ageing session that 'we should view the ageing issue from a development perspective'.[73] It re-iterated this in 2014 and 2015, stating that '[a]chieving development is the foundation for the resolution of issues related to aging'[74] and that 'addressing the issue of ageing should be based on economic development'.[75] A representative of the government of Botswana, which has been ambivalent on the issue of a convention,[76] also referred to older persons as a 'social development' issue.[77] China and Botswana, as countries of the global South, have traditionally focused on development-related priorities, sometimes at the expense of supporting human rights-based approaches. More broadly, the subject of older persons, including a proposed convention, has been discussed in the Third Committee of the UN General Assembly under the agenda item 'social development' rather than the 'human rights' agenda item, which suggests the strength of the development frame and the support it

---

72 We recognise that many states which support a human rights frame of older persons' rights also approach the issue through a social development frame in other fora, but a social development frame that is human rights-based. The critical difference is how one views the persons who are the beneficiaries of social development—whether as participating rights-holders or the beneficiaries of discretionary policy decisions by the state to confer benefits.

73 Zhang Dan, 'Statement Made by Ms Zhang Dan at the First Session of the UN Open-Ended Working Group on Ageing' (People's Republic of China, 18 April 2011) 2.

74 Yao Shaojun, 'Statement Made by Counsellor Yao Shaojun at the Fifth Session of the GA Open-Ended Working Group on Ageing' (People's Republic of China, 30 July 2014).

75 Yao Shaojun, 'Statement Made by Counsellor Yao Shaojun at the Sixth Session of the GA Open-Ended Working Group on Ageing' (People's Republic of China, 15 July 2015).

76 For example, Botswana abstained in the vote on *Towards a Comprehensive and Integral International Legal Instrument to Promote and Protect the Rights and Dignity of Older Persons*, UN Doc A/RES/67/139 (n 14) calling for states to consider proposals on a convention (UN General Assembly 2012), nor has it made any statements at the Working Group on Ageing.

77 Field notes, Open-Ended Working Group on Ageing, United Nations, New York, 2016.

THE HUMAN RIGHTS OF OLDER PERSONS   271

receives among the Group of 77, the largest intergovernmental coalition representing developing countries in the UN.[78]

Some states from the global North can be seen adopting both frames of older persons. For example, the European Commission's *2018 Ageing Report* sounded alarm bells on the upward pressure that population ageing will put on public spending. Framing older persons as an economic liability, the report states that 'there is considerable uncertainty as to future developments of age-related public expenditure, related to future GDP growth prospects ... and to the challenge to cope with trend increases in public spending in particular on health care and long-term care'.[79] At the same time, in its *Fundamental Rights Report 2018* the European Union Agency for Fundamental *Rights* endorsed the shift from thinking about old age in terms of 'deficits' that create 'needs' to a more comprehensive one encompassing a 'rights-based' approach towards ageing.[80] Although neither of these reports was presented at the Working Group on Ageing, they may contribute to explaining the competing ideas behind the EU's reluctance to support a convention and their more recent constructive engagement in the Working Group on Ageing process.[81] There are also examples, however, of states using this 'hybrid' frame at the Working Group on Ageing. At the very first session of the Working Group on Ageing, for instance, the delegate of Pakistan stated that the government was sympathetic to the idea of drafting a convention,[82] but clarified that it 'prefer[red] taking an approach on the subject that is development oriented'.[83]

In summary, while there is a minority of states that are still framing the challenges facing older persons as one of social development and even a few that are merging these two frames, the dominant problem frame that has emerged is one of human rights. In this article we are analysing the framing battles taking place at the international level to better understand the political support the convention is (not) receiving and to consider ways of increasing this support. Once one accepts that a human rights framework is a necessary part of

---

78   An exception was in 2016 when the resolution that addressed ageing was presented under the 'human rights' agenda item.

79   European Commission, *The 2018 Ageing Report: Economic & Budgetary Projections for the 28 EU Member States (2016–2070)*, (Institutional Paper 079, May 2018) 6.

80   European Union Agency for Fundamental Rights, *Fundamental Rights Report 2018* (June 2018).

81   Johan ten Geuzendam, 'Closing Statement by European Union at the Open-Ended Working Group on Ageing' (European Union, 15 December 2016).

82   Pakistan, 'Pakistan's Statement during the Concluding Session of the UN Open-Ended Working Group on Ageing' (Pakistan, 21 April 2011).

83   Pakistan, 'Pakistan's Opening Statement during Open-Ended Working Group on Ageing' (Pakistan, 18 April 2011).

addressing the challenges facing older persons, then the question arises: what causes this problem and how might it be resolved? This gives rise to a further set of competing frames that have been part of recent discussions about a convention to which we now turn.

5 The Cause of the Problem

Even within a human rights frame on older persons, the debates over the desirability of a new treaty have been marked by diagnostic frames that are sometimes in tension with each other. This section explores the different ways that participants in the Working Group on Ageing have framed the cause of the widespread violation of the rights of older persons around the world. Some state advocates have argued that the failure of international human rights treaties to explicitly address the situation of older persons in a comprehensive way means that there is a 'normative gap' that needs to be filled by a new set of binding treaty norms, and that closing the 'normative gap' would contribute to the better enjoyment of rights. Opponents, however, argue that there is no 'normative gap', but are rather 'implementation, monitoring, and information gaps', and that existing international norms and implementation mechanisms simply need more vigorous, focused and effective implementation and enforcement to ensure the enjoyment by older persons of their rights. Civil society, from quite an early stage in the Working Group on Ageing, appeared to recognise the futility of exclusively framing the cause of the problem solely in terms of 'normative' gaps and, instead, invoked multiple diagnostic frames in their efforts to demonstrate the need for a convention.

5.1 Normative Gaps versus Other Gaps: the Ongoing Deadlock

In its influential background paper prepared for the Working Group on Ageing in 2012, the Office of the United Nations High Commissioner for Human Rights ('OHCHR') argued that the lack of protection of the rights of older persons is partly due to so-called normative gaps in international human rights law. Specifically, the report stated that 'there is a demonstrable inadequacy of protection arising from normative gaps, as well as fragmentation and a lack of coherence and specificity of standards' on older persons.[84] An official from

---

84   United Nations Office of the High Commissioner for Human Rights, *Normative Standards in International Human Rights Law in Relation to Older Persons* (Analytical Outcome Paper, August 2012) 3. In an earlier report the concept was described as 'where the current provisions fail to provide specific guidance on how to give content and effect to existing

THE HUMAN RIGHTS OF OLDER PERSONS 273

the OHCHR said that the term 'normative gaps' refers to 'the lack of specific ... attention to some issues ... [it is] a combination of lack of sensitivity of existing instruments to the specific issue and then some gaps regarding the lack of coverage of some issues that are important for older persons ...'[85]. HelpAge International has described the concept of normative gap in different ways. In 2009 it explained as the following: 'Human rights are intended to formally define the thresholds that identify situations in which human dignity is threatened or violated. A normative gap exists when there is no such definition [in existing human rights law] or where the definition is inadequate.'[86]

Subsequently in 2017 HelpAge articulated a broader, more elaborate definition of the term. In a presentation at the Global Alliance for National Human Rights Institutions ('GANHRI') working group in Korea, Senior Rights Adviser, Bridget Sleap, said that: 'A normative gap exists when persistent acts, circumstances and institutional factors depriving a person of their dignity are not provided for, or are inadequately provided for, in existing international human rights law'.[87] In its advocacy material, HelpAge refers to the example of the right to palliative care, which it insists is mostly invisible in international human rights law, though it can be derived from the right to health and other existing rights.[88] The group's 2012 report argues that a normative gap exists because international law fails to provide adequate remedies for a failure to ensure the enjoyment of this right.[89]

The 'normative gap' diagnosis of the widespread violations of the rights of older persons around that world was picked up by key states advocating for a convention. Perhaps the most adamant advocate of the normative gap frame was the first Chair of the Working Group on Ageing, Deputy Permanent Representative of Argentina to the United Nations in New York Mateo Estrémé. He said: 'We already know that the Covenants are not enough. This is not a problem about implementation of existing norms at international level but is

---

       norms and to address adequately ongoing practice which denies rights': *Follow-Up Report to the Second World Assembly on Ageing*, UN Doc A/64/127 (n 13) [18].

85   Interview with UN official (Annie Herro, 12 November 2016).

86   HelpAge International, *International Human Rights Law and Older People: Gaps, Fragments and Loopholes* (Report, 2012) 2 (citations omitted) <https://social.un.org/ageing-working -group/documents/GapsinprotectionofolderpeoplesrightsAugust2012.pdf>.

87   Bridget Sleap, 'A New UN Convention on the Rights of Older Persons: Why We Need It and What Should Be in It' (Speech, Global Alliance for National Human Rights Institutions Working Group on Ageing, 18 September 2017).

88   Frank Brennan, 'Palliative Care as an International Human Right' (2007) 33(5) *Journal of Pain and Symptom Management* 494.

89   HelpAge International (n 86) 10.

a problem of a normative gap that we have to really focus on.'[90] Others using this argument included states from Latin America and the Caribbean, for example Guatemala, which referred to gaps in the international legal regime ['*lagunas en el marco jurídico internacional*'],[91] as well as other states that support a convention such as Bangladesh.[92] A number of these states saw normative gaps, lack of specificity of existing norms, and fragmentation and lack of cohesion of general standards that could be interpreted to protect older persons' rights as critical elements of the problem, and a specific convention as an important part of the solution.[93]

Opponents of a convention on the rights of older persons have challenged the normative gap frame.[94] They argue that the rights of older persons were being violated not because of gaps in international law but rather because of the failure to implement *existing* international human rights laws and norms, as well as gaps in monitoring international agreements and in information on older persons. As the EU delegation argued at the Working Group on Ageing in 2014, 'although it is important to discuss the implementation and protection gaps, they are not of a normative nature'.[95] At the ninth session of the Working Group on Ageing in 2018, the representative of Germany called on advocates to demonstrate that there were indeed normative gaps.[96] This position represents the view that while many rights have been articulated in a general way and do not explicitly address older persons or their situations, these general guarantees are capable of being so interpreted and applied. Accordingly, the priority should be to extend the existing human rights to older persons

---

90 Personal communication Mateo Estrémé to Annie Herro, 6 October 2016.

91 Ministerio de Relaciones Exteriores, Guatemala [Ministry of Foreign Affairs, Guatemala], 'Cuarta Sesión del Grupo de Trabajo de Composición Abierta sobre Envejecimiento' [Statement of the Representative of Guatemala at the Fourth Session of the Open-Ended Working Group on Ageing] (12–15 August 2013) [10] <https://social.un.org/ageing-work ing-group/documents/fourth/statements/Guatemala.pdf>.

92 Samia Anjum, 'Statement by Ms Samia Anjum, Counsellor at the General Debate of the Sixth Session of the Open-Ended Working Group on Ageing' (Bangladesh, 14 July 2015) <http://statements.unmeetings.org/media2/7650774/bangladesh.pdf>.

93 Miguel Camilo Ruiz Blanco, 'Quinto Periodo de Sesiones del Grupo de Trabajo de Composición Abierta sobre el Envejecimiento' [Fifth Session of the UN Open-Ended Working Group on Ageing] (Colombia, 30 July 2014) 2–3 <https://social.un.org/ageing -working-group/documents/fifth/Colombia.pdf>.

94 See, eg, Pit Koehler, 'Opening Statement by the European Union' (Fifth Session of the UN Open-Ended Working Group on Ageing, 30 July 2014–1 August 2014) <https://social .un.org/ageing-working-group/documents/fifth/European%20Union_Opening%20 Statement.pdf>.

95 Ibid.

96 Field notes taken by Andrew Byrnes (United Nations, New York, 2018).

THE HUMAN RIGHTS OF OLDER PERSONS

in practice rather than spend time and energy on the formulation of more detailed articulations of these broad rights in treaty form. Other states in the EU, such as Norway, Sweden, Albania and Switzerland all made similar arguments. For example, Switzerland, a staunch opponent of a convention, argued that: 'Switzerland ... does not see normative gaps in the protection of the human rights of older persons. But we do acknowledge that there may well be an *implementation, monitoring and information* gap regarding the respect and promotion of their human rights.'[97]

A 'monitoring gap' refers to the absence of an independent body or mechanism to ensure states comply with their treaty obligations, while information gaps refer to the lack of disaggregated data and statistics on older persons.[98] These counter-frames have been used to slow down pre-negotiations and to divert effort into existing treaty regimes and other policy frameworks. But, according to Estrémé, 'those that were against the possibility of having an international legal instrument devoted to older persons would have found any kind of argument in order to stop the process'.[99] In other words, it has been used by some as an argumentative strategy to block a new instrument.

A similar contestation over the meaning and existence of a 'normative gap' has recently taken place in the context of debates over the desirability of a new international convention on the elimination of violence against women. Some advocates of a new convention have argued that, since there is no United Nations treaty that explicitly addresses violence against women, there is a 'normative gap' that should be filled by a new gendered violence-specific convention.[100] They have seen the demonstration of the existence of a normative gap as a pre-emptive argument, designed to head off states' resistance to new norms on the ground that there are already enough, indeed perhaps too many, relevant norms.

Others, while not necessarily arguing against a new treaty, have contested the existence of the alleged 'normative gap', pointing to the extensive interpretive practice of treaty bodies and states parties under various treaties that make it clear that as a matter of treaty law and probably customary international law there are binding obligations to eliminate violence against women.[101] While there are differences between the normative landscape in the

---

97 Dettling (n 39) (emphasis added).

98 HelpAge International (n 86) 2.

99 Interview with Mateo Estrémé (Annie Herro, New York, 6 October 2016).

100 Rashida Manjoo and Jackie Jones (eds), *The Legal Protection of Women from Violence: Normative Gaps in International Law* (Routledge, 2018).

101 International Women's Rights Action Watch Asia Pacific, 'Gender-Based Violence Against Women and International Human Rights Law: Options for Strengthening the International

two areas, the strategy adopted by advocates of new conventions in each case was to seek to frame the existing law as involving a normative gap which could only effectively be filled by new norms, has been strikingly similar. The critical issue is not whether there are normative gaps, but whether a more detailed and focused treaty would contribute to the more effective fight to eliminate violence against women.

Despite the insistence of some state and civil society advocates that there are indeed normative gaps which a new treaty on the rights of older persons would address, even from the outset civil society, while not abandoning the argument about the existence of a normative gap, sought to engage with opponents on their own ground. As a HelpAge International representative put it, 'there's a lot of discussion around whether there is or isn't a normative gap which isn't useful to our case'.[102] Even in its early advocacy material, HelpAge International recognised, and implicitly endorsed, the view that there were multiple protection gaps—normative, implementation etc.[103] The normative gap frame was also mentioned in one of the first significant publications formally submitted to the Working Group on Ageing in 2011 released by principal NGOs, such as AARP, HelpAge International and the International Association of Homes & Services for the Ageing (now Global Ageing Network). However, that report also recognised implementation gaps to show that existing international law was not being used to protect the rights of older persons and could have been better used for that purpose.[104]

The participants in the 2017 civil society workshop held prior to the eighth session of the Working Group on Ageing acknowledged that '[t]here are normative, protection, data and information gaps' and that '[a] comprehensive legal instrument is necessary to tackle definitional issues'.[105] Civil society advocates have thus recognised that when those resisting a convention

---

Framework' (Discussion Paper, 2015) <http://www.ohchr.org/Documents/Issues/Women/SR/Framework/2.IWRAW-AsiaPacificDiscussionPaperOptionInternationalMechnisms.pdf>; Andrew Byrnes, 'Whose International Law Is It? Some Reflections on the Contributions of Non-State Actors to the Development and Implementation of International Human Rights Law' (2016) 59 *Japanese Yearbook of International Law* 14, 34–43.

102 Personal communication, 9 May 2017.

103 HelpAge International (n 86).

104 INPEA et al, *Strengthening Older People's Rights: Towards a UN Convention* (19 March 2020, Report) <https://social.un.org/ageing-working-group/documents/Coalition%20to%20Strengthen%20the%20Rights%20of%20Older%20People.pdf>; See also *Follow-Up Report to the Second World Assembly on Ageing*, UN Doc A/64/127 (n 13) [18].

105 Ellen Graham, *Civil Society Workshop: Preparing for a Substantive Debate at the 8th Open-Ended Working Group on Ageing* (Summary Report, 3 July 2017) 2 <http://www

THE HUMAN RIGHTS OF OLDER PERSONS   277

characterise the barriers to full enjoyment of rights as resulting from a range of
different gaps (but not from a normative gap that needs new norms to fill it),
they must respond to those characterisations on their own terms. That means
demonstrating that a convention would contribute significantly to the elimination of implementation, monitoring and information gaps, even if other
measures might also assist. These responses are discussed further below.

There is therefore a tension between those arguing that there is a normative
gap in international law and those arguing that there is no normative gap but
rather implementation and other gaps that have not yet been overcome. In
Section 7, we propose an alternative frame of the 'relative invisibility' of older
persons, which could contribute to overcoming the stalemate in the debate
that we have just outlined. But before we do this, we discuss how this stalemate
has consequences for the solutions frame as each diagnostic frame leads to
different positions on the desirability of a proposed convention on the rights
of older persons.

6   The Solutions Proposed

Advocates and opponents have responded to the question of whether a new
convention is necessary with conflicting frames, which correspond to the previously discussed framing tensions. On the one hand, advocates maintain a
new treaty is needed to respond to normative and other gaps in international
law; on the other, opponents insist that strengthening the *current* system of
international human rights law to respond to the information, implementation and other gaps is all that is required to address the problems identified.

6.1   *New Treaty versus Making the System Work Better: Further Deadlock*
Those who argue that there are normative gaps in existing human rights instruments insist that the 'only remedy is to negotiate a legal instrument'.[106] The
Independent Expert on human rights of older persons, Rosa Kornfeld-Matte,
has also called on states to 'consider the various proposals that have been made,
notably the elaboration of a convention on the rights of older persons'.[107]

Conversely, states which argue that normative gaps do not exist have proposed different solutions. Albania, for example, said it is important to use

---

.rightsofolderpeople.org/wp-content/uploads/2017/08/Civil-Society-Workshop-Summary
-Report-Final.pdf>.
106   Interview with Mateo Estrémé (Annie Herro, 6 October 2016).
107   Kornfeld-Matte (n 2) [125].

existing mechanisms and MIPAA to implement the rights of older persons,[108] while Switzerland suggested strengthening the Human Rights Council and its role in the implementation of the rights of older persons.[109] The EU suggested a range of measures to address the various gaps it identified, including compiling the existing human rights standards in one document to improve access to existing norms and encouraging the Independent Expert to contribute to systematically assess the implementation of existing international instruments.[110]

Some members of civil society organisations, for their part, advocated a number of solutions to the various gaps they and others identified.[111] They argued that an implementation gap could only be closed if a variety of measures were adopted. Some of those were practical implementation measures and policy changes at the domestic level, but they insisted that these would be significantly enhanced by the adoption of more detailed normative standards in a new treaty (and presumably the establishment of a new monitoring mechanism).[112] These new binding standards would help to focus advocacy efforts and the minds of policymakers and decision makers at the national level, as had been the case under the CRPD.[113] In this way, they have sought to reconcile the proposed solutions put forward by states on either end of the spectrum by advocating a suite of measures, including the creation of a new convention, to address various gaps in the human rights system.

To summarise, the discussion above shows that violations of the human rights of older persons and, by extension, the prospect of establishing a convention on the rights of older persons are viewed by states, UN actors and civil society through a number of frames, which are sometimes in competition with one another. Specifically, while the challenges faced by older persons have been viewed through competing human rights and social development frames, the former has come to dominate thanks to the adoption of various global policies, the establishment of the Working Group on Ageing and advocacy around it, and other legal developments. This has given rise to an additional tension surrounding the 'normative gap' diagnostic frame which, in turn, corresponds with conflicting ideas about the proposed solutions: that is, the establishment of a new treaty to fill the normative gaps as a critical part of

---

108   Albania, 'Opening Statement—Albania' (4th Session of the UN Open-Ended Working Group on Ageing, New York, 12–15 August 2013) <https://social.un.org/ageing-working -group/documents/fourth/statements/Albania.pdf>.

109   Dettling (n 39).

110   ten Geuzendam (n 81) 2.

111   INPEA et al (n 104).

112   Ibid.

113   HelpAge International (n 86).

THE HUMAN RIGHTS OF OLDER PERSONS 279

an overall strategy to improve the enjoyment by older people of their human rights versus arguments that what is needed, legally speaking, is better implementation of existing rights, to be achieved strengthening the engagement of existing human rights bodies with older person' rights ('the implementation gap' frame). Put differently, this analysis highlights where the central 'sticking points' are in the international discourse surrounding the creation of a convention on the rights of older persons. The next section offers an alternative diagnostic frame—the invisibility frame—in an attempt to overcome this bottleneck to establishing a convention.[114]

7 Reconciling and Moving beyond Current Frames

This section draws on lessons from the CRPD pre-negotiation process[115] to propose an alternative diagnostic frame to the ones currently utilised. We have noted that some members of civil society have tried to circumvent the current impasse by insisting that there is a range of gaps, including a normative one, and by advocating a suite of proposed measures, including the creation of a new convention, to address them.[116] While this seems like a very sensible tactic, it has so far not broken the deadlock between state proponents and opponents of a convention[117]—some opponents have simply not conceded that normative gaps have been shown to exist. In fact, in 2016, to avoid the seemingly never-ending debate about a normative gap and a convention or not, the Chair of the Working Group on Ageing proposed that states should focus on substantive discussions about specific areas of human rights where the protection of older people's rights requires greater attention; this also afforded the opportunity to identify deficiencies in existing norms and their application that might persuade those looking for normative gaps that there were indeed a number. This moved the focus away from the question whether

---

114 We acknowledge that it is possible that the normative gap, the implementation and the invisibility frames could be complementary rather than exclusive and that we could be confronting all of these problems at once; therefore, there is a degree of artificiality in the opposition between 'camps'. We thank the anonymous reviewer for pointing this out.

115 See Annie Herro, 'The Pre-Negotiation of UN Human Rights Treaties: The Case of the Convention on the Rights of Persons with Disabilities' (2019) 24(2) *International Negotiation* 240.

116 United Nations Office of the High Commissioner for Human Rights, 'Human Rights of Older Persons: International Human Rights Principles and Standards' (Background Paper, Open-Ended Working Group on Ageing, 18–21 April 2011).

117 United Nations, *Report of the Open-Ended Working Group on Ageing on its Tenth Working Session*, UN GAOR, 10th sess, UN Doc A/AC.278/2019/2 (20 May 2019) [33].

and why a convention was feasible/desirable to what the rights of older persons might look like.[118] Nevertheless, in the 2019 Working Group on Ageing session, discussions resumed among states about whether or not there was a 'normative gap'.[119]

The definition of a 'normative gap' is of course both a conceptual and semantic exercise: it is certainly defensible to define a 'normative gap' as including a pattern of failure to interpret general norms to apply to the specific circumstances of older persons. But it is questionable whether reliance on such a frame as the principal argument for a convention is tactically viable in light of the strength of the counter-frames used by opponents.

In his reflections on the international process to establish a convention on the rights of older persons, the prominent Irish disability law scholar, Gerard Quinn, who co-authored with German disability law scholar Theresia Degener a report for the OHCHR on the treatment of the rights of persons with disabilities within the UN human rights treaty body system, argued that 'the search for 'normative gaps' to justify creation of a new thematic treaty is a wild goose chase ... There are no normative gaps ... if the universal scheme of rights is both comprehensive and universal.'[120] In other words, Quinn was suggesting the international human rights framework applies to everyone including older persons and that all rights are to be enjoyed without discrimination on the basis of age.

A similar assumption underpinned Quinn and Degener's 2002 report for OHCHR, in which they invoked an 'invisibility' thesis, which meant that, although persons with disabilities were conceptually within the frame of existing rights, they were practically invisible.[121] To use their words:

> The problem is not the values themselves or the system of basic freedoms that they postulate but the fact that they are either not applied or are applied differently to people with disabilities. This is a legacy of the past,

---

118   United Nations, *Report of the Open-Ended Working Group on Ageing on its Ninth Working Session*, UN GAOR, 9th sess, UN Doc A/AC.278/2018/2 (24 August 2018) [38].

119   Personal observation by author (Byrnes) at tenth session of the Working Group on Ageing, New York, June 2019.

120   Gerard Quinn, 'The Anatomy of the Treaty Drafting Process: Lessons for the Age Treaty from the Drafting of the UN Disability Treaty' in Ralph Ruebner, Teresa Do and Amy Taylor (eds), *International and Comparative Law on the Rights of Older Persons* (Vandeplas Publishing, 2015) 4.

121   Gerard Quinn and Theresia Degener, Office of the United Nations High Commissioner on Human Rights, *Human Rights and Disability: The Current Use and Future Potential of United Nations Human Rights Instruments in the Context of Disability* (United Nations, 2002).

THE HUMAN RIGHTS OF OLDER PERSONS 281

when people with disabilities were often virtually invisible citizens of many societies.[122]

Quinn and Degener also integrated the heterogeneity of persons with disability into their invisibility thesis. Under the sub-heading, '[d]ouble invisibility—some are more invisible than others', they argued that:

Children with disabilities have traditionally been seen as less worthy of social investment (for example through education) than other children. Women with disabilities often suffer double discrimination. Other minority groups, including racial and ethnic minorities, fare little better. People with intellectual disabilities find it difficult in many societies to make progress—or at least as much progress as other groups with disabilities.[123]

According to Quinn and Degener, the invisibility of persons with disabilities in international law did not mean that the existing treaties (and the rights they guaranteed) could *not* be interpreted to apply to the particular experiences of people with disabilities but that they *were* not and that this would be unlikely without the added spur of a specific legal instrument. In their report, the authors did not advocate for a new treaty in order to create and insulate an outlier group and endow them with new rights; rather they did so on the assumption that a new instrument would have a catalysing effect and bring about the application of all other existing human rights treaties to persons with disabilities: 'The answer to invisibility is an insistence on the *equal* application of all human rights to persons with disabilities.'[124]

The Quinn/Degener report offered a detailed examination of the limited extent to which the existing system dealt with the rights of persons with disabilities. It analysed the track record of the existing array of UN human rights treaty bodies and found that there was relatively little attention paid to the rights of persons with disabilities and that this was, on the whole, sporadic and not systematic. This provided the basis for an argument that these bodies, which were already overburdened with a large volume of work and confronted a range of competing issue priorities, were unlikely to be able to devote the level of attention and expertise to disability issues required to make a difference at the international and national levels. Accordingly, a new treaty and

---

122   Ibid 23.
123   Ibid.
124   Ibid 27 (emphasis in original).

related monitoring body were both required to dispel the invisibility and address the implementation and monitoring gaps. The question of whether or not there were 'normative gaps' was rendered largely irrelevant. The existing system had not been able to deploy its interpretive and institutional resources to coherently and systematically address the rights of persons with disabilities and there was no realistic prospect that major changes could be made in this regard. Accordingly, a new treaty and monitoring body was the best way to ensure that the human rights system engaged properly with these issues.

In many ways, this argument is similar to that advanced by many civil society advocates—the invisibility of the human rights of older persons is partly a result of implementation and information gaps (and normative gaps if one defines those as the failure to apply general norms to older persons' specific issues). This approach was touched on in the 2012 OHCHR report analysing the current status of the human rights of older person in the international human rights system. However, it was not the central argument of that analysis: while the report expressly uses the language of (relative) invisibility of older persons on a number of occasions, these references are intertwined with arguments about normative gaps and fragmented and incoherent coverage. Moreover, as demonstrated earlier, it is the normative gap frame that has received the most attention from state advocates so, despite the language of invisibility of older persons, this was neither the dominant frame in the report, nor the one that was picked up by proponents of a convention as their main argument. But, as mentioned, the major difference is that civil society's frame, while seeking to transcend the normative gap debate, still encompasses it.[125] Given that this is such a contentious issue for opponents—and one, according to Quinn, that is philosophically flawed—we argue that consensus on starting to draft a new convention will only be possible once the frame is changed from one of normative gaps to one of relative invisibility that will only be dispelled by the stimulus and focus that a new dedicated convention can bring.

The case can be made that the rights of older persons are relatively invisible in the work of the UN human rights treaty bodies.[126] There has already been some documentation of the 'relative invisibility' of older persons in the existing UN human rights system. A search by HelpAge conducted in 2015 for 'older persons' as an affected group listed in the UN's Universal Human Rights Index retrieved only 115 specific recommendations on the rights of older

---

125　Graham (n 105) 2.

126　See, eg, the relatively small number of references to the rights of older persons in the period from 2000–2008 in figures presented in United Nations. See *Follow-Up Report to the Second World Assembly on Ageing*, UN Doc A/64/127 (n 13) [19].

THE HUMAN RIGHTS OF OLDER PERSONS 283

people across all the Special Procedures and Treaty Bodies since 1999. A more recent assessment by the OHCHR put that figure in 2019 at about 1% of all recommendations.[127] Many of those are references to age in a list of prohibited criteria for discrimination and do not reflect any focused substantive engagement with older persons' rights.

Another area where the extent of engagement of treaty bodies with older persons' rights issue can be tested is in the list of issues sent to states parties to the treaties under the reporting procedures. Where states parties have already reported, the relevant committee will send the state a list of issues to which it must respond in writing before the consideration of the state's report. Where states have not yet reported but opted for the so-called 'simplified reporting procedure', the committee sends the state a 'list of issues prior to reporting', which form the basis of the written documentation that the committee considers in its meeting with the state party representatives. The latter type of question in particular reflects the priority that the committee gives to specific issues generally and in the context of the particular state.

Looking at a randomly selected recent set of questions issued to six states parties in 2018 by the Committee on Economic, Social and Cultural Rights (which has adopted an important *General Comment* on the economic, social and cultural rights of older persons),[128] one sees relatively little attention given to older persons' rights. Two sets of questions do not refer to age or older persons at all. In addition, the failure to request information around the broader issues relating to the situation of older persons (apart from pensions and the age of retirement) leads in most cases to the absence of any specific recommendations to the state party by the committee in its final comments on the situation in the state. As a result, there is no stimulus for action on these issues coming from the international level to the domestic level.[129]

Notwithstanding the increasing level of attention that is being paid within the UN system and elsewhere to ageing issues, the problem persists of sporadic and non-systematic consideration of these from a human rights perspective and, with few exceptions, the bodies engaging with these issues do not

---

127   *Activities to Support States' Efforts to Promote and Protect the Human Rights of Older Persons*, UN Doc A/HRC/41/32 (n 23) [42].

128   Committee on Economic, Social and Cultural Rights, *General Comment No 6 (1995): The Economic, Social and Cultural Rights of Older Persons*, UN ESCOR, 13th sess, 39th mtg, UN Doc E/C.12/1995/18 (24 November 1995) annex IV.

129   See states' lists of issues and lists of issues prior to reporting from the 63rd pre-sessional working group of the Committee on Economic, Social and Cultural Rights (15–19 October 2018), available at the following URL: <https://tbinternet.ohchr.org/_lay outs/15/treatybodyexternal/SessionDetails1.aspx?SessionID=1264&Lang=en>.

have any particular expertise in relation to ageing or older persons and their human rights.

While international human rights law is not a panacea and far from the only source of change and rights protection at the national level, the premise of the international human rights system—backed by empirical studies—is that its standards and procedures can play an important role in stimulating change at the domestic level under certain conditions. To achieve this for the rights of older persons, those engaged in the implementation of international human rights standards must first understand the specificities of the violations of older persons' rights and conceptualise them as falling within the existing guarantees. But they must also put time, energy and resources into ensuring that these issues are given informed, coherent and systematic attention— something which is difficult to achieve within already overcrowded agendas occupying the attention of committees whose members do not necessarily have particular expertise in relation to the rights of older persons.

8   Conclusion

Winning over states that are currently opposed or ambivalent to a convention is more than simply a re-framing exercise: some states deploy oppositional frames strategically as a ploy to hinder the Working Group on Ageing process and to disguise more fundamental concerns about a convention such as its assumed cost. In these cases, reformulating the frames is unlikely to prompt them to shift their position. Other states may genuinely be open to persuasion and demonstration that the adoption of a new treaty can make a unique and significant contribution to addressing the monitoring, implementation or information gaps—or remedying the relative invisibility of older persons and their human rights in existing norms and practice. Acceptance of that position would mean a significant adjustment of the prognosis and solution frames. While ultimately the primary catalyst for change to bring about a convention will be political pressure, especially at the national level, arguments about how the problem is framed are part of that debate. Changing the framing of the issues has the potential to persuade governments that are genuinely open to evidence-based argument that a new convention is a critical component of improving our communities' responses to the widespread failures to respect, protect and ensure the rights of older persons around the world.

Notes

∴

Revisiting *Lockerbie*: How a General Principle of Judicial Review Could Promote United Nations Security Council Reform

*Kate Renehan**

1 Introduction[1]

Despite its position at the centre of world politics, the United Nations ('UN') is at a crossroads. Not only is the popularity of multilateralism in decline,[2] but the structure and work of its most famous organ, the United Nations Security Council ('the Council'), is the subject of increasing scrutiny and calls for reform.[3] Three major criticisms dominate discussions about Council reform. First, the Council's inability to deal with mass atrocities due to the stifling effect of the veto power.[4] Second, how permanent membership is manifestly unrepresentative of modern power blocs at the UN, particularly Africa, Asia and the Middle East.[5] Third, the inadequate working methods of the Council, predominantly regarding transparency of process, the Council's post-Cold War expansion of power, and the lack of compliance to legal limitations.[6] This has led to concerted efforts in recent times to reform the Council. However, given the splintering of beliefs within the UN membership regarding how reform should proceed,[7] meaningful reform is unlikely to occur in the immediate future.

---

* BIR, LLB (Hons) (ANU).

1 The author is currently Tipstaff to the Honourable Justice Peter Garling RFD. This note was submitted as part of the author's candidacy for Honours in law at the Australian National University. The author wishes to thank Professor Donald Rothwell for his insightful assistance when writing this note.

2 G John Ikenberry, 'The End of Liberal International Order?' (2018) 94(1) *International Affairs* 7, 8.

3 Shashi Tharoor, 'Security Council Reform: Past, Present, and Future' (2011) 25(4) *Ethics and International Affairs* 397, 397.

4 Richard Butler, 'Reform of the United Nations Security Council' (2012) 1(1) *Penn State Journal of Law and International Affairs* 23, 34.

5 Matthew Gould and Matthew D Rablen, 'Reform of the United Nations Security Council: Equity and Efficiency' (2017) 173(1–2) *Public Choice* 145, 147; Yehuda Z Blum, 'Proposals for UN Security Council Reform' (2005) 99(3) *American Journal of International Law* 632, 638.

6 Daniel Moeckli and Raffael N Fasel, 'A Duty to Give Reasons in the Security Council: Making Voting Transparent' (2017) 14(1) *International Organizations Law Review* 13, 15, 24.

7 Brian Cox, 'United Nations Security Council Reform: Collected Proposals and Possible Consequence' (2009) 6(1) *South Carolina Journal of International Law and Business* 89, 105–12.

© KONINKLIJKE BRILL NV, LEIDEN, 2021 | DOI:10.1163/26660229_03801013

Whilst veto and membership reform will require amendments to the *Charter of the United Nations ('Charter')*, it is arguable that working methods reform could be at least partially addressed through alternate means. Namely, it is timely to consider whether judicial review of Council resolutions by the International Court of Justice ('the Court'), when raised in a broader dispute between states, would go some way to reforming the Council's working methods. The Court did not determine whether it has such a power of judicial review when it considered the question over two decades ago in *Questions of Interpretation and Application of the 1971 Montreal Convention Arising from the Aerial Incident at Lockerbie*,[8] and this issue has divided academic literature ever since. Criticism of the Council's working methods, particularly the alleged disregard of legal limitations,[9] could be remedied at least in part if resolutions could be subject to judicial review to ensure procedural validity, and deal with accusations of resolutions being ultra vires.

However, recent attempts by other UN organs to deal with the Council's failures to act have been subject to criticism. For example, the 2016 establishment of the International, Impartial and Independent Mechanism for the Syrian Arab Republic by the United Nations General Assembly ('the Assembly') after the Council failed to establish an accountability mechanism for Syria was met with fierce criticism from some states, due to the perception that the Assembly went outside its jurisdiction to achieve political ends.[10] This exemplifies the difficulty of addressing Council inadequacies through other UN organs: whilst it can be an effective and creative way to deal with the lack of progress in reform efforts,[11] to do so without clear and unambiguous jurisdiction can lead to serious legitimacy questions which complicate any progress.

Accordingly, this note aims to reconsider the question of judicial review in light of these recent discussions regarding Council reform. In conducting this analysis, this note proceeds on the basis that the Court could play a part

---

8 (*Libya v United Kingdom*) (*Preliminary Objections*) [1998] ICJ Rep 9 ('*Lockerbie Preliminary Objections*'). See also *Lockerbie* (*Libya v United States of America*) (*Preliminary Objections*) [1998] ICJ Rep 115. Given the cases have identical judgments, citations used in this note refer to the former.

9 Ian Hurd, 'The UN Security Council and the International Rule of Law' (2014) 7(3) *Chinese Journal of International Politics* 361, 369.

10 See, eg, *Prevention of Armed Conflict*, UN GAOR, 71st sess, 66th plen mtg, Agenda Item 31, UN Doc A/71/PV.66 (21 December 2016): at 21–2 (Syria); at 23 (Russia); at 24 (Venezuela); at 25 (Cuba); at 26 (South Africa); at 27 (Iran); at 28 (Algeria); Christian Wenaweser and James Cockayne, 'Justice for Syria?: The International, Impartial and Independent Mechanism and the Emergence of the UN General Assembly in the Realm of International Criminal Justice' (2017) 15(2) *Journal of International Criminal Justice* 211, 218.

11 Alex Whiting, 'An Investigation Mechanism for Syria: The General Assembly Steps into the Breach' (2017) 15(2) *Journal of International Criminal Justice* 231, 237.

in revitalising the Council's working methods if it had the power to review the validity of Council resolutions when raised within broader disputes in its contentious jurisdiction. However, the Court could only retain legitimacy in undertaking such review if a clear jurisdictional basis was established and the rights of both parties to the case were duly respected.

This note will not consider whether advisory opinions could play a role in judicial review of the Council. Furthermore, this note does not contend that the validity of a Council resolution could be directly appealed to the Court in its contentious jurisdiction. Rather, this note will consider whether there is any jurisdiction to consider a question of validity if it is raised as part of a broader dispute litigated between states.

This note consists of three sections. The first section explores the powers of the Council and the Court, and the current relationship between the two organs. The second section considers whether any legal basis exists upon which the Court could base jurisdiction for judicial review. Here, this note will show a gap exists in art 36(1) of the *Statute of the International Court of Justice* ('*Statute*'), specifically regarding the exact boundaries of the Court's jurisdiction when faced with judicial review of a Council resolution. Consequently, this section concludes that the jurisdictional gap could be filled by a general principle of judicial review. Building upon this, the third section develops a model to guide judicial discretion in applying this general principle, with a focus on maximising the legitimacy of the Court by ensuring judicial review remains within the confines of the *Charter* system.

2   The Landscape of Judicial Review

This section explores the established relationship between the Court and the Council by considering three defining aspects: (a) the powers of the two organs; (b) how the Court defines its relationship with the Council; and (c) the scholarly debate regarding judicial review.

2.1   *Relevant Powers of the Court and the Council*
2.1.1   Powers of the Council
The Council was created to provide the UN with greater enforcement power than its predecessor, the League of Nations.[12] Because of this, the *Charter* confers upon the Council broad and largely unfettered powers to fulfil its primary

---

12   Jean-d'Amour K Twibanire, 'The United Nations Security Council: Imbalance of Power and the Need for Reform' (2016) 2(1) *International Journal of Political Science and Diplomacy* 106, 106.

responsibility of maintaining international peace and security.[13] Council resolutions override treaty obligations for states,[14] meaning the Council is placed at a 'supreme position' in international law.[15]

The strongest powers of the Council are contained in ch VII, which enables the Council to take either provisional, diplomatic or forceful action against a declared threat to international peace and security in order to maintain or restore peace.[16] States have a legal obligation to carry out such decisions from the Council.[17] Whilst these powers were conferred on the Council to guarantee the UN had the requisite enforcement power to ensure longevity,[18] they have in the modern day become the aspects of the Council's work which are most readily accused of being ultra vires.[19] Thus, a large proportion of reform discussions for the Council concern either the alleged misuse of ch VII powers,[20] or criticism of the inability to invoke ch VII in cases of mass atrocity due to the veto power.[21] For this reason, any consideration of potential judicial review of Council decisions will most readily concern ch VII decisions.

2.1.2 Limitations on the Council

The Council's largely unfettered power is limited only by certain requirements imposed by the *Charter* and *jus cogens* norms.

First, the *Charter* imposes structural limitations. The five permanent members possess a veto power,[22] yet resolutions supported by the permanent

---

13   *Charter of the United Nations* art 24(1) ('*Charter*'); Anna Spain, 'The UN Security Council's Duty to Decide' (2013) 4(2) *Harvard National Security Journal* 320, 329.

14   *Charter* (n 13) arts 25, 103.

15   Devon Whittle, 'The Limits of Legality and the United Nations Security Council: Applying the Extra-Legal Measures Model to Chapter VII Action' (2015) 26(3) *European Journal of International Law* 671, 674.

16   *Charter* (n 13) arts 39, 40, 41, 42; Jared Schott, 'Chapter VII as Exception: Security Council Action and the Regulative Ideal of Emergency' (2007) 6(1) *Northwestern Journal of International Human Rights* 24, 26.

17   *Charter* (n 13) art 48.

18   Matthew D Stephen, 'Legitimacy Deficits of International Organizations: Design, Drift, and Decoupling at the UN Security Council' (2018) 31(1) *Cambridge Review of International Affairs* 96, 107.

19   Eric Rosand, 'The Security Council As "Global Legislator": Ultra Vires or Ultra Innovative?' (2004) 28(3) *Fordham International Law Journal* 542, 544.

20   Hitoshi Nasu, 'Chapter VII Powers and the Rule of Law: The Jurisdictional Limits' [2007] 26 *Australian Year Book of International Law* 87, 96.

21   Graham Melling and Anne Dennett, 'The Security Council Veto and Syria: Responding to Mass Atrocities through the "Uniting for Peace" Resolution' (2017) 57(3–4) *Indian Journal of International Law* 285, 287.

22   *Charter* (n 13) art 27(3).

members can be defeated if other Council members vote against them.[23] Thus, the Council's structure gives the permanent five the ability to restrict the Council's agenda,[24] but not the power to force action without broader agreement. This provides an inherent limitation to the Council's power to take forceful action. Second, the *Charter* imposes procedural rules on the Council. For example, if the Council holds a debate concerning a dispute between states, the Council must include all parties to the dispute in the meeting.[25] This prevents the Council from acting without due consideration of all perspectives. Third, the Council must act in accordance with the purposes and principles of the UN.[26] The *travaux préparatoires* of the *Charter* confirm that the principles and purposes were intended to meaningfully govern the conduct of the Council, despite their breadth.[27] Nevertheless, the generality of this restriction means that in practice, the Council has relative freedom under international law. This largely unobstructed power is by design, as the framers deliberately opted to create a body which would not be restricted in its ability to respond quickly to issues.[28]

Council powers are also limited by *jus cogens* norms, which are fundamental rules of international law which bind all states and from which no derogation is permitted.[29] *Jus cogens* norms are considered superior to the law of treaties,[30] and therefore must also limit the acts of organs created by treaty.[31] Thus, though some do argue the Council could theoretically mandate a breach of a

---

23   Ibid art 27.

24   Blessing Nneka Iyase and Sheriff Folami Folarin, 'A Critique of Veto Power System in the United Nations Security Council' (2018) 11(2) *Acta Universitatis Danubius: Relationes Internationales* 104, 106.

25   *Charter* (n 13) art 32.

26   Ibid arts 1, 2, 24(2).

27   Leland M Goodrich, Edvard Hambro and Anne Patricia Simons, *Charter of the United Nations: Commentary and Documents* (Colombia University Press, 3rd rev ed, 1969) 23; Nicholas Tsagourias, 'Security Council Legislation, Article 2(7) of the UN Charter, and the Principle of Subsidiarity' (2011) 24(3) *Leiden Journal of International Law* 539, 550.

28   CL Lim, 'The Great Power Balance, the United Nations and What the Framers Intended: In Partial Response to Hans Köchler' (2007) 6(2) *Chinese Journal of International Law* 307, 318.

29   *Vienna Convention on the Law of Treaties*, opened for signature 23 May 1969, 1155 UNTS 331 (entered into force 27 January 1980) art 53 ('*VCLT*').

30   Ibid.

31   Alexander Orakhelashvili, 'The Acts of the Security Council: Meaning and Standards of Review' (2007) 11(1) *Max Planck Yearbook in United Nations Law* 143, 178.

jus cogens norm,[32] it is the more widely accepted view that *jus cogens* norms bind the Council.[33]

2.1.3   Powers of the Court

The Court is the principal judicial organ of the UN.[34] It has the power to deliver two types of judicial decisions. First, the Court can adjudicate contentious cases between states,[35] with the resulting judgment binding only between the parties.[36] In this contentious jurisdiction, all issues that the parties refer to the Court are justiciable, as well as those provided for in the *Charter* or other treaties.[37] If a party is non-compliant with a judgment, the Council is empowered to take measures to give effect to the Court's decision.[38] Second, the Court has the power to deliver non-binding advisory opinions when requested by UN organs to clarify a point of law.[39] This function is not an appellate jurisdiction, rather a form of legal advice to assist other UN organs.[40] Though neither contentious judgments or advisory opinions are universally binding in the international system, both are influential in the development of international law.[41] Certainly, the Court itself frequently refers to its previous decisions, even if the decision comes from the alternate jurisdiction (that is, the Court will

---

32   Gabriël H Oosthuizen, 'Playing the Devil's Advocate: The United Nations Security Council is Unbound by Law' (1999) 12(3) *Leiden Journal of International Law* 549, 559.

33   See, eg, *Prosecutor v Tadić* (*Judgment*) (International Criminal Tribunal for the Former Yugoslavia, Appeals Chamber, Case No IT-94-1-A, 15 July 1999) [296]; *Application of the Convention on the Prevention and Punishment of the Crime of Genocide* (*Bosnia & Herzegovina v Yugoslavia*) (*Provisional Measures*) [1993] ICJ Rep 325, 440 (Judge Lauterpacht) ('*Genocide Case*'); Dire Tladi, Special Rapporteur, *Third Report on Peremptory Norms of General International Law* (*Jus Cogens*), UN Doc A/CN.4/714 (12 February 2018); Alexander Orakhelashvili, 'The Impact of Peremptory Norms on the Interpretation and Application of United Nations Security Council Resolutions' (2005) 16(1) *European Journal of International Law* 59, 63.

34   *Charter* (n 13) art 92.

35   *Statute of the International Court of Justice* art 34 ('*Statute*').

36   Ibid art 59.

37   Ibid art 36.

38   *Charter* (n 13) art 94(2).

39   *Statute* (n 35) art 65.

40   Teresa F Mayr and Jelka Mayr-Singer, 'Keep the Wheels Spinning: The Contributions of Advisory Opinions of the International Court of Justice to the Development of International Law' [2016] 76 *Heidelberg Journal of International Law* 425, 427.

41   S Gozie Ogbodo, 'An Overview of the Challenges Facing the International Court of Justice in the 21st Century' [2012] 18 *Annual Survey of International and Comparative Law* 93, 99–105.

REVISITING LOCKERBIE

reference previous advisory opinions when adjudicating contentious cases and vice-versa).[42]

Despite having separate roles, the jurisdictions of the Court and Council have intersected on past occasions.[43] It is therefore vital to consider how the Court has conceptualised its relationship with the Council when jurisdictions intersect.

2.2 Relationship between the Council and the Court

Previously, the Court has considered two questions regarding its relationship with the Council: whether the Court has jurisdiction to consider an issue concurrently with the Council, and whether the Court has capacity to review the Council.

2.2.1 Concurrent Consideration of Issues

Concurrent consideration of issues by the Council and the Court was first considered in *Corfu Channel*,[44] where the Court stated that the Council 'undoubtedly intended that the whole dispute should be decided by the Court'.[45] However, concurrent consideration has not always been this clear cut. On multiple subsequent occasions, questions have been raised about how, and when, issues can be concurrently considered by the Council and other UN organs.[46] On all such occasions, the Court has remained steadfast to one basic principle: whilst the *Charter* provides the Council with primary responsibility over maintaining international peace and security, the Council is not conferred sole responsibility.[47] Consequently, when there is requisite competence to do so, other UN organs do have the capacity to consider issues concurrently

---

42   See, eg, *Gabčikovo—Nagymaros Project (Hungary v Slovakia) (Judgment)* [1997] ICJ Rep 7, 41, quoting *Legality of the Threat or Use of Nuclear Weapons (Advisory Opinion)* [1996] ICJ Rep 226.

43   Despite not being a court, it is common in literature to refer to the Council's 'jurisdiction': see, eg, Simon Chesterman, Thomas M Franck and David M Malone, *Law and Practice of the United Nations* (Oxford University Press, 2008), 105.

44   *(United Kingdom v Albania) (Merits)* [1949] ICJ Rep 4.

45   Ibid 26.

46   See, eg, *Certain Expenses of the United Nations (Article 17, paragraph 2 of the Charter) (Advisory Opinion)* [1962] ICJ Rep 151 ('*Certain Expenses*'); *United States Diplomatic and Consular Staff in Tehran (United States of America v Iran) (Jurisdiction)* [1980] ICJ Rep 3 ('*Tehran Case*'); *Military and Paramilitary Activities in and against Nicaragua (Nicaragua v United States of America) (Jurisdiction)* [1984] ICJ Rep 392 ('*Nicaragua*').

47   See, eg, *Certain Expenses* (n 46) 165; *Tehran Case* (n 46) 22 [40]; *Nicaragua* (n 46) 434–5 [95].

to the Council.[48] However, this power of concurrent consideration does not extend to areas where the *Charter* has conferred sole power to the Council.[49]

In its advisory capacity, the Court has recommended this interpretation for concurrent consideration of issues by the Assembly and the Council.[50] In its contentious jurisdiction, the Court has confirmed its own competence to adjudicate matters concurrently before the Council on multiple occasions.[51] The Court has further held it retains its competence even after the Council has made a declaration that a situation is a threat to international peace and security, stating:

> The Council has functions of a political nature assigned to it, whereas the Court exercises purely judicial functions. Both organs can therefore perform their separate but complementary functions with respect to the same events.[52]

The Court, through such cases, has clearly set out its view that it sits alongside the Council in the *Charter* system,[53] performing a separate function which is not subservient to, nor directly influenced by, political decisions made concurrently by the Council.[54]

(ii)   Judicial Review of Council Resolutions

This question is divided into two separate but related considerations: whether the Court can review the validity of Council process, and whether the Court can review the validity of Council action.

Regarding review of process, the Court has shown some willingness in its advisory capacity to review procedural validity of resolutions. In both *Legal*

---

48   Kathleen Renée Cronin-Furman, 'The International Court of Justice and the United Nations Security Council: Rethinking a Complicated Relationship' (2006) 106(2) *Columbia Law Review* 435, 442.

49   *Certain Expenses* (n 46) 165.

50   Michael Ramsden, '"Uniting for Peace" In the Age of International Justice' (2016) 42(1) *Yale Journal of International Law Online* 1, 21.

51   *Tehran Case* (n 46) 22 [40]; *Nicaragua* (n 46) 434–5 [95]; *Armed Activities on the Territory of the Congo (Democratic Republic of the Congo v Uganda) (Provisional Measures)* [2000] ICJ Rep 111, 126 [36].

52   *Nicaragua* (n 46) 434–5 [95].

53   Henry G Schermers and Neils M Blokker, *International Institutional Law: Unity within Diversity* (Martinus Nijhoff, 5th rev ed, 2011) 171.

54   Vera Gowlland-Debbas, 'The Relationship Between the International Court of Justice and the Security Council in the Light of the Lockerbie Case' (1994) 88(4) *American Journal of International Law* 643, 648.

Consequences for States of the Continued Presence of South Africa in Namibia (South-West Africa) Notwithstanding Security Council Resolution 276 (1970)[55] and *Legal Consequences of the Construction of a Wall in the Occupied Palestinian Territory*,[56] the Court considered the procedural validity of the resolution requesting the advisory opinion to confirm its own jurisdiction.[57]

However, these instances do not necessarily mean that the Court has opened the door to review of Council process in its contentious jurisdiction.[58] In both *Namibia* and the *Wall Opinion,* the disputed resolutions formed the basis of the Court's jurisdiction, and thus procedural review was required to determine the Court's ability to issue the advisory opinion.[59] Indeed, after conducting procedural review in *Namibia*, the Court went on to state that '[u]ndoubtedly, the Court does not possess powers of judicial review or appeal in respect of the decisions taken by the United Nations organs concerned'.[60]

Namibia is a key opinion in consideration of judicial review power. On the one hand, the Court's willingness to review procedural issues to confirm its advisory jurisdiction may indicate an openness by the Court to reviewing a resolution's procedural compliance in its contentious jurisdiction.[61] On the other hand, the subsequent dismissal in *Namibia* of the notion of using the Court for judicial review suggests that the Court is generally unwilling to review the substantive decisions of other UN organs. Given the dismissal of judicial review in *Namibia* was to the Court being a body of direct appeal through advisory opinions, the nuance of whether ancillary review in the Court's contentious jurisdiction is acceptable remains unresolved.[62]

Additionally, these advisory opinions do not cover the second, and far more contentious, aspect of this question: to what extent, if any, can the Court directly review a question the Council has already ruled on, thus questioning

---

55   (*Advisory Opinion*) [1971] ICJ Rep 16 ('*Namibia*').

56   (*Advisory Opinion*) [2004] ICJ Rep 136 ('*Wall Opinion*').

57   *Namibia* (n 55) 22 [21]–[25]; *Wall Opinion* (n 56) 148–52 [24]–[35].

58   Dapo Akande, 'The International Court of Justice and the Security Council: Is there Room for Judicial Control of Decisions of the Political Organs of the United Nations?' (1997) 46(2) *International and Comparative Law Quarterly* 309, 326.

59   Michelle Burgis, 'Discourses of Division: Law, Politics and the ICJ Advisory Opinion on the Legal Consequences of the Construction of a Wall in the Occupied Palestinian Territory' (2008) 7(1) *Chinese Journal of International Law* 33, 41.

60   *Namibia* (n 55) 45 [89].

61   Matthew Happold, 'Reviewing the Security Council' [2009] 103 *Proceedings of the Annual Meeting (American Society of International Law)* 481, 481.

62   Eric Zubel, 'The Lockerbie Controversy: Tension Between the International Court of Justice and the Security Council' (1999) 5(1) *Annual Survey of International and Comparative Law* 259, 280, 282.

the validity of the ruling made by the Council? This was the question faced by the Court in *Lockerbie*, and ultimately left unanswered due to diplomatic resolution of the dispute before the merits phase.[63] This question has not arisen again and thus, remains unresolved.

In the absence of a *Lockerbie* merits judgment, it is the various dissenting opinions from the provisional measures and preliminary objections phases of *Lockerbie* that have inspired a wealth of academic literature on this topic. This is primarily because multiple different judges across these two phases present polarising, disparate and conflicting opinions on the extent of the Court's power. A consideration of these judicial opinions and the academic arguments they inspired is therefore vital to lay the foundation for later consideration by this note of whether a legal basis for review exists.

2.3 *Arguments in Literature*

The most prominent arguments for and against judicial review of the Council by the Court tend to fall into two theoretical camps: realists and legalists.

(i) Realist School

A consistent principle underpins arguments posited by realist scholars: given that the *Charter* does not provide the Court with the power to review the Council, any such review would be outside the jurisdiction of the Court.[64] Judicial foundation for this realist perspective is found within the dissenting opinions from the preliminary objections phase of *Lockerbie*. Of particular note is the dissenting opinion of President Schwebel, which states:

---

63   M Plachta, 'The Lockerbie Case: The Role of the Security Council in Enforcing the Principle *Aut Dedere Aut Judicare*' (2001) 12(1) *European Journal of International Law* 125, 135.

64   For scholars who advocate a realist perspective: see, eg, W Michael Reisman, 'The Constitutional Crisis in the United Nations' (1993) 87(1) *American Journal of International Law* 83; Gregory H Fox, 'Discussion' in Jost Delbrück (ed), *New Trends in International Law-Making: International 'Legislation' in the Public Interest* (Duncker & Hamblot, 1997) 319; Deborah D'Angelo, 'The Check on International Peace and Security Maintenance: The International Court of Justice and Judicial Review of Security Council Resolutions' [1999–2000] 23 *Suffolk Transnational Law Review* 561; Jaroslav Ušiak and Ľubica Saktorová, 'The International Court of Justice and the Legality of UN Security Council Resolutions' (2014) 5(3) *DANUBE* 201; Scott S Evans 'The Lockerbie Incident Cases: Libyan-Sponsored Terrorism, Judicial Review and the Political Question Doctrine' (1994) 18(1) *Maryland Journal of International Law and Trade* 21, 76; Edward McWhinney, 'The International Court as Emerging Constitutional Court and the Co-Ordinate UN Institutions (Especially the Security Council): Implications of the Aerial Incident at Lockerbie' [1992] 30 *Canadian Yearbook of International Law* 261, 271; Michael J Matheson, 'ICJ Review of Security Council Decisions' (2004) 36(3) *George Washington International Law Review* 615, 622.

> The texts of the Charter of the United Nations and of the Statute of the Court furnish no shred of support for a conclusion that the Court possesses a power of judicial review in general, or a power to supervene the decisions of the Security Council in particular.[65]

Realist scholars tend to approach this argument in three ways. First, the *Charter* is a treaty, not a constitution.[66] Thus, unlike domestic courts which have 'read in' a judicial review power to constitutional documents,[67] the Court can only rely upon powers established by agreed sources of international law. Second, the *Charter* system prioritises international security, and thus a Council with broad powers and no legal 'straightjacket' is consistent with the intentions of the drafters of the *Charter*.[68] To implement judicial review would inhibit the powers of a body that necessarily requires quick and unencumbered action at its disposal to achieve its overall purpose of maintaining international peace and security. Third, the restrictions imposed on the Council by the *Charter* are broad in nature, and thus any attempt to use them as a basis for judicial review will necessarily require the Court to reconsider the original issue before the Council.[69] This would amount to appellate jurisdiction, and would see the Court engage in political decision making.[70] This politicisation of the Court would not only be outside the Court's powers, but undermine the standing of the Court in the international community.

Many realist scholars also point to the fact that Belgium proposed that the Court have a power of review over Council action during the drafting of the *Charter*. This proposal was ultimately rejected.[71] To some, this renders arguments regarding judicial review pointless, as member states already considered the possibility and rejected it. However, when the United States ('US') voted against the proposal, it specifically noted that states would retain the right to bring cases which 'might properly be before the court'.[72] This implies that the US at the time did not see the rejection of a *direct* avenue for judicial review as a rejection of the Court having any recourse to judicial review under certain

---

65   *Lockerbie (Preliminary Objections)* (n 8) 75 (President Schwebel).

66   See, eg, Matheson (n 64) 622.

67   *Marbury v Madison* 5 US 137, 170 (1803) ('*Marbury v Madison*').

68   See, eg, D'Angelo (n 64) 590.

69   See, eg, Reisman (n 64) 93.

70   *Statute* (n 35) art 36.

71   Summary Report of Seventh Meeting of Committee III/2, *Documents of the United Nations Conference on International Organization Volume XII*, UN Doc 433, III/2/1513 (19 May 1945) 49 ('UNCIO').

72   Ibid.

circumstances. Thus, it would be disingenuous to view the rejection of a direct appellate power as equivalent to rejecting ancillary review when it is part of a larger question properly brought before the Court.

(ii)   Legalist School

On the other hand, the opposing legalist school argues that the Court does possess a power of review,[73] as the very existence of restrictions on the Council in the *Charter* is evidence that states did not intend for the system to have an unaccountable, all powerful body at its helm. This is the view shared by the dissenting judges in the provisional measures phase, perhaps most famously by Judge Weeramantry:

> But it by no means follows from these propositions that the Court when properly seised of a legal dispute should co-operate with the Security Council to the extent of desisting from exercising its independent judgment on matters of law properly before it.[74]

---

73   For scholars who advocate a legalist perspective: see, eg, James Crawford, '*Marbury v Madison* at the International Level' (2004) 36(3) *George Washington International Law Review* 505, 512; Jose E Alvarez, 'Judging the Security Council' (1996) 90(1) *American Journal of International Law* 1; Bernd Martenczuk, 'The Security Council, the International Court and Judicial Review: What Lessons from Lockerbie' (1999) 10(3) *European Journal of International Law* 517; Ken Roberts, 'Second-Guessing the Security Council: The International Court of Justice and its Powers of Judicial Review' (1995) 7(2) (Spring) *Pace International Law Review* 281; Bernhard Graefrath, 'Leave to the Court What Belongs to the Court: The Libyan Case' (1993) 4(2) *European Journal of International Law* 184; Geoffrey R Watson, 'Constitutionalism, Judicial Review and the World Court' (1993) 34(1) (Winter) *Harvard International Law Journal* 1; Robert Kolb, *The International Court of Justice* (Hart Publishing, 2013); Mohammed Bedjaoui, *The New World Order and the Security Council: Testing the Legality of its Act* (Martinus Nijhoff Publishers, 1994); Thomas M Franck, 'The "Powers of Appreciation": Who Is the Ultimate Guardian of UN Legality?' (1992) 86(3) *American Journal of International Law* 519, 523; Matthias J Herdegen, 'The "Constitutionalization" of the UN Security System' (1994) 27(1) *Vanderbilt Journal of Transnational Law* 135, 156; Robert F Kennedy, '*Libya v United States*: The International Court of Justice and the Power of Judicial Review' (1993) 33(4) (Summer) *Virginia Journal of International Law* 899, 924; Derek Bowett, 'The Impact of Security Council Decisions on Dispute Settlement Procedures' (1994) 5(1) *European Journal of International Law* 89; Kamrul Hossain, 'Legality of the Security Council Action: Does the International Court of Justice Move to Take up the Challenge of Judicial Review' (2009) 5(17) *Review of International Law and Politics* 133, 159.

74   *Interpretation and Application of the* 1971 Montreal Convention *Arising from the Aerial Incident at Lockerbie* (*Libya v United Kingdom*) (*Provisional Measures*) [1992] ICJ Rep 3, 59 (Judge Weeramantry).

Legalists argue that as the principal judicial body, the Court is properly placed to enforce such limitations. Different justifications are promulgated to support this stance. Some frame the argument as constitutional in nature, analogising the situation to that seen in *Marbury v Madison*.[75] Many also point to the fact that the Court has in the past reviewed the validity of action from other bodies of the UN.[76] Therefore, judicial review of the Council is not outside the purview of what the Court has already deemed itself competent to do. Others point to the changing context of the world: whilst in 1945, the primary concern was effectiveness of the Council and longevity of the organisation, these concerns no longer define the UN.[77] Rather, the organisation in the modern day has greater regard for compliance with the *Charter* system of laws, the legitimacy of Council decisions, and checking the powers of the permanent five members.

An issue with many legalist arguments is the reliance on theoretical or political ideas rather than identifying a specific legal basis for extending the Court's jurisdiction. Whilst the changing nature of the world is certainly a valid criticism of the modern UN system, it does not give the Court the ability to unilaterally change the powers conferred upon it within the UN system. Similarly, the argument that the Court has chosen in the past to review the actions of other bodies also fails to hold much weight without any legal grounding. If the Court has in the past gone beyond its jurisdiction, this is not an argument for the Court to continue doing so without seeking a basis for such action. This would only further damage the standing of the Court and its legitimacy. As the principal judicial body, the Court must above all else be the standard bearer for compliance to the *Charter*. A Court which does not hold itself to its own *Charter* limitations can hardly review other bodies for going beyond their own limitations with any level of legitimacy.

This is not to say the legalist school is necessarily incorrect. Rather, it is imperative that any future action by the Court which seeks to review Council action is grounded in law, not politics. It is therefore necessary to explore whether an acceptable legal basis exists upon which the Court could base an ancillary review of Council resolutions.

---

75   See, eg, Watson (n 73) 19; Roberts (n 73) 286–7; Franck (n 73) 519.

76   See, eg, Crawford (n 73) 510–11; Watson (n 73) 14–28.

77   See, eg, Kolb (n 73) 884; Roberts (n 73) 315.

3   Legal Basis for Judicial Review

This section will consider what legal basis the Court could rely upon to undertake ancillary review. Article 36(1) of the *Statute* provides the Court's jurisdiction, and thus serves as the starting point for any discussion.

However, if art 36(1) neither provides nor precludes requisite jurisdiction in a case, and thus contains a gap (*lacuna*) in the law, what is the Court to do? Neither the *Charter* nor the *Statute* provides the power for judges of the Court to employ unfettered discretion to fill such gaps.[78] Rather, looking to the discussions of the original Committee of Jurists for the *Statute of the Permanent Court of International Justice* ('*PCIJ Statute*'), 'general principles of international law' were originally included as a source of law in art 38(3) to allow judges to use limited judicial discretion to apply generally accepted legal principles to fill such *lacunae*.[79] This was intended to prevent the Court being forced to declare itself incompetent due to a lack of applicable rules (*non liquet*).[80] Art 38(3) of the *PCIJ Statute* concerning general principles of law was then reproduced verbatim as art 38(1)(c) in the modern *Statute*.

Using a general principle of law to fill *lacunae* in jurisdiction or procedure is consistent with the Court's previous conception of its competence. Both the current Court and its predecessor, the Permanent Court of International Justice ('PCIJ'), have relied on art 38(3) of the *PCIJ Statute* and art 38(1)(c) of the *Statute* respectively to bridge procedural or jurisdictional gaps. For example, Judge Anzilotti of the PCIJ explicitly cited art 38(3) when looking to use civil procedure from domestic jurisdictions in *Interpretation of Judgments No 7 and 8 (The Chorzow Factory)*.[81] Similarly, in *Application of the Convention on the Prevention and the Punishment of the Crime of Genocide*,[82] Judge Weeramantry cites art 38(1)(c) to establish that interlocutory measures are binding (though ultimately does not rely on this finding).[83] There have also been multiple occasions where judges of the Court have filled procedural gaps or determined

---

78   The Committee of Jurists for the Permanent Court of International Justice discussed and rejected proposals regarding using judicial discretion to fill gaps in the law. See Permanent Court of International Justice: Advisory Committee of Jurists, *Procès-Verbaux of the Proceedings of the Committee, June 16th–July 24th 1920 with Annexes* (Van Langenhuysen, 1920) 286.

79   Lord Phillimore, 'Scheme for the Permanent Court of International Justice' [1920] 6 *Transactions of the Grotius Society* 89, 94.

80   Committee of Jurists (n 78) 296.

81   (*Germany v Poland*) (*Interpretation*) [1927] PCIJ (ser A) No 13, 27 (Judge Anzilotti).

82   (*Bosnia and Herzegovina v Serbia and Montenegro*) (*Provisional Measures*) [1993] ICJ Rep 325.

83   Ibid 378 (Judge Weeramantry).

the limits of jurisdiction by invoking a principle or rule precisely because it is found in a number of domestic jurisdictions.[84] Though not an explicit invocation of art 38(1)(c),[85] or art 38(3),[86] these judgments can be similarly viewed as instances where the Court used general principles of law to fill procedural or jurisdictional gaps.

Accordingly, the following section will consider whether there is any basis for jurisdiction found in art 36(1), and if a *lacuna* is identified, whether a general principle of judicial review could form the basis of jurisdiction.

3.1   *Article 36(1)*

Article 36(1) of the *Statute* provides: 'The jurisdiction of the Court comprises all cases which the parties refer to it and all matters specially provided for in the Charter of the United Nations or in treaties and conventions in force.'

As a preliminary point, art 36(1) provides no clear jurisdiction to review Council action. There are no bilateral or multilateral treaties, including the *Charter*, that expressly provide the Court the power to consider the validity of a Council resolution. Thus, a jurisdictional basis for review could only be *directly* founded on art 36(1) if all parties included the validity of a Council resolution within a broader dispute they submit to the Court.

It could be argued that art 36(1) provides the extent of the Court's jurisdiction, and thus, excluding the unlikely scenario of parties conferring jurisdiction by special agreement, no jurisdiction for judicial review exists.[87] However, this note argues that whilst art 36(1) provides the basis of jurisdiction, it does not provide the boundaries of jurisdiction in all cases. Does 'all matters ... in Treaties and Conventions' refer to only the aspects of a dispute that fall within the strict boundaries of a treaty, or does it refer to all aspects of a dispute based on a treaty? The issue of ancillary judicial review of the Council starkly demonstrates this ambiguity in art 36(1).

Consider a scenario where two states, Alpha and Omega, have a bilateral treaty which prohibits the use of armed force between the parties and provides the Court as the mechanism of dispute resolution. The two states

---

84   For examples of filling jurisdictional gaps see: *Mavrommatis Palestine Concessions (Greece v Britain) (Judgment)* [1924] PCIJ (ser A) No 2, 57–8 (Judge Moore); *Free Zones of Upper Savoy and the District Of Gex (France v Switzerland) (Judgment)* [1932] PCIJ ser A/B No 46, 202 (Judge Dreyfus). For an example of filling procedural gaps see: *Certain Phosphate Lands in Nauru (Nauru v Australia) (Preliminary Objections)* [1992] ICJ 240, 270 (Judge Shahabuddeen).

85   *Statute* (n 35).

86   *Statute of the Permanent Court of International Justice.*

87   See, eg. *Lockerbie (Preliminary Objections)* (n 8) 75 (President Schwebel).

become embroiled in an escalating dispute, and Alpha bombs the territory of Omega. Omega brings this breach of the bilateral treaty to the Court, but Alpha argues that the action was authorised by Council Resolution x. Omega in turn argues that Resolution x is invalid. In this situation, the jurisdiction of the Court is ambiguous. On the one hand, art 36(1) does not provide expressly that the Court can review Council resolutions. On the other hand, Resolution x changes the obligations of Alpha under the bilateral treaty, and thus the validity of Resolution x is the central legal issue in a case brought under art 36(1).

Scholars approach this ambiguity regarding the Court's jurisdiction in several ways. Some argue that the very existence of limitations on the Council in the *Charter* means such a right of review implicitly exists, and the Court can therefore 'read in' this review power.[88] This note rejects this notion because, even though the *Charter* is the constitutive document of the UN, it remains a multilateral treaty. Thus, any interpretation must comply with the rules of treaty interpretation. Under art 31 of the *Vienna Convention on the Law of Treaties*,[89] which reflects customary international law and thus applies to *Charter* interpretation,[90] treaty clauses are afforded their ordinary meaning in light of context, object and purpose. Treaty interpretation rules, therefore, do not provide the ability to 'read in' extra powers and obligations.

Others argue that the *Charter* provides the extent of jurisdiction, and the Court should therefore refuse to consider a question which requires judicial review.[91] However, as shown by the hypothetical above, such cases often have a valid basis for jurisdiction. Accordingly, such refusal could realistically be seen as the Court declaring *non liquet*, which the Commission of Jurists saw as deeply undesirable.[92] Thus, it is appropriate to consider whether an applicable general principle of law exists to fill the gap, as intended by the Committee of Jurists.

3.2   *General Principles of Law*

3.2.1   What is a General Principle of Law?

Article 38(1)(c) of the *Statute* provides that the Court can rely upon 'general principles of law as recognized by civilised nations' as a source of law. Three initial issues arise: what is a 'principle', what is the relevance of 'as recognized by civilized nations', and how binding is a general principle?

---

88   Martenczuk (n 73) 527.

89   Opened for signature 23 May 1969, 1155 UNTS 331 (entered into force 27 January 1980).

90   *Arbitral Award of 31 July 1989 (Guinea-Bissau v Senegal) (Judgment)* [1991] ICJ Rep 53, 69–70 [48].

91   See, eg, D'Angelo (n 64) 589.

92   Phillimore (n 79) 94.

The definition of 'principle' has been subject to scholarly debate. Some posit that general principles must have a significant level of conceptual generality, and thus only broad principles may constitute general principles of law.[93] Others argue that more specific rules can constitute general principles of law, provided there is requisite general acceptance amongst states.[94] These views are not, however, mutually incompatible: as suggested by Saunders, the most principled position seems to be that a dual model of art 38(1)(c) exists, encompassing both fundamental principles which define legal systems, and specific rules which share commonality across states.[95]

Considering the meaning of 'civilized nations', the requirement here has softened over time.[96] Though early work had Western-centric overtones when looking to which legal systems are 'civilized',[97] modern scholarship does not see 'civilized' as a substantive requirement. The overwhelming consensus amongst scholars from the late 20th century onwards is that 'civilized nations' are simply the UN member states.[98]

---

93   Bin Cheng, 'Comments' in Harold C Gutteridge, 'The Meaning and Scope of Article 38(l)(c) of the Statute of the International Court of Justice' [1952] 38 *Transactions of the Grotius Society* 125, 132; Oscar Schachter, *International Law in Theory and Practice* (Martinus Nijhoff Publishers, 1991), 54–5; Frances T Freeman Jalet, 'The Quest for the General Principles of Law Recognized by Civilized Nations—A Study' (1962–1963) 10 *UCLA Law Review* 1041, 1046; Dino Kritsiotis, 'On the Possibilities of and for Persistent Objection' (2010) 21(1) *Duke Journal of Comparative and International Law* 121, 125–6.

94   Rudolf B Shlesinger, 'The Common Core of Legal Systems: An Emerging Subject of Comparative Study' in Kurt H Nadelmann, Arthur T Von Mehren, and John N Hazard (eds), *XXth Century Comparative and Conflicts Law: Legal Essays in Honor of Hessel E Yntema* (AW Sythoff, 1961) 65, 79; Michael Akehurst, 'Equity and General Principles of Law' (1976) 25(4) *International and Comparative Law Quarterly* 801, 814–15.

95   Imogen Saunders, 'General Principles as a Source of International Law: Article 38(1)(c) of the Statute of the International Court of Justice' (PhD Thesis, the Australian National University, 2012) 370–3.

96   Margaret White, 'Equity: A General Principle of Law Recognised by Civilised Nations' (2004) 4(1) *Queensland University of Technology Law and Justice Journal* 103, 108.

97   Martti Koskenniemi, 'International Law in the World of Ideas' in James Crawford and Martti Koskenniemi (eds), *The Cambridge Companion to International Law* (Cambridge University Press, 2012) 47, 54.

98   Akehurst (n 94) 818–19; Hanna Bokor-Szegő, 'General Principles of Law' in Mohammaed Bedjaoui (ed), *International Law: Achievements and Prospects* (UNESCO, 1991) 213, 215; David J Bederman, *The Spirit of International Law* (University of Georgia Press, 2002) 30; M Cherif Bassiouni, 'A Functional Approach to "General Principles of International Law"' (1990) 11(3) *Michigan Journal of International Law* 768, 768; Hermann Mosler, *The International Society as a Legal Community* (Sijthoff & Noordhoff, 1980) 122.

Regarding the status of general principles as 'law', the *Statute* denotes that art 38(1)(c) is a formal source of law.[99] Whilst acknowledging there is some discussion as to whether it is a subsidiary source of law,[100] this note takes the view that the ordinary meaning of art 38(1)(c) in the context of art 38 is that general principles of law are a formal source of law.[101]

3.2.2   How is a General Principle of Law Established?

The common view is that widespread representation across many municipal legal systems will allow a principle or rule to become a general principle of law.[102] Though some have argued general principles are brought into existence by their inherently moral character,[103] this has not garnered widespread acceptance. This note will consider breadth of representation in municipal sources as the key measure for establishing a general principle. This elicits two further questions: what constitutes 'widespread representation', and does content of the principle have any bearing on its establishment as a general principle of law?

There is not a concrete answer as to what constitutes 'widespread representation'. The only 'threshold' that has ever been posited is by Judge Tanaka in *South West Africa*,[104] where he noted that 73% of national constitutions had clauses regarding equality, which in his view was sufficient to establish

---

99   Catherine Redgwell, 'General Principles of International Law' in Stefan Vogenauer and Stephen Weatherill (eds), *General Principles of Law: European and Comparative Perspectives* (Hart Publishing, 2017) 5, 11.

100   Bokor-Szegö (n 98) 217; Neha Jain, 'Judicial Lawmaking and General Principles of Law in International Criminal Law' (2016) 57(1) (Winter) *Harvard International Law Journal* 111, 125, 150.

101   Sir Robert Jennings and Sir Arthur Watts (eds), *Oppenheim's International Law: Volume 1 Peace* (Oxford University Press, 9th ed, 2008) 40.

102   See, eg, *Lighthouses Case (France v Greece) (Merits)* [1934] PCIJ (ser A/B) No 62, 49 (Judge Séfériadés); *Diversion of Water from the Meuse (Netherlands v Belgium) (Merits)* [1937] PCIJ (ser A/B) No 70, 76–7 (Judge Hudson); *Namibia* (n 55) 157 (Judge Dillard); *Certain Phosphate Lands in Nauru* (n 84) 289 (Judge Shahabuddeen); *Aerial Incident of 10 August 1999 (Pakistan v India) (Jurisdiction)* [2000] ICJ Rep 12, 57 (Judge Al-Khasawneh); *Oil Platforms (Iran v United States of America) (Merits)* [2003] ICJ Rep 161, 331 (Judge Simma); Wolfgang Friedmann, 'The Uses of "General Principles" in the Development of International Law' (1963) 57(2) *American Journal of International Law* 279, 282; Akehurst (n 94) 814.

103   *SS 'Lotus' (France v Turkey) (Merits)* [1927] PCIJ (ser A) No 10, 35 (Judge Loder); Cheng (n 93) 132.

104   *(Ethiopia v South Africa) (Judgment)* [1966] ICJ Rep 6, 250 (Judge Tanaka).

REVISITING LOCKERBIE
305

a general principle of law.[105] Whilst this percentage may not be a concrete benchmark, it serves as a helpful threshold when considering what level of generality is expected. A rule or principle should also be represented in the different legal systems of the world,[106] including and beyond common and civil law systems,[107] and should be represented across different geographic regions.[108]

Concerning the content of the principle, it is relevant insofar as it impacts the ability for the principle to be transposed from domestic jurisdictions to an international context.[109] However, this requirement does not necessarily mean that a domestic rule must be able to be mirrored exactly in international law. As stated by Judge McNair:

> The way in which international law borrows from [municipal legal systems] is not by means of importing private law institutions 'lock, stock and barrel', ready-made and fully equipped with a set of rules ... [municipal laws are] as an indication of policy and principles rather than as directly importing these rules and institutions.[110]

Similarly, Judge Fitzmaurice has stated that domestic rules 'may be less capable of vindication if strictly applied when transposed onto the international level'.[111] This is consistent with the practice of international courts, which have on multiple occasions identified the broader principle behind a specific rule in order to allow it to fit more reasonably in an international context.[112] Scholars

---

105 Ibid 299.

106 H Patrick Glenn, *Legal Traditions of the World: Sustainable Diversity in Law* (Oxford University Press, 5th ed, 2014), 60, 98, 132, 180, 236, 287, 319.

107 CG Weeramantry, *Universalising International Law* (Martinus Nijhoff Publishers, 2004) 188.

108 Jaye Ellis, 'General Principles and Comparative Law' (2011) 22(4) *European Journal of International Law* 949, 957.

109 American Law Institute, *Restatement (Third) of Foreign Relations Law of the United States of America* (1987) § 102 Reporters' Note 7; Jerome B Elkind, *Interim Protection: A Functional Approach* (Martinus Nijhoff Publishers, 1981) 12.

110 *International Status of South-West Africa (Advisory Opinion)* [1950] ICJ Rep 128, 148 (Judge McNair) ('*Status South-West Africa*').

111 *Barcelona Traction, Light & Power Company (Belgium v Spain) (Judgment)* [1970] ICJ Rep 3, 67 [5] (Judge Fitzmaurice).

112 See, eg, *Right of Passage over Indian Territory (Portugal v India) (Merits)* [1960] ICJ Rep 6, 66–7 [26] (Judge Wellington Koo), 134 [34] (Judge Fernandes); *Prosecutor v Tadić (Decision on the Defence Motion for Interlocutory Appeal on Jurisdiction)* (International Criminal Tribunal for the Former Yugoslavia, Appeals Chamber, Case No IT-94-1-A, 2 October 1995)

have also recognised the legitimacy of using judicial discretion to ensure that a domestic principle is applied appropriately in an international context.[113]

Accordingly, a general principle is established if it is contained in a sufficiently diverse critical mass of municipal legal systems, and the principle is broadly capable of being applied in an international context. What therefore must be considered is whether there is sufficient evidence that a general principle of judicial review exists.

3.2.3 A General Principle of Judicial Review?

First and foremost, a large number of municipal legal systems contain some form of judicial review. According to a study undertaken by Ginsburg and Versteeg in 2011, 83% of UN member states provide for constitutional review in their constitutions.[114] Furthermore, as this study concerned judicial review of constitutionality, only constitutionally provided judicial review was discoverable. Consequently, states like the US, which have judicial review as a result of the common law,[115] or Australia, which primarily sources constitutional review from common law and statute,[116] were not included in the 83% figure. The number of states which recognise constitutional review is, therefore, higher than 83%. When considering this number against the 73% figure used by Judge Tanaka, it appears that, at least numerically, there would be a sufficient number of states which recognise a rule of judicial review for a general principle to arise.

Regarding the level of diversity within this group of states, judicial review power can be found in the municipal legal systems of all geographic regions

---

[43]; *Prosecutor v Furundžija* (*Judgment*) (International Criminal Tribunal for the Former Yugoslavia, Trial Chamber, Case No IT-95-17/1-T, 10 December 1998) 69–72 [177]–[181].

113 Georg Schwarzenberger, *International Law as Applied by International Courts and Tribunals* (Stevens & Sons, 3rd ed, 1957) vol 1, 46; Jean d'Aspremont, *Formalism and the Sources of International Law: A Theory of the Ascertainment of Legal Rules* (Oxford University Press, 2011) 171.

114 Tom Ginsburg and Mila Versteeg, 'Why Do Countries Adopt Constitutional Review?' (2014) 30(3) *Journal of Law, Economics, and Organization* 587, 587.

115 *Marbury v Madison* (n 67) 170.

116 For statute, see: *Administrative Decisions (Judicial Review) Act 1977* (Cth); *Judiciary Act 1903* (Cth). For common law, see, eg, *Attorney General (NSW) v Quin* (1990) 170 CLR 1, 35–6 (Brennan J).

of the world.[117] There is judicial review found in common law,[118] civil law,[119] Asian,[120] and Islamic systems.[121] Judicial review is also found in systems that blend with Hindu,[122] Talmudic,[123] or Chthonic law.[124] Thus, it appears the principle of judicial review has requisite generality across systems of law and the regions of the world to establish a general principle.

3.2.4 Can this Principle Transpose to International Law?

The existence of a general principle of judicial review was considered by Erika de Wet in 2000.[125] De Wet identifies two elements which, in her view, prevent a general principle of judicial review transposing to international law: that judicial review generally does not concern national security decisions, and that

---

117 See, eg, *Constitution of the Republic of South Africa Act 1996* (South Africa) ch 2 ss 33, 38 (Southern Africa); *Law 48 of 1979 Governing the Operations of the Supreme Constitutional Court of Egypt* (Egypt) art 25 (North Africa); *Constitution of Kenya 2010* (Kenya) art 47 (East Africa); *Constitution of the Gabonese Republic 1991* (Gabon) art 83 (Central Africa); *Lardan v Attorney-General (No 2)* (1957) 2G & G 98 (Ghana) (West Africa); *Constitution of the Federative Republic of Brazil 2010* (Brazil) art 97 (South America); *Political Constitution of the Republic of Costa Rica 1949* (Costa Rica) art 10 (Central America); *Constitution Act 1982* (UK) (Canada) c 11, sch B pt 1 art 24(1) (North America); *Constitution of the Republic of Trinidad and Tobago 1976* (Trinidad and Tobago) ch 1 pt v art 14 (Caribbean); *Constitution of the Republic of Korea 1948* (Republic of Korea) ch vi art 111 (East Asia); *Constitution of the Republic of Kazakhstan 1995* (Kazakhstan) art 72 (Central Asia); *Constitution of Nepal 2015* (Nepal) pt 11 art 133 (South Asia); *Chan Hiang Leng Colin v Public Prosecutor* [1994] 3 slr(R) (209 (High Court of Singapore) (Southeast Asia); *Lebanese Constitution 1926* (Lebanon) pt 11 ch 1 art 19 (Middle East); *Constitution of the Republic of the Marshall Islands 1979* (Marshall Islands) art 1 s 4 (Oceania); *Federal Constitutional Law No 1 on the Judicial System of the Russian Federation 1996* (Russia) arts 3–4 (Eastern Europe); *Grundgesetz für die Bundesrepublik Deutschland* [Basic Law for the Federal Republic of Germany] art 93 (Western Europe).

118 *Council of Civil Service Unions v Minister for the Civil Service* [1985] AC 374 (United Kingdom).

119 *Constitution of Austria 1920* (Austria) ch vii s D arts 137–42.

120 *Constitution of the Kingdom of Thailand 2017* (Thailand) ch xi s 210.

121 *Constitution of the Islamic Republic of Pakistan 1973* (Pakistan) pt vii ch 1 art 175.

122 *Constitution of India 1950* (India) pt iii s 32.

123 *United Mizrahi Bank Ltd v Migdal Cooperative Village* [1995] IsrLR 1, 260–77 (Supreme Court of Israel).

124 *Constitution of the Islamic Republic of Afghanistan 2004* (Afghanistan) art 121.

125 Erika de Wet, 'Judicial Review as an Emerging General Principle of Law and its Implications for the International Court of Justice' (2000) 47(2) *Netherlands International Law Review* 181.

the *Charter* does not sufficiently mirror a domestic constitution to allow transposal from a domestic to an international context.[126]

Regarding national security, de Wet argues that recognising a general principle of judicial review 'would not take account of the fact that [domestic judicial review] does not necessarily extend to decisions concerning national security'.[127] She argues the principle cannot apply in the international context, as the Council deals almost exclusively with threats to international peace and security. There are two arguments against this point. First, as noted by Kotuby and Sobota, 'the inclusion of a principle in the written laws of many legal systems is itself validation of the principle'.[128] Thus, how the principle is specifically utilised from jurisdiction to jurisdiction may not be a barrier to transposal. Second, de Wet relies on an unsubstantiated assumption, as she does not provide examples of judicial review powers being restricted against national security decisions, nor address examples where national security decisions were subject to judicial review.[129] For example, passport cancellations predicated on national security concerns may be the subject of judicial review in certain countries.[130] Cases have also arisen in the wake of the 'war on terror', which have seen invocations of executive power based on national security concerns reviewed by domestic and regional courts.[131] Thus, in the absence of a clear trend establishing that judicial review is widely inapplicable to national security decisions, this issue does not appear to be a barrier to transposal.

Regarding constitutional similarity, de Wet argues that 'judicial review is a phenomena of modern constitutionalism' and thus 'the *Charter* must possess

---

126   Ibid 209.

127   Ibid.

128   Charles T Kotuby Jr and Luke A Sobota, *General Principles of Law and International Due Process: Principles and Norms Applicable in Transnational Disputes* (Oxford University Press, 2017) 28, citing *Texaco Overseas Petroleum Company v Libya (Award)* (1978) 17 ILM 1, 24.

129   See, eg, *Church of Scientology v Woodward* (1982) 154 CLR 25 (Australia); *Anonymous (Lebanese citizens) v Minister of Defence* [2000] 54(1) PD 721 (Israel); David Scharia, *Judicial Review of National Security* (Oxford University Press, 2014) 5.

130   *Abdelrazik v Canada (Minister of Foreign Affairs and International Trade)* [2010] 1 FCR 267 (Canada); *R (XH) v Secretary of State for the Home Department* [2018] QB 355 (UK); *Habib v Commonwealth* (2010) 183 FCR 62 (Australia); Conseil constitutionnel [French Constitutional Court], decision n° 96–377 DC, 16 July 1996 reported in JO, 23 July 1996, 11108 (France).

131   *Boumediene v Bush,* 553 US 723 (2008) (United States). See also decisions of regional courts: *Al-Skeini v United Kingdom* [2011] IV Eur Court HR 99; *Kadi and Al Barakaat International Foundation v Council and Commission* (C-402/05) [2008] ECR I-6351[343]–[344]; *Kadi v European Commission* (T-85/09) [2010] ECR II-5177 [134].

a constitutional character not unlike that of municipal constitutions'[132] for a general principle of judicial review to be applicable in international law. As already observed, this note views the *Charter* as a multilateral treaty rather than a constitution. Nevertheless, it is accepted that for a principle of judicial review to transpose from a domestic to an international context, broad structural similarities between the systems must exist. However, this need not be the *Charter* mirroring a domestic constitution. As discussed above, principles from domestic jurisdictions need not be transposed to international law 'lock, stock and barrel'.[133] Moreover, not all domestic jurisdictions derive the power of judicial review directly from the national constitution.[134] Rather, the link between judicial review and constitutionalism is more accurately stated as follows: judicial review is exercised within a separation of powers system defined by the national constitution. Thus, the more appropriate determinant of the ability for judicial review to transpose is whether the structure of the UN system is generally equivalent to the separation of powers found in municipal systems. As the Court is the 'judiciary' of the system,[135] this question hinges on whether the Council is sufficiently 'executive' in nature.

There are arguments for and against the Council being the executive body of the UN system. On the one hand, the Council's mandate has elements of judicial, legislative and executive power.[136] Furthermore, in contrast to the existence of domestic police, the Council cannot force compliance to its resolutions without assistance from states. On the other hand, the Council does possess relatively extensive powers to enforce the peace, such as the ability to authorise the use of force by states.[137] Furthermore, the *Charter* does quite clearly delineate power between the Assembly, the Council and the Court.[138] As de Wet states, even the rudimentary separation of powers seen in the UN system remains a separation of powers.[139]

Given a separation of powers does exist, there is no barrier to transposing a general principle of judicial review to the international system. However, it would need to be tempered in its application for two reasons. First, given the

---

132 De Wet (n 125) 185.

133 *Status South-West Africa* (n 110) 148 (Judge McNair).

134 See (n 116–17) and accompanying text.

135 *Charter* (n 13) art 92.

136 Whittle (n 15) 671.

137 *Charter* (n 13) ch VII; Pascal Teixeira, *The Security Council at the Dawn of the Twenty-First Century: To What Extent is it Willing and Able to Maintain International Peace and Security?* UNIDIR/2003/36 (December 2003) 88.

138 *Charter* (n 13) chs IV–VI, VIII, XIV.

139 De Wet (n 125) 195.

principle is intended to fill a *lacuna* found within art 36(1), it would only be applicable within the Court's established boundaries provided by the *Charter* and the *Statute*. Second, judicial review could only be used to determine compliance of other UN organs to *Charter* limitations. The principle of judicial review could in no way empower review of the merits of political decisions made by other UN organs, as the *Charter* dictates such decisions are solely within the jurisdiction of political organs, not the Court.

For this reason, the use of a general principle of judicial review by the Court would require the use of judicial discretion, to keep its application within the boundaries of the law. This note will now propose a model for the Court to follow that would guide such discretion.

4   Model for Conducting Review

The Court retains an inherent discretion to refuse to exercise jurisdiction in cases it deems inappropriate.[140] This note argues that, although on a case by case basis the Court *may* decide to refuse to exercise jurisdiction on a variety of bases,[141] there is one scenario where the Court must always limit its jurisdiction when relying upon a general principle of judicial review: where a generous application of the general principle would undo established boundaries of the law.

Given general principles are, at most, equal to treaty and custom as a source of law,[142] and arguably a lesser source,[143] a general principle cannot vary the requirements set out in a treaty. If that treaty is the *Charter*, this is true to an even greater extent, as the *Charter* sits above other treaties in the hierarchy of

---

140   See, eg, *Nuclear Tests (Australia v France) (Jurisdiction)* [1974] ICJ Rep 253, 259 [23]; *Nottebohm Case (Liechtenstein v Guatemala) (Preliminary Objections)* [1953] ICJ Rep 111, 119.

141   *Monetary Gold Removed from Rome in 1943 (Italy v France, United Kingdom and United States of America) (Preliminary Question)* [1954] ICJ Rep 19, 32 ('*Monetary Gold*'); Dinah Shelton, 'Form, Function, and the Powers of International Courts' (2009) 9(2) *Chicago Journal of International Law* 537, 547.

142   Schwarzenberger (n 113) 55–6; Johan G Lammers, 'General Principles of Law Recognized by Civilised Nations' in Frits Kalshoven, Pier Jan Kuyper and Johan G Lammers (eds), *Essays on the Development of the International Legal Order: In Memory of Haro F van Panhuys* (Sijthoff & Noordhoff, 1980) 53, 65.

143   See, eg, Cheng (n 93) 132; Georg Schwarzenberger and ED Brown, *A Manual of International Law* (Professional Books, 6th ed, 1976) 27; Michael Bogdan, 'General Principles of Law and the Problem of Lacunae in the Law of Nations' (1977) 46(1–2) *Nordic Journal of International Law* 37, 44; Ulrich Fastenrath, 'Relative Normativity in International Law' (1993) 4(1) *European Journal of International Law* 305, 328.

REVISITING LOCKERBIE

international law by virtue of art 103.[144] Consequently, it is legally necessary for the Court to employ discretion to limit a general principle if its broad application would contradict the terms of the *Charter*. Not only is this legally required to safeguard the *Charter* system, but using discretion to limit the application of a general principle to comply with the *Charter* legitimises any subsequent decision of the Court. This legitimacy is vital to allow the Court to continue to function effectively in the context of fraught contemporary international relations.

There are three ways a general principle of judicial review may clash with the Court's established legal boundaries under the *Charter* system. First, the *Charter* provides the Council with sole jurisdiction over certain questions, and thus the Court cannot conduct merits review of Council decisions.[145] Second, as the *Statute* provides that the Court must only consider 'legal disputes',[146] any purely political decisions taken by the Council would only be reviewable insofar as a legal question arises. Third, the *Charter* imposes obligations on states. Thus, any application of a general principle of judicial review that renders state compliance to the *Charter's* obligations impossible would be antithetical to the function of the *Charter*. This would be tantamount to the Court acting outside the limits of its constitutive document.

Essentially, the Court must be careful to not use the assertion of the existence of a broad general principle of judicial review as a 'trojan horse' that allows indiscriminate review of Council decisions. Doing so would not only irrevocably hurt the legitimacy and standing of the Court amongst states, but it would also overstep the jurisdictional limits inherent in the systems of laws set up by the *Charter*. Thus, this note proposes a model, consisting of three rebuttable presumptions, that should guide the Court in any application of this general principle. These rebuttable presumptions are: (a) that the question is an exclusively political question; (b) that the resolution is valid; and (c) that an invalid resolution is voidable, rather than void ab initio.

4.1   *Rebuttable Presumption of Exclusively Political Question*
This first rebuttable presumption protects the Court from overstepping its jurisdictional boundaries. As international law is inherently political,[147] this presumption seeks only to stop the Court from considering *exclusively* political

---

144   Rudolf Bernhardt, 'Article 103' in Bruno Simma et al (eds), *The Charter of the United Nations: A Commentary* (Oxford University Press,1st ed, 1994) 1117–24.

145   *Charter* (n 13) art 11(2).

146   *Statute* (n 35) art 36(2).

147   Sir Robert Y Jennings, 'The Proper Work and Purposes of the International Court of Justice' in AS Muller, D Raič and JM Thuránszky (eds), *The International Court of Justice: Its Future Role after Fifty Years* (Kluwer Law International, 1997) 33, 43.

questions. To rebut this presumption, an applicant state must show that there exists a legal question to answer.

This note proposes that, in its approach to this first presumption, the Court take inspiration from the political questions doctrine adopted in US constitutional law. Whilst the Court has no legal requirement to utilise this doctrine, the merit of the US approach is twofold. First, the US doctrine was developed in an analogous situation: the judiciary considering the validity of decisions from political bodies, with the power of review not conferred by the constitutive document. The US approach therefore has functionality in an international context. Second, it provides a systematic approach to identifying political questions, which will afford consistency to judicial decisions when the Court is faced with the same issue in different contexts.

Some scholars argue that the Court has rejected applying a political question doctrine due to its past consideration of questions with political elements,[148] or that are politically controversial.[149] However, this note argues that the Court should aim to exclude judicial consideration of *exclusively* political questions, not questions with political elements.[150] Using this framing, there is judicial support for applying the political questions doctrine.[151] Perhaps most importantly, a political questions doctrine is necessary in the context of judicial review, as the Court will be directly considering the decisions of a political body. Thus, unlike other considerations of the Court which may have political overtones, the Court here will be directly inserting itself into political territory. Thus, clear and structured protection for the Court against accusations of political activity is required.

The US political questions doctrine states that questions that are fundamentally political are not justiciable.[152] The leading authority, *Baker v Carr*,[153]

---

148   See, eg, Gowlland-Debbas (n 54) 651–2, citing *Tehran Case* (n 46), *Nicaragua* (n 46); Jose E Alvarez, *International Organizations as Law-makers* (Oxford University Press, 2005) 71.

149   See, eg, Michla Pomerance, 'The ICJ's Advisory Jurisdiction and the Crumbling Wall between the Political and the Judicial' (2005) 99(1) *American Journal of International Law* 26, 33, citing *Wall Opinion* (n 56) 148–52 [24]–[35].

150   See, eg, politically controversial US cases deemed justiciable when applying the political questions doctrine: *Davis v Bandemer* 478 US 109 (1986) (regarding gerrymandering); *Immigration and Naturalization Service v Chadha* 462 US 919 (1983) (regarding relationship between legislature and executive); *Powell v McCormack* 395 US 486 (1969) (regarding qualification for members of Congress).

151   *Nicaragua* (n 46) 220–37 (Judge Oda).

152   John Harrison, 'The Political Question Doctrines' (2017) 67(2) *American University Law Review* 457, 473.

153   369 US 186 (1962).

REVISITING LOCKERBIE 313

lists six characteristics that indicate a political question.[154] This note proposes two such characteristics are directly relevant in an international context and should form the basis of this presumption: that there is a demonstrated textual commitment that a political body has sole power in the area;[155] and that there is a lack of judicially discoverable standards against which to judge the question.[156] The first characteristic indicates whether there is a legal character to the question, and the second asks for legal criteria for review.

For example, a case regarding compliance of a resolution to the *Charter* would rebut this presumption. It is not a question solely for another body, and the relevant articles of the *Charter* would be the legal criteria for review. Conversely, the decision to authorise the use of force is one exclusively given to the Council.[157] Whilst the compliance of this decision to established *Charter* rules may be justiciable, the content of the decision itself is a political question. Thus, any merits review of the decision would be non-justiciable. By requiring the applicant state to show that its question is not one solely for a political body, and that legally acceptable standards exist upon which to base judgment, the Court is protected from overstepping its legal boundaries when wading into inherently politicised territory.

4.2 *Rebuttable Presumption of Validity*

This presumption is framed by the fact the *Charter* gives the Council extensive power to take action to maintain international peace and security, and this power is deliberately unencumbered.[158] It must be recalled that a direct power of review was rejected for the very reason that litigation is seen as a hindrance to effective action.[159] Whilst this rejection should not prevent the Court from relying on a general principle of judicial review to fill the *lacuna* present in art 36(1), it should inform how the Court views such power. The *Charter* system deliberately did not give the Court extensive power over the Council. Thus, there should be a high threshold for invalidation of Council decisions.

A presumption of validity protects this system, as it puts the onus of proof on the state asserting invalidity. By requiring the Court to rule that a resolution is valid unless the presumption is rebutted, successful cases are limited to clear, unequivocal cases of invalidity. This provides recourse for instances where defective Council working methods cause an egregious breach of state

---

154 Ibid 217.
155 Ibid.
156 Ibid.
157 *Charter* (n 13) art 42.
158 Lim (n 28) 218.
159 UNCIO (n 71) 49.

314 AUSTRALIAN YEAR BOOK OF INTERNATIONAL LAW VOLUME 38

rights that clearly falls outside the gambit of the *Charter*, without undermining the division of power between UN organs upon which the entire system depends.

4.3 Rebuttable Presumption of Voidability

The first two presumptions ensure the Court adheres to the separation of powers between UN organs within the *Charter*. This third presumption ensures the Court does not unintentionally vary the obligations of states under the *Charter*.

When faced with an invalid resolution, the Court has two options. It could declare the resolution voidable, meaning it considers the resolution void and therefore the Council should officially nullify it for the international community going forward.[160] As the Court's judgment only applies between parties to the case,[161] it does not have the power to nullify a resolution for the entire community. Alternatively, the Court could declare a resolution void ab initio, meaning it considers the resolution retrospectively null and void and thus inapplicable as a defence to action taken by a state in the case before it.[162]

This is a difficult issue for the Court. On the one hand, a void ab initio declaration favours an applicant state that desires accountability for action taken against it due to an invalid resolution. This also complies with the argument that a resolution made outside the boundaries of the law is void from its inception.[163] On the other hand, a declaration of void ab initio risks disrupting the rights of the respondent state, as actions taken under authorisation of the Council would be retroactively rendered indefensible. As there is a legal obligation on states to carry out the decisions of the Council, this is particularly problematic.[164] Essentially, a declaration of void ab initio does not hold the Council accountable for invalidity, but rather holds a state accountable for following a Council authorisation which subsequently was declared invalid.

Thus, any move to declare resolutions void ab initio would fundamentally change the way states approach their legal obligation to implement decisions of the Council. It would be tantamount to legally requiring states to follow Council resolutions, but also requiring states to bear the consequences of invalidity. Thus, void ab initio declarations would at least in practice change how

---

160 The Assembly dissolved the Maritime Safety Committee following a declaration by the Court that the Assembly had formed the committee contrary to its constitutive document in *Constitution of the Maritime Safety Committee of the Inter-Governmental Maritime Consultative Organization* (*Advisory Opinion*) [1960] ICJ Rep 150, 171.

161 Gowlland-Debbas (n 54) 670.

162 Alvarez, 'Judging the Security Council' (n 73) 7.

163 *Certain Expenses* (n 46) 221 (Judge Morelli).

164 *Charter* (n 13) art 25.

states approach their obligations under the *Charter*. As established, the Court cannot use a general principle of law to vary the obligations established by the *Charter*. Thus, it is proper that invalid resolutions are presumed to be merely voidable. This is also consistent with the approach taken to treaty invalidity, where acts performed in conformity with a treaty later declared invalid are not themselves considered invalid.[165]

Nevertheless, this note accepts that (in admittedly limited circumstances) it should be possible to rebut this presumption. Kolb has argued that action taken under a resolution by a state with a 'legitimate expectation' that the resolution is valid should not be unlawful due to subsequent nullity.[166] This implies an illegitimate expectation would lead to liability. Thus, for the Court to declare a resolution void ab initio, this note proposes that the applicant state would need to show that any expectation of validity from the respondent state was illegitimate: essentially, that the respondent state acted in bad faith.

The circumstances under which bad faith could be proven are limited. Realistically, only in cases where there is evidence that the state in question knew, or ought to have known, that the resolution was invalid would the presumption be rebuttable. For example, if there is evidence the state in question had, or should have had, knowledge of potential invalidity. Similarly, any action by a state that would amount to a breach of a *jus cogens* norm. This cannot be a good faith use of a Council authorisation, as breaches of *jus cogens* norms cannot be authorised by the Council.[167]

Importantly, given a judgment is only binding between the parties,[168] a declaration of void ab initio in one case does not automatically make the same resolution void ab initio in subsequent cases. Given the Court will not exercise jurisdiction over a case where a third party's legal interest forms the subject matter of the decision,[169] the Court could not declare a resolution void ab initio for all subsequent cases. Rather, the conduct of the parties in each case would determine whether the same resolution is declared voidable or void ab initio across different cases.

Whilst the imposition of three presumptions to guide judicial discretion may weigh any cases requesting review in favour of validity, it is the only way to ensure the application of the general principle does not unintentionally vary the function of the *Charter*.

---

165   Erika de Wet, *The Chapter VII Powers of the United Nations Security Council* (Hart Publishing, 2004) 60.
166   Kolb (n 73) 912.
167   *Genocide Case* (n 33) 441 (Judge Lauterpacht).
168   *Statute* (n 35) art 59.
169   *Monetary Gold* (n 141) 32.

4.4 *Hypothetical Case*

To highlight how the three presumptions work, it is appropriate to consider the hypothetical case used previously between states Alpha and Omega.

4.4.1 Presumption of Exclusively Political Question

To rebut this first presumption, Omega must simply assert a legal question and demonstrate legal criteria against which the Court can determine its answer. Importantly, the allegation of invalidity need not be proven at this stage.

If Omega argued that Resolution x does not comply with procedural rules set down by the *Charter*, this would rebut the presumption. Considering compliance with procedural rules is not power solely conferred on a political body, and the rules themselves are the criteria for review.

Similarly, if Omega argued Resolution x is ultra vires art 24(2), as it does not comply with a specific principle of the UN, this would rebut the presumption. This is similarly a question of compliance with the *Charter*, and the principle specified is the standard against which it can be judged.

Conversely, if Omega argued that Resolution x is invalid because Omega disputes the Council's assessment that the situation is a threat to international peace and security, this would not rebut the presumption. A declaration of a threat to international peace and security is the sole responsibility of the Council.[170] Article 39 also has within it no criteria the Council must follow, nor any need for the Council to provide reasons. This indicates an art 39 determination is an exclusively political question, meaning it would be non-justiciable.

Similarly, if Omega asserted the resolution at hand is ultra vires ch VII generally, this would only rebut one half of the presumption. Whilst this is broadly a legal question, asserting a resolution has gone beyond an entire chapter of the *Charter* does not provide specific legal criteria against which the Court may determine the question at hand.

4.4.2 Presumption of Validity

Once a legal question and criteria are established under the first presumption, the Court can move on to the substantive determination. For this stage, assume Resolution x required Alpha to impose sanctions on Omega, in violation of a bilateral free-trade treaty. Certain actions would rebut the presumption of validity. For example, if Omega was not given the chance to participate in the Council debate on Resolution x this would likely rebut the presumption

---

170　*Charter* (n 13) art 39; Malcolm N Shaw, *International Law* (Cambridge University Press, 7th ed, 2014) 898–901.

of validity, as the *Charter* explicitly requires the Council to invite parties to a dispute to participate.

Alternatively, if Omega argues that the imposition of sanctions was ultra vires art 24(2), the presumption of validity would require Omega to show the imposition of the sanctions clearly conflicts with one of the purposes and principles of the UN. This is not impossible, but it is a deliberately high bar. As discussed above, this high bar safeguards the integrity of the *Charter* system.

4.4.3 Presumption of Voidability

In very few circumstances should this presumption be rebuttable. First, assume Alpha is a permanent member of the Council and Omega was not invited to participate in debate for Resolution x concerning the dispute, rendering the resolution procedurally invalid. Given Alpha is a permanent member of the Council, any action taken by Alpha under the procedurally invalid resolution can be deemed to have been taken in bad faith, as it is a clear and unambiguous requirement that the Council provide Omega with the opportunity to participate. As a permanent member of the Council, Alpha ought to have known this requirement, and thus should have had a legitimate expectation that the resolution was invalid.

Second, assume Alpha is a member of the Council and Resolution x is ultra vires art 24(2). Article 24(2) is a more subjective requirement than procedural obligations, and therefore rebutting the presumption is harder. It cannot be readily assumed that a Council member would know that the resolution was invalid when such an assessment is inherently subjective. Distinctions can therefore be made: for example, is Alpha a permanent or non-permanent member? A permanent member would conceivably understand more precisely the rules regarding adherence to principles and purposes due to accumulated knowledge over time. Has Alpha indicated in past Council debates a cognisance of art 24(2) requirements? This may similarly bolster the ability to make out a case that Alpha followed an ultra vires resolution in bad faith.

Third, assume Resolution x called upon states to use 'all means necessary' to rid Omega of nuclear weaponry, and this resolution was subsequently found to be invalid. If Alpha used this authorisation to not only use force against Omega to neutralise a nuclear threat but also to use force systematically against an ethnic minority in Omega amounting to genocide, this action cannot be said to be used with the legitimate expectation that it was authorised under Resolution x. There can be no legitimate expectation that a Council resolution endorses the breach of a *jus cogens* norm.

5   Conclusion

By employing the model presented above, the Court can apply a general principle of judicial review without compromising the rights of state parties or its own legitimacy. What this model provides is a valid legal avenue to ensure Council accountability. In an age where Council reform is a dominant debate at the UN, a valid legal avenue for review which does not require *Charter* amendment could be a key path to a different kind of reform. Whilst any move by the Court to review the Council may lead to politically charged criticism, basing such review on an identifiable, valid source of law provides at the very least protection for the Court against criticism regarding the legality of its action.

Moreover, by basing jurisdiction in a general principle of judicial review, both realist and legalist arguments regarding the Court's ability to review the Council are addressed. On the one hand, for legalists, this model provides the Court with a jurisdictional basis to hold the Council to its established boundaries. On the other hand, for realists, this note has not only identified a valid legal source of jurisdiction, but has done so by using a mechanism originally envisioned by the Committee of Jurists to fill gaps in the law. Utilising a general principal of judicial review to fill a gap in art 36, as set out by the above model, provides a solution to a question that has divided scholars since *Lockerbie*.

The model sets a high bar for findings of invalidity. Consequently, there is potential that few cases would rebut all three presumptions. Nevertheless, this should not displace the value of the model. Realistically, the Court can only act within the boundaries of the law, and these boundaries are reinforced through the three presumptions. The model therefore creates a mechanism which deals with particularly egregious breaches of the *Charter* by the Council without imposing extensive judicial oversight. Thus, the Court both ensures it does not overstep its jurisdictional boundaries and avoids declaring *non liquet*.

It is also arguable the proposed model for judicial review may only make minimal inroads in reforming how the Council acts, as the Council may elect to not enforce judgments which invalidate Council resolutions.[171] However, the mere presence of a review mechanism may equally see self-imposed reform by the Council to ensure working methods are to a higher standard. Moreover, the Council will lose legitimacy in the long term if it continuously defies reasonable judgment from the Court regarding its failures to abide by legal limitations. By utilising the proposed model, the Court can adjudicate cases involving Council resolutions whilst also ensuring it remains within the

---

171   *Charter* (n 13) art 94(2).

boundaries of the *Charter*. By respecting its own legal limitations, the Court retains legitimacy when undertaking such review, which in turn neutralises the weight of any subsequent Council criticism.

Disputes within the UN membership regarding Council reform remain fraught, divisive and without a workable solution in sight. The Court may not be the solution to this division, but the role it can play in holding the Council to its *Charter* limitations could see a revitalisation of the Council's working methods, and act as a stepping stone to wider *Charter* reform.

Book Reviews

Edited by
Amy Maguire

∴

The Greening of Antarctica: Assembling an International Environment

Alessandro Antonello
(Oxford University Press, 2017, 262 pp)

December 1, 2019 marked the sixtieth anniversary of the adoption of the *Antarctic Treaty*[1] and it will be soon the sixtieth anniversary of its entry into force. The treaty is a remarkable instrument which arose as a response to particular historical contingences.[2] The *Antarctic Treaty* has allowed demilitarisation of the continent and directed human presence on the continent towards peaceful use and scientific research.[3] It is therefore sometimes referred to as an 'arms control' or 'peace treaty'.[4]

However, environmental protection was not a concern during the negotiations of the treaty. The word 'environment' is not mentioned even once in the instrument. The working document that came out of the Antarctic Treaty preparatory meetings held in Washington, in 1958 and 1959, under the leadership of US Ambassador Paul Daniels, 'does not include anything that comes near to it'.[5] The closest reference to environmental protection in the *Antarctic Treaty*

---

1   *The Antarctic Treaty,* signed 1 December 1959, 402 UNTS 71 (entered into force 23 June 1961) ('*Antarctic Treaty*').

2   Shirley Scott, 'Ingenious and Innocuous? Article IV of the Antarctic Treaty as Imperialism' (2011) 1(1) *The Polar Journal* 51.

3   Marcus Haward and Tom Griffiths (eds), *Australia and the Antarctic Treaty System: 50 Years of Influence* (University of New South Wales Press, 2011).

4   See Paul Berkman et al (eds), *Science Diplomacy: Antarctica, Science, and the Governance of International Spaces* (Smithsonian Institution, 2011).

5   Alfred van der Essen, 'Chapter 1: Welcome' in Joe Verhoeven, Philippe Sands and Maxwell Bruce (eds), *The Antarctic Environment and International Law* (Kluwer Law International, 1992) 1.

© KONINKLIJKE BRILL NV, LEIDEN, 2021 | DOI:10.1163/26660229_03801014

is in art IX(f), which establishes a meeting of the Contracting Parties and indicates they might recommend measures to their respective governments on 'preservation and conservation of living resources in Antarctica'. However, this article is directed at 'living resources', rather than environmental protection per se.

While the *Antarctic Treaty* initially sought to put on hold competing sovereignty claims and promote further international scientific cooperation, issues concerning conservation of the Antarctic environment began to be considered even before the treaty entered into force in 1961. This idea was first raised by the biologist and ecologist Robert Carrick from the Scientific Committee on Antarctic Research ('SCAR') who worked for the Commonwealth Scientific and Industrial Research Organisation ('CSIRO'), Australia's national science agency. Carrick's paper, titled 'Nature Conservation in the Antarctic', was delivered during a 1959 symposium convened to disseminate and discuss the results of the International Geophysical Year.[6]

With the later adoption of a set of related international treaties on conservation of seals,[7] conservation of Antarctic marine living resources[8] and environmental protection,[9] Antarctic law and governance is recognised as a leading success story in the field of international environmental law.[10] The *Antarctic Treaty* and these related international treaties, plus the measures in effect under those instruments, are defined and commonly referred to as the Antarctic Treaty System ('ATS').[11] The result is a comprehensive conservation and environmental protection regime which governs key activities undertaken on the Antarctic continent and the surrounding Southern Ocean.[12]

---

6   Robert Carrick, 'Conservation of Nature in the Antarctic' (1960) (6) *SCAR Bulletin* 299.

7   *Convention for the Conservation of Antarctic Seals*, opened for signature 1 June 1972, 1080 UNTS 175 (entered into force 11 March 1978) ('*CCAS*').

8   *Convention on the Conservation of Antarctic Marine Living Resources*, opened for signature 20 May 1980, 1329 UNTS 47 (entered into force 7 April 1982) ('*CCAMLR*').

9   *Protocol on Environmental Protection to the Antarctic Treaty*, opened for signature 4 October 1991 (entered into force 14 January 1998).

10   Oran Young, *Institutional Dynamics: Emergent Patterns in International Environmental Governance* (MIT Press, 2010) 81.

11   The term 'The Antarctic Treaty System' is defined by art 1(e) of the 1991 Madrid Protocol. It was first used by the Argentine scholar and diplomat Robert Guyer in his 1973 lecture at The Hague Academy of International Law: see R Guyer, 'The Antarctic Treaty System' (1973) *Hague Recueil des Cours, Vol 139–II* 149, 156; R Scully, 'The Antarctic Treaty as a System' (1991) in R Herr, M Hall and MG Haward (eds), *Antarctica's Future: Continuity or Change?* (Australian Institute of International Affairs, 1990) 96–7.

12   Jeffrey McGee and Marcus Haward, 'Antarctic Governance in a Climate Changed World' (2019) 11(2) *Australian Journal of Maritime & Ocean Affairs* 78, 78–9.

BOOK REVIEWS

323

Much has been previously written on the ATS and protection of the Antarctic environment.[13] However, one important aspect has been largely overlooked. That is, how during the second half of the twentieth century, human understanding of Antarctica changed from that of a sterile and abiotic frozen continent to that of a living, fragile, and pristine region including the globally significant ecosystem of the Southern Ocean. In providing a careful and nuanced analysis of this changed human understanding, Antonello's *The Greening of Antarctica* offers an important new contribution to the literature on Antarctic law, history and governance.[14]

The Greening of Antarctica focuses on the two decades from the 1960s to the late 1970s which served as the foundation period for the contemporary ATS. The book highlights the historical importance of negotiations carried out by diplomats, scientists and non-governmental actors in conceptualising Antarctica as an environmental space requiring protection. As Antonello comments, the book provides 'for the first time, critical histories of the negotiations of three central Antarctic documents—the *Agreed Measures for the Conservation of Antarctic Fauna and Flora* (AMCAFF), the *Convention for the Conservation of Antarctic Seals* (CCAS), and the *Convention on the Conservation of Antarctic Marine Living Resources* (CCAMLR)—and of the first phase of the minerals debate, as well as how the agreements articulated the linked contest for power and the formation of environmental sensibilities'.[15] Therefore, the aim of the book is to analyse how an understanding of Antarctica as an area of environmental protection developed during the period between the adoption of the *Antarctic Treaty* in 1959 and the signing of the landmark *CCAMLR* in 1980.

Antonello describes how two interrelated drivers during the 1960s and 1970s shaped the idea of the 'greening of Antarctica'. On one hand, there was a new ecological understanding of the Antarctic region which was shaped by the activities and worldviews of scientists from the biological sciences. On the other, there was negotiation of the suite of international treaties and associated

---

13   See, eg, Gillian Triggs and Anna Riddell (eds), *Antarctica: Legal and Environmental Challenges for the Future* (British Institute of International and Comparative Law, 2007); Davor Vidas (ed), *Implementing the Environmental Protection Regime for the Antarctic* (Springer, 2000); Christopher Joyner, *Governing the Frozen Commons: The Antarctic Regime and Environmental Protection* (University of South Carolina Press, 1998); Joe Verhoeven, Philippe Sands and Maxwell Bruce (eds), *The Antarctic Environment and International Law* (Kluwer Law International, 1992).

14   Alessandro Antonello, *The Greening of Antarctica: Assembling an International Environment* (Oxford University Press, 2019).

15   Ibid 171.

binding measures directed towards conservation and management of marine resources and protection of the Antarctic environment.

In an insightful introduction to the book, Antonello introduces the history of post-1945 Antarctic politics, including the adoption of the 1959 *Antarctic Treaty* by the seven claimant states and five other countries involved in Antarctic science during the 1957–58 International Geophysical Year. The first chapter outlines the history of negotiations for the first environmental protection measures in Antarctica, the '*AMCAFF*'.[16] As previously mentioned, from 1959 there was scientific concern that there was no framework to protect the Antarctic environment from the impacts of human activities, including scientific work and associate activities at research bases.[17] Even before the *Antarctic Treaty* entered into force in 1961, diplomats and biologists working within SCAR therefore became concerned about growing human impact and the necessity for rules for conservation of Antarctic flora and fauna. Nevertheless, Antonello argues that the adoption of the *AMCAFF* by the *Antarctic Treaty* parties not only permitted diplomats to introduce environmental rules to Antarctica, but also enhanced the authority and institutional standing of scientists (particularly the life scientists) within the Antarctic scientific community.

However, there is one matter that might have made a useful addition to chapter 1. The chapter makes no reference to art V of the *Antarctic Treaty* (ie prohibiting all nuclear explosions, both peaceful and nuclear, and disposal of nuclear waste), which some claim is an environmental protection provision in the text of the Treaty.[18] An interesting perspective on the negotiation of art V is found in Alfred van der Essen's work. The former Belgian diplomat explains that the (now alarming) idea of the use of 'peaceful' nuclear explosions to remove the ice cap in some Antarctic regions to allow mining activities was headed off, thanks primarily to the advocacy of Argentina and Australia.[19]

---

16   *Agreed Measures for the Conservation of Antarctic Fauna and Flora*, signed 2 June 1964, 17 UST 996, TIAS 6058 (1965), modified in 24 UST 1802, TIAS 7692 (1973) (entered into force 1 November 1982) ('*AMCAFF*').

17   Carrick (n 6).

18   *Antarctic Treaty* (n 1) art 1: '1. Any nuclear explosions in Antarctica and the disposal there of radioactive waste material shall be prohibited. 2. In the event of the conclusion of international agreements concerning the use of nuclear energy, including nuclear explosions and the disposal of radioactive waste material, to which all of the Contracting Parties whose representatives are entitled to participate in the meetings provided for under Article IX are parties, the rules established under such agreements shall apply in Antarctica'.

19   Van der Essen (n 5) 1.

BOOK REVIEWS

Chapter 2 discusses the adoption of the CCAS in 1972 which allowed the *Antarctic Treaty* parties to expand the geographical scope of Antarctic governance. After the AMCAFF were adopted in 1964, scientists and diplomats realised that animals located in the ocean were not covered by the AMCAFF [20] and hence, a new international instrument on sealing was needed to fill this gap. This concern for the Southern Ocean seal populations for the first time lifted the gaze of Antarctic governance offshore to the waters and marine systems of the Southern Ocean.

With the awakening of a new environmental concern in the late 1960s, international interest in commercial sealing diminished. Nevertheless, the *Antarctic Treaty* parties and scientists within SCAR continued to pursue a convention on the conservation of seals. In chapter 2, Antonello shows that the CCAS should be viewed not only as an opportunity used by the parties to the *Antarctic Treaty* to expand the effective area of Antarctic governance, but also as a tool of power used to mark their authority and respective positions for the governance of the Antarctic.

In the late 1960s, the *Antarctic Treaty* parties became concerned when several mineral and oil companies began investigating whether Antarctica could be exploited and there was no legal framework to manage such activities. Antonello's third chapter describes how debates surrounding possible exploitation of minerals in Antarctica between 1969 and 1977 shaped understandings of the value of Antarctica and what constituted its resources. The deliberations of what Antonello calls 'the first phase of the Antarctic minerals debate' concluded in the 1977 London Antarctic Treaty Consultative Meeting. Even though the parties to the *Antarctic Treaty* only agreed on a temporary freeze on mining activities, while they negotiated a comprehensive minerals regime, the chapter highlights how the debates set a precedent for future negotiation of the 1991 *Protocol on Environmental Protection to the Antarctic Treaty*,[21] which emphasises the value of the Antarctic as a source of scientific knowledge for the world. In addition, during these discussions a key concept emerged for the protection of Antarctica—the notion of 'environmental impact' entered Antarctic policy discourse.

Since the late 1960s, the Soviet Union had given special attention to the potential value of krill fishing in Antarctica. Prevention of the over-exploitation

---

20   See AMCAFF (n 16) art 1.1: 'These Agreed Measures shall apply to the same area to which the Antarctic Treaty is applicable, namely the area south of 60° South Latitude, including all ice shelves'.

21   *Protocol on Environmental Protection to the Antarctic Treaty*, opened for signature 4 October 1991, 2941 UNTS 3 (entered into force 14 January 1998). Commonly referred to as the 'Madrid Protocol'.

of krill was the key driver for some parties to the *Antarctic Treaty* and environmentalist NGOs to push for the formation of CCAMLR, a treaty governing marine living resources in the Southern Ocean. Chapter 4 describes the negotiations behind the adoption of the CCAMLR in 1980. This convention was a landmark treaty in international law and constructed the idea of Antarctica and the surrounding Southern Ocean as a living region. For the first time in international law, a marine resources convention provided for the protection of an entire ecosystem (ie the biophysical system located South of the Antarctic convergence). Nevertheless, Antonello claims again that with the adoption of CCAMLR, the parties to the *Antarctic Treaty* not only furthered their incremental transformation of understanding of the continent, but also continued underpinning their historic links with the region in political, scientific, and cultural terms.

The final chapter 5 shifts the focus of the book to how the *Antarctic Treaty* parties managed the tensions over sovereignty claims in the context of the 1970s discussions on mineral and marine living resources. During this period, the ATS faced significant external challenges. It was subject to external criticism from forums and states outside the treaty, including the Non-Aligned Movement,[22] the Food and Agriculture Organization of the United Nations, and growing international environmental NGOs. For example, the *Antarctic Treaty* parties (especially the seven claimant States) were concerned that the emerging concept of 'common heritage of mankind',[23] promoted by developing countries seeking a 'New International Economic Order'[24] could undermine

---

22   The Non-Aligned Movement is a political forum established in 1961 during the midst of the collapse of the colonial system and the emancipatory struggle of the oppressed peoples of Africa, Asia, Latin America, the Caribbean and other regions of the world, and at the heights of the Cold War. The purpose of the organisation was enumerated in the Havana Declaration of 1979 to ensure 'the national independence, sovereignty, territorial integrity and security of non-aligned countries' in their struggle against imperialism, colonialism, neo-colonialism, racism, and all forms of foreign subjugation. Currently, it is composed of 120 Member States from the developing world. In addition, there are also 17 countries and 10 International Organizations that hold an Observer status.

23   The idea of the common heritage of mankind was launched in a memorable speech made at the United Nations General Assembly on 1 November 1967 by the representative of Malta, Mr Arvid Pardo. It represents the notion that certain global commons or elements regarded as beneficial to humanity as a whole should not be unilaterally exploited by individual states or their nationals, nor by corporations or other entities, but rather should be exploited under some sort of international arrangement or regime for the benefit of mankind as a whole.

24   The New International Economic Order was a set of proposals put forward during the 1970s by some developing countries through the United Nations Conference on Trade and Development to replace the Bretton Woods system and promote an international

BOOK REVIEWS

existing sovereignty claims. However, Antonello argues that the parties to the *Antarctic Treaty* banded together to manage these external threats and maintain their positions as the States with greatest interests in Antarctica.

On the other hand, Antonello describes how the ATS also faced significant internal challenges during this period. The new international regime for the oceans, developed in the 1970s through the Third United Nations Conference on the Law of the Sea,[25] created tensions between the Antarctic claimant and non-claimant states. The Antarctic claimant states intended to use the provisions under the new law of the sea regime to claim maritime jurisdiction, such as the 200 nautical mile Exclusive Economic Zone, which might be applied off the Antarctic coastline. Through his exploration of the rich stories behind these negotiations, Antonello shows how the *Antarctic Treaty* parties effectively managed to avoid collapse of the ATS and further their ideas about sovereignty and territory in the region.

All histories are written in particular temporal and cultural contexts, so the following comments are offered in the spirit of friendly critique. Even though *The Greening of Antarctica* largely avoids the problem of 'polar orientalism' that it expressly seeks to avoid,[26] there are one or two areas where a non-Western and non-English speaking perspective might have strengthened Antonello's account. For example, a South American perspective would have bolstered Antonello's discussion of how the extension of the *CCAMLR* area beyond 60°S latitude challenged the understanding of the area of Antarctic governance. When Antonello explains that some subantarctic islands north of 60°S such as Heard island, the Kerguelen and Crozet islands, the Prince Edward islands, Bouvet island, and the South Georgia, South Sandwich, and South Orkney island groups, would also be covered by *CCAMLR*, he is not completely clear in explaining the legal status of some of these islands. To clarify, the South Georgia (*Georgias del Sur*) islands are not the only groups of islands subject to a sovereignty dispute between Argentina and the United Kingdom. Among

---

      economic system in favour of developing countries. See HW Singer, 'The New International Economic Order: An Overview' (1978) 16(4) *The Journal of Modern African Studies* 539.

25   Between 1973 and 1982 the Third United Nations Conferences on the Law of the Sea discussed the establishment of a 'Constitution for the Oceans'. The conferences concluded with the adoption of the *United Nations Convention on the Law of the Sea,* opened for signature 10 December 1982, 1833 UNTS 397 (entered into force 16 November 1994).

26   Polar orientalism is considered as 'a scholarly and political strategy of delegitimizing the ideas and efforts of non-Western and non-English-speaking states' in Klaus Dodds and Alan D Hemmings, 'Britain and the British Antarctic Territory in the Wider Geopolitics of the Antarctic and the Southern Ocean' (2013) 89(6) *International Affairs* 1429.

others, the South Sandwich (*Sandwich del Sur*) and the South Orkney (*Orcadas del Sur*) islands are also claimed as the sovereign territory of both States.

In concluding the book, the 'Epilogue' briefly considers two relevant topics. The first of these links the 1960–1970s period (or as the author calls 'the greening of Antarctica') with the failed ratification of the 1988 *Convention on the Regulation of Antarctic Mineral Resource Activities*[27] and successful negotiations of the 1991 *Protocol on Environmental Protection to the Antarctic Treaty*.[28] The second issue raised in the Epilogue is how the regulation of ice has been overlooked by diplomats and scientists. Although ice dominates the landscape of Antarctica, it has not been a central concern of the ATS. Antonello argues that more attention should be given to ice since it might affect future Antarctic diplomacy and geopolitics due to the severe impacts of climate change in the Southern region.

The Greening of Antarctica is a major addition to the international law and history literature on the ATS. The protection regime for the Antarctic environment is frequently taken as an example for other international environmental problems.[29] *The Greening of Antarctica* allows us to better understand the important roles played by diplomats, scientists and nongovernmental actors in shifting the human understanding of Antarctica that underpins the key agreements of the ATS. As Antonello comments, 'their thoughts and actions have profoundly shaped our continuing engagement with the Antarctic'.[30] The book also helps us rethink the current and future challenges faced in governance of the Antarctic environment. It should find a place on the bookshelves of all scholars interested in the history of Antarctica and international environmental law.

Bruno Arpi
PhD Candidate, Faculty of Law, Institute for Marine and Antarctic Studies, University of Tasmania

Jeffrey McGee
Associate Professor, Faculty of Law, Institute for Marine and Antarctic Studies, University of Tasmania

---

27 Opened for signature 25 November 1988, 27 ILM 868 (not yet in force).

28 More about the importance of the Madrid Protocol is available at: Donald R Rothwell, 'Polar Environmental Protection and International Law: The 1991 Antarctic Protocol' (2000) 11(3) *European Journal of International Law* 591.

29 See Berkman et al (n 4).

30 Antonello (n 14) 174.

Solving the Internet Jurisdiction Puzzle

Dan Jerker B Svantesson
(Oxford University Press, 2017, 246 pp)

This is an important book because it advances knowledge about the question of 'internet jurisdiction', but also the related matters of applicable law, the possibilities of declining jurisdiction, and the matters of recognition and enforcement. In the preface to his book, Svantesson seeks to overcome the difficulties of internet jurisdiction: that there is no prospect of solutions; and that the current law is so entrenched that we cannot in fact hope to change it. He presents a framework for jurisdiction that builds on well-established principles, and he is hopeful that his framework can be a rallying point for a diverse range of interests.[1]

Courts around the world have been grappling with the question of which state may properly exercise jurisdiction over the parties to cyberspace transactions and, through court decisions, the jurisdictional principles applicable to the internet are gradually emerging.[2]

Certain characteristics and features of the internet (such as being borderless, anonymous, digital, ubiquitous and instantaneous) challenge not only traditional areas of law such as contract and intellectual property but also fundamental concepts like 'jurisdiction'.

Svantesson quickly identifies the problem which he wants to discuss and solve in the introductory chapter to the book, namely:

> The problem with Internet jurisdiction is the difficulty in finding an appropriate balance of the various interests at stake, and to express that balance in a sufficiently clear and precise manner so as to provide adequate guidance for those expected to act in accordance with the expressed balance.[3]

---

1 Dan Jerker B Svantesson, *Solving the Internet Jurisdiction Puzzle* (Oxford University Press, 2017) xiii.
2 B Fitzgerald et al, *Internet and E-Commerce Law: Technology, Law and Policy* (Thomson Reuters, 2007) 34.
3 Svantesson (n 1) 1.

© KONINKLIJKE BRILL NV, LEIDEN, 2021 | DOI:10.1163/26660229_03801015

He argues that one of the key problems that needs to be addressed in relation to internet jurisdiction is that 'present thinking on jurisdiction is anchored in an unhelpful adherence to territoriality'.[4]

The book is divided into 13 chapters. Given that the title of the book invokes the fundamental dilemma of technological developments out-pacing the law, Svantesson arranges the chapter themes extremely well by interspersing the discussion of the positive and normative legal approaches with the role and impact of technology. Chapter two deals with 'the tyranny of territoriality', which is the problem, whilst chapter three presents the 'New Jurisprudential Framework for Jurisdiction' that is the recommended solution to the problem.

The remaining chapters deal with topics such as the history of the internet (chapter four), jurisdictional interoperability (chapter five), understanding the functions of jurisdictional law (chapter six), the vagueness of the law and the importance of interpretation (chapter seven), the impact of our categorisation of types of jurisdiction (chapter eight), scope of remedial jurisdiction (chapter nine), a layered approach to jurisdiction (chapter ten), the role of geo-location technologies (chapter 11), a doctrine of selective legal compliance (chapter 12) and final remarks (chapter 13).

In chapter two, Svantesson discusses in detail his theme that we are being ruled by 'territoriality' in a tyrannical fashion and that we are restricted by its hard hand. He goes on to analyse and dissect in surgical detail the two most commonly cited sources of territoriality: the 1927 *Lotus Case*[5] and the 1935 'Harvard Draft Convention on Jurisdiction with Respect to Crime' ('Harvard Draft').[6] After reproducing the majority opinion in full in the *Lotus Case*, Svantesson extrapolates the rules from this opinion, including the default rule that a state may not exercise its power in any form in the territory of another state, and the proviso that this rule may be departed from only where there is a permissive rule, derived from international custom or from a convention to the contrary.[7] Svantesson argues that leading scholars[8] have questioned whether the *Lotus Case* decision remains good law, particularly since the Court

---

4   Ibid 3.

5   *SS 'Lotus' (France v Turkey) (Judgment)* [1927] PCIJ (ser A) No 10 ('*Lotus Case*').

6   Supplement, 'Draft Convention on Jurisdiction with Respect to Crime' (1935) 29 (Supplement) *American Journal of International Law* 439 ('Harvard Draft').

7   Svantesson (n 1) 17.

8   See Cedric Ryngaert, *Jurisdiction in International Law* (Oxford University Press, 2nd ed, 2015) 34; Harold G Maier's 'Jurisdictional Rules in Customary International Law' in Karl M Meessen (ed), *Extraterritorial Jurisdiction in Theory and Practice* (Kluwer Law International, 1996) 64, 66.

BOOK REVIEWS 331

did not discuss what these permissive rules might look like.[9] Turning to the Harvard Draft, Svantesson says the legacy of this document is that it articulates a set of five principles (or grounds of jurisdiction), including the territory, nationality, protective, universality and passive principles. He says that these principles have been accepted as the definitive statement of when states may exercise prescriptive and adjudicative jurisdiction under international law.[10] Notwithstanding this wide acceptance of the Harvard Draft, Svantesson correctly argues that the principles 'are no longer part of any solution' and that 'they have become a part of the problem' with territoriality.[11] He says these 'principles are unrealistically mechanical'; and that they 'validate a dated and rigid focus on territoriality that makes impossible any progress in relation to the complexities associated with Internet jurisdiction'.[12] These are valid criticisms which set the basis for Svantesson postulating a 'New Jurisprudential Framework for Jurisdiction' in chapter three.

In order to go forward, Svantesson says 'we must first ... identify the jurisprudential core principles for which the "Harvard Draft's" jurisdictional principles act as proxies'.[13] He says the two core principles emanating from the Harvard Draft are:

1.   There is a substantial connection between the matter and the state seeking to exercise jurisdiction; and

2.   The state seeking to exercise jurisdiction has a legitimate interest in the matter.

He then advances a third principle; namely:

3.   The exercise of jurisdiction is reasonable given the balance between the state's legitimate interests and other interests.[14]

Svantesson says that this 'third principle completes the picture' and that these principles 'are "old wine"'.[15] He gives an explanation of fundamental terms: substantial connection, legitimate interest and interest balancing. More importantly, he explains the role of the new framework. The aim of his proposal is to raise the issue (the territoriality principle) and to advocate a particular solution. He says that 'this can help put the matter on the agenda and create a

---

9   Svantesson (n 1) 17.
10   Ibid 24, 26.
11   Ibid 29.
12   Ibid 55.
13   Ibid 59.
14   Ibid 60–1.
15   Ibid 61.

legal, and political, discussion that over time can facilitate the sought-after paradigm shift'.[16]

Svantesson makes the audacious claim that '[i]f we accept the three principles' he advances they will bring the disciplines of public international law and private international law together into one discipline.[17] Obviously, only the passage of time will tell if this claim materialises.

Svantesson's analysis of the history of the internet jurisdiction in chapter four is comprehensive and intuitive because, amongst other things, he explains well some of the targeting test for jurisdiction case law, such as the 'sliding scale test' laid down in *Zippo Manufacturing Company v Zippo.com Inc*;[18] and the decision of the High Court of Australia in *Dow Jones & Company Inc v Gutnick*,[19] where it was decided that the mere accessibility of a website was the basis for jurisdiction.

Chapters one to four inclusive explain what the problem and solution are for the Internet jurisdiction whilst the subsequent chapters, five to 12, explain how to implement the solution. In chapter five, Svantesson says the most appropriate way forward is to focus on the concept of 'jurisdictional interoperability' as part of 'legal interoperability'. He references the work of Palfrey and Gasser to outline their observations regarding legal interoperability such as that 'we need not pursue "the goal to create one uniform 'world law'"', and that '[w]e need to aim for interoperability among legal systems at an optimal, rather than maximum, level'.[20]

The questions of Internet jurisdiction are dealt with in a philosophical context in chapter six by discussing 'What is law?', including the balancing of law, facts and interests, and market sovereignty. In relation to market sovereignty, Svantesson mentions that instead of focusing on the location of persons, acts or things (for jurisdictional purposes) we should turn our attention to marketplace control (which he calls 'market sovereignty').[21]

In chapters seven and eight, Svantesson briefly discusses the vagueness of the law and the importance of interpretation and notes that there is a considerable diversity of views on how to categorise jurisdictional claims, with no

---

16   Ibid 83.

17   Ibid 89.

18   952 F Supp 1119 (WD Pa, 1997).

19   (2002) 210 CLR 575.

20   Svantesson (n 1) 119, quoting John Palfrey and Urs Gasser, *Interop: The Promise and Perils of Highly Interconnected Systems* (Basic Books, 2012) 179.

21   Svantesson (n 1) 144.

BOOK REVIEWS

real consensus discernible as to what the categories are, how they relate to each other or how to identify the underlying jurisdictional thresholds.[22]

There are two dimensions to 'jurisdiction'; namely, personal jurisdiction (the court's ability to adjudicate matters directed against a particular party) and subject-matter jurisdiction (the substantive areas of law in which the courts may adjudicate matters). In chapter nine, Svantesson proposes a 'third dimension' which he calls the 'scope of jurisdiction' or the 'scope of remedial jurisdiction', which is about the 'appropriate geographical scope of orders rendered by a court that has personal jurisdiction and subject-matter jurisdiction'.[23] He says that issues of scope of jurisdiction are controversial 'in the context of removal, blocking, or delisting of Internet content' since 'a court's order in State A that content be removed from the internet directly affects what content people in other states can access online'.[24] To deal with these issues, Svantesson offers the following five factors as a comprehensive framework for dealing with them:

a.   the strength of the connection to the forum;
b.   the connection between the party and the dispute;
c.   the impact on other countries and persons in other countries;
d.   the type and effectiveness of the order compared to alternatives; and
e.   the level of fault of the party.[25]

Svantesson says in chapter 10 that 'lawmakers have a tendency to approach the question of jurisdiction in an overly simplistic, indeed naïve, manner'[26] and refers to the example of the European Union's *General Data Protection Regulation*.[27] In light of this alleged simplicity and naïvity on the part of lawmakers, he outlines a 'layered approach' under which the substantive law rules are broken up into different layers (the abuse-prevention layer, the rights layer and the administrative layer) and how different jurisdictional thresholds may then be applied to each such layer.[28]

In chapter 11, he explores his interest in geo-location technologies and concludes that the impact of such technologies on jurisdictional issues in

---

22   Ibid 169.
23   Ibid 171.
24   Ibid 174.
25   Ibid 181.
26   Ibid 191.
27   *Regulation (EU) 2016/679 of the European Parliament and of the Council of 27 April 2016 on the Protection of Natural Persons with Regard to the Processing of Personal Data and on the Free Movement of Such Data* [2016] OJ L 119 ('*General Data Protection Regulation*').
28   Svantesson (n 1) 199.

a particular case must be determined in the light of the individual facts of that case.

Svantesson discusses in chapter 12 the possibility of selective legal compliance to protect internet intermediaries, given their role in the operation of the internet. He argues that, since the law already takes some steps towards protecting internet intermediaries,[29] the expansion into selective legal compliance is a 'natural development' and that it would be helpful for establishing jurisdictional interoperability.[30]

In his 'Final Remarks' in chapter 13, Svantesson concludes that his book is about solving the internet jurisdiction puzzle. He has definitely gone a long way to solve this puzzle by proposing new concepts (such as the jurisdictional interoperability, scope of (remedial) jurisdiction, and the layered approach) and new frameworks (such as the 'jurisdictional principles' and 'the doctrine of selective legal compliance').

This book excels in its depth of analysis and the solutions it provides for the internet jurisdiction problem. I agree that his solutions and frameworks will be a rallying point for a diverse range of interests.

Timothy Beale
Postgraduate Student, ANU College of Law, Australian National University

---

29   See, eg, *Communications Decency Act of 1996* 47 USC (1996).

30   Svantesson (n 1) 223.

The Oxford Handbook of International Law in Asia and the Pacific

Simon Chesterman, Hisashi Owada and Ben Saul (eds)
(Oxford University Press, 2019, 912 pp)

Producing a book covering the topic of 'international law in Asia and the Pacific' is an ambitious undertaking. As mentioned in the opening paragraph of *The Oxford Handbook of International Law in Asia and the Pacific* ('*Handbook*'), the Asia-Pacific covers almost one third of the world's land area, spans vast maritime areas across the Pacific and Indian Oceans, and is home to around 60% of the world's population.[1] It is unsurprising that 'no book has so far attempted to survey in depth the whole field of international law across Asia and the Pacific'.[2]

As the editors of the *Handbook* note, existing scholarship on international law in Asia and the Pacific is more circumscribed. It usually focuses on the experience of a particular state with international law or on the application of a particular 'branch' of international law in the region. As the editors note, there has to date been:

> no major book covering how Asian and Pacific states (a) as a whole participate in each of the main specialized branches of international law; (b) individually contribute to the making and application of international law on the international plane; and (c) individually implement international law in their national legal systems.[3]

It is these gaps in the literature that the *Handbook* sets out to fill.

The *Handbook* tackles this task in three parts. Part I on 'Themes, Institutions, and History' deals with cross-cutting issues. After an introductory chapter by the editors, Part I contains chapters on 'Asia's Ambivalence about International Law' by Simon Chesterman (drawing on his 2016 *European Journal of*

---

1 Simon Chesterman, Hisashi Owada and Ben Saul, 'Introduction' in Simon Chesterman, Hisashi Owada and Ben Saul (eds), *The Oxford Handbook of International Law in Asia and the Pacific* (Oxford University Press, 2019) 3 ('*Handbook*').
2 Ibid.
3 Ibid 6.

International Law article on the same topic),[4] 'Regional Organizations' by Tan Hsien-Li and 'Asia in the History and Theory of International Law' by Antony Anghie.

Part II deals with the first gap in the literature identified by the editors. Across seven chapters, each dealing with a different branch of international law, the contributors consider how Asian and Pacific States as a whole participate in each of the selected branches of international law. Part II contains chapters on 'Regional Peace and Security' by Waheguru Pal Singh Sidhu, 'Human Rights' by Hurst Hannum, 'International Humanitarian Law and International Criminal Law' by Suzannah Linton, 'International Environmental Law' by Ben Boer, 'Law of the Sea and Asian States' by Robert Beckman, 'International Economic Law and Asia' by Wang Jiangyu and 'International Dispute Settlement' by Hisashi Owada and Samuel H Chang.

Part III deals with the second and third gaps identified by the editors. It contains 21 chapters, most of which are dedicated to an individual state (the exceptions being the chapters dedicated to 'Central Asian States' collectively and to 'South Pacific Island States' collectively). The chapters consider how the relevant states individually contribute to the making and application of international law and implement international law domestically. Part III is arranged in four subparts: (i) on 'East Asia', with chapters on 'China' by Li Zhaojie, 'Japan' by Mogami Toshiki and 'South Korea' by Seokwoo Lee and Hee Eun Lee; (ii) on 'Southeast Asia', with chapters on 'Thailand' by Vitit Muntarbhorn, 'Indonesia' by Hikmahanto Juwana and Anbar Jayadi, 'The Philippines' by Romel Regalado Bagares, 'Singapore' by Li-ann Thio and Kevin YL Tan, 'Malaysia' by Abdul Ghafur Hamid and Khin Maung Sein, 'Viet Nam' by Trinh Hai Yen, 'Cambodia' by Mahdev Mohan and 'Myanmar' by Catherine Renshaw; (iii) on 'South and Central Asia', with chapters on 'India' by BS Chimni, 'Pakistan' by Ahmer Bilal Soofi, 'Bangladesh' by Kamal Hossain and Sharif Bhuiyan, 'Nepal' by Pratyush Nath Upreti and Surya P Subedi, 'Sri Lanka' by Amrith Rohan Perera, 'Afghanistan' by Veronica L Taylor and 'Central Asian States' by Marina Girshovich; and (iv) on 'The Pacific (including Oceania and Australasia)', with chapters on 'South Pacific Island States' by Jennifer Corrin, 'Australia' by Ben Saul and 'New Zealand' by Kenneth Keith.

The *Handbook* 'seeks to broaden the discourse of international law in search of a richer understanding of perspectives *from* the region, *about* the region and including authors *of* the region'.[5] Without a doubt, the *Handbook* does

---

4 Simon Chesterman, 'Asia's Ambivalence about International Law and Institutions: Past, Present and Futures' (2016) 27(4) *European Journal of International Law* 945.

5 Chesterman, Owada and Saul (n 1) 15.

BOOK REVIEWS

337

this. The book also achieves its more specific aims: to cover in one text how Asian and Pacific States as a whole participate in the main branches of international law and how Asian and Pacific States individually contribute to the making, application and domestic implementation of international law. The book is certainly not exhaustive. As the editors acknowledge, there are additional branches of international law that could have been included in Part II. Similarly, some Asian and Pacific States are not covered in Part III (namely, the Democratic People's Republic of Korea, Mongolia, Brunei Darussalam, Laos, Bhutan, Maldives, Marshall Islands, Micronesia, Palau and Timor-Leste). But there are limits to what can be covered in one book and the scope of the *Handbook* is impressively broad, covering seven branches of international law and 33 states (five in the chapter on Central Asian States and nine in the chapter on South Pacific Island States).

As is to be expected from an edited collection, there is some variation in how the individual contributors have approached the aims of the book. For example, while the editors nominate 28 states as falling within 'Asia',[6] some contributors employ different conceptions of 'Asia', including broader conceptions that also encompass the Middle East.[7] This is understandable. As the editors note, the definition of 'Asia' is debated.[8] When reading a chapter, one simply needs to be mindful of how the particular contributor is using the label 'Asia'. As another example, some chapters in Part III (such as the chapters on China and Japan) focus almost exclusively on how the relevant state contributes to the making and application of international law, rather than also addressing how the relevant state implements international law domestically. These chapters are nonetheless still very interesting to read. The chapter on China argues, for example, that while China still sees international law as a tool for enhancing its own interests, rather than as a normative framework governing international relations, China is seeking to act within and incrementally

---

6   Ibid 8. The editors nominate 15 states as falling within the 'Pacific', for a total of 43 states in the Asia-Pacific.

7   See, eg, Waheguru Pal Singh Sidhu, 'Regional Peace and Security' in Simon Chesterman, Hisashi Owada and Ben Saul (eds), *The Oxford Handbook of International Law in Asia and the Pacific* (Oxford University Press, 2019) 95, 95: 'For this chapter: "Asia" includes the fifty-five members of the Asia-Pacific group at the United Nations (UN), stretching from Cyprus in the west, to Kiribati in the east, and from Kazakhstan in the north to Tonga in the south, plus Australia, New Zealand and the United States (ANZUS), and Russia. Though not part of the UN Asia-Pacific group, ANZUS countries and Russia are included by virtue of their geographical location and their peace and security role in the region.'

8   Chesterman, Owada and Saul (n 1) 7.

reform the international legal system (a system that it did not play a significant part in creating).[9]

Indeed, a number of chapters of the book go beyond providing a survey of their allocated topic and make interesting arguments of their own. The chapter on international dispute settlement by Owada and Chang,[10] for example, challenges the perception that Asian States eschew international dispute settlement, and the chapter on regional organisations by Tan argues against the assumption that international organisations should be assessed based on their degree of legalisation and institutionalisation,[11] a metric against which Asia-Pacific regional organisations do not fare well. The most important contribution made by the *Handbook*, however, is the collection of chapters in Part III dedicated to the relationships that each of the smaller states in the region has with international law as a whole.

The *Handbook* is likely to be particularly useful for those looking at the domestic implementation of international law in the region, especially those interested in the implementation of international law in multiple jurisdictions. The *Handbook* would also be useful for readers looking for an overview of one of the topics covered in the book—in a particular state's relationship with international law or in the region's interaction with a particular branch of international law. To say that the book would be useful for those looking for an 'overview' of these topics is not a criticism. The editors, and multiple contributors, stress that the intention was not to provide encyclopaedic coverage of the various topics dealt with in the *Handbook*. Rather, the chapters of the book provide high-quality yet accessible surveys or overviews of the various topics. In particular, the chapter by Anghie provides an informative and easy-to-read overview of the history of Asia's engagement with international law.[12] As a general matter, the *Handbook* would likely be most useful for those concerned with Asia, as opposed to the Pacific. Beyond the chapters dealing with Australia and New Zealand, Part III of the book only contains one chapter

---

9   Li Zhaojie, 'China' in Simon Chesterman, Hisashi Owada and Ben Saul (eds), *The Oxford Handbook of International Law in Asia and the Pacific* (Oxford University Press, 2019) 299.

10   Hisashi Owada and Samuel H Chang 'International Dispute Settlement' in Simon Chesterman, Hisashi Owada and Ben Saul (eds), *The Oxford Handbook of International Law in Asia and the Pacific* (Oxford University Press, 2019) 267.

11   Tan Hsien-Li, 'Regional Organizations' in Chesterman, Owada and Saul Simon Chesterman, Hisashi Owada and Ben Saul (eds), *The Oxford Handbook of International Law in Asia and the Pacific* (Oxford University Press, 2019) 37.

12   Antony Anghie, 'Asia in the History and Theory of International Law' in Simon Chesterman, Hisashi Owada and Ben Saul (eds), *The Oxford Handbook of International Law in Asia and the Pacific* (Oxford University Press, 2019) 68.

BOOK REVIEWS 339

devoted to the Pacific, and a number of the chapters in Parts I and II focus primarily on Asian States.

There is no concluding chapter tying together the various contributions in the *Handbook*, but readers can see for themselves that a number of ideas recur across the chapters of the book. One theme that emerges from multiple chapters is the incredible diversity of the Asia-Pacific—between Asian States and Pacific States, between the different subregions of Asia, between individual states and between the approaches of states (individually and collectively) to the different branches of international law. Another issue highlighted by multiple chapters, and with which a number of chapters grapple, is the economic and political rise of states in Asia—states that historically have been 'rule takers'—and how this will affect the international legal order.[13] The *Handbook* is intended to be 'a survey that stimulates discussion'.[14] Whether one is interested in broader themes such as those mentioned above, or is simply interested in a topic covered in one of the discrete chapters, the reader will find the *Handbook* to be thought-provoking, a catalyst for discussion and likely also a catalyst for future research.

Callista Harris
University of Sydney

13   Chesterman, Owada and Saul (n 1) 3.
14   Ibid 14.

Maritime Legacies and the Law: Effective Legal Governance of WWI Wrecks

Craig Forrest
(Edward Elgar Publishing, 2019, 332 pp)

On 28 June 1914 the heir to the throne of Austria-Hungary, Archduke Franz Ferdinand, was assassinated during an official visit to Sarajevo. This act changed the course of history. It triggered a chain of events that ultimately led to the outbreak of World War I ('WWI'). Spanning four years, this global conflict pitted Germany, Austria-Hungary and the Ottoman Empire against Great Britain, France, Russia, Italy, Japan and the United States. It saw more than 65 million soldiers mobilised from over 30 nations and caused unprecedented carnage, death and destruction.[1] By the end of the war in 1918 over 16 million people—combatants and civilians—had been killed.[2] Craig Forrest's book, *Maritime Legacies and the Law: Effective Legal Governance of WWI Wrecks*, pays tribute to those who lost their lives during the oft-ignored war at sea and the stock of 'legacy wrecks' (naval and auxiliary ships, merchant vessels, passenger liners, fishing boats and small crafts) that sank during WWI. These wrecks are scattered across the seabed of the world's oceans and provide an invaluable link between the past and the present. Remarkably, even though it is more than a century since the end of WWI, the protection of this underwater legacy remains a complicated and controversial issue. Forrest's work offers a way forward, one that relies upon the widespread ratification of the 2001 *Convention on the Protection of the Underwater Cultural Heritage* ('*UCH Convention*').[3] As the overriding objective of the *UCH Convention* is to provide a protective and regulatory system for all underwater cultural heritage, Forrest lays out a strong and convincing argument for why the *UCH Convention* is the most promising and appropriate mechanism to protect WWI legacy wrecks.

While the iconic battles on land during WWI, such as the Somme and the Gallipoli campaign, are well documented, less attention has been paid to the battles waged at sea.

---

1 Alan Taylor, 'World War I in Photos: Introduction', *The Atlantic* (Web Page, 27 April 2014) <https://www.theatlantic.com/photo/2014/04/world-war-i-in-photos-introduction/507185/>.

2 History.com Editors, 'World War I' *History* (Web Page, 29 October 2009) <https://www.history.com/topics/world-war-i/world-war-i-history>.

3 *Convention on the Protection of the Underwater Cultural Heritage*, opened for signature 2 November 2001, 2562 UNTS 3 (entered into force 2 January 2009) ('*UCH Convention*').

BOOK REVIEWS

Forrest begins his text by reviewing the losses of the war at sea. His purpose is not to provide an exhaustive analysis or catalogue of losses, as this has been extensively treated elsewhere, rather, it is to illustrate 'the sunken legacy of WWI' (wrecked vessels, aircraft and objects) and to situate these losses within their historical context.[4] Using the great naval battles of WWI as analytical tools, Chapter 1 provides a detailed overview of the geographical diversity of WWI naval engagements, the belligerent states involved, the nature of the naval and merchant fleets and the rate and extent of losses, including the human death toll.

Chapter 3 introduces the 'complex matrix'[5] of national and international law that currently governs WWI legacy wrecks. Drawing on extensive research, Forrest undertakes a thorough examination of private law rights, including the acquisition, transfer and loss of ownership as well as the rights of insurers and re-insurers. Before turning to the public international law framework, Forrest examines the international law of sovereign immunity and the fundamental role it continues to play in states' rights to legacy wrecks. Attention is then directed to the numerous international conventions that have an impact upon or address (either intentionally or unintentionally) WWI wrecks, including the 1982 *United Nations Convention on the Law of the Sea* and the instruments adopted under the branches of salvage,[6] environmental[7] and cultural heritage law.[8] From the outset, it is clear that Forrest wishes to avoid a dry critique of the current legal framework. Accordingly, in order to frame his narrative in subsequent chapters, Forrest uses Chapter 2 to introduce the physical legacy of WWI wrecks and the values they embody. Recognising that these values have changed over time, Forrest traces their evolution from initially being seen

---

4   Craig Forrest, *Maritime Legacies and the Law: Effective Legal Governance of WWI Wrecks,* (Edward Elgar Publishing, 2019) 6.

5   Ibid 74.

6   *International Convention on Salvage,* opened for signature 28 July 1989, 1953 UNTS 165 (entered into force 14 July 1996).

7   *International Convention Relating to Intervention on the High Seas in Cases of Oil Pollution Casualties,* opened for signature 29 November 1969, 970 UNTS 211 (entered into force 6 May 1975); *Nairobi International Convention on the Removal of Wrecks,* opened for signature 18 May 2007, 46 ILM 697 (entered into force 14 April 2015).

8   *Convention for the Protection of Cultural Property in the Event of Armed Conflict,* opened for signature 14 May 1954, 249 UNTS 215 (entered into force 7 August 1956); *Convention on the Means of Prohibiting and Preventing the Illicit Import, Export and Transfer of Ownership of Cultural Property,* opened for signature 14 November 1970, 823 UNTS 231 (entered into force 24 April 1972); *Convention for the Protection of the World Cultural and Natural Heritage,* opened for signature 16 November 1972, 1037 UNTS 151 (entered into force 17 December 1975); *UCH Convention* (n 3); *Convention for the Safeguarding of the Intangible Cultural Heritage,* opened for signature 17 October 2003, 2368 UNTS 3 (entered into force 20 April 2006).

as navigational hazards and sources of scrap metal to objects of enormous archaeological and historical value. Of course, legacy wrecks are also now often thought of as sacred sites, being memorials and the maritime war graves of those lost at sea.

Chapters 4 to 7 address each of the four values identified in Chapter 2. Chapter 4 begins by considering legacy wrecks as objects of salvage. Forrest argues that salvage law poses the greatest threat to WWI wrecks. In support of his argument, Forrest provides an historical account of the law of salvage and reviews its problematic application to legacy wrecks before identifying its weaknesses as a regulatory regime. Forrest illustrates the extent of irregular, illegal and unreported salvage and pilfering through a number of case studies including the iconic and historically important Jutland Wrecks, the Live Bait Squadron (HMS *Aboukir*, HMS *Cressy* and HMS *Hogue*), the Dardanelles Wrecks, the *Lusitania* and the German Fleet at Scapa Flow. Chapter 5 considers the various threats legacy wrecks pose. This includes their ability to hinder the navigation of other ships as well as the dangers they pose to the marine environment and its biodiversity due to the nature of the cargo or munitions they carried at the time of their sinking. Forrest examines and critiques the legal regimes that apply to the removal of hazardous wrecks situated both within and outside national jurisdiction, highlighting gaps and limitations within the current legal framework. In Chapter 6 Forrest considers the value of legacy wrecks as historical and archaeological sites. Due to significant advancements in science and technology, access to historic wrecks is easier than ever before. Consequently, in recent decades there has been a marked increase in the amount of activity taking place at WWI wrecks, including unregulated salvage and recreational sports diving. In turn, this has led to calls for a 'consistent and informed protective regime for historically and archaeologically important wrecks in both national and international waters',[9] ultimately resulting in the adoption of the *UCH Convention*. Chapter 6 provides a detailed overview of the *UCH Convention*, including its main set of archaeological principles and practises which are applied to all activities directed at underwater cultural heritage. Forrest argues that the widespread ratification of the *UCH Convention* will enable all states to approach the regulation of legacy wrecks on an even keel, working from the same common set of rules and standards. He expresses frustration with a bloc of powerful states, including the United States, Russia, the Netherlands and Germany, all of which hold stakes in the protection of legacy wrecks but have failed to join the *UCH Convention*. Forrest contends that the United Kingdom's resistance to the *UCH Convention* is most troubling

---

9   Forrest (n 4) 193.

BOOK REVIEWS

of all, for two reasons. Firstly, the United Kingdom has one of the greatest interests in legacy wrecks, given its maritime history and the number and geographical spread of its wrecks.[10] Secondly, the United Kingdom has adopted a complex interpretation of the *UCH Convention* which has, to date, prevented it from ratifying the instrument. The complex relationship the United Kingdom shares with the *UCH Convention* is addressed in Chapter 8 and is a consistent theme running throughout Forrest's text.

The final and arguably most significant value of legacy wrecks is considered in Chapter 7. This chapter focuses on the important role historic wrecks play in the memorialisation of WWI, oftentimes being the final resting place of those who lost their lives at sea. Forrest laments the fact that the concept of a 'maritime war grave' does not exist in international law and ardently promotes the use of the *UCH Convention* as a powerful protective tool in this regard. Forrest also examines the national legislation adopted by a number of states in an effort to protect maritime war graves, including the United Kingdom's *Protection of Military Remains Act 1986* (UK). In Chapter 8, Forrest uses legacy wrecks as a medium for exploring the United Kingdom's objections to the *UCH Convention*. He challenges and effectively debunks each objection before strongly encouraging the United Kingdom to revisit the *UCH Convention* and reform its legislative framework concerning WWI wrecks. By way of comparison, Forrest also provides a range of perspectives on the *UCH Convention* from other states, including Germany, France, Belgium, the Netherlands, Denmark, Ireland and the United States.

The centenary of WWI generated renewed interest in legacy wrecks and as time passes the value of these underwater relics will only increase, be it as objects of historical and archaeological interest or as sacred sites or memorials to those who perished at sea. As this underwater heritage provides a window into the past, it is essential for WWI wrecks to be protected and preserved for future generations. Forrest's book makes for compelling reading. It offers a unique insight into this complex and niche area of international law. As there is a limited amount of literature on this topic, Forrest's book is a notable addition and one that will be of interest to practitioners, scholars, and students alike with a keen interest in the law of the sea, cultural heritage law and marine issues.

Sarah Lothian
PhD Student, The University of Sydney Law School

---

10   Ibid 295.

Oil under Troubled Water: Australia's Timor Sea Intrigue

Bernard Collaery
(Melbourne University Press, 2020, xxi + 466pp)

Australia's relationship with Timor-Leste has been through numerous highs and lows. Some are well known and understood, such as the events of 1975 leading up to the Indonesian intervention in Portuguese East Timor. Likewise, the 1999 Australian military intervention in East Timor immediately following the United Nations sponsored ballot on the future of the territory. A continuous thread running through the relationship has been the shared interest in the Timor Sea, the need for the settlement of maritime boundaries, and the oil and gas reserves in the area. The international law dimensions of that relationship are numerous and include multiple dimensions ranging from treaties and other international instruments between Australia and Indonesia, the United Nations and Timor-Leste concerning the Timor Sea, to litigation before the International Court of Justice and arbitral tribunals arising from those treaties. Those international law issues and associated disputes have, to a degree, been brought to an end by a conciliation process under the framework of the 1982 *United Nations Convention on the Law of the Sea*[1] ('*LOSC*'), which resulted in the 2018 *Treaty between Australia and the Democratic Republic of Timor-Leste Establishing Their Maritime Boundaries in the Timor Sea*[2] ('2018 *Timor Sea Treaty*') between Australia and Timor-Leste. However, while the 2018 *Timor Sea Treaty* is a landmark in the bilateral relationship and is something of a win-win for both countries,[3] the history leading to its negotiation is troubled and contested.

Bernard Collaery is a prominent Canberran, law graduate from the University of Sydney where Julius Stone was one of his lecturers, former member of the Australian Capital Territory ('ACT') Legislative Assembly, former ACT Attorney-General and legal advisor to the East Timorese for over 30 years both prior to and after their 2002 independence. Collaery is also the

---

1 *United Nations Convention on the Law of the Sea*, opened for signature 10 December 1982, 1833 UNTS 397 (entered into force 16 November 1994) ('*LOSC*').
2 Opened for signature 6 March 2018, [2019] ATS 16 (entered into force 30 August 2019) ('2018 *Timor Sea Treaty*').
3 See, eg, 'Timor Sea Treaty Agora' (2018) 36 *Australian Year Book of International Law* 23–72.

© KONINKLIJKE BRILL NV, LEIDEN, 2021 | DOI:10.1163/26660229_03801018

BOOK REVIEWS

subject of proceedings in the ACT courts arising out of his relationship with a client, known only as Witness K, which directly relate to certain allegations over Australia's conduct during the negotiation of the *Treaty between Australia and the Democratic Republic of Timor-Leste on Certain Maritime Arrangements in the Timor Sea*[4] (*'CMATS'*) in 2004.[5] While this matter is not the subject of discussion in this book, it is alluded to, and provides additional context to the matters Collaery writes about.

Oil Under Troubled Waters is a personal account by Collaery of his legal journey with the East Timorese. While the reader is informed by Collaery's personal recollections, the work is much more than just a series of recollections. Collaery has written a work that documents Australia's engagement with the international world order starting with HV Evatt at the San Francisco Conference in 1945, and the aspirations Australia had for a United Nations founded on respect for international law. With that background, the reader is taken to the early development of the modern law of the sea, notably the First United Nations Conference on the Law of the Sea in 1958, and into the 1960s when Australia gained an initial appreciation of the potential significance of the mineral resources of the Timor Sea continental shelf. This was the genesis for Australia's efforts to negotiate the seabed boundaries in the Timor Sea first with Indonesia and then with Portugal. While Indonesia was willing to reach an agreement, Portugal was not, resulting in the so-called 'Timor Gap' in Australia's maritime boundaries in the Timor and Arafura Seas to the south of Timor. The Whitlam government's dealings with Indonesia in 1974–75 are assessed unfavourably but are not dwelt upon given the author was not personally engaged in those matters. Likewise, the 1989 *Treaty between Australia and the Republic of Indonesia on the Zone of Cooperation in an Area between the Indonesian Province of East Timor and Northern Australia*[6] ('1989 *Timor Gap Treaty*') and subsequent proceedings brought by Portugal in the International Court of Justice[7] are only briefly assessed.

---

4   Opened for signature 12 January 2006, [2007] ATS 12 (entered into force 23 February 2007) (*'CMATS'*).

5   Mong Palatino, 'East Timor-Australia Spying Scandal', *The Diplomat* (online, 16 December 2013) <https://thediplomat.com/2013/12/east-timor-australia-spying-scandal/>; Christopher Knaus, 'Witness K and the "Outrageous" Spy Scandal that Failed to Shame Australia', *The Guardian* (online, 10 August 2019) <https://www.theguardian.com/australia-news/2019/aug/10/witness-k-and-the-outrageous-spy-scandal-that-failed-to-shame-australia>.

6   Opened for signature 11 December 1989, [1991] ATS 9 (entered into force 9 February 1991) ('1989 *Timor Gap Treaty*').

7   *Case Concerning East Timor (Portugal v Australia)* [1995] ICJ Rep 90.

The narrative becomes more personal, reflective and engaged when discussing the lead up to the 1999 ballot, and the international law issues that arose during the period of administration of East Timor from 1999–2002 under the United Nations Transitional Administration in East Timor ('UNTAET'). A unique feature of those arrangements was an Exchange of Notes between Australia and UNTAET to maintain the key features of the 1989 *Timor Gap Treaty* for an interim period,[8] and that Australia and UNTAET—with significant Timorese involvement—set about negotiating a new treaty arrangement for the Timor Sea. With the signature of the 2002 *Timor Sea Treaty between the Government of East Timor and the Government of Australia*[9] ('2002 *Timor Sea Treaty*') on Timor's independence on 20 May 2002, another Exchange of Notes was entered into between Australia and the newly independent Timor-Leste[10] to put into place interim arrangements pending the entry into force of the treaty. It was in these 2002 instruments that Collaery argues a significant omission arose with respect to helium which was to the benefit of the existing Timor Sea oil and gas operators, but was a significant loss to Timor and Australia.

While the role of the Australian military in coming to the aid of the Timorese in 1999 is acknowledged, Australian foreign policy and its international law consequences for the Timorese are the subject of severe critique. In particular, Australia is portrayed as seeking to ensure that it gained as much access to the Timor Sea as possible, and that the incoming Timorese government was subjected to considerable political pressure to enter into the 2002 *Timor Sea Treaty*. Collaery does not question the international legal validity of that treaty, though he certainly details its highly unusual negotiation and eventual settlement. In the process, he highlights the internal political dynamics within the Timorese leadership of the day, especially between Xanana Gusmão and Mari Alkatiri.

---

8 *Exchange of Notes Constituting an Agreement between the Government of Australia and the United Nations Transitional Administration in East Timor (UNTAET) Concerning the Continued Operation of the Treaty between Australia and the Republic of Indonesia on the Zone of Cooperation in an Area between the Indonesian Province of East Timor and Northern Australia of 11 December 1989*, opened for signature 10 February 2000, [2000] ATS 9 (entered into force 10 February 2000 with effect from 25 October 1989).

9 Opened for signature 20 May 2002, [2003] ATS 13 (entered into force 2 April 2003) ('2002 *Timor Sea Treaty*').

10 *Exchange of Notes Constituting an Agreement between the Government of Australia and the Government of the Democratic Republic of East Timor Concerning Arrangements for Exploration and Exploitation of Petroleum in an Area of the Timor Sea between Australia and East Timor*, opened for signature 20 May 2002, [2002] ATS 11 (entered into force 20 May 2002).

BOOK REVIEWS

347

From the perspective of international law, the strongest critique is reserved for Australia's position regarding its March 2002 modification of its art 36(2) *Statute of the International Court of Justice* declaration,[11] and its art 298 *LOSC* declaration.[12] Those declarations, which in 2020 were the subject of an Australian Senate inquiry that post-dated this book,[13] effectively ensured that an independent Timor-Leste was unable to commence compulsory proceedings against Australia in either the International Court of Justice or before an arbitral tribunal. While Timor did commence arbitral proceedings against Australia on separate grounds under the 2002 *Timor Sea Treaty*,[14] it was not until 2016, with the commencement of compulsory conciliation against Australia under the *LOSC*, that a seabed dispute between Timor and Australia was brought before a third party. As has been recorded in the *Australian Year Book of International Law*, the outcome of that ground-breaking conciliation, which for the first time utilised the procedures under annex V of the *LOSC*, paved the way for the conclusion of the 2018 *Timor Sea Treaty* and dissolution of the prior 2002 *Timor Sea Treaty*. It is unfortunate that the historical significance of the conciliation is underplayed, especially given that Timor had finally been able to bring Australia before a compulsory dispute resolution process after many years. In that respect, it must be observed that art 298(1)(a)(ii) of the *LOSC* anticipates States will 'negotiate an agreement on the basis of' a report of the Conciliation Commission. Nevertheless, Australia and Timor-Leste, with the guidance of the conciliators, were able to negotiate the 2018 *Timor Sea Treaty* prior to the formal conclusion of the conciliation.

Collaery's principal critique of Australia is that it acted 'opportunistically to continue exploitation of Timor Sea petroleum resources'[15] from 1999 onwards and that, as a result, Australia's actions during that time 'may influence other states, thereby undermining respect in international law'.[16]

---

11   *Declaration under the Statute of the International Court of Justice Concerning Australia's Acceptance of the Jurisdiction of the International Court of Justice*, [2002] ATS 5 (signed and entered into force 21 March 2002).

12   *Declaration under the United Nations Convention on the Law of the Sea Concerning the Application to Australia of the Dispute Settlement Provisions of that Convention*, [2002] ATS 6 (signed and entered into force 21 March 2002).

13   Senate Standing Committee on Foreign Affairs, Defence and Trade, Parliament of Australia, *Australia's Declarations Made under Certain International Laws* (Report, February 2020).

14   *Arbitration under the Timor Sea Treaty (Timor-Leste v Australia) (Procedural Order No 1)* (Permanent Court of Arbitration, Case No 2013–16, 6 December 2013).

15   Bernard Collaery, *Oil Under Troubled Waters: Australia's Timor Sea Intrigue* (Melbourne University Press, 2020) 384.

16   Ibid.

This work certainly sheds additional light on Australian foreign policy and its interpretation of international law with respect to the Timor Sea over a 60 year period beginning in the 1960s. It is the product of extensive research in places and is an important scholarly contribution to the voluminous literature that has been generated on the Australia—Timor bilateral relationship over the decades. However, the critique is written from a Timorese perspective. Not much weight is given to the legitimate entitlements that Australia has under *LOSC* to be able to exploit the resources of the continental shelf, and that States can have well founded differences as to how maritime boundaries are to be negotiated and settled. Likewise, while there are a range of international law mechanisms for the resolution of maritime boundary disputes, Australia sought to legitimately avail itself of options available to it in order to place emphasis on negotiation of maritime boundary agreements rather than utilise third party dispute settlement. Notwithstanding Australia's position on this matter, Timor was still successful in commencing compulsory conciliation against Australia and reaching settlement through that process of a permanent maritime boundary. A distinctive set of arrangements have also been agreed to regarding the Greater Sunrise area. This may not have been the outcome that Timor envisaged when the conciliation was commenced, however Timor has endorsed that outcome and is moving forward with the new permanent maritime boundaries. Collaery is right to question Australia's actions with respect to the negotiation of *CMATS*. Analysis of the specifics of the allegations against Australia will hopefully be the subject of future scholarly investigation.

Oil Under Troubled Waters is an important work by someone who was not only an observer, but a participant, in key aspects of the Australia—Timor international law relationship with respect to the Timor Sea since 1989. It makes for uncomfortable reading and ultimately challenges the notion of Australia as the good international citizen. It is not, however, the last word on the subject, and legal scholars should be encouraged to pursue further the issues Collaery raises.

Donald R Rothwell
General Editor, Australian Year Book of International Law

Research Handbook on Feminist Engagement with International Law

Susan Harris Rimmer and Kate Ogg (eds)
(Edward Elgar Publishing, 2019, 592 pp)

The book under review provides a diverse and ambitious analysis of feminist engagement with international law. The editors, Susan Harris Rimmer and Kate Ogg, curate a meticulous investigation of the past, present and imagined future of feminism's interaction with international law and its ultimate effect.

One question the book seeks to answer, posed at its beginning, is '[how to] make feminist ideas more inclusive, diverse and influential?'[1] In answering this question, the editors and authors undertake a complex yet streamlined approach, weaving a way between the 'hope and despair'[2] which marks the trajectory of feminist international legal scholarship.

Four objectives for the future of feminist engagement with international law are identified from the outset, to which the four parts of the book and their respective chapters respond. Part one is composed of chapters that consider feminist engagement in new horizons of international law, such as climate change law and international disaster law. Part two groups together chapters examining how feminist ideas have and can gain a greater hold in mainstream legal thinking and international institutions. Part three addresses how feminist scholarship may make meaningful change in women's lives through exploring policy and law. Part four positions feminist scholarship within other, intersecting critical theories in order to overcome a recognised critique of feminism's exclusivity and enable new debate. Due to the span of the book, this review considers only part two.

The object of part two is contained within its tongue-in-cheek title, 'Making Feminist Engagement with International Law More Influential: Not Just Talking to Ourselves', in an echo of Hilary Charlesworth's comment on what feminist scholarship amounts to when ignored by others in the academic field and

---

1   Kate Ogg and Susan Harris Rimmer, 'Introduction to the *Research Handbook on Feminist Engagement with International Law*' in Susan Harris Rimmer and Kate Ogg (eds), *Research Handbook on Feminist Engagement with International Law* (Edward Elgar Publishing, 2019) 1, 2.

2   Ibid 7, quoting Dianne Otto, 'Feminist Approaches to International Law' in Anne Orford and Florian Hoffman (eds), *Oxford Handbook of the Theory of International Law* (Oxford University Press, 2016) 488, 489.

beyond.[3] Chapter 11 concerns feminist engagement with refugee law. Author Kate Ogg argues that this popular area of feminist scholarship has yet to move from the margins to the centre. Ogg suggests this may be achieved through feminist approaches to non-gendered issues in refugee law. She demonstrates the possibilities and merits of this practice to refugee law's doctrine and theory through two examples.

The first is an analysis of art 1F of the *Convention Relating to the Status of Refugees* ('*Refugee Convention*'),[4] which provides that a person may be excluded from the protection of the Convention on the ground of criminality. Ogg here applies a feminist methodological approach to the increasing reliance on this provision among states. Ogg identifies case examples of women who have been excluded from protection due to actions committed in highly coercive circumstances, where their experience of human rights abuses was connected to their commission of excludable crimes. Ogg analyses how international criminal law principles (such as mens rea), when used to determine whether art 1F is met, 'can truncate the full narrative [of] the protection claimant' in not considering the wider context which may compel a claimant's actions.[5] Ogg uses these case examples to indicate how feminist theory and methodology can raise otherwise unknown or ignored gender issues in refugee law, and stimulate necessary reform to law and/or practice.

Ogg's second example applies a feminist approach to the theoretical concept of surrogate state protection. Ogg here refers to Martha Fineman and Jennifer Nedelsky's theories on the relationship between the state and the individual to deconstruct gendered assumptions embedded in United Nations High Commissioner for Refugees models of surrogate state protection. The neoliberal-endorsed relationship between refugee and surrogate state as self-reliant and isolated is interrogated through the application of Nedelsky's theory of relational autonomy and Fineman's argument that dependency (and not autonomy) is the natural state. This re-envisages the relationship between refugee and surrogate state. Ogg here provides an alternate, feminist reading of the *Refugee Convention*—its text and drafting history—as a text which

---

3 Hilary Charlesworth, 'Talking to Ourselves? Feminist Scholarship in International Law' in Sari Kouvo and Zoe Pearson (eds), *Feminist Perspectives on Contemporary International Law: Between Resistance and Compliance?* (Hart Publishing, 2014) 37.

4 *Convention Relating to the Status of Refugees*, opened for signature 28 July 1951, 189 UNTS 137 (entered into force 22 April 1954) art 1F ('*Refugee Convention*').

5 Kate Ogg, 'The Future of Feminist Engagement with Refugee Law: From the Margins to the Centre and Out of the "Pink Ghetto"?' in Susan Harris Rimmer and Kate Ogg (eds), *Research Handbook on Feminist Engagement with International Law* (Edward Elgar Publishing, 2019) 174, 184.

BOOK REVIEWS

normalises reliance on welfare rights. Ogg's analysis demonstrates how feminist theory can raise otherwise ignored gender concerns, trigger new areas of research, suggest alternate interpretations of primary legal texts, and provide alternate visions of law and policy.

Chapter 12 examines the relationship between women and the International Court of Justice ('ICJ'). Ekaterina Yahyaoui Krivenko analyses the ICJ's engagement with women's rights and *Convention on the Elimination of All Forms of Discrimination against Women*[6] by reference to the only case in the Court's history to directly address both, *Case Concerning Armed Activities on the Territory of the Congo*.[7] The chapter considers the role of female judges sitting on the ICJ, pointedly asking: 'Do women judges make a difference?'[8] and 'Does the presence of judges with more sensitivity to feminist approaches make a difference?'.[9] Surprisingly, the first question delivers an uncertain answer. Krivenko, after collecting data on judges' gender and judgment record, found female judges delivered no more separate or dissenting opinions in comparison to male judges. The second question is investigated through a lens of judgments on *jus cogens* that apply methods common to feminist scholarship: contextualising the individual, intersectionality, and deconstructing binaries and hierarchies. Krivenko finds that judgments employing such approaches are present only in dissenting or separate opinions from a minority of the court. Overall, Krivenko depicts the ICJ as a judicial body—consciously or not—disengaged from gender issues. The author calls for an acknowledgement and reversal of this historic behaviour, to enable gender awareness and engagement from the institution.

Chapter 13 considers gender-just judging in the past, present, and future of international criminal courts. The authors, Rosemary Grey and Louise Chappell argue judges can use their positions to be 'agents of "gender-justice"'[10] and make visible the experiences of marginalised groups, challenge gender biases in the interpretation and application of law, and support gender equality

---

6   *Convention on the Elimination of All Forms of Discrimination against Women*, signed 18 December 1979, 1249 UNTS 13 (entered into force 3 September 1981).

7   *Armed Activities on the Territory of the Congo (Democratic Republic of the Congo v Uganda) (Judgment)* [2005] ICJ Rep 168.

8   Ekaterina Yahyaoui Krivenko, 'Women and the International Court of Justice' in Susan Harris Rimmer and Kate Ogg (eds), *Research Handbook on Feminist Engagement with International Law* (Edward Elgar Publishing, 2019) 196, 202.

9   Ibid.

10   Rosemary Grey and Louise Chappell, '"Gender-Just Judging" in International Criminal Courts: New Directions for Research' in Susan Harris Rimmer and Kate Ogg (eds), *Research Handbook on Feminist Engagement with International Law* (Edward Elgar Publishing, 2019) 213, 213.

through their work. The authors review definitions of gender justice from Anne-Marie Goetz and Nancy Fraser[11] and consider the concept with respect to the objective of international criminal courts. In order to assess judicial contributions to gender-justice, the authors propose a framework of qualitative indicators. These include '[d]rawing out evidence of sexual violence', '[p]rotecting the welfare of victims and witnesses', and '[e]nsuring reparations are non-discriminatory'.[12] Drawing on case examples from the International Criminal Court, International Criminal Tribunal for the Former Yugoslavia and International Criminal Tribunal for Rwanda, the authors demonstrate how their proposed framework may be used. Finally, the chapter hopefully considers how the framework may be adapted for the future study of international court judgments (criminal and otherwise) and how the indicators of assessment may enable new research on the contributory role of judges to gender justice.

Chapter 14, 'Revisiting the Category "Women"', asks whether and how the category 'women' can be used to create an inclusive future for international law—in lawmaking, adjudication, and governance. The author, Jaya Ramji-Nogales investigates the history of the category 'women', employing Judith Butler's definition of the category as 'produced and restrained by the power structures from which emancipation is sought'.[13] She undertakes nuanced assessment of its 'promise and perils' with respect to the question posed.[14] Ramji-Nogales strategises for a new approach to the category 'women' as a political (rather than essential) categorisation which engages in a critical approach to international law. This chapter also acknowledges that a theory which emphasises inclusion of multiple perspectives does risk a lesser impact or domination of the theory by one perspective. However, the author remains encouraged that, through analysing and subverting structures of power as we know them, we may transform them. She exhorts women in lawmaking and

---

11 Anne-Marie Goetz, 'Gender Justice, Citizenship and Entitlements: Core Concepts, Central Debates, and New Directions for Research' in Maitrayee Mukhopadhyay and Navsharan Singh (eds), *Gender Justice, Citizenship and Development* (Zubaan, 2007) 15; Nancy Fraser, *The Scales of Justice: Reimagining Political Space in a Globalised World* (Columbia University Press, 2009); Nancy Fraser, 'Feminist Politics in the Age of Recognition: A Two-Dimensional Approach to Gender Justice' (2007) *Studies in Social Justice* 1(1) 23.

12 Grey and Chappell (n 10) 222.

13 Jaya Ramji-Nogales, 'Revisiting the Category "Women"' in Susan Harris Rimmer and Kate Ogg (eds), *Research Handbook on Feminist Engagement with International Law* (Edward Elgar Publishing, 2019) 240, 243, citing Judith Butler, *Gender Trouble: Feminism and the Subversion of the Identity* (Routledge, 1990) 1.

14 Ramji-Nogales (n 13) 242.

BOOK REVIEWS   353

law reform to identify and support the inclusion of marginalised people within legal and power structures.

Chapter 15 attends to what the author, Dorothy Estrada-Tanck, identifies as a gap in feminist scholarship on human security from the perspective of international law. The author proposes a human security framework around which to orient feminist approaches to international law theories and practices. She demonstrates this through an analysis of the experience of undocumented migrant women and girls. Estrada-Tanck suggests the potential of a feminist human security—human rights lens to analyse women's engagement with international law and catalyse progressive interpretations of human rights texts for women.

Chapter 16 is concerned with the future of feminist engagement with international law from within the institutions which produce its scholarship and teaching. The author, Ntina Tzouvala examines the consequences of the neoliberalisation of universities for teaching, learning, research and writing in this field. She argues such neoliberalisation is detrimental for the position of women within the discipline and the development of feminist orientations. Tzouvala first reflects on the teaching of international law in universities as an academic discipline, maps the transformation of the academic environment since the submission of universities to neoliberal objectives, and examines the impact of these evolutions on feminist legal scholarship.

Chapter 17 uses the International Labour Organization ('ILO') as a case study to analyse what the author, Jane Aeberhard-Hodges, terms 'women's invisibility' in international treaty making.[15] The chapter examines the continuation of gender-based inequality even where efforts have been made for women's inclusion. The author assesses the ILO's attempts to improve the involvement of women over the past decade.

These chapters each offer the reader a different perspective on and insight into an area of feminism's engagement with international law. Though varying from feminist interpretations of refugee law and policy to examination of women's contributions to treaty making at the ILO, each chapter carries an undercurrent of 'hope and despair'.[16] However, the combined value and contribution of these engagements undoubtedly leaves the reader with greater hope than despair. More broadly, this book is remarkable in its span across the

---

15   Jane Aeberhard-Hodges, 'Women and International Treaty Making—The Example of Standard Setting in the International Labour Organization' in Susan Harris Rimmer and Kate Ogg (eds), *Research Handbook on Feminist Engagement with International Law* (Edward Elgar Publishing, 2019) 286, 286.

16   Otto (n 2) 489.

discipline and, as a result, is sometimes challenging to read. Readers will gain from multiple engagements with the various chapters.

The book is impressively self-aware, acknowledging the shortfalls of feminist scholarship in representing a diversity of perspectives from different 'cultures, religions, economic backgrounds, nationalities and races'.[17] Ogg acknowledges that feminist scholarship can be a space largely occupied by First World feminists.[18] Contributors to this volume do an admirable job of recognising and incorporating this risk into their analyses, and the editors have sought to overcome historic under-representation through their conscious curation of authors from a diversity of backgrounds.

For lawyers, academics, and those who aspire to a body of international law that acknowledges and incorporates feminist concerns into its theory, policy, and practice, this book serves as an example of both how this may be achieved and why it is such a worthwhile goal. It is an offering to international law of the capabilities of feminist thought in the space, by moving it into imaginative new directions and imbuing it with an energy of hope and potential.

Kate Slowey
Law Student, University of Newcastle Law School

17   Ogg (n 5) 187.
18   Ibid.

Regular Features

Cases before Australian Courts and Tribunals concerning Questions of Public International Law 2019

Mary Crock,* Rowan Nicholson,** Kailin Chen, Seric Han, Marcus Lee, Francis Manuel, John McCrorie, Edward Wu and Gordon Yen

1 Act of State Doctrine[1]

Public International Law—Act of State Doctrine—Whether Commercial Acts of Respondent Airline had Sovereign Aspect to Them

Public International Law—Where Respondent Submitted Injunctions and Pecuniary Penalties Would be Contrary to Customary International Law—Where Respondent Argued Customary International Law Relevant to Court's Discretion and Power to Grant Remedies—Where Respondent Argued Relevance of Principles of 'Accommodation, Mutuality and Proportionality'

Australian Competition and Consumer Commission v PT Garuda Indonesia Ltd
(2019) 370 ALR 637
Federal Court of Australia
Perram J

1.1 *Background and Litigation History*

In 2008 and 2009, the Australian Competition and Consumer Commission ('the Commission') commenced proceedings against 15 international airlines including PT Garuda Indonesia Ltd ('Garuda'), for price fixing in the supply of cargo services. At trial, Garuda was found to have reached and implemented a

---

* Professor of Public Law at The University of Sydney Law School and Co-Director of the Sydney Centre for International Law ('SCIL').

** Lecturer at The University of Sydney Law School and Co-Director of the SCIL.

1 The summaries that follow were prepared by Professor Crock, Dr Nicholson and SCIL interns Kailin Chen, Seric Han, Marcus Lee, Francis Manuel, John McCrorie, Edward Wu and Gordon Yen. We wish to thank Kate Bones, Chester Brown, Andrew Edgar for their comments and suggestions. Mary is happy to be accountable for any errors that remain.

© KONINKLIJKE BRILL NV, LEIDEN, 2021 | DOI:10.1163/26660229_03801020

number of understandings with other international airlines to impose various pre-determined surcharges on the supply of air cargo services from overseas ports to ports in Australia.[2] In 2017, the High Court of Australia found that Garuda's conduct contravened s 45(2) of the *Trade Practices Act* 1974 (Cth) ('*TPA*'), which prohibits a corporation arriving at an understanding which has the purpose, or has or is likely to have the effect, of substantially lessening competition.[3] In this case, the Commission applied to the Court for remedial orders for Garuda's contraventions, including to declare that Garuda's conduct was unlawful, to restrain it from engaging in the conduct again and to impose upon it a civil penalty.[4]

1.2 *The Act of State Doctrine*

Garuda submitted that while the act of state doctrine does not prevent the Court from making findings on the 'bare question of liability', it requires the Court not to impose the remedies of injunction or civil liability upon it.[5] Garuda's argument had two elements. First, it argued that Garuda was an emanation of the Republic of Indonesia and therefore the act of state doctrine applied.[6] Secondly, Garuda argued that any price-fixing was engaged in for the purpose of performing a public function of a state and was thus subject to the act of state doctrine.[7]

Perram J rejected both arguments. He noted that for a commercial activity to be protected by the act of state doctrine, one must show that the activity has a sovereign element to it.[8] In the present case, Garuda had failed to establish what the sovereign element was.[9] Perram J observed that commercial activities that merely benefit the public by providing services and fulfilling the needs of the Indonesian people differ from activities that advance the interests of the Indonesian state, and thus Garuda's actions in conducting a commercial airline were not an act of the state of the Republic of Indonesia.[10] He further held that the Indonesian Government's role in addressing Garuda's precarious

---

2   *Australian Competition and Consumer Commission v Air New Zealand Ltd* (2014) 319 ALR 388.

3   *Air New Zealand Ltd v Australian Competition and Consumer Commission* (2017) 262 CLR 207.

4   *Australian Competition and Consumer Commission v PT Garuda Indonesia Ltd* (2019) 370 ALR 637.

5   Ibid 647.

6   Ibid 649.

7   Ibid.

8   Ibid 650.

9   Ibid.

10   Ibid 648.

financial situation and financially 'rescuing the company' by injecting about $48 million into the company was not enough to establish the sovereign nature of the airline.[11] Perram J held that the role of the government in the present case was no different from that of shareholders who were obliged to inject further funds to keep a company going.[12]

1.3 *Other International Law Considerations*

1.3.1 Discretion and Power

Garuda submitted that the Court should decline to grant the relief sought by the Commission in the exercise of its discretion because the remedies sought were exorbitant under customary international law.[13] However, Perram J rejected the notion that the extraterritorial reach of the TPA would breach customary international law, as long as a territorial nexus exists.[14] He found that s 5(1) of the TPA provided a sufficient territorial nexus as it stated that 'Part IV, Part IVA, Part V (other than Division 1AA), Part VB and Part VC extend to the engaging in conduct outside Australia by bodies corporate incorporated or carrying on business within Australia'.[15] The Court would not exercise its discretion to decline to grant relief on the basis that the relief would breach customary international law.

1.3.2 Accommodation, Mutuality and Proportionality

Garuda submitted that there was a competition law in Indonesia at the relevant time which was being enforced and that the Supreme Court of Indonesia had held that agreements to fix surcharges did not contravene Indonesian competition law. Garuda argued on this premise that the Court should exercise its discretion in accordance 'with the principles of accommodation, mutuality and proportionality'.[16] Perram J rejected this submission. He found that the Supreme Court of Indonesia did not hold that an agreement to fix fuel surcharges did not infringe Indonesian competition law and hence that the premise for this submission was not established.[17]

Garuda also submitted that granting a civil penalty would result in the judicial power of the Commonwealth being extended into an area of jurisdiction which according to the comity of nations belonged to another sovereign.

---

11   Ibid 650.
12   Ibid.
13   Ibid.
14   Ibid 651.
15   Ibid.
16   Ibid 652.
17   Ibid.

Perram J rejected this submission, repeating that the only jurisdictional requirement is that there be a territorial nexus; the comity of nations had no consequences for the present issue.[18]

1.4   *Held*
The Court upheld the Commission's application and made orders for Garuda to pay the Commonwealth of Australia pecuniary penalties of $19 million.

2   Anti-Terrorism, Money Laundering

> **Criminal Practice—Forfeiture of Tainted Property—Where Appellants Remitted Money to Australia Using Money Remitters or Money Changers in Foreign Country—Where Large Number of Cash Deposits, Usually Each Less than $10,000, Made into Appellants' Bank Accounts in Australia in Process Known as 'Cuckoo Smurfing'—Where Deposits Proceeds or Instrument of Structuring Offence under s 142 of *Anti-Money Laundering and Counter-Terrorism Financing Act 2006* (Cth)—Where Commissioner of Australian Federal Police Successfully Applied for Restraining Orders over Appellants' Bank Accounts under s 19 of *Proceeds of Crime Act 2002* (Cth) ('*POCA*')—Where Appellants Applied under ss 29 and 31 of *POCA* to have Property Excluded from Orders—Whether Property 'Ceased' to be Proceeds or Instrument of Offence under s 330(4) of *POCA*—Whether Property Acquired by Third Party for Sufficient Consideration without Third Party Knowing, and in Circumstances that Would Not Arouse Reasonable Suspicion, that Property Proceeds or Instrument under s 330(4)(a) of *POCA***

Lordianto v Commissioner of the Australian Federal Police
(2019) 374 ALR 58
High Court of Australia
Kiefel CJ, Bell, Keane, Gordon and Edelman JJ

The High Court heard two appeals together: *Lordianto v Commissioner of the Australian Federal Police* ('*Lordianto*') was an appeal from the Court of Appeal of the Supreme Court of New South Wales, and *Kalimuthu v Commissioner*

---

18   Ibid.

CASES CONCERNING QUESTIONS OF PUBLIC INTERNATIONAL LAW 2019   361

of the Australian Federal Police ('Kalimuthu') was appealed from the Court of Appeal of the Supreme Court of Western Australia.

The appellants, Mr Lordianto, Ms Koernia, Mr Ganesh and Mrs Ganesh, transferred money to Australia through the use of remitters or money changers in a foreign country.[19] They were involved in 'cuckoo smurfing', a form of money laundering that involved the following process:

> [A] person offshore who wishes to transfer funds to a bank account in Australia using a money remitter [is identified]. The remitter withholds amounts corresponding to the amount of money he has been told is to be laundered in Australia. The customer's bank account details are provided to people in Australia. A team of depositors in Australia deposits cash into the bank account, generally at a series of bank branches and below the threshold for reporting transactions involving physical currency. The account holder sees deposits that match the amounts they intended to remit. Because the amounts of each deposit are below the threshold, there is generally no record that could enable regulatory agencies to intervene.[20]

The relevant offence was a structuring offence contrary to s 142(1) of the *Anti-Money Laundering and Counter-Terrorism Financing Act 2006* (Cth).[21] The Commissioner of the Australian Federal Police ('AFP') had successfully applied, under s 19 of the *Proceeds of Crime Act 2002* (Cth) ('POCA'), for orders that 'restrain[ed] the disposal of, or any dealing with, [the appellants'] specific bank accounts'.[22] The appellants applied under ss 29 and 31 of the POCA to exclude from the restraining orders their interest in their choses in action in respect of their various bank accounts.[23] The choses in action entitled them to be paid by the bank, in part or in full, the amount credited to their accounts.[24] In order to be successful, the appellants had to prove on the balance of probabilities that their choses in action had ceased to be proceeds or an instrument of an offence under s 330(4)(a) of the POCA.[25] Section 330(4)(a) provides:

---

19 *Lordianto v Commissioner of the Australian Federal Police* (2019) 374 ALR 58, 60 [1] (Kiefel CJ, Bell, Keane and Gordon JJ) ('*Lordianto*').
20 Ibid.
21 Ibid 61 [3] (Kiefel CJ, Bell, Keane and Gordon JJ).
22 Ibid 61 [2] (Kiefel CJ, Bell, Keane and Gordon JJ).
23 Ibid 61 [4]–[5] (Kiefel CJ, Bell, Keane and Gordon JJ).
24 Ibid 61 [5] (Kiefel CJ, Bell, Keane and Gordon JJ).
25 Ibid.

(4) Property only ceases to be *proceeds* of an offence or an *instrument* of an offence:

> (a) if it is acquired by a third party for sufficient consideration without the third party knowing, and in circumstances that would not arouse a reasonable suspicion, that the property was proceeds of an offence or an instrument of an offence (as the case requires)[.]

In the majority, Kiefel CJ, Bell, Keane and Gordon JJ (with Edelman J largely in agreement) explained that s 330(4)(a) raises four issues, namely:

1. What is the 'property' restrained by the order which a person seeks to have excluded from that order?
2. Did the applicant for an exclusion order acquire the property 'for sufficient consideration'?
3. Was the property acquired in circumstances that would not arouse a 'reasonable suspicion' that the property was proceeds of an offence or an instrument of an offence? and
4. How is the reference to 'a third party' to be understood?[26]

The majority held that all four issues had to be construed together in the context of the operation of the *POCA* as a whole.[27] The purpose of the *POCA* is to 'undermine the profitability of criminal enterprises.'[28] This is achieved through a 'confiscation scheme' that deprives people of property when there are reasonable grounds to suspect that the property is a proceed or instrument of offences.[29] The majority held that the inquiry under s 330(4)(a) is similar to the question of whether a person is a bona fide purchaser for value without notice.[30] The following summary examines in turn the majority's finding in respect of each of the four issues identified.

1. What is the 'property' restrained by the order which a person seeks to have excluded from that order?

The 'property' in this case was the appellants' *choses in action* in respect of their bank accounts that entitled them to be paid by the bank, in part or in full, the amount credited to their accounts.[31]

---

26 Ibid 62 [8] (Kiefel CJ, Bell, Keane and Gordon JJ).
27 Ibid 62 [8], 72 [61] (Kiefel CJ, Bell, Keane and Gordon JJ).
28 Ibid 62 [9] (Kiefel CJ, Bell, Keane and Gordon JJ).
29 Ibid 62 [9]–[10] (Kiefel CJ, Bell, Keane and Gordon JJ).
30 Ibid 72 [63] (Kiefel CJ, Bell, Keane and Gordon JJ).
31 Ibid 73 [66] (Kiefel CJ, Bell, Keane and Gordon JJ).

CASES CONCERNING QUESTIONS OF PUBLIC INTERNATIONAL LAW 2019

2. Did the applicant for an exclusion order acquire the property 'for sufficient consideration'?

Section 338 of the POCA states that 'an acquisition or disposal of property is for sufficient consideration if it is for a consideration that is sufficient and that reflects the value of the property, having regard solely to commercial considerations'.[32] The majority held that the inquiry into whether the applicant acquired the property 'for sufficient consideration' is objective and takes into account the circumstances in which the applicant acquired the property.[33] A non-exhaustive list of factors need to be taken into account. These are: what the property is, how the applicant acquired the property, the form in which the applicant provided the consideration, the amount of the consideration, and when and how the applicant provided the consideration.[34] The majority ruled that the inquiry into whether an applicant acquired the property 'for sufficient consideration' forms part of the next question of whether the property was acquired in circumstances that would not arouse a 'reasonable suspicion' that the property was proceeds or an instrument of an offence.[35]

The majority discussed the commercial considerations to be taken into account when the property is choses in action in respect of bank accounts. They held it was not necessary for the appellants to prove that the funds that were deposited into their bank accounts were their own funds, or that they had a direct connection with the people who deposited the funds into their bank accounts, or that the remitters in the foreign country had a contractual relationship with the people who deposited the funds into their bank accounts.[36] Their Honours held that 'the consideration must be by way of exchange but may not be direct.'[37] With regard to bank transfers, instructions from a buyer to the appellants' bank to reduce their account balance and to correspondingly increase the balance of the vendor's account would be enough evidence to establish the required connection.[38]

3. Not knowing and in circumstances that would not arouse a reasonable suspicion

The majority found that the inquiry into whether the property was acquired in circumstances that would not arouse a 'reasonable suspicion' is an objective

---

32   *Proceeds of Crime Act 2002* (Cth) s 338.
33   *Lordianto* (n 19) 73 [69] (Kiefel CJ, Bell, Keane and Gordon JJ).
34   Ibid 74 [71] (Kiefel CJ, Bell, Keane and Gordon JJ).
35   Ibid.
36   Ibid 75 [79]–[80] (Kiefel CJ, Bell, Keane and Gordon JJ).
37   Ibid 76 [82] (Kiefel CJ, Bell, Keane and Gordon JJ).
38   Ibid 76 [82]–[83] (Kiefel CJ, Bell, Keane and Gordon JJ).

test.[39] A reasonable suspicion must be based on fact: 'It is a positive feeling and more than a mere idle wondering'.[40] Subjective ignorance of the law is not a defence and there does not need to be a 'reasonable suspicion' that the property was proceeds or an instrument of the *specific* offence committed. What is required is a 'reasonable suspicion' that the property was proceeds or an instrument of *an* offence.[41]

4. *How is the reference to 'a third party' to be understood?*

The majority ruled that a 'third party' is 'simply a person who satisfies s 330(4)(a)', namely, a party who acquires proceeds or an instrument for sufficient consideration without knowing that the property was proceeds or an instrument of an offence, and in circumstances that would not arouse a reasonable suspicion that this was the case.[42]

2.1 *The* Lordianto *Appeal*

The property in question was Mr Lordianto and Ms Koernia's choses in action in respect of their bank accounts.[43] The majority held that Mr Lordianto and Ms Koernia did not prove that they had acquired their choses in action for sufficient consideration and in circumstances that would not have aroused a reasonable suspicion that the property was proceeds or an instrument of an offence. The court held that was because the pair were 'financially sophisticated', had experience transferring large sums of money into foreign countries, were familiar with currency controls and national disclosure requirements, and had knowledge of the advantageous rates that were offered by the remitters that they used to transfer their funds.[44]

Edelman J agreed with the reasons in the majority in the *Lordianto* appeal.[45] Appeal dismissed.

2.2 *The* Kalimuthu *Appeal*

In this case the property in question was Mr and Mrs Ganesh's choses in action in respect of their bank accounts.[46] The majority held that Mr Ganesh did not prove that he had acquired his choses in action for sufficient consideration and

---

39   Ibid 77 [89] (Kiefel CJ, Bell, Keane and Gordon JJ).
40   Ibid.
41   Ibid 77 [90], 78 [92] (Kiefel CJ, Bell, Keane and Gordon JJ).
42   Ibid 78 [93] (Kiefel CJ, Bell, Keane and Gordon JJ).
43   Ibid 81 [109] (Kiefel CJ, Bell, Keane and Gordon JJ).
44   Ibid 82 [111] (Kiefel CJ, Bell, Keane and Gordon JJ).
45   Ibid 84 [120], 88 [142] (Edelman J).
46   Ibid 82 [112] (Kiefel CJ, Bell, Keane and Gordon JJ).

CASES CONCERNING QUESTIONS OF PUBLIC INTERNATIONAL LAW 2019   365

in circumstances that would not have aroused a reasonable suspicion that the property was proceeds or an instrument of an offence, because of his knowledge that 'the very large amounts of cash he provided to [the remitter] were not leading to deposits in corresponding amounts, but rather to a number of deposits of considerably smaller amounts'.[47]

In respect of Mrs Ganesh, the majority ruled that she was not a third party who acquired the choses in action for sufficient consideration. Rather, she was a volunteer as she had provided no value, and thus she also did not satisfy the requirements of s 330(4)(a) of the *POCA*.[48] The majority dismissed the appeal.

Edelman J agreed generally with the majority in the *Kalimuthu* appeal, dissenting on the ruling in respect of Mrs Ganesh.[49] He held that Mrs Ganesh should not be treated as a volunteer as it is 'contrary to an assumption made at trial' which was continued before the Court of Appeal of the Supreme Court of Western Australia.[50] His Honour found 'it is a matter as to which in this Court there was no notice of contention, no written or oral argument, and no questions from the bench'.[51]

Appeal dismissed.

3   Aviation

In 2019, there were two major Australian cases concerning international aviation conventions. *Heli-Aust Pty Limited v Civil Aviation Safety Authority*,[52] which has not been extracted here, concerns the rules of discovery in relation to the communications between the Civil Aviation Safety Authority ('CASA') and the Australian Transport Safety Bureau ('ATSB'). After considering the *Transport Safety Investigation Act 2003* (Cth) and the general rules regarding privileges, the Court ultimately refused to order the production and inspection of these documents. In reaching its decision, the Court took annex 13 of the *Convention on International Civil Aviation* ('the *Chicago Convention*') into account.[53] Paragraph 5.12 of annex 13 states that all statements taken from persons by the investigation authorities during the course of their investigation, cockpit

---

47   Ibid 82–83 [114] (Kiefel CJ, Bell, Keane and Gordon JJ).
48   Ibid 83 [117] (Kiefel CJ, Bell, Keane and Gordon JJ).
49   Ibid 84 [121], 89 [143] (Edelman J).
50   Ibid 84 [121] (Edelman J).
51   Ibid.
52   *Heli-Aust Pty Limited v Civil Aviation Safety Authority* [2019] NSWSC 506.
53   *Convention on International Civil Aviation*, opened for signature 7 December 1944, 15 UNTS 295 (entered into force 4 April 1947) ('the *Chicago Convention*').

airborne image recordings and any part of transcripts from such recordings, and opinions expressing the analysis of information including flight recorder information, shall not be disclosed by the State conducting the investigation of an accident unless the appropriate authority for administration of justice in that State determines that their disclosure outweighs the adverse domestic and international impact such action may have on that or any future investigation.[54] The Court reaffirmed that s 11 of the *Civil Aviation Act 1998* (Cth) requires CASA to perform its functions 'in a manner consistent with the obligations of Australia' under all relevant treaties.[55] In other words, it is consistent with Australia's obligations under the *Chicago Convention* for CASA to maintain the confidentiality of information received from, provided to, or otherwise collected for the purpose of assisting the ATSB and thus, the order to produce and inspect was refused.

The second case, *Di Falco v Emirates (No 2)*,[56] extracted and summarised below, examined the meaning of an 'accident' in art 17(1) of the *Convention for the Unification of Certain Rules for International Carriage by Air* ('the *Montreal Convention*').[57] The meaning of an 'accident' is crucial in a personal injury claim on board an aircraft because under art 17 (1) of the *Montreal Convention*, a carrier incurs strict liability for damage sustained in case of death or bodily injury of a passenger 'upon condition only that the accident which caused the death or injury took place on board the aircraft or in the course of any of the operations of embarking or disembarking.'[58]

> **Carriage by Air—Strict Liability Claim against Air Carrier for Injuries Sustained During Aircraft Accident—Whether *Civil Aviation (Carriers' Liability) Act 1959* (Cth) Applies—Whether Failure to Provide Hydration Capable of Constituting an 'Accident'—Circumstances Leading to Dehydration Not Unusual or Unexpected—Plaintiff's Claim Dismissed—*Montreal Convention***

---

54   *Heli-Aust Pty Limited v Civil Aviation Safety Authority* [2019] NSWSC 506, [40] (Harrison AsJ), citing the *Chicago Convention* annex 13.

55   *Heli-Aust Pty Limited v Civil Aviation Safety Authority* [2019] NSWSC 506, [42] (Harrison AsJ).

56   *Di Falco v Emirates (No 2)* [2019] VSC 654.

57   *Convention for the Unification of Certain Rules for International Carriage by Air*, opened for signature 28 May 1999, 2242 UNTS 309 (entered into force 4 November 2003) ('the *Montreal Convention*').

58   *Di Falco v Emirates (No 2)* [2019] VSC 654, [7] (Forbes J), quoting the *Montreal Convention* art 17(1).

CASES CONCERNING QUESTIONS OF PUBLIC INTERNATIONAL LAW 2019   367

Art 17(1)—*Warsaw Convention* Art 7, *Vienna Convention* Art 3, *Civil Aviation (Carriers' Liability) Act 1959* (Cth) s 9E

Di Falco v Emirates (No 2)
[2019] VSC 654
Supreme Court of Victoria
Forbes J

3.1   *Factual Background*

The plaintiff was a passenger on an Emirates flight. She made four requests for water in the span of approximately four to five hours but none of the requests were met. The plaintiff felt nauseous shortly after the first meal service and got up from her seat to go to the bathroom. At the bathroom doorway, she fainted and as a result, fractured her ankle in the stall. The plaintiff alleged that the reason for her faint was that she was dehydrated. She commenced proceedings against Emirates seeking damages for her injuries under the *Civil Aviation (Carriers' Liability) Act 1959* (Cth).

3.2   *Liability under the* Civil Aviation *(Carriers' Liability) Act 1959* (Cth)

Section 9E of the *Civil Aviation (Carriers' Liability) Act 1959* (Cth) provides that 'the liability of a carrier under the [*Montreal Convention*], in respect of personal injury suffered by a passenger that has not resulted in the death of the passenger, is *in substitution for any civil liability of the carrier under any other law in respect of the injury*' (emphasis added). Article 17(1) of the *Montreal Convention* sets out that '[t]he carrier is liable for damage sustained in cases of death or bodily injury of a passenger upon condition only that the accident which caused the death or injury took place on board the aircraft or in the course of any of the operations of embarking or disembarking'. In other words, if an 'accident' has occurred, liability of the carrier is strict.

3.3   *The Meaning of an Accident*

The key issue in this case is whether the failure to supply adequate hydration amounts to an 'accident' under the Convention. Forbes J reviewed three cases[59] and provided a succinct summary on the principles that can be applied

---

59   Forbes J began with reviewing *Air France v Saks*, 470 US 392 (1985) which first defined an accident under the *Montreal Convention* to be an 'unexpected or unusual event or happening that is external to the passenger'. Then her Honour reviewed the case of *Olympic Airways v Husain*, 540 US 644 (2004) which held that a failure to act could constitute an event. Lastly, her Honour reviewed the Australian High Court case of *Povey v Qantas*

to determine whether an accident has occurred under the meaning of the *Montreal Convention*.[60] The principles are extracted below:

1. A passenger's own internal reaction to the usual, normal and expected operation of the aircraft is not an accident;
2. An accident that is a cause of an injury is different to the occurrence of injury itself;
3. It is necessary to identify an event or happening that is external to the passenger;
4. An event may arise from acts, *omissions* or from a combination of acts and omission;
5. The event must be unexpected or unusual;
6. There may be a chain of events that lead to injury;
7. It is sufficient that some link in the chain of casual events was an unexpected or unusual event external to the passenger;
8. If the event is described as inaction or as a failure to do something, the absence of action will not amount to an event *unless it can be shown to be an omission by reference to some legal standard requiring action*;
9. Common law notions of actions or failure to act arising from a duty of care owed to passengers are irrelevant; [and]
10. Whether an accident has occurred is a question of fact.[61]

3.4 *Held*

Forbes J held that there was no 'accident' as defined by art 17 of the *Montreal Convention* and so no liability of Emirates pursuant to s 9E of the *Civil Aviation (Carriers' Liability) Act 1959* (Cth) in respect of the personal injury suffered by the plaintiff. Her Honour rejected the plaintiff's argument that the event was unusual or unexpected merely because adequate hydration was not supplied to her when she had an expectation of access to adequate hydration on board and expected it would be supplied.[62] Her Honour stated that the unusualness and the unexpectedness of an external event is measured by reference to objective standards of normal aircraft operation, not by reference to the subjective expectation of the passenger.[63] Her Honour ruled that the way in which the plaintiff's requests were dealt with were in accordance with the usual

---

Airways Ltd (2015) 223 CLR 189, which accepted that an accident can be a result of omissions as well as acts or by some combination of the two.

60   *Di Falco v Emirates (No 2)* [2019] VSC 654, [18].
61   Ibid (emphasis added).
62   Ibid [44].
63   Ibid.

CASES CONCERNING QUESTIONS OF PUBLIC INTERNATIONAL LAW 2019   369

practice of attendants and were not in disregard of or contrary to airline policy.[64] Therefore, her Honour found that nothing unusual or unexpected occurred on the flight and no accident as defined by art 17 of the *Montreal Convention* occurred.

Plaintiff's claim was dismissed.

4   Criminal Law—Child Abduction

Hague Convention on Child Abduction

Family Law—Children—Final Parenting—Making Orders Enforceable in Turkey Following Agreed Withdrawal of a Hague Return Proceeding—Jurisdiction Curtailed Where *Convention on Jurisdiction, Applicable Law, Recognition, Enforcement and Co-operation in Respect of Parental Responsibility and Measures for the Protection of Children* has Entered into Force

Kubat v Kubat
[2019] FamCA 671
Family Court of Australia
Bennett J

Ms Kubat ('the mother') and Mr Kubat ('the father') had four children—X, Y, Z ('the children') and W.[65] After telling the father that she wanted to separate, the mother brought the children to Australia on 15 November 2018, while W remained in the care of the father in Turkey.[66] The State Central Authority for Victoria brought a Hague return application seeking the return of the children to Turkey under the *Family Law (Child Abduction Convention) Regulations 1986* (Cth) when the mother failed to return them to Turkey by an agreed date, 31 March 2019.[67] The Hague return proceeding was dismissed upon mutual consent by the parents.[68] Leave was granted to the mother and father to make a mutual joint application for final parenting orders pursuant to Part VII of the *Family Law Act 1975* (Cth) ('the Act').

---

64   Ibid [45].
65   *Kubat v Kubat* [2019] FamCA 671, [1].
66   Ibid [3].
67   Ibid [1].
68   Ibid [3].

370   AUSTRALIAN YEAR BOOK OF INTERNATIONAL LAW VOLUME 38

The Judge predicated the Court's jurisdiction on art 5 of the *Convention on Jurisdiction, Applicable Law, Recognition, Enforcement and Co-operation in Respect of Parental Responsibility and Measures for the Protection of Children* ('the 1996 Convention').[69] Bennett J ruled that the children were habitual residents in Australia, or alternatively, on the more doubtful basis that they were habitual residents in Turkey.[70] She found that art 7 of the 1996 Convention was not an obstacle to her ability to make orders because the father had acquiesced in the retention of the children in Australia.[71] Her Honour's orders in relation to the children were to be recognised as operation of law in Turkey by virtue of art 23(1) of the 1996 Convention.[72]

However, her Honour ruled that she had no jurisdiction to make orders with respect to W. This was because of W's presence and habitual residence in Turkey at the time of the application.[73] The Judge noted that the 1996 Convention entered into force between Australia and Turkey on 1 February 2017. This meant that both countries 'curtailed their jurisdiction to make orders in relation to children who were not habitually resident in that country.'[74] Bennett J noted that this curtailment is expressed in s 111CD(1)(c) of the Act.[75] Article 9(3) of the 1996 Convention provides that:

> The authority initiating the request may exercise jurisdiction in place of the authority of the Contracting State of the habitual residence of the child *only if* the latter authority has accepted the request.[76]

Pursuant to art 9 of the 1996 Convention, Bennett J noted that an Australian Court may request a court in Turkey to authorise it to exercise jurisdiction to take necessary measures of protection if the Australian Court considers itself to be better placed to assess a child's best interests.[77] The Judge was satisfied that this pre-requisite was met in W's case.[78] Both parents were participating in the proceedings in Australia. W was interviewed in Turkey by a Family Consultant

---

69   *Convention on Jurisdiction, Applicable Law, Recognition, Enforcement and Co-operation in Respect of Parental Responsibility and Measures for the Protection of Children,* opened for signature 19 October 1996, [2003] ATS 19 (entered into force 8 January 2003) art 5 ('the 1996 Convention').

70   *Kubat v Kubat* [2019] FamCA 671, [9].

71   Ibid.

72   Ibid [17].

73   Ibid [11].

74   Ibid.

75   *Family Law Act 1975* (Cth) s 111CD(1)(c).

76   1996 Convention (n 69) art 9(3) (emphasis added).

77   *Kubat v Kubat* [2019] FamCA 671, [12].

78   Ibid [13].

from the Court's Child Dispute Services Section. This section includes expert psychologists and highly trained social workers who are experienced in child development and parenting after separation and divorce.[79]

A request by the Court to assume jurisdiction also required W to have substantial connection to Australia.[80] The Judge was also satisfied that this pre-requisite was met.[81] W was an Australian citizen by virtue of his birth in the country in 2003.[82] Article 8(2) of the 1996 Convention therefore enabled Australia to exercise jurisdiction, allowing a request to Turkey for a transfer of jurisdiction to be made.[83]

In relation to W, Bennett J's order would have to be re-instated *nunc pro tunc* following a successful request granted by Turkey.[84] As the Court lacked the requisite jurisdiction under ch 11 of the 1996 Convention during the application,[85] her Honour remarked that there was a possibility that recognition of her orders could be refused pursuant to art 23(2)(a) of the 1996 Convention. Moreover, the Judge observed that 'recognition [did] not equate to enforceability'.[86] The parents' intention was for her Honour's parenting orders to be enforceable in Australia and Turkey.[87]

Child Abduction—Prima Facie Case of Wrongful Retention Admitted—Whether Return will Expose Child to Grave Risk of Harm or Expose Him to an Intolerable Situation

Jurisdiction—Orders Made for Parenting Arrangements Immediately on Return—Recognition by Operation of Law under Art 11 of *Convention on Jurisdiction, Applicable Law, Recognition, Enforcement and Co-operation in Respect of Parental Responsibility and Measures for the Protection of Children*

State Central Authority v Rilling
[2019] FamCA 74
Family Court of Australia
Bennett J

---

79   Ibid.
80   Ibid [14].
81   Ibid.
82   Ibid.
83   1996 Convention art 8(2).
84   *Kubat v Kubat* [2019] FamCA 671, [16].
85   Ibid [17].
86   Ibid.
87   Ibid.

This is a Hague return case where the State Central Authority brought an application under reg 16(1) of the *Family Law (Child Abduction Convention) Regulations 1986* (Cth) ('the Regulations')[88] for the return of X ('the child') at the request of the child's mother ('the mother').[89] The respondent was the child's father, Mr Shilling ('the father').[90] The Regulations give effect to the *Convention on the Civil Aspects of International Child Abduction* ('the 1980 Convention')[91] in Australian domestic law.[92]

The child was a citizen and habitual resident of the United Kingdom ('UK').[93] The mother, who had rights of custody over the child,[94] agreed for the father to have the child in his care in Australia between July 2018 and 1 September 2018.[95] However, the father did not return the child to the UK on 1 September 2018 or thereafter.[96] The father's retention of the child in Australia from 1 September 2018 contravened the mother's rights of custody.[97] The father conceded that his retention of the child was thus 'wrongful' within the meaning of art 3 of the 1980 Convention.[98] The Court was prima facie required to order the return of the child to the UK under reg 16(1) of the Regulations. Reg 16(1) provides:

(1)   Subject to subregulations (2) and (3), on application under regulation 14, a court must make an order for the return of a child:

  (a)   if the day on which the application was filed is less than 1 year after the day on which the child was removed to, or first retained in, Australia; or

  (b)   if the day on which the application was filed is at least 1 year after the day on which the child was removed to, or first retained in, Australia unless the court is satisfied that the child is settled in his or her new environment.[99]

---

88   *Family Law (Child Abduction Convention) Regulations 1986* (Cth) reg 16(1) ('the Regulations').

89   *SCA v Rilling* [2019] FamCA 74 [3].

90   Ibid.

91   *Convention on the Civil Aspects of International Child Abduction*, opened for signature 25 October 1980, [1987] ATS 2 (entered into force 1 January 1987) ('the 1980 Convention').

92   *SCA v Rilling* [2019] FamCA 74 [2].

93   Ibid [3].

94   Ibid [6].

95   Ibid [14].

96   Ibid.

97   Ibid [33].

98   Ibid.

99   *Family Law (Child Abduction Convention) Regulations 1986* (Cth) reg 16(1).

However, the Court could refuse to make an order for the child's return if the father was able to establish before the Court one of the exceptions pursuant to reg 16(3) of the Regulations.[100] The father, alleging that the child's mother and her partner had physically mistreated the child, relied on reg 16(3)(b),[101] whereby 'there [was] a grave risk that the return of the child to the country in which he or she habitually resided immediately before the removal or retention would expose the child to physical or psychological harm or otherwise place the child in an intolerable situation'.[102]

The Judge was not satisfied on the evidence that the child's return to the UK would amount to the situation outlined in reg 16(3)(b).[103] This meant that the child's return was mandatory.[104] Her Honour concluded that the risk of harm did not reach the requisite 'gravity' to qualify as an exception to the child's return.[105] Evidence suggested that, inter alia, only the mother herself had engaged in acts of physical chastisement, which were limited to hitting the child on the bottom, and that such acts had been a form of parental discipline rather than unfounded physical abuse.[106] Furthermore, the evidence did not indicate that the child remembered occasions of his mother's physical chastisement as being brutal or hurtful.[107]

Bennett J observed that 'it [was] not in the child's best interests, nor in the spirit of the 1980 Convention, for the child's time in Australia to be prolonged.'[108] During his time in Australia, the evidence suggested that the child was regressing in his behaviour, wetting his bed and engaging in attention-seeking behaviour. The Judge found that he was 'becoming increasingly unsettled due to the uncertainty about his return to the United Kingdom and to his mother's care'.[109]

In relation to parenting arrangements post-return of the child, her Honour noted that one of the inherent purposes of the 1980 Convention is to ensure the return of the child to his home state 'as easy and as child-focussed as possible.'[110] To this end, the Judge emphasised the Court's subordinate jurisdiction pursuant to art 11 of the Convention on Jurisdiction, Applicable

---

100   *SCA v Rilling* [2019] FamCA 74, [6]–[7].
101   Ibid [6].
102   *Family Law (Child Abduction Convention) Regulations 1986* (Cth) reg 16(3).
103   *SCA v Rilling* [2019] FamCA 74, [52].
104   *Family Law (Child Abduction Convention) Regulations 1986* (Cth) reg 16(1).
105   *SCA v Rilling* [2019] FamCA 74, [52].
106   Ibid [51].
107   Ibid.
108   Ibid [58].
109   Ibid [57].
110   Ibid [60].

374 AUSTRALIAN YEAR BOOK OF INTERNATIONAL LAW VOLUME 38

Law, Recognition, Enforcement and Co-operation in Respect of Parental Responsibility and Measures for the Protection of Children.[111] This rendered her Honour's orders valid in the UK by operation of law until the courts in that country made orders of their own.[112] After reviewing the evidence, Bennett J concluded that it was in the child's best interests to have a settling-in period with the mother, with regular periods of seeing his father, until the UK court ordered otherwise.[113]

> **Family Law—Child Abduction—Hague Convention—Children Brought to Australia from New Zealand—Whether Father Consented to Children's Removal—*Family Law Act 1975* (Cth) s 111B–*Family Law (Child Abduction Convention) Regulations 1986* (Cth)—Regulation 16—Return Order**

> *State Central Authority v Kejah*
> [2019] FamCA 391
> Family Court of Australia
> Williams J

This case concerned an application to have two children, X and Y, returned to New Zealand under the *Family Law (Child Abduction Convention) Regulations 1986* (Cth) ('the Regulations').[114] The State Central Authority submitted the application at the request of Mr B, the father of X and Y, on the basis that they were wrongfully taken away from him by their mother, Ms Kejah (a pseudonym). The mother and the State Authority agreed that the matter came within the ambit of regs 16(1) and (1A) of the Regulations.[115] The Authority asserted that, as both minors and New Zealand nationals, X and Y were removed against the father's custodial rights and wishes.[116]

Ms Kejah claimed that she took the children to Australia[117] with their father's consent. She conceded that she communicated with Mr B on

---

111 *Convention on Jurisdiction, Applicable Law, Recognition, Enforcement and Co-operation in Respect of Parental Responsibility and Measures for the Protection of Children*, opened for signature 19 October 1996, [2003] ATS 19 (entered into force 8 January 2003) art 11.

112 *SCA v Rilling* [2019] FamCA 74 [52].

113 Ibid [62].

114 *State Central Authority & Kejah* [2019] FamCA 391, [1].

115 *Family Law (Child Abduction Convention) Regulations 1986* (Cth) ss 16(1), 16(1A).

116 *State Central Authority & Kejah* [2019] FamCA 391, [3].

117 Ibid [4].

CASES CONCERNING QUESTIONS OF PUBLIC INTERNATIONAL LAW 2019   375

13 February 2019,[118] notifying him that she would not let the children return to New Zealand. Further, she initially applied to the court for an order allowing the children to stay in Australia[119] pursuant to reg 16(3).[120] However, in the pre-trial stage, Ms Kejah discontinued this request.[121] At trial, she focused only on proving that her husband had permitted her to take the children away from New Zealand.[122]

Mr B has lived in New Zealand since 2004. Ms Kejah moved there to live with him in 2007. In 2014, she became a New Zealand citizen.[123] Both X and Y were New Zealand citizens by birth.[124] The first signs of tension in the home arose in October 2018, when Ms Kejah expressed disdain about living with Mr B's parents.[125] Following this, on 25 January 2019, she travelled to Australia with her children.[126] In the following month, Mr B flew to Australia to see the children but was unable to take them back to New Zealand with him.[127] Ms Kejah, X and Y have lived in Australia since January 2019, with the father residing away from them in New Zealand.[128]

Section 111B of the *Family Law Act 1975* (Cth) operates to incorporate into Australia's domestic laws keys elements of the *Convention on the Civil Aspects of International Child Abduction*.[129] This Hague Convention provides a way to remedy the wrongful deprivation of children who are purported to have been taken away from their home countries.

Williams J found that the onus of proof rested on Ms Kejah to prove that her husband, Mr B, consented to the children moving to Australia with her on a permanent basis.[130]

Ms Kejah tendered affidavit evidence that Mr B allowed the children to relocate, relying on supporting evidence from her brother, Mr L, and of a friend, Mr N.[131] Williams J found that Ms Kejah could only provide vague evidence of

---

118   Ibid [5].
119   Ibid [6].
120   *Family Law (Child Abduction Convention) Regulations 1986* (Cth) s 16(3).
121   *State Central Authority & Kejah* [2019] FamCA 391, [10].
122   Ibid [12].
123   Ibid [15].
124   Ibid [16].
125   Ibid [20].
126   Ibid [21].
127   Ibid [22].
128   Ibid [23].
129   Opened for signature 25 October 1980, [1987] ATS 2 (entered into force 1 January 1987) ('the Hague Convention'); *State Central Authority & Kejah* [2019] FamCA 391, [40].
130   Ibid [48]; *Re H (Abduction: Habitual Residence: Consent)* [2000] 2 FLR 294, 301 (Holman J).
131   *State Central Authority and Kejah* [2019] FamCA 391, [50].

Mr B's consent. She acknowledged that she had made false statements about purchasing uniforms for the children and that she had lied about Mr B having paid for them. This led Williams J to discredit multiple affidavits by Ms Kejah in which she contradicted herself about when Mr B had spoken to her about returning the children to New Zealand.[132] Further, Williams J expressed doubts about claims raised by Mr L, Ms Kejah's brother,[133] whom the Judge believed was trying to present his sister in the best possible light against her husband, Mr B.[134]

In addition, the claims made by Mr N, a family friend, were different from those made by Ms Kejah as to what she said about the reluctant agreement of Mr B allowing X and Y to resettle in Australia.[135] Ms Kejah could not explain this,[136] and as a result, Williams J viewed both her and the friend's evidence as misleading.[137]

Ms Kejah did not satisfy the onus of proof and the statements given in cross-examination by both witnesses, Mr N and Mr L, were inconsistent with her own claims. Williams J ruled that it had not been proven that Mr B had given his precise consent for the removal and relocation of X and Y from New Zealand to Australia.[138]

Williams J found the father, Mr B, more persuasive.[139] Even after lengthy cross-examination by counsel for Ms Kejah, Mr B's remained resolute and consistent in his claims.[140] His Honour found that Mr B never consented to the emigration of both X and Y.[141]

Williams J made orders for the return of both X and Y to New Zealand in accordance with the application of the State Central Authority and the Regulations.[142]

---

132   Ibid [53].
133   Ibid [59].
134   Ibid [60].
135   Ibid [65].
136   Ibid [66].
137   Ibid [67].
138   Ibid [72].
139   Ibid [68].
140   Ibid [70].
141   Ibid [73].
142   Ibid [76].

CASES CONCERNING QUESTIONS OF PUBLIC INTERNATIONAL LAW 2019

5   Criminal Law—Crimes against Humanity

Criminal Law—Criminal Procedure—Private Prosecution—
Authority to Prosecute—Where Private Citizen Sought to
Commence Criminal Proceeding for Offence of Crime against
Humanity Contrary to s 268.11 of *Criminal Code* (Cth)—Where
s 268.121(1) Provides Proceedings under Div 268 Must Not be
Commenced Without Attorney-General's Written Consent—Where
Attorney-General Did Not Consent—Where s 268.121(2) of *Criminal
Code* Provides Offence against Div 268 'May Only be Prosecuted
in the Name of Attorney-General'—Where s 13(a) of *Crimes Act
1914* (Cth) Provides Any Person May 'Institute Proceedings for
Commitment for Trial of Any Person in Respect of Any Indictable
Offence against Law of Commonwealth' unless Contrary Intention
Appear—Whether s 268.121(2) Expresses Contrary Intention
for Purpose of s 13(a)—Whether s 268.121(2) Precludes Private
Prosecution of Offence against Div 268—*Crimes Act 1914* (Cth)
s 13(a)—*Criminal Code* (Cth) ss 268.11, 268.121—*Judiciary Act 1903*
(Cth) ss 68, 69

Taylor v Attorney-General of the Commonwealth
[2019] HCA 30
High Court of Australia
Kiefel CJ, Bell, Gageler, Keane, Nettle, Gordon and Edelman JJ

This is a case where a private citizen attempted to bring a private prosecution against Myanmar's de facto head of government Aung San Suu Kyi, alleging that she had committed a crime against humanity in contravention of s 268.11 of the *Criminal Code* (Cth). The plaintiff sought the Australian Attorney-General's consent to prosecute. The Attorney-General refused to give consent.

On 16 March 2018, the plaintiff, a private citizen, lodged a charge-sheet together with a draft summons, alleging that Aung San Suu Kyi, the Minister of the Office of the President and Foreign Minister of the Republic of the Union of Myanmar, had committed a crime against humanity in contravention of s 268.11 of the *Criminal Code* (Cth).[143] The plaintiff lodged the charge-sheet and summons in purported reliance on s 13(a) of the *Crimes Act 1914* (Cth) and attempted to commence private prosecution proceedings. Section 13 of the *Crimes Act* provides:

---

143   *Taylor v Attorney-General (Cth)* [2019] HCA 30, [1].

378 AUSTRALIAN YEAR BOOK OF INTERNATIONAL LAW VOLUME 38

Unless the contrary intention appears in the Act or regulation creating the offence, any person may:

(a) institute proceedings for the commitment for trial of any person in respect of any indicatable offence against the law of the Commonwealth; or

(b) institute proceedings for the summary conviction of any person in respect of any offence against the law of the Commonwealth punishable on summary conviction.[144]

On the same day, the plaintiff sent an email to the defendant, the Attorney-General of the Commonwealth, requesting his consent under s 268.121(1) of the *Criminal Code* to commencement of the prosecution. Section 268.121 provides:

(1) Proceedings for an offence under this Division must not be commenced without the Attorney-General's written consent.

(2) An offence against this Division may only be prosecuted in the name of the Attorney-General.

(3) However, a person may be arrested, charged, remanded in custody, or released on bail, in connection with an offence under this Division before the necessary consent has been given.[145]

The defendant communicated to the plaintiff his decision not to prosecute three days later. The plaintiff sought a writ of certiorari quashing the defendant's decision.

The majority (Kiefel CJ, Bell, Gageler and Keane JJ) disallowed the application. After reviewing the legislative history, their Honours held that s 268.121(2) of the *Criminal Code* derives immediately from s 12 of the *War Crimes Act 1945* (Cth). The Explanatory Memorandum to this Act made clear that the nature of the offences in the *War Crimes Act* made it desirable to exclude the possibility of private prosecutions.[146] Their Honours found s 268.121 (2) exhibits a contrary intention for the purpose of s 13 of the *Crimes Act* and thus precluded the plaintiff from commencing a private prosecution of an offence against Div 268 of the *Criminal Code*.[147]

---

144 *Crimes Act 1914* (Cth) s 13.
145 *Criminal Code Act 1995* (Cth) s 268.121.
146 *Taylor v Attorney-General (Cth)* [2019] HCA 30, [34].
147 Ibid [10].

The Court also rejected the plaintiff's argument that the exclusory operation of s 268.121(2) of the *Criminal Code* was confined to the indictment stage, thus allowing private prosecution to proceed, with the consent of the Attorney-General, up to the committal stage.[148] Instead, the Court affirmed that the prosecution to which s 268.121(2) refers is the *'totality of the prosecutorial process beginning with the commencement of proceedings for an offence against Div 268'*.[149]

Their Honours added that this construction of s 268.121(2) does not render the consent requirement in subsection (1) redundant.[150] This is because such requirements ensure that proceedings are brought consistently with subsection (2), including requiring that proceedings brought by the Commonwealth Director of Public Prosecutions in the name of the Attorney-General are commenced with the consent of the Attorney-General.[151]

The Court acknowledged that the principal object of Div 268 of the *Criminal Code* and the *International Criminal Court (Consequential Amendments) Act 2002* (Cth) is to facilitate Australia's compliance with its obligations to exercise criminal jurisdiction over those responsible for international crimes under the *Rome Statute*.[152] Nonetheless, the Court disagreed that it would advance the legislative purpose of facilitating the exercise of Australia's international rights to allow a private citizen to bring a private summary prosecution or a private prosecution up to the committal stage.[153] Their Honours found that such a course would have the real potential to embarrass Australia internationally.[154]

However, Nettle and Gordon JJ were in dissent. Their Honours argued that s 13 of the *Crimes Act* requires an express term or at least necessary implication to exclude the right of private prosecution.[155] Their Honours suggested that s 268.121 of the *Criminal Code* does not expressly prohibit a private person from commencing a proceeding for an offence against Div 268 of the *Code*, nor does it necessarily imply as much.[156] In fact, their Honours held that the requirement in s 268.121(1) for the Attorney-General to provide written consent before a private party commences proceedings actually implies that a private person

---

148 Ibid [38].
149 Ibid [39].
150 Ibid [41].
151 Ibid.
152 Ibid [11].
153 Ibid [42].
154 Ibid.
155 Ibid [53].
156 Ibid [54].

may bring proceedings, as long as the person first obtains the consent of the Attorney-General.[157]

Justices Nettle and Gordon also compared and contrasted the Australian provisions with provisions in the United Kingdom, New Zealand and Canada to determine the drafters' intentions. Their Honours suggested that the Australian drafters opted for the UK and New Zealand wording of the provision, namely that proceedings must not begin without the consent of the Attorney-General, as opposed to requiring that proceedings must be 'conducted *only* by the Attorney-General' as the Canadian provision does. This shows that the drafters intended to retain the private right of prosecution while subjecting it to a requirement to first to obtain the Attorney-General's consent.[158]

Justice Edelman was also in dissent. Like Nettle and Gordon JJ, his Honour compared and contrasted the Australian provisions with the provisions in the United Kingdom, New Zealand and Canada and concluded that the choice of expression by the Commonwealth Parliament indicated an intention to allow the Attorney-General to completely control the proceedings without abolishing the prospect of a commencement of proceedings by a private person.[159] In other words, a 'relator' prosecution brought in the name of the Attorney-General, and controlled by the Attorney-General, would satisfy the requirement of a prosecution brought 'in the name of the Attorney-General'.[160]

6   Human Rights

> Statutes—Construction—Where s 45(1)(a) of *Crimes Act 1900*
> (NSW)—Female Genital Mutilation—Two Respondents Charged
> with having 'Mutilated the Clitoris' of the Complainants—Where
> One Respondent Charged with Assisting the Other Respondents
> with Commission of Offences—Defence Claimed Procedure was
> Merely Ritualistic—Whether Trial Judge Misdirected Jury as to
> Meaning of 'Mutilate' and 'Clitoris'—Where Relevance of Extrinsic
> Material Discussed—Where International Instruments were
> Related to the Offences

---

157   Ibid [55].
158   Ibid [79].
159   Ibid [101].
160   Ibid [150].

CASES CONCERNING QUESTIONS OF PUBLIC INTERNATIONAL LAW 2019   381

The Queen v A2
The Queen v Magennis
The Queen v Vaziri
[2019] HCA 35
High Court of Australia
Kiefel CJ, Bell, Gageler, Keane, Nettle, Gordon and Edelman JJ

In this case the High Court allowed three appeals from the New South Wales Court of Criminal Appeal ('CCA'), overruling the lower Court's construction of the term 'otherwise mutilates' in s 45(1)(a) of the *Crimes Act 1900* (NSW). The court held that the prohibition of female genital mutilation ('FGM') in this section gives the phrase 'otherwise mutilates' an extended meaning that requires consideration of the cultural context of an act. A majority of the High Court held further that the term 'clitoris' in s 45(1)(a) encompasses the clitoral hood or prepuce.

Section 45(1)(a) of the *Crimes Act* provides that a person who 'excises, infibulates or otherwise mutilates the whole or any part of the labia majora or labia minora or clitoris of any person' is liable to imprisonment. A2 and Magennis were charged and found guilty upon indictment of mutilating the clitoris of two minor children, C1 and C2 in the course of performing a cultural ceremony called 'khatna'. Vaziri was charged with assisting A2 and Magennis. Found guilty by the trial Judge of two counts of FGM contrary to s 45(1)(a),[161] the trio succeeded in having their convictions overturned by the CCA. The CCA upheld the respondents' arguments that the operations performed did not amount to mutilation because they did not do permanent damage to the children involved. It ruled that the word 'mutilates' should be given its ordinary meaning for the purposes of s 45(1)(a), requiring the Crown to demonstrate that some imperfection or irreparable damage had been caused.[162] The Court also ruled that the term 'clitoris' did not include the clitoral hood or prepuce. Overall, it concluded that the jury's verdict in the case was unreasonable or not supported by the evidence.

The Crown appealed to the High Court against the findings in all three cases. The High Court agreed with the Crown's argument that the term 'mutilation' should not be given its 'ordinary' meaning. Rather, it should be constructed broadly so as to encompass conduct that amounted to a 'cut' or 'nick' of the clitoris. A majority also ruled that the term 'clitoris' should be

---

161   See *A2 v The Queen* [2018] 174 NSWCCA 157. Vaziri was found guilty of two counts of being an accessory to those offences.
162   *A2 v The Queen* [2018] 174 NSWCCA 157, [521]–[522] ('*A2 v The Queen*').

constructed to include the clitoral hood (where the mutilation was alleged to have occurred).[163]

The FGM provisions in the *Crimes Act* (NSW)[164] were created in part in response to obligations assumed by Australia under the *UN Convention on the Rights of the Child*,[165] the *Universal Declaration of Human Rights*,[166] the *Convention on the Elimination of All Forms of Discrimination Against Women*,[167] the *Declaration on the Elimination of Violence Against Women*,[168] and the 1951 Convention and 1967 Protocol relating to the Status of Refugees.[169] Most relevantly, the *Convention on the Rights of the Child* provides that State parties 'take all effective and appropriate measures with a view to abolishing traditional practices prejudicial to the health of children'.[170]

6.1   *The Use of Extrinsic Materials*

In reaching its decision, the High Court made extensive reference to extrinsic materials to resolve ambiguities expressed by the terms 'mutilation' and 'clitoris'.[171] A central piece of extrinsic material referred to by the Court was a 1994 Family Law Council ('FLC') report.[172] This report included comments about the adequacy of FGM laws in Australia, recommendations about how these laws could be improved and a general discussion of how FGM is categorised.[173]

---

163   *The Queen v A2* [2019] 35 HCA 18, [56]–[58].

164   *Crimes Act 1900* (NSW) s 45.

165   *Convention on the Rights of the Child*, opened for signature 20 November 1989, 1577 UNTS 3 (entered into force 2 September 1990).

166   *Universal Declaration of Human Rights*, GA Res 217A (III), UN GAOR, UN Doc A/810 (10 December 1948).

167   *Convention of the Elimination of All Forms of Discrimination against Women*, opened for signature 18 December 1979, 1249 UNTS 13 (entered into force 3 September 1981).

168   *Declaration on the Elimination of Violence against Women*, GA Res 48/104, UN Doc A/RES/48/104 (20 December 1993).

169   *Convention Relating to the Status of Refugees*, opened for signature 28 July 1951, 189 UNTS 150 (entered into force 22 April 1954); Protocol Relating to the Status of Refugees, 606 UNTS 267(entered into force 4 October 1967).

170   *Convention on the Rights of the Child* (n 166) art 24(3).

171   Ibid 3 [13]–[30], 21 [67].

172   Family Law Council, *Female Genital Mutilation: A Report to the Attorney-General prepared by the Family Law Council* (Report, June 1994).

173   *A2 v the Queen* (n 163) 3 [13]–[18], 6 [21]–[24].

6.2 *The Construction of Terms*

In reference to the FLC report (and other extrinsic materials such as the relevant Second Reading Speech and Explanatory Note), the Court came to the conclusion that the purpose of s 45(1)(a), was to:

> criminalise the carrying out of [female genital mutilation] on female children. Its wider purpose may be taken to be its cessation.[174]

The Court noted that the FLC report identified 'ritualised circumcision' as being included under the 'collective name' of FGM. Further support for this approach to the definition was found in other extrinsic materials.[175] The Court ruled that these extrinsic materials supported both a broad construction of the term 'mutilation' and also the criminalisation of all conduct which amounted to mutilation.[176] It noted that a construction which promotes the purpose of a statute is to be preferred. In the result, a broad construction of 'mutilation' was adopted by the Court. The Respondents' conduct was found to be captured by s 45(1)(a).[177]

In this case the High Court did not refer directly to relevant international instruments such as the *Convention on the Rights of the Child*. However, international law was referenced heavily in critical pieces of extrinsic material referenced by the Court in the process of constructing a legal definition of the terms 'mutilate' and 'clitoris'. The extrinsic materials argued that relevant international laws encouraged a broad interpretation of these terms, ultimately supporting the conclusion that the conduct engaged in by the Respondents was criminal in nature.

Appeal allowed.

7 International Arbitration—UNCITRAL

International Arbitration—1965 *Convention on the Settlement of Investment Disputes*—Recognition and Enforcement of an Award of the International Centre for Settlement of Investment Disputes—Application for a Stay of Proceedings under s 35(4) of the *International Arbitration Act 1974* (Cth)

---

174   Ibid 14 [44].
175   Ibid 6 [21]–[22], 14 [42].
176   Ibid 18 [56]–[58].
177   Ibid 13 [37]; *Interpretation Act 1987* (NSW) s 33; *Crimes Act* (n 145) s 45(1)(a).

Infrastructure Services Luxembourg SÀRL v Kingdom of Spain
[2019] FCA 1220
Federal Court of Australia
Stewart J

On 15 June 2018, a tribunal of the International Centre for Settlement of Investment Disputes ('ICSID') issued an arbitration award in favour of Infrastructure Services Luxembourg SÀRL and Energia Solar Luxembourg SÀRL ('the applicants') against the Kingdom of Spain ('Spain').[178] The tribunal found that Spain had breached its obligations under the Energy Charter Treaty to accord fair and equitable treatment to the applicants, and required Spain to pay €101 million as compensation. The ICSID award was made under the 1965 *Convention on the Settlement of Investment Disputes between States and Nationals of other States* ('the Convention').[179]

Australia, which has implemented the Convention in Part IV of its *International Arbitration Act 1974* (Cth) ('IAA'), was chosen by the applicants as a jurisdiction in which to seek recognition and enforcement of the ICSID award. On 17 April 2019, the applicants commenced proceedings in the Federal Court of Australia, invoking s 35(4) of the IAA in an attempt to have the award enforced as if it were a judgment of the Court itself.[180] However, on 23 May 2019, and prior to any substantive matters being heard in the Federal Court, Spain applied to the Secretary-General of ICSID for an annulment of the award on grounds contained in art 52(1) of the Convention.[181] Spain additionally made a request from the Secretary-General for a stay of the enforcement of the award under art 52(5), until the annulment matter had been resolved.[182] The Secretary-General granted a provisional stay on 23 May 2019.[183]

Then, on 15 July 2019, the applicants interrupted their own proceedings in the Federal Court by filing an interlocutory application for a stay of those proceedings, so as to avoid any conflict with ICSID's provisional stay of the

---

178   *Antin Infrastructure Services Luxembourg SÀRL and Antin Enerfia Termosolar B.V. v The Kingdom of Spain* (Decision on Rectification of the Award) (ICSID Arbitral Tribunal, Case No ARB/13/31, 29 January 2019).

179   *Convention on the Settlement of Investment Disputes between States and Nationals of Other States*, opened for signature 18 March 1965, 575 UNTS 159 (entered into force 14 October 1966).

180   *Infrastructure Services Luxembourg SÀRL v Kingdom of Spain* [2019] FCA 1220.

181   Ibid [12].

182   Ibid.

183   Ibid [13].

enforcement of the award.[184] This development prompted Stewart J to consider the interplay between arts 52(5) and 54(1), the latter of which obliges Australia, as a contracting State, to recognise and enforce any pecuniary obligations imposed by an ICSID award.[185] As Stewart J noted, art 54(1) 'might be seen to oblige the Court to progress the proceeding and not stay it.'[186] However, since such an obligation would be at odds with the provisional stay of enforcement under art 52(5), his Honour concluded that obligations under art 54(1) are subject to art 52(5), meaning that a provisional stay of enforcement also suspends a contracting State's obligations under art 54(1).[187] According to his Honour, 'that is the only logical way of reading [the articles] in harmony.'[188] In reaching this conclusion, Stewart J expressly adopted the reasoning of the ad hoc committee in *Maritime International Nominees Establishment v Republic of Guinea*,[189] which had similarly been tasked with considering the relationship between arts 52(5) and 54(1).[190]

A short while after the Federal Court proceedings had successfully been stayed by the applicants, an ad hoc committee created by ICSID lifted the provisional stay of the award against Spain,[191] opening the way for the applicants to re-commence their enforcement proceedings in Australia. The final outcome of those proceedings is still pending. If the applicants are ultimately successful in having the ICSID award enforced, Australian courts may face a growing number of claimants seeking to have their awards enforced in Australia.

Infrastructure Services Luxembourg SÀRL v Kingdom of Spain (NSD 602 of 2019)[192] proceeded in parallel with another application for recognition and enforcement of an ICSID award (*Eiser Infrastructure Ltd v Spain*,[193] which is NSD 601 of 2019). Both cases are before Stewart J of the Federal Court of Australia. The hearing on the merits of the applications for recognition and enforcement in both cases was held on 29 October 2019.

---

184 Ibid [18]–[19].
185 Ibid [26]–[30].
186 Ibid [28].
187 Ibid.
188 Ibid [30].
189 (*Interim Order*) (ICSID Committee, Case No ARB/84/4, 12 August 1988).
190 *Infrastructure Services Luxembourg SÀRL v Kingdom of Spain* [2019] FCA 1220, [29]–[30].
191 *Infrastructure Services Luxembourg SÀRL. and Energia Termosolar BV v Kingdom of Spain* (*Decision on the Continuation of the Provisional Stay of the Enforcement of the Award*) (ICSID Committee, Case No ARB/13/31, 21 October 2019).
192 [2019] FCA 1220.
193 [2020] FCA 157.

Domestic and International Commercial Arbitration—UNCITRAL Model Law—Proper Approach to the Construction of Arbitral Clauses

Rinehart v Hancock Prospecting Pty Ltd
Rinehart v Rinehart
[2019] HCA 13
High Court of Australia
Kiefel CJ, Gageler, Nettle, Gordon and Edelman JJ

Ms Rinehart and Mr Hancock ('the appellants') brought proceedings in the Federal Court of Australia against Mrs Rinehart, Hancock Prospecting Pty Ltd and others ('the respondents') regarding the diminishment of trust assets of which the appellants were beneficiaries. The respondents made interlocutory applications seeking an order that the proceedings be dismissed or permanently stayed, and that the matters the subject of the proceedings be referred to arbitration instead. These applications were refused, with the primary judge reasoning that where an arbitral clause in a deed provides for arbitration in the event of disputes arising 'under this deed', then certain disputes about the validity of the deed itself may be beyond the scope of that arbitral clause.[194]

In *Hancock Prospecting Pty Ltd v Rinehart*,[195] the Full Court (Allsop CJ, Besanko and O'Callaghan JJ) disagreed with the reasoning of the primary judge and granted a stay, allowing for the matters to be resolved through arbitration. In handing down its judgment, the Full Court took the opportunity to consider whether the decision of the House of Lords in *Fiona Trust & Holding Corporation v Privalov* ('*Fiona Trust*')[196] should be followed in Australia. In *Fiona Trust*, a fresh approach to the construction of arbitral clauses was taken, 'leaving behind some verbal distinctions (on the language of particular arbitration clauses) which', according to Lord Walker, 'few commercial men would regard as significant'.[197] Hence, English commercial law no longer draws distinctions between phrases such as 'under this deed', 'out of this deed', 'in relation to this deed' etc when determining the scope of an arbitral clause. Such clauses are now construed in accordance with the presumption that parties are likely to have intended any dispute arising out of their agreement (or purported

---

194 *Rinehart v Rinehart (No 3)* (2016) 257 FCR 310, [579]–[587] (Gleeson J).
195 (2017) 257 FCR 442.
196 [2007] 4 All ER 951.
197 Ibid [37].

agreement) to be referred to arbitration. This presumption can only be displaced using very clear language indicating a contrary intention.[198]

According to Lord Hoffman, this liberal presumptive approach was 'firmly embedded as part of the law of international commerce',[199] and the Lords of Appeal all agreed that this approach would give full effect to the legislative purpose of s 7 of the *Arbitration Act 1996* (UK).[200] Section 7 enshrines the separability principle—ie, the principle that the invalidity of a contract does not automatically entail the invalidity of an arbitral clause in that contract. The implementation of this principle was especially significant to Lord Hoffman, as it 'show[ed] a recognition by Parliament that ... businessmen frequently do want the question of whether their contract was valid, or came into existence, or has become ineffective, submitted to arbitration and that the law should not place conceptual obstacles in their way.'[201]

The separability principle is a key tenet of the United Nations Commission on International Trade Law ('UNCITRAL') Model Law,[202] which was implemented in Australia via an integrated statutory framework comprising the *Commercial Arbitration Act 2010* (NSW) and the *International Arbitration Act 1974* (Cth). In *Hancock Prospecting Pty Ltd v Rinehart*,[203] the Full Court made reference to Lord Hoffman's remarks about the separability principle and observed that the presumption laid down in *Fiona Trust* 'has a real role to play' in the construction of arbitral clauses in Australia.[204]

On 8 May 2019, the High Court of Australia unanimously dismissed an appeal from the Full Court regarding the order for a stay of proceedings. However, their Honours did not endorse the liberal presumptive approach taken by the Full Court in order to uphold that order. As stated by Kiefel CJ, Gageler, Nettle and Gordon JJ (with Edelman J agreeing), such matters 'can be resolved in the application of orthodox principles of interpretation, which require consideration of the context and purpose of the Deeds, without reference to *Fiona Trust*.'[205] Moreover, their Honours observed that the separability principle is 'not determinative of the issues in these appeals and it is not necessary to resort to [it]'.[206] By instead focusing on the context and purpose of

---

198   Ibid [7] (Lord Hoffman).
199   Ibid [31].
200   Ibid [12] (Lord Hoffman), [37] (Lord Walker).
201   Ibid [10].
202   See art 16.
203   (2017) 257 FCR 442.
204   Ibid [182] (Allsop CJ, Besanko and O'Callaghan JJ).
205   *Rinehart v Hancock Prospecting Pty Ltd* [2019] HCA 13, 5 [18].
206   Ibid 4 [13].

the deeds, it became clear to the Court that the parties had agreed to avoid public scrutiny as much as possible, and it was inconceivable that either party had intended that future validity claims raising allegations of undue influence were not to be determined through confidential arbitration.[207]

As a result of this decision, Australian courts may continue to face similar disputes about the scope of arbitral clauses, with future litigants having to base unique arguments on the surrounding circumstances and objectives of their agreements. Alternatively, as noted by the High Court, '[t]he approach adopted in *Fiona Trust* may not assume so much importance for courts in the future given the likelihood that arbitral clauses such as the UNCITRAL Arbitration Clause in different and arguably wider terms are now recommended for use by commercial parties.'[208] Hence, as regards arbitration clauses that have indeed been formulated in such a way as to accord with UNCITRAL's recommendation, there are now important obiter dicta to the effect that such clauses will cause any related validity claims to be resolved through arbitration instead of litigation.

8   Migration Protection Visa/Refugee

Migration—Request for Revocation of Mandatory Visa Cancellation under s 501CA(4) of the *Migration Act 1958* (Cth)— Non-Refoulement Obligation—*Convention on the Rights of Persons with Disabilities*—Respondent Claimed Harm if He were Returned to His Country of Origin on Account of the Treatment Afforded to People with Mental Illness—Assistant Minister's Failure to Engage in an Active Intellectual Process with the Representation— Amended Notice of Contention Upheld—Appeal Dismissed, with Costs

Minister for Home Affairs v Omar
[2019] FCAFC 188
Federal Court of Australia
Allsop CJ, Bromberg, Robertson, Griffiths and Perry JJ

This case concerned a decision of the Assistant Minister of Home Affairs ('the Assistant Minister') to refuse to revoke a mandatory cancellation of a partner

---

207   Ibid 13 [48].
208   Ibid 6 [21].

visa held by Mr Omar ('the Respondent'), in the process declining to consider issues relating to the Respondent's protection claims. The Respondent arrived in Australia from Somalia in 2001 (aged 15) as a dependant on his aunt's partner visa. He had been orphaned and then recruited at the age of eight as a child soldier. Rescued by family members, he fled to Kenya where he lived in a refugee camp for six years.[209] His visa was cancelled under the mandatory cancellation provision in s 501(3A) of the *Migration Act 1958* (Cth) ('the Act') as he had a 'substantial criminal record' and was serving a term of imprisonment.[210] It was accepted by the parties and the court that the Respondent had mental health problems and intellectual disability, which were referred to as 'severe'. There was uncontested evidence that if he was to be deported to Somalia, he would be subjected to harmful living conditions on account of his mental health issues.[211]

The primary Federal Court judge ruled that the Assistant Minister had considered the risks associated with removing the Respondent, but that his refusal to consider representations relating to Australia's non-refoulement obligations amounted to failure to perform a statutory task required by s 501CA of the Act.[212] The Assistant Minister had proceeded on the basis that non-refoulement obligations did not need to be considered because the Respondent could subsequently apply for a protection visa and have protection claims considered in that process. The Assistant Minister appealed the decision to a Full Bench of the Federal Court, whereupon the Chief Justice elected to constitute a bench of five justices.

The central issue for the Court was whether the Assistant Minister had made a jurisdictional error by failing to properly consider representations made by the Respondent as reasons for revoking the visa cancellation. In a unanimous judgement, the Court found that the trial judge erred in ruling that the Assistant Minister had considered the risk of harm to the Respondent if he were returned to Somalia.[213] As such, the Assistant Minister had failed to perform a statutory duty in their decision-making process and the Minister's appeal was dismissed. Determining the appeal on this basis, the Full Court did not address the issue that was determinative in the primary judgement, that is, whether the Assistant Minister was required to consider representations

---

209   *Minister for Home Affairs v Omar* [2019] FCAFC 188, [6] ('*Omar*').
210   Ibid 23; *Migration Act 1958* (Cth) s 501 ('the Act').
211   *Omar* (n 210) [6]–[7], [8].
212   Ibid [27].
213   Ibid.

concerning Australia's non-refoulement obligations.[214] Instead the Court focused on matters better described as process (what constitutes consideration).

8.1 Summary of Relevant Legal Principles

The Respondent's convictions led to the mandatory cancellation of his visa under s 501(3A) of the Act, and he sought revocation of that cancellation. Under s 501CA(3) of the Act, the Minister must invite the visa-holder to provide representations as to why the cancellation should be revoked.[215] The representations as a whole are a mandatory consideration for the Assistant Minister in their decision making process, and must be properly referenced in the statement of reasons.[216] Moreover, the Assistant Minister has a statutory duty to 'consider' whether they are satisfied that the representations give rise to 'another reason' which compels revocation of the cancellation.[217] Otherwise explained, the Assistant Minister must have a 'requisite state of satisfaction to revoke the cancellation in reference to the material in the representations'.[218] In determining whether there is 'another reason' why a visa should be cancelled under s 501(CA)(4)(b)(ii), the Assistant Minister must consider those representations which are clearly articulated and significant—including the potential of harm if sent back to their country of origin.[219] The Assistant Minister's consideration of representations relating to the Respondent's potential return to Somalia were of central importance to the Court.

For the Assistant Minister to have properly 'considered' representations made by the Respondent, they must engage in an 'active intellectual process' where they apply their own mind to the facts presented to them.[220]

---

214 Ibid [29], [47].

215 Ibid [34]; *Migration Act 1958* (Cth) s 501CA(3).

216 *Omar* (n 210) [34]. Under s 501G of the Act, the Assistant Minister is required to give written notice to those affected by a non-revocation decision; providing a 'Statement of Reasons' for the decision, explaining findings on material questions of fact, and referring to evidence on which those findings were based. See generally, *Acts Interpretation Act 1901* (Cth) s 25D; and *Goundar v Minister of Immigration and Border Protection* [2016] FCA 1203, [56] (Robertson J); *Minister of Immigration and Border Protection v BHA17* (2018) 260 FCR 523, [139] (Robertson, Moshinsky and Bromwich JJ); *Viane v Minister of Immigration and Border Protection* (2018) 263 FCR 531, [70]–[72] (Colvin J); *Minister of Home Affairs v Buadromo* (2018) 237 FCR 316, [41] (Besanko, Barker and Bromwich JJ).

217 *Omar* (n 210) [36]; *Migration Act 1958* (Cth) s 501CA(4); *Carrascalao v Minister for Immigration and Border Protection* (2017) 346 ALR 173.

218 *Omar* (n 210) [34]; *Viane v Minister for Immigration and Border Protection* (2018) 263 FCR 531, [66] (Colvin J).

219 *Omar* (n 210) [34]; *BCR16 v Minister for Immigration and Border Protection* (2017) 248 FCR 456, [70]–[73] (Bromberg and Mortimer JJ).

220 *Omar* (n 210) [36]; *Tickner v Chapman* [1995] FCA 1726, [495] (Kiefel J).

CASES CONCERNING QUESTIONS OF PUBLIC INTERNATIONAL LAW 2019   391

8.2   *Failure to 'Consider' Certain Representations*
The Court explained in view of the above principles:

> Giving meaningful consideration to a clearly articulated and substantial or significant representation on risk of harm independently of a claim concerning Australia's non-refoulement obligations, requires more than the Assistant Minister simply acknowledging or noting that the representations have been made.[221]

Relevant representations made by the Respondent included his diagnosis of schizophrenia and accompanying intellectual disability.[222] These mental conditions were relevant to the non-revocation decision, as evidence showed that the Respondent would be likely to experience inhumane and degrading treatment.[223] The Respondent contended that the cancellation of his visa could amount to refoulement in contravention of art 3 of the *Convention against Torture* or the *Convention on the Rights of Persons with Disabilities*.[224] The Court held that the Assistant Minister was required to make findings of fact in relation to these serious and significant matters, to 'assess the veracity and gravity of the risks of harm'.[225] As the Assistant Minister had a statutory duty to determine whether there is 'another reason' as to why the cancellation should be revoked, a failure to consider these representations can—and did— give rise to a jurisdictional error.[226]

Consequently, the Court ruled that the primary judge erred in finding that the Assistant Minister had:
- adequately examined the risks associated with sending Mr Omar back to Somalia;
- appropriately accepted that there would be harm, but that other factors outweighed the risks of sending Mr Omar back to Somalia; and
- properly accepted, at a factual level, the difficulties Mr Omar would face if returned to Somalia.[227]

---

221   *Omar* (n 210) [39].
222   Ibid [6], [8], [10], [12], [15], [19]–[20], [22].
223   Ibid [10]–[12], [20]–[22], [40], [43].
224   Ibid [33]; *Convention against Torture and Other Cruel, Inhuman or Degrading Treatment or Punishment*, opened for signature 10 December 1984, 1465 UNTS 85 (entered into force 26 June 1987); *Convention on the Rights of Persons with Disabilities*, opened for signature 30 March 2007, 2515 UNTS 3 (entered into force 3 May 2008).
225   *Omar* (n 210) [43].
226   Ibid [41]; *Migration Act 1958* (Cth) s 501(CA)(4)(b)(ii).
227   *Omar* (n 210) [42].

The Court found that the Assistant Minister 'merely noted' some matters raised in the Respondent's representations and failed to make findings on certain representations relating to how the Respondent would be treated if returned to Somalia.[228] Consequently, the Assistant Minister failed to properly consider the representations made by the Respondent—thereby failing to perform the statutory duty to determine if there was 'another reason' to revoke mandatory cancellation and falling into jurisdictional error.[229]

The case recognises an important distinction between the consideration of representations on risk of harm—as a factual matter—and representations that those circumstances engage Australia's non-refoulement obligations.[230]

Appeal dismissed.

> **Migration—Appeal from a Judgment Dismissing the Appellant's Application for Judicial Review of a Decision Made under s 501BA(2) of the *Migration Act 1958* (Cth) ('the Act') to Cancel the Appellant's Class BC Subclass 100 Partner (Migrant) Visa—Whether the Assistant Minister Understood s 501BA(2) as Precluding Him from Providing the Appellant with Natural Justice—Whether the Minister had Conflated Australia's Possible International Non-Refoulement Obligations in Respect of the Appellant with the Claimed Protection Obligations under s 36(2)(a) of the Act—Whether the Errors were Material so as to be Jurisdictional—Appeal Allowed**

Ibrahim v Minister for Home Affairs
[2019] FCAFC 89
Federal Court of Australia
White, Perry and Charlesworth JJ

This case concerned an appeal of the decision of the Assistant Minister for Home Affairs ('the Assistant Minister') to dismiss Mr Ibrahim's ('the appellant's) application for judicial review following a visa cancellation decision made under s 501BA(2) of the *Migration Act 1958* (Cth) ('the Act').[231] The appellant was a Nigerian national who came to Australia in 2008 as the holder of a partner visa. In 2015, while the appellant was in custody serving a sentence imposed in 2014, a delegate of the Assistant Minister cancelled his visa,

---

228 Ibid [29].
229 Ibid [36], [41], [43]–[44] and [46].
230 Ibid [44], [34(f)] citing *DOB18 v Minister for Home Affairs* [2019] FCAFC 63 at [185]–[186].
231 *Migration Act 1958* (Cth) s 501BA(2).

pursuant to s 501(3A) of the Act ('the Cancellation Decision').[232] Subsequently, in 2016, another delegate of the Minister, acting under s 501CA(4) of the Act,[233] revoked the Cancellation Decision ('the Revocation Decision'). In May 2017, the Assistant Minister for Immigration and Border Protection set this decision aside and again cancelled the appellant's visa, pursuant to s 501BA(2).[234] On 13 October 2017, the Court made orders quashing the decision the then Assistant Minister made in May 2017.[235] The new Assistant Minister for Home Affairs then considered again the exercise of the power under s 501BA(2) to set aside the revocation of the Cancellation Decision.[236] On 26 February 2018, the new Assistant Minister made a decision to do so and cancelled the appellant's visa, which led to this appeal.

According to the Assistant Minister, the appellant's visa was cancelled because he did not satisfy the character test by reason of having a 'substantial criminal record', as the Assistant Minister considered that the cancellation was in national interest.[237] It was accepted by both parties that the appellant had a 'substantial criminal record', but there was strong evidence that if returned to Nigeria, the appellant would have a fear of being persecuted for reasons of race, religion, nationality, membership of a particular social group or political opinion.[238]

The power of an Assistant Minister to set aside a revocation order and to cancel a visa depends on the Assistant Minister being satisfied of the matters specified in s 501BA(2).[239] The Assistant Minister's state of mind has to be formed on a correct understanding of the law and of the legal consequences of his decision. If a visa cancellation is revoked under s 501CA, the Minister has power under s 501BA to set aside that revocation and to cancel the visa.[240] The rules of natural justice are obligations which are imposed, on a proper construction of the empowering statute, on decision-makers and are entitlements vested in the persons whose rights and interests are affected by that decision.[241]

---

232 Ibid s 501(3A).

233 Ibid s 501CA(4).

234 Ibid s 501BA(2).

235 *Ibrahim v Minister for Immigration and Border Protection (No 2)* (2017) 256 FCR 50.

236 *Migration Act 1958* (Cth) s 501BA(2).

237 Ibid s 501(6)(a), s 501(7)(c).

238 *Ibrahim v Minister for Home Affairs* [2019] FCAFC 89, [90] ('*Ibrahim v Minister for Home Affairs*').

239 Ibid [12].

240 Ibid.

241 Ibid [46]–[50]; *R v MacKellar; Ex parte Ratu* (1977) 137 CLR 461, 475; *Kioa v West* (1985) 159 CLR 550, 594.

The appellant submitted three distinct grounds on which the Assistant Minister's decision was affected by jurisdictional error. The judges considered each of these three grounds.[242]

8.3 *Ground 1*

The appellant contended that the Assistant Minister had proceeded on a misunderstanding of the effect of s 501BA(3) in that he could not afford natural justice to the appellant, not just that he was not required to do so.[243] The appellant's counsel submitted that the Assistant Minister had not thought to allow the appellant the opportunity to make submissions concerning the exercise of the power under s 501BA(2), giving rise to jurisdictional error.[244] The primary judge rejected this submission at first instance and was not satisfied that the Assistant Minister had been bound to consider providing natural justice to the appellant.[245]

There was a misunderstanding on the part of the Assistant Minister, whose Notice of Contention was rejected for a few reasons.[246] First, the Assistant Minister thought he could only proceed under s 501BA(2) *or* provide natural justice.[247] Next, the Assistant Minister thought that s 501BA(2) was blocking him from allowing the appellant to make submissions.[248] Finally, there was no reason for the Assistant Minister to weigh the disadvantages to the appellant against the proceeding under s 501BA(2) if the appellant could fix them.[249] The Court defined jurisdictional error from *Wei v Minister for Immigration and Border Protection*[250] as requiring consideration of whether a material breach of an express or implied condition exists[251] from the power conferred by s 501BA(2).[252] The Assistant Minister's misunderstanding had affected the validity of his decision and treated his power to act under s 501BA(2)[253] as *conditioned* on him not affording a hearing to the Appellant.[254] The judges said that the Assistant Minister did not accord procedural fairness in exercising

---

242   *Ibrahim v Minister for Home Affairs* (n 241) [8]–[10].
243   *Migration Act 1958* (Cth) s 501BA(3).
244   Ibid s 501BA(2).
245   *Ibrahim v Minister for Home Affairs* (n 241) [18].
246   Ibid [63].
247   *Migration Act 1958* (Cth) s 501BA(2).
248   Ibid.
249   Ibid.
250   (2015) 257 CLR 22, 6 [23] (Gageler and Keane JJ).
251   *Ibrahim v Minister for Home Affairs* [51].
252   *Migration Act 1958* (Cth) s 501BA(2).
253   Ibid.
254   *Re Patterson; Ex parte Taylor* (2001) 207 CLR 391.

statutory power under s 501BA(2),[255] which constituted jurisdictional error, because precluding the appellant from natural justice due to the Act was a fundamental misunderstanding by the Assistant Minister.[256]

Ground 1 upheld.

8.4 *Ground 2*

The appellant argued that the Assistant Minister failed to understand that it was necessary to consider non-refoulement obligations in making his decision because he assumed that obligations of that kind would be considered in the context of an application for a protection visa, which the Appellant would be able to make if he wished.[257] The appellant relied on the decision in *BCR16*, in which the Minister claimed that the appellant could make a valid application for a protection visa and non-refoulment obligations would be considered.[258] Direction 75, under s 499 of the Act, dictated that decision-makers should assess whether the refugee and protection criteria are met before considering ineligibility grounds that may diminish the possibility of acquiring a protection visa.[259] This was sufficient to indicate that the Assistant Minister did not have a misunderstanding regarding the 26 February 2018 decision.

Ground 2 failed.

8.5 *Ground 3*

The appellant argued that the Assistant Minister had not understood that the content of Australia's non-refoulement obligations differs in material respects from the criteria contained in s 36 of the Act.[260] Specifically, that the Assistant Minister conflated Australia's non-refoulment obligations with protection obligations considered on an application for a protection visa as present in s 36(2)(a) of the Act.[261] The Assistant Minister misapprehended this belief because only the criteria in s 36 are to be considered, creating a jurisdictional error in line with the majority opinion in *BCR16*.[262] The appellant was granted leave to argue Ground 3.

Ground 3 upheld.

---

255   *Migration Act 1958* (Cth) s 501BA(2).
256   *Ibrahim v Minister for Home Affairs* [59].
257   Ibid [97].
258   *BCR16 v Minister for Immigration and Border Protection* (2017) 248 FCR 456 ('*BCR16*').
259   *Ministerial Direction No.75—Refusal of Protection visas relying on section 36(1C) and section 36(2C)(b),* made under s 499 of the *Migration Act 1958 (Cth)* on 6 September 2017.
260   *Migration Act 1958* (Cth) s 36.
261   Ibid s 36(2)(a).
262   *BCR16* (n 272) [72].

The appeal was allowed, and a writ of certiorari was issued to the Assistant Minister for Home Affairs quashing the decision made on 26 February 2018 to cancel Mr Ibrahim's visa.[263]

> **Migration—Whether the Primary Judge Erred in Concluding that the Minister had not Fallen into Jurisdictional Error in Reasoning that it was Unnecessary to Determine Whether Non-Refoulement Obligations were Owed in Respect of the Appellant—Whether the Primary Judge Erred in Reaching the Conclusion that Non-Refoulement Considerations Would be (Necessarily, as a Matter of Law) Considered in Any Future Protection Visa Application that the Appellant Might Bring, Even if the Application were Determined by the Minister Personally— Considering Whether or Not, if the Appellant Made a Protection Visa Application, Non-Refoulement Obligations Would then be Fully Considered**

DOB18 v Minister for Home Affairs
[2019] FCAFC 63
Federal Court of Australia
Rares, Logan, and Robertson JJ

The appellant, a Bangladeshi national, has lived in Australia since 2000. On 16 November 2006 he was granted a Class XA subclass 785 temporary protection visa on grounds that he feared persecution by reason of his homosexuality.[264] This visa was replaced by a (permanent) subclass 851 resolution on November 2009.[265] On 27 April 2016, the appellant's visa was cancelled by a delegate of the Minister of Home Affairs following the appellant's conviction of drug offences, being the 'supply of prohibited drug greater than indictable quantity (not cannabis)'.[266] The appellant was sentenced to imprisonment for two years and eight months. The nature of the offence meant that cancellation of the appellant's visa was mandatory, although subject to an application to have the decision revoked.[267] Another delegate decided against the appellant's request for revocation, whereupon the appellant

---

263   *Ibrahim v Minister for Home Affairs* (n 241) [120].
264   *DOB18 v Minister of Home Affairs* [2019] FCAFC 63, [98] (*'DOB18'*).
265   Ibid [100].
266   Ibid [101].
267   *Migration Act 1958* (Cth) ss 501(3A), 501CA.

CASES CONCERNING QUESTIONS OF PUBLIC INTERNATIONAL LAW 2019   397

lodged an appeal to the Administrative Appeals Tribunal ('AAT'). The AAT set aside the delegate's decision on 24 November 2016 and ordered the revocation of the visa cancellation decision.[268] The appellant was released from immigration detention. Nonetheless, the Minister proceeded to cancel the appellant's visa on 15 February 2018 under s 501BA of the *Migration Act 1958* (Cth) ('the Act').

The appellant sought judicial review of this decision and the application was denied on 17 October 2018. He then appealed to the Full Federal Court, constituted by Rares, Logan and Robertson JJ, who delivered separate judgments. Logan and Robertson JJ were in substantive agreement (the majority), with Rares J in dissent.

8.6   *The Minister's Decision*

The Minister found that the appellant failed to pass the character test and that it was in the national interest to cancel his visa.[269] The Minister also accepted the appellant's claim that the latter would face hardship were he to return to Bangladesh.[270] The Minister contended that it was unnecessary to determine whether non-refoulement obligations are owed in respect of the appellant for the purpose of the decision to cancel his visa under s 501.[271] On the other hand, the Minister reasoned that non-refoulement obligations could be fully considered if and when the appellant made a valid application for a protection visa (which he was entitled to do).[272]

The appellant argued that the primary judge erred in two respects:

> [First,] in reaching the conclusion that non-refoulement considerations would be (necessarily, as a matter of law) considered in any future protection visa application that the appellant might bring, even if the application were determined by the Minister personally; [and]
>
> [second], in relying upon the different stages of decision-making under the Act. That reasoning had no regard to the qualitatively different role that non-refoulement obligations might play in the context of determining a protection visa application, compared to the role they might play in relation to a determination under s 501BA(2).[273]

---

268   *DOB18* (n 281) [101].
269   Ibid [103].
270   Ibid [106.82].
271   Ibid [106.80].
272   Ibid.
273   Ibid [114].

Robertson J and Logan J rejected both arguments, finding no error in the reasoning of the primary judge. Their Honours held that in determining issues around the cancellation of the appellant's visa on character grounds, the Minister was not bound to consider whether Australia had non-refoulement obligations in respect of the appellant.[274] Both judges accepted the Minister's assertion that these matters could be assessed in a future process after the appellant lodged an application for a protection visa.

In relation to the proposition that the appellant's options would be limited if the Minister were to make a decision personally, Robinson J found:

> The appellant appears to accept that the Minister made no jurisdictional error if as a matter of fact any future application for a protection visa is to be decided by persons other than the Minister, such as by officers of the Department.
>
> Since I have concluded that the Minister, at [80]–[81] of his reasons, was not setting out a legal proposition but a factual proposition as to the future if a protection visa application was made by the appellant, in my opinion it would be for the appellant at trial to show both that it was likely the Minister personally would make a decision on the protection visa application and that as a matter of fact the Minister would not consider the application of the protection specific criteria before proceeding with any consideration of other criteria. The appellant has not done this.[275]

Robertson J considered and distinguished the case of *BCR16*.[276] His Honour reasoned that no jurisdictional error had been committed in the way the Minister had acted. He found the Minister had appropriately completed his statutory task through his acceptance and consideration of the appellant's history, including the hardship he would face if returned to Bangladesh.[277] Moreover, his Honour ruled that where the Minister has assessed the prospect that an appellant is likely to apply for protection visa, references to non-refoulement obligations will not constitute a jurisdictional error.[278]

---

274   Ibid [38].

275   Ibid [168]–[169].

276   *BCR16 v Minister for Immigration and Border Protection* (2017) 248 FCR 456 ('*BCR16*').

277   *DOB18* (n 281) [193].

278   Ibid [185].

CASES CONCERNING QUESTIONS OF PUBLIC INTERNATIONAL LAW 2019   399

Logan J agreed with Robertson J and found that nothing in s 501BA of the Act expressly requires the Minister to take into account the subject of non-refoulement.[279]

In dissent, Rares J held that the Minister's failure to consider non-refoulement obligations in respect of the appellant did constitute a jurisdictional error.[280] His Honour reasoned that non-refoulement obligations necessarily arose in the consideration of national interest.[281]

The appeal was dismissed.

> **Migration—Whether the Meaning of 'a National' as Appears in the Definition of 'Receiving Country' in s 5 of the *Migration Act 1958* (Cth) Applies to a Person who Does Not Have a Present Status of a Citizen of Another Country but is Capable of Acquiring that Status—Meaning Does Not Apply in Such a Circumstance**
>
> **Practice and Procedure—Discretion of Judge Not to Grant Relief Notwithstanding Jurisdictional Error being Established—Whether Appeal Governed by Principles in *House v The King* (1936) 55 CLR 499—Error of Principle Established**
>
> *FER17 v Minister for Immigration, Citizenship and Multicultural Affairs*
> [2019] FCAFC 106
> Federal Court of Australia Full Court
> Kerr, White and Charlesworth JJ

The substantive issue in this case concerns the construction of the phrase 'a national' as it applies to the assessment of protection visas. It is the first Full Court of the Australian Federal Court ('FCAFC') to construe the term following the enactment of the *Migration and Maritime Powers Legislation Amendment (Resolving the Asylum Caseload Legacy) Act 2014* (Cth).[282] In a joint judgment, the Full Court determined that the scope of 'a national' does not extend to non-nationals who have the immediate capacity to acquire the status of a national. 'A national' means a person holding the status of citizen at a relevant time.

---

279   Ibid [39].
280   Ibid [34].
281   Ibid [19].
282   Refugee Legal, *Refugee Legal: Digest* (Digest No 5 of 2019) 40.

8.7 *Background*

The appellant arrived in Australia by boat in 2013 and thereafter applied for a Safe Haven Enterprise Visa ('SHEV').[283] His parents had fled the Sri Lankan civil war to India, where he was born in 1998. He claimed that during his upbringing in India, as a Tamil, he had suffered racial discrimination and was afraid to leave home other than to attend school.[284] The appellant also claimed that he did not hold Sri Lankan citizenship and had never resided in Sri Lanka.[285] He expressed fears that, were he to be returned to Sri Lanka, he would suffer political persecution, his father having previously been imprisoned in India for five years on suspicion of being a member of the Tamil Tigers.[286]

The appellant's claim was dismissed by a delegate of the Minister for Immigration, Citizenship and Multicultural Affairs (first respondent) on the basis that the circumstances did not rise to a level that would engage protection obligations.[287] The application was then automatically transferred for review to the Immigration Assessment Authority ('IAA') under Pt 7AA of the *Migration Act 1958* (Cth) ('the Act').[288] The IAA, satisfied that the appellant was born to Sri Lankan citizen parents, affirmed the delegate's decision, but did so on the basis that the appellant was a Sri Lankan national and that Sri Lanka was his 'receiving country'.[289]

Upon judicial review of the IAA's decision in the Federal Circuit Court of Australia ('FCCA'), the primary judge accepted the appellant's submission that the IAA had fallen into jurisdictional error.[290] The primary judge held that by recognising the appellant as a Sri Lankan national the IAA had misconstrued the *Citizenship Act 1948* (Sri Lanka) ('Citizenship Act'). Under s 5 of the Citizenship Act, persons born outside Sri Lanka must register their birth in a prescribed manner if they are to attain Sri Lankan citizenship.[291] The appellant's birth had not been so registered. The IAA had made an error material to its findings—hence, the jurisdictional error.

Nonetheless, the primary judge refused relief on discretionary grounds.[292] The primary judge determined that the appellant had failed to make any

---

283   *FER17 v Minister for Immigration, Citizenship and Multicultural Affairs* [2019] FCAFC 106, [5] (Kerr, White and Charlesworth JJ) ('*FER17*').
284   Ibid.
285   Ibid.
286   Ibid [6].
287   Ibid [7]–[8].
288   Ibid [9].
289   Ibid [10]–[13].
290   Ibid [14]–[15], [19]–[20].
291   *Citizenship Act 1948* (Sri Lanka) s 5.
292   *FER17* (n 300) [15], [22].

CASES CONCERNING QUESTIONS OF PUBLIC INTERNATIONAL LAW 2019   401

'substantial claims' with respect to India before the IAA. Therefore, by submitting to the FCCA that India ought to have been the 'receiving country' instead of Sri Lanka, the appellant's application for judicial review was regarded as lacking in 'genuineness or good faith'—hence, the discretionary decision.

This case concerned the appellant's appeal against the primary judge's decision to refuse relief on discretionary grounds and the Minister's cross-appeal in relation to the primary judge's determination that the IAA had fallen into jurisdictional error.

8.8   *The Appellant's Appeal—Allowed*

The FCAFC held that the primary judge had erred in principle when making a discretionary decision to refuse relief.[293] There was no basis for the primary judge to find that the appellant's application for judicial review had lacked 'genuineness or good faith'.[294] First, it was not open to the primary judge to characterise the appellant's claims with respect to India as 'belated'.[295] The plain fact was that *all* the appellant's claims were submitted, as they appeared before the Minister's delegate, to the IAA.[296] Second, even if it were accepted that the appellant had taken advantage of the IAA's error, it was not an error that the appellant had induced.[297] Therefore, given that the primary judge had acted upon a wrong principle, the discretionary decision to refuse relief was overturned.

8.9   *The Minister's Cross-Appeal—Dismissed*

The Minister's core contention was that the scope of 'a national', as it appears within the definition of 'receiving country' in s 5 of the Act, refers not only to existing nationals but to persons who possess the immediate capacity to acquire the status of a national.[298] Based on this construction of 'a national', the Minister submitted that the IAA had not committed a jurisdictional error when it equated the appellant's immediate capacity to attain Sri Lankan citizenship with existing Sri Lankan citizenship.[299]

The FCAFC rejected the Minister's construction of 'a national', affirming instead that the ordinary and natural grammatical meaning of 'a national' does not extend to persons who do not presently possess the status of a national,

---

293   Ibid [105].
294   Ibid [96]–[98].
295   Ibid [102].
296   Ibid.
297   Ibid [103].
298   Ibid [40]–[45].
299   Ibid.

even if such persons have the immediate means to become a national.[300] Therefore, the FCAFC upheld the primary judge's determination that the IAA had fallen into jurisdictional error by proceeding on the fundamentally mistaken basis that the appellant was a Sri Lankan national.

Whilst the Minister also submitted that the ambit of 'nationality' is wider than that of 'citizenship', the FCAFC expressed that it was neither necessary nor desirable to offer a concluded view on the matter.[301] However, in obiter dicta, the FCAFC noted that the correctness of such a proposition is not self-evident.[302]

Migration—Protection Visa—Complementary Protection Claim— Distinction between Personal Risk and Risk for General Population—*Migration Act 1958* (Cth), ss 36(2)(aa), 36(2B)(a), 36(2B)(c)

BCX16 v Minister for Immigration and Border Protection
[2019] FCA 465
Federal Court of Australia
Charlesworth J

The appellant was a citizen of Afghanistan and a former resident of Kabul. On 13 November 2012, the appellant applied to the Australian Government for a Protection (Class XA) visa ('visa') under the *Migration Act 1958* (Cth) ('the Act'). A delegate of the Minister for Immigration and Border Protection refused to grant the appellant a visa. On 8 January 2014, the appellant applied to the Administrative Appeals Tribunal ('the AAT') for merits review of the delegate's decision. The AAT affirmed the delegate's decision. On 16 February 2018, an application for judicial review of the AAT's decision was dismissed by the Federal Circuit Court ('FCC'). On appeal from the FCC to the Federal Court, the appellant succeeded in arguing that the AAT had committed jurisdictional error in its application of a carve-out provision in the Act relating to Australia's complementary protection obligations.

Where a person does not meet the definition of 'refugee' under the Act, the person may nevertheless receive a protection visa pursuant to the complementary protection criterion in s 36(2)(aa), namely, if the Minister is satisfied that Australia has protection obligations because there is a real risk that the person

---

300   Ibid [64].
301   Ibid [77].
302   Ibid.

will suffer significant harm if removed to a receiving country. This provision was introduced by the *Migration Amendment (Complementary Protection) Act 2011* (Cth) to give effect to Australia's non-refoulement obligations under the *International Covenant on Civil and Political Rights* ('ICCPR') and the *Convention Against Torture, and other Cruel, Inhuman, or Degrading Treatment or Punishment* ('UNCAT').[303] A carve-out provision, s 36(2B), was introduced alongside s 36(2)(aa). That section provides as follows:

> there is taken not to be a real risk that a non-citizen will suffer significant harm in a country if the Minister is satisfied that:
> (a) it would be reasonable for the non-citizen to relocate to an area of the country where there would not be a real risk that the non-citizen will suffer significant harm; or
> (b) the non-citizen could obtain, from an authority of the country, protection such that there would not be a real risk that the non-citizen will suffer significant harm; or
> (c) the real risk is one faced by the population of the country generally and is not faced by the non-citizen personally.

The appeal before Charlesworth J in the Federal Court concerned, amongst other things, a rather narrow question of construction regarding the exclusionary effect of s 36(2B)(c) of the Act. At the hearing before the AAT, the applicant had contended that he faced a real risk of significant harm owing to his place of residency in Kabul, where he would be caught in the middle of ongoing sectarian violence.[304] The AAT rejected this contention by invoking s 36(2B)(c), reasoning that the risk faced by the Appellant was a risk 'faced by the population generally, not by the applicant personally in this generalised violence context in that city'.[305]

Justice Charlesworth interpreted the AAT's reference to 'the population generally' as a reference to the population of Kabul and not the whole of Afghanistan, meaning that the AAT had failed to undertake the required task of comparing the circumstances of the appellant as a resident of Kabul with the circumstances of the population of the whole country.[306] According to her Honour, '[a] risk to which a person is exposed because of the circumstance

---

303   See Explanatory Memorandum, Migration Amendment (Complementary Protection and Other Measures) Bill 2015 (Cth).
304   *BCX16 v Minister for Immigration and Border Protection* [2019] FCA 465, [28].
305   Ibid [30].
306   Ibid [37]–[42].

404   AUSTRALIAN YEAR BOOK OF INTERNATIONAL LAW VOLUME 38

that he or she resides in a specific area of the country is ... a risk that is faced by the person personally, notwithstanding that other persons residing in the same area are exposed to the same risk'.[307] Her Honour reached this conclusion by reading s 36(2B)(c) together with s 36(2B)(a), the latter of which contemplates the possibility of different areas within a particular country posing different levels of risk to the general population.[308]

By only turning its mind to the level of violence faced by the population of Kabul, and not the whole of Afghanistan, the AAT misapplied s 36(2B)(c). On the basis of that jurisdictional error, Charlesworth J quashed the decision of the AAT and ordered the matter to be re-heard on its merits by a differently constituted AAT.

> **Migration—Where Minister Personally Refused Grant of Protection Visa under s 501(1) of the *Migration Act 1958* (Cth) because Applicant was Unacceptable Risk to Australian Community s 501(6)(d)(v)—Where Minister Found Applicant to be a Refugee and Australia Owed Applicant Protection Obligations—Where Minister Did Not Consider Legal Consequences of Refusal or What Would Happen if Refouled in Accordance with ss 197C and 198 of the *Migration Act 1958* (Cth)—Whether Minister Failed to Engage in an Intellectual Process—Where Applicant Had No Realistic Prospect of being Granted Another Visa—Material Jurisdictional Error—Whether General Powers under s 501 and Pt 9 of the *Migration Act 1958* (Cth) and Prescription of Public Interest Criteria (PIC) 4001 in cl 785.226 of *Migration Regulations 1994* (Cth) are Inconsistent with Specific Power in s 36(1C) of the *Migration Act 1958* (Cth)—Where Enactment of ss 36(1C) and 197C Intended to Codify Australia's Non-Refoulement and Protection Obligations under Arts 32 and 33 of the *Refugee Convention***

> *BAL19 v Minister for Home Affairs*
> [2019] FCA 2189
> Federal Court of Australia
> Rares J

The applicant, a Sri Lankan national of Tamil ethnicity, arrived in Australia by boat on 20 March 2010.[309] The applicant had been in detention since his date

---

307   Ibid [37].
308   Ibid.
309   *BAL19 v Minister for Home Affairs* [2019] FCA 2189, [1].

of arrival. He suffered from serious physical and mental health issues which included an eye condition that rendered him legally blind.[310] The Minister for Home Affairs ('Minister') accepted that Australia owed the applicant non-refoulement obligations.[311] However, on 12 July 2019, the Minister personally refused to grant the applicant a Temporary Protection (Subclass 785) visa ('protection visa') pursuant to the Minister's power under s 501(1) of the *Migration Act 1958* (Cth) ('the Act').[312]

8.10 *The Minister's Decision*

The Minister refused the applicant's protection visa application on grounds of bad character under s 501 of the Act.[313] The Minister acknowledged that the decision was made by him personally and that regard had been had to non-disclosable information. Section 501G(1)(e) of the Act provided that the Minister did not need to give the applicant the non-disclosable information. The Minister found that, 'if the applicant engaged, in the future, in some of his past behaviours, that may result in significant harm to members of the Australian community'.[314]

In refusing the visa, the Minister relied on the criterion provided in s 501(6) (d)(v) of the Act. He considered that factors in favour of refusal outweighed the factors in favour granting the visa.[315] This decision was reached by the Minister while he accepted that the applicant was a refugee who was also owed non-refoulement obligations.[316] In addition, the Minister acknowledged that the continuing detention of the applicant had attracted criticism from the Australian Human Rights Commission (AHRC) and the UN Working Group on Arbitrary Detention.[317]

The applicant applied for Constitutional writ relief at the Federal Court of Australia ('FCA') in respect to the Minister's decision.[318]

8.11 *Issues of the Case*

Justice Rares described the first issue (the failure to consider issue) as follows:

---

310   Ibid [17].
311   Ibid [1].
312   Ibid.
313   Ibid [14]. Section 501 of the *Migration Act 1958* (Cth) read together with relevant Public Interest Criteria (PIC) in Schedule 4 of the *Migration Regulations 1994* (Cth).
314   Ibid [15]. See also [16]–[18].
315   Ibid [22].
316   Ibid [24], setting out paras 91–7 of the Minister's reasons. See also [26].
317   Ibid [25].
318   Ibid [1].

whether the Minister failed to consider and weigh the legal and or practical consequences of removing the applicant from Australia when deciding to refuse to grant him the visa.[319]

The second broad question concerned the potential inconsistency between the rules governing public interest and criminal conduct in Part 9 of the Act, and Australia's protection obligations in s 36(1C) of the same Act (the inconsistency issue). Finally, the FCA considered 'whether there was any basis other than s 501 on which the Minister could have refused to grant the visa given that the applicant had satisfied the criterion in s 36(1C) and the Minister had found him to be a refugee (the outstanding criteria issue).[320]

8.12   *The Failure to Consider Issue*

The first issue concerned the extent, nature, and timing of the Minister's obligation to consider matters that were relevant to the applicant's refoulement under international law. The Minister contended that s 501(1) mandated consideration of the direct and immediate consequences of his decision in refusing the visa—but nothing more.[321] The Minister also argued that he was not obliged to consider remote and practical consequences that might flow from the legal consequences of his decision.[322] He disputed the applicant's assertion that the Minister was bound to consider the 'precise nature of the potential harm' faced by the applicant. This included, as the applicant mentioned, the possibility of being killed or seriously mistreated if returned to Sri Lanka.[323]

The complexity of the Act lay in the inclusion of Ministerial powers to override adverse decisions, and the presumption in ss 197C and 198 that the removal process would not involve consideration of non-refoulement obligations outside of a visa application process.

Justice Rares characterised the Minister's contentions (and the outcome they produced) as a 'Catch-22'.[324] Because the Minister found that the applicant failed to satisfy the s 50 character test, the Minister was unable to grant the applicant another visa (ie a bridging visa). The Minister was also unable to exercise his non-compellable power under s 48B to permit an application for

---

319   Ibid [3].

320   Ibid.

321   Ibid [28], citing *Taulahi v Minister for Immigration and Border Protection* (2016) 246 FCR 146 at 168 [84] and *NBMZ v Minister for Immigration and Border Protection* (2014) 220 FCR 1, 4–5 [6]–[10].

322   *BAL19 v Minister for Home Affairs* [2019] FCA 2189 [28].

323   Ibid.

324   Ibid [43].

another protection visa. This resulted in a situation where the applicant could not be returned to his country of origin due to non-refoulement obligations, while ss 197C and 198 operated to require his removal from Australia as soon as reasonably practicable.[325]

His Honour explained:

> The Minister referred to his awareness of the theoretical possibility that the applicant could apply for, *first*, a bridging visa and, *secondly*, if he (The Minister) exercised his compellable power under ss 48B and 195A, another visa. However, the grant of a bridging visa would not prevent ss 197C and 198 operating to require the removal of the applicant as soon as reasonably practicable, because it is not a substantive visa.[326]

Justice Rares found that outcome constituted a failure to engage in an 'active intellectual process' and a material error of law. His Honour found that the Minister was required to consider the legal and practical consequences of his decision. The failure to properly consider Australia's non-refoulement obligations to the applicant meant that this did not occur.[327]

8.13 *The Inconsistency Issue*

The Minister argued that s 36(1C) of the Act did not affect s 501 and its analogues in Part 9 of the Act as a source of power to refuse or cancel a protection visa.[328] Justice Rares disagreed. His Honour ruled that there would be no 'intelligible statutory purpose' in the creation of s 36(1C) and its mandatory criteria if the Minister could elect to bypass the section and apply the less stringent criteria in s 501(1) and its analogues.[329] Such a circumstance would mean that the non-refoulement obligations enshrined in s 36 would be of no useful function and would breach Australia's obligations under arts 32 and 33 of the *Convention relating to the Status of Refugees* ('the Refugees Convention').[330] After examining in detail amendments to the Act in and after 2014, Rares J ruled first that 'PIC 4001 is broader than s 36(1C) and, therefore, like PIC 4002

---

325 Ibid [44].
326 Ibid [41].
327 Ibid [49].
328 Ibid [57].
329 Ibid [67].
330 Ibid [71]. See *Convention relating to the Status of Refugees*, opened for signature 28 July 1951, 189 UNTS 150 (entered into force 22 April 1954) ('Refugee Convention'); *Protocol relating to the Status of Refugees*, opened for signature 31 January 1967, 606 UNTS 267 (entered into force 4 October 1967) ('Refugee Protocol').

in *Plaintiff M47* [2012] HCA 46; 251 CLR 1, is inconsistent with s 36(1C)'.[331] His Honour concluded further that the general provisions in s 501 did not vest the Minister with a power to refuse or grant or cancel a protection visa. He said:

> As the majority held in *Plaintiff M47* [2012] HCA 46; 251 CLR 1, prior to the 2014 Amendments, s 501 gave power to the Minister that was consistent with Arts 1F, 32 and 33 of the *Refugees Convention* **because** those articles were not statutory criteria for the grant of protection visa. But that position is no longer the case, as I have explained. Now, for the reasons I have given, s 501(6)(d)(v) (and PIC 4001 for that matter) is inconsistent with the specific criteria for a protection visa in s 36(1C).
>
> I am of opinion that, since 2014 Amendment, s 501(1) is not, and is not intended or expressed to be, relevant to determining whether or not a person, in accordance with ss 35A(6) and 36, is entitled to (or may be refused) under s 65(1) a protection visa as a refugee (as now defined in the Act) or to whom Australia otherwise owes protection obligations. Rather, s 36(1C) is a specific criterion applicable only to an applicant for a protection visa and it precludes the Minister using s 501(1) or its analogues as a basis to refuse to grant a protection visa: *Anthony Hordern* 47 CLR at 7; *Nystrom* 228 CLR at 571–572 [2].[332]

8.14   *The Outstanding Criteria Issue*

Justice Rares found against the Minister on whether there was any basis (with the exception of s 501) on which the Minister could refuse the grant of a visa given that the applicant satisfied the criterion in s 36(1C) and therefore was found to be a refugee. His Honour ruled that the Minister had failed to assess the national interest criterion in cl 785.227 of the *Migration Regulations 1994* (Cth).[333] His Honour stated:

> [T]his conclusion is another reason why the Minister's decision is invalid independently of my finding on the failure to consider issue. *Prima facie*, the application for the protection visa must be assessed in accordance only with the mandatory criteria in s 36 and cl 785.227 and the Minister cannot refuse the grant of the visa under s 501(1) or any other provision in Pt 9 of the Act. That is because the Minister has found that the applicant is a refugee having met the criteria in s 36 and is, subject to any relevant

---

331   Ibid [86].
332   Ibid [87]–[88].
333   Ibid [3].

CASES CONCERNING QUESTIONS OF PUBLIC INTERNATIONAL LAW 2019   409

application of cl 785.227, entitled to be granted a protection visa in accordance with s 65(1).[334]

Justice Rares held that the Minister's decision under s 501 of the Act be quashed and the Minister be required to make a prompt decision on the application for a visa according to law. His Honour also held that the Minister must pay the applicant's costs.[335]

9   Taxation

Taxation—Double Tax Agreement—Tax Free Threshold—Working Holiday Makers—Definition of Tax Resident

Addy v Commissioner of Taxation (Cth)
[2019] FCA 1768
Federal Court of Australia
Logan J

Applicant Catherine Addy ('the applicant') was a British citizen who was granted a Working Holiday (Temporary) (Class TZ) (Subclass 417) visa ('working holiday visa') in two instances.[336] The first grant permitted her to remain to Australia until July 2016, while the second gave her until August 2017. The Commissioner of Taxation ('Commissioner') issued to the applicant a series of notices of assessment—the last of which stated that the applicant was not entitled to the tax-free threshold she claimed.[337] The applicant lodged an objection with the Commissioner on the basis of Part 1 of Schedule 7 of the *Income Tax Rates Act 1986 (Cth)* ('Tax Rates Act') and art 25 of the Double Tax Agreement between Australia and the United Kingdom ('Double Tax Agreement').[338] For Australian tax residents Part 1 of Schedule 7 of the Tax Rates Act provides for a significant tax free threshold ($18,200) and then a graduated rate scale. Part III

---

334   Ibid [90].
335   Ibid [91].
336   *Addy v Commissioner of Taxation* [2019] FCA 1768, [1] ('*Addy*').
337   Ibid [12]–[13].
338   *Convention between the Government of Australia and the Government of the United Kingdom of Great Britain and Northern Ireland for the avoidance of double taxation and the prevention of fiscal evasion with respect to taxes on income and on capital gains and the exchange of notes relating to that convention,* signed 21 August 2003, [2003] ATS 22 (entered into force 17 December 2003) ('Double Tax Agreement').

410   AUSTRALIAN YEAR BOOK OF INTERNATIONAL LAW VOLUME 38

of this Act applies to working holiday makers and allows for no tax-free threshold; instead, a 15% tax rate applies to all income.

The applicant claimed that she was entitled to the tax-free threshold and reasoned that the 15% rate that was applied to her income was inconsistent with art 25(1) of the Double Tax Agreement. The applicant contended that 15% was a rate that was 'other or more burdensome' than the taxation that would be levied on a citizen of Australia who is also a tax resident.[339] The Commissioner disallowed the applicant's objection.[340] The applicant appealed to the Federal Court of Australia ('FCA') against the Commissioner's decision to disallow her objection. The FCA considered first whether the applicant was an Australian resident for income tax purposes and, secondly, whether the special working holiday maker rate scale was contrary to the principle of non-discrimination found in art 25 of the Double Tax Agreement.

Article 25(1) of the Double Tax Agreement provides:

> Nationals of a Contracting State shall not be subjected in the other Contracting State to any taxation or any requirement connected therewith, which is *other or more burdensome than the taxation* and connected requirement to which *nationals* of that other State in the same circumstances, in particular with respect to *residence*, are or may be subjected. (emphasis added)

Justice Logan considered the *Vienna Convention on the Law of Treaties* ('Vienna Convention') in giving meaning to the provision above.[341] His Honour identified arts 31(1) and 32 of the Vienna Convention as the principles that are better suited to interpret art 25(1) of the Double Tax Agreement.[342] In analyzing the ordinary meaning of the terms in light of its object and purpose, his Honour found that the evident purpose of art 25(1) is to prevent forms of discrimination—one of which is discrimination based entirely on one's nationality. In addition, his Honour made use of supplementary materials such as the Organisation for Economic Co-Operation and Development ('OECD') Model Tax Convention to further interpret the meaning of art 25(1).[343] His

---

339   *Addy* (n 353) [14].
340   Ibid [15].
341   *Vienna Convention on the Law of Treaties*, opened for signature 23 May 1969, 1155 UNTS 331 (entered into force 27 January 1980) ('Vienna Convention').
342   *Addy* (n 353) [89].
343   Ibid [96].

Honour agreed with the OECD commentary on the Model Convention,[344] confirming that the purpose of art 25(1) was to prevent discrimination between two individuals who are residents of the same State but are treated differently entirely due to difference in nationality.[345]

Ultimately, Logan J identified the case at hand as a situation where a non-citizen resident can hold a certain type of visa such as the working holiday visa (a visa that only non-citizens can hold) and is consequently taxed differently as her passport was not issued by the taxing State.[346] His Honour considered this a form of taxation discrimination based on nationality, which art 25(1) expressly prohibits.[347] The Court held that the applicant's tax must not be assessed at a 15% rate as provided in Part III of Schedule 7 of the Tax Rates Act, but rather Part I should apply. The effect of art 25(1) of the Double Taxation Agreement was to prevent a non-citizen resident from being taxed at a more burdensome rate than what would be levied on a citizen of Australia solely on the basis of nationality.[348]

> Taxation—Foreign Income Tax Offset—s 770–10 of the *Income Tax Assessment Act 1997* (Cth)—Where Taxpayer Paid Tax in the United States on Gains Made from the Sale of Certain Assets in that Country—Where Gains were Also Taxable in Australia—Where Gains were Derived on Capital Account for Australian Tax Purposes—Where 50% Capital Gains Tax Discount Applied—Where Commissioner Denied the Taxpayer a Foreign Income Tax Offset against His Tax Liability in Australia on the Gains to the Extent of Half of the Tax Paid in the United States—Whether the Capital Gains before the Application of Capital Losses and the Capital Gains Tax Discount were 'Included in' the Taxpayer's Assessable Income for the Purposes of s 770–10—Whether the Full Tax Paid in the United States on the Gains Was Paid 'in Respect of' the Australian Net Capital Gain for the Purposes of s 770–10

> Taxation—Treaty Interpretation—Art 22(2) of the Double Tax Convention between Australia and the United States—Where Art 22(2) of the Double Tax Convention between Australia and

---

344 Organisation for Economic Co-Operation and Development, *Commentaries on the Articles of the Model Tax Convention*, 21 November 2017, 332.

345 *Addy* (n 353) [102].

346 Ibid [104].

347 Ibid [101].

348 Ibid [116].

the United States Requires Australia to Allow as a Credit against Australian Tax the United States Tax Paid 'in Respect of Income Derived from Sources in the United States'—Whether the Gain Constitutes 'Income Derived from Sources in the United States'— Whether the Gain 'in Respect of' Which Tax is Paid Refers to the Whole of the Gain Taxed in the United States or the Discounted Gain Taxed in Australia—Where the Double Tax Convention was Incorporated into Australian law Pursuant to s 5 of the *International Tax Agreements Act 1953* **(Cth)—Whether There is an Inconsistency between Art 22(2) and s 770–10 of the** *Income Tax Assessment Act 1997* **(Cth)**

Burton v Commissioner of Taxation (Cth)
(2019) 372 ALR 293
Federal Court of Australia
Logan, Steward, and Jackson JJ

For the income years of 2011 and 2012, Australian tax resident and appellant Craig Burton derived capital gains from investments he made in the United States of America ('United States') as a trustee for an oil and gas company. The entirety of the capital gains was taxed under United States law and the tax was subsequently paid by the appellant.[349] However, due to the appellant's Australian residence, the gains were also subject to tax in Australia. Under the *Income Tax Assessment Act 1997* (Cth), the appellant was entitled to a 50% discount on his capital gains.[350] The appellant decided nonetheless to return the discounted gains in his income tax return and claim full credit for the amount of tax he paid in the United States. The appellant claimed entitlement of credit either as a foreign income tax offset ('FITO') under s 770–10 of the *Income Tax Agreements Act 1997* (Cth), or as a foreign tax credit ('FTC') under art 22(2) of the *Convention between the Government of Australia and the Government of the United States of America for the Avoidance of Double Taxation and the Prevention of Fiscal Evasion with respect to Taxes on Income* ('Convention'),[351] incorporated into Australian law under s 5 of the *International Tax Agreements Act 1953* (Cth).

Article 22(2) of the Convention states:

---

349   *Burton v Commissioner of Taxation* (2019) 372 ALR 293, [1] ('Burton').

350   *Income Tax Assessment Act 1997* (Cth), s 770–10.

351   *Convention between the Government of Australia and the Government of the United States of America for the Avoidance of Double Taxation and the Prevention of Fiscal Evasion with respect to Taxes on Income*, signed 6 August 1982, [1983] ATS 16, (entered into force 31 October 1983) ('Convention').

Subject to paragraph (4), *United States tax paid* under the law of the United States and in accordance with this Convention, other than United States tax imposed in accordance with paragraph (3) of Article 1 (Personal Scope) solely by reason of citizenship or by reason of an election by an individual under United States domestic law to be taxed as a resident of the United States, *in respect of income derived from sources in the United States by a person who, under Australian law relating to Australian tax, is a resident of Australia shall be allowed as a credit against Australian tax payable in respect of the income. The credit shall not exceed the amount of Australian tax payable on the income* or any class thereof or on income from sources outside Australia. Subject to these general principles, the credit shall be in accordance with the provisions and subject to the limitations of the law of Australia as that law may be in force from time to time.[352]

The appellant considered that on the basis of art 22(2) of the Convention, he was entitled to a full tax credit against his Australian tax liability. He reasoned that the purpose of the Convention was to avoid double taxation. However, the Commissioner of Taxation ('Commissioner') did not accept this assertion. The Commissioner maintained that the Convention's purpose in avoiding double taxation was achieved by the granting of a FITO or FTC of 50% of the US tax paid.[353] The appellant appealed against the Commissioner's decision to the Full Court of the Federal Court of Australia ('FCA').[354]

Justices Logan, Steward, and Jackson of the Full Court affirmed the approach of looking to the context of the treaty discussed in the case of *Thiel v Commissioner of Taxation*.[355] Their Honours referred to art 31 of the *Vienna Convention on the Law of Treaties* ('Vienna Convention'),[356] and considered that despite the United States not being a party to the Vienna Convention, its provisions on statutory interpretation still reflect customary rules of interpreting treaties.[357] Their Honours deemed it proper to have regard to the terms and context of the Convention in question, in light of its object and purpose.

---

352 Ibid (emphasis added).

353 *Burton* (n 366) [4].

354 *Taxation Administration Act 1953* (Cth) s 14zz.

355 (1990) 171 CLR 338.

356 *Vienna Convention on the Law of Treaties*, opened for signature 23 May 1969, 1155 UNTS 331 (entered into force 27 January 1980) ('Vienna Convention').

357 *Burton* (n 366) [49].

Justice Logan particularly identified avoidance of double taxation as one purpose of the Convention.[358] His Honour held that the appellant was entitled to the full credit for the US tax under art 22(2). Although Logan J concluded that the construction adopted by the primary judge in relation to s 770–10 that limited the offset was correct, art 22(2) still had primacy.[359] His Honour held that appeal should be allowed on those grounds.[360] Nevertheless, Steward J and Jackson J both rejected all grounds of appeal.

Justice Steward rejected the submission of the appellant and considered that the term 'double taxation' was not understood by the appellant in line with the Convention's context. His Honour found that in the context of art 22(2), double taxation occurs when the same amount is taxed by the different countries twice.[361] Furthermore, an instance will be considered as double taxation only when the two countries pursue taxing the same thing. Consequently, in a situation where one country taxes more aspects of a singular transaction than the other country, as contemplated in this case, double taxation does not exist.

Justice Jackson agreed with both Logan J and Steward J that the grounds of appeal regarding s 770–10 should not be upheld. In addition, His Honour also agreed with Steward J that the appellant's grounds of appeal regarding art 22(2) should be denied—to which Logan J dissented. The Full Court dismissed the appellant's appeal.[362]

---

358   Ibid [50].
359   Ibid [78].
360   Ibid [95].
361   Ibid [121].
362   Ibid [174].

Cases before International Courts and Tribunals concerning Questions of Public International Law Involving Australia 2019

Mary Crock,* Rowan Nicholson,** Corinne Lortie, Seric Han, Francis Manuel, Hae-Soo Park, Hannah Place and Gordon Yen

1 International Centre for Settlement of Investment Disputes (ICSID)—*Convention on the Settlement of Investment Disputes between States and Nationals of Other States (ICSID Convention)*—Article 52(1)(d)—Serious Departure from a Fundamental Rule of Procedure—Article 52(1)(b)—Manifest Excess of Power—Article 52(1)(e)—Failure to State Reasons[1]

Churchill Mining Plc and *Planet Mining Pty Ltd v Republic of Indonesia*
Decision on Annulment
ICSID Case No ARB/12/14 and ARB/12/40
Members of the *ad hoc* Committee
Judge Dominique Hascher, President
Professor Dr Karl-Heinz Böckstiegel
Ms Jean Kalicki
18 March 2019

On 18 March 2019, the *ad hoc* Committee ('Committee') issued its decision on an application for annulment of the Award rendered by the Tribunal on 6 December 2016 in the arbitration proceedings between Churchill Mining plc and its wholly owned Australian subsidiary, Planet Mining Pty Ltd (together

---

* Professor of Public Law at The University of Sydney Law School and Co-Director of the Sydney Centre for International Law ('SCIL').

** Lecturer at The University of Sydney Law School and Co-Director of the SCIL.

1 The summaries that follow were prepared by Professor Crock, Dr Nicholson and Sydney Law School students and SCIL interns Corinne Lortie, Seric Han, Francis Manuel, Hae-Soo Park, Hannah Place, and Gordon Yen. We wish to thank Chester Brown, Jeanne Huang, Ron McCallum, David Thorpe and Brett Williams for their comments and suggestions. Mary is happy to be accountable for any errors that remain.

© KONINKLIJKE BRILL NV, LEIDEN, 2021 | DOI:10.1163/26660229_03801021

the 'Applicants'), and the Republic of Indonesia (the 'Respondent', and together with the Applicants, the 'Parties').[2]

The Applicants through an Indonesian company undertook a mining project called the East Kutai Coal Project ('EKCP') in the Regency of East Kutai, Indonesia, in partnership with other Indonesian companies ('Ridlatama Companies').[3] The dispute in the arbitration proceedings arose out of the revocation of the Ridlatama coal exploitation licences.[4] There were initially two proceedings. The first proceedings were brought by Churchill Mining plc under the *Agreement between the Government of the United Kingdom of Great Britain and Northern Ireland and the Government of the Republic of Indonesia for the Promotion and Protection of Investments ('UK-Indonesia BIT')* and the *Convention on the Settlement of Investment Disputes between States and Nationals of Other States ('ICSID Convention')*. The second proceedings were brought by Planet Mining Pty Ltd under the *Agreement between the Government of Australia and the Government of the Republic of Indonesia for the Promotion and Protection of Investments ('Australia-Indonesia BIT')* and the *ICSID Convention*. The two proceedings were subsequently joined.[5] In an Award of 6 December 2016, the Tribunal which was constituted to determine the Applicants' claims found that 'a fraudulent scheme permeated the Claimants' investments in the EKCP'.[6] More specifically, the Tribunal concluded that the claims were 'based on documents forged to implement a fraud aimed at obtaining mining rights'.[7] As a result, the Tribunal held that all the claims before it were inadmissible.[8]

The Applicants applied for annulment of the Award on three grounds:

1. that the Tribunal seriously departed from a fundamental rule of procedure (Article 52(1)(d) of the *ICSID Convention*);

2. that the Tribunal manifestly exceeded its powers (Article 52(1)(b) of the *ICSID Convention*); and

3. that the Tribunal failed to state the reasons on which the Award was based (Article 52(1)(e) of the *ICSID Convention*).[9]

---

2 *Churchill Mining plc v Indonesia (Annulment)* (ICSID Arbitral Tribunal, Case No ARB/12/14 and ARB/12/40, Decision on Annulment, 18 March 2019) [1] ('*Churchill (Annulment)*').

3 Ibid [4].

4 Ibid.

5 Ibid [3].

6 *Churchill Mining plc v Indonesia (Annulment)* (ICSID Arbitral Tribunal, Case No ARB/12/14 and ARB/12/40, Award of 6 December 2016) [507].

7 Ibid [528].

8 Ibid [528]; *Churchill (Annulment)* (n 2) [6], [233].

9 *Churchill (Annulment)* (n 2) [7].

CASES CONCERNING QUESTIONS OF PUBLIC INTERNATIONAL LAW 2019

1.1 *Article 52(1)(d) of the ICSID Convention—Serious Departure from a Fundamental Rule of Procedure*

The 'right to be heard' and 'equal treatment of the parties' are fundamental rules of procedure.[10] The Committee held that in interpreting Article 52(1)(d), other sources including Article 17 of The United Nations Commission on International Trade Law ('UNCITRAL') Arbitration Rules (as revised in 2010) can be considered.[11] Article 17 states 'the parties are [to be] treated with equality and ... each party is [to be] given a reasonable opportunity of presenting its case'.[12] Following from this, the Committee stated that the right to be heard is not an absolute right and is subject to possible limitations that are 'reasonable and proportional to the aim to be achieved'.[13]

A serious departure from a fundamental rule of procedure is a departure that is 'substantial' and 'deprive[s] a party of the benefit of the protection which the rule was intended to provide'.[14] The Committee held that there is no requirement to prove that the departure has resulted in a different outcome in the case.[15]

The Applicants argued that the Tribunal seriously departed from fundamental rules of procedure in six respects, which are set out below; the Respondent argued that this was not the case.[16]

1.1.1 The *Minnotte* Direction

After the 2015 Hearing, the Tribunal had issued the *Minnotte* Direction, which instructed the Parties to provide their views on the Award in *Minnotte v Poland*,[17] a decision which none of the Parties had previously relied on, in relation to specific international law issues.[18] The specific issues were:

1. the admissibility in international law of claims tainted by fraud or forgery where the alleged perpetrator is a third party,
2. the lack of due care or negligence of the investor to investigate the factual circumstances surrounding the making of an investment, and
3. the deliberate closing of the eyes to indications of serious misconduct or crime, or an unreasonable failure to perceive such indications.[19]

---

10   Ibid [177].
11   Ibid [178].
12   Article 17 of the UNCITRAL Arbitration Rules (as revised in 2010).
13   *Churchill (Annulment)* (n 2) [178].
14   Ibid [180].
15   Ibid.
16   Ibid [114], [151].
17   *Minnotte v Poland (Award)* (ICSID Arbitral Tribunal, Case No ARB(AF)/10/1, 16 May 2014).
18   *Churchill (Annulment)* (n 2) [89], [152].
19   Ibid [183].

The Applicants argued that the theory underlying *Minnotte* had been excluded from the scope of the document authenticity phase, and thus the Tribunal surprised the Parties with issues that neither had anticipated.[20] As the Tribunal stated that the Parties could only provide their views on the basis of the existing evidence in the record, the Applicants claimed that the Tribunal precluded them from filing necessary further evidence and failed to provide them with an opportunity to present their case on the *Minnotte* factors.[21]

The Applicants had previously submitted evidence on due care and this evidence was included in the existing record.[22] The Applicants alleged the evidence was partial and not exhaustive because it had not been submitted in relation to the *Minnotte* Award.[23] However, the Committee stated that the fact that the Applicants had submitted evidence indicated they had the opportunity to do so, and as the Tribunal was satisfied the existing record contained sufficient evidence of the Applicants' due care, there was no obligation on the Tribunal to allow the Applicants to file further evidence.[24]

The Applicants argued that the existing record contained 'virtually no evidence' of 'wilful blindness' or the deliberate closing of the eyes to the fraud being perpetrated.[25] However, the Tribunal had not agreed, and had determined there was such evidence. The Committee stated that it could not review questions relating to the evaluation of evidence under Article 52 of the *ICSID Convention*.[26]

The Applicants also argued that the Tribunal should have inquired about the estoppel issue and the Applicants' good faith.[27] The Committee held that due to the seriousness of the forgery of the Ridlatama licences, the Tribunal did not need to hear about these issues.[28]

1.1.2   Whether Mr Noor's evidence was Re-Admitted and Given Weight

Another issue on which the Applicants sought to rely in their application under Article 52(1)(d) was the Tribunal's treatment of the evidence of one of the witnesses, Mr Noor. The Applicants claimed that the Tribunal had re-admitted and given weight to Mr Noor's witness statement, without notifying

---

20   Ibid [118].
21   Ibid [118], [181], [183], [185].
22   Ibid [119].
23   Ibid.
24   Ibid [186], [189].
25   Ibid [188].
26   Ibid.
27   Ibid [189].
28   Ibid [200].

or consulting with the Parties, when reaching its view that the Ridlatama Exploitation Licences had been signed on a 'misguided assumption'.[29] The Applicants also argued that the Tribunal had treated the Parties unequally because the Tribunal handled Mr Noor's evidence in this way, but favoured Indonesia by accepting their claim of privilege with respect to the production of Police Files.[30]

The Committee held that the Tribunal could have reached their view based only on Ridlatama's conduct, without resort to Mr Noor's witness statement. Thus the Committee ruled that it did not need to address whether the Tribunal notified or consulted with the Parties on the witness statement.[31] Regarding the claim of privilege, the Committee acknowledged that 'the obligation of the parties to cooperate with each other and with the tribunal in the production of evidence is a general principle of international arbitration'.[32] However, the Committee held that the 'duty to disclose evidence is ... not absolute, and national law concerns, such as the secrecy of criminal investigations relied on by Indonesia, can be put forward to limit full adversarial proceedings'.[33] The Tribunal did not unequally treat the Parties by accepting Indonesia's claim of privilege.[34]

1.1.3 The Burden of Proof in Relation to Fraud and Deception and the *Minnotte* Factors

Another ground for the Applicants' application under Article 52(1)(d) was its allegation that the Tribunal had reversed the burden of proof by placing the burden on the Applicants to disprove forgery and to prove the *Minnotte* factors.[35] In response, the Committee stated that it was an established principle of international law that each party bears the burden of proving the facts relied on in supporting their case.[36] However, the Committee also held that once a party proves the facts supporting their claim, the opposing party is then required to present proof supporting their denial of this claim.[37] The Committee stated that this is what had happened in the arbitration proceedings.[38]

---

29   Ibid [123]–[124], [207].
30   Ibid [210].
31   Ibid [209].
32   Ibid [211].
33   Ibid.
34   Ibid.
35   Ibid [126]–[127], [129], [213].
36   Ibid [215].
37   Ibid
38   Ibid.

1.1.4 The Infection Issue

The Applicants also sought to argue that the award should be annulled under Article 52(1)(d) because the Tribunal had, by denying them the right to be heard on the *Minnotte* factors, also denied their right to be heard on the Infection Issue. That is: 'whether the Exploitation Licences were stand-alone legal title instruments that, under Indonesian law, remained valid even if the underlying documents were forged'.[39] But the Committee held that the Applicants were not denied the right to be heard on the *Minnotte* factors and stated that the Tribunal had decided the case on grounds for which evidence of Indonesian law was not required.[40] Thus, the Applicants were not denied the right to be heard.[41]

1.1.5 Denial of Justice

Further, the Applicants also submitted that the Award should be annulled under Article 52(1)(d) because they had been denied the opportunity to argue that they had suffered a denial of justice before the Indonesian courts.[42] However, the Committee held that due to the fraudulent nature of the EKCP, the Tribunal was not required to hear this claim.[43]

1.1.6 State Responsibility

Finally as regards Article 52(1)(d), the Applicants argued that they were denied the opportunity to present arguments on State responsibility in relation to whether the State was complicit in the fraudulent scheme.[44] The Committee also rejected this claim, finding that the Applicants were not precluded from presenting evidence on State responsibility and that regardless, the Tribunal was not required to consider the international law of State responsibility as the Tribunal had determined that any possible assistance from a Regency insider would not excuse the fraud of Ridlatama, the principal actor.[45]

Thus, the Committee held that the Tribunal did not seriously depart from a fundamental rule of procedure.[46]

---

39 Ibid [130].
40 Ibid [225].
41 Ibid.
42 Ibid [133].
43 Ibid [226].
44 Ibid [134], [227]–[228].
45 Ibid [228]–[229].
46 Ibid [204].

1.2 *Article 52(1)(b) of the* ICSID Convention—*Manifest Excess of Powers*

A Tribunal manifestly exceeds its powers if it exercises its powers 'beyond the limits of its constituent instrument'.[47] The Tribunal's powers in these arbitration proceedings arose from the arbitration clause in the BITs, the *ICSID Convention* and the UNCITRAL Arbitration Rules (as revised in 2010).[48] The Committee stated that international arbitrators 'possess inherent powers for conducting the arbitration through procedural orders and directions' and that in accordance with Article 44 of the *ICSID Convention*, the Tribunal could decide on questions of procedures not covered by the agreement of the parties, *ICSID Convention* or UNCITRAL Arbitration Rules (as revised in 2010).[49] The Committee held there is 'a heavy threshold for demonstrating a manifest excess of powers with respect to the determination, interpretation and application of procedural rules by the tribunal'.[50] The Committee agreed with the *ad hoc* Committees in *Wena v Egypt*[51] and *Repsol v Petroecuador*[52] that the manifest excess of powers 'must be self-evident rather than the result of elaborate interpretation'.[53]

The Applicants argued the Tribunal manifestly exceeded its powers because of its failure to:

1. apply Indonesian Law to the Infection Issue,
2. apply the international law of State responsibility when deciding the case, and
3. address the Claimants' unjust enrichment claim and apply the international law of unjust enrichment.[54]

The Committee held that as all claims relating to the EKCP were inadmissible due to the fraudulent nature of the investment, the Tribunal did not need to address the Infection Issue or the unjust enrichment claim.[55] Regarding the State responsibility issue, the Committee stated that it was the Tribunal's role, and not the Committee's role, to determine the relevance of this issue.[56] The Committee held that as the Tribunal seemed to have implicitly considered

---

47   Ibid [239].
48   Ibid.
49   Ibid.
50   *Churchill (Annulment)* (n 2) [239].
51   *Wena Hotels Ltd v Egypt (Annulment)* (ICSID Arbitral Tribunal, Case No ARB/98/4, 5 February 2002).
52   *Repsol YPF Ecuador S.A v Empresa Estatal Petróleos del Ecuador (Petroecuador) (Annulment)* (ICSID Arbitral Tribunal, Case No ARB/01/10, 8 January 2007).
53   *Churchill (Annulment)* (n 2) [239].
54   Ibid [137].
55   Ibid [233].
56   Ibid [235].

422   AUSTRALIAN YEAR BOOK OF INTERNATIONAL LAW VOLUME 38

the Applicants' arguments on State responsibility and then rejected them, the Tribunal was not required to expressly consider the arguments.[57] Furthermore, the Committee stated that by arguing the Tribunal should still have expressly considered the arguments, the Applicants were in effect 'challeng[ing] ... the Tribunal's approach to admissibility' and this was not for the Committee to review.[58]

Thus, the Committee held that the Tribunal did not manifestly exceed its powers.[59]

1.3   *Article 52(1)(e) of the* ICSID Convention—*Failure to State Reasons*

The Applicants argued that the Tribunal failed to state the reasons on which the Award was based, with the result that the award was tainted by annullable error contrary to Article 52(1)(e), while the Respondent argued that this was not the case.[60] The Applicants advanced six issues under this ground for annulment, as follows:

First, the Applicants alleged that the Tribunal failed to state the reasons for re-admitting Mr Noor's evidence, but the Committee held that the Tribunal did not use Mr Noor's evidence to begin with.[61]

Secondly, the Applicants argued that the Tribunal failed to state the reasons for their dismissal of the Infection Issue, but the Committee held that 'there was no necessity to address the validity of the Exploitation Licences as a matter of Indonesian law, because the forgery was too serious'.[62]

Thirdly, the Applicants claimed that the Tribunal's award was arbitrary as it did not explain the standard against which the Applicants' due diligence was assessed.[63] However, the Committee held that the standard was explained.[64]

Fourthly, the Applicants argued that the Tribunal failed to state the reasons why they accepted Indonesia's claim of privilege with respect to the production of Police Files without drawing adverse inferences against Indonesia.[65] The Committee held that the Tribunal did not have to provide reasons for their decision to not draw adverse inferences because 'the reasonableness of

---

57   Ibid.
58   Ibid.
59   Ibid [240].
60   Ibid [142], [175]–[176].
61   Ibid [241].
62   Ibid [243].
63   Ibid [145], [244].
64   Ibid [244].
65   Ibid [145].

adverse inferences depends on the discretion of the tribunal' and it was indeed difficult for Indonesia to produce Police Files due to national law concerns.[66]

Fifthly, the Applicants claimed that the Tribunal dismissed their arguments on State responsibility without stating reasons.[67] However, the Committee held that the Tribunal implicitly considered the arguments and their analysis 'can reasonably be inferred from the terms in the decision'.[68]

Sixthly, and finally, the Applicants claimed that the Tribunal had dismissed their alternative claims—IP, denial of justice and substitute claims—without stating reasons.[69] The Committee held that the Tribunal provided reasons.[70] It was not a problem that the reasoning was brief as 'Article 52(1)(e) allows arbitrators a discretion as to the way they express their reasoning' as long as it is understandable by the parties.[71]

Thus, the Committee held that the Tribunal did not fail to state the reasons on which the Award was based.[72]

1.4   *Conclusion*

As the Committee held that the Tribunal did not seriously depart from a fundamental rule of procedure, manifestly exceed its powers or fail to state the reasons on which the Award was based, the Committee dismissed the Annulment Application in its entirety. The Stay of Enforcement of the Award was terminated pursuant to Article 52(5) of the *ICSID Convention* and Rule 54(3) of the ICSID Rules of Procedure for Arbitration Proceedings (Arbitration Rules) 2006.

2   **Investor-State Dispute Settlement—ICSID Arbitration— Australia—Pakistan BIT—Standard of Compensation for Unlawful Expropriation and Other Breaches—Causation—Standard and Burden of Proof—Income-Based Valuation Method for Loss of Profits in Mining Projects**

Tethyan Copper Company Pty Limited v Islamic Republic of Pakistan (Award)

---

66   Ibid [211], [245].
67   Ibid [145].
68   Ibid [249].
69   Ibid [250].
70   Ibid [254].
71   Ibid.
72   Ibid [257].

ICSID Case No ARB/12/1
ICSID Arbitral Tribunal
12 July 2019

This case concerned a dispute between Tethyan Copper Company Pty Limited ('Tethyan'), a company incorporated in Australia, and the Islamic Republic of Pakistan ('Pakistan'). The dispute related to Tethyan's investment in a mining project (the 'Reko Diq Project') in Pakistan.

On 28 November 2011, Tethyan submitted the dispute to the International Centre for Settlement of Investment Disputes ('ICSID'),[73] invoking the *Agreement between Australia and Pakistan on the Promotion and Protection of Investments ('Australia-Pakistan BIT')*[74] and the *Convention on the Settlement of Investment Disputes between States and Nationals of Other States ('ICSID Convention').*[75]

On 10 November 2017, the ICSID Tribunal ('Tribunal') determined that it had jurisdiction to hear the claims and that the claims were thus admissible.[76] It also found that by denying the Mining Lease Application to Tethyan's subsidiary in Pakistan in order to allow instead the provincial government to implement its own mining project, Pakistan had breached its obligations under three provisions of the *Australia-Pakistan BIT*. Pakistan had:

1. breached its obligation to accord Tethyan fair and equitable treatment under Article 3(2);

2. carried out a measure having effect equivalent to expropriation that did not comply with the requirements for a lawful expropriation under Article 7(1); and

3. impaired the use of Tethyan's investment in violation of Article 3(3).[77]

The Award issued on 12 July 2019 concerned the quantum phase of the proceeding.

The principal issues in the quantum phase arose from the fact that Tethyan's investment in the Reko Diq Project had not yet entered the operational stage

---

73   *Tethyan Copper Company Pty Ltd v Pakistan (Award)* (ICSID Arbitral Tribunal, Case No ARB/12/1, 12 July 2019) [9].

74   *Agreement between Australia and the Islamic Republic of Pakistan on the Promotion and Protection of Investments*, signed 7 February 1998, [1998] ATS 23 (entered into force 14 October 1998).

75   *Convention on the Settlement of Investment Disputes between States and Nationals of Other States*, opened for signature 18 March 1965, 575 UNTS 159 (entered into force 14 October 1966).

76   *Tethyan Copper Company Pty Ltd v Pakistan (Jurisdiction and Liability)* (ICSID Arbitral Tribunal, Case No ARB/12/1, 10 November 2017) [688].

77   Ibid [1373].

CASES CONCERNING QUESTIONS OF PUBLIC INTERNATIONAL LAW 2019 425

at the time of Pakistan's breaches of the *Australia-Pakistan BIT*. This generated considerable uncertainty over the feasibility and profitability of the Reko Diq Project. Against this backdrop, the parties disagreed in the quantum phase on several key issues including:

1. the standard of compensation;
2. causation;
3. the standard and burden of proof; and
4. the appropriate valuation method for determining the value of Tethyan's investment and accordingly the amount of compensation to which Tethyan was entitled.[78]

The Tribunal first addressed the relevant legal issues before moving on to analyse the factual matters.

2.1 *Applicable Standard of Compensation*

There was common ground between the parties that Tethyan's losses should be quantified on the basis of the 'market value' of Tethyan's investment as of the date on which the breach was committed.[79] However, as to the determination of that market value, the parties disagreed on whether the applicable standard of compensation should be that provided for under Article 7(2) of the *Australia-Pakistan BIT* or the standard of full reparation under customary international law.[80]

Although the Tribunal indicated its agreement with Tethyan that the wording of Article 7(2) suggests that the provision is at least primarily intended to apply to calculating compensation under the legality requirements set out in Article 7(1), it reserved its opinion on whether the provision should further apply to the calculation of compensation for an unlawful expropriation or other breaches.[81] Based on its interpretation of Article 7(2), the Tribunal found that the two standards would lead to substantive differences only if the so-called 'modern DCF'[82] valuation method favoured by Tethyan did not produce a 'readily ascertainable' result.[83] Following further analysis, it concluded that

---

78 *Tethyan (Award)* (n 73) [189].
79 Ibid [272]–[274].
80 Ibid [276].
81 Ibid.
82 Ibid [216].
83 Ibid [279]; Article 7(2) provides:

2. The compensation referred to in paragraph 1(c) of this Article shall be computed on the basis of the market value of the investment immediately before the expropriation or impending expropriation became public knowledge. Where that value cannot be readily ascertained, the compensation shall be determined in accordance with generally recognised principles of valuation and equitable principles taking into account the capital

in the circumstances of this case the said method was 'the most appropriate measure to value [Tethyan]'s investment'.[84] However, the Tribunal nonetheless decided to use the standard favoured by Pakistan—which translates into the past-transaction-based valuation method relied on by Pakistan[85]—to verify whether the result produced by Tethyan's modern DCF method was reconcilable with the amount of Tethyan's invested capital.[86]

2.2 *Causation*

There was no dispute that Tethyan had to prove the casual relationship between Pakistan's breaches of the *Australia-Pakistan BIT* and its loss,[87] and that Tethyan was entitled to compensation equal to the value that its investment would have had but for Pakistan's breaches.[88] However, Tethyan contended that causation had already been established in the liability phase.[89]

Having recalled its relevant finding in the liability phase,[90] the Tribunal concluded that although '[Pakistan]'s conduct has deprived [Tethyan] of the value of its investment and had thereby caused a loss that is equal to the value that [Tethyan]'s investment would have had' but for Pakistan's breaches, no finding had been made as to 'specific aspects of causation.'[91] These aspects included, inter alia, the feasibility of the Reko Diq Project, and the assumptions made by Tethyan and its valuation expert, including in the feasibility studies completed prior to the commencement of the ICSID arbitral proceeding.[92] The Tribunal also pointed out the need to determine whether a mineral agreement regarding the exploitation of the relevant mineral resources would have been concluded after the valuation date and, if so, on what terms.[93]

2.2 *Standard and Burden of Proof*

It was not disputed that Tethyan bore the onus of proving its loss,[94] but the parties disagreed on the applicable standard of proof.[95] Tethyan contended

---

  invested, depreciation, capital already repatriated, replacement value, and other relevant factors.

84 *Tethyan (Award)* (n 73) [281], [303]–[365].
85 Ibid [112].
86 Ibid [281].
87 Ibid [282].
88 Ibid [275], [286].
89 Ibid [282].
90 Ibid [283].
91 Ibid [284].
92 Ibid.
93 Ibid [285].
94 Ibid [287].
95 Ibid [288].

CASES CONCERNING QUESTIONS OF PUBLIC INTERNATIONAL LAW 2019   427

that a distinction should be drawn between the fact of the loss and the quantum of the loss—the 'normal standard of the balance of probabilities' applies to the former, whereas a 'reasonable basis' would be sufficient for the latter.[96] Pakistan's position was less clear. It submitted that Tethyan must prove both the fact and the quantum of its losses 'with reasonable, or sufficient, certainty.'[97] It might also have argued that Tethyan had to meet a higher standard of 'absolute certainty' due to the fragility of the modern DCF model,[98] but the Tribunal rejected this higher standard as it was not supported by any authority and practically near-impossible to satisfy.[99]

The Tribunal closely examined the arguments made and authorities[100] cited by the legal experts on both sides, and concluded that 'the standards invoked by the Parties are in fact not too far apart',[101] and the real dispute concerned the appropriateness of the modern DCF method in this case—in other words, whether 'the valuation method used by [Tethyan] and its expert yields results that are not "too speculative" or "too uncertain" but rather enable the Tribunal to assess [Tethyan]'s damages "with reasonable confidence" and reach a "reliable" conclusion.'[102]

Another issue in contention was whether the Tribunal should consider the extent to which any uncertainties in the valuation resulted from Pakistan's breaches.[103] The tribunals in *Crystallex International Corporation v Venezuela* ('*Crystallex*')[104] and *Gemplus SA v Mexico*[105] had indicated that this might or should be a consideration,[106] but Pakistan's legal expert disagreed and argued that certain 'fundamental uncertainties' must be 'resolved in favour of [Tethyan] on the basis of the applicable standard of proof' before the DCF method can be relied on.[107]

---

96 Ibid.
97 Ibid.
98 Ibid [289].
99 Ibid [290].
100 See *Crystallex International Corporation v Venezuela* (*Award*) (ICSID Arbitral Tribunal, Case No ARB(AF)/11/2, 4 April 2016) [869]–[871], [873]–[876] ('*Crystallex*'); *Lemire v Ukraine* (*Award*) (ICSID Arbitral Tribunal, Case No ARB/06/18, 28 March 2011) [246], [248] ('*Lemire*').
101 *Tethyan* (*Award*) (n 73) [296].
102 Ibid [298].
103 Ibid [299].
104 *Crystallex* (n 100).
105 *Gemplus SA v Mexico* (*Award*) (ICSID Arbitral Tribunal, Case No ARB(AF)/04/3, 16 June 2010) [13]–[99].
106 *Tethyan* (*Award*) (n 73) [299].
107 Ibid [300].

The Tribunal refused to discuss this point in the abstract, but indicated that in the specific context of certain risks and uncertainties, it would consider whether there was 'an evidentiary uncertainty which has been caused by [Pakistan] and might therefore justify alleviating [Tethyan]'s burden of proof.'[108] It further concluded that there were no 'fundamental uncertainties' that would preclude the application of the modern DCF model.[109]

2.4 *Appropriate Valuation Method*

The practical effect of the contentions over the above-mentioned legal issues, in particular the standard of compensation and the standard of proof, largely boiled down to whether the income-based 'modern DCF model' relied on by Tethyan or the 'past-transaction-based method' used by Pakistan was the appropriate valuation method in the circumstances of the case. The valuation results of the Reko Diq Project presented by the parties applying the two methods respectively have a significant difference of USD$8.3508 billion.[110] As Pakistan's past-transaction-based valuation was intended 'to challenge, and not to cure' Tethyan's valuation,[111] the Tribunal decided to first assess the appropriateness of the modern DCF model; if the Tribunal accepted the appropriateness of that model, it would then make its own conclusion on the value of the Reko Diq Project on the basis of that method.[112] Finally, the Tribunal explained that it would assess whether any reasonable grounds existed for any remaining differences from the result produced by Pakistan's method.[113]

The Tribunal began its assessment of the appropriateness of the modern DCF model by first considering whether it was appropriate to value the Reko Diq Project based on a projection of future cash flows. The Tribunal agreed with the parties that this question 'cannot be answered in the abstract, ie, for any given development-stage project at a certain defined stage',[114] but must be answered 'on a case-by-case basis'.[115] Having reviewed several comparable cases,[116] the Tribunal concluded that an income-based valuation method

---

108 Ibid [301]. Note that the Tribunal later applied this principle in the context of determining whether a mineral agreement would have been concluded: at [414].

109 *Tethyan (Award)* (n 73) [301].

110 Tethyan put the value at USD 8.5 billion plus interest whereas Pakistan submitted it should not exceed USD 149.2 million: see *Tethyan (Award)* (n 73) [86], [127].

111 *Tethyan (Award)* (n 73) [305].

112 Ibid [306].

113 Ibid.

114 Ibid [309].

115 Ibid [310].

116 *Gold Reserve Inc v Venezuela (Award)* (ICSID Arbitral Tribunal, Case No ARB(AF)/09/1, 22 September 2014) [830]–[834] ('*Gold Reserve*'); *Crystallex* (n 100) [878]–[884], [896];

was appropriate for a project that had not entered the operational stage if: (i) but for the respondent's breaches the project would have become operational and also profitable;[117] and (ii) the inputs for the calculation presented by the parties provide 'a reasonable basis to determine the future cash flows of [the investment] with a reasonable amount of confidence.'[118]

The Tribunal further explained that it would first look at whether there were 'fundamental uncertainties' in light of which it was 'not convinced that the project would have reached the operational stage and would have been able to generate profits'.[119] If such 'fundamental uncertainties' existed, the DCF method would not be applicable, otherwise it would proceed to assess the inputs provided by the parties' experts.[120] If the Tribunal was not convinced by those inputs, 'it may conclude that it cannot apply the DCF method or it may conclude that certain deductions have to be made to account for additional risks or uncertainties faced by the project.'[121]

Based on the facts, the Tribunal concluded that no fundamental uncertainties existed that would prevent the Reko Diq Project from becoming operational and profitable,[122] and that the inputs presented by Tethyan's expert provided the Tribunal with a reasonable basis to determine the project's future cash flows (although certain adjustments had to be made to such inputs).[123] Accordingly, the Tribunal found that a forward-looking DCF method was appropriate in this case.[124]

The Tribunal then discussed whether Tethyan's 'modern DCF model', which was different from a traditional DCF method,[125] was appropriate in this case. The Tribunal noted that this approach had not yet been adopted by any

---

Rusoro Mining Ltd v Venezuela (*Award*) (ICSID Arbitral Tribunal, Case No ARB(AF)/12/5, 22 August 2016) [758]–[760], [785]–[786] (*'Rusoro'*); *Khan Resources Inc v Mongolia* (*Award on the Merits*) (Permanent Court of Arbitration, Case No 2011–09, 2 March 2015) [390]–[393] (*'Khan Resources'*); *Bear Creek Mining Corporation v Peru* (*Award*) (ICSID Arbitral Tribunal, Case No ARB/14/21, 30 November 2017) [599]–[600] (*'Bear Creek'*); *Compañía de Aguas del Aconquija SA and Vivendi Universal v Argentina* (*Award*) (ICSID Arbitral Tribunal, Case No ARB/97/3, 20 August 2007) [8.3.4]–[8.3.5], [8.3.7]–[8.3.8], [8.3.10] (*'Vivendi'*).

117 *Tethyan* (*Award*) (n 73) [330].
118 Ibid [334].
119 Ibid [330].
120 Ibid.
121 Ibid.
122 Ibid [331]–[333].
123 Ibid [334]–[335].
124 Ibid [335].
125 One of the key differences is that instead of using a constant risk-adjusted discount rate for all future cash flows of a project, the modern DCF model applies at-source pricing of

investment arbitration tribunal for a mining project.[126] However, it considered that 'the absence of investment treaty jurisprudence—affirmative or negative—does not in itself constitute a valid ground for rejecting a valuation method if the Tribunal is otherwise convinced' that the method is appropriate.[127] Having considered the evidence—giving particular weight to an explanatory letter by the Special Committee of the Canadian Institute of Mining, Metallurgy and Petroleum on Valuation of Mineral Properties[128]—the Tribunal concluded that the modern DCF method was appropriate in the case of the Reko Diq Project, subject to necessary changes to risk adjustments.[129] The Tribunal also reiterated that it would verify the result of the modern DCF method with other alternative approaches.[130]

2.4 Risks, Adjustments and Verification

Having determined the above legal issues and adopted the modern DCF model, the Tribunal went on to examine a wide range of issues, risks and uncertainties raised by Pakistan challenging the feasibility and profitability of the Reko Diq Project.[131] Following this extensive analysis,[132] the Tribunal found that Tethyan would have concluded a mineral agreement with the local and national governments of Pakistan and further that the feasibility and profitability of the Reko Diq Project was established.[133] However, due to several differences between the Tribunal's findings and the relevant assumptions in Tethyan's valuation, Tethyan's damages were reduced by an amount of USD$1,843 million.[134] The Tribunal further considered systematic and asymmetric risks affecting the Reko Diq Project[135] and made a further reduction of USD$2.560 million to fully account for such risks.[136]

As foreshadowed, having made its own conclusion on the value of the Reko Diq Project applying the modern DCF model, the Tribunal then used

---

      risk at the level of each income stream, coupled with a risk-free discount rate for cash flows so adjusted: see *Tethyan (Award)* (n 73) [341]–[343].

126   *Tethyan (Award)* (n 73) [359].

127   Ibid [360].

128   This is because the Tribunal considers it 'good evidence of the valuation methodology likely in practice to have been used by an actual buyer in the limited market for large-scale mining enterprises at the relevant time': *Tethyan (Award)* (n 73) [348].

129   Ibid [361]–[364].

130   Ibid [365].

131   Ibid [366]–[1420].

132   It takes up 355 pages of the *Award*.

133   *Tethyan (Award)* (n 73) [1421].

134   Ibid [1422].

135   Ibid [1423]–[1599].

136   Ibid [1600].

CASES CONCERNING QUESTIONS OF PUBLIC INTERNATIONAL LAW 2019   431

alternative methods—including Pakistan's past-transaction-based approach and an expansion pre-feasibility study—to verify that result,[137] and it concluded that the deviations can be explained through reasonable grounds.[138]

2.6   Award

Finally, the Tribunal made the last determinations on interests and costs and awarded Tethyan USD$4.087 billion as the principal amount of compensation, along with interest and costs.[139]

3   **Geographic Location of Mauritius in the Indian Ocean—Chagos Archipelago, Including the Island of Diego Garcia, Administered by the United Kingdom During Colonization as a Dependency of Mauritius—Adoption on 14 December 1960 of the Declaration on the Granting of Independence to Colonial Countries and Peoples (General Assembly Resolution 1514 (XV))—Establishment of the Special Committee on Decolonization ('Committee of Twenty-Four') to Monitor the Implementation of Resolution 1514 (XV)—Lancaster House Agreement between the Representatives of the Colony of Mauritius and the United Kingdom Government regarding the Detachment of the Chagos Archipelago from Mauritius—Creation of the British Indian Ocean Territory ('BIOT'), Including the Chagos Archipelago—Agreement between the United States of America and the United Kingdom Concerning the Availability of the BIOT for Defence Purposes—Adoption by the General Assembly of Resolutions on the Territorial Integrity of Non-Self-Governing Territories—Independence of Mauritius—Forcible Removal of the Population of the Chagos Archipelago—Request by Mauritius for the BIOT to be Disbanded and the Territory Restored to It—Creation of a Marine Protected Area around the Chagos Archipelago by the United Kingdom—Challenge to the Creation of a Marine Protected Area by Mauritius before an Arbitral Tribunal and Decision of the Tribunal**

Legal Consequences of the Separation of the Chagos Archipelago from Mauritius in 1965
(Advisory Opinion)

---

137   Ibid [1602]–[1742].
138   Ibid [1693]–[1742].
139   Ibid [1743]–[1858].

[2019] ICJ Rep 169
Present: President Yusuf; Vice-President Xue; Judges Tomka, Abraham, Bennouna, Cançado Trindade, Donoghue, Gaja, Sebutinde, Bhandari, Robinson, Gevorgian, Salam, Iwasawa; Registrar Couvreur
25 February 2019

On 22 June 2017, the United Nations General Assembly ('UNGA') adopted Resolution 71/292, requesting the International Court of Justice ('ICJ') to render an advisory opinion on the following questions:

1. Was the process of decolonisation of Mauritius lawfully completed when Mauritius was granted independence in 1968, following the separation of the Chagos Archipelago from Mauritius and having regard to international law, including obligations reflected in General Assembly resolutions 1514 (XV) of 14 December 1960, 2066 (XX) of 16 December 1965, 2232 (XXI) of 20 December 1966 and 2357 (XXII) of 19 December 1967?

2. What are the consequences under international law, including obligations reflected in the above-mentioned resolutions, arising from the continued administration by the United Kingdom of Great Britain and Northern Ireland of the Chagos Archipelago, including with respect to the inability of Mauritius to implement a programme for the resettlement on the Chagos Archipelago of its nationals, in particular those of Chagossian origin?

3.1   *Background*

The Chagos Archipelago consists of a number of islands and atolls located 2,200 km northeast of the main island of Mauritius. It was administered by the United Kingdom ('UK') as a dependency of the colony of Mauritius between 1814 and 1965. In 1964, the UK began discussions with the United States of America and the Premier of Mauritius separately regarding the detachment of the Chagos Archipelago from Mauritius and allowing the US to establish military facilities on the Chagos Archipelago. These discussions led to an agreement in 1965, known as the Lancaster House agreement, in which the Premier of Mauritius agreed to detach the Chagos Archipelago from Mauritius. While Mauritius became an independent State in 1968, the Chagos Archipelago formed part of a new UK colony known as the British Indian Ocean Territory ('BIOT'). The inhabitants of the Chagos Archipelago were forcibly removed from the islands and prevented from returning to the islands. US military facilities were installed on the main BIOT island, Diego Garcia. At the time the advisory opinion was delivered in February 2019, the Chagossians remained dispersed in several countries. By virtue of UK laws, they have been prevented from returning to the Chagos Archipelago. The case represents a significant development following the failure of a series of challenges made through UK domestic courts.[140]

3.2 Australia's Challenge on ICJ's Jurisdiction and Discretion

Australia, along with numerous other states, made submissions during the proceedings before the ICJ. On 27 February 2018, Australia argued in its written statement that the ICJ did not have jurisdiction to give an advisory opinion on the questions raised in this case. It contended that while the questions ostensibly concerned decolonisation, their true purpose and effect was to seek the ICJ's adjudication of a question of sovereignty. Australia argued that there was a lack of clarity in the 'legal question' upon which the opinion of the Court is sought, such that it had no jurisdiction to determine the matter.[141] Even if the ICJ had jurisdiction, Australia urged that the ICJ should exercise its discretion and refuse to give an advisory opinion because:

1. both the UK and Mauritius had not consented to the ICJ to resolve the dispute;
2. the UNGA lacked a sufficient interest in the subject matter of the opinion sought; and
3. the factors previously identified weighing in favour of providing an advisory opinion were not present.[142]

The ICJ rejected both arguments. In relation to the Court's jurisdiction, the Court observed that the two questions were genuine legal questions on which the Court's opinions were sought.[143] Even if the questions were unclear, the Court reaffirmed that it could depart from the language of the question when giving its opinion.[144] In relation to the Court's discretion, the Court did not find that there were any compelling reasons for it to decline to give the opinion.[145]

---

140 See, eg, *Chagos Islanders v The Attorney General* [2003] EWHC 2222 (QB), *R (Bancoult) v Secretary of State for Foreign and Commonwealth Affairs (No 2)* [2008] UKHL 61; [2009] AC 453 and most recently in *R (Bancoult) v Secretary of State for Foreign and Commonwealth Affairs (No 4)* [2016] UKSC 35; [2017] AC 300.

141 'Written Statement of the Government of Australia', *Legal Consequences of the Separation of the Chagos Archipelago from Mauritius in 1965 (Advisory Opinion)* [2019] ICJ Pleadings, 4.

142 Ibid 6.

143 *Legal Consequences of the Separation of the Chagos Archipelago from Mauritius in 1965 (Advisory Opinion)* [2019] ICJ Rep 169.

144 Ibid [134].

145 Ibid [91].

3.2.1 Question One: Was the Process of Decolonisation of Mauritius Lawfully Completed in 1968?

In order to answer this question, the ICJ first had to determine the applicable international law, namely the nature, content and scope of the right to self-determination, at the time Mauritius was granted independence. The Court considered that the adoption of Resolution 1514 (XV) of 14 December 1960 in the UNGA represents a defining moment in the consolidation of state practice and *opinio juris* on decolonisation and thus its content represents the scope and content of the right to self-determination as customary international law at the time in question.[146]

The Court emphasised that Resolution 1514 (XV) not only affirms the right to self-determination, but it also provides that the transfer of powers to the peoples of non-self-governing territories should be 'without any conditions or reservations' and that any attempt aimed at the partial or total disruption of the national unity and territorial integrity of a country is incompatible with the purposes and principles of the *Charter of the United Nations*.[147] In other words, both state practice and *opinio juris* at the time confirmed the customary law character of the right to territorial integrity as a corollary of the right to self-determination.[148] It followed that unless the detachment of part of a non-self-governing territory is based on the freely expressed and genuine will of the people of the territory concerned, it is contrary to the right to self-determination.

A review of historical records clearly indicated that the Chagos Archipelago was an integral part of Mauritius in 1965.[149] The Court held that the Lancaster House agreement in 1965 was invalid.[150] This was because the Court considered that it is impossible to treat the agreement as an international agreement when one of the parties to it was under the authority of the other.[151] Thus, the detachment of the Chagos Archipelago and its incorporation into the new colony, BIOT, as a result of the Lancaster House agreement was not based on a free and genuine expression of the will of the Mauritian people and the process of decolonisation of Mauritius was not lawfully completed in 1968.[152]

---

146   Ibid [150].
147   Ibid [153].
148   Ibid [160].
149   Ibid [170].
150   Ibid [172].
151   Ibid.
152   Ibid [174].

CASES CONCERNING QUESTIONS OF PUBLIC INTERNATIONAL LAW 2019   435

3.2.3   Question Two: the Consequences of the United Kingdom's
         Continued Administration of the Chagos Archipelago

As the Court found in relation to question one that the decolonisation of Mauritius was conducted in a manner inconsistent with the customary international law right to self-determination, the UK's continued administration of the Chagos Archipelago constitutes a wrongful act entailing international responsibility.[153] Accordingly, the UK is under an obligation to bring an end to its administration of the Chagos Archipelago, thereby enabling Mauritius to complete the decolonisation of its territory in a manner consistent with the right of peoples to self-determination. The Court regarded the resettlement on the Chagos Archipelago of Mauritian nationals, including those of Chagossian origin, as a matter related to the protection of human rights, and it left the matter to be addressed by the UNGA during the completion of the decolonisation of Mauritius.[154]

4   World Trade Organization (WTO)—*Marrakesh Agreement Establishing the World Trade Organization*—Dispute Settlement Understanding—General Agreement on Tariffs and Trade 1994— Inconsistency with WTO Obligations

China—Tariff Rate Quotas for Certain Agricultural Products
Panel Report
WTO Doc WT/DS517/R
Complainant: United States
Respondent: China
Third Parties (original proceedings): Australia; Brazil; Canada, Ecuador; European Union: Guatemala: India; Indonesia: Japan; Kazakhstan; Korea, Republic of; Norway; Russian Federation; Singapore; Chinese Taipei; Ukraine; Viet Nam
18 April 2019

On 15 December 2016,[155] pursuant to the *Dispute Settlement Understanding* (*'DSU'*)[156] and of the *General Agreement on Tariffs and Trade 1994* (*'GATT*

---

153   Ibid [177].
154   Ibid 181.
155   *China—Tariff Rate Quotas for Certain Agricultural Products*, WTO Docs WT/DS517/1 and G/L/1171 (21 December 2016) (Request for Consultations by the United States).
156   *Marrakesh Agreement Establishing the World Trade Organization*, opened for signature 15 April 1994, 1867 UNTS 3 (entered into force 1 January 1995) annex 2 (*'Understanding on Rules and Procedures Governing the Settlement of Disputes'*) arts 1, 4.

1994'),[157] the United States of America ('US') requested consultations with the Government of the People's Republic of China ('China') with regard to the latter's administration of its tariff-rate quotas ('TRQs') involving agricultural products such as wheat, rice, and corn.

The US alleged that China had acted inconsistently with its World Trade Organization ('WTO') obligations. Under the Accession Protocol,[158] the US claimed that China failed to administer each TRQ in a transparent, predictable, or fair basis that uses clearly specified administrative procedures. The US asserted that the lack of clarity in the legal instruments utilized by China violates the latter's obligation to administer the TRQs in a manner that would not inhibit the filling of each TRQ. The US further argued that under the *GATT 1994*,[159] China failed to administer each TRQ in a reasonable manner. Moreover, under Article XIII:3(b),[160] the US alleged that China violated its WTO obligations for failing to provide public notice of quantities, or changes in quantities that are permitted to be imported under each TRQ.

On 22 December 2016 the European Union[161] and Australia[162] requested to join the consultations. Pursuant to Article 4.11 of the *DSU*, Australia expressed its desire to join in the consultations due to its substantial trade and commercial interests in the matter. Australia submitted that in 2015, China was assessed as Australia's largest agricultural market with the value of exports estimated at AUD$9.8 billion—this was composed of AUD$466 million in wheat and about AUD$544 million in the export of other cereals.[163]

---

157 *Marrakesh Agreement Establishing the World Trade Organization*, opened for signature 15 April 1994, 1867 UNTS 3 (entered into force 1 January 1995) annex 1A (*'General Agreement on Tariffs and Trade 1994'*) art XXII.

158 *Accession of the People's Republic of China*, WTO Doc WT/L/432 (23 November 2001) (Decision of 10 November 2001) [1.2].

159 *Marrakesh Agreement Establishing the World Trade Organization*, opened for signature 15 April 1994, 1867 UNTS 3 (entered into force 1 January 1995) annex 1A (*'General Agreement on Tariffs and Trade 1994'*) art X:3(a).

160 *Marrakesh Agreement* annex 1A (*'General Agreement on Tariffs and Trade 1994'*) (n 157).

161 *China—Tariff Rate Quotas for Certain Agricultural Products*, WTO Doc WT/DS517/3 (6 January 2017) (Request to Join Consultations—Communication from the European Union).

162 *China—Tariff Rate Quotas for Certain Agricultural Products*, WTO Doc WT/DS517/2 (6 January 2017) (Request to Join Consultations—Communication from Australia).

163 Ibid.

CASES CONCERNING QUESTIONS OF PUBLIC INTERNATIONAL LAW 2019 437

In response to the request from the US,[164] the Dispute Settlement Body ('DSB') established a panel.[165] On 18 April 2019, the panel report was circulated to the WTO members.[166] The Panel mostly agreed with the contentions made by the US—and on the basis of their findings of a violation, concluded that China's administration of its TRQs were inconsistent with its obligations. One of the more interesting findings was the formulation by China of vague eligibility criteria required from applicants requesting a TRQ allocation. The Panel held that possession of a 'good integrity situation' and fulfilment of 'social responsibilities' as eligibility criteria were inconsistent with China's obligation to administer TRQs on a transparent basis.[167] Notwithstanding the aforementioned positive findings, the Panel found that the US had not satisfactorily demonstrated two of its claims—first, the claim that the extent of public notice provided in connection with the administration of some of the TRQs breached China's obligations,[168] and second, the claim that China's usage requirements for imported rice used in China's TRQ for rice was inconsistent with China's obligation to administer TRQs in a manner that would not inhibit the filing of each TRQ (though the US had established a similar claim in respect of usage requirements for imported wheat and corn used in administration of its TRQs for wheat and corn).[169]

On 28 May 2019, the DSB adopted the panel report where it was recommended that China amend the administration of its TRQs to comply with its WTO obligations.[170] China expressed its intention[171] to implement the recommendations and the ruling of the DSB and was given until 29 February 2020 to implement such recommendations in a manner consistent with its WTO obligations.[172]

---

164   *China—Tariff Rate Quotas for Certain Agricultural Products*, WTO Doc WT/DS517/6 (21 August 2017) (Request for the Establishment of a Panel by the United States).

165   *China—Tariff Rate Quotas for Certain Agricultural Products*, WTO Doc WT/DS517/7 (12 February 2018) (Constitution of the Panel Established at the Request of the United States).

166   Panel Report, *China—Tariff Rate Quotas for Certain Agricultural Products*, WTO Doc WT/DS517/R (18 April 2019).

167   Ibid [7.30].

168   Ibid [7.127].

169   Ibid [7.112].

170   Ibid [8.3].

171   *China—Tariff Rate Quotas for Certain Agricultural Products*, WTO Doc WT/DS517/10 (4 July 2019) (Agreement under Article 21.3(B) of the DSU).

172   *China—Tariff Rate Quotas for Certain Agricultural*, WTO Doc WT/DS517/11 (20 January 2020) (Modification of the Agreement under Article 21.3(B) of the DSU).

438 AUSTRALIAN YEAR BOOK OF INTERNATIONAL LAW VOLUME 38

5   Court of Arbitration for Sport—International Association
for Athletics—Arbitral Award—Human Rights—
Non-Discrimination—Eligibility of Females with Hyperandrogeny
to Compete in International Sporting competitions—
Hyperandrogenism Regulations—International Association of
Athletics *Eligibility Regulations for Female Classification (Athletes
with Differences of Sex Development)*

*Mokgadi Caster Semenya v International Association of Athletics
Federations*
CAS 2018/O/5794
Athletics South Africa v International Association of Athletics Federations
CAS 2018/O/5798
Arbitral Award delivered by the Court of Arbitration for Sport
Sitting in the following composition
The Hon Dr Annabelle Bennett AO SC, President
The Hon Hugh L Fraser
Dr Hans Nater
Ad hoc Clerk: Mr Edward Craven

5.1   *Overview of the Case*

The ruling was delivered on 1 May 2019, and full award with reasons released
shortly thereafter. This case concerned the International Association of
Athletics Federations (IAAF) *Eligibility Regulations for Female Classification
(Athletes with Differences of Sex Development)* (*'DSD Regulations'*),[173] which
came into effect on 1 November 2018.[174] The Court of Arbitration for Sport
('CAS') dismissed both requests for arbitration made respectively by Mokgadi
Caster Semenya ('Semenya') and Athletics South Africa ('ASA'), (collectively,
the 'Claimants').

5.2   *Factual Background*

The parties to the proceedings were Semenya, a female athlete of South African
nationality, competing in middle distance running; the ASA, the national

---

173   'Book of Rules, Book C: C3.6—Eligibility Regulations for the Female Classification', *World
Athletics* (Rule Book) <https://www.worldathletics.org/about-iaaf/documents/book-of
-rules> ('Book of Rules C3.6').

174   *Mokgadi Caster Semenya v International Association of Athletics Federations (Award)*
(Court of Arbitration for Sport, Case No 2018/O/5794, 30 April 2019); *Athletics South Africa
v International Association of Athletics Federations (Award)* (Court of Arbitration for Sport,
Case No 2018/O/5798, 30 April 2019) [13] ('*Semenya case*').

governing body for the sport of athletics in South Africa; and the IAAF, the international governing body of athletics. The *DSD Regulations* here contested were in response to the challenge brought by Indian sprinter Dutee Chand in 2014.[175] Chand challenged the *IAAF Regulations Governing Eligibility of Females with Hyperandrogenism to Compete in Women's Competition* ('*Hyperandrogenism Regulations*') after being instructed to take androgen-suppressive drugs to be eligible to continue competing.[176] According to the IAAF, they were introduced to ensure fair competition within the female category, but Chand contended that they were unfairly discriminatory 'against women who naturally produced higher levels of testosterone.'[177] The *Hyperandrogenism Regulations* relied on the existence of a performance-enhancing effect of high levels of endogenous testosterone, a finding that, Chand argued, lacked scientific support.[178] It was on this second ground that the CAS ordered upon delivering their decision July 2015 that the regulations be suspended pending further research and evidence to validate the requirements.[179] The IAAF was given two years to substantiate the regulations,[180] a window later extended.[181]

In March 2018, the IAAF opted instead to withdraw the *Hyperandrogenism Regulations*, and replace them with the *DSD Regulations* which narrowed the field of applicability.[182] The new requirements of these regulations include the prevention of athletes with 46 XY DSD[183] with testosterone concentrations of more than 5 nmol/L and androgen sensitivity[184] from competing in 'restricted events', namely the 400-metre, 400-metre hurdles, 800-metre, 1500-metre, and 1-mile races.[185] To be eligible to compete, those affected women or 'relevant

---

175   *Dutee Chand v Athletics Federation of India (Interim Award)* (Court of Arbitration for Sport, Case No 2014/A/3759, 24 July 2015) ('*Dutee Case*').

176   Ibid 2.

177   Simon Franklin, Jonathan Ospina Betancurt and Silvia Camporesi, 'What Statistical Data of Observational Performance Can Tell Us and What They Cannot: The Case of *Dutee Chand v AFI & IAAF*' (2018) 52(7) *British Journal of Sports Medicine* 420, 420.

178   Arne Ljungqvist, 'Sex Segregation and Sport' (2018) 52(1) *British Journal of Sports Medicine* 3, 3.

179   *Dutee Case* (n 175) 160.

180   Ibid 160.

181   'Semenya, ASA and IAAF: Executive Summary', Court of Arbitration for Sport (Executive Summary, 1 May 2019) <https://www.tas-cas.org/fileadmin/user_upload/CAS_Executive_Summary__5794_.pdf> ('CAS Executive Summary') [9].

182   Ibid [4]–[5].

183   Ibid [6]. DSD conditions are where the affected individual has XY chromosomes. Accordingly, no individuals with XX chromosomes are subjected to any restrictions or eligibility conditions under the DSD Regulation.

184   A 'material androgenizing effect': ibid [7].

185   Book of Rules C3.6 (n 173) s 2.2 (2.2.2).

athletes', must be recognised at law as female or intersex, reduce their blood testosterone concentration to below 5 nmol/L for a continuous period of at least six months, and thereafter maintain the lowered level for as long as they want to remain eligible.[186] Semenya was found to be a relevant athlete, and was thus deemed ineligible to compete for the second time in her career.[187]

5.3   *Submissions as Presented by the Parties*

5.3.1   Claimants

The Claimants' submissions focused on refuting that the *DSD Regulations* are necessary, reasonable and proportionate. It was submitted that the *DSD Regulations* are discriminatory on a myriad of grounds that included sex/gender, physical appearance and female athletes who compete in specific events.[188] The Claimants contended that there is no sensible scientific basis for distinguishing between DSD and other genetic variations and mutations that positively impact on athletic performance.[189] Further, the Claimants stated that the studies relied on by the IAAF in support of the *DSD Regulations* are flawed and unreliable. Three grounds are provided for this assertion, first, that the studies were produced by individuals that not only have conflicts of interest, but also feature 'bias (conscious or subconscious) against women who do not conform to a particular socio-cultural view of femininity'.[190] Subsequently, that the studies are 'rudimentary and lack rigour', as substantiated by expert evidence which finds that 'the IAAF has deviated from commonly recognised best practices, leading to unreliable results that are an inadequate basis for regulation'.[191] The Claimants' experts equally identified the presence of significant errors in the data utilised. Were the studies to be accepted, they would fail nevertheless to establish necessity as there was a lack of rational connection between their findings and the stated aim of ensuring fair competition within the female classification.

The Claimants submitted that if the panel were to find the *DSD Regulations* necessary, they would nonetheless be irrational and arbitrary and thus unreasonable.[192] Their argument was based, inter alia, on the contention that the selected 'restricted events' do not in actuality reflect the findings of the

---

186   Ibid s 2.3; Cara Tannenbaum and Sheree Bekker, 'Sex, Gender, and Sports' (2019) 364 *British Medical Journal* 1120, 1120.

187   Having previously been barred from competition in 2009 and reinstated in 2010.

188   *Semenya case* (n 174) [51].

189   Ibid [53].

190   Ibid [54].

191   Ibid.

192   Ibid [57].

study and that the threshold of 5 nmol/L is arbitrary given the lack of empirical data to support it.[193] They also contended that women with other conditions (eg polycystic ovarian syndrome), who may surpass this threshold, are not covered by the *DSD Regulations*, an important point given the IAAF's contention that testosterone is the critical factor conferring a performance advantage.[194] This supported the submission that the *DSD Regulations* 'rely entirely on a subjective assessment of the androgenising effect of elevated testosterone', and that it will likely 'produce uncertain, inconsistent and arbitrary outcomes.'[195]

If the IAAF were to succeed in establishing that the *DSD Regulations* are necessary and reasonable, the Claimants submitted that they would nonetheless be disproportionate. The policy objective was outweighed by the significant and irreparable harm that would befall affected female athletes, which according to Semenya is 'of a magnitude ... unprecedented in sport.'[196]

Accordingly, the Claimants sought an award from the CAS declaring the *DSD Regulations* as unlawful and preventing them from being brought into force on the grounds summarised above, and thus that they 'violate the IAAF Constitution, the Olympic Charter, the laws of Monaco, the laws of jurisdictions in which international athletics competitions are held, as well as universally recognised fundamental human rights.'[197]

5.3.2   IAAF

The IAAF in response maintained that the *DSD Regulations* were necessary, reasonable and a proportionate means of achieving a legitimate aim. They stated that the *Regulations* 'respect the gender identity and dignity of affected athletes while simultaneously protecting the right of female athletes to fair and meaningful competition.'[198] In respecting gender identity, they contended nonetheless that 'there are some contexts where biology has to trump identity.'[199] To this end, they asserted that the evidence was clear in supporting the position that athletes with 5-ARD have a significant performance advantage when competing in the female category.[200] This assertion was grounded in their submission that athletes with 5-ARD are 'biologically

---

193   Ibid [58]–[59].
194   Ibid [60].
195   Ibid [61].
196   Ibid [65].
197   CAS Executive Summary (n 181) [9].
198   *Semenya case* (n 174) [286].
199   Ibid [289].
200   Ibid.

indistinguishable' from males save for 'the size and shape of their external genitals', a factor 'which has no impact on athletic performance.'[201]

They argued accordingly that to allow 5-ARD athletes (or transgender male-to-female athletes) to compete in the female category based on their female legal sex or gender identity is arbitrary, and irrational as it ignores the fundamental separation of male/ female competition categories.[202] This fundamental separation equally grounded the need for distinct treatment of 46 XY DSD from other natural physical characteristics, as these characteristics do not have different competition categories.[203] They therefore contended that the *DSD Regulations* do not discriminate, and that even supposing they do, it is necessary discrimination.[204] It was equally proportionate given the IAAF's contention that the *DSD Regulations* comprise very narrow restrictions, and 'do not exceed what is necessary in order to achieve equality of opportunity.'[205]

They ultimately concluded 'that the *DSD Regulations* have a strong scientific, legal and ethical foundation',[206] and that without them, female athletes would be denied 'an equal chance to excel in sport.'[207]

5.4   Merits

The Panel was 'faced with regulations that are dealing with an agreed binary division of athletes for competition, namely male and female, in a world that is not so neatly divided'.[208] It had to be acknowledged that they were only tasked with determining the validity and therefore legal enforceability of the *DSD Regulations*. The Panel was 'restrained in its task, due to the strict framework of the arbitration'.[209]

The Panel by majority 'were unable to establish that the DSD were invalid'.[210] The Panel Members accepted that they were discriminatory,[211] but that the discrimination was 'a necessary, reasonable and proportionate means

---

201   Ibid.
202   Ibid.
203   Ibid [298].
204   Ibid [300].
205   Ibid [302].
206   Ibid [311].
207   Ibid.
208   Ibid [625].
209   'CAS Arbitration: Caster Semenya, Athletics South Africa (ASA) and International Association of Athletics Federations (IAAF): Decision', *Court of Arbitration for Sport* (Media Release, 1 May 2019) 2 <https://www.tas-cas.org/fileadmin/user_upload/Media _Release_Semenya_ASA_IAAF_decision.pdf> ('CAS Media Release').
210   Ibid.
211   *Semenya case* (n 174) [547].

of achieving the IAAF's aim of preserving the integrity of female athletics in the Restricted Events'.[212] The Panel's decision thus included an analysis of the discrimination which legally would be permissible if the IAAF could discharge its burden of proving that the Regulations were a necessary, reasonable and proportionate means of attaining a legitimate objective.[213]

The objective, according to the IAAF, was to ensure consistent treatment and preserve fair and meaningful competition.[214] The IAAF maintained that the *DSD Regulations* are 'a justified and proportionate means of ensuring' that objective within the female classification.[215] There was thus an imperative that to ensure this aim 'competition has to be organised within categories that create a level playing field and ensure that success is determined by talent, dedication, hard work, and the other values and characteristics that the sport embodies and celebrates'.[216]

The IAAF 'does not want to risk discouraging those aspirations by having unfair competition conditions that deny athletes a fair opportunity to succeed'.[217] The Panel did not consider whether segregated competition was an issue, as it was not raised by the parties.[218]

Despite this conclusion, the Panel did raise some serious concerns with the *DSD Regulations* and their future application.[219] Three main issues were emphasised. The first was the potential inability or difficulty for an athlete to comply with the requirements. The strict liability of the provision around maximum permitted levels of testosterone could result in consequences through unintentional non-compliance.[220] Secondly, there were issues around the lack of and the strength of existing evidence available to support the submission that a significant athletic advantage exists in the 1500-metre and 1-mile events. The Panel therefore questioned their inclusion in the restricted events, and suggest they be removed pending further study. And finally, further evidence was required around the potential side effects of hormonal treatment. With greater understanding, these are factors that could tip proportionality.[221]

---

212   CAS Media Release (n 209) 2.
213   *Semenya case* (n 174) [547]–[548].
214   Ibid [415].
215   Ibid.
216   Book of Rules C3.6 (n 173) s 1.1.1.
217   Ibid s 1.1.1(a).
218   *Semenya case* (n 174) [461].
219   Ibid [620].
220   Ibid [621]–[624].
221   Ibid.

Regardless of these reservations, it was noted that 'evidence … so far has not established that those concerns negate the conclusion of *prima facie* proportionality, this may change in the future unless constant attention is paid to the fairness of how the Regulations are implemented'.[222] The Panel strongly encouraged the IAAF to heed these concerns, and remember that the policy is a 'living document' capable of revision. Implementation and experience will likely prove helpful in improving the *Regulations*.[223]

Semenya filed an appeal in the Swiss Federal Supreme Court.[224] Her lawyers have foreshadowed that the appeal will focus on 'fundamental principles of Swiss public policy'.[225]

United Nations Treaty Body Concluding Observations on Australia's Compliance with Human Rights Obligations 2019

As a party to the United Nations ('UN') *Convention on the Rights of the Child*[226] and the UN's *Convention on the Rights of Persons with Disabilities*[227] the Australian Government must periodically report to the respective treaty monitoring bodies. The Committee on the Rights of the Child ('CRC')[228] and Committee on the Rights of Persons with Disabilities ('CRPD')[229] assess implementation and compliance with treaty obligations and provide recommendations moving forward. In 2019 Australia received concluding observations from both Committees after belated reporting. The two conventions overlap to some extent. For example, certain concerns and recommendations relating to children with disabilities were reiterated by both the CRC and the CRPD, making it a notable area of concern.

---

222   CAS Media Release (n 209) 2.

223   *Semenya case* (n 174) [624].

224   '"The IAAF will not drug me or stop me being who I am": Semenya appeals against Cas ruling', *The Guardian* (News Article, 30 May 2019) <http://www.theguardian.com/sport/2019/may/29/caster-semenya-appeals-against-cas-ruling-over-iaaf-s-testosterone-levels>.

225   Ibid.

226   *Convention on the Rights of the Child*, opened for signature 20 November 1989, 1577 UNTS 3 (entered into force 2 September 1990) ('*Convention on the Rights of the Child*').

227   *Convention on the Rights of Persons with Disabilities*, opened for signature 30 March 2007, 2515 UNTS 3 (entered into force 3 May 2008) ('*Convention on the Rights of Persons with Disabilities*').

228   *Convention on the Rights of the Child* (n 226) art 44.

229   *Convention on the Rights of Persons with Disabilities* (n 227) art 35.

6 Committee on the Rights of the Child: Concluding Observations on the Combined Fifth and Sixth Periodic Reports of Australia

UN CRC 82nd session
CRC/C/AUS/CO/5–6
1 November 2019

6.1 *Commendations*

Australia was commended for the creation of the position of Assistant Minister for Children and Families in 2018, the establishment of the National Children's Commission within the Australian Human Rights Commission in 2012 and the Royal Commission into the Detention and Protection of Children in the Northern Territory in 2016.[230]

The CRC included recommendations about the impact of climate change on the rights of the child, demonstrating a notable shift in rights thinking and discourse. The CRC acknowledged that climate change is impacting children's 'right to life, survival, development, non-discrimination, health and standards of living.'[231] Furthermore the CRC endorsed childhood advocacy and the positive right children have to express their views and to be listened to by the State. The recommendations recognise children as the ultimate bearers of current climate related policy outcomes and placed pressure on the Government to be more receptive and to fulfil obligations under the *Paris Agreement*[232] promptly.

6.2 *Areas of Concern*

The CRC expressed its concern about Australia's compliance with the *Convention* across several areas including violence, sexual violence, abuse and neglect,[233] children deprived of a family environment,[234] mental health,[235] and administration of child justice.[236] The Committee noted that some of its previous recommendations had not been implemented.[237] It continued to be

---

230 Committee on the Rights of the Child, *Concluding observations on the combined fifth and sixth periodic reports of Australia,* 82nd sess, UN Doc CRC/C/AUS/CO/5–6 (1 November 2019) [3].

231 Ibid [40].

232 *Paris Agreement,* opened for signature 22 April 2016, [2016] ATS 24 (entered into force 4 November 2016).

233 *Concluding observations on the combined fifth and sixth periodic reports of Australia* (n 230) [29].

234 Ibid s E.

235 Ibid [37]–[38].

236 Ibid [48].

237 Ibid [47].

seriously concerned about mandatory minimum criminal sentencing laws in Western Australia and the Northern Territory that were applicable to children and about the co-imprisonment of minors and adults,[238] alongside '[r]eports that children in detention are frequently subjected to verbal abuse and racist remarks, deliberately denied access to water, restrained in ways that are potentially dangerous and excessively subjected to isolation'.[239]

A common thread throughout the concluding observations was concern for Aboriginal and Torres Strait Islander children and asylum-seeker, refugee and migrant children. The report reiterates that children belonging to minority groups facing marginalisation are particularly vulnerable. Concern for their rights are multifaceted and inter-related. The report is a reminder that an inability to access and enjoy rights has a cascading effect on many other aspects of children's lives.

6.2.1   Aboriginal and Torres Strait Islander Children

The Committee expressed continued concern for the rights and outcomes of Aboriginal and Torres Strait Islander children across a number of areas. Recommendations addressed the exposure of children to family violence,[240] overrepresentation in alternative care,[241] homelessness,[242] and poor mental health in particular among children living in rural areas.[243] The Committee recognised that many educational targets reflected in the Government's 'Closing the Gap' scheme remain unmet.[244] Aboriginal and Torres Strait Islander parents and children remain overrepresented in the criminal justice system.[245] It recommended greater Indigenous involvement in working to overcome these issues and an increase in online resources which target, and can be accessed by, children.[246]

6.2.2   Asylum-Seeking, Refugee and Migrant Children

Australia's treatment of asylum-seeker, refugee and migrant children attracted eight major expressions of concern and nine recommendations making it the lengthiest individual section of the report.[247] The CRC expressed particular

---

238   Ibid [47](e)–(f).
239   Ibid [47](c).
240   Ibid [29](e).
241   Ibid [33](b).
242   Ibid [42].
243   Ibid [38](b).
244   Ibid [43](a).
245   Ibid [47](b).
246   Ibid [38](d).
247   Ibid [44]–[46].

concern for children caught up in Australia's offshore and regional processing regime and the detention and treatment of children under the *Migration Act 1958* (Cth) and *Maritime Powers Act 2013* (Cth).

The Committee expressed its disapproval of the fact that:

> The best interests of the child is not a primary consideration in asylum, refugee and migration processes, leading to children going through lengthy assessment and determination procedures, and that the 286 children transferred from Nauru and the many thousands of children before them (the 'legacy caseload') 'will not be settled in Australia and are encouraged to engage in third country migration options' ... leaving them in limbo for an undetermined period of time ...[248]

The CRC recommendations call for the *Migration Act 1958* (Cth) to be amended so as 'to prohibit the detention of asylum-seeking, refugee and migrant children'[249] and to prohibit 'the detention of children and their families in regional processing countries'.[250]

In addition, the Committee expressed grave concern about the fact that migration laws policies still allow disability to be the basis for rejecting an immigration request.[251]

Concerns for asylum-seeking, refugee and migrant children was not limited to their treatment in the resettlement processes but extended to their education, mental health, freedom of expression and freedom from discrimination as individuals within the community. A greater appreciation of cultural and linguistic diversity in the provision of services to children was encouraged overall.

7   **Committee on the Rights of Persons with Disabilities: Concluding Observations on the Combined Second and Third Periodic Reports of Australia**

UN CRPD 22nd session
UN Doc CRPD/C/AUS/CO/2–3
15 October 2019

---

248   Ibid [44](e) (citations omitted).
249   Ibid [45](b).
250   Ibid [45](d).
251   Ibid [44](g).

7.1 *Commendations*

The CRPD Committee commended Australia on the following:

The adoption of the *National Disability Insurance Scheme Act 2013*;

1. The adoption of states' and territories' legislation and policies such as the *Disability Inclusion Act 2018*, the *Disability Services Act 1986*, the disability justice plans and the *Disability Discrimination Act 1992* action plans;
2. The adoption of the disability inclusion strategy for development assistance Development for All 2015–20;
3. The adoption of the new National Disability Employment Framework;
4. The adoption of the Australian Government Plan to Improve Outcomes for Aboriginal and Torres Strait Islander People with Disability;
5. The establishment of the Royal Commission into Violence, Abuse, Neglect and Exploitation of People with Disability, in 2019;
6. The establishment of the National Disability and Carers Advisory Council;
7. The commitment to introduce a 7 per cent employment target for persons with disabilities in the public service;
8. The endorsement of a new national disability data set bringing together Commonwealth, state and territory data from across multiple sources and systems to provide a more complete picture of the requirements of persons with disabilities.[252]

The *Convention on the Rights of Persons with Disabilities* not only seeks to improve the lives of those with disabilities but also aims to bring awareness to the diversity amongst persons living with disabilities. Overall, the CRPD Committee recommendations sought to encourage comprehensive systems which adequately reflect international legal obligations. Emphasis was placed on individuals exposed to multiple types of disadvantage including children, women, Aboriginal and Torres Strait Islander people, asylum-seekers and refugees, cultural and linguistically diverse individuals and the LGBTQI community. Recommendations frequently encouraged the meaningful engagement of persons with disabilities either directly or through representative organisations in working towards solutions to systemic and structural barriers often experienced by persons with disabilities.

In relation to Australia's international aid initiative—Development for All—the Committee expressed concern about the absence of appropriate mechanisms to measure the impact of development cooperation efforts on persons with disabilities. It also lamented the lack of information about the

---

252 Committee on the Rights of Persons with Disabilities, *Concluding observations on the combined second and third periodic reports of Australia*, 22nd sess, UN Doc CRPD/C/AUS/CO/2–3 (15 October 2019) [4].

CASES CONCERNING QUESTIONS OF PUBLIC INTERNATIONAL LAW 2019   449

'effective involvement of organizations of persons with disabilities as development cooperation partners.'[253]

The CRPD Committee called for improvements in data collection, noting 'the lack of information on the representation of women with disabilities, particularly Aboriginal and Torres Strait Islander women with disabilities, in political and public life',[254] along with 'no national disaggregated data on students with disabilities, including on the use of restrictive practices and cases of bullying',[255] and the '[a]bsence of national data disaggregated by disability at all the stages of the criminal justice system, including data on the number of persons unfit to plead who are committed to custody in prison and other facilities.'[256]

7.2   *National Disability Insurance Scheme ('NDIS')*

Although Australia was commended on the creation of the NDIS, the CRPD Committee recommended changes to the scheme to address the following concerns:

> The disability assessment that individuals must undergo in order to be eligible to receive services through the National Disability Insurance Scheme, which still relies heavily on the medical model of disability and does not provide older persons with disabilities, persons with disabilities from culturally and linguistically diverse backgrounds, Aboriginal and Torres Strait Islander persons with disabilities and persons with intellectual or psychosocial disabilities with equal opportunities;
>
> The inaccessibility of the National Disability Insurance Scheme due to complex procedures, limited publicly available and accessible information and the lack of services in remote areas ...[257]

7.3   *Access to Justice*

The CRPD Committee discussed at length access to justice, participation within the justice system and the related issues of liberty and security of the person.[258] In particular the Committee expressed concern for the number of grounds or circumstances in which individuals with 'cognitive and

---

253   Ibid [59].
254   Ibid [53].
255   Ibid [45](c).
256   Ibid [25](f).
257   Ibid [5](e)–(f).
258   Ibid [27]–[29].

450 AUSTRALIAN YEAR BOOK OF INTERNATIONAL LAW VOLUME 38

mental impairment' may find themselves detained indefinitely.[259] It noted in particular:

> The reported abuse of young Aboriginal and Torres Strait Islander persons with disabilities by fellow prisoners and prison staff, the use of prolonged solitary confinement, particularly of persons with intellectual or psychosocial disabilities, and the lack of safe and accessible channels for making complaints ...[260]

7.4 Liberty of Movement and Nationality (Art 18)

The Committee expressed concern over the discrimination against people with disabilities under the *Migration Act 1958* (Cth) and *The Disability Discrimination Act 1992* (Cth) which exempts certain provisions within the *Migration Act 1958* (Cth). These result in the exclusion of persons with disabilities. The 10-year qualifying period for certain migrants to access the Age Support Pension and the Disability Support Pension was lamented, as was 'the transfer of refugees and asylum seekers with disabilities to Nauru, Papua New Guinea and other "regional processing countries".[261] The CRPD Committee recommended that Australia:

1. Review and amend its migration laws and policies to ensure that persons with disabilities do not face discrimination in any of the formalities and procedures relating to migration and asylum and, especially, remove the exemption in the *Disability Discrimination Act 1992* to certain provisions of the *Migration Act 1958*;

2. Remove the 10-year qualifying period for migrants to access the Age Support Pension and the Disability Support Pension;

3. Cease the transfer of refugees and asylum seekers, particularly persons with disabilities, to Nauru, Papua New Guinea and other 'regional processing countries', as requested by the Office of the United Nations High Commissioner for Refugees in a factsheet on the protection of so-called 'legacy caseload' asylum seekers, and establish a minimum standard of health care and support for persons with disabilities held in immigration detention.[262]

---

259 Ibid [27].
260 Ibid [29](b).
261 Ibid [35].
262 Ibid [36].

CASES CONCERNING QUESTIONS OF PUBLIC INTERNATIONAL LAW 2019   451

7.5   *Living Independently and Being Included in the Community (Art 19)*
A matter of concern to the CRPD Committee was the number of young persons with disabilities in Australia forced to live in residential aged care. It recommended the closure of all disability specific residential institutions and preventing 'transinstitutionalization, including by addressing how persons with disabilities not eligible for the National Disability Insurance Scheme can be supported to transition from living in an institution to living independently in the community'.[263] The CRPD Committee called for an increase in the range, affordability and accessibility of public and social housing for persons with disabilities, and for a revision of the Younger People in Residential Aged Care action plan, setting 2025 as a target date for ensuring that no person under 65 years of age enters or lives in residential aged care.[264]

7.6   *Education*
The CRPD Committee recommended that a robust review be conducted into the disability standards for education and to develop a national action plan for inclusive education.[265]

7.7   *Work and Employment*
The CRPD Committee recommended that a comprehensive review be undertaken of Australian Disability Enterprises (sheltered workshops), and that Australia

> [i]mplement measures to address systemic and structural barriers experienced by persons with disabilities, particularly by women with disabilities, Aboriginal and Torres Strait Islander persons with disabilities, persons with disabilities from culturally and linguistically diverse backgrounds and refugee and asylum-seeking persons with disabilities.'[266]

7.8   *Participation in Political and Public Life*
The CRPD Committee reiterated its 2013 recommendation that the *Electoral Act 1918* (Cth) be amended to ensure that all persons with disabilities be entitled to vote.[267]

---

263   Ibid [38].
264   Ibid [38](b)–(c).
265   Ibid [46].
266   Ibid [50](c).
267   Ibid [54]. Note that s 93(8) of that Act does not permit persons 'of unsound mind' to vote.

7.9 *Other Recommendations*

Overall, the Committee called on Australia to better appreciate diversity and to work on accommodating every person's abilities as well as disadvantages either associated with their disability and/or age, gender, location and ethnicity.

The Committee noted that the daily lives of many persons with disabilities in Australia could be improved in simple ways. Examples include:

– implementing recommendations of better infrastructure including afford-able housing options;[268]
– improving access to public transport;[269] and
– enacting 'legally binding information and communications standards so that information, particularly all information about significant changes to laws, policies, systems and obligations, is provided in accessible modes, means and formats, including Braille, Easy Read and sign language (Auslan)'.[270]

United Nations Treaty Body Jurisprudence on Individual Complaints 2019

Mandatory reporting procedures are not the only supervisory mechanisms available to treaty bodies; the individual complaints mechanism provided for within optional protocols to multiple international human rights treaties pro-vides an evolving body of useful jurisprudence on questions of international law and access to justice for many.

8 *International Convention on Civil and Political Rights* **Human Rights Committee—The Right to Life—Climate Change—Non-Refoulement Admissibility—Manifestly Ill-Founded—Victim Status**

Views adopted by the Committee under article 5(4) of the Optional Protocol
Communication No 2728/2016
UN Doc CCPR/C/127/D/2728/2016
Human Rights Committee
Views adopted 24 October 2019

---

268   Ibid [38](b).
269   Ibid [17](a).
270   Ibid [42].

CASES CONCERNING QUESTIONS OF PUBLIC INTERNATIONAL LAW 2019   453

Communication submitted by:	Ioane Teitiota (represented by counsel, Michael J Kidd)
Alleged victim:	The author
State party:	New Zealand
Date of communication:	15 September 2015 (initial submission)
Document reference:	Decision taken pursuant to former rule 97 of the Committee's rules of procedure, transmitted to the State party on 16 February 2016 (not issued in document form)
Date of adoption of Views:	24 October 2019
Subject matter:	Deportation to the Republic of Kiribati
Procedural issues:	Admissibility—manifestly ill-founded; admissibility—victim status
Substantive issue:	Right to life
Article of the Covenant:	6(1)
Articles of the Optional Protocol:	1 and 2

The *International Covenant on Civil and Political Rights*[271] ('ICCPR') forms the backbone of the international human rights system and the expert Human Rights Committee responsible for its oversight has an impressive catalogue of jurisprudence aiding the evolution of international human rights law.[272] '[I]t is generally for the organs of States parties to examine the facts and evidence of the case ... unless it can be established that this assessment was clearly arbitrary or amounted to a manifest error or a denial of justice' the Commission will not accept complaints.[273] In keeping with the requirement that there be an exhaustion of local remedies, the case of Ioane Teitiota made its way through the New Zealand judicial hierarchy from 2013 to 2015. The complex and novel questions pertaining to how individuals desiring resettlement due

---

271   *International Covenant on Civil and Political Rights*, opened for signature 16 December 1966, 999 UNTS 171 (entered into force 23 March 1976).

272   Wouter Vandenhole, *The Procedures Before the UN Human Rights Treaty Bodies: Divergence or Convergence?* (Intersentia, 2004) 195.

273   See, eg, Human Rights Committee, *Views adopted by the Committee under article 5 (4) of the Optional Protocol, concerning comunicación No 2345/2014*, UN Doc CCPR/C/125/D/2345/2014 (18 April 2019) 14 [8.4] (*M.M v Denmark*); Human Rights Committee, *View adopted by the Committee under article 5 (4) of the Optional Protocol concerning communication No 3041/2017*, UN Doc CCPR/C/125/D/3041/2017) (6 June 2019) 10–11 [7.3] (*BDK v Canada*). See also Human Rights Committee, *General Comment No 32, Article 14: Right to equality before courts and tribunals and to a fair trial*, 90th sess, UN Doc CCPR/C/GC/32 (23 August 2007).

to their land, property, housing, food, health and personal security rights being adversely affected by climate change and rising sea levels raised significant questions under international human rights law, principally the right to life in art 6(1) of the ICCPR and refugee status under the Refugee Convention. Increased social instability and occurrences of violence were found by the Tribunal to 'not amount to fear of prosecution; and the lack of 'evidence that [the author] had no access to potable water, or that the environmental conditions that he faced or would face on return were so perilous that his life would be jeopardized'[274] saw the author fail to be recognized as a 'refugee' under the Refugee Convention.[275] The question therefore shifted to the scope of the right to life and whether the author had substantiated claims that upon deportation he faced a real risk of irreparable harm to his right to life through the adverse effects of climate change in the Republic of Kiribati.

The New Zealand adjudicative system and the Committee both recognised that 'environmental degradation, climate change and unsustainable development constitute some of the most pressing and serious threats to the ability of present and future generations to enjoy the right to life.'[276] However, none of the grounds put forward by the author, namely the general situation of violence, lack of access to potable water, deprivation of subsistence through crop destruction, concerns of overpopulation, intense flooding and breaches of sea walls, reached the threshold necessary for the Committee to find the author's right to life had been jeopardized to such an extent as to render the New Zealand authorities assessment arbitrary or erroneous, permitting it to be overturned.[277] There was no failure on New Zealand's behalf to provide:

> an individualized assessment of [the author's] need for protection and took note of all of the elements provided by the author when evaluating the risk he faced when the State party removed him to the Republic of Kiribati in 2015, including the prevailing conditions in Kiribati, the foreseen risks to the author and the other inhabitants of the islands, the time left for the Kiribati authorities and the international community to intervene [10 to 15 years before the island becomes uninhabitable] and

---

274 Human Rights Committee, *Views adopted by the Committee under article 5 (4) of the Optional Protocol, concerning communication No 2728/2016* CCPR/C/127/D/2728/2016 5 [2.8] (*'Ioane Teitiota v New Zealand'*).

275 Ibid.

276 Ibid 10 [9.4].

277 Ibid 11 [9.9].

CASES CONCERNING QUESTIONS OF PUBLIC INTERNATIONAL LAW 2019 455

the efforts already underway to address the very serious situation of the islands.[278]

On these facts the Committee found no violation under article 6(1) of the ICCPR. However:

> The Committee is of the view that without robust national and international efforts, the effects of climate change in receiving states may expose individuals to a violation of their rights under articles 6 or 7 of the Covenant, thereby triggering the *non-refoulement* obligations of sending states. Furthermore, given that the risk of an entire country becoming submerged under water is such an extreme risk, the conditions of life in such a country may become incompatible with the right to life with dignity before the risk is realized.[279]

The relationship between the right to life and environmental degradation and climate change has not been addressed in the past but since its first mention in the Committee's General Comments No 36 on the right to life,[280] and communications such as the case at hand, it can be expected to be commonly addressed in the Committee's recommendations to States.

The right to life has always been interpreted broadly albeit with the requirement that the the risk of a violation of the Covenant be 'imminent'.[281] This requirement was elaborated on:

> The Committee considers that in the context of attaining victim status in cases of deportation or extradition, the requirement of imminence primarily attaches to the decision to remove the individual, whereas the imminence of any anticipated harm in the receiving state influences the assessment of the real risk faced by the individual.[282]

Although the requisite immanency was lacking for Mr Teitiota's claim, the recognition of climate change related environmental disturbances as a real risk to individual's enjoyment of the non-derogable right to life under article 6(1)

---

278 Ibid 12 [9.13].

279 Ibid 12 [9.11].

280 See, Human Rights Committee, *General Comment No 36. Article 6: right to life,* UN Doc CCPR/C/GC/36 (3 September 2019) 13 [62].

281 Human Rights Committee, *Aalbersberg et al. v the Netherlands Decision,* 87th sess, UN Doc CCPR/C/87/D/1440/2005 (12 July 2006).

282 *Ioane Teitiota v New Zealand* (n 274) 8–9 [8.5].

will have profound effects on all ICCPR signatory States. States', including Australia's, *non-refoulement* obligations are derived in part from article 6(1) and 'States parties must allow all asylum seekers claiming a real risk of a violation of their right to life in the State of origin access to refugee or other individualized or group status determination procedures that could offer them protection against *refoulement*'.[283] Moreover, the Committee cautioned that '[t]he obligation not to extradite, deport or otherwise transfer pursuant to article 6 of the Covenant may be broader than the scope of the principle of *non-refoulement* under international refugee law, since it may also require the protection of aliens not entitled to refugee status'.[284] For millions of people living in poverty the decision represents an expansion of opportunities for access to justice.

Australia and New Zealand are both likely to experience changes in migration patterns as many neighbouring island nations risk becoming uninhabitable. The remarks of the Committee are a reminder that climate change is not only an issue of international concern due to global environmental destruction but a catalyst and promulgator of human rights concerns reinforcing the need for pragmatic action and signposting potential changes in international migration law in the future.

8.1 Individual Opinion of Committee Member Vasilka Sancin (Dissenting)

The principal concern for Vasilka Sancin related to the majority's findings relating to potable water. The finding that there was insufficient evidence to support claims of a lack of access to potable water was influential in the majority decision and tended to suggest that it was 'unestablished that [the author] faced a risk of an imminent, or likely, risk of arbitrary deprivation of life upon return to Kiribati'.[285]

Sancin cautioned that access to potable water should not be equated to a finding that the author is able access safe drinking water, and the burden on New Zealand 'to demonstrate that the author and his family would in fact enjoy access to safe drinking (or even potable) water in Kiribati'[286] remains to be discharged. Until this shortfall is remedied the authors claim concerning the lack of access to safe drinking water is not substantiated, rendering the

---

283   Ibid 9 [9.3].
284   Ibid.
285   Ibid 13 [4].
286   Ibid 13 [5].

CASES CONCERNING QUESTIONS OF PUBLIC INTERNATIONAL LAW 2019   457

State Party's assessment of the author's and his family's situation arbitrary or manifestly erroneous.[287]

8.2   *Individual Opinion of Committee Member Duncan Laki Muhumuza (Dissenting)*

Duncan Laki Muhumuza was unable to find himself in the majority due to feeling 'an unreasonable burden of proof on the author to establish the real risk and danger of arbitrary deprivation of life'.[288] Although it was uncontroversial that the risk to a person expelled or otherwise removed must be personal— not deriving from general conditions, except in extreme cases—the threshold should not be too high and unreasonable.[289] The following extract reflects this position:

> In my view, the author faces a real, personal and reasonably foreseeable risk of a threat to his right to life as a result of the conditions in Kiribati. The considerable difficulty in accessing fresh water because of the environmental conditions, should be enough to reach the threshold of risk, without being a complete lack of fresh water. There is evident significant difficulty to grow crops. Moreover, even if deaths are not occurring with regularity on account of the conditions ... it should not mean that the threshold has not been reached. It would indeed be counterintuitive to the protection of life, to wait for deaths to be very frequent and considerable; in order to consider the threshold of risk as met. It is the standard upheld in this Committee, that threats to life can be a violation of the right, even if they do not result in the loss of life. It should be sufficient that the child of the author has already suffered significant health hazards on account of the environmental conditions. It is enough that the author and his family are already facing significant difficulty in growing crops and resorting to the life of subsistence agriculture on which they were largely dependent. Considering the author's situation and his family, balanced with all the facts and circumstances of the situation in the author's country of origin, reveals a livelihood short of the dignity that the Convention seeks to protect.[290]

---

287   Ibid 13 [6]
288   Ibid 15 [1]
289   Ibid 15 [3]
290   Ibid 20–1[5]

458 AUSTRALIAN YEAR BOOK OF INTERNATIONAL LAW VOLUME 38

To Laki Muhumuza the decision of the majority could be simply summed up: 'New Zealand's action is more like forcing a drowning person back into a sinking vessel, with the "justification" that after all there are other voyagers on board. Even as Kiribati does what it takes to address the conditions; for as long as they remain dire, the life and dignity of persons remains at risk'.[291]

9   *United Nations Convention on the Rights of Persons with Disabilities*

Committee on the Rights of Persons with Disabilities—Access to Court—Intellectual and Psychosocial Disability—Exercise of Legal Capacity—Deprivation of Liberty—Discrimination on the Ground of Disability—Restrictions of Rights—Exhaustion of Domestic Remedies

Views adopted by the Committee under article 5 of the Optional Protocol
Communication No 18/2013
UN Doc CRPD/C/22/D/18/2013
Committee on the Rights of Persons with Disabilities
Views adopted 30 August 2019

Communication submitted by:	Manuway (Kerry) Doolan (represented by counsel, Phillip French and Mark Patrick, Australian Centre for Disability Law)
Alleged victim:	The author
State party:	Australia
Date of communication:	19 September 2013 (initial submission)
Document references:	Decision taken pursuant to rule 70 of the Committee's rules of procedure, transmitted to the State party on 22 November 2013 (not issued in document form)
Date of adoption of Views:	30 August 2019
Subject matters:	Institutionalization of person with intellectual and psychosocial impairment; right to enjoy legal capacity on an equal basis with others

---

291   Ibid 21 [6].

CASES CONCERNING QUESTIONS OF PUBLIC INTERNATIONAL LAW 2019   459

Procedural issue:	Exhaustion of domestic remedies
Substantive issues:	Access to court; intellectual and psychosocial disability; exercise of legal capacity; deprivation of liberty; discrimination on the ground of disability; restrictions of rights
Articles of the Convention:	5, 12, 13, 14, 15, 19, 25, 26 and 28
Article of the Optional Protocol:	2

The author of the communication, Manuway (Kerry) Doolan, was an Aboriginal national of Australia, born on 12 March 1989 claiming to be a victim of violations by Australia of articles 5, 12, 13, 14, 15, 19, 25, 26 and 28 of the *Convention on the Rights of Persons with Disabilities.*[292] The author had intellectual and psychosocial impairments.

Following his arrest on charges of common assault and damage to property in a circumstance of aggravation on 14 August 2008, the author was remanded in custody and incarcerated in a high-security section of Alice Springs Correctional Centre. He was brought before the Northern Territory Supreme Court on an indictment dated 8 October 2008.[293] In view of his intellectual impairment, on 21 May 2009, with the consent of both counsel for the Director of Public Prosecution and the author, a judge of the Northern Territory Supreme Court determined that the author was unfit to stand trial on the basis of his mental impairment and applied the provisions of part II.A of the *Criminal Code Act 1983* (NT) (Northern Territory Criminal Code) dealing with mental impairment and unfitness to be tried.[294] The Court also determined that there was no reasonable prospect of the author becoming fit to be tried for these offences within 12 months.[295] These determinations required the Court to conduct a special hearing before a jury. The jury found the author not guilty of the offences with which he had been charged by reason of his mental impairment.[296] As a consequence of the verdict, the Court had to determine if the author ought to be released unconditionally or if he ought to be liable to supervision. On 29 October 2009, the Northern Territory Supreme

---

292   *Convention on the Rights of Persons with Disabilities,* opened for signature 13 December 2006, 2515 UNTS 3 (entered into force 3 May 2008).

293   Committee on the Rights of Persons with Disabilities, *Views adopted by the Committee under article 5 of the Optional Protocol, concerning communication No 18/2013,* UN Doc CRPD/C/22/D/18/2013 (17 October 2019) 2 [2.1] (*'Manuway Doolan v Australia'*).

294   Ibid 2 [2.2],[2.3].

295   Ibid 2 [2.3].

296   Ibid.

Court placed the author under a custodial supervision order and committed him to custody in prison.[297] The Court was required to fix a term appropriate for the offence concerned and to specify that term in the order.[298] The Court would have imposed a sentence of 9 months of imprisonment for the offence of assault and 6 months of imprisonment for the offence of unlawfully damaging property had the author been held guilty for the offences, to be served cumulatively for a total period in custody of 12 months;[299] however, the author returned to the high-security unit at Alice Springs Correctional Centre and remained there until April 2013. In total the author spent four years and nine months in custody in prison, almost five times the period of custody he would have been required to serve had he been convicted of the offences with which he was charged.[300] In April 2013, the author was transferred to Kwiyernpe House, a custodial facility built in 2013 by the Northern Territory Government and operated by the Aged and Disability Program of the Northern Territory Department of Health.[301]

9.1 *Article 5—Equality and Non-Discrimination*

The Committee permitted the complaint under article 5 despite Australia's contestation that local remedies, namely redress through bodies established under the *Anti-Discrimination Act 1992* (NT), had not been exhausted.[302] The Committee considered that the procedures before the Northern Territory Anti-Discrimination Commissioner and the Australian Human Rights Commission did not give rise to any enforceable remedy for violations of human rights as they had no effect on the laws of the Northern Territory and could not, therefore, be considered as effective remedies.[303] Moreover as the author noted in his submissions responding to Australia's observations, neither the Government of Australia nor the Government of the Northern Territory has a constitutional or statutory bill of rights that might be invoked by the author to invalidate part II.A of the Northern Territory Criminal Code, further limiting access to remedies.[304]

The author submitted that a person without a disability should not be committed to indefinite custody in prison without having been convicted of an

---

297 Ibid 2 [2.4].
298 Ibid.
299 Ibid.
300 Ibid 3 [2.4].
301 Ibid 3 [2.7].
302 Ibid 11–12 [7.4].
303 Ibid.
304 Ibid 9 [5.3].

offence and in that sense, part II.A of the Northern Territory Criminal Code is a discriminatory law which only applies to persons with disabilities.[305] Australia on the other hand insisted 'that the Northern Territory Criminal Code does not treat persons any differently because of their disabilities, but provides for the differential treatment of people found "unfit to stand trial".[306] The Code was likely to disproportionately affect those who may meet those criteria for reasons associated with a disability, but such differential treatment was legitimate and well-established in international law in relation to both direct and indirect forms of discrimination.[307]

As clarified in paragraph 16 of the Committee's general comment No 6 (2018) on equality and non-discrimination, the term 'equal benefit of the law' means that States parties must eliminate barriers to gaining access to all of the protections of the law and the benefits of equal access to the law and justice to assert rights.[308] Throughout the author's detention (between 2008 and 2017) judicial procedure focused on his mental capacity to stand trial without giving him any possibility to plead not guilty or to respond to the charges against him.[309] The Committee therefore considered that part II.A of the Criminal Code resulted in the discriminatory treatment of the author's case, in violation of article 5 (1) and (2) of the Convention.[310]

Moreover the Committee noted that, according to the information provided, the author was not consulted at any stage of the procedures regarding his custody and accommodation and considered that confining the author to live in a special institution on account of his disability from April 2013 to February 2017 amounted to a violation of article 5 of the Convention.[311]

9.2   *Article 12—Equal Recognition before the Law and Article 13—Access to Justice*

On the issue of admissibility, the Committee remarked:

> [D]omestic remedies need not be exhausted if they objectively have no prospect of success. In this connection, the Committee notes the author's argument that, for his appeal to have any chance of success, he would have had to demonstrate that the Court's decisions were in error, while in fact

---

305   Ibid 12 [8.2].
306   Ibid 6 [4.11].
307   Ibid.
308   Ibid 13 [8.4].
309   Ibid.
310   Ibid.
311   Ibid 13 [8.5].

462   AUSTRALIAN YEAR BOOK OF INTERNATIONAL LAW VOLUME 38

they were adopted in compliance with the Northern Territory Criminal Code. The Committee notes that this appreciation relies on the law itself, alleging that it violates the author's rights under the Convention, and it does not correspond to a question of interpretation or application of the legislation by domestic courts. In view thereof, the Committee considers that no additional effective remedies were available to the author and that his claims under articles 12, 13 and 14 are admissible.[312]

The author's alleged that his rights under 12 (2) and (3) and 13 (1) of the Convention were violated due to the decision that he was unfit to stand trial depriving him of the possibility to exercise his legal capacity to answer the charges against him.[313] The Committee emphasised that a person's status as a person with disabilities or the existence of an impairment must never be grounds for denying legal capacity or any of the rights provided for in article 12.[314] Moreover, under article 12 (2), States parties have the obligation to recognise that persons with disabilities enjoy legal capacity on an equal basis, and under article 12 (3), States parties must provide access to the support that persons with disabilities may require to exercise their legal capacity.[315] The Committee also recalled that, under article 13 (1), States parties must ensure effective access to justice for persons with disabilities on an equal basis with others.[316]

Being deemed unfit to stand trial resulted in the denial of the author's right to exercise his legal capacity to plead not guilty and to test the evidence against him.[317] The Committee considered that no adequate form of support or accommodation was provided by the State party's authorities to enable the author to stand trial and exercise legal capacity.[318] He therefore never had the opportunity to have the criminal charges against him determined. In view of this, the situation under review amounted to a violation of the author's rights under articles 12 (2) and (3) and 13 (1) of the Convention.[319]

9.3   Article 14—Liberty and Security of Person
On the facts provided to the Committee the following conclusion was reached:

---

312   Ibid 12 [7.5].
313   Ibid 13–14 [8.6].
314   Ibid.
315   Ibid.
316   Ibid.
317   Ibid 14 [8.7].
318   Ibid.
319   Ibid.

The author's detention ... decided on the basis of the assessment by the State party's authorities of potential consequences of his intellectual disability, in the absence of any criminal conviction, thereby convert[ed] his disability into the core cause of his detention. The Committee therefore considers that the author's detention amounts to a violation of article 14 (1)(b) of the Convention, according to which the existence of a disability shall in no case justify a deprivation of liberty.[320]

9.4 Article 15—Freedom from Torture, Cruel, Inhuman or Degrading Treatment or Punishment

For the purposes of admissibility, the Committee was satisfied that the author had substantiated his claims under article 15, 19, 25, 26 and 28.[321]

The author submitted that he was detained in maximum security, held in custody with convicted persons, subjected to involuntary treatment and also acts of violence from other prisoners.[322] The State party admitted that the author was not separated at all times from convicted offenders, was temporarily held in isolation and was sometimes subjected to involuntary treatment.[323] Additionally, the Committee noted that the author was committed to custody, first in Alice Springs Correctional Centre and then in a secure care facility, for more than nine years, without having any prior indication as to the expected duration of his detention. The Committee considered the author's custody indefinite even if in compliance with section 43ZC of part II.A of the Northern Territory Criminal Code.[324]

Through a consideration of the irreparable psychological effects that indefinite detention may have on a detained person, the Committee considered that the indefinite custody to which the author was subjected amounts to inhuman and degrading treatment.[325] Even though the author did not demonstrate that he was subjected to violence from other prisoners, a violation of article 15 was founded on the indefinite character of his custody, his detention in a correctional centre without being convicted of a criminal offence, his periodic isolation, his involuntary treatment and his detention together with convicted offenders.[326]

---

320 Ibid 14 [8.8].
321 Ibid 12 [7.7].
322 Ibid 15 [8.10].
323 Ibid.
324 Ibid.
325 Ibid.
326 Ibid.

9.5 Article 19—Living Independently and Being Included in the Community; Article 25—Health. Article 26—Habitation and Rehabilitation and Article 28 Adequate Standard of Living and Social Protection

The author's complaints under article 19 were considered by the Committee to be moot due to a decision on 9 February 2017 to grant the author the possibility of living in a community residence in Alice Springs.[327] As for further complaints submitted under articles 25, 26 and 28 the statement of facts received from the author and Australia were too inconsistent for the Committee to make findings as to the Convention's violation on these points.[328]

9.6 Conclusions and Recommendations

The Committee concluded with the view that Australia had failed to fulfil its obligations under articles 5, 12, 13, 14 and 15 of the Convention. In addition to requests that the author be provided with an effective remedy the Committee made the following recommendations:

1. Amend part IIA of the Northern Territory Criminal Code and all equivalent or related federal and State legislation, in close consultation with persons with disabilities and their representative organizations, in such a way as to comply with the principles of the Convention and with the Committee's guidelines on the right to liberty and security of persons with disabilities;

2. Ensure without delay that adequate support and accommodation measures are provided to persons with intellectual and psychosocial disabilities to enable them to exercise their legal capacity before the courts whenever necessary;

3. Protect the right to live independently and be included in the community by taking steps, to the maximum of its available resources, to create community residences in order to replace any institutionalized settings with independent living support services;

4. Ensure that appropriate and regular training on the scope of the Convention and its Optional Protocol, including on the exercise of legal capacity and access to justice, is provided to staff working with persons with intellectual and psychosocial disabilities, members of the Law Reform Commission and Parliament, judicial officers and staff involved in facilitating the work of the judiciary, and avoid using high-security

---

327 Ibid 15 [8.11].
328 Ibid 15 [8.12].

CASES CONCERNING QUESTIONS OF PUBLIC INTERNATIONAL LAW 2019   465

institutions for the confinement of, persons with intellectual and psycho-social disabilities.[329]

10   **Committee on the Rights of Persons with Disabilities—Access to Court—Intellectual and Psychosocial Disability—Exercise of Legal Capacity—Deprivation of Liberty—Discrimination on the Ground of Disability—Restrictions of Rights—Exhaustion of Domestic Remedies**

Views adopted by the Committee under article 5 of the Optional Protocol
Communication No 18/2013
UN Doc CRPD/C/22/D/17/2013
Committee on the Rights of Persons with Disabilities
Views adopted 30 August 2019

Communication submitted by:	Christopher Leo (represented by counsel, Phillip French and Mark Patrick, Australian Centre for Disability Law)
Alleged victim:	The author
State party:	Australia
Date of communication:	19 September 2013 (initial submission)
Document references:	Decision taken pursuant to rule 70 of the Committee's rules of procedure, transmitted to the State party on 21 November 2013 (not issued in document form)
Date of adoption of Views:	30 August 2019
Subject matters:	Institutionalization of person with intellectual and psychosocial impairment; right to enjoy legal capacity on an equal basis with others
Procedural issue:	Exhaustion of domestic remedies

---

329   Ibid 16 [9].

Substantive issues:	Access to court; intellectual and psychosocial disability; exercise of legal capacity; deprivation of liberty; discrimination on the ground of disability; restrictions of rights
Articles of the Convention:	5, 12, 13, 14, 15, 19, 25, 26 and 28
Article of the Optional Protocol:	2

The view of the committee offered in the case of *Manuway Doolan v Australia*[330] were reiterated almost identically in the case of *Christopher Leo v Australia*,[331] decided at the same time. Leo, also an Aboriginal man with intellectual impairment arising from a brain injury, epilepsy and mental illness spent a total of 5 years and 10 months in custody in prison, which was almost six times the period of custody he would have been required to serve had he been convicted of the offences with which he was charged after being found unfit to stand trial due to his mental impairment. He too was dealt with under the provisions of part IIA of the *Criminal Code Act 1983* (NT). His claims under articles 5, 12, 13, 14 and 15 were successful, and insufficient evidence was adduced to deal with complaints under articles 19, 25, 26 and 28. The same recommendations were made by the Committee.

11   *United Nations Convention against Torture and Other Cruel, Inhuman or Degrading Treatment or Punishment*
Committee against Torture—Risk to Life and Risk of Torture or Ill-Treatment in the Event of Deportation to Country of Origin— Lack of Substantiation of Claims—Non-Exhaustion of Domestic Remedies

Decision adopted by the Committee under article 22 of the Convention
Communication No 749/2016
UN Doc CAT/C/66/D/749/2016
Committee against Torture
Views adopted 3 May 2019

---

330   *Manuway Doolan v Australia* (n 293).

331   Committee on the Rights of Persons with Disabilities, *Views adopted by the Committee under article 5 of the Optional Protocol, concerning communication No 17/2013* UN Doc CRPD/C/22/D/17/2013 (18 October 2019) ('*Christopher Leo v Australia*').

Communication submitted by:	X (represented by counsel, John Phillip Sweeney)
Alleged victim:	The complainant
State party:	Australia
Date of complaint:	22 April 2016 (initial submission)
Document references:	Decision taken pursuant to rule 115 of the Committee's rules of procedure, transmitted to the State party on 10 May 2016
Date of present decision:	3 May 2019
Subject matter:	Deportation to Sri Lanka
Procedural issues	Lack of substantiation of claims; non-exhaustion of domestic remedies
Substantive issues:	Risk to life and risk of torture or ill-treatment in the event of deportation to country of origin
Article of the Convention:	3

Article 3 of the *Convention against Torture, Cruel, Inhuman or Degrading Treatment or Punishment* forms parts of Australia's non-refoulement obligations and prohibits the return of individuals 'to another State where there are substantial grounds for believing that he would be in danger of being subjected to torture'.[332] The Committee against Torture receives individuals' complaints under article 22 of the Convention.[333]

The complainant in this case was born in Sri Lanka and worked as a private gem trader in Sri Lanka and several other countries from 1993 to 2011.[334] In Sri Lanka he lived as a pious Muslim who supported the United National Party and was asked to run as a candidate in the 2010 parliamentary elections.[335] Upon refusing an offer to run with the opposing United People's Freedom Party Alliance the complainant received threats from a sitting Alliance Party

---

332 *Convention against Torture, Cruel, Inhuman or Degrading Treatment or Punishment*, opened for signature 10 December 1984, 1465 UNTS 85 (entered into force 26 June 1987), art 3.

333 Ibid art 22.

334 Committee against Torture, *Decision adopted by the Committee under article 22 of the Convention, concerning communication No 749/2016*, UN Doc CAT/C/66/D/749/2016 (2 September 2019) 2.1 ('*X v Australia*').

335 Ibid 2 [2.2].

Member of Parliament, Y.[336] Threats materialised and the complaint claims he was assaulted and locked in the United People's Freedom Party Alliance office for three days during which time he was tied to a concrete post and tortured, his hands were burned, and he was not given any food.[337] After release the claimant was treated at the National Hospital in Colombo.[338] With the threats continued and fearing that he would be killed, the complainant left Sri Lanka for Australia.[339]

On 23 October 2011 the claimant entered Australia on a short stay visa, and on 22 November 2011[340] he commenced his application for a protection visa, which was rejected on 6 February 2013 due to a lack of substantial grounds for believing that the complainant would suffer a real risk of significant harm on return to Sri Lanka.[341] The complainant appealed to the Refugee Review Tribunal, but the original decision was upheld; he then appealed to the Federal Circuit Court of Australia.[342] However, a new barrister took the case and advanced the opinion that there were 'no prospects of success', and on 8 March 2016 the complainant withdrew this application.[343]

On 9 March, the complainant appealed to the Minister for Immigration and Border Protection to intervene on his behalf, but his request was rejected on 6 April.[344] The complainant maintained that he had thus exhausted all available domestic remedies and made his application the Committee against Torture. The complainant referred to section 486I of the Migration Act 1958[345] to say that an appeal to the Federal Circuit Court would not have a reasonable prospect of success, but the Committee held that

---

336   Ibid 2 [2.3].
337   Ibid 2 [2.5].
338   Ibid.
339   Ibid.
340   Ibid 2 [2.7].
341   Ibid 2 [2.8].
342   Ibid 2 [2.9].
343   Ibid.
344   Ibid.
345   Section 486I reads as follows:
       Lawyer's certification
       (1) A lawyer must not file a document commencing migration litigation, unless the lawyer certifies in writing that there are reasonable grounds for believing that the migration litigation has a reasonable prospect of success.
       (2) A court must refuse to accept a document commencing migration litigation if it is a document that, under subsection (1), must be certified and it has not been.

there is nothing in section 486I of the Migration Act to suggest that an appeal submitted in good faith will not be considered. In the present case, it was the personal conclusion of the lawyer rather than the lack of effectiveness of the remedy that prevented the complainant from exhausting domestic remedies. The Committee recalls its consistent jurisprudence that mere doubt about the effectiveness of a remedy does not dispense with the obligation to exhaust it.[346]

With the case failing on grounds of admissibility, the Committee did not deem it necessary to comment on other facts of the case including the correctness of the conclusions reached by the State party that there was a lack of evidence that the complainant was currently or would be someone targeted by Y if returned to Sri Lanka[347] and the finding that a 'diagnosis ticket' from the National Hospital of Sri Lanka indicating assault and injury to the head was fraudulently created.[348]

12   **Committee against Torture—Risk of Torture in the Event of Deportation to Country of Origin (Non-Refoulement) Admissibility—Manifestly Ill-Founded**

Decision adopted by the Committee under article 22 of the Convention
Communication No 723/2015
UN Doc CAT/C/67/D/723/2015
Committee against Torture
Views adopted 2 August 2019

Communication submitted by:	VM (represented by counsel, John Sweeney)
Alleged victim:	The complainant
State party:	Australia
Date of complaint:	30 December 2015 (initial submission)

---

346   *X v Australia* (n 334) 5 [7.3].

347   Ibid 4 [4.7].

348   Ibid 4 [4.6].

Document references:	Decision taken pursuant to rule 115 of the Committee's rules of procedure, transmitted to the State party on 30 December 2015 (not issued in document form)
Date of adoption of decision:	2 August 2019
Subject matter:	Deportation to Sri Lanka
Procedural issue:	Admissibility—manifestly ill-founded
Substantive issue:	Risk of torture in the event of deportation to country of origin (non-refoulement)
Article of the Convention:	3

The case put forward by the complainant, a national of Sri Lanka born in 1967, was that he was at significant risk of being subject to torture by the Sri Lanka Army and Navy if returned to Sri Lanka due to several incidents that were traceable back to his Tamil ethnicity.[349] His primary fear was being targeted as a witness of war crimes and other acts of torture committed by the army.[350] There was also fear regarding how he would be treated if returned as a failed asylum seeker.[351] It was claimed that the denial by Australia of his asylum visa was a breach of obligations under article 3 of the *Convention against Torture* ('CAT').[352]

The claim was admissible as all domestic avenues had been appropriately exhausted; however, the Committee shared the same concerns as Australian authorities regarding the credibility of the complaint's submissions.[353] The committee supported Australia's submission that considering the available country information, it could not be satisfied that ethnic Tamils were subject to a real chance of persecution by the authorities of Sri Lanka on account of their ethnicity alone, or that the complainant was subject to a real chance of persecution because of his status as a failed asylum seeker.[354] Overall the Committee accepted the State party's submission regarding the complainant's claim of witnessing war crimes: that such claim was surprisingly not raised

---

349 Committee against Torture, *Decision adopted by the Committee under article 22 of the Convention, concerning communication No 723/2015*, UN Doc CAT/C/67/D/723/2015 (4 September 2019) (*'VM v Australia'*).

350 Ibid 2 [3.1].

351 Ibid 3 [3.2].

352 Ibid 2 [3.1].

353 Ibid 8 [7.5].

354 Ibid.

before the domestic authorities and in any event, it was implausible that the complainant resided in Sri Lanka for another three years after the alleged incident without being identified or targeted by the Sri Lanka Army.[355]

The complainant failed to adduce sufficient evidence and to adequately substantiate his contention that the alleged past events would attract the real interest of the authorities of Sri Lanka.[356] The Committee therefore held that the complainant had not adduced sufficient grounds to enable it to believe that he would run a real, foreseeable, personal and present risk of being subjected to torture upon his return to Sri Lanka.[357]

355   Ibid.
356   Ibid 9–10 [7.8]
357   Ibid 10 [8].

Australian Legislation concerning Matters of International Law 2019

Angad Keith, Malithi Karunaarachchi, Chiara Angeloni, Asha Belkin, Sarah Grant, Andrea Gronke, Kryssa Karavolas, Hayley Keen, Guy Kelleher, Fatima Malik, Pranamie Mandalawatta, Kate O'Connell, Caitlin O'Rourke, Amparo Santiago, Navina Vijaysegaran, Emma Wiggins and Phoebe Winch

1 Acts 2019

1.1 *Combatting Child Sexual Exploitation Legislation Amendment Act 2019* (Cth) (No 72 of 2019)

This Act amends the *Criminal Code Act 1995* (Cth) ('*Criminal Code*'), the *Crimes Act 1914* (Cth) ('*Crimes Act*'), the *Customs Act 1901* (Cth) ('*Customs Act*'), the *Telecommunications (Interception and Access) Act 1979* (Cth) and the *Surveillance Devices Act 2004* (Cth) to strengthen the laws protecting children from sexual abuse.

The amendments give further effect to Australia's obligations under arts 19 and 34 of the *Convention on the Rights of the Child*,[1] to, among other matters, undertake to protect children from all forms of sexual exploitation and abuse, including by taking all appropriate legislative, administrative, social and educational measures. In particular, the Act criminalises the possession of a child-like sex doll under the *Criminal Code* and makes a child-like sex doll 'child abuse material' for the purposes of the *Criminal Code* and the *Customs Act*. The amendments aim to criminalise purported sexual abuse of children through the use of child-like sex dolls in order to reduce the risks that these behaviours may escalate the risk posed to real children.

The Act also updates the terminology used for child sexual abuse offences in Commonwealth legislation, by repealing references to 'child pornography material' and reconstituting the current definitions of 'child abuse material' and 'child pornography material' into a single definition of 'child abuse material'. It does this to reflect the gravity of these crimes, the harm that is inflicted on the children involved, and shifts in national and international best practice (including as reflected in international instruments, such as the United

---

1   Opened for signature 20 November 1989, 1577 UNTS 3 (entered into force 2 September 1990).

AUSTRALIAN LEGISLATION

Nations' Commission on Crime Prevention and Criminal Justice 2019 resolution 'Countering Child Sexual Exploitation and Sexual Abuse Online').[2]

This Act commenced on 20 September 2019.

1.2 Customs Amendment (Immediate Destruction of Illicit Tobacco) Act 2019 (Cth) (No 76 of 2019)

This Act amends the Customs Act to allow the Comptroller-General of Customs to cause tobacco products seized as prohibited imports to be dealt with in a manner he or she considers appropriate, including the immediate destruction of the goods. The amendments support the implementation of Australia's obligations under the World Health Organisation's Framework Convention on Tobacco Control ('Framework Convention'),[3] under which Australia has committed to implement policies to adopt measures for preventing and reducing tobacco consumption, nicotine addiction and exposure to tobacco smoke. In particular, art 15(4) of the Framework Convention requires Australia to enact or strengthen legislation against illicit trade in tobacco products, and take appropriate steps to ensure that confiscated tobacco products are destroyed or disposed of in accordance with national law.[4]

This Act commenced on 3 October 2019.

1.3 Industrial Chemicals Act 2019 (Cth) (No 12 of 2019)

This Act establishes a new risk-based national regulatory scheme for industrial chemicals in Australia. Part 9 of the Act implements certain obligations of Australia under the Rotterdam Convention on the Prior Informed Consent Procedure for Certain Hazardous Chemicals and Pesticides in International Trade ('Rotterdam Convention').[5] The Rotterdam Convention aims to promote shared responsibility and cooperative efforts among States Parties in the international trade of certain hazardous chemicals by facilitating information exchange about the characteristics of such chemicals, by providing for a national decision-making process on their import and export and by disseminating these decisions to Parties.[6]

For example, s 159 of the Act implements Australia's obligation under art 5(1) of the Rotterdam Convention by making the Executive Director of the

---

2 Commission on Crime Prevention and Criminal Justice, Combatting Child Sexual Exploitation and Sexual Abuse Online, UN GAOR, 3rd Comm, 74th sess, Agenda Item 106 UN Doc A/C.3/74/L.6 (23 September 2019).

3 Opened for signature 16 June 2003, 2302 UNTS 166 (entered into force 27 February 2005).

4 Ibid art 15(4).

5 Opened for signature 10 September 1998, 2244 UNTS 337 (entered into force 24 February 2004).

6 Ibid art 1.

Australian Industrial Chemicals Introduction Scheme responsible for notifying Australia's designated national authority when laws are made, or actions are taken, that have the effect of banning or severely restricting the introduction or use of an industrial chemical. Australia's designated national authority is then responsible for providing this information to the Secretariat. Part 9 also regulates the processes for prohibiting, or imposing conditions on, the introduction or export of industrial chemicals, where Australia is a party to an international agreement or an arrangement that deals with such prohibitions or restrictions.

Sections 1 and 2 of the Act commenced on 12 March 2019; ss 3–180 will commence on 1 July 2020.

1.4 *National Disability Insurance Scheme Amendment (Worker Screening Database) Act 2019* (Cth) (No 82 of 2019)

This Act amends the *National Disability Insurance Scheme Act 2013* (Cth) ('*NDIS Act*') to establish a database for nationally consistent worker screening, for the purpose of minimising the risk of harm to people with disability from those who work closely with them. The database will provide and maintain current and accurate information relating to worker screening checks. The database will also be administered by the National Disability Insurance Scheme ('NDIS') Quality and Safeguards Commissioner, assisted by the NDIS Quality and Safeguards Commission.

This Act supports the protection of the rights of people with disability in Australia consistent with the *Convention on the Rights of Persons with Disabilities* ('CRPD'),[7] particularly art 16 which requires States Parties to take all appropriate legislative, administrative, social, educational and other measures to protect persons with disabilities from all forms of exploitation, violence and abuse. The measures contained in the *NDIS Act* protect the rights of people with disability by reducing the potential for NDIS providers to employ workers who pose an unacceptable risk of harm to people with disability; prohibiting those persons who have a history of harm against people with disability from having more than incidental contact with people with disability when working for a registered NDIS provider; and deterring individuals who pose an unacceptable risk of harm from seeking work in the sector.

This Act commenced on 3 October 2019.

---

7 Opened for signature 13 December 2006, 2515 UNTS 3 (entered into force 3 May 2008).

AUSTRALIAN LEGISLATION

1.5   *National Sports Tribunal Act 2019* (Cth) (No 68 of 2019)
       *National Sports Tribunal (Consequential Amendments and
       Transitional Provisions) Act 2019* (Cth) (No 69 of 2019)

The *National Sports Tribunal Act 2019* (Cth) ('*NST Act*') establishes the National
Sports Tribunal ('Tribunal') to ensure the Australian sporting community has
access to effective, efficient, transparent and independent specialist sports
dispute resolution services. The Tribunal will have an Anti-Doping Division,
a General Division and an Appeals Division. The *NST Act* gives effect to
Australia's obligation under the *International Convention against Doping in
Sport*[8] to adopt appropriate measures which are consistent with the principles
of the World Anti-Doping Code,[9] particularly in relation to hearing of matters
in the Anti-Doping and Appeals divisions. The Tribunal may resolve disputes
through mediation, conciliation or case appraisal, and will not exercise judicial power.

The *National Sports Tribunal (Consequential Amendments and Transitional
Provisions) Act 2019* (Cth) ('*NST Amendments Act*') amends Commonwealth
legislation to address consequential and transitional matters arising from the
enactment of the *NST Act*. For example, the *NST Amendments Act* amends the
Australian Sports Anti-Doping Authority Act 2006 (Cth) such that the National
Anti-Doping Scheme is required to authorise the Chief Executive Officer of
the Australian Sports Anti-Doping Authority, in certain circumstances, to present certain assertions and information at hearings of the Tribunal. The *NST
Amendments Act* also amends the *Freedom of Information Act 1982* (Cth) ('*FOI
Act*') to exempt material from requirements to release imposed by the *FOI Act*,
to align with s 72 of the *NST Act*.

These Acts commenced on 19 March 2020.

1.6   Implementation of the *Treaty between Australia and the
       Democratic Republic of Timor-Leste Establishing Their Maritime
       Boundaries in the Timor Sea*
       *Timor Sea Maritime Boundaries Treaty Consequential Amendments
       Act 2019* (Cth) (No 57 of 2019)
       *Passenger Movement Charge Amendment (Timor Sea Maritime
       Boundaries Treaty) Act 2019* (Cth) (No 58 of 2019)

The Acts partially implement the *Treaty between Australia and the Democratic
Republic of Timor-Leste Establishing Their Maritime Boundaries in the Timor Sea*
('*Timor Sea Maritime Boundaries Treaty*').[10]

---

8   Opened for signature 19 October 2005, 2419 UNTS 201 (entered into force 1 February 2007).
9   Ibid art 3(a).
10   Signed 6 March 2018, [2019] ATS 16 (entered into force 30 August 2019).

The *Timor Sea Maritime Boundaries Treaty* establishes permanent maritime boundaries between Australia and Timor-Leste and also establishes the Greater Sunrise Special Regime in the Special Regime Area. The Special Regime Area is an area extending over the Sunrise and Troubadour gas and condensate fields, collectively known as the Greater Sunrise Fields. Under art 9 of the *Timor Sea Maritime Boundaries Treaty*, upon its entry into force the *Timor Sea Treaty between the Government of East Timor and the Government of Australia ('Timor Sea Treaty')*[11] and the *Agreement between the Government of Australia and the Government of Timor-Leste relating to the Unitisation of the Sunrise and Troubadour Fields ('Greater Sunrise Unitisation Agreement')*[12] ceased to be in force, including the Joint Petroleum Development Area established under art 3 of the *Timor Sea Treaty*.[13]

The *Timor Sea Maritime Boundaries Treaty Consequential Amendments Act 2019* (Cth) amends Commonwealth legislation to, among other matters, reflect the new permanent continental shelf boundary and the exclusive economic zone boundary between Australia and Timor-Leste; establish and define the Greater Sunrise Special Regime in the Special Regime Area to give effect to the Treaty; establish an administrative and governance framework for the joint development, exploitation and management of petroleum in the Special Regime Area, and to provide for the exercise of jurisdiction with respect to environmental protection, vessels and criminal law matters. This Act commenced in August 2019.

The *Passenger Movement Charge Amendment (Timor Sea Maritime Boundaries Treaty) Act 2019* (Cth) makes consequential amendments to the *Passenger Movement Charge Act 1978* (Cth) by removing references to the Joint Petroleum Development Area and inserting references to the Greater Sunrise Special Regime. This Act commenced in August 2019.

1.7   *Treasury Laws Amendment (Timor Sea Maritime Boundaries Treaty) Act 2019* (Cth) (No 59 of 2019)

This Act amends the *Income Tax Assessment Act 1997* (Cth) to give effect to tax arrangements required to support the *Timor Sea Maritime Boundaries Treaty*.[14] In particular, this Act fulfils Australia's obligation under the Treaty to provide 'conditions equivalent' to participants in transitioned petroleum activities

---

11   Signed 20 May 2002, [2003] ATS 13 (entered into force 2 April 2003).
12   Signed 6 March 2003, [2007] ATS 11 (entered into force 23 February 2007).
13   *Timor Sea Maritime Boundaries Treaty* (n 10) art 10(a).
14   *Timor Sea Maritime Boundaries Treaty* (n 10).

affected by the *Timor Maritime Boundary Treaty* in respect of their taxation affairs.[15]

The *Timor Sea Maritime Boundaries Treaty* affects two classes of petroleum activities. First, projects in the Joint Petroleum Development Area, which were subject to Australian income tax on 10 per cent of the taxable income and to Timorese income tax on 90 per cent of an equivalent Timorese amount, but following the entry into force of the *Timor Sea Maritime Boundaries Treaty*, transferred to being entirely within Timorese jurisdiction. Second, the portion of Australian exploration permit WA-523-P, which was within Australian jurisdiction and also transitioned to be within Timor-Leste's jurisdiction. The primary effect of the jurisdictional transition on the tax affairs of these projects is that they cease to generate Australian assessable income and instead generate Timorese income. The amendments ensure that taxation arrangements applying to transitioning petroleum activities in the Timor Sea will continue in accordance with annex D to the *Timor Sea Maritime Boundaries Treaty*, including providing 'conditions equivalent' to disadvantaged taxpayers.

The amendments commenced on 30 August 2019.

1.8 *Wine Australia Amendment (Trade with the United Kingdom) Act 2019* (Cth) (No 11 of 2019)

Currently, trade in wine between Australia and the United Kingdom ('UK') is regulated by the *Agreement between Australia and the European Community on Trade in Wine ('Wine Agreement')*.[16] However, the UK has now left the EU and the *Wine Agreement* will cease to apply to the UK at the end of the transition period agreed between the UK and the EU. This Act amends the *Wine Australia Act 2013* (Cth) (*'Wine Australia Act'*), which gives effect to the *Wine Agreement*, to ensure that the UK continues to be treated as an 'agreement country' for the purposes of the *Wine Australia Act*. These amendments will enable the continued trade in wine between Australia and the UK during any transition period.

The Act commenced on 13 March 2019.

---

15   Ibid annex D (*'Transitional Provisions'*) art 4(2).
16   Signed 1 December 2008, [2010] ATS 19 (entered into force 1 September 2010).

478　AUSTRALIAN YEAR BOOK OF INTERNATIONAL LAW VOLUME 38

2　Regulations 2019

2.1　*Air Navigation (Gold Coast Airport Curfew) Amendment (Technical Measures) Regulations 2019* (Cth) (F2019L01249)

These regulations are made under the *Air Navigation Act 1920* (Cth), which implements the *Convention on International Civil Aviation* (*'Chicago Convention'*)[17] and the *International Air Services Transit Agreement*[18] into Australian law.

The regulations amend the *Air Navigation (Gold Coast Airport Curfew) Regulations 2018* (Cth) to: define helicopter and maximum take-off weight to align definitions in similar legislation, add a provision to permit aircraft to only land and not take-off during the curfew period (11pm to 6am daily), and clarify that non-emergency helicopters are not permitted to operate during the curfew period. In particular, the regulations insert a definition of 'helicopter' to clarify that the term has the same meaning as in annex 16 vol 1 to the *Chicago Convention*.

The regulations commenced on 24 September 2019 and were repealed on 6 December 2019 by operation of ch 3 pt 3 div 1 of the *Legislation Act 2003* (Cth) (*'Legislation Act'*).

2.2　*Air Services Regulations 2019* (Cth) (F2019C00814)

These regulations are made under the *Air Services Act 1995* (Cth) (*'Air Services Act'*), which establishes Airservices Australia—a corporate Commonwealth entity that provides services to promote the safety, regularity and efficiency of air navigation, consistent with Australia's obligations under the *Chicago Convention*. The regulations replace the *Air Services Regulations 1995* (Cth), which were due to sunset on 1 April 2019, ensuring continuity of the law, and enabling Airservices Australia to continue to carry out its functions.

The regulations note that—as established by s 9 of the *Air Services Act*—Airservices Australia must perform its functions in a manner that is consistent with Australia's obligations under the *Chicago Convention*. Consistent with these obligations: regs 14 and 15 contain obligations in relation to the publication of aeronautical information, reg 16 provides for the functions of rescue and fire-fighting services, reg 20 stipulates the functions of Airservices Australia in providing services and facilities to assist in emergencies and other circumstances, reg 28 stipulates the provision of meteorological information and reg 40 provides that messages extracted from the Aeronautical

---

17　Opened for signature 7 December 1944, 15 UNTS 295 (entered into force 4 April 1947).

18　Opened for signature 7 December 1944, 84 UNTS 389 (entered into force 30 January 1945).

AUSTRALIAN LEGISLATION 479

Fixed Telecommunication Network, as referred to in annex 10 to the *Chicago Convention*, may be used as evidence of flight by an aircraft.

The regulations commenced on 6 November 2019.

2.3 *Australian Human Rights Commission Regulations 2019* (Cth) (F2019L01188)

These regulations are made under the *Australian Human Rights Commission Act 1986* (Cth).

The purpose of the regulations is to remake the *Australian Human Rights Commission Regulations 1989* (Cth), which were due to sunset on 1 October 2019, to ensure that they remain fit-for-purpose and in line with community and stakeholder expectations.

The regulations promote the right to equality and non-discrimination under art 26 of the *International Covenant on Civil and Political Rights*[19] and art 5 of the CRPD.[20] The regulations replace the three disability-related grounds with a single ground of 'disability', which ensures that all forms of disability are captured without distinguishing between different types of disability. This aligns the treatment of disability discrimination issues with the more contemporary concepts and terminology employed in the *Disability Discrimination Act 1992* (Cth). Regulation 6 of the regulations also replaces the 'criminal record' attribute with 'an irrelevant criminal record', which provides further guidance to employers and prospective employees about when job applications can be rejected from people with criminal records— striking a better balance between allowing those with criminal records to find employment, while ensuring employers can refuse to employ someone where their criminal record makes them unsuitable in the position for which they have applied.

The regulations commenced on 1 October 2019.

2.4 Regulations Made under the *Charter of the United Nations Act 1945* (Cth)

Section 6 of the *Charter of the United Nations Act 1945* (Cth) ('*UN Charter Act*') permits the making of regulations to give effect to sanctions (not involving the use of force) adopted by the United Nations Security Council ('UNSC') under ch VII of the *Charter of the United Nations* ('*UN Charter*'). Regulations made under this authority in 2019 are outlined below.

---

19   Opened for signature 19 December 1966, 999 UNTS 171 (entered into force 23 March 1976).
20   CRPD (n 7).

**2.5   Charter of the United Nations (Sanctions—South Sudan)
Amendment (2019 Measures No 1) Regulations 2019 (Cth)
(F2019L00112)**

These regulations amend the *Charter of the United Nations (Sanctions—South Sudan) Regulation 2015* (Cth) (*'Principal Regulation'*) to implement Australia's international obligations under UNSC *Resolution 2428*[21] to impose an arms embargo in relation to South Sudan. *Resolution 2428* was adopted in the context of continued hostilities and violations[22] of the *Agreement on the Resolution of the Conflict of the Republic of South Sudan*,[23] the *Agreement on the Cessation of Hostilities, Protection of Civilians and Humanitarian Access*[24] and the *Khartoum Declaration of Agreement between Parties of the Conflict of South Sudan.*[25]

Specifically, the regulations amend the *Principal Regulation* to prevent the direct or indirect supply, sale or transfer to South Sudan of arms or related materiel, by an Australian or from Australia territory. Arms or related materiel include: weapons, ammunition, military vehicles and equipment, paramilitary equipment, as well as spare parts for these items.[26] The regulations also prohibit the provision of technical, training and financial assistance related to military activities or the provision of arms or related materiel to the territory of South Sudan.[27] There are some limited exceptions, for example a supply intended solely for the support of United Nations ('UN') personnel.[28]

The regulations commenced on 12 February 2019 and were repealed on 2 August 2019 pursuant to ch 3 pt 3 div 1 of the *Legislation Act.*

**2.6   Charter of the United Nations Legislation Amendment (2019
Measures No 1) Regulations 2019 (Cth) (F2019L00404)**

Schedule 1 pt 1 of the regulations repeal the *Charter of the United Nations (Sanctions—Eritrea) Regulations 2010* (Cth) pursuant to UNSC *Resolution 2444*,[29] which requires all Member States to lift UN-mandated sanctions in

---

21   SC Res 2428, UN Doc S/RES/2428 (13 July 2018), para 4.

22   Ibid Preamble para 5(1).

23   Signed 17 August 2015.

24   Signed 21 December 2017.

25   Signed 27 June 2018.

26   *Charter of the United Nations (Sanctions—South Sudan) Amendment (2019 Measures No 1) Regulations 2019* (Cth) sch 1 s 2, amending *Principal Regulation* s 4.

27   Ibid sch 1 s 4, amending *Principal Regulation* s 4.

28   Ibid sch 1 s 7, amending *Principal Regulation* pt 2.

29   SC Res 2444, UN Doc S/RES/2444 (14 November 2018), para 4.

AUSTRALIAN LEGISLATION   481

relation to Eritrea originally imposed by UNSC *Resolution 1907*,[30] *Resolution 2023*,[31] *Resolution 2060*[32] and *Resolution 2111*.[33] Schedule 1 pt 2 of the regulations also make consequential amendments to the *Charter of the United Nations (Dealing with Assets) Regulations 2008* (Cth) and update the reference to the 'United Nations Consolidated Appeal for Somalia' in the *Charter of the United Nations (Sanctions—Somalia) Regulations 2008* (Cth) consistently with *Resolution 2444*.

The regulations commenced on 27 March 2019 and were repealed on 12 September 2019 by operation of ch 3 pt 3 div 1 of the *Legislation Act*.

2.7 *Charter of the United Nations (Sanctions—Central African Republic) Amendment (2019 Measures No 1) Regulations 2019* (Cth) (F2019L00576)

These regulations amend the *Charter of the United Nations (Sanctions— Central African Republic) Regulation 2014* (Cth) in order to give effect to UNSC *Resolution 2399*,[34] continued in *Resolution 2454*.[35]

The regulations implement measures in *Resolution 2399* and set out the circumstances where arms and related materiel can be supplied, sold or transferred to the Central African Republic ('CAR'). The regulations update the exceptions to the arms embargo to: update the list of international forces providing support to the CAR; enable the supply of non-lethal equipment and technical assistance or training for use in the CAR process of security reform in coordination with the UN Multidimensional Integrated Stabilization Mission ('MINUSCA'); enable the supply of arms to Chadian or Sudanese forces solely for use in international patrols to enhance security in the common border areas, in cooperation with MINUSCA; require advance notification of the supply of arms to the UNSC CAR Sanctions Committee in certain circumstances; and clarify that 'CAR security forces' includes State civilian law enforcement institutions.

The regulations commenced on 9 April 2019 and were repealed on 17 September 2019 by operation of ch 3 pt 3 div 1 of the *Legislation Act*.

---

30   SC Res 1907, UN Doc S/RES/1907 (23 December 2009).
31   SC Res 2023, UN Doc S/RES/2023 (5 December 2011).
32   SC Res 2060, UN Doc S/RES/2060 (25 July 2012).
33   SC Res 2111, UN Doc S/RES/2111 (24 July 2013).
34   SC Res 2399, UN Doc S/RES/2399 (30 January 2018).
35   SC Res 2454, UN Doc S/RES/2454 (31 January 2019).

2.8 Regulations Made under the *Civil Aviation Act 1988* (Cth)
Civil Aviation Safety Amendment (Operations Definitions) Regulations 2019 (Cth) (F2019L00557)

The *Civil Aviation Safety Amendment (Operations Definitions) Regulations 2019* (Cth) (*'Operations Definitions Regulations'*) are made under the *Civil Aviation Act 1988* (Cth) (*'Civil Aviation Act'*). Sub-section 98(1)(c) of the Act provides that the Governor-General may make regulations for the purpose of carrying out or giving effect to provisions of the *Chicago Convention*[36] relating to safety.

Schedule 1 of the regulations includes amendments to the *Civil Aviation Safety Regulations 1998* (Cth) (*'CASR'*) to insert new terms and their definitions in pts 1 and 2 of the Dictionary in the *CASR*, and repeal and/or replace other defined terms. The new definitions of 'air traffic service' and 'aviation distress signal' directly incorporate definitions contained in the *Chicago Convention* by reference to annex 11 as well as s 1.1 of app 1 to annex 2 respectively. The amendments are consequential to the making of the flight operations suite of the *CASR* in December 2018, comprising Parts 91, 119, 121, 133, 135 and 138, which will commence on 25 March 2021. The *Civil Aviation Legislation Amendment (Parts 103, 105 and 131) Regulations 2019* (Cth) also make consequential amendments to Part 91 of the *CASR*, and amend the *Operations Definitions Regulations* by replacing certain definitions in those regulations. The *Operations Definitions Regulations* will also commence on 25 March 2021, and will be repealed on 26 March 2021 by operation of ch 3 pt 3 div 1 of the *Legislation Act*.

2.9 *Civil Aviation Safety Amendment (Part 139) Regulations 2019* (Cth) (F2019L00176)

These regulations are made under the *Civil Aviation Act*. The Civil Aviation Safety Authority ('CASA'), in consultation with industry, has undertaken a post-implementation review of pt 139 ('Aerodromes') of the *CASR*. The review found that, among other matters, in some cases aerodrome standards are not aligned with international standards and current industry best practice.

The regulations amend pt 139 of the *CASR* by repealing existing pts 139.A to 139.F in the *CASR* and replacing them with new pts 139.A to 139.E. The amendments update the regulatory framework by recognising development in technology and international standards since pt 139 of the *CASR* was first made in 2003. For example, the International Civil Aviation Organisation ('ICAO') has proposed changes to annex 14 vol 1 to the *Chicago Convention* that provide relief to aerodrome operators based on refined physical characteristics for the movement area. ICAO has published a new document,

---

36   *Chicago Convention* (n 17).

AUSTRALIAN LEGISLATION

PANS-Aerodromes (ICAO Doc 9981), which provides guidance on certification of aerodrome, safety management systems, aerodrome manuals, compatibility of aerodrome operations and infrastructure with aircraft that exceed the existing reference characteristics of the aerodrome. The new document will become applicable in November 2020. However, these changes are not yet reflected in current Australian requirements.

'The regulations commenced on 22 August 2020 and were repealed on 23 August 2020 by operation of ch 3 pt 3 div 1 of the *Legislation Act*'.

2.10 *Crimes (Biological Weapons) Regulations 2019* (Cth) (F2019L00468)

These regulations are made under the *Crimes (Biological Weapons) Act 1976* (Cth) (*'Biological Weapons Act'*), which gives effect to the *Convention on the Prohibition of the Development, Production and Stockpiling of Bacteriological (Biological) and Toxin Weapons and on their Destruction*.[37]

Schedule 1 repealed the *Crimes (Biological Weapons) Regulations 1980* (Cth), which were due to sunset on 1 April 2019. The regulations continue in a substantively similar manner the arrangements relating to the procedures and requirements to be followed in relation to the notification, storage, labelling and disposal of biological substances which are prohibited items under the Act. They also enable a person charged with an offence under the *Biological Weapons Act* to seek an independent analysis of a sample of the substance relevantly alleged to be a biological agent or toxin. Minor changes in the regulations include updates to outdated references.

The regulations commenced on 30 March 2019.

2.11 *Customs (Prohibited Imports) Amendment (Collecting Tobacco Duties) Regulations 2019* (Cth) (F2019L00352)

These regulations are made under the *Customs Act*.

They amend the *Customs (Prohibited Imports) Regulations 1956* (Cth) to prohibit the importation of tobacco products into Australia without permission, with limited exemptions. The amendments are part of a broader Government initiative to address recommendations of the October 2017 Black Economy Taskforce Final Report in which the Government announced a range of measures to address illicit tobacco trade in Australia. The regulations also give effect to Australia's commitments made under the World Health Organisation

---

37 Opened for signature 10 April 1973, 1015 UNTS 163 (entered into force 26 March 1975).

Framework Convention,[38] which, among other matters, requires parties to implement measures to prevent the illicit trade in tobacco products.

The regulations commenced on 1 July 2019 and were repealed on 18 October 2019 by operation of ch 3 pt 3 div 1 of the *Legislation Act*.

2.12 *Family Law Legislation Amendment (Miscellaneous Measures) Regulations 2019* (Cth) (F2019L00344)

Family Law Legislation Amendment (Miscellaneous Measures) Regulations 2019 (Cth) ('*Family Law Amendment Regulations*') are made under the *Family Law Act 1975* (Cth) ('*Family Law Act*'). The regulations make minor amendments to the *Family Law Regulations 1984* (Cth) ('*Family Law Regulations*'), *Family Law (Child Abduction Convention) Regulations 1986* (Cth) ('*Abduction Regulations*') and the *Family Law (Child Protection Convention) Regulations 2003* (Cth) ('*Protection Regulations*').

The *Family Law Amendment Regulations* make amendments to the *Family Law Regulations* to update inaccurate and out-dated references. The *Family Law Amendment Regulations* also update sch 2 of the *Family Law Regulations*, which prescribes a list of countries to which Australia owes international child and spousal maintenance obligations. The *Abduction Regulations* implement the *Hague Convention on the Civil Aspects of International Child Abduction* ('*Abduction Convention*')[39] into Australian law. The *Family Law Amendment Regulations* repeal the existing meaning of 'convention countries' in reg 10 of the *Abduction Regulations*, and introduce a single definition of 'convention country' to sub-reg 2(1), that being any country in respect of which the *Abduction Convention* has entered into force with Australia. The regulations also amend sch 3 to the *Abduction Regulations* to repeal two prescribed forms, providing instead for these forms to be approved in writing by the Minister in order to allow them to be updated more efficiently.

The *Protection Regulations* implement the *Hague Convention on Jurisdiction, Applicable Law, Recognition, Enforcement and Co-operation in Respect of Parental Responsibility and Measures for the Protection of Children* ('*Protection Convention*').[40] The *Family Law Amendment Regulations* correct typographical errors in the *Protection Regulations*, and repeal the list of countries in sch 1 in the *Protection Regulations* in respect of which the *Protection Convention* is in force with Australia. This list was deemed unnecessary, given s 111CA(1) of the

---

38   *Framework Convention* (n 3).

39   Opened for signature 25 October 1980, 1343 UNTS 89 (entered into force 1 December 1983).

40   Opened for signature 19 October 1996, 2204 UNTS 95 (entered into force 1 January 2002).

Family Law Act provides an authoritative definition of 'Convention country' for the purposes of the *Protection Regulations*.

The regulations commenced on 23 March 2019 (with the exception of sch 1 item 26), and were repealed on 12 September 2019 by operation of ch 3 pt 3 div 1 of the *Legislation Act*.

2.13 *Great Barrier Reef Marine Park Regulations 2019* (Cth) (F2019L00166)

These regulations are made under the *Great Barrier Reef Marine Park Act 1975* (Cth) ('*Great Barrier Reef Act*'). They repeal the *Great Barrier Reef Marine Park (Aquaculture) Regulations 2000* (Cth), which were due to sunset on 1 October 2019, and the *Great Barrier Reef Marine Park Regulations 1983* (Cth), which were due to sunset on 1 April 2019. The regulations enable the continued operation of the *Great Barrier Reef Act* by prescribing all matters required or permitted by the Act to be prescribed or necessary to be prescribed for carrying out or giving effect to the Act. The *Great Barrier Reef Act* establishes the Great Barrier Reef Marine Park Authority and makes provision for and in relation to the establishment, control, care and development of a marine park in the Great Barrier Reef Region. One of the objects of the *Great Barrier Reef Act* is to assist in meeting Australia's international responsibilities in relation to the environment and protection of world heritage,[41] especially Australia's responsibilities under the *World Heritage Convention*.[42]

The regulations give effect to the objects of the *Great Barrier Reef Act* by regulating the use of the Great Barrier Reef Marine Park. Regulation 5(1) incorporates the following international instruments by reference: ch VII of the annex to the *International Convention for the Safety of Life at Sea*;[43] the *International Code for the Safe Carriage of Packaged Irradiated Nuclear Fuel, Plutonium and High level Radioactive Wastes on Board Ships*;[44] and the *International Convention for the Prevention of Pollution from Ships*.[45]

The regulations commenced on 1 April 2019.

---

41 *Great Barrier Reef Act*, s 2A(2)(c).

42 Opened for signature 16 November 1972, 1037 UNTS 151 (entered into force 17 December 1975).

43 Opened for signature 1 November 1974, 1185 UNTS 2 (entered into force 25 May 1980).

44 Maritime Safety Committee, *Adoption of the International Code for the Safe Carriage of Packaged Irradiated Nuclear Fuel, Plutonium and High-Level Radioactive Wastes on Board Ships*, Res MSC.88(71) (27 May 1999).

45 Opened for signature 17 February 1978, 1340 UNTS 61 (entered into force 2 October 1983).

2.14   *Intellectual Property Laws Amendment (PCT Translations and Other Measures) Regulations 2019* (Cth) (F2019L00376)

These regulations are made under the *Designs Act 2003* (Cth) and the *Patents Act 1990* (Cth).

The regulations amend the *Patents Regulations 1991* (Cth) ('*Patents Regulations*') and the *Designs Regulations 2004* (Cth) to, among other matters, ensure Australia's compliance with international obligations. Australia is a Party to the *Patent Cooperation Treaty* ('*PCT*'),[46] which assists applicants in seeking patent protection internationally. Schedule 1 to the regulations amends the *Patents Regulations* to clarify the translation requirements for patent applications amended under arts 19 and 34 of the *PCT* to enter the national phase in Australia and provides greater flexibility for applicants when filing translated documents. Schedule 2 pt 2 of the regulations amends the *Patents Regulations* to ensure that Australia continues to meet its obligation under the *PCT* to apply reductions to the international filing fee and handling fee payable for the benefit of the International Bureau of the World Intellectual Property Organisation.

Schedule 2 to the regulations commenced on 26 March 2019. Schedule 1 commenced on 25 September 2019. The regulations were repealed on 26 September 2019 by operation of ch 3 pt 3 div 1 of the *Legislation Act*.

2.15   *International Transfer of Prisoners (United Arab Emirates) Regulations 2019* (Cth) (F2019L01277)

These regulations are made under the *International Transfer of Prisoners Act 1997* (Cth) ('*ITP Act*').

The regulations give effect in Australian domestic law to the *Treaty between the Government of Australia and the Government of the United Arab Emirates concerning Transfer of Sentenced Persons*.[47] The Treaty ensures that Australia can accept applications from prisoners for transfer to or from the United Arab Emirates ('UAE') in accordance with mutually agreed terms. The Treaty also strengthens Australia's international crime cooperation relationship with the UAE.

Schedule 1 to the regulations sets out the terms of the Treaty. The regulations also declare the UAE a 'transfer country', as required under sub-s 8(1) of the *ITP Act*, and allow the *ITP Act* to apply to the UAE subject to the Treaty. As a result, upon entry into force of the Treaty, every prisoner transfer between Australia and the UAE will require the consent of the prisoner, the Australian

---

46   Opened for signature 19 June 1970, 1160 UNTS 231 (entered into force 24 January 1978).

47   Signed 9 May 2018, [2018] ATNIF 35 (not yet in force).

AUSTRALIAN LEGISLATION 487

and UAE Governments, and in certain cases, the relevant Australian state or territory government.

The regulations will commence on the day the Treaty comes into force for Australia.

2.16 National Measurement Legislation (SI Redefinition) Regulations 2019 (Cth) (F2019L00559)

The regulations are made under the *National Measurement Act 1960* (Cth).

Schedule 1 to the regulations updates Australia's legal units of measurement in the *National Measurement Regulations 1999* (Cth) (*'NM Regulations'*) to align it with the International System of Units of Measurement. The regulations insert a new definition for the term 'SI definition', referencing app 3 to *Resolution 1* adopted by the General Conference on Weights and Measures ('CPGM').[48] The Resolution revises the definition of the base units of the SI system. The amendments to the *NM Regulations*, which implement revised definitions of the base units of the SI system are necessary to maintain international harmonisation and meet Australia's obligations under the *Metre Convention*,[49] which establishes the CPGM and serves as the basis of international agreement on units of measurement.

The regulations commenced on 20 May 2019 and were repealed on 17 September 2019 by operation of ch 3 pt 3 div 1 of the *Legislation Act*.

2.17 Ombudsman Amendment (National Preventive Mechanism) Regulations 2019 (Cth) (F2019L00591)

These regulations are made under the *Ombudsman Act 1976* (Cth).

The regulations amend the *Ombudsman Regulations 2017* (Cth) to confer on the Commonwealth Ombudsman the roles and functions of the National Preventive Mechanism ('NPM') Coordinator and of the NPM Body. This gives effect to Australia's obligations to establish a system of independent monitoring for places of detention in order to prevent torture and other cruel, inhuman or degrading punishment or treatment under the *Optional Protocol to the Convention against Torture and Other Cruel, Inhuman or Degrading Treatment or Punishment* ('OPCAT').[50] Australia ratified the OPCAT on 21 December 2017. Pursuant to that instrument, Australia is obligated to set up, designate or

---

48 International Bureau of Weights and Measures, General Conference on Weights and Measures, *On the Revision of the International System of Units (SI)*, Res 1, 26th meeting, 13–16 November 2018.

49 Signed 20 May 1875.

50 Opened for signature 18 December 2002, 2375 UNTS 237 (entered into force 22 June 2006).

maintain an NPM, and facilitate visits to Australia, including places of detention under Australia's jurisdiction and control, by the UN Subcommittee on the Prevention of Torture and other Cruel, Inhuman or Degrading Treatment or Punishment ('SPT').

As the NPM Coordinator, the Ombudsman is responsible for coordinating a network of Commonwealth, State and Territory inspectorates responsible for inspecting and making recommendations about places of detention within their jurisdiction. As the NPM Body, the Ombudsman is also responsible for undertaking inspections of places of detention under the Commonwealth's jurisdiction and control. This includes inspections of immigration detention facilities, Australian Defence Force facilities and Australian Federal Police cells in Australia's external territories. The amendments make clear that the function of the NPM Coordinator includes communicating with, and giving information to, the SPT.

The regulations commenced on 10 April 2019 and were repealed on 17 September 2019 by operation of ch 3 pt 3 div 1 of the *Legislation Act*.

2.18 *Shipping Registration Regulations 2019* (Cth) (F2019L00206)

These regulations are made under the *Shipping Registration Act 1981* (Cth). They replace and have the same effect as the *Shipping Registration Regulations 1981* (Cth), which were due to sunset on 1 April 2019.

The regulations implement Australia's obligations under art 91 of the *United Nations Convention on the Law of the Sea*,[51] which requires each State Party to fix the conditions for the grant of its nationality to ships, for the registration of ships in its territory, and for the right to fly its flag. The effect of these regulations is that they provide a mechanism for the registration of ships on the Australian General Shipping Register and the Australian International Shipping Register, permitting ships to be granted Australian nationality and allowing for Australian ships to fly the Australian National Flag or the Australian Red Ensign.

The regulations commenced on 1 April 2019.

2.19 *Timor Sea Legislation Amendment (Maritime Boundaries Treaty) Regulations 2019* (Cth) (F2019L01049)

These regulations are made under the *Export Charges (Imposition—Customs) Act 2015* (Cth), the *Export Charges (Imposition—General) Act 2015* (Cth), the *International Organisations (Privileges and Immunities) Act 1963* (Cth), the *Maritime Powers Act 2013* (Cth), the *Radiocommunications Act 1992*

---

51   Opened for signature 10 December 1982, 1833 UNTS 3 (entered into force 16 November 1994).

AUSTRALIAN LEGISLATION 489

(Cth), the *Telecommunications Act 1997* (Cth), and the *Transport Safety Investigation Act 2003* (Cth).

The regulations amend Commonwealth regulations to partially implement the *Timor Sea Maritime Boundaries Treaty*.[52] The regulations make technical amendments to multiple Acts. For example, the amendments remove references to the *Timor Sea Treaty*[53] where they are no longer required, or replace with references to the *Timor Sea Maritime Boundaries Treaty*. The regulations also repeal the *International Organisations (Privileges and Immunities—Timor Sea Proceedings) Regulations 2017* (Cth) and the *Timor Sea Treaty Designated Authority (Privileges and Immunities) Regulations 2003* (Cth), as they have become redundant following the entry into force of the *Timor Sea Maritime Boundaries Treaty*.

The regulations commenced on 30 August 2019 and were repealed on 15 November 2019 by operation of ch 3 pt 3 div 1 of the *Legislation Act*.

2.20 *Transport Security Legislation Amendment (2019 Measures No 1) Regulations 2019* (Cth) (F2019L00829)

These regulations are made under the *Aviation Transport Security Act 2004* (Cth) and the *Maritime Transport and Offshore Facilities Security Act 2003* (Cth). The Acts establish a regulatory framework to safeguard against unlawful interference with civil aviation and maritime transport and offshore oil and gas facilities, respectively. The Acts respectively set out the minimum security requirements for the civil aviation and maritime industries by imposing obligations on persons engaged in such activities.

The regulations amend the *Aviation Transport Security Regulations 2005* (Cth) and the *Maritime Transport and Offshore Facilities Security Regulations 2003* (Cth) to enhance transport security and ensure consistency with Australia's international obligations. In particular, reg 25 amends the *Aviation Transport Security Regulations 2005* (Cth) by removing the current exemption from clearance for certain checked baggage transferring from an inbound international air service to a screened air service in Australia. This amendment ensures Australia's ongoing compliance with its obligations under the *Chicago Convention*.[54]

The regulations commenced on 18 June 2019 and were repealed on 17 September 2019 by operation of ch 3 pt 3 div 1 of the *Legislation Act*.

---

52   *Timor Sea Maritime Boundaries Treaty* (n 10).
53   *Timor Sea Treaty* (n 11).
54   *Chicago Convention* (n 17).

2.21 Trans-Tasman Mutual Recognition Amendment (Permanent Exemption for Emissions-Controlled Products) Regulations 2019 (Cth) (F2019L00314)

These regulations are made under the *Trans-Tasman Mutual Recognition Act 1997* (Cth) ('*TTMR Act*'). The regulations give effect to the *TTMR Act* in the implementation of mutual recognition principles between Australia and New Zealand with respect to the sale of goods and the registration of occupations. Schedule 1 amends the *TTMR Act* by permanently exempting propulsion marine engines and non-road spark ignition engines from the operation of the Act. This is to ensure consistency with emissions-controlled products in Rules made under the *Product Emissions Standards Act 2017* (Cth) ('*PES Act*'), which regulates emissions from these engines to address the adverse impacts of air pollution on human health and the environment.

New Zealand does not have an emissions standards legislation regulating the supply and import of emissions-controlled products similar to the *PES Act*. Consequently, the regulations give an exemption under the *TTMR Act* so that uncertified engines that can be imported and supplied in New Zealand, cannot be legally imported or supplied in Australia.

The regulations commenced on 20 March 2019.

2.22 Wine Australia Amendment (Trade with United Kingdom) Regulations 2019 (Cth) (F2019L00438)

These regulations are made under the *Wine Australia Act*.

The purpose of the regulations is to enable Australia to give domestic effect to the *Agreement on Trade in Wine between the Government of Australia and the Government of the United Kingdom of Great Britain and Northern Ireland* ('*AU—UK Wine Agreement*')[55] and to ensure continuity of trade in wine with the UK post-Brexit.

Sub-section 3(d) of the *Wine Australia Act* states that one of the objects of the Act is to enable Australia to fulfil its obligations under prescribed wine-trading agreements and other international agreements. The regulations amend the *Wine Australia Regulations 2018* (Cth) to declare the *AU—UK Wine Agreement* as a prescribed wine-trading agreement for the purposes of sub-s 4(1)(b) of the *Wine Australia Act*. The effect of this amendment is that the UK will be recognised as an 'agreement country' for the purposes of the *Wine Australia Act*, while the *AU—UK Wine Agreement* remains in force. The regulations will commence at the same time as the *AU—UK Wine Agreement* enters into force for Australia.

---

55   Signed 18 January 2019, [2019] ATNIF 9 (not yet in force).

Australian Practice in International Law 2019

Contents

1 **Introduction** 495
2 **International Rules-Based Order** 495
   2.1 *Confronting Challenges and Advancing an International Rules-Based Order* 495
3 **Accountability** 509
   3.1 *Downing of MH17* 509
   3.2 *Murder of Jamal Khashoggi* 510
   3.3 *Rule of Law* 512
   3.4 *Crimes against Humanity* 513
   3.5 *Criminal Accountability of UN Officials and Experts on Mission* 514
   3.6 *Universal Jurisdiction* 516
   3.7 *Jurisdiction of the International Criminal Court* 517
   3.8 *International Residual Mechanism for Criminal Tribunals* 519
   3.9 *Responsibility of States for Internationally Wrongful Acts* 521
4 **State Sovereignty and Territorial Integrity** 522
   4.1 *Ukraine including Crimea* 522
5 **International Peace and Security** 523
   5.1 *Cyberspace* 523
   5.2 *Missile Testing in the Democratic People's Republic of Korea (DPRK)* 528
   5.3 *Protests in Hong Kong* 529
   5.4 *Turkish Military Action in Northeastern Syria* 531
   5.5 *Territorial Defeat of Dae'esh* 532
   5.6 *Terrorism: Countering Terrorism and Violent Extremism* 533
   5.7 *Responsibility to Protect* 539
   5.8 *Protection of Civilians* 545
   5.9 *Women, Peace and Security* 547
   5.10 *Role of Reconciliation in Maintaining International Peace and Security* 549
   5.11 *Autonomous Sanctions and International Law* 551
   5.12 *Democratic People's Republic of Korea Sanctions* 552
   5.13 *Ukraine Sanctions* 553
   5.14 *United Nations Counter-Terrorism Sanctions* 554

© DEPARTMENT OF FOREIGN AFFAIRS AND TRADE, COMMONWEALTH OF AUSTRALIA, 2021
DOI:10.1163/26660229_03801023

	5.15	*United Nations Sanctions in respect of South Sudan, Eritrea, Somalia and the Central African Republic* 556
6	**Climate Change** 559	
	6.1	*25th United Nations Climate Change Conference of Parties (COP25)* 559
7	**International Human Rights** 561	
	7.1	*Australia's 2018–2020 Term on the Human Rights Council* 561
	7.2	*Freedom of Expression* 566
	7.3	*Freedom of Religion or Belief* 568
	7.4	*Human Rights and Autonomous Sanctions* 570
	7.5	*Death Penalty* 570
	7.6	*Human Rights in the Pacific* 573
	7.7	*Human Rights of Older Persons* 574
	7.8	*Detention of Dr Yang Hengjun* 576
	7.9	*Detention of Mr Alek Sigley* 579
	7.10	*Detention of Mr Hakeem al-Araibi* 579
	7.11	*Release of Mr Tim Weeks* 581
	7.12	*Environmental Human Rights Defenders* 581
	7.13	*Elections—Bougainville* 582
	7.14	*Elections—Venezuela* 583
	7.15	*Gender Equality, Human Rights and Ending Violence against Women* 584
	7.16	*Equal Human Rights for Lesbian, Gay, Bisexual, Transgender and Intersex (LGBTI) Persons* 602
	7.17	*Human Rights Online, including the Right to Privacy* 606
	7.18	*Human Rights Situations—Belarus* 613
	7.19	*Human Rights Situations—Burundi* 613
	7.20	*Human Rights Situations—Cambodia* 615
	7.21	*Human Rights Situations—Central African Republic* 615
	7.22	*Human Rights Situations—China* 617
	7.23	*Human Rights Situations—Congo* 620
	7.24	*Human Rights Situations—The Democratic People's Republic of Korea* 622
	7.25	*Human Rights Situations—Eritrea* 624
	7.26	*Human Rights Situations—Georgia* 624
	7.27	*Human Rights Situations—Libya* 626
	7.28	*Human Rights Situations—Mali* 627
	7.29	*Human Rights Situations—Myanmar* 627
	7.30	*Human Rights Situations—Nicaragua* 633

AUSTRALIAN PRACTICE IN INTERNATIONAL LAW 2019

7.31   *Human Rights Situations—Saudi Arabia*   634

7.32   *Human Rights Situations—Somalia*   637

7.33   *Human Rights Situations—South Sudan*   637

7.34   *Human Rights Situations—Sri Lanka*   639

7.35   *Human Rights Situations—Syria*   640

7.36   *Human Rights Situations—The Sudan*   643

7.37   *Human Rights Situations—Ukraine*   645

7.38   *Human Rights Situations—Venezuela*   648

7.39   *Human Rights Situations—Yemen*   649

7.40   *Human Right to an Adequate Standard of Living*   651

7.41   *Multilateral Approaches to Human Rights*   651

7.42   *National Human Rights Institutions*   652

7.43   *Right to Development*   653

7.44   *Rights of Persons with Disabilities*   654

7.45   *The Rights of the Child*   657

7.46   *The Rights of Indigenous Peoples including the United Nations Permanent Forum on Indigenous Issues (UNFII) and the Expert Mechanism on the Rights of Indigenous Peoples (EMRIP)*   660

7.47   *The Situation of Human Rights Defenders, and Torture and Other Cruel, Inhuman or Degrading Treatment or Punishment*   666

7.48   *Universality and Equality of Human Rights*   668

7.49   *Xenophobia and Hate Speech*   671

7.50   *Cultural Rights and the Promotion and Protection of Human Rights and Fundamental Freedoms while Countering Terrorism*   672

7.51   *Countering Trafficking and Modern Forms of Slavery*   674

8   **Development of International Law Jurisprudence**   678

8.1   *General Principles of International Law*   678

8.2   *Administration of Justice at the United Nations*   679

8.3   *Immunity of State Officials from Foreign Criminal Jurisdiction*   681

8.4   *International Law Commission's Work on Peremptory Norms of International Law*   682

9   **Transnational Crime**   685

9.1   *Combatting Transnational Crime in Southeast Asia*   685

9.2   *Countering the Use of Information and Communications Technologies for Criminal Purposes*   688

10   **International Environment Law and Law of the Sea**   690

10.1   *Antarctica*   690

10.2   *Japanese Whaling*   691

10.3   *Sustainability of Oceans*   691

10.4 *South China Sea* 693

10.5 *Australia—Timor-Leste Maritime Boundary Treaty* 693

10.6 *Freedom of Navigation* 694

10.7 *Protection of the Environment in the Context of Armed Conflict* 696

10.8 *Sea-Level Rise* 696

11 International Trade and Investment Law 700

11.1 *UK—Australia Trade Agreements* 700

11.2 *Signing and Ratification of Indonesia—Australia Comprehensive Economic Partnership Agreement, Australia—Hong-Kong Free Trade and Investment Agreement, and Peru—Australia Free Trade Agreement* 702

11.3 *Vietnam Bilateral Investment Treaty* 703

11.4 *Uruguay Bilateral Investment Treaty* 703

11.5 *WTO—Digital Trade Negotiations* 705

11.6 *WTO—Sugar Dispute* 710

11.7 *WTO—Aid for Trade* 712

12 Arms Control, Nuclear Non-Proliferation and Disarmament 713

12.1 *Chemical Weapons* 713

12.2 *Anti-Personnel Mine Ban Convention* 715

12.3 *Arms Trade Treaty* 716

12.4 *Conference on Disarmament* 718

12.5 *Iran—Joint Comprehensive Plan of Action (JCPOA)* 721

AUSTRALIAN PRACTICE IN INTERNATIONAL LAW 2019 495

1 Introduction

This compilation contains extracts of publicly available materials that evidence Australia's state practice of international law in 2019. This compilation aims to assist in the dissemination of Australian thinking and practice on matters of international law and serve as a work of reference for legal advisers, practitioners, academics as well as anyone interested in international law.

The range of public sources drawn upon for this compilation include the following:

- speeches and media releases by the Australian Prime Minister, Minister for Foreign Affairs, Minister for Trade, Attorney-General, Minister for Defence, other ministers, and relevant senior officials;
- statements and answers to questions by Ministers in Parliament;
- statements made by relevant Ministers or officials at meetings of international organisations, such as the United Nations Security Council, Human Rights Council and World Trade Organisation.

Significant events in 2019 included in this compilation:

- Publication of Australia's position on the application of international law to State conduct in cyberspace
- Signing and ratification of free trade agreements by Australia with Indonesia, Hong Kong and Peru
- Freedom of Bahraini refugee Mr Hakeem Al-Araibi from detention in Thailand, after extensive diplomatic efforts by Australia

2 International Rules-Based Order

2.1 *Confronting Challenges and Advancing an International Rules-Based Order*

On 23 September 2019, Australia's Prime Minister, the Hon. Scott Morrison MP delivered a speech concerning Australia's role in the world and its relationship with the United States at the Chicago Council on Global Affairs in Chicago. An excerpt of that speech follows:

> [...]
> Ladies and gentlemen, we are grappling with the end of one era now and really what is the dawn of another.
>
> Like [Teddy Roosevelt (TR)] more than 100 years ago, we confront a changing economic order and transformative technological change. This isn't fresh news. Like TR, we should approach this challenge with confidence, resolve and clearly articulated principles to guide us. And this is

the central focus of what my Government and Australia is doing in the Indo-Pacific.

It is the region where we live, it's our neighbourhood. It's the region that will continue to shape our prosperity, our security, our destiny and, increasingly, our global balance of power.

Our engagement with the Indo-Pacific will be shaped by five key principles. Firstly, a commitment to open markets and the free flow of trade based on rules, not power. Respect for sovereignty of nations, their independence, irrespective of their size. From the smallest Pacific nation to the largest economies in the world.

A commitment to burden-sharing with strong and resilient regional architecture. Respect for international law and the peaceful resolution of disputes. And a commitment to work together to resolve challenges of common interest including particularly on our oceans—we're the biggest island continent in the world, our oceans impact heavily not just on our economy, on our security, but how we do life in Australia and always have not just in modern times but going down in over 60,000 years of the oldest living culture in the world, our Indigenous Australians. Oceans, climate, illegal fishing and plastics pollution. Practical issues that need addressing.

We also need to work together to find ways to reduce trade tensions that have developed over recent years.

China's economic growth is welcomed by Australia and we recognise the economic maturity that it has now realised as a newly developed economy. This was the point of the world's economic engagement with China. Having achieved this status, it is important that China's trade arrangements, participation in addressing important global environmental challenges like the ones I just mentioned, that there is transparency in their partnerships and support for developing nations, all of this needs to reflect this new status and the responsibilities that go with it as a very major world power.

The world's global institutions must adjust their settings for China, in recognition of this new status. That means more will be expected of course, as has always been the case for nations like the United States who've always had this standing.

So it is also true that China's economic expansion was made possible by the stability underwritten by US strategic engagement and the international community who built the global trading system and welcomed China's accession to the WTO.

We should remember that it was 75 years ago—at Bretton Woods— that the United States led the way in the creation of financial institutions and economic forums that established equitable rules to stabilise the international economy and remove the points of friction that had contributed to two world wars.

That was the dividend of peace. And investing that dividend of peace in a new world order. And I agree with the assessment made in the President's 2017 *National Security Strategy* that while the global economic system continues to serve our interests, it needs some reform. We cannot pretend that rules that were written a generation ago remain appropriate for today. Why would that be true in this area and not in any other?

It is clear that global trade rules are no longer fit for purpose. In some cases, the rules were designed for a completely different economy in another era, one that simply doesn't exist anymore. In other cases, our rules are not comprehensive. And it is clear that our rules are not keeping pace with technological change that is happening at an unprecedented pace. But we do need the rules, we do need the rules. A study by Accenture estimated that digital commerce now drives 22 per cent of the world economy, you know these figures. A separate study by McKinsey Global Institute showed that data flows grew by a factor of 45 in the decade to 2016.

But there are many existing obstacles and many emerging barriers to the expansion of the digital economy. Left to proliferate, such barriers will distort and choke the global economy and the great benefits that have flowed to all nations. That's why Australia is taking a leading role in developing e-commerce rules at the WTO. That's a practical thing to do.

There is a broader imperative at work. We must demonstrate that collectively we have not lost our ability to adapt and adjust our trading system to new realities.

When there were 144 members of the WTO, the Director General at the time likened the WTO to a vehicle that had one accelerator and 143 brakes.

We cannot allow that to continue. We can no longer move at the speed of the lowest common denominator. It is time for the system to catch up with the world. And we intend to help that process in a practical way, making our contribution based on our experience and I've got to say we're positive about it. The world has just reached a change point, that's all. There's no need to catastrophise it, there's a need to understand it to adjust the institutions and the rules to accommodate it. There's no need to engage in a heavily polarised debate on this issue, there's a much more practical issue at the heart of all this and we just have to reset to ensure that can provide the same peace and stability and prosperity that will last. We're totally up to it, we still have the wisdom and capability to achieve it and so Australia won't be a bystander in that process, we'll be involved. We'll be rolling our sleeves up, we'll be playing our part and just in case you think we're doing that because we're terribly friendly and wonderfully affable people, which we are, the real issue is it's in our national interest.

The reason we're here today is it's a great Council, it's a great institution, I'm here today because one in five Australian jobs depends on trade and our connection with the rest of the world depends on that. I'm here today because what's happening with plastics in our oceans is bad news for our local environment in Australia so we need to do something about it. I'm here today because of our friends in the Pacific, our family in the Pacific, people are stealing their fish, that's got to stop if they want to have a secure future for their families and their people. And these issues are the things we need to move the dial on.

[...]

On 25 September 2019, Australia's Prime Minister, the Hon. Scott Morrison MP delivered his National Statement at the United Nations General Assembly in New York. The full text of the statement follows:

Much has changed since the United Nations was established.

Australia was there in the beginning. And we are here today because we continue to believe that differences can be resolved through dialogue and mutual respect.

Because we believe that an international rules-based order is essential for global stability, security and prosperity.

Because we know that you can't have prosperity without peace.

The world today is complex and contested. Many fatalistically see a polarised world where countries feel pushed to make binary choices. Australia will continue to resist this path.

Australia will continue to seek to honestly maintain our great alliances and comprehensive partnerships in good repair, from our great and powerful friends to our smallest Pacific Island family neighbours.

Approaching its 75th anniversary next year, the UN must reform and evolve to respond effectively to the challenges of the 21st Century.

And to fulfil its core mandate, the UN must be ever mindful of the principles and values that have always been foundational to the UN's efforts.

Peaceful settlement of disputes in accordance with international law. Respect for the sovereignty and independence of all states. Open markets that facilitate the free flow of trade, capital and ideas. Freedom of faith, freedom of expression. Respect for human rights, and combatting disadvantage, discrimination and persecution based on disability, gender, religion, sexuality, age, race or ethnicity.

These are the liberal democratic values which underpinned the UN at its inception. These are Australia's values. We believe they should remain the guiding principles and values for the UN into the future.

The alternate path of lowest common denominator transactionalism and relativism is a dead end.

The UN is the prime custodian of the rules-based order. It is also the custodian of mechanisms for dialogue and adjudication which buttress them.

It has a challenging task ahead of it.

For Australia's part, we will continue to practice what we preach.

Last month, Australia ratified a maritime treaty setting out a new sea boundary with Timor-Leste.

This followed the first-ever conciliation initiated under the UN Convention on the Law of the Sea.

This demonstrates that the UN and its norms are central to a cooperative rules-based approach to global challenges.

In the Pacific, we are also stepping up.

Australia is the single largest development partner for Pacific Island nations.

This is an instinctive response for Australia, consistent with our clear national interest and our commitment to our Pacific family, our vuvale, our whanau.

Our goal is simple—a Southwest Pacific that is secure strategically, stable economically, sovereign politically and sustainable environmentally.

The UN's work in partnership with Australia has also helped to build a more sustainable and resilient Pacific: to support local climate change actions and resilience, to strive for gender equality through the empowerment of women and girls, to support continuing improvement in health outcomes and to bolster regional peace, including through the Bougainville Referendum Support Project.

Today I want to take the opportunity to speak about Australia's response to the great global environmental challenges.

Firstly how Australia is acting to protect our oceans.

Australia is an island continent.

Australia has the world's third largest maritime jurisdiction, stretching from the great Southern Ocean to the vast Pacific and Indian oceans.

Over 85 per cent of Australia's population lives within just 50 kilometres of the coast.

Australia's Indigenous peoples have been linked to the land and sea for more than 65,000 years.

Our oceans connect Australia with the world. Ninety nine per cent of Australia's trade by volume is carried by sea. By 2025, marine industries will contribute around $100 billion each year to our economy.

Our prosperity and security rely on the established laws that govern freedom of navigation, be it in the Strait of Hormuz or closer to home.

Protecting our oceans is also one of the world's more pressing environmental challenges.

To protect our oceans, Australia is committed to leading urgent action to combat plastic pollution choking our oceans; tackle over-exploitation of our fisheries, prevent ocean habitat destruction and of course take action on climate change.

Scientists estimate that in just 30 years' time the weight of plastics in our oceans will exceed the weight of the fish in those oceans.

Recently, I announced that Australia will ban exports of waste plastic, paper, glass and tyres, and we anticipate that starting in 2020. That's about 1.4 million tonnes of potent recyclable material.

Australia is also leading on practical research and development into recycling—turning recycled plastic and glass into roads, manufacturing 100% recycled PET bottles and capturing methane and waste to create energy.

New technologies are coming on line with the potential to recycle used plastics into valuable new plastics—creating a circular plastics economy.

These include innovations like 'bioplastics'—compostable plastic replacements and technologies like the 'Catalytic Hydrothermal Reactor'—an innovative Australian designed technology that converts end of life plastics into waxes, diesel and new plastics.

These innovations show us a truly circular economy is not only possible, but is achievable. And it's of course, essential. And Australia intends to do more.

Australia will invest $167 million in an Australian Recycling Investment Plan.

Our focus is to create the right investment environment so that new technologies are commercialised—preventing pollution from entering our oceans, and creating valuable new products.

Australia supports the High Level Panel for a Sustainable Ocean Economy and we are working through the International Maritime Organization to address the way shipping contributes to plastics pollution in our oceans.

Australia supports the G20 work on marine plastic debris and the Osaka Blue Ocean Vision led of course by Prime Minister Abe.

We welcome the contributions and leadership from business and the private sector to address these challenges, including Australia's own Minderoo Foundation. Industry led mechanisms for investing in new recycling technologies and mitigating plastic waste in rivers, beaches and oceans on a global scale is absolutely essential.

We must also act to safeguard the sustainability of our fisheries. This means cracking down on illegal fishing.

There are too many nations standing by while their nationals are thieving the livelihoods of their neighbours.

Australia is acting not only in our own interest but helping Pacific Island family to reduce illegal fishing which depletes the fish stocks Pacific Islanders rely on for jobs, revenue and their food security.

We have also worked together with Indonesia, and I congratulate President Widodo, we have been co-committed to an action plan to combat illegal fishing in Southeast Asia and thank Indonesia for their regional leadership.

And we are working with regional organisations to improve fisheries governance.

As well, we are providing patrol boats to 13 countries supported by aerial surveillance through our Pacific Maritime Security Program in Pacific Island nations to help them police illegal fishing in their waters.

We are leading efforts to preserve natural habitats and biodiversity, including through partnerships with other countries to protect migratory birds and their habitats.

And we have worked hard to prevent commercial whaling and to end whaling in the Southern Ocean.

Australia set up the International Partnership for Blue Carbon in 2015 with the aim of protecting and conserving mangroves, tidal marshes and seagrasses for climate change mitigation and adaptation.

And our Great Barrier Reef remains one of the world's most pristine areas of natural beauty. Feel free to visit it. Our reef is vibrant and resilient and protected under the world's most comprehensive reef management plan.

The UNESCO World Heritage Committee has found that Australia's management of our reef is 'highly sophisticated' and is considered by many as the 'gold standard' for large scale marine protected areas.

Australia's $2 billion Reef 2050 Long Term Sustainability Plan is based on the best available science and draws on 40 years of analysis, underpinned by the Great Barrier Reef Marine Park Authority.

Australia's continued support for reef, coral and water quality science will ensure that the Great Barrier Reef remains one of the best managed World Heritage sites in the world.

Now, Australia is also taking real action on climate change and we are getting results.

We are successfully balancing our global responsibilities with sensible and practical policies to secure our environmental and our economic future.

Australia's internal and global critics on climate change willingly overlook or perhaps ignore our achievements, as the facts simply don't fit the narrative they wish to project about our contribution.

Australia is responsible for just 1.3 per cent of global emissions. Australia is doing our bit on climate change and we reject any suggestion to the contrary.

By 2020 Australia will have overachieved on our Kyoto commitments, reducing our greenhouse gas emissions by 367 million tonnes more than required to meet our 2020 Kyoto target. Now there are few member countries, whether at this forum or the OECD who can make this claim.

Our latest estimates show both emissions per person and the emissions intensity of the economy are at their lowest levels in 29 years.

In 2012, it was estimated Australia would release some 693 million tonnes of emissions in 2020. As of 2018, this estimate has fallen to 540 million tonnes.

Australia's electricity sector is producing less emissions. In the year to March 2019, emissions from Australia's electricity sector were 15.7 per cent lower than the peak recorded in the year to June 2009.

While we are a resource rich country, it is important to note that Australia only accounts for around 5.5 per cent of the world's coal production.

Having met and we will exceed our Kyoto targets, Australia will meet our Paris commitments as well and we stand by them.

We are committed to reducing greenhouse gas emissions by 26 to 28 per cent below 2005 levels by 2030.

This is a credible, fair, responsible and achievable contribution to global climate change action. It represents a halving of our emissions per person in Australia, or a two thirds reduction in emissions per unit of GDP.

At the centre of our domestic efforts is a $3.5 billion Climate Solutions Plan that I successfully took to our recent national election—supporting practical projects like capturing methane from waste, revegetation of degraded land and soil carbon.

Through our Climate Solutions Plan, we are supporting the transition to renewable energy—with projects such as Snowy 2.0, the largest pumped hydro station project in the Southern Hemisphere.

And we are investing significantly in research and development to use the best science and business expertise to commercialise new renewable technologies and integrate renewables into our electricity grid.

Australia now has the highest per capita investment in clean energy technologies of anywhere in the world and one in five Australian households has rooftop solar systems.

In 2018, $13.2 billion was invested in clean energy technologies in Australia. This builds on the estimated $10 billion invested in 2017.

We are also doing the right thing by our neighbours.

We recently committed to invest a further 500 million Australian dollars over five years from 2020 for renewable energy, climate change and resilience in the Pacific.

We have decided to invest this directly from within our international overseas development programme, rather than through additional budget commitments to the Global Green Climate Fund.

This enables us to target our support directly to Pacific Island nations, ensuring they receive this support more directly, in a more timely and targeted fashion.

At the same time, it provides greater transparency, fairness and accountability to Australian taxpayers who rightly demand attention and support from Government to address challenges at home, in particular boosting drought resilience through our investment in our national water grid infrastructure.

Australia is also committed with other countries to the Montreal Protocol, an agreement that will help protect the world from ozone depletion and combat climate change.

Under the Montreal Protocol, Australia will further accelerate its efforts and will use 60 per cent less HCFCs than permitted. I can proudly inform you that Australia is on track to fulfil our commitments and I urge all other countries to fulfil their commitments.

All of this adds up to significant and comprehensive action by Australia in response to the world's greatest environmental challenges.

Australia is under no illusions about the challenges the global community confronts in the years ahead.

Today I want to reassure all members that Australia is carrying its own weight and more, just as we always have.

We are a generous nation playing our part in securing our shared future.

Reforming the rules of global governance, setting common standards to ensure global connectivity in the future, preventing conflict, building the capacity of developing nations, supporting essential health projects, protecting our oceans and taking action on climate change and getting results.

Like many leaders here, I get many letters from children in Australia concerned about their future.

I take them very seriously and I deeply respect their concerns and indeed I welcome their passion, especially when it comes to the environment.

My impulse is always to seek to respond positively and to encourage them. To provide context, perspective and particularly to generate hope.

To focus their minds and direct their energies to practical solutions and positive behaviour that will deliver enduring results for them.

To encourage them to learn more about science, technology, engineering and maths—because it's through research, innovation and enterprise that the practical work of successfully managing our very real environmental challenges is achieved.

We must respect and harness the passion and aspiration of our younger generations, we must guard against others who would seek to compound or, worse, facelessly exploit their anxiety for their own agendas. We must similarly not allow their concerns to be dismissed or diminished as this can also increase their anxiety. What parent could do otherwise?

Our children have a right not just to their future but to their optimism.

Above all, we should let our children be children, let our kids be kids, let our teenagers be teenagers—while we work positively together to deliver the practical solutions for them and their future.

I am confident, once again, that Australia stands with you and together we have the wit and the capacity to surmount the challenges that come our way. Just as those who have come before us in this place have done, consistent with the values that have made that possible.

On 3 October 2019, Australia's Prime Minister, the Hon. Scott Morrison MP delivered a speech on global challenges facing Australia and the manner in which Australia is responding to such challenges, titled 'In Our Interest' for the Lowy Institute in Sydney. An excerpt of the speech follows:

[...]

Ladies and gentlemen, we are living in a world in transition that former US Treasury Secretary, Hank Paulson, has described as 'an unusually delicate moment in time'.

A new economic and political order is still taking shape.

We have entered a new era of strategic competition—a not unnatural result of shifting power dynamics, in our modern, more multi-polar world and globalised economy.

It is a time of technological disruption, some of which is welcomed, some resented and feared.

A time when global supply chains have become integrated to an unprecedented degree, and more of our economies are dependent on global trade than at any other time, including the major economic powers of the United States, China, Japan and Europe.

There is both the promise and the threat of automation and artificial intelligence.

There are fears, overstated in my opinion, of technological bifurcation—a sort of economic 'Iron Curtain' coming down.

It is also an era of continuing security threats from terrorism, extremist Islam, anti-Semitism, white supremacism, and evil on a local and global level.

An era where pragmatic international engagement, based on the cooperation of sovereign nation states, is being challenged by a new variant of globalism that seeks to elevate global institutions above the authority of nation states to direct national policies.

Of polarisation within and between societies.

An era in which elite opinion and attitudes have often become disconnected from the mainstream of their societies, and a sense of resentment and disappointment has emerged.

An era of insiders and outsiders, threatening social cohesion, provoking discontent and distrust.

Whether directly or indirectly, these changes impact Australians.

On our jobs, what we earn, our living standards and the essential services we rely on, that depend on a strong budget and strong economy.

On our environment, our oceans, our coasts, our grazing and pasture lands, our water resources, our soil, that depend upon our practical conservation.

On our safety, that depends on our national security, afforded by our alliances, our defence, diplomatic and intelligence capabilities, our adherence to the rule of law and our ability to enforce the law.

On our freedom, that depends on our dedication to national sovereignty, the resilience of our institutions, and our protections from foreign interference.

Dealing with uncertainty is not new.

This is not the first time our children have grown up in a time of global tension and disruption. This is a context and perspective I fear is too often missing in our contemporary discussion of global issues.

My generation grew up under the threat of nuclear Armageddon, hoping as Sting put it, that 'the Russians loved their children too'.

My parents' generation grew up during the greatest global conflict in world history, including the Holocaust, the invasion of what was then Australian soil in New Guinea, the bombing of Darwin and Japanese subs in Sydney Harbour sinking ferries.

My grandparents grew up during the war to end all wars, where every neighbourhood knew the cost as 60,000 Australians were killed out of a population of not even five million; who then went on to endure the Great Depression, before backing up to fight to defend our freedom in the Middle East and the Pacific.

Those generations recognised the challenges of their time, and responded with a practical resilience, optimism and resolve, rather than the anxiety inducing moral panic and sense of crisis evident in some circles today.

And at every stage Australia has played its part as a force for good, in partnership with those who shared our outlook and our values.

The key to progress was individual, like-minded sovereign nations acting together with enlightened self-interest.

The Marshall Plan.

The rebuilding of Japan.

The Colombo Plan.

A co-operative and respectful internationalism.

On occasion these efforts were forged through international institutions established to serve the states that formed them.

On other occasions, the work was done by looser coalitions of partners.

But in all cases, it was the principled actions of nation states, most often led by the United States, binding together the liberal democracies of the western world.

And in all cases these actions were underpinned by common values that anchor these societies.

As I recently reminded the United Nations General Assembly, these shared values filled the vacuum to win peace, provide stability, achieve prosperity and extend liberty essential for the human spirit to thrive.

We can never be complacent or take comfort that such achievements are permanent. They require eternal vigilance.

To preserve this legacy in the face of the uncertainties of our modern world, we must approach the future with the same optimism, confidence and resolve, of previous generations, and through our commitment to the values and beliefs that have always guided our way.

The approach my Government is taking to these challenges is straightforward.

Know who we are and what we stand for, and allow this to guide our constructive engagement in and expectations of our international cooperation, including global institutions, and ensure that our national interests remain paramount.

Build a strong open economy at home, connected to global prosperity, enabling our capacity to protect and pursue our national interests.

Know where we live and work to promote stability, prosperity and engagement in our region by championing the common interest of sovereignty and independence as the natural antidote to any possible threat of regional hegemony.

And maintain our unique relationships with the United States—our most important ally—and China—our comprehensive strategic partner—in good order, by rejecting the binary narrative of their strategic competition and instead valuing and nurturing the unconflicted benefit of our close association.

Knowing who we are and what we stand for is as true today as it ever was.

We will continue to bring clear objectives and enduring values to our international engagement.

Freedom of thought and expression [...] of spirit and faith [...] of our humanity, including inalienable human rights.

Freedom of exchange, free and open markets, free flow of capital and ideas.

Freedom from oppression and coercion, freedom of choice,

These have never been more important.

And they are under threat, not just from the direct challenge of competing worldviews, but the complacency of western liberal democratic societies that owe their liberty and prosperity to these values.

Australia does and must always seek to have a responsible and participative international agency in addressing global issues. This is positive and practical globalism. Our interests are not served by isolationism and protectionism.

But it also does not serve our national interests when international institutions demand conformity rather than independent cooperation on global issues.

The world works best when the character and distinctiveness of independent nations is preserved within a framework of mutual respect. This includes respecting electoral mandates of their constituencies.

We should avoid any reflex towards a negative globalism that coercively seeks to impose a mandate from an often ill-defined borderless global community. And worse still, an unaccountable internationalist bureaucracy.

Globalism must facilitate, align and engage, rather than direct and centralise. As such an approach can corrode support for joint international action.

Only a national government, especially one accountable through the ballot box and the rule of law, can define its national interests. We can never answer to a higher authority than the people of Australia.

And under my leadership Australia's international engagement will be squarely driven by Australia's national interests.

To paraphrase former Prime Minister John Howard, as Australians, 'we will decide our interests and the circumstances in which we seek to pursue them.'

This will not only include our international efforts to support global peace and stability and to promote open markets based on fair and transparent rules, but also other global standards that underpin commerce, investment and exchange.

When it comes to setting global standards, we've not been as involved as we could be.

We cannot afford to leave it to others to set the standards that will shape our global economy.

I'm determined Australia will play a more active role in standards setting.

I have tasked the Department of Foreign Affairs and Trade to come back to me with a comprehensive audit of global institutions and rule-making processes where we have the greatest stake.

And I want to send a message here tonight that we will be looking to tap Australian expertise as part of our efforts.

Ladies and gentlemen, the foundation for robust and credible Australian engagement abroad is a strong economy at home.

Without a strong economy, we cannot protect the living standards of our people.

Without a strong economy we cannot keep our people safe, protect and preserve our environment, guarantee the essential services Australians rely on and invest in national defence and global order.

[...]

AUSTRALIAN PRACTICE IN INTERNATIONAL LAW 2019

3 Accountability

3.1 *Downing of MH17*

On 19 June 2019, Australia's Minister for Foreign Affairs, Senator the Hon. Marise Payne, released a media statement regarding the announcement in the Netherlands of the prosecution of four individuals for their alleged roles in the downing of Malaysia Airlines Flight MH17 on 17 July 2014. The full text of that media release follows:

> Australia welcomes today's announcement in the Netherlands of the prosecution of four individuals for their alleged roles in the downing of Malaysia Airlines flight MH17.
>
> This is a significant step in the Dutch prosecution towards justice and accountability for the victims of the downing and their loved ones.
>
> The downing of MH17 was a despicable act and the Australian Government has not stopped in the pursuit of justice for the 298 victims, including 38 Australians.
>
> The Australian Government remains committed to holding the perpetrators to account. We have allocated $50.3 million over four years to support the Dutch prosecution and ensure that Australian families have meaningful access to the proceedings, including through translation services.
>
> Australia thanks the Netherlands for conducting these prosecutions on behalf of the international community. Australia has full confidence in the integrity of the process.
>
> While we cannot take away the grief of those who lost loved ones, we will continue to do everything possible to ensure justice prevails.

On 17 July 2019, Australia's Minister for Foreign Affairs, Senator the Hon. Marise Payne, released a media statement regarding the fifth anniversary of the downing of MH17. The full text of that media release follows:

> Today marks the fifth anniversary of the downing of Malaysia Airlines flight MH17, resulting in the tragic deaths of 298 passengers and crew, including 38 Australians.
>
> Our thoughts remain with those who perished on board, and their families and loved ones.
>
> While nothing can bring back those who lost their lives, the Australian Government remains resolute in its commitment to pursuing accountability for the downing and to achieving justice for the victims and their loved ones.

We pay tribute to the Australian Federal Police whose officers travelled to Ukraine and the Netherlands to investigate the crash, bring the victims home and continue to work to uncover the truth.

The announcement by the Joint Investigation Team (JIT) on 19 June of the indictment of four individuals for their alleged roles in the downing is a significant step towards justice and accountability and the Government commends the ongoing meticulous work of the JIT, which involves authorities from Australia, Belgium, Malaysia, the Netherlands and Ukraine.

Together with the Netherlands we are engaging in talks with the Russian Federation arising out of our joint assertion on 25 May 2018 of Russia's state responsibility for its role in the downing.

Australia has committed $50.3 million over four years to support the prosecution and ongoing investigation and to ensure the victims' families and loved ones can meaningfully participate in the Dutch court proceedings.

3.2   *Murder of Jamal Khashoggi*

On 15 February 2019, Australia's Minister for Foreign Affairs, Senator the Hon. Marise Payne, released a media statement noting the preliminary observations of the UN Special Rapporteur regarding the killing of Jamal Khashoggi. The full text of that statement follows:

> Australia notes the preliminary observations of the UN Special Rapporteur on Extrajudicial, Summary or Arbitrary Executions regarding her inquiry into the killing of Saudi journalist Jamal Khashoggi.
>
> We welcome all efforts to establish full accountability for those responsible for the killing.
>
> We await the outcome of the investigations underway, including those undertaken by the Special Rapporteur.

On 26 June 2019, during the 41st session of the United Nations Human Rights Council in Geneva, Australia delivered a national statement at the Clustered Interactive Dialogue with the Special Rapporteur on the extrajudicial killings, summary or arbitrary executions and the Special Rapporteur on the right to education. An extract of that statement follows:

> [...]
>
> We remain concerned at allegations of extra-judicial killings around the world. The mandate of the Special Rapporteur on extrajudicial

killings, summary or arbitrary executions is now more important than ever.

Australia expresses its sincere gratitude to the Special Rapporteur for her detailed and important investigation into the murder of Jamal Khashoggi on consular premises, protected by the Vienna Convention on Consular Relations. Her report is a valuable contribution to transparency and accountability.

The Australian Government has urged Saudi Arabia to cooperate with all efforts to determine facts and secure justice. At the 40th session of this Council, we joined 35 other states to call again for Saudi Arabia's cooperation. As Dr Callamard has noted in her report, that cooperation was not evident.

The Special Rapporteur's report raises serious, unanswered questions about the deplorable circumstances of Mr Khashoggi's death, including how consular premises came to be used in the commission and cover up of this crime. Truth and accountability must be established, for Mr Khashoggi's family and for the international community.

Dr Callamard's report is a critical step towards these objectives.

[...]

On 24 December 2019, Australia's Acting Minister for Foreign Affairs, the Attorney-General, the Hon. Christian Porter MP, released a media statement noting sentences had been handed down for the killing of Jamal Khashoggi. The full text of that statement follows:

The Australian Government has repeatedly expressed its condemnation of Mr Khashoggi's brutal murder at the Saudi consulate in Istanbul in 2018, and its deep concern at the open abuse of the Vienna Conventions caused by the commission and concealment of this terrible crime.

The Australian Government has been consistent in calling on the government of Saudi Arabia to conduct an independent, transparent investigation into the murder, including cooperating with Dr Agnes Callamard, the UN's Special Rapporteur on extrajudicial, summary or arbitrary executions, so that those responsible can be held to account and such an egregious act can never be allowed to happen again.

In light of the sentencing of 11 of those charged with involvement in Mr Khashoggi's murder, we again call on the Saudi authorities to provide a detailed clarification of what happened at the Saudi consulate on 2 October 2018 and the location of Mr Khashoggi's remains.

While this represents another step on the long road to justice for Mr Khashoggi's family, we continue to support calls for transparency, accountability and disclosure. Australian officials will consult our international partners on this development, including through our embassies and the United Nations.

As a matter of principle, Australia opposes the use of the death penalty in all circumstances, for all people. Australia strongly supports the principles of a free press and the safety of journalists. We continue to advocate actively for the protection of journalists around the world.

3.3   *Rule of Law*

On 10 October 2019, New Zealand made a statement to the Sixth Committee of the United Nations General Assembly in New York, on the rule of law, delivered on behalf of Canada, Australia and New Zealand (CANZ). The full text of that statement follows:

Mr. Chairman

I have the honour of speaking to you today on behalf of Canada, Australia and my own country, New Zealand.

This year marks the 70th anniversary of the Geneva Conventions. These treaties and additional protocols were signed by States in the aftermath of the horrors of the Second World War. They and other key instruments of the rules-based international order, including the *UN Charter*, the *Universal Declaration of Human Rights*, the *General Agreement on Tariffs and Trade*, and the *Nuclear Non-Proliferation Treaty*, laid the foundation for a relatively stable and prosperous post-war period. The rule of law is embedded in the Charter and is an essential ingredient for just and effective governance at the domestic and international level.

The Geneva Conventions also illustrate our capacity to achieve consensus and agree on fundamental, universal obligations that are legally binding. They reflect the lessons of a global tragedy and deal with the enormous humanitarian challenges posed by warfare.

It is our generation's task to deal with the global challenges of our time. CANZ countries thank the Secretary General for clearly identifying global trends that concern the rule of law in his report on strengthening and coordinating United Nations rule of law activities. The challenges we face now are of an enormous scope, scale and complexity.

Many of today's challenges are not constrained by national borders. Some stem from new and rapidly developing technologies and inhabit unseen virtual spaces. Non-traditional actors are in play. The degree of interconnectedness between people, communities, organisations, and States is greater than ever before. Unprecedented events are occurring with increasing frequency and are transmitted across the globe instantly. These challenges bring uncertainty.

But the international rules-based system, with the rule of law at its heart, provides an anchor. New and emerging threats can be addressed and constrained through the application of existing international law. Unlawful cyber activity; terrorism and violent extremism online; security challenges in space: while these and other issues may raise new and difficult questions for legal experts and policy makers, they can and should be addressed through the prism of existing international law, with the Charter at its core.

CANZ countries urge States to cleave to the rule of law at both national and international levels to help ensure stability, freedom and prosperity for all. We encourage all States to both initiate and welcome dialogue about the rule of law and to focus on what adherence to the rule of law means in practice. This includes sharing ideas and best practice at every opportunity.

The United Nations system is instrumental in translating the rule of law into practical measures to materially improve lives. The Secretary General's report canvases the enormous scope of work undertaken. The United Nations has contributed to ensuring the effective, inclusive and functioning justice institutions, ensuring accountability for violations of human rights, curbing corruption and making justice accessible. CANZ countries encourage all states to engage in this important work. We acknowledge the work of the Rule of Law Unit. We also acknowledge the Law Coordination and Resources Group. The Group's remit includes taking into account the emergence of new realities and actors in the field of the rule of law.

In engaging in this work, and with one another, we should be guided by the purposes and principles of the Charter. We should be heartened by our proven ability to achieve consensus and agree to be legally bound by our commitments and we should reflect on the benefits that the international rules-based order has and will continue to deliver.

Thank you.

3.4 *Crimes against Humanity*

On 28 October 2019, Australia made a statement to the Sixth Committee of the United Nations General Assembly in New York, on the work of the International Law Commission (ILC). Extracts from that statement follow:

Chair

Australia welcomes the adoption by the Commission of its draft articles on crimes against humanity.

We extend our thanks to the Special Rapporteur for his leadership, for taking into careful account the views of states and for the extensive effort he has put into crafting the draft articles.

As we consider the substance of the draft articles, we are mindful of the Commission's recommendation that States elaborate a Convention on the basis of the draft articles and the potential benefit such a convention may bring.

We recognise the role such an instrument could play in closing the gap in the current structure of conventions regarding serious international crimes and we are open to continuing a conversation with other States in this regard.

3.5 Criminal Accountability of UN Officials and Experts on Mission

On 10 October 2019, Canada made a statement to the Sixth Committee of the United Nations General Assembly in New York, on criminal accountability of UN officials and experts on mission delivered on behalf of Canada, Australia and New Zealand (CANZ). The full text of that statement follows:

I have the honour today of speaking on behalf of Australia, New Zealand, and my own country, Canada.

UN Officials and experts on mission play an important role in creating the conditions for lasting peace. Every day, tens of thousands of individuals from countries across the globe are engaged in maintaining peace and security, delivering humanitarian assistance and helping to rebuild societies, and supporting development, all in the name of the United Nations. These people are trusted to use their positions of relative influence and power to advance the purposes and principles of the United Nations, and often to assist thousands of the most vulnerable people in the world. CANZ commends their important work.

However, the deplorable acts of a few UN officials and experts, and the failure to hold them accountable, intensifies and proliferates suffering among the people they are mandated to help and protect. It undermines the reputation, credibility, and integrity and impartiality of UN Missions, and the United Nations as a whole.

In closing the impunity gap, it is therefore important that Member States and the UN develop a culture in which individuals are encouraged and supported to report misconduct and alleged crimes and establish appropriate safeguards against retaliation.

We recognize the leadership demonstrated by the Secretary-General of the UN in responding to this grave problem, notably through its adoption of the zero-tolerance policy and we commend the UN for its increased commitment to transparency and reporting on wrongdoing within the organization. Understanding the scope of the problem is critical to bringing about the change that is required.

We are concerned that sexual exploitation and abuse, corruption, fraud and other financial crimes are committed by UN officials and experts too frequently. We note that for the first two quarters of this year, 75 allegations of sexual exploitation or abuse involving UN personnel have been reported. We urge the UN to ensure that all of these allegations are investigated in an impartial, thorough, and timely manner, and to ensure that substantiated cases are appropriately dealt with, whether through disciplinary measures or through referral to home states.

We also continue to encourage the UN to undertake analysis of the cases, to better understand the dynamics giving rise to these crimes.

It is also useful to have the updated table of national provisions regarding Member States' establishment of jurisdiction over their nationals for relevant criminal offences. In this regard, we thank the Secretary-General for the latest update of the table as of June 2019. We would encourage all Member States to contribute to this table to provide clarity on where jurisdiction can be established and where gaps remain.

CANZ is acutely aware that all Member States need to do more to address the criminal accountability of UN officials and experts on mission. Member States have the primary responsibility to prevent misconduct and crimes from occurring by instilling a culture of zero tolerance for sexual exploitation and abuse. Corruption, fraud and related financial crimes must be in our sight. Member States also have a responsibility to implement measures including pre-deployment training and screening. Member States need to do more, to investigate and prosecute credible allegations of criminal misconduct by our nationals. We urge Member States that have not yet done so to consider establishing jurisdiction over serious crimes committed by their nationals while serving as UN officials or experts on mission. We stress that all Member States should investigate allegations of criminal conduct by their nationals, cooperate with other Member States in these criminal matters, and hold perpetrators accountable according to their domestic criminal law. We also encourage Member States to share information on any obstacles to effective prosecution they may encounter, whether jurisdictional, evidentiary, or otherwise.

If our commitment to the rules based order is to be more than rhetoric, the UN and its Member States must lead by example. We encourage the international community to hold to account those individuals who commit crimes while on mission. Such deplorable conduct undermines the work of the United Nations. We therefore support, in principle, the proposal for a convention that would require Member States to exercise criminal jurisdiction over their nationals participating in UN operations abroad. We would welcome further discussions on the feasibility of such a convention.

In closing, let us reiterate our unwavering support to the zero-tolerance policy of the Secretary-General. No one, including UN officials and experts on mission, who are the 'face' of the United Nations to the world, should be above or outside the law.

3.6 *Universal Jurisdiction*

On 15 October 2019, Australia made a statement to the United Nations General Assembly in New York, on the scope and application of the principle of universal jurisdiction, delivered on behalf of Canada, Australia and New Zealand (CANZ). The full text of that statement follows:

Mr President,

I have the honour of speaking today on behalf of Canada and New Zealand, as well as my own country, Australia.

CANZ welcomes the opportunity to engage in a dialogue on the scope and application of universal jurisdiction. We thank Member States for their contributions to the Secretary-General's report on this important topic.

CANZ recognises universal jurisdiction as a well-established principle of international law. Universal jurisdiction vests in every State the competence to exercise criminal jurisdiction over individuals responsible for the most serious crimes of international concern, regardless of where the conduct occurs and the nationality of the perpetrator. It offers a complementary framework to ensure that perpetrators are held to account in circumstances where the territorial State is unwilling or unable to exercise jurisdiction.

Australia, Canada and New Zealand have recognised universal jurisdiction over the most serious international crimes: genocide, crimes against humanity, war crimes, slavery, torture and piracy. Impunity for such crimes is unacceptable.

Given the complementary nature of the framework, CANZ reiterates that, as a general rule, primary responsibility for investigating and

AUSTRALIAN PRACTICE IN INTERNATIONAL LAW 2019

prosecuting these international crimes rests with the State in which the conduct occurs and the State of nationality of the perpetrator. Those States are often in the best position to achieve justice, given their access to evidence, witnesses and victims, and their ability to enforce sentences. They are also likely to be best placed to deliver the 'justice message' to perpetrators, victims, and affected communities.

CANZ wishes to emphasise the paramount importance of exercising universal jurisdiction in good faith and consistently with all principles and rules of international law, including laws related to diplomatic relations and privileges and immunities. This is essential to ensure that the goal of ending impunity does not in itself generate abuses of the human rights of the accused or conflict with other existing rules of international law. It is also important that judicial independence and impartiality is maintained to ensure that the principle of universal jurisdiction is not manipulated for political ends.

Canada, Australia and New Zealand all have legislation establishing universal jurisdiction in respect of the most serious international crimes. Such crimes attack the interests of all States; and as such it is in the interests of all States to ensure they are prosecuted. We applaud the work of those States that have incorporated into their domestic legislation universal jurisdiction over serious international crimes, and encourage others to do the same.

We look forward to continuing the valuable discussion on the scope and application of the principle of universal jurisdiction and reiterate our willingness to work constructively with other States on this important issue. By working cooperatively and collaboratively we can ensure that perpetrators of such grave crimes do not receive safe haven anywhere in the world.

Thank you.

3.7   *Jurisdiction of the International Criminal Court*

Australia's representative, HE Matthew Neuhaus, Ambassador to The Netherlands, made a statement at the 18th Session of the Assembly of States Parties of the International Criminal Court, held from 2–6 December 2019 in The Hague. Extracts from his statement follow:

[...]

As a strong supporter of accountability, and a longstanding supporter of the International Criminal Court, Australia remains firm in its conviction that accountability for atrocity crimes is critical to sustaining peace and supporting reconciliation in post-conflict situations.

The Court is a key element in the system of international criminal justice that helps deliver that accountability; designed to ensure that those responsible for the most serious crimes of concern to the international community face justice, where States that would otherwise have jurisdiction are unable or unwilling to exercise it.

Australia welcomes the important work undertaken this year—under your leadership Mr President—to strengthen the Court and Rome Statute system. We support a State-driven process to identify ways in which we can focus the Court on its core mandate. The Court must continue to find ways to deliver robustly, effectively and efficiently within the reality of finite resources. Prioritisation of cases and the expeditious resolution of situations under preliminary examination—where it is in the interests of justice and accountability—is key to achieving this objective.

An independent expert review that delivers concrete, achievable and actionable recommendations would be an important first step in this process.

But we cannot just leave it to others. We as States Parties must recommit ourselves to the responsibilities that fall to us. We should improve the ways in which we work—for example, streamlining the omnibus resolution and negotiations.

And, critically, it is our responsibility as States Parties to ensure that only the most qualified individuals are appointed to the leadership posts at the Court.

We must support the Court to consolidate around its core mandate.

[...]

The primary responsibility to investigate and, where appropriate, prosecute those responsible for serious international crimes rests with States. And properly so.

The ICC's role is as a critical court of *last resort* where States that would otherwise have jurisdiction are unable or unwilling to exercise it. To investigate and, where appropriate, to prosecute. This complementary nature of the ICC's jurisdiction is, of course, crucial to the Court's success.

As co-focal point with Romania on complementarity, Australia is pleased to facilitate dialogue on significant issues such as admissibility, States' obligations and the role of national jurisdictions. We encourage all States to participate in this dialogue.

[...]

In the words of the Preamble of the Statute, 'effective prosecution must be ensured by taking measures at the national level and by enhancing international cooperation'. In a world where, tragically, grave crimes and atrocities still occur, much still remains to be done.

[...]

At the 18th Session of the Assembly of States Parties of the International Criminal Court, held from 2–6 December 2019 in The Hague, Australia delivered an explanation of position following the adoption of an amendment to Article 8 of the Rome Statute inserting the crime of the use of deliberate starvation of civilians as a method warfare in non-international armed conflict. The full text of the explanation follows:

Australia welcomes the adoption of this amendment to Article 8, to insert into the Rome Statute the crime of the use of the deliberate starvation of civilians as a method of warfare in non-international armed conflict: a method we have seen employed, with horrendous consequences, in contemporary non-international armed conflicts.

Australia's support for this amendment to Article 8 is based on our commitment to the humanitarian objectives underpinning the substance of the amendment. It is Australia's understanding that the amendment is directed at conduct that deliberately and intentionally results in the starvation of the civilian population as a method of warfare.

We also reiterate our concern about amendments that seek to criminalise specific means or methods of warfare, including specific weapons or technologies, as opposed to conduct or behaviour in armed conflict that results in intolerable outcomes. We remain concerned that a possible consequence of identifying the use of certain means or methods of warfare as war crimes is to create an inference that the use of those means or methods of warfare not so identified is condoned. This is surely not our collective intention—and risks taking us away from the foundations of the Rome Statute.

3.8   *International Residual Mechanism for Criminal Tribunals*

On 23 October 2019, Australia made a statement to the United Nations General Assembly in New York, on the International Residual Mechanism for Criminal Tribunals, delivered on behalf of Canada, Australia and New Zealand (CANZ). The full text of that statement follows:

Mr President
President Agius, thank you for your report.

I have the honour to speak today on behalf of Canada, New Zealand and my own country, Australia.

CANZ continues to strongly support the important work of the International Residual Mechanism for Criminal Tribunals. This Mechanism safeguards and continues the legacy of the ad hoc tribunals for the Former Yugoslavia and for Rwanda.

Part of this legacy is the critical impact these tribunals have had on international criminal law's development. These Tribunals paved the way for the contemporary international criminal justice architecture, under which we now hold perpetrators of serious international crimes to account. This architecture is a key component of the international community's collective response in the face of mass atrocities.

CANZ remains steadfast in our commitment to accountability for serious international crimes. We recognise accountability's role in sustaining peace. We are active supporters of international criminal justice mechanisms, and believe that the Mechanism, and other international courts, are cornerstones of the rules-based international order.

CANZ would like to take this opportunity to welcome Judge Carmel Agius, who assumed office in January 2019, as the new President of the Mechanism. We also wish to thank the outgoing President, Judge Thedore Meron, for his service in that role since 2012. We pay tribute to the significant contribution he has made, as the inaugural President.

Mr. President,

International criminal Courts and Tribunals rely on sustained international support to fulfil their mandates, which continue long past the point at which the crimes themselves no longer occupy our headlines.

As the work of the tribunals themselves and of this Mechanism illustrate, the closing stages of a case are as important as the opening stages in ensuring justice is done. We have witnessed this most recently in the *Karadzić* and *Ngirabatware* cases.

We commend the Mechanism's commitment to concluding its remaining judicial work and fulfilling its mandate as efficiently and effectively as possible, while ensuring that fundamental procedural safeguards are met.

We are also particularly pleased to see proactive steps being taken on gender issues within the Mechanism, including efforts to combat sexual harassment and discrimination and address the significant gender imbalance.

Mr. President,

AUSTRALIAN PRACTICE IN INTERNATIONAL LAW 2019 521

The Mechanism relies on the support and cooperation of Member States. CANZ urges States to enhance their cooperation to secure the arrest and surrender of the eight fugitives, indicted by the ICTR, who are at large. We remain hopeful that these individuals will be held to account.

The Mechanism undertakes critical work in support of national jurisdictions. CANZ notes the almost ten-fold increase in documents provided to such jurisdictions in the past year. We acknowledge that staff and resources are required to respond to assistance requests.

Thank you.

3.9   *Responsibility of States for Internationally Wrongful Acts*

On 15 October 2019, Australia made a statement to the United Nations General Assembly in New York, on the responsibility of States for internationally wrongful acts, delivered on behalf of Canada, Australia and New Zealand (CANZ). The full text of that statement follows:

Mr President

I have the honour to speak today on behalf of Canada and New Zealand as well as my own country, Australia.

The draft Articles on the Responsibility of States for Internationally Wrongful Acts continue to play a valuable role as a persuasive statement on international law for governments and courts around the world.

Since the General Assembly first took note of the Articles in 2001 and commended them to the attention of governments, without prejudice to any future action, international legal bodies, as well as Governments, have increasingly referred to the authority of the Articles, including as a reflection of custom, to guide their decisions.

The Secretary-General's useful updated compilation of decisions of international courts, tribunals and other bodies referring to the Articles supports our assessment.

We are grateful to the Secretariat for its continued work to support Member States' consideration of the Articles.

We have carefully considered the views of other Member States on what future action, if any, should be taken regarding the Articles.

However, we have not heard a compelling reason articulated as to why there would be a need to alter the status quo.

The Articles, as they now stand, reflect widespread consensus on most issues and have a proven track record of application.

Opening up the Articles in a diplomatic negotiation would risk enlivening disagreement between Member States over different aspects of the Articles.

No matter how well intentioned, such an approach could dilute and undermine the influence of the Articles and the significant achievement of the International Law Commission, after many decades of careful deliberation.

We believe that the Articles, in their current form, provide the most viable framework for guiding international bodies and governments in their consideration of state responsibility issues.

We look forward to participating in the Working Group to be convened by this Committee to discuss the question of a convention or other appropriate action on the basis of the Articles.

However, until a compelling need has been identified, we consider the risks of negotiating a convention are too great.

But we would support the adoption of a resolution endorsing the Articles as they currently stand and attaching them as an annex.

Such an approach would maintain the integrity of the Articles and facilitate the progressive development of their content, without undermining them.

Thank you.

4 State Sovereignty and Territorial Integrity

4.1 *Ukraine including Crimea*

On 18 March 2019, Australia's Minister for Foreign Affairs, Senator the Hon. Marise Payne, released a media statement accounting new financial sanctions and travel bans in response to Russia's continued aggression against Ukraine. The full text of that media release follows:

Australia stands united with our partners in opposition to Russia's continued aggression against Ukraine, five years after its illegal annexation of Crimea.

Together with the United States, the United Kingdom and other European Union member states, and Canada, we are strong supporters of Ukraine's sovereignty and territorial integrity.

Today I announce targeted financial sanctions and travel bans against seven Russian individuals for their role in the interception and seizure of Ukrainian naval vessels that were attempting to pass through the Kerch

Strait. Australia is concerned by this escalation of tensions in the Sea of Azov in November 2018.

Australia condemns the aggression and calls on Russia to release the detained Ukrainian sailors and seized vessels without delay. We also call on Russia to allow free and unencumbered passage of Ukrainian and international ships through the Kerch Strait and the Sea of Azov.

Australia does not recognise any actions seeking to legitimise the annexation of Crimea or the secession of parts of Ukraine's Donetsk and Luhansk regions.

I have therefore also imposed targeted financial sanctions and travel bans against three 'leaders' from separatist-controlled parts of the Donetsk and Luhansk regions of Ukraine following so-called elections in November 2018.

Details of these 10 individuals are in DFAT's Consolidated List of individuals and entities subject to targeted sanctions under Australian law.

We call on Russia to respect Ukraine's sovereignty and territorial integrity within its internationally recognised borders, including its territorial waters.

5   International Peace and Security

5.1   *Cyberspace*

On March 2019, Australia's Department of Foreign Affairs and Trade published the Supplement to Australia's Position on the Application of International Law to State Conduct in Cyberspace. This forms part of Australia's International Cyber Engagement Strategy. The full publication follows:

> In the International Cyber Engagement Strategy (2017) (Strategy), Australia committed to periodically publish its position on the application of relevant international law to state conduct in cyberspace. The first such publication appeared in Annex A to the Strategy. This document is the second publication and is aimed at further elaborating Australia's position on applicable international law as expressed in the Strategy. As such, it should be read as a supplement to that document.

> **Application and development of international law**
> The Strategy recognised the well-established position that existing international law—including the UN Charter in its entirety—provides the framework for responsible state behaviour in cyberspace. The

international community, including the permanent members of the United Nations (UN) Security Council, recognised this in the 2013 and 2015 reports of the *UN Group of Governmental Experts on the use of Information Communications Technologies in the Context of International Security* (UNGGE), as adopted by the UN General Assembly. Australia also acknowledged that activities conducted in cyberspace raise new challenges for how international law applies. To deepen understandings and set clear expectations, Australia encourages states to be transparent in how they interpret existing international law as it applies to state conduct in cyberspace. The Strategy, and this supplement, form part of Australia's ongoing effort to make its views on the applicability of international law public.

The law on the use of force (jus ad bellum) and the principle of non-intervention

The *United Nations Charter* (Charter) and associated rules of customary international law apply to activities conducted in cyberspace. Article 2(3) of the Charter requires states to seek the peaceful settlement of disputes and Article 2(4) prohibits the threat or use of force by a state against the territorial integrity or political independence of another state, or in any manner inconsistent with the purposes of the UN. In the Strategy, Australia made clear that these obligations—and the UN Charter in its entirety, including those obligations—apply in cyberspace as they do in the physical realm.

A use of force will be lawful when the territorial state consents, it is authorised by the Security Council under Chapter VII of the UN Charter or when it is taken pursuant to a state's inherent right of individual or collective self-defence in response to an armed attack, as recognised in Article 51 of the Charter. Australia considers that the thresholds and limitations governing the exercise of self-defence under Article 51 apply in respect of cyber operations that constitute an armed attack and in respect of acts of self- defence that are carried out by cyber means. Thus if a cyber operation—alone or in combination with a physical operation—results in, or presents an imminent threat of, damage equivalent to a traditional armed attack, then the inherent right to self-defence is engaged. The rapidity of cyber attacks, as well as their potentially concealed and/or indiscriminate character, raises new challenges for the application of established principles. These challenges have been raised by Australia in explaining its position on the concept of imminence and the right of self-defence in the context of national security threats that have evolved as a result of technological advances (see Figure 1).

Figure 1—Imminence and cyber operations

'[A] state may act in anticipatory self-defence against an armed attack when the attacker is clearly committed to launching an armed attack, in circumstances where the victim will lose its last opportunity to effectively defend itself unless it acts.

This standard reflects the nature of contemporary threats, as well as the means of attack that hostile parties might deploy.

Consider, for example, a threatened armed attack in the form of an offensive cyber operation (and, of course, when I say 'armed attack', I mean that term in the strict sense of Article 51 of the Charter). The cyber operation could cause large-scale loss of human life and damage to critical infrastructure. Such an attack might be launched in a split-second. Is it seriously to be suggested that a state has no right to take action before that split-second?'

Attorney-General, Senator the Hon. George Brandis QC,
University of Queensland, 11 April 2017

Harmful conduct in cyberspace that does not constitute a use of force may still constitute a breach of the duty not to intervene in the internal or external affairs of another state. This obligation is encapsulated in Article 2(7) of the Charter and in customary international law. A prohibited intervention is one that interferes by coercive means (in the sense that they effectively deprive another state of the ability to control, decide upon or govern matters of an inherently sovereign nature), either directly or indirectly, in matters that a state is permitted by the principle of state sovereignty to decide freely. Such matters include a state's economic, political, and social systems, and foreign policy. Accordingly, as former UK Attorney-General Jeremy Wright outlined in 2018, the use by a hostile State of cyber operations to manipulate the electoral system to alter the results of an election in another State, intervention in the fundamental operation of Parliament, or in the stability of States' financial systems would constitute a violation of the principle of non-intervention.

International humanitarian law (jus in bello) and international human rights law

The Strategy and the 2015 Report of the *UN Group of Governmental Experts on Developments in the Field of Information and*

Telecommunications in the Context of International Security (A/70/174), discussed the applicability of international humanitarian law (IHL) to cyber operations in armed conflict, including the principles of humanity, military necessity, proportionality and distinction. Australia considers that, if a cyber-operation rises to the same threshold as that of a kinetic 'attack' (or act of violence) under IHL, the rules governing such attacks during armed conflict will apply to those kinds of cyber operations. Applicable IHL rules will also apply to cyber operations in an armed conflict that do not constitute or rise to the level of an 'attack', including the principle of military necessity and the general protections afforded to the civilian population and individual civilians with respect to military operations.

International human rights law (IHRL) also applies to the use of cyberspace (see eg, Figure 2). States have obligations to protect relevant human rights of individuals under their jurisdiction, including the right to privacy, where those rights are exercised or realised through or in cyberspace. Subject to lawful derogations and limitations, states must ensure without distinction individuals' rights to privacy, freedom of expression and freedom of association online.

Figure 2—Commonwealth Cyber Declaration

'Recognising the potential for a free, open, inclusive and secure cyberspace to promote economic growth for all communities and to act as an enabler for realisation of the Sustainable Development Goals across the Commonwealth, we: ...

5. Affirm that the same rights that citizens have offline must also be protected online.'

Commonwealth Heads of Government Declaration
20 April 2018

General principles of international law, including the law on state responsibility

In the Strategy, Australia recognised that the law on state responsibility, much of which is reflected in the International Law Commission's *Articles on the Responsibility of states for Internationally Wrongful Acts*, applies to state behaviour in cyberspace. Under the law on state responsibility, there will be an internationally wrongful act of a state when its conduct in cyberspace—whether by act or omission—is attributable to it and constitutes a breach of one of its international obligations.

Australia will, in its sole discretion, and based on its own judgement, attribute unlawful cyber operations to another state. In making such decisions, Australia relies on the assessments of its law enforcement and intelligence agencies, and consultations with its international partners (see eg, Figure 3). A cyber operation will be attributable to a state under international law where, for example, the operation was conducted by an organ of the state; by persons or entities exercising elements of governmental authority; or by non-state actors operating under the direction or control of the state.

As outlined in the Strategy, if a state is a victim of malicious cyber activity which is attributable to a perpetrator state, the victim state may be able to take countermeasures (whether in cyberspace or through another means) against the perpetrator state, under certain circumstances. Countermeasures are measures, which would otherwise be unlawful, taken to secure cessation of, or reparation for, the other state's unlawful conduct. Countermeasures in cyberspace cannot amount to a use of force and must be proportionate. States are able to respond to other States' malicious activity with acts of retorsion, which are unfriendly acts that are not inconsistent with any of the State's international obligations.

If a state is the victim of harmful conduct in cyberspace, that state could be entitled to remedies in the form of restitution, compensation or satisfaction. In the cyber context, this may mean that the victim-state could for example seek replacement of damaged hardware or compensation for the foreseeable physical and financial losses resulting from the damage to servers, as well as assurances or guarantees of non-repetition.

Figure 3—Australian Government Attribution of Cyber Incidents to Russia

'Today, the Australian Government has joined international partners to condemn a pattern of malicious cyber activity by Russia targeting political, business, media and sporting institutions worldwide.

Based on advice from Australian intelligence agencies, and in consultation with our partners and allies, the Australian Government has determined that the Russian military, and their intelligence arm 'the GRU', is responsible for this pattern of malicious cyber activity ...

Cyberspace is not the Wild West. The International Community— including Russia—has agreed that international law and norms of responsible state behaviour apply in cyberspace.

By embarking on a pattern of malicious cyber behaviour, Russia has shown a total disregard for the agreements it helped to negotiate ...

Australia's International Cyber Engagement Strategy recognises that there must be consequences for those who act contrary to the consensus on international law and norms.'

The Hon Scott Morrison MP, Prime Minister & Senator the Hon. Marise Payne, Minister for Foreign Affairs,
Joint Media Release, 4 October 2018

5.2 *Missile Testing in the Democratic People's Republic of Korea (DPRK)*

On 24 August 2019, Australia's Minister for Foreign Affairs, Senator the Hon. Marise Payne, released a media statement condemning North Korea's repeated missile tests. The full text of that media release follows:

> The Australian Government condemns North Korea's repeated missile launches since May 2019. Short-range ballistic missile launches are a clear violation of UN Security Council resolutions.
>
> Australia calls on North Korea to cease provocative actions that increase tensions on the Korean Peninsula and in the wider region. Such provocations do nothing for regional peace and stability, and increase the risk of miscalculation.
>
> Australia once more calls on North Korea to choose the path of dialogue. We commend the commitment demonstrated by the United States and the Republic of Korea to continue talks with North Korea.
>
> Australia joins with many other nations in seeking permanent peace on the Korean Peninsula, including the complete, verifiable and irreversible denuclearisation of North Korea.
>
> In the meantime, we remain committed to maintaining sanctions and other measures until North Korea takes clear steps towards denuclearisation.
>
> The Australian Government calls on all countries to assist in maintaining sanctions, including by fully implementing UN Security Council resolutions against North Korea.

On 1 November 2019, Australia's Minister for Foreign Affairs, Senator the Hon. Marise Payne, released a media statement again condemning North Korea's repeated missile tests. The full text of that media release follows:

> The Australian Government strongly condemns North Korea's repeated ballistic missile launches, most recently on 31 October.
>
> North Korea's ballistic missile launches are in clear contravention of multiple UN Security Council resolutions. The persistence with which North Korea engages in this destabilising behaviour is of increasing concern.

Australia calls on North Korea to cease provocative actions that increase tensions on the Korean Peninsula and undermine regional peace and stability.

Australia once more calls on North Korea to comply with the clear views of the international community on its nuclear, other weapons of mass destruction and ballistic missile programs, as expressed through UN Security Council resolutions.

We commend the commitment demonstrated by the United States and the Republic of Korea to continue talks with North Korea. Our support for diplomacy should not be seen by North Korea as silent approval of its ballistic missile launches.

Australia joins with many other nations in seeking permanent peace on the Korean Peninsula, including the complete, verifiable and irreversible denuclearisation of North Korea.

In the meantime, we remain committed to maintaining sanctions and sanctions enforcement measures against North Korea. The Australian Government calls on all countries to do likewise, including by fully implementing UN Security Council resolutions against North Korea.

The Australian Government supplements UN Security Council sanctions against North Korea with our own autonomous sanctions. We keep our autonomous sanctions regime under constant review.

5.3 *Protests in Hong Kong*

On 12 June 2019, Australia's Minister for Foreign Affairs, Senator the Hon. Marise Payne, released a media statement regarding the ongoing protests in Hong Kong. The full text of that media release follows:

> Australia has a substantial interest in Hong Kong's success, home to one of our biggest expatriate communities globally and our largest commercial presence in Asia.
>
> There is intense public interest and international community concern at events in Hong Kong.
>
> Australia supports the right of people to protest peacefully and to exercise their freedom of speech, and we urge all sides to show restraint and avoid violence.
>
> The Australian Government believes it is important that any changes to Hong Kong's extradition arrangements are pursued in keeping with regular processes of government and resolved in a way that fully respects Hong Kong's high degree of autonomy and upholds the rights and

freedoms enshrined in Hong Kong's Basic Law under the 'one country, two systems' framework.

The Australian Consul-General in Hong Kong has raised concerns about the proposed amendments at senior levels within the Hong Kong government and with the Executive and Legislative Councils.

DFAT keeps its travel advisories under close review. On 12 June, DFAT issued an update to the travel advice for Hong Kong, advising Australian citizens that they may encounter demonstrations or protests in Hong Kong and to avoid large public gatherings.

On 16 June 2019, Australia's Minister for Foreign Affairs, Senator the Hon. Marise Payne, released a media statement regarding the suspension of the extradition bill in Hong Kong. The full text of that media release follows:

Australia welcomes the announcement by Hong Kong Chief Executive Carrie Lam to suspend legislative consideration of the Fugitive Offenders and Mutual Legal Assistance in Criminal Matters Legislation (Amendment) Bill 2019.

Australia values Hong Kong's unique advantages and freedoms under 'One Country, Two Systems', the rule of law and its independent judiciary.

Australia supports freedom of speech and peaceful protest.

On 14 November 2019, Australia's Minister for Foreign Affairs, Senator the Hon. Marise Payne, released a media statement regarding the ongoing protests in Hong Kong. The full text of that media release follows:

We are deeply concerned by the violence in Hong Kong and the increasing divide between the authorities and Hong Kong people.

We reiterate our view that it is crucial for all sides—police and protestors—to exercise restraint and take genuine steps to de-escalate tensions. It is essential that the police respond proportionately to protests.

Australia continues to urge genuine efforts by all parties to find an effective political solution that supports and upholds Hong Kong's freedoms and advantages, an open and accountable law enforcement and the professional and unbiased application of justice.

A statement by the international expert panel providing advice to Hong Kong's Independent Police Complaints Council (IPCC) has identified limitations in the capability of the IPCC to oversee the police. It suggested there should be a further independent investigation into police

AUSTRALIAN PRACTICE IN INTERNATIONAL LAW 2019   531

responses to the protests. Australia encourages the Hong Kong authorities to address the panel's recommendations.

These steps are essential for any meaningful dialogue and restoring the trust of Hong Kong's people.

Our Consul-General in Hong Kong continues to raise our concerns with the Hong Kong authorities at the highest levels. Consulate staff are working closely with Australian business and community members in Hong Kong.

Australia has a substantial stake in Hong Kong's success. The city is home to one of our biggest expatriate communities globally and our largest commercial presence in Asia.

5.4   *Turkish Military Action in Northeastern Syria*

On 10 October 2019, the Hon. Scott Morrison MP and Minister for Foreign Affairs, Senator the Hon. Marise Payne, released a media statement regarding Turkey's military operation into northeastern Syria. The full text of that media release follows:

The Australian Government is deeply troubled by Turkey's unilateral military operation into northeastern Syria.

Actions of this nature will have grave consequences for regional security and could significantly undermine the gains made by the international coalition in its fight against Da'esh, which remains a serious threat to regional peace and security despite its territorial defeat.

It will cause additional civilian suffering, lead to greater population displacement, and further inhibit humanitarian access.

While Turkey has legitimate domestic security concerns, unilateral cross-border military action will not solve these concerns.

We have expressed this view directly to the Turkish Government.

The Government remains in close contact with our US, European, Middle East and other allies and security partners, including through our Embassies and other officials.

We urge restraint and call on all parties to the conflict in Syria to avoid escalatory or opportunistic actions that cause further instability and humanitarian suffering.

The Australian Government notes that the Syrian Democratic Forces (SDF) have been steadfast partners for the international Coalition in the fight against Da'esh, and have borne a significant share of the sacrifice.

They have also helped the international community by providing security support at Internally Displaced Persons camps.

The full implications of the Turkish military operation on these camps and the people residing in them are difficult to assess at this early stage and will depend, in part, on subsequent actions taken by Turkey and the Kurds.

The Government remains concerned for the Australians in these camps but, as we have previously stated, the situation is dangerous and unpredictable, and we will not put Australian officials and the public in danger.

5.5 *Territorial Defeat of Dae'esh*

On 24 March 2019, Australia's Prime Minister, the Hon. Scott Morrison MP, Minister for Foreign Affairs, Senator the Hon. Marise Payne and Minister for Defence, Senator the Hon. Linda Reynolds CSC, released a joint media statement regarding the territorial defeat of Da'esh by the Syrian Democratic Forces. The full text of that media release follows:

> The Australian Government welcomes the announcement by the Syrian Democratic Forces of the territorial defeat of Da'esh.
>
> The last remaining civilians under Da'esh control in the Middle Euphrates River Valley have been liberated, and the task of removing Da'esh's control of territory in Iraq and Syria has been completed.
>
> The territorial defeat of Da'esh has been achieved through the tremendous courage and sacrifice of Iraqi Security Forces and Syrian Democratic Forces, who have operated with Coalition backing. Civilians in Syria and Iraq have displayed incredible resilience to overcome the brutality of Da'esh occupation.
>
> The Government commends the professionalism and dedication of Australia's deployed forces who have made an important contribution to operations against Da'esh forces as part of the 79-member Global Coalition to Defeat Da'esh.
>
> Since September 2014, Australia has made one of the most significant contributions to the Global Coalition. Since the start of operations, on average, around 600 Australian Defence Force personnel are deployed at any one time to the Middle East as part of our support to the coalition.
>
> Despite the significance of the milestone represented by this territorial defeat, it does not represent the end of the fight against Da'esh nor the extremism it embodies. Da'esh continues to pose a security threat in the Middle East region and beyond, including through the propagation of its extreme ideology.

AUSTRALIAN PRACTICE IN INTERNATIONAL LAW 2019

Australia continues to assist the Iraqi Security Forces, at the request of the government of Iraq, to address the continuing threat from Da'esh. This includes Australia's training mission at Taji near Baghdad, where Australian and New Zealand soldiers have to date trained more than 42,000 members of the ISF in their fight against Da'esh.

Australia will continue to work closely with Coalition partners and the wider international community, using a range of measures, to counter Da'esh.

5.6   Terrorism: Countering Terrorism and Violent Extremism

On 26 February 2019, Australia's Minister for Foreign Affairs, Senator the Hon. Marise Payne, released a media statement regarding the deterioration of relations between India and Pakistan following terrorist attacks in Jammu and Kashmir. The full text of that media release follows:

> The Australian government is concerned about relations between India and Pakistan following the horrific terrorist attack in Jammu and Kashmir on 14 February, which Australia has condemned.
>
> India's Foreign Secretary has stated that India has now conducted operations targeting terrorist groups based in Pakistan.
>
> Pakistan must take urgent and meaningful action against terrorist groups in its territory, including Jaish-e-Mohammed which has claimed responsibility for the 14 February bombing, and Lashkar-e-Taiba.
>
> Pakistan must do everything possible to implement its own proscription of Jaish-e-Mohammed. It can no longer allow extremist groups the legal and physical space to operate from its territory.
>
> These steps would make a substantial contribution to easing tensions and resolving the underlying causes of conflict.
>
> Australia urges both sides to exercise restraint, avoid any action which would endanger peace and security in the region and engage in dialogue to ensure that these issues are resolved peacefully.

On 2 April 2019, HE Gillian Bird, Permanent Representative of Australia to the United Nations, presented the following Explanation of Vote on Combatting terrorism and other acts of violence based on religion or belief:

> Australia is pleased to support the resolution. Australians share their deepest sympathies for those affected by the devastating terrorist attack in Christchurch and share the grief of Muslim communities all over the

world. As our Prime Minister has said, Australia condemns in absolute terms the abhorrent attack of 15 March 2019.

We stand together with New Zealand and all countries that condemn the hatred and intolerance behind this extremist attack. Australia condemns acts of terrorism, as well as the racism, xenophobia and intolerance that fuels them, in the strongest terms.

We condemn all forms of violent extremism and its manifestations. This includes far right violent extremism. We will always defend and protect the right of all Australians to practice their religion peacefully and without fear. Australia is a successful immigrant nation, based on a harmonious multicultural society. Almost half of our current population was either born overseas or has at least one parent born overseas, from every nation, culture and faith. While peaceful protest is a fundamental right, the Australian Government does not and will not tolerate anyone who incites violence and hatred within our community.

Australia supports the call for strengthened international efforts to promote a culture of tolerance and peace at all levels, based on respect for human rights, freedom of religious worship, and for the diversity of religions and beliefs. Australia welcomes the call for all States to work together to protect individuals against acts of violence, discrimination and hate crimes based on religion, racism, racial discrimination, xenophobia, and related intolerance. We must continue to build cohesive societies that are resilient to messages of extremism.

Terrorism remains a global challenge, which requires a sustained and strengthened global response from all members of the international community in partnership. Australia stands strengthened in our resolve to work together to promote tolerance and openness following the terrorist attack in Christchurch.

On 23 September 2019, the Hon. Scott Morrison MP, Prime Minister, delivered a speech at the Leaders' Dialogue on Strategic Responses to Terrorist and Violent Extremist Narratives at the UN Headquarters, New York. Excerpts from that speech follow:

[...]

Terrorists and violent extremists are weaponising the internet by spreading hate. And we have a simple rule that says that our expectations of behaviour in the physical world should be the same as our expectations for behaviour in the digital world. Similarly, the rules of the physical world should equally apply in the rules of the digital world. There should be no leave passes or different tolerances for different types of behaviour along the lines that exist in real space. So we cannot allow the internet to be weaponised by violent extremists.... The industry is taking steps to prevent this abhorrent content being streamed and uploaded, re-uploaded on digital platforms. And it must. This hadn't been the priority before. But I'm glad it is quickly becoming one now. Through the shared terrorist violent extremist Christchurch protocol, government and industry will now work in lockstep to respond to a live-streamed attack. That's good. And we endorsed these guidelines and strategy.

[...]

Australia, New Zealand and the OECD are developing voluntary transparency reporting protocols on the major platforms. This will set the first global reporting standards for industry to meet. And I welcome the support of all of those who have sought to shape these protocols. We'll start by delivering a benchmark to practice. Defining metrics and creating a common network so that we can measure progress and take action together. These are the practical steps that are necessary. And I think there is a widespread agreement about the need to take action. But we've got to keep checking up on ourselves to make sure it actually happens. Or we'll let down everybody outside this room who depends on it.

In Australia we're working with industry to combat violent extremist content, including introducing new criminal offences to ensure that it is expeditiously removed and reported to the police. The industry built this new digital world and we have to work closely with them to ensure we can deal with the technologies that can help protect us from this digital world as well. Without the industry's deep and engaged involvement in this, as committed to solving this problem as they are to pursuing the commercial objectives for which they were formed, then it will be very difficult to overcome. One thing is clear though, digital platforms must not be used to facilitate terrorism and violent extremism. Our shared sense of humanity must and will prevail. And the rules of the physical world must apply in the digital. So Australia stands with all those here today, to expect the public trust in the digital environment continue. Thank you.

On 8 October 2019, Canada made a statement to the Sixth Committee of the United Nations General Assembly in New York, on measures to eliminate international terrorism, delivered on behalf of Canada, Australia and New Zealand (CANZ). The full text of that statement follows:

Thank you, Chair.

I have the honour to speak on behalf of Australia, New Zealand and my own country, Canada, on the agenda item Measures to Eliminate International Terrorism. I would like to congratulate you, Chair, and other members of the Bureau. We know we are in safe hands.

At the outset, let me reiterate our absolute condemnation of terrorism and violent extremism, wherever it takes place and in whatever form. This year, once again, we have all too many examples of terrorist acts and the devastating impact they can have on victims, communities and societies at large. This includes the devastating terrorist attack against the Muslim community in Christchurch on March 15 and the Easter attacks in Sri Lanka on April 21, both this year.

I also would like to reconfirm our full support for the holistic and preventative approach of the Secretary-General's Plan of Action to Prevent Violent Extremism, as well as the Global Counter-Terrorism Strategy. Only through joint actions—taken with conviction and in compliance with the UN Charter, Security Council resolutions, as well as the relevant principles and rules of international law—can the international community credibly respond to the global terrorist threat.

Let me also convey CANZ's appreciation to Under-Secretary-General Vladimir Voronkov, Assistant Secretary-General Michèle Coninsx and the Counter-Terrorism Committee Executive Directorate (CTED), for their ongoing work to encourage Member States to comply and fully implement Security Council resolutions 1373 (2001) and 1624 (2005) on measures to eliminate international terrorism.

Through concerted efforts, we have made real progress in preventing acts of terrorism being committed, and suppressing and combating international terrorism. In that regard, we welcome the efforts made towards implementation of counter-terrorism conventions, and we encourage all Member States to ratify and implement the various international instruments concerning international terrorism.

CANZ believes collaborative, multi-stakeholder efforts between governments, online service providers, civil society and non-governmental organisations focussed on protecting a free, open and secure internet, are crucial in addressing terrorist and violent extremist use of the internet, as well as to address online hate and abuse. In the wake of the 15 March terrorist attack on the Muslim community in Christchurch, CANZ members were pleased to join Government and tech industry leaders in adopting the Christchurch Call to Action. The Christchurch Call to Action gives us a road map to eliminate terrorist and violent extremist content online.

We are also working in support of the development of the OECD Voluntary Transparency Reporting Protocols (VTRP). This project will establish a common global reporting standard—starting by delivering a benchmark of existing practices by online platforms, establishing metrics to measure progress, and developing a common voluntary reporting protocol. We encourage online platforms to accelerate their efforts to prevent and remove terrorist and violent extremist content on the Internet. To achieve long term sustainable results, we will need to find better ways to combat the spread of hateful online messages, while upholding our commitment to human rights, the rule of law, democratic principles, inclusion and diversity.

CANZ countries encourage Member States to comply and fully implement Security Council resolution 2396 (2017). Better coordination on border protection, information sharing and detection are making it increasingly difficult for foreign terrorist fighters to travel to conflict zones.

Denying terrorist groups access to resources, both human and financial, is a prerequisite for success. The evolving and highly sophisticated use of block-chain technology to mask the movement of illicit funds is a worrying phenomenon, which requires immediate attention. Australia is pleased to be hosting the No Money For Terror Ministerial Conference on Counter-Terrorism Financing in Melbourne on 7–8 November 2019, which will include a focus on the risk of emerging technologies, such as blockchain, being exploited to finance terrorism.

CANZ encourages Member States that have not done so to implement all UNSC resolutions addressing international terrorism, along with the various international instruments. We remind Member States of our continuing commitments and obligations under Resolutions 1373, 2178, and their successor resolutions, pertaining to the effective investigation and prosecution of all acts of terrorism. Through collective action we have succeeded in depriving Da'esh of its territory in Iraq and Syria—an essential step towards its defeat. Nonetheless, the group remains a threat in the region, and its expanding influence in Afghanistan, sub-Saharan Africa and South East Asia are particularly concerning. Al Qa'eda also remains a threat. We must remain alert, vigilant, and prepared to act together.

Member States are also grappling with the challenges of returning foreign terrorist fighters and their families. For those who return from the conflict zone, and are not subject to arrest and prosecution, finding enduring solutions for their successful rehabilitation and reintegration into society requires the coordinated involvement of governments and civil society. To be effective, our approaches need to be trauma-informed, age and gender appropriate, and address the many complex needs that stem from witnessing and/or experiencing violence. Children taken to the conflict zone or born there are particularly at risk of trauma-impact. CANZ applauds the many women's organizations working on the front lines in prevention, early warning, and responses to international terrorism. They are key partners in building resilience in local communities.

The international community also has a responsibility to address the plight of the victims of terrorism. CANZ members are proud to support the recently-formed Group of Friends of Victims of Terrorism, including in its focus on victims' rights and needs, on giving them a voice internationally, and on promoting their role in countering terrorist and violent extremist ideology. We also recognise our collective obligation to bring terrorists to justice, and support calls for coordinated action by governments, civil society and the private sector to share best practices and lessons learned in the areas of prosecution and correction—for those who can be successfully charged and tried, and in monitoring, rehabilitation and reintegration, for those who cannot.

Please allow me in conclusion to reiterate CANZ's unwavering commitment to support and work with all others engaged in countering terrorism and violent extremism, including through the work of the Global Counter Terrorism Forum which Canada will be co-chairing with the Kingdom of Morocco for the next two years, from 2019 to 2021.

Thank you.

On 28 October 2019, Australia's Prime Minister, the Hon. Scott Morrison MP, Minister for Foreign Affairs, Senator the Hon. Marise Payne and Minister for Defence, Senator the Hon. Linda Reynolds CSC, released a joint media statement welcoming the death of ISIS leader Abu Bakr al-Baghdadi. The full text of that media release follows:

> The announcement by US President Donald Trump confirming the death of ISIS leader Abu Bakr al-Baghdadi is welcomed by Australia.
>
> Al-Baghdadi died in a US-led raid on his hideout in northwest Syria on 26 October.
>
> He led a murderous, terrorist group responsible for widespread misery and destruction across large parts of Iraq and Syria.
>
> He also inspired or directed cowardly attacks by ISIS followers against innocent civilians around the world, some of whom were Australian.

He was responsible for ordering ethnic cleansing, sexual slavery, and other crimes against humanity.

Al-Baghdadi's death is a significant blow to ISIS and another important step in preventing its revitalisation. It is important to remember his death does not represent the end of the campaign to defeat this terrorist group and the extremism it embodies.

ISIS and its perverted ideology continue to pose security threats in the Middle East region and beyond.

Australia remains an active contributor to the 79-member Global Coalition to Defeat ISIS, and is committed to playing our part in the evolving counter-terrorism fight. Keeping Australians safe from terrorist attacks remains a foremost priority for the Government.

Australian Defence Force personnel continue to support Coalition operations against ISIS.

The Australian Government thanks Australian and Coalition military forces who, for many years, have helped in the efforts to defeat ISIS.

We honour the courage and sacrifice of Iraqi Security Forces in the liberation of their land from the ruthless occupation of ISIS.

We also restate our deep respect for the Syrian Democratic Forces, who have been steadfast and courageous security partners in the counter-ISIS coalition.

Australia will continue to work closely with Coalition partners and the wider international community to counter ISIS, including by stemming their financing, and stopping terrorist groups using the internet as a tool of recruitment and propaganda.

5.7 *Responsibility to Protect*

On 7 March 2019, during the 40th session of the United Nations Human Rights Council in Geneva, Australia joined a Joint Statement of the Group of Friends on the Responsibility to Protect. Extracts of that statement follow:

[...]

Fourteen years ago, the principle of the Responsibility to Protect populations from genocide, war crimes, crimes against humanity and ethnic cleansing was unanimously adopted by all UN member states. Too often, the ongoing disrespect for human rights can serve as an early warning sign of situations that may escalate into mass atrocity crimes. This is why the Group of Friends on R2P strongly believes that Geneva-based human rights mechanisms play a fundamental role in upholding our individual and shared commitment to mass atrocity prevention.

Mr. President,

The High Commissioner and her office play an important role in promoting and strengthening early warning and early action to respond to human rights violations and prevent mass atrocity crimes. The High Commissioner's reports and regular updates on country specific situations are particularly well suited to mobilize action when witnessing an emerging risk of mass atrocity crimes. Therefore, we strongly encourage the High Commissioner and her office, in accordance with her mandate, to continue in assisting the international community to uphold R2P.

In addition to OHCHR, special procedures mandate holders—both thematic and country specific—represent a key mechanism to assist states in upholding and deepening their commitment to R2P in the early and imminent stages of atrocity prevention, including through strengthening their compliance with obligations under international human rights law.

The Universal Periodic Review provides a unique opportunity for mainstreaming and institutionalizing structural prevention, both through strengthening national capacities for atrocity risk analysis as well as through mobilizing international support through technical assistance and capacity building.

We further believe that in order to achieve a systematic integration of human rights into wider discussions and policies of prevention, greater coordination between Geneva-based human rights mechanisms and other UN agencies and organs as well as regional organizations and mechanisms is fundamental for developing a comprehensive prevention framework.

Mr President,

In conclusion, the Group of Friends believes that the international community can and should lay the ground for the prevention of mass atrocity crimes through strengthening and deepening its engagement with Geneva-based human rights mechanisms.

[...]

On 25 June 2019, during the 41st session of the United Nations Human Rights Council in Geneva, Australia joined a Joint Statement of the Group of Friends on the Responsibility to Protect. An extract of that statement follows:

[...]

The Group of Friends of R2P thanks the High Commissioner for her update. Over the past years, the Group of Friends of R2P has continuously emphasized the link between the Responsibility to Protect and Geneva-based human rights mechanisms and institutions. As the primary international human rights body, the Human Rights Council, through its procedures and mechanisms, is particularly well suited to apply preventive measures in situations where early warning signs of possible atrocities arise. Preventing widespread violations and abuses of human rights is crucial to avoid them developing into mass atrocities. It is our individual and collective responsibility to prevent that from happening. We further thank the High Commissioner for highlighting the link between human rights violations and impunity.

In this regard, we would like to thank the High Commissioner and her office for their preventive efforts in promoting human rights including through the World Programme of Human Rights Education as well as in highlighting violations and abuses of human rights and identifying patterns of systematic discrimination against individuals and groups. The identification of risk factors and early warning signs is essential to prevent widespread violations and abuses of human rights that could potentially lead to mass atrocities. We therefore encourage the Office of the High Commissioner to continue to provide regular information to the Human Rights Council and the UN General Assembly, and to provide briefings to the UN Security Council, within her mandate. The promotion of a coherent and comprehensive approach to mass atrocity prevention across the different UN bodies is key in upholding our responsibility to protect. We further encourage the Office of the High Commissioner for Human Rights to continue and strengthen the engagement with the Special Advisers on the Prevention of Genocide and the Responsibility to Protect.

Besides regular HRC sessions, special procedures, treaty bodies and the Universal Periodic Review are also key mechanisms for atrocity prevention and have often contributed to the early warning of atrocity crimes. In addition, Human Rights Council-mandated investigative mechanisms can play an instrumental role in documenting patterns of widespread human rights violations, identify perpetrators of possible mass atrocity crimes, and strengthen accountability processes. Together, this can have an important deterrence effect to prevent the recurrence of atrocities.

In addition, the Human Rights Council and its procedures plays a crucial role in strengthening states' individual efforts to prevent mass atrocity crimes. By providing timely and targeted technical assistance and capacity building measures, states are able to strengthen respect for the rule of law and good governance and consolidate effective and accountable national institutions, which are key elements for effective atrocity prevention. Côte d'Ivoire, which has previously benefitted from technical assistance and capacity building by an Independent Expert, serves as an example of how the HRC can contribute to strengthening domestic institutions and national processes for structural prevention and guarantees of non-recurrence.

In line with the recommendations from the latest SG report on the Responsibility to Protect, we underscore the importance of enhancing prevention efforts at grassroots level, for which assisting domestic, regional and local actors and institutions remains vital. Furthermore, partnerships and cooperation between UN human rights mechanisms, within their mandates, and national actors can ensure that atrocity prevention is both a bottom-up and top-down process. All in all, the variety of human rights mechanisms and institutions allow for context specific and comprehensive preventive action.

However, where early warning signs and risk factors are being identified, timely and sustained action should follow in accordance with the UN charter. The international community must increase efforts when it comes to early action, as outlined in the Secretary General's 2018 and 2019 reports on the Responsibility to Protect.

We strongly believe that this Council, and all UN Member States, can, and should do more to make the responsibility to protect a living reality.

[...]

On 27 June 2019, HE Gillian Bird, Australia's Ambassador and Permanent Representative to the United Nations, made a statement to the United Nations General Assembly in New York, in relation to the Responsibility to Protect. The full text of that statement follows:

Australia was proud to partner with Ghana to propose last year's important debate on the Responsibility to Protect—the first in this Assembly for a decade.

Well over one hundred states—from all regions—participated.

Support for the R2P principle and its implementation were overwhelming.

As was the desire for ongoing dialogue, in this Assembly, on how we can better protect populations from mass atrocities.

Such a response was fitting. After all, when our leaders agreed the R2P principle in 2005 they envisaged a leading role for this Assembly.

We also appreciated the opportunity to hear those who have questions, or harbour misgivings.

Let me reaffirm that the R2P principle is not a stalking horse for other agendas.

Nor is not an attempt to reinterpret the UN Charter.

It is about reinforcing the need to work collectively and in line with the Charter, to protect populations from mass atrocities.

Mr President,

Australia agrees with the Secretary-General that regional organisations are essential to operationalising R2P.

Pacific Islands Forum leaders—via the Declarations in Biketawa in 2000 and in Boe in 2018—have long recognised our collective vulnerability and the need to address such challenges at the regional level, as the Permanent Representative of the Marshall Islands has just reminded us.

The Biketawa Declaration served as the foundation for regional assistance efforts, including a successful mission to Solomon Islands—'RAMSI'—that ended in 2017. An example of Pillar 2 in action.

The 2018 Boe Declaration reaffirms the critical importance of a rules-based international order, with the UN Charter at its heart.

It commits to strengthen regional security and stability, including by:
- identifying and addressing emerging security challenges; and
- improving early warning mechanisms.

Regional organisations can learn much from each other in their respective atrocity prevention efforts.

This is why Australia supports innovative regional initiatives, such as the Asia-Pacific Partnership on Atrocity Prevention.

Australia will host the first Regional Meeting of Asia Pacific R2P Focal Points later this year.

Such collaboration is bolstered by global forums, like the Global Network of R2P Focal Points, in which Australia is active.

With 61 focal points, this Network shares ideas, policies and builds capacity for implementing R2P.

Mr President,

Australia thanks the Secretary-General's Chef de Cabinet for the insightful remarks today and for this year's report, of the Secretary-General, on R2P.

We pay tribute to the efforts of the Special Advisers for the Prevention of Genocide and R2P, Mr Adama Dieng and Ms Karen Smith.

We agree that the UN's principal organs, and its member states, have a critical role in implementing R2P.

But it is important also to evaluate the role of the Secretariat.

Recent independent reviews have highlighted, in situations of mass atrocities, the critical importance of UN officials speaking for the UN as a whole.

It is also essential that the Secretariat ensure that reporting from the field provides an accurate and complete picture of developments on the ground.

In this regard, we wholeheartedly support the Secretary-General's ongoing reform agenda.

Mr President,

The Charter endows the Security Council with unique powers. With such powers come special responsibilities.

That is why we joined 118 others to support the Accountability, Coherence and Transparency Group's Code of Conduct. A commitment to refrain from vetoing Security Council action in cases of mass atrocities.

We also encourage all states—but especially current and prospective Security Council members—to join Australia and 100 other states supporting the France/Mexico initiative on veto restraint.

In instances where a permanent member blocks Council action in cases of mass atrocities, or atrocity risk, we believe we should explore possible ways to use this Assembly for further dialogue.

On 10 September 2019, during the 42nd session of the United Nations Human Rights Council in Geneva, Australia joined a Joint Statement of the Group of Friends on the Responsibility to Protect. An extract of that statement follows:

[...]

We would like to thank the High Commissioner Madame Bachelet and her Office for their tireless endeavours in preventing the continuation of human rights violations, engaging with Governments to secure respect for all human rights, and enhancing international cooperation to protect human rights, including through reporting of gross human rights violations around the world. We further thank her for the oral update to the Council.

The work of the High Commissioner, the Human Rights Council and its mechanisms is vital to fulfilling the Responsibility to Protect populations from genocide, war crimes, crimes against humanity and ethnic cleansing. Geneva-based human rights mechanisms are fundamental to uphold our individual and shared commitment to mass atrocity prevention.

Mr. President,

The High Commissioner's reports on country situations are particularly relevant in supporting international efforts to address the risks of mass atrocity crimes, since they help raise awareness and can mobilize effective preventive and responsive action at an early stage. Further, OHCHR plays a crucial role in addressing factors which facilitate systematic human rights violations and can, through the wider Geneva-system, contribute to provide technical assistance and capacity building to strengthen domestic atrocity prevention.

Furthermore, we highlight the importance of special procedures mandate holders, the Universal Periodic Review and other mechanisms of the Council that assist States to fulfil their international obligations. States also have an individual responsibility to protect their populations from mass atrocities and, where unable or unwilling to do so, the responsibility lies with the international community to act through the United Nations. Lastly, we highlight the importance of streamlining the United Nations system in the field of human rights to more effectively prevent gross human rights violations.

Mr. President,

It is clear that the key to effective action in preventing mass atrocity crimes is raising awareness of situations at risk. We therefore urge the High Commissioner to continue to shed light on systematic human rights violations and mobilize support to take action. Towards this end, we call upon the international community to better utilize this knowledge to act in a timely and decisive manner when early warning signs of possible atrocity situations emerge.

[...]

5.8 Protection of Civilians

On 23 May 2019, HE Gillian Bird, Australia's Ambassador and Permanent Representative to the United Nations, made a statement to the United Nations Security Council in New York, in relation to the protection of civilians ('POC'). The full text of that statement follows:

Mr President,

Let me begin by commending Indonesia for its successful Presidency of the Council and for the focus you have given to this important issue.

The protection of civilians is the primary responsibility of states, a fundamental principle of international humanitarian law, and a critical benchmark by which the UN's performance is judged.

Emerging in response to the international community's failures to prevent mass atrocities in Rwanda and the Balkans in the 1990s, the UN's protection of civilians agenda has become a critical component of the Security Council's work to maintain international peace and security.

While a solid normative POC framework has been established, under international law and through Council practice, realities on the ground often paint a different picture.

The majority of casualties in armed conflict are civilians. Vast numbers are killed, maimed, raped, starved or forced to flee. Civilians are often indiscriminately targeted.

Mr President,

Let me make a few points about what more we could do to ensure the protection of civilians.

First, the Council must be more systematic, comprehensive and consistent in addressing protection concerns within and across conflict situations.

Where peaceful means are inadequate and national authorities manifestly fail to protect their populations, the Council must uphold the international community's responsibility to protect populations from mass atrocities.

We urge all states to sign the Accountability, Coherence and Transparency Group Code of Conduct and support the France-Mexico initiative on veto restraint, to ensure Council resolutions designed to prevent or halt mass atrocities are not blocked.

Second, the credibility and legitimacy of UN peacekeeping depends on the Council's capacity to act when civilians are under threat.

Effective POC requires comprehensive and trusted engagement with local communities to understand and respond to their protection needs.

We welcome the expansion of Community Liaison Alert Networks and recognise the indispensable role of women and child protection advisers in combatting sexual violence and recruitment of child soldiers.

We urge Council members to explore further the unarmed civilian protection methodologies employed by a number of organisations. Community engagement is central to the success of these efforts.

Uniformed components need to be well trained and equipped for POC tasks that require a proactive posture. New POC performance assessments will help address shortcomings and strengthen accountability.

We encourage all troop-contributing countries to endorse the *Kigali Principles on the Protection of Civilians*.

AUSTRALIAN PRACTICE IN INTERNATIONAL LAW 2019   547

Third, we need to enhance and ensure respect for international humanitarian and human rights law in conflict.

We welcome the development of national POC policies to ensure international obligations are met and protection strategies are effective. In 2015, we adopted the *Australian Guidelines for the Protection of Civilians*.

We applaud the ongoing engagement with states and non-state armed groups to deepen understanding and respect for international law, including ongoing efforts to end the recruitment and use of child soldiers.

Finally, we support more robust and innovative approaches to accountability, including through sanctions and independent investigative mechanisms, to help bring justice and deter future crimes.

5.9   *Women, Peace and Security*

On 11 April 2019, HE Gillian Bird, Ambassador and Permanent Representative of Australia to the United Nations delivered a national statement at the United Nations Security Council in New York, on United Nations Peace Operations: Women in Peacekeeping. Extracts from the statement follow:

[...]

Gender parity in peace operations has vast potential to improve effectiveness, capability and credibility. We have made pledges to do better and set targets to go higher. But, in the field, the number of uniformed women remains extremely low and the rate of change has, speaking frankly, been glacial. This failing is undermining UN efforts to fulfil mandates and sustain peace.

Australia welcomes the Secretary-General's firm commitment to gender equality, supported by the Uniformed Gender Parity Strategy. We support the Elsie Initiative which aims to accelerate the pace of change and enhance the deployment of women as peacekeepers. The appointment of women into senior leadership positions is crucial, yet continues to face the greatest barriers.

Australia is committed to the full inclusion of women in our defence and police forces and to mainstreaming a gender perspective across operations. It is fundamental to strengthen our workforce capability and improve operational effectiveness. The same applies to UN peacekeeping missions. We have translated this commitment at the UN by achieving and exceeding the uniformed women targets. We have provided gender advisers to UN missions and stress the importance of adequately resourcing these positions in all missions. We also fund the participation of female peacekeepers at UN training courses to increase the numbers, qualifications and readiness of women for a peacekeeping deployment.

[...]

On 23 April 2019, HE Gillian Bird, Ambassador and Permanent Representative of Australia to the United Nations delivered a national statement at the United Nations Security Council in New York, on Sexual Violence in Conflict. Extracts from the statement follow:

[...]

In order to eradicate sexual violence in conflict we need to address all four pillars of the Women, Peace and Security agenda, not just protection. This is not simply an issue of protection. These are issues of prevention and accountability.

Protection starts with prevention.

Sexual violence in conflict is part of a continuum of violence, primarily against women and girls, which is rooted in gender inequality. Research clearly shows that gender inequality, including violence against women in peacetime, is a direct cause of sexual violence in conflict. Indeed, gender inequality is the strongest indicator of a country's risk of conflict.

While this debate naturally focuses on violence during conflict, we must not forget the fundamental route to prevention relies in addressing the fundamental cause: gender inequality in all its forms.

Sexual violence is not an inevitable occurrence in the ordinary course of conflict. It is not something we should ever accept. Australia is outraged by the persistent and widespread occurrence of sexual violence in armed conflict. A climate of impunity discourages reporting, undermines assistance, and abets further violations.

We acknowledge the central importance of sexual and reproductive health and rights for all people in conflict situations, but particularly survivors of rape and sexual violence. Access to the full range of quality reproductive and sexual health care, services and information is critical for the recovery of survivors and for the restoration of their dignity and bodily autonomy. Sexual and reproductive health and rights are vital human rights. Respecting and upholding these rights, particularly the right to services and information, can be the difference between life and death.

In addressing sexual based violence in conflict, we need to identify solutions and approaches that are context specific, inclusive, and informed by experience, especially that of survivors. Our actions must be survivor-centred and recognise diversity of experience and need.

AUSTRALIAN PRACTICE IN INTERNATIONAL LAW 2019 549

We emphasise the importance of ensuring that our military, police and service providers develop positive internal cultures that are gender-sensitive and do not tolerate violence. Further, we encourage the use of gender advisers in peacekeeping, the military and police and note that the representation of women is not the same as gender expertise.

Finally, diverse women must be involved in all aspects of our efforts to end sexual violence and in the design and implementation of services to survivors of sexual violence in conflict. Australia commends the extraordinary work of survivor-advocates, civil society organisations and human rights defenders. We call on member states to listen to their voices and support their work.

[...]

On 5 December 2019, Australia's Minister for Foreign Affairs and Minister for Women, Senator the Hon. Marise Payne, delivered a speech at the Bali Democracy Forum, which included reference to women, peace and security. Extracts from the statement follow.

[...]

Enabling women's full and meaningful participation is fundamental to preventing conflict and achieving global peace and stability. [...]

I'm a former defence minister in Australia. I'm very committed to UN Security Council Resolution 1325. [...]

Women, peace, and security makes a difference [...] When women are included in the peace process, the statistical assessment is that there is a 35 per cent greater chance that a peace agreement will last at least 15 years. So providing a safe and secure environment for women is paramount. As violence is not only a gross violator of human rights, but it undermines the country's social fabric, and it prevents women from achieving social and economic equality. It has a profound and devastating impact on victims, on families, on societies, and frankly, it costs economies billions of dollars.

[...]

5.10 Role of Reconciliation in Maintaining International Peace and Security

On 19 November 2019, HE Mr Mitch Fifield Ambassador and Permanent Representative of Australia to the United Nations, delivered a statement at the United Nations Security Council Open Debate on the Role of Reconciliation in Maintaining International Peace and Security in New York. The full text of that statement follows:

Thank you President.

We thank the United Kingdom for convening this debate. President, reconciliation is fundamental to building and sustaining peace. And must be seen as central to member States' Sustaining Peace agenda and to the SDGs.

The Security Council and the General Assembly decided in the Sustaining Peace resolutions that sustaining peace is a shared task and responsibility. It is to be fulfilled by Government and all other national stakeholders. It flows through all three pillars of the UN's engagement at all stages of conflict and in all its dimensions.

Further, all nations are working towards the Sustainable Development Goals and particularly SDG16 on the establishment, protection and maintenance of peace, justice and strong institutions. This requires putting reconciliation at the centre. An inclusive approach to national conversations is essential in efforts to build and sustain peace.

Australia prioritises reconciliation when working with partners in the context of its overseas development program, as well as in our own national policies and strategies, bringing stakeholders and affected communities together.

Reconciliation isn't just a concept or a practice for countries with recent experience of conflict. It is a work in progress in different contexts for all countries.

Domestically, Australia is walking the path of reconciliation between Indigenous and non-Indigenous Australians. Australia's framework—known as 'Closing the Gap'—includes a number of measures to bridge this divide, including economic opportunities for Indigenous Australians through an Indigenous Procurement Policy. This seeks to leverage the government's annual multi-billion dollar procurement spend. This drives demand for Indigenous goods and services, stimulates Indigenous economic development and grows the Indigenous business sector.

The private sector also plays an important role in reconciliation. The Business Council of Australia and major corporations are to be applauded for creating the 'Raising the Bar' program. This aims to see more than $3 billion spent by major corporations with Indigenous suppliers over the next five years.

The Australian government also supports work with the corporate sector to deliver Reconciliation Action Plans. These Plans support organisations to consider how they can contribute to reconciliation between Indigenous and non-indigenous Australians. This delivers jobs, culturally

AUSTRALIAN PRACTICE IN INTERNATIONAL LAW 2019 551

aware workplaces and businesses, and helps to develop future generations of Indigenous leaders.

Reconciliation is a key focus of Australia's international efforts. An
example is our support to peacebuilding in Bougainville, as part of our
bilateral partnership with Papua New Guinea. Working in partnership,
the role of community leaders, faith based organisations, and ensuring women's involvement has been key in advancing reconciliation and
building and sustaining peace. For example, the Nazareth Centre for
Rehabilitation has been an important contributor to the ongoing peace
and reconciliation process, and Australia has been proud to be a long
term supporter.

We urge that UN assistance to member States focuses on and inte-
grates reconciliation needs, including in the context of comprehensive
analysis which member States have decided should be delivered under
the sustaining peace agenda and UN reform. And we welcome the use of
the PBC and other UN forums to learn lessons from national experiences
and provide a platform for discussion of effective approaches to reconciliation for the purposes of sustaining peace.

We look forward to continuing to promote reconciliation, nationally
and internationally, in partnership with the UN, its member states and
civil society, to further efforts to achieve SDG16 and the Sustaining Peace
agenda.

5.11 Autonomous Sanctions and International Law

On 21 March 2019, at the 40th session of the UN Human Rights Council in
Geneva, Australia voted against a resolution entitled 'Human Rights and
Unilateral Coercive Measures' (resolution L.5). The full text of the explanation
of vote follows:

Australia does not agree with resolution L.5 and the inference that autonomous sanctions are inherently unjust or contrary to international law.
Targeted sanctions can be a powerful tool to promote human rights and
hold accountable those who violate or abuse them. L.5 mischaracter-
ises international law. We believe that sanctions can be an appropriate,
effective and legitimate measure that is fully compliant with international law and the United Nations Charter. The nature and content of
this draft resolution focuses on the relations between States instead of on
the human rights of individuals. Australia does not believe the Human
Rights Council is the appropriate forum to address this issue. Australia

has concerns that the aim of certain countries is to pursue political goals within this resolution. This is unacceptable.

For these reasons, Australia cannot support resolution L.5 and will vote against.

5.12 Democratic People's Republic of Korea Sanctions

On 4 December 2019, the Minister for Foreign Affairs and Minister for Women, Senator the Hon. Marise Payne, made the *Autonomous Sanctions (Designated and Declared Persons—Democratic People's Republic of Korea) Continuing Effect Declaration and Designation Instrument 2019* (the Instrument). The Instrument continued in effect the designation for targeted financial sanctions and declarations for travel bans of 18 persons, and designations for targeted financial sanctions of 14 entities, made in May and December 2016. An extract of the Explanatory Statement for the instrument follows:

> […]
>
> Autonomous sanctions are punitive measures not involving the use of armed force which a government imposes as a matter of foreign policy— as opposed to an international obligation under a United Nations Security Council decision—in situations of international concern. Such situations include threats to regional peace and stability posed by the Democratic People's Republic of Korea's (DPRK) nuclear, other weapons of mass destruction and ballistic missile programs, and related proliferation activities.
>
> The *Autonomous Sanctions Regulations 2011* (the Regulations) make provision relating to, amongst other things, the proscription of persons or entities for autonomous sanctions. The Regulations enable the Minister for Foreign Affairs (the Minister) to designate a person or entity for targeted financial sanctions and/or declare a person for the purposes of a travel ban, if they satisfy a range of criteria, as set out in regulation 6.
>
> The purpose of a designation is to subject the designated person or entity to targeted financial sanctions. There are two types of targeted financial sanctions under the Regulations:
>
> - the designated person or entity becomes the object of the prohibition in regulation 14 (which prohibits directly or indirectly making an asset available to, or for the benefit of, a designated person or entity, other than as authorised by a permit granted under regulation 18); and
> - an asset owned or controlled by a designated person or entity is a 'controlled asset', subject to the prohibition in regulation 15 (which requires a person who holds a controlled asset to freeze that asset,

by prohibiting that person from either using or dealing with that asset, or allowing it to be used or dealt with, or facilitating the use of or dealing with it, other than as authorised by a permit granted under regulation 18).

The purpose of a declaration is to prevent a person from travelling to, entering or remaining in Australia.

Designated and declared persons, and designated entities, in respect of the DPRK are listed in the *Autonomous Sanctions (Designated Persons and Entities—Democratic People's Republic of Korea) List 2012*.

The *Autonomous Sanctions (Designated and Declared Persons— Democratic People's Republic of Korea) Continuing Effect Declaration and Designation Instrument 2019* (the 2019 Instrument) gives effect to a review of the designations and declarations of 18 persons and the designation of 14 entities that were either made or continued in effect by the Minister in May and December 2016. These listings were made on the basis that the person or entity met the criteria mentioned in the table in subregulation 6(1) as it then was, that is: a person the Minister is satisfied is associated with the DPRK's weapons of mass destruction or missiles program. Under subregulation 9(1) of the Regulations, these designations and declarations cease to have effect three years after the date on which they took effect or were renewed unless the Minister declares they are to continue.

The 2019 Instrument continues under subregulation 9(3) of the Regulations, and designates under subregulation 6(1) of the Regulations, the designations and declarations made in 2016. The Minister made the declarations and designations being satisfied that each of the persons and entities listed in Schedules 1 and 2 of the 2019 Instrument is a person or entity that:

- is, or has been, associated with the DPRK's weapons of mass destruction program or missiles program; or
- is assisting, or has assisted, in the violation, or evasion, by the DPRK of UN Security Council Resolutions 825, 1540, 1695, 1718, 1874, 1887, 2087, 2094, 2270 or 2321, or a subsequent resolution with respect to the DPRK.

[...]

5.13 *Ukraine Sanctions*

On 15 March 2019, the Minister for Foreign Affairs, Senator the Hon. Marise Payne, made the *Autonomous Sanctions (Designated and Declared Persons— Ukraine) Amendment List 2019* (the instrument). The instrument gives effect to designations for targeted financial sanctions and declarations for travel bans in respect of 10 individuals, made on the basis of the Minister being satisfied that the individuals are responsible for, or complicit in, the threat to the sovereignty and territorial integrity of Ukraine. An extract of the Explanatory Statement for the instrument follows:

> [...]
> Autonomous sanctions are punitive measures not involving the use of armed force which a government imposes as a matter of foreign policy—as opposed to an international obligation under a United Nations Security Council decision—in situations of international concern. Such situations include threats to a country's sovereignty and territorial integrity.
>
> The *Autonomous Sanctions Regulations 2011* (the Regulations) facilitate the conduct of Australia's relations with other countries including Ukraine and with specific persons or entities outside Australia, through the imposition of autonomous sanctions in relation to the threat to the territorial integrity and sovereignty of Ukraine, and through targeting those persons and entities.
>
> The Regulations also enable the Minister for Foreign Affairs (the Minister) to designate a person or entity for targeted financial sanctions and/or declare a person for the purposes of a travel ban, if they satisfy a range of criteria, as set out in regulation 6.
> [....]
> Designated and declared persons, and designated entities, in respect of Ukraine are listed in the *Autonomous Sanctions (Designated Persons and Entities and Declared Persons—Ukraine) List 2014.*
>
> Each person listed in Schedule 1 of the *Autonomous Sanctions (Designated and Declared Persons—Ukraine) Amendment List 2019* (the 2019 List) is designated by the Minister pursuant to paragraph 6(1)(a) of the Regulations, and declared by the Minister pursuant to paragraph 6(1)(b) of the Regulations, on the basis that the person meets the criteria mentioned in Item 9 of the table in subregulation 6(1); that is, they are a person that the Minister is satisfied is:
> – responsible for, or complicit in, the threat to the sovereignty and territorial integrity of Ukraine.
> [...]

5.14 United Nations Counter-Terrorism Sanctions

United Nations Security Council Resolution 1373 (2001) imposes obligations on UN Member States to prevent and suppress terrorism. Australia implements its obligations under Resolution 1373 to freeze the assets of terrorists through

Part 4 of the *Charter of the United Nations Act 1945* (the Act) and the *Charter of the United Nations (Dealing with Assets) Regulations 2008*. These laws make it a criminal offence to use or deal with the assets of persons or entities designated under Part 4, and prohibit making assets available to them. Non-citizens listed under Part 4 of the Act are also banned from travelling to or remaining in Australia under the *Migration Act 1958*. In 2019, the Minister for Foreign Affairs and Minister for Women, Senator the Hon. Marise Payne, listed or renewed the listings of 29 individuals and 38 entities for targeted financial sanctions and/or travel bans under Part 4 of the Act. In 2019, the listing of six individuals under Part 4 of the Act lapsed.

On 28 March 2019, HE Gillian Bird, Permanent Representative of Australia to the United Nations, made a statement to the United Nations Security Council entitled 'Preventing and Combating the Financing of Terrorism'. An extract of the statement follows:

> [...]
> Madam President,
> At the outset, I would like to express on behalf of all Australians our deepest sympathies for those affected by the devastating terrorist attack in Christchurch.
> Events in New Zealand are a painful reminder that our protective systems must continue to be flexible and evolve to address the ever-changing threat environment with which we are all confronted.
> Terrorists need money to carry out their atrocities—money for weapons and explosives, for supplies, for travel and for shelter. Terrorists, like criminals, constantly adapt how and where they move their funds in order to circumvent safeguards that countries have put in place. The evolution of financial payment systems, while fostering economic growth and efficiencies, provides ever more alternatives for terrorists and their supporters to finance their senseless attacks.
> Global bodies such as the Financial Action Task Force agree that we need to take concerted action urgently to strengthen global counter-terrorist financing regimes to combat the financing of serious terrorist threats, and contribute to strengthening the financial and economic system.
> Australia has a robust and dynamic anti-money laundering and counter-terrorism financing system built upon close relationships between law enforcement and intelligence agencies, policy makers, industry and our international counterparts.

Australia is committed to upholding our obligations under the Terrorist Financing Convention, UNSC Resolution 1373, the ISIL/Al Qaida and Taliban sanctions regimes as well as the Financial Action Task Force's standards and best practices in this area. We are continually reviewing our domestic laws to further strengthen these systems and enhance compliance with our international obligations and the FATF standards.

[...]

5.15 United Nations Sanctions in respect of South Sudan, Eritrea, Somalia and the Central African Republic

On 7 February 2019, the Australian Government amended the *Charter of the United Nations (Sanctions—South Sudan) Regulation 2015* to implement United Nations Security Council Resolution (UNSCR) 2428 (2018). UNSCR 2428 imposes an arms embargo in relation to South Sudan. An extract of the Explanatory Statement for the amending instrument (the *Charter of the United Nations (Sanctions—South Sudan) Amendment (2019 Measures No 1) Regulations 2019*) follows:

[...]

The Regulations amend the principal Regulations to implement the decision of the UNSC in paragraph 4 of UNSCR 2428 to impose an arms embargo in relation to South Sudan. Paragraph 4 of UNSCR 2428 requires Australia to prevent the direct or indirect supply, sale or transfer to South Sudan of arms or related materiel, by an Australian or from Australian territory. It also requires Australia to prevent the provision to South Sudan, by an Australian or from Australian territory, of technical assistance, training, financial or other assistance, related to military activities, or the provision, maintenance or use of arms or related materiel, including the provision of armed mercenary personnel whether or not originating in Australian territory. Paragraph 5 of UNSCR 2428 outlines several narrow exemptions to the arms embargo allowing provision of otherwise sanctioned goods and services in a limited range of circumstances.

The Regulations provide in subsection 4B(2) that strict liability applies to the circumstance where the making of the sanctioned supply is not authorised by a permit. The proposed Regulations would provide in subsection 4D(2) that strict liability applies to the circumstance where the provision of the sanctioned service is not authorised by a permit.

[...]

The Act has the legitimate objective of giving domestic effect to UNSC resolutions and providing a foreign policy mechanism for the Australian Government to address situations of international concern. The exclusion of merits review in relation to sanctions-related decisions is warranted by the seriousness of the foreign policy and national security considerations involved, as well as the potentially sensitive nature of the evidence relied on in reaching those decisions. Where the UNSC has resolved that there will be limitations on engagement with a sanctioned regime, Australia, as a member of the United Nations, must comply with these international obligations. While merits review is unavailable for a decision by the Minister under the Regulations, an applicant can still seek judicial review of a decision.

[...]

On 21 March 2019, the Australian Government amended the *Charter of the United Nations (Sanctions—Eritrea) Regulations 2010*, the *Charter of the United Nations (Dealing with Assets) Regulations 2008*, and the *Charter of the United Nations (Sanctions—Somalia) Regulations 2008* to implement United Nations Security Council Resolution 2444 (2018). Resolution 2444 lifts sanctions on Eritrea and refers to the United Nations Humanitarian Response Plan for Somalia, rather than the United Nations Consolidated Appeal for Somalia. An extract of the Explanatory Statement for the amending instrument (the *Charter of the United Nations Legislation Amendment (2019 Measures No 1) Regulations 2019*) follows:

[...]

The *Charter of the United Nations Legislation Amendment (2019 Measures No 1) Regulations 2019* (the Regulations) amend the *Charter of the United Nations (Sanctions—Eritrea) Regulations 2010* (the Principal Eritrea Regulations) and the *Charter of the United Nations (Sanctions— Somalia) Regulations 2008* (the Principal Somalia Regulations) to implement UNSC Resolution 2444 (2018) (UNSCR 2444) to lift sanctions in relation to Eritrea, and to update references in relation to the Somalia sanctions regime, consistent with Australia's international obligations.

The preamble to UNSCR 2444 notes that the Security Council was acting under Chapter VII of the Charter. Decisions of the Security Council contained in UNSCR 2444 are binding on Australia.

UNSCR 2444 was adopted on 14 November 2018 in the context of positive developments towards peace, stability and reconciliation in the region. It requires all Member States to lift UN-mandated sanctions in relation to Eritrea.

Section 8 of the Act provides that regulations giving effect to a particular decision of the UNSC cease to have effect when Article 25 of the Charter ceases to require Australia to carry out that decision. Consequently, the Principal Eritrea Regulations expired on 14 November 2018.

The Regulations repeal the expired Principal Eritrea Regulations, and effect a consequential amendment to the *Charter of the United Nations (Dealing with Assets) Regulations 2008* to remove reference to Eritrea.

The Regulations amend the Principal Somalia Regulations to update the reference to the United Nations Consolidated Appeal for Somalia, to reflect paragraph 48 of UNSCR 2444, which instead refers to the United Nations Humanitarian Response Plan for Somalia. The Regulations also remove outdated and unnecessary notes from the Principal Somalia Regulations.

[...]

On 9 April 2019, the Australian Government amended the *Charter of the United Nations (Sanctions—Central African Republic) Regulation 2014* (the Regulations) to give effect to certain provisions of United Nations Security Council Resolution 2399 (2018). Resolution 2399, affirmed by Resolution 2454 (2019), continued the arms embargo in place for the Central African Republic (CAR). The amendments to the Regulations updated the exemptions to the arms embargo for the CAR. An extract of the Explanatory Statement for the amending instrument (the *Charter of the United Nations (Sanctions—Central African Republic) Amendment (2019 Measures No 1) Regulations 2019*) follows:

[...]

The UNSC has determined that the situation in the Central African Republic (CAR) continues to constitute a threat to international peace and security in the region, and that existing sanctions imposed in respect to CAR should continue, with some modifications to the exceptions to the arms embargo. The Regulations would implement measures in UNSC Resolution 2399 that sets out the circumstances where arms and related materiel can be supplied, sold or transferred to the CAR. The Regulations update the exceptions to the arms embargo to:
  - update the list of international forces providing support to the CAR;
  - enable the supply of non-lethal equipment and technical assistance or training for use in the CAR process of security reform

in coordination with the UN Multidimensional Integrated Stabilization Mission (MINUSCA);

– enable the supply of arms to Chadian or Sudanese forces solely for use in international patrols to enhance security in the common border areas, in cooperation with MINUSCA;

– require advance notification of the supply of arms to the UN Security Council CAR Sanctions Committee in certain circumstances;

– clarify that 'CAR security forces' includes State civilian law enforcement institutions.

[...]

6 Climate Change

6.1 *25th United Nations Climate Change Conference of Parties (COP25)*

On 10 December 2019, at the COP25 High Level Segment in Madrid, The Hon. Angus Taylor MP, Minister for Energy and Emissions Reduction, delivered a National Statement. An extract of that statement follows:

[...]

The Paris Agreement sent a powerful signal to the world that countries are serious about climate change.

Australia is committed to the Paris Agreement. We are already on track to meet and beat the target we have set for 2030, just as we are meeting and beating our Kyoto targets.

Our recently released forecasts say that we expect to beat our 2020 targets by 411 million tonnes, which is around 80% of a full year of emissions.

Strong messages and targets alone won't address climate change, no matter how ambitious.

The world needs action to reduce emissions and Australia believes technology is central to achieving this.

We can only reduce emissions as fast as the deployment of commercially viable technologies allow.

This means we need to get the right technology to the marketplace when and where it is needed.

In Australia, we are developing a Technology Investment Roadmap.

The roadmap will establish an enduring, strategic approach to Australia's low emissions technology investment.

We will continue to work closely with our industry, researchers, and our international partners to find commercially viable deployment pathways for these priority technologies.

An example of a priority technology is hydrogen. Last month we released our National Hydrogen Strategy. The strategy outlines actions for the development of a hydrogen industry that offers enormous benefits for our economy and could, through our exports, assist other countries to reduce their emissions.

We recognise that international collaboration will be crucial to achieving our technology vision. We are an active participant in Mission Innovation, particularly in the hydrogen, heating and cooling, and smart grids challenges. I welcome the recently formed Leadership Group for Industry Transition and am pleased to announce the Australia will join that initiative.

Australia provides an important perspective as one of the world's biggest, and most trusted energy suppliers.

In Australia, an unprecedented wave of low emissions energy investment is already underway.

Last year, renewable investment was Australia's highest on record at AU$14.1 billion, which is world leading investment given our population.

Renewables are now more than 25% of our electricity supply in our National Electricity Market.

Australia's Clean Energy Finance Corporation, the world's most successful green bank, has mobilised over $20 billion in new investments.

The Australian Renewable Energy Agency has provided $1.4 billion to improve the affordability and increase the supply of renewable energy in Australia.

Australia has the world's highest uptake of household solar panels, with around two million, or one in five, Australian households now having solar panels.

This increase has not been without issues and one of our challenges is to ensure energy remains affordable and reliable as these changes occur. We cannot move faster than the technology allows.

Our long term strategy to reduce emissions is focused on deploying cost effective technologies and we will be releasing a more detailed technology strategy next year.

The strategy will build on the $3.5 billion Climate Solutions Package announced earlier this year, which has provided the pathway to meet or exceed our 2030 target, as we have done for our previous targets.

AUSTRALIAN PRACTICE IN INTERNATIONAL LAW 2019

As well as reducing emissions at home, Australia is focused on working with our developing country partners to address climate challenges, particularly our Pacific neighbours.

We are delivering on our $1 billion climate finance commitment from 2015 to 2020.

We have announced an additional $500 million over five years from 2020 to help Pacific nations invest in clean energy and climate and disaster resilience.

Acknowledging the importance of continuing to build resilience, Australia is pleased to be hosting the Asia Pacific Ministerial on Disaster Risk Reduction in Brisbane in June 2020.

We will also invest $140 million to mobilise private sector investments in low emissions, climate-resilient solutions for the Pacific and Southeast Asia.

Like our Pacific neighbours, we recognise oceans are critical to health, wealth and survival. We are a world leader in ocean protection and sustainable use. We play a leading role in the International Partnership for Blue Carbon to improve understanding and management of coastal blue carbon.

Mr President.

Here in Madrid, we need to finalise arrangements for Paris Agreement carbon markets that give us confidence that traded carbon units represent genuine emissions reductions.

A clear path forward on Article 6 arrangements will help countries deliver on our Paris Agreement goals and signal commitment to Paris Agreement implementation.

[...]

7 International Human Rights

7.1 Australia's 2018–2020 Term on the Human Rights Council

On 25 February 2019, Australia's Minister for Foreign Affairs, Senator the Hon. Marise Payne, delivered Australia's National Statement at the High Level Segment of the 40th session of the United Nations Human Rights Council in Geneva. Excerpts of that statement follow:

[...]

The indivisibility, universality and inalienability of human rights are principles that Australia has consistently championed—through the efforts of Australian Doc Evatt in the drafting of the United Nations Charter during the San Francisco Conference, as an advocate for the Universal Declaration, and as a supporter of the creation of this august body in 2006.

Democracy, the rule of law, individual freedom and the right to all to dignity and respect—these values have guided Australians for generations. And these are the values which Australia has sought to promote as a member of the UN Human Rights Council.

Five fundamental principles are guiding our advocacy on this Council:
1. Gender equality;
2. Freedom of expression and association, freedom of religion;
3. Good governance and robust democratic institutions;
4. The rights of Indigenous peoples, including Aboriginal and Torres Strait Islander Australians; and
5. Strong national human rights institutions.

I will focus some of my remarks today on freedom of expression and freedom of religion and belief. As a proud multicultural nation these tenets are an inherent part of Australia's national identity.

We're a country in which one in four of us was born overseas—from all corners of the globe. According to our most recent national census, over 130 religious traditions are observed in Australia. This diversity brings richness and strength but it also brings challenges that require our vigilance to ensure the indivisible and universal nature of the human rights of all Australians continue to be respected.

Religious freedom and tolerance are fundamental to open, multicultural and resilient societies. Sadly, however, in 2019, there is no region globally—nor any single religious tradition—that does not experience some degree of religious intolerance or abuse. In different parts of the world, persecuted religious communities exist—communities following Christianity, Islam, Judaism, Buddhism and a myriad of belief systems and religions.

We are deeply concerned by this intolerance. We are disturbed by the use of blasphemy laws to discriminate against religious belief or practice, targeting individuals and communities in order to settle personal scores and grievances.

And we are alarmed by restrictions—or worse—placed on populations based solely on their religious adherence, where the rights of whole communities are infringed.

The right to freedom of thought, conscience, belief and faith are not only inherent rights but rights which makes our societies richer, deeper and ultimately more compassionate.

As part of our longstanding commitment to these inalienable rights, Australia will also maintain our focus on supporting the work of this Council in response to situations of human rights concern as we have highlighted in our considered Universal Periodic Review statements, informed and complemented by direct bilateral and regional engagement with our friends and counterparts on these issues.

I want to reinforce that we are consistent and clear in our approach to these matters.

Sadly they are broad ranging but to name a few of recent concern: we welcome the ultimate release of Asia Bibi; we note the challenges facing democracy in Venezuela; we note the critical situation of the Rohingya in Myanmar and Bangladesh; we note concerns in relation to the rights of women in Saudi Arabia, and the murder of Jamal Khashoggi; we note the chilling restrictions placed on journalists and therefore the erosion of the free press in multiple locations; the treatment of Uighurs in China, and the horrific humanitarian toll of conflict in Yemen and Syria.

Mr President,

Consistent with our view that a strong, accountable and credible United Nations contributes to peace, stability and dignity worldwide, Australia will continue to work with all States to strengthen this Council.

Part of these efforts must be to ensure a balanced agenda which considers the human rights challenges of all member states. As has been our longstanding position since the inception of the Human Rights Council in 2006, for over 12 years, Australia opposes in principle the existence of Item 7 of the Agenda of the Council. It is our firm view that a separate agenda item focussing on a single country situation—in this case Israel—is inappropriate. It does not occur in any other context, for any other country.

Australia continues to advocate for international efforts which enhance prospects for a two-state solution where Israel and a future Palestinian state exist side-by-side in peace within internationally recognised borders.

Another critical element of ensuring consideration of the full range of human rights challenges before us is the actual diversity of the membership of this Council.

We warmly welcome Fiji in joining the Council this year, the first ever Pacific Island member, and we welcome the Republic of Marshall Islands' candidacy for 2020.

I want to acknowledge the presence of Fijian Prime Minister, Frank Bainimarama, here today and his remarks to the Council.

A voice from the Pacific region is an important part of this Council's deliberations. One year into our term we are pleased to have been able to engage closely with our Pacific island neighbours to promote the interests and concerns of our region.

We have brought focus on the particular barriers faced by people with disabilities in the region and the valuable work of the Pacific to increase women's participation in public life, especially those who live in rural and remote communities. During this session we are working with our neighbours to highlight the important issue of modern slavery in the fishing industry.

We also believe that respecting fundamental human rights and freedoms, and building them into the fabric of society, makes Australia and the world safer and more secure.

We seek to maintain and build on the rules and institutions that have provided the basis upon which universal human rights are protected and promoted.

Global abolition of the death penalty, ending discrimination on the basis of sexual orientation and the protection of the rights of LGBTI people, freedom of religion, advancing Indigenous peoples rights globally, championing the rights of people with disabilities, promoting gender equality and supporting the role of civil society and national human rights institutions will continue to be priorities for us for the remainder of our term and beyond.

I can assure you, Mr President, that Australia's commitment to human rights goes to the core of who we are as a nation and we look forward to advancing these values on this Council in 2019.

[...]

On 18 October 2019, at the 74th Session of the UN General Assembly Third Committee in New York, Australia delivered a national statement during the General Discussion on Promotion and Protection of Human Rights. An extract of that statement follows:

[...]

As the end of Australia's second year on the Human Rights Council approaches, it is timely to reflect on the contributions we have made as a member of the Council and the goals we continue to strive for.

Australia has continued to focus our efforts on our priority areas for advancing human rights: gender equality; freedom of expression;

freedom of religion or belief; good governance; the rights of indigenous peoples; strong national human rights institutions; the death penalty; the rights of LGBTI persons; the rights of persons with disabilities; and civil society engagement.

But today I would like to highlight some of the key achievements Australia has made during the last year.

Australia is proud to continue our leadership in amplifying the voices of Pacific countries. We warmly welcomed Fiji in joining the Human Rights Council this year, the first ever Pacific Island member, and we welcome the Republic of Marshall Islands' candidacy for the Human Rights Council in 2020. Voices from the Pacific region have an important place in discussions about human rights. We are pleased to have been able to engage closely with our Pacific island neighbours to promote the interests and concerns of our region in New York and Geneva, including by developing joint statements.

Gender equality and the rights of women and girls are also key priorities for Australia. Australia continues to advocate for gender equality and women and girls' empowerment, including in discussions on economic empowerment, gender-based violence and discrimination; through national statements and strong support for resolutions. At HRC 41 we were proud to partner with other countries to lead a new resolution to promote equal pay for work of equal value. Australia also signed a joint statement on Accountability for the Rights of Women and Girls in Humanitarian settings. Australia is proud to be a Vice Chair of the Bureau of the Commission on the Status of Women and the UN Women Board.

We promoted the rights of indigenous women and girls by working with Australia's Aboriginal and Torres Strait Islander Social Justice Commissioner [Ms June Oscar] on a photographic exhibition in New York titled 'Hear us, See us', documenting Ms Oscar's Women's Voices project; and hosted an event just last month on women's empowerment and gender equality with Elizabeth Broderick—Deputy Chair of the UN Working Group on Discrimination against Women and Girls.

Australia will continue to work for the promotion and protection of human rights, both at home and abroad. At the highest levels, we have underscored our longstanding commitment to human rights principles and our commitment to the international rules-based order. We look forward to working with all UN member states during UNGA74 to further the promotion and protection of human rights.

On 10 December 2019, Australia's Minister for Foreign Affairs, Senator the Hon. Marise Payne, released a statement for International Human Rights Day. The full text of that media release follows:

> Today marks International Human Rights Day, commemorating the adoption of the Universal Declaration of Human Rights by the United Nations General Assembly in 1948.
>
> Human rights matter and should apply to all people. The Australian Government will continue to speak honestly and consistently for their promotion and protection internationally. As a proud, liberal democracy, we believe in the indivisibility, universality and inalienability of individual rights.
>
> Nations that uphold principles domestically are more likely to cooperate in ways that promote the common good. Respecting fundamental human rights and freedoms, and building them into the fabric of society, makes Australia and the world safer and more secure.
>
> The right of all people to dignity and respect means that we will continue to combat disadvantage, discrimination and persecution based on disability, gender, religion, sexuality, age, race or ethnicity. Our strong commitment to the rule of law means Australia will continue to stand up for the rights of all Australians, including due process and access to lawyers for our citizens detained abroad.
>
> I have instructed Australia's Ambassadors and High Commissioners to ensure engagement on human rights issues is a core part of the fabric of our bilateral relationships.
>
> Australia will also continue to speak up for individual rights through our membership of the UN Human Rights Council. We will continue advocating for the improvement, application and enforcement of the rules and institutions that have provided the basis for universal human rights for more than 70 years.

7.2   *Freedom of Expression*

On 8 March 2019, during the 40th session of the United Nations Human Rights Council in Geneva, Australia joined a Joint Statement (delivered by Canada and the Netherlands) on freedom of expression. The full text of that statement follows:

> We take this opportunity to highlight our concerns relating to violations of the rights to freedoms of opinion and expression. Not since 2009 has this Council adopted a substantive resolution relating to the rights to freedoms of opinion and expression.

The importance of Article 19 of the International Covenant on Civil and Political Rights is well known but the deepening crisis for freedom of expression worldwide, both online and offline requires us to ask for public attention. Digital technologies are pervasive in our everyday lives. As a result, the rights to freedoms of opinion and expression is increasingly mediated through digital contexts.

As this Council has previously agreed, the effective exercise of those freedoms is an important indicator of the level of protection of all other human rights and freedoms. It is also essential for democracy.

As fundamental rights, they are essential elements of a full range of human rights as well as Agenda 2030, which seeks to achieve sustainable development for all, and in particular Goal 16.

We insist on the centrality of information for democracy and the importance of a free, independent and pluralistic media as a conveyer of reliable news.

Yet it remains under sustained attack, through both assaults on freedom of the press and encroachments on the rights of ordinary citizens to freedoms of opinion and expression. According to data collected by Freedom House, freedom of expression has declined each year over the last 13 years, with sharper drops since 2012.

The recent emergence of a new generation of digital technologies—from Artificial Intelligence to the Internet of Things—can enhance human development. At the same time, there are broader implications from the use, and possible misuse of these technologies, for the core values of democratic societies, including equality and fairness. We stress the need for states to ensure that AI developments occur safely and for the benefit of all and in line with international human rights standards.

In 2018 dozens of journalists were killed. These deadly attacks are just the tip of the iceberg. Journalists and media workers whose work enables individuals to enjoy their right to information are increasingly at risk of intimidation and judicial harassment, violence and arbitrary detention, leading to self-censorship and undermining the public debate, the bedrock of democracy. Increasing demonization of the media by political leaders is also a worrying trend that contributes to this climate.

In many cases the perpetrators are not held accountable for their crimes. This climate of impunity perpetuates the cycle of violence against journalists, media workers and the media itself. We urge states to stem the violence, intimidation and harassment against media outlets, journalists and media workers and bring all perpetrators to justice.

We are concerned about gender-based discrimination, including sexual and gender-based violence, threats, intimidation, harassment and incitement to hatred against women, including journalists, media workers and human rights defenders, both online and offline. Further, as this Council has previously agreed, such harms in online contexts prevent women and girls from fully enjoying their human rights and fundamental freedoms, including the rights to freedoms of opinion and expression.

We are also concerned over the shrinking of online space. The internet continues to gain importance as a sphere to enjoy the same human rights as offline, including the rights to freedom of opinion and expression, privacy, association and assembly, as well as a means to receive and seek information. However, this reality has been met by an increased call for state control over the online space, abuse of big data and the multiplication of legislations criminalizing free speech. Our countries are committed to drawing the attention of the Council to continued violations and abuses regarding these aspects.

In this respect, we stress the need for greater emphasis on prevention measures and the creation of enabling legal frameworks for freedom of expression to ensure a safe and enabling environment for journalists and media workers.

We invite the Council to continue addressing such issues in relation to freedoms of opinion and expression and address the situations of persons whose rights are violated in this regard and to ensure accountability for such violations.

7.3 *Freedom of Religion or Belief*

On 5 March 2019, at the 40th session of the United Nations Human Rights Council in Geneva, Australia delivered a national statement at the Clustered Interactive Dialogue with Special Rapporteur on Freedom of Religion or Belief ('FoRB') and Special Rapporteur on the Sale and Sexual Exploitation of Children. Extracts of that statement follow:

> [...]
> We welcome the report of the Special Rapporteur on freedom of religion or belief on the mutually reinforcing relationship between FoRB and Freedom of Expression. We join the Special Rapporteur in viewing these freedoms within a framework of universal, inalienable, indivisible, inter-dependent and inter-related rights.
>
> We welcome the report's analysis of common limitations on expression involving religion or belief from around the world, and examination of real-life cases. These examples illustrate clearly the full impact of legislation and regulation.

As a proud multicultural nation, freedom of religion or belief is an inherent part of Australia's national identity. We continue to advocate for individuals in all countries to enjoy this fundamental human right, including by manifesting their religion, in line with international human rights law.

Noting the Special Rapporteur's comments on societal actors (para 65), how does the SR envisage religious leaders at the international level promoting understanding and countering hatred?

[...]

On 3 July 2019, at the 41st session of the United Nations Human Rights Council in Geneva, Australia delivered a national statement in the general debate on Item 4. An extract of that statement follows:

[...]

Australia objects to the oppression of individuals and communities based on their religious adherence. Australia condemns violence and persecution based on religious belief in all circumstances.

[...]

On 19 July 2019, Minister for Foreign Affairs of Australia, the Hon. Marise Payne, published a media release about the second Ministerial to Advance Religious Freedom, held in Washington DC from 16–18 July. The full text of that statement follows:

The forum brought together governments, international organisations, religious groups and other civil society representatives to discuss opportunities to promote and protect freedom of religion or belief internationally.

The Australian Government is a committed advocate for freedom of religion or belief for all individuals worldwide. It is a fundamental human right, and we firmly believe that its protection contributes to stable, cohesive societies.

Australia seeks out every possible avenue to advocate for those experiencing religious intolerance or abuse.

We advocate on this issue directly with states, in bilateral, multilateral and regional settings, through our development program, and in partnership with civil society.

The promotion and protection of human rights underpins sustainable peace and prosperity for individuals, communities and societies as a whole.

570   AUSTRALIAN YEAR BOOK OF INTERNATIONAL LAW VOLUME 38

> Australia looks forward to continuing to work with our international partners to advance human rights globally, including the right to freedom of religion or belief.

7.4 *Human Rights and Autonomous Sanctions*

On 12 July 2019, during the 41st session of the United Nations Human Rights Council in Geneva, Australia delivered an explanation of vote on the Resolution for enhancement of international cooperation in the field of human rights. An extract of that statement follows:

> [...]
>
> We continue to reject the inference in this resolution that autonomous sanctions are unjust or contrary to international law. Targeted sanctions can be a powerful tool to promote human rights and to hold accountable those who violate or abuse them. Such sanctions can be an effective and legitimate tool of foreign policy, and are fully compliant with international law. We are also concerned at ongoing efforts in this resolution to elevate certain rights over others, an effort which is incompatible with the principle that human rights are universal, indivisible and inalienable.
>
> We deeply regret these ongoing attempts to use this resolution to introduce concepts entirely unrelated to international cooperation, which diverge from core principles of international human rights law.
>
> [...]

7.5 *Death Penalty*

On 26 February 2019, at the 40th session of the United Nations Human Rights Council, Australia delivered a national statement at the High Level Panel Discussion on the Death Penalty. An extract of that statement follows:

> [...]
>
> Australia opposes the death penalty in all circumstances for all people. Our steadfast opposition is built on four fundamental principles, some of which the panel has highlighted today:
> - the death penalty is irrevocable and no legal system is free of error
> - it denies any possibility of rehabilitation to the convicted individual
> - there is no convincing evidence that it is a more effective deterrent than long-term or life imprisonment
> - finally, it is deeply unfair. We know that the death penalty is used disproportionately against the poor, people with disabilities, and minority groups. It is an affront to justice when those who are most

in need of the protection of the law, should find themselves needing protection *from* the law.

We regret some countries continue to see the death penalty as an acceptable form of punishment, including for crimes that do not meet the threshold of 'most serious crimes', such as apostasy, blasphemy, adultery, and consensual same-sex relationships.

We urge all states to heed this Council's call for abolition. We further call on states that still use the death penalty to ensure it is not applied on the basis of discriminatory laws, or as a result of discriminatory or arbitrary application of the law.

The Secretary-General's report makes clear that transparency around use of the death penalty is critical to ensure human rights standards are being upheld. We call on all countries that use the death penalty to publish full and accurate execution data.

[…]

On 13 September 2019, at the 42nd session of the United Nations Human Rights Council in Geneva, Australia delivered a national statement during the Item 3 general debate on the abolition of the death penalty. The full text of that statement follows:

This year marks 30 years since the adoption of the Second Optional Protocol to the International Covenant on Civil and Political Rights (ICCPR), aiming at the abolition of the death penalty.

Since its adoption, the world has experienced a steady and welcome trend towards abolition. Some states have abolished the death penalty by removing it from domestic legislation. Others have ratified the Second Optional Protocol to signal their commitment. And some have introduced formal moratoria on executions. All these moves are to be applauded. They are signs of progress towards a world free of the death penalty.

Despite these positive steps, more than 15 countries have used this most final and unforgiving punishment this year. States give many reasons for their use of the death penalty. They say the public supports it, and yet research shows that public support for the death penalty inevitably wanes after abolition. They say it deters crime, and yet there is no compelling evidence to suggest this is the case. They say it is their sovereign right to manage their own justice systems. Indeed; and yet sovereignty does not absolve states of their obligations under international law.

We deplore the death penalty in all circumstances, and most particularly as a sentence for non-violent conduct, such as consensual same-sex relations, blasphemy, economic crimes and drugs offences.

Australia opposes the death penalty for all people, in all circumstances. We call on all states to continue progress towards global abolition and to support efforts by those leaders moving their communities towards a death penalty-free future.

On 24 October 2019, at the 74th Session of the UN General Assembly Third Committee in New York, Australia delivered an intervention in the Interactive Dialogue with the Special Rapporteur on extrajudicial, summary or arbitrary executions. The full text of that intervention follows.

As set out in our Strategy for Abolition of the Death Penalty, Australia opposes the death penalty in all circumstances for all people.

We agree with the Special Rapporteur that, as an important part of progress towards global abolition, states should take steps to protect persons from the imposition of the death penalty outside their territory.

We thank the Special Rapporteur for highlighting the vital importance of consular assistance in potential death penalty cases.

Australians facing, or potentially facing, the death penalty receive high priority, targeted and sensitive consular assistance.

We call upon States to meet their obligations under Article 36 of the Vienna Convention on Consular Relations in relation to communication with and access to nationals of sending States.

We join the Special Rapporteur in encouraging states to ensure national laws on extradition and deportation do not facilitate the imposition of the death penalty.

Australia will not surrender a person to a foreign country where there is a risk that the death penalty will be carried out upon the person, unless the foreign country provides an undertaking that the death penalty will not be applied.

As a matter of policy, and consistent with our international obligations, Australia does not deport or return individuals to situations where they face a real risk of the application of the death penalty.

It is also important that states do not deliberately or inadvertently share information which may contribute to the imposition of the death penalty

Australia's federal police force applies safeguards to control information-sharing in situations where a person may face the death penalty.

AUSTRALIAN PRACTICE IN INTERNATIONAL LAW 2019   573

In the case of formal government-to-government requests for assistance, Australian legislation prohibits the provision of assistance to a foreign country if this assistance may result in the death penalty being imposed, unless special circumstances apply.

Australia asks the Special Rapporteur: How can we support other states to introduce reforms to ensure they do not directly or indirectly facilitate the imposition of the death penalty abroad?

7.6   *Human Rights in the Pacific*

On 7 March 2019, during the 40th session of the United Nations Human Rights Council in Geneva, Australia delivered a joint statement on 'Human rights in the fishing industry, including modern slavery and trafficking in persons' on behalf of 15 Pacific nations, in the Item 3 General Debate. The full text of that statement follows:

I have the pleasure of delivering this statement on behalf of nations of the Pacific: Australia, Cook Islands, Federated States of Micronesia, Fiji, Kiribati, Marshall Islands, Nauru, New Zealand, Niue, Palau, Papua New Guinea, Samoa, Tonga, Tuvalu and Vanuatu.

Fisheries play a key role in supporting sustainable economic development in the Pacific. We want to ensure fishing operations in our waters and beyond are conducted fairly, responsibly, safely, and in a manner consistent with international human rights law.

All Pacific nations take seriously our international human rights law obligations and commitments. We condemn the abhorrent criminal practices of forced labour, modern slavery, human trafficking and child labour, including in the fishing industry.

Pacific island countries have demonstrated a commitment to action. At the Forum Fisheries Committee Ministers' Meeting in July 2018, Pacific Ministers underlined the importance of addressing human rights abuses on fishing vessels operating in the Pacific region. In December 2018, the Western and Central Pacific Fisheries Commission resolved to encourage implementation of measures to support improved labour standards for crew.

Member states of the *Bali Process on People Smuggling, Trafficking in Persons and Related Transnational Crime*, including many in the Pacific, are also working alongside the business community to combat human trafficking.

We recognise the need to address these challenges in line with Target 8.7 of the Sustainable Development Goals, and Articles 6 and 8 of the *1995*

574   AUSTRALIAN YEAR BOOK OF INTERNATIONAL LAW VOLUME 38

FAO Code of Conduct for Responsible Fisheries, and resolve to ensure safeguards against forced labour, smuggling, trafficking, modern day slavery, and sexual exploitation and abuse. We further recognise the importance of increasing inclusion and empowerment of women in the fishing industry.

We encourage all states to take steps to end slavery-like practices in the fishing industry.

7.7   *Human Rights of Older Persons*

On 24 June 2019, during the 41st session of the United Nations Human Rights Council in Geneva, Australia delivered a national statement in the Clustered Interactive Dialogue with the Special Rapporteur for Health and Special Rapporteur for Leprosy. An extract of that statement follows:

[…]

We welcome the focus of the report by the Special Rapporteur for Health on the critical role of the social and underlying determinants of health in realising the right to mental health.

Australia promotes the right of everyone to achieve the highest attainable standard of mental health.

Australia is firmly committed to ensuring people of all ages and backgrounds who experience mental disorders and other mental health conditions receive the treatment, care and support they need.

We recognise the importance of the psychosocial, political, economic and physical environments in building and sustaining mental health and well-being. We are committed to addressing the broad determinants of mental disorders and other mental health conditions.

Australia is prioritising mental health and suicide prevention by implementing: the Fifth National Mental Health and Suicide Prevention Plan; targeted programs to support Indigenous Australians, who suffer unacceptably high levels of suicide; and national mental health reforms to improve access to appropriate treatments and reduce stigma. Public discussion on mental health is encouraged through initiatives like 'R U OK' Day and supporting youth ambassadors.

As noted by the Special Rapporteur for Health, older persons can experience particular challenges to their mental health. Could the Special Rapporteur share some examples of innovative programs which help promote and protect the rights of older persons?

AUSTRALIAN PRACTICE IN INTERNATIONAL LAW 2019 575

On 10 July 2019, during the 41st session of the United Nations Human Rights Council in Geneva, Australia delivered a national statement in the Item 10 Annual Thematic Discussion on Technical Cooperation—Human Rights of Older Persons. The full text of that statement follows:

> Australia welcomes a discussion on innovative ways to promote and protect the rights of older persons to their independence as well as active and healthy ageing.
>
> Australia has developed a suite of policy measures to uphold older persons' rights, with investments that take a human rights-based approach to ageing. These investments include measures to improve the provision of mental health support, more comprehensive palliative care to older Australians in residential care, and targeted investments for people living with dementia.
>
> A Royal Commission into Australia's aged care system is being held in Australia. The Royal Commission into Aged Care Quality and Safety will help us to better understand the challenges and the opportunities of delivering aged care services now and into the future. The Royal Commission will also help to build a national culture of respect for senior Australians and Australians as they age.
>
> Australia has made significant progress since November 2018 to better support the rights of older Australians in care. Australia has established an independent Aged Care Quality and Safety Commission, new Aged Care Quality Standards, a single Charter of Aged Care Rights and an Aged Care Diversity Framework.
>
> We made a commitment to protect the rights of older persons, and will work to deliver the level of care they deserve as valued members of our society.

On 11 September 2019, at the 42nd session of the United Nations Human Rights Council in Geneva, Australia delivered a national statement at the Interactive Dialogue with the Independent Expert on the rights of older persons. An extract of that statement follows:

> [...]
> Australia recognises older persons' experiences of disasters and humanitarian crises can be different to other groups in their communities, due to physical, sensory and social reasons.

These challenges are often compounded when they intersect with other potential vulnerabilities or inequities, such as gender, a disability, health issues, or caregiving responsibilities.

Australia also recognises that older persons play important roles in disaster risk reduction, conflict prevention, and post-crisis management, bringing a wealth of experience, knowledge and influence to on-the-ground humanitarian action.

Australia supports international and local humanitarian organisations to take a comprehensive victim-centred approach when supporting people affected by armed conflict and disasters, including older persons. We require our humanitarian partners to collect age, sex and disability disaggregated data in order to identify and target those in greatest need, during a crisis.

We also expect humanitarian agencies to be accountable to the people they are assisting, including by ensuring the participation of older people in decisions affecting the assistance that they receive.

This approach ensures all community members are heard and enabled in response efforts, and no one is left behind.

[...]

7.8   *Detention of Dr Yang Hengjun*

On 24 January 2019, Australia's Minister for Foreign Affairs, Senator the Hon. Marise Payne, released a media statement regarding the detention of Australian Mr Yang Hengjun, detained in China. The full text of that media release follows:

> The Chinese authorities gave formal notification to our Embassy in Beijing last night that they have detained Mr Yang Hengjun, an Australian citizen. We will continue to make representations to China to ensure that this matter is dealt with transparently and fairly.
>
> Our Embassy in Beijing will meet with Chinese authorities this morning to seek further clarification of the nature of this detention and to arrange consular access at the earliest possible opportunity, in accordance with the bilateral consular agreement.

On 19 July 2019, Australia's Minister for Foreign Affairs, Senator the Hon. Marise Payne, released a media statement regarding the detention of Australian Dr Yang Hengjun in China. The full text of that statement follows:

> The Australian Government is deeply disappointed that Australian citizen and academic Dr Yang Hengjun (Dr Yang Jun) has been transferred to

criminal detention in China. Dr Yang has been detained since 19 January this year.

Formal notification was received today from Chinese authorities of his criminal detention.

The Australian Government has raised its concerns about Dr Yang's case regularly with China at senior levels. Australian Embassy officials have visited Dr Yang six times, most recently on 27 June, in accordance with our bilateral consular agreement with China. I have written twice to China's Foreign Minister, State Councilor Wang Yi, to request a fair and transparent resolution to this matter and that Dr Yang be granted access to his lawyers. This has not occurred.

The Government has expressed concern about Dr Yang's welfare and the conditions under which he is held. And we have asked for clarification regarding the reasons for Dr Yang's detention. If he is being detained for his political views, then he should be released.

We have worked tirelessly and in good faith with the Chinese Government to advocate for Dr Yang's interests since he was detained. We expect basic standards of justice and procedural fairness to be met.

The Australian Government is concerned by this development in relation to an Australian citizen. We will continue to press Chinese authorities for fair and humane treatment, in accordance with international norms. Our thoughts are with Dr Yang and his family during this difficult period.

On 27 August 2019, Australia's Minister for Foreign Affairs, Senator the Hon. Marise Payne, released a media statement regarding the formal arrest of Australian Dr Yang Hengjun in China. The full text of that media release follows:

The Government is very concerned and disappointed to learn that Australian citizen and academic Dr Yang Hengjun (Dr Yang Jun) was formally arrested in China on suspicion of espionage on 23 August and will continue to be criminally detained. Our thoughts are with Dr Yang and his family at this very difficult time.

Dr Yang has been held in Beijing in harsh conditions without charge for more than seven months. Since that time, China has not explained the reasons for Dr Yang's detention, nor has it allowed him access to his lawyers or family visits.

I have discussed this twice with China's Foreign Minister, State Councilor Wang Yi, and have written to him three times, stating my concerns, and those of the Australian government and people. We have serious concerns for Dr Yang's welfare, and about the conditions under which he is being held. We have expressed these in clear terms to the Chinese authorities.

It is important, and we expect, that basic standards of justice and procedural fairness are met. I respectfully reiterate my previous requests that if Dr Yang is being held for his political beliefs, he should be released.

We expect Dr Yang to be treated in accordance with international human rights law, including the Universal Declaration of Human Rights, with special attention to those provisions that prohibit torture and inhumane treatment, guard against arbitrary detention and that protect the right to freedom of thought, conscience and religion.

Australian Embassy officials have visited Dr Yang seven times since his detention, most recently on 25 July, in accordance with our Bilateral Consular Agreement with China. We expect this to continue for the duration of Dr Yang's detention, and have a visit approved for today, Tuesday 27 August.

I will continue to advocate strongly on behalf of Dr Yang to ensure a satisfactory explanation of the basis for his arrest, that he is treated humanely and that he is allowed to return home.

On 2 November 2019, Australia's Minister for Foreign Affairs, Senator the Hon. Marise Payne, released a media statement regarding the continuing detention of Australian Dr Yang Hengjun in China. The full text of that media release follows:

I am very concerned by reports from a recent consular visit to Australian citizen Dr Yang Hengjun, who remains in criminal detention in China.

His circumstances of detention include increased isolation from the outside world, with restrictions on his communications with family and friends, and the resumption of daily interrogation, including while shackled.

This is unacceptable.

We have made repeated requests to the Chinese authorities for an explanation of the charges against Dr Yang. We have also made repeated requests for him to be afforded basic standards of justice, procedural fairness and humane treatment, in line with international norms, including access to his lawyers and to his family, both of which continue to be denied to him.

This has not led to any substantive changes in his treatment

We will continue to express our expectations in clear terms to the Chinese authorities—both in Beijing and in Canberra—including that

AUSTRALIAN PRACTICE IN INTERNATIONAL LAW 2019

Dr Yang be released and that, while his detention continues, he be treated fairly and humanely.

7.9 Detention of Mr Alek Sigley

On 4 July 2019, Australia's Prime Minister, the Hon. Scott Morrison MP and Minister for Foreign Affairs, Senator the Hon. Marise Payne, released a joint media statement regarding the freeing of Mr Alek Sigley from detention in the Democratic People's Republic of Korea (DPRK). The full text of that media release follows:

We are pleased to announce that Mr Alek Sigley has today been released from detention in the Democratic People's Republic of Korea (DPRK). He is safe and well.

Swedish authorities advised the Australian Government that they met with senior officials from the DPRK yesterday and raised the issue of Alek's disappearance on Australia's behalf.

Earlier this morning we were advised that the DPRK had released Alek from detention, and he has now safely left the country.

On behalf of the Australian Government, I would like to extend my deepest gratitude to Swedish authorities for their invaluable assistance in securing Alek's prompt release.

This outcome demonstrates the value of the discreet, behind the scenes work of officials in resolving complex and sensitive consular cases, in close partnership with other governments.

We couldn't be more pleased that we not only know where Alek is, but that he is safe.

7.10 Detention of Mr Hakeem al-Araibi

On 5 February 2019, Australia's Minister for Foreign Affairs, Senator the Hon. Marise Payne, released a media statement regarding the Government's call for Thailand to release Mr Hakeem Alaraibi. The full text of that media release follows:

The Australian Government reiterates its calls for the Thai Government to release Hakeem Alaraibi home to Australia to be with his friends and family following his extradition hearing.

Thailand's office of the Attorney-General has publicly confirmed that Thailand's Extradition Act allows for executive discretion in such cases. This was also confirmed by the prosecutor in the context of yesterday's hearing.

Mr Alaraibi is a refugee and a permanent resident of Australia and the Government remains deeply concerned by his ongoing detention in Thailand.

The Australian Government continues to advocate on behalf of Mr Alaraibi at the highest levels in both Thailand and Bahrain.

Both governments are aware of the importance of this matter to the Australian Government and Australian people.

The Australian Government welcomes the many messages of support and concern that have been expressed for Mr Alaraibi, including from the UN High Commissioner for Refugees, other governments, the Football Federation of Australia, FIFA, the IOC and Mr Alaraibi's local community in Melbourne.

On 12 February 2019, Australia's Prime Minister, the Hon. Scott Morrison MP and Minister for Foreign Affairs, Senator the Hon. Marise Payne, released a joint media statement regarding the freeing of Mr Hakeem Alaraibi from detention. The full text of that media release follows:

Hakeem al-Araibi is home.

We welcome the Thai Government's decision to allow Mr al-Araibi to return to Australia.

We know all Australians will deeply appreciate the decision, allowing him to return to his wife, family and friends.

The outpouring of support—from the Pascoe Vale Football Club, to the advocacy of Craig Foster and the Football Federation of Australia and so many others—is a testament to how deeply Mr al-Araibi's situation touched Australians.

We also appreciate the efforts of Australian officials and diplomats in working towards this outcome.

We commend Thailand's commitment to due process and human rights, which had led the Thai Government to take this decision.

The people of Australia have a great affection for Thailand and the Thai people.

Australia and Thailand enjoy a long, deep and enduring partnership. We look forward to continuing to strengthen the friendship and partnership between our two nations.

We also acknowledge the constructive dialogue that we have had with Bahrain in helping to resolve this issue. Australia and Bahrain share an important and longstanding relationship, which we will continue to build upon.

AUSTRALIAN PRACTICE IN INTERNATIONAL LAW 2019 581

7.11 Release of Mr Tim Weeks

On 19 November 2019, Australia's Prime Minister, the Hon. Scott Morrison MP and the Minister for Foreign Affairs, Senator the Hon. Marise Payne, released a joint media statement announcing the release of Mr Tim Weeks from three years of detention by the Taliban. The full text of that media release follows:

> The Australian Government offers its deepest appreciation to President Trump and the United States for their immeasurable assistance and cooperation, without which we would not be able to welcome Tim back today.
>
> We also convey our deepest appreciation to the Government of Afghanistan, led by President Ghani, for its invaluable assistance with this case over the past three years.
>
> We regard this release as one of a series of confidence-building measures that are taking place in Afghanistan. We hope that such measures will set the stage for a ceasefire and intra-Afghan dialogue.
>
> The Australian Government has provided consular support to Tim's family throughout this case. Several Australian agencies—including diplomatic, security and military personnel—were closely involved in efforts to secure his release.
>
> Tim's family has asked for privacy. They have asked the Australian Government to convey their relief that their long ordeal is over, and their gratitude to all those who have contributed to Tim's safe return.
>
> For privacy and operational reasons, the Australian Government will not comment further on the details of this case.

7.12 Environmental Human Rights Defenders

On 21 March 2019, during the 40th session of the United Nations Human Rights Council in Geneva, Australia delivered a general comment on the Resolution on environmental human rights defenders. An extract of that statement follows:

> […]
>
> Human Rights Defenders make a vital contribution to the promotion and protection of human rights, to peace and security, and to the achievement of sustainable development for all.
>
> We welcome this resolution's contribution to our understanding of the challenges faced by environmental human rights defenders.
>
> We particularly note the intersectional dimensions of challenges faced by environmental human rights defenders who are also women, indigenous peoples, rural and marginalized communities, and persons belonging to minorities.

582 AUSTRALIAN YEAR BOOK OF INTERNATIONAL LAW VOLUME 38

We reiterate L.22's call for states to provide a safe and enabling environment for human rights defenders, and to combat impunity for attacks or reprisals against them.

[…]

7.13 Elections—Bougainville

On 20 November 2019, Australia's Minister for Foreign Affairs, Senator the Hon. Marise Payne, released a media statement regarding the deployment of an Australian Observer Team for the Bougainville referendum. The full text of that media release follows:

> An 11-member Australian Observer Team will observe Referendum voting and counting processes across Bougainville during the upcoming Referendum at the invitation of the Papua New Guinea and Autonomous Bougainville governments.
>
> Former Federal Parliamentarian Hon Jane Prentice will lead Australia's team, which also includes serving Federal MPs Ken O'Dowd and Sharon Claydon.
>
> The Team includes former Federal MPs, Ewen Jones, Hon Harry Jenkins and Gai Brodtmann, current NSW Parliamentarians, Hon Shayne Mallard MLC and Hon Gregory Donnelly MLC, former senior diplomats James Batley and Ann Harrap, and former Assistant Commissioner of the Australian Electoral Commission, Marie Neilson.
>
> Australia has also deployed two Australian Federal Police officers as part of the New Zealand-led Regional Police Support Mission. The unarmed mission will provide neutral advisory support to the Bougainville Police Service to assist in ensuring a safe and inclusive Referendum.
>
> The Bougainville Referendum marks an important milestone for the 2001 Bougainville Peace Agreement.
>
> Australia's observation mission will complement observer groups from eight other foreign nations and organisations.
>
> We look forward to the peaceful conduct of the Referendum, and the announcement of the result in mid-December 2019.
>
> Under the Peace Agreement the result is non-binding, with both Papua New Guinea and Bougainville required to consult on the outcome. Australia offers our support as appropriate.

On 12 December 2019, Australia's Minister for Foreign Affairs, Senator the Hon. Marise Payne, released a media statement on the successful conduct of the

Referendum on the future political status of Bougainville. The full text of that media release follows:

> Australia congratulates the Papua New Guinea and Autonomous Bougainville governments, and the people of Bougainville, on the successful conduct of the Referendum on the future political status of Bougainville.
>
> The work of the independent Bougainville Referendum Commission, ably chaired by former Irish Prime Minister Bertie Ahern, was integral to the credibility of the polling process.
>
> The polling period ran from 23 November to 7 December, with over 800 polling locations in Bougainville and across Papua New Guinea, Australia and Solomon Islands: a significant achievement by the Papua New Guinea and Autonomous Bougainville governments. I welcome in particular the effort to achieve an inclusive vote, including ensuring women and people with a disability were able to cast their vote unhindered.
>
> Australia was pleased to be among five nations that witnessed the signature of the Bougainville Peace Agreement. New Zealand, Solomon Islands, Fiji and Vanuatu also played roles. I acknowledge the valuable contribution of the 11-strong Australian Observation Mission, led by the Hon Jane Prentice. The Australian observer team's interim assessment is that the Referendum process was free, fair and credible.
>
> Australia was pleased to support the preparations and conduct of the Referendum, alongside the United Nations and other international partners and donors. The successful conduct of the Referendum concludes one of the three pillars of the 2001 Bougainville Peace Agreement.
>
> As Prime Minister Marape stated yesterday, under the Agreement, the outcome of the Referendum is non-binding and will be subject to consultations between the two governments.
>
> Australia looks forward to continued productive engagement as the Bougainville Peace process enters its next stage.

7.14   Elections—Venezuela

On 28 January 2019, Australia's Minister for Foreign Affairs, Senator the Hon. Marise Payne, released a media statement recognising and supporting the President of the Venezuelan National Assembly, Juan Guaidó. The full text of that media release follows:

> Australia recognises and supports the President of the National Assembly, Juan Guaidó, in assuming the position of interim president, in accordance

584 AUSTRALIAN YEAR BOOK OF INTERNATIONAL LAW VOLUME 38

with the Venezuelan constitution and until elections are held. Australia calls for a transition to democracy in Venezuela as soon as possible.

Australia supported the Lima Group's early call for Nicolas Maduro to refrain from assuming the presidency on 10 January, relayed through our non-resident Ambassador to Venezuela.

We now urge all parties to work constructively towards a peaceful resolution of the situation, including a return to democracy, respect for the rule of law and upholding of human rights of the Venezuelan people.

7.15 *Gender Equality, Human Rights and Ending Violence against Women*

On 28 February 2019, Australia delivered a national statement at the 40th Session of the Human Rights Council in Geneva, during the Clustered Interactive Dialogue with the Special Rapporteur on the situation of human rights defenders and the Special Rapporteur on torture and other cruel, inhuman or degrading treatment or punishment, including a focus on women human rights defenders. That statement is excerpted in Section 7.47, below.

On 7 March 2019, Australia delivered a national statement in the 40th Session of the Human Rights Council in Geneva, during the Interactive Dialogue with the UN High Commissioner for Human Rights, which included reference to human rights applying to all. An extract from that statement follows:

> [...]
> Human rights apply to all, regardless of sexual orientation or gender identity ... We call on all countries to protect the rights of LGBTI persons
> [...]

On 8 March 2019, Australia's Minister for Women, the Hon. Kelly O'Dwyer MP released a media statement to mark International Women's Day 2019 and the 63rd Session of the Commission on the Status of Women. Extracts from the statement follow:

> [...]
> This International Women's Day marks another year of the Coalition Government continuing to deliver practical measures to give women greater choices about their lives, build financial security for them and their families, and grow the Australian economy.
> 'In the last 12 months we have seen the gender pay gap fall to a record low of 14.2 per cent, women's workforce participation rise to the record

high of 60.7 per cent, and women's employment reach a record high of almost 6 million, with more women in full-time work than ever before,' Minister O'Dwyer said.

'Whether it is keeping women and children safe from domestic and family violence, or giving women greater choices about their lives so they can build greater financial security for themselves and their families, the Coalition Government is focussed on improving the lives of Australian women.'

This week, the Coalition Government announced the single largest ever Commonwealth investment of $328 million for prevention and frontline services to support the Fourth Action Plan of the National Plan to Reduce Violence against Women and their Children 2010–2022.

In November 2018 Minister O'Dwyer also delivered the first ever Women's Economic Security Statement, with more than $100 million dedicated to practical measures to help give women greater life choices, build financial security and grow the Australian economy.

The last twelve months has also seen the percentage of women on Australian Government boards increase to 45.8 per cent—the highest overall result since public reporting began.

Minister O'Dwyer will also travel to New York today to speak at the United Nations and lead the Australian delegation to the sixty-third session of the Commission on the Status of Women, which will take place at United Nations Headquarters.

'I look forward to sharing with my international colleagues Australia's world-leading approach to women's economic security, eSafety, and addressing issues of sexual harassment in the workforce,' she said.

'Everyone has an important role to play in advancing gender equality—women, men, government, community organisations and businesses are all vital partners in gender equality.'

[...]

On 24 June 2019, Australia delivered a national statement at the 41st Session of the Human Rights Council in Geneva, during the Clustered Interactive Dialogue with the Independent Expert on sexual orientation and gender identity and the Special Rapporteur on the independence of judges and lawyers. Extracts from the statement follow:

[...]

The Australian Government believes all individuals are entitled to respect, dignity, and the opportunity to participate in society and receive the protection of the law regardless of their sexual orientation or gender identity.

We welcome the Independent Expert's recognition of the crucial role played by civil society, human rights defenders and national human rights institutions in providing an evidence base for public policy. Civil society and governments can work together to increase awareness of the importance of collecting and using data on sexual orientation and gender identity to challenge preconceptions and ensure more effective protections.

[...]

On 25 June 2019, Australia delivered a national statement at the 41st Session of the Human Rights Council in Geneva, during the Item 2 General Debate, which included a focus on eliminating all forms of discrimination against women, the prevalence of violence against women, human rights defenders and discrimination against LGBTI persons. Extracts from the statement follow:

[...]

This year we mark the 40th anniversary of the Convention on the Elimination of All Forms of Discrimination Against Women. Much work remains to be done to implement the rights articulated in the convention around the world.

Australia is concerned by the prevalence of violence against women around the world, particularly conflict-related sexual violence against women [...]

Civil society plays a critical role in promoting and protecting the human rights of women [...] Australia is concerned by the increasing use of regulations and other measures to create barriers for civil society organisations [...]

Australia believes that human rights are universal, indivisible and inalienable. Dignity and respect should apply to everyone, which is why Australia is deeply concerned by persistent discrimination against LGBTI persons.

[...]

On 27 June 2019, Australia delivered a national statement in the 41st Session of the Human Rights Council in Geneva during the Annual full-day discussion on the human rights of women (Panel 1: Violence against women in the world of work). Extracts from the statement follow:

[...]

Australia condemns all forms of violence against women and is committed to dismantling the structural inequalities and social norms that underpin gender-based violence.

[...]

Violence in the workplace has devastating consequences and impacts women's ability to work. It can result in loss of livelihood, silencing of women's voices and limiting of their contributions in the workplace. Effects are more severe for women experiencing intersectional disadvantage. There is a strong business case to support women's participation in the workforce.

Australia welcomes the recent adoption of the International Labour Organization's standard on Ending Violence and Harassment in the World of Work, and notes the overwhelming majority support that the Convention and Recommendation received. This signifies an important step towards achieving the elimination of violence against women universally.

As States, we have the responsibility to protect workers from violence, and to ensure perpetrators are held to account. Workplaces should be places of safety for people experiencing violence at home, a factor which can impact on women's ability to work and increase their vulnerability to violence in the workplace.

In December 2018, Australia legislated leave entitlements to help workers deal with the impacts of family and domestic violence. This legislation supports people to retain their employment and financial independence at a critical time.

[...]

On 28 June 2019, Australia delivered a national statement in the 41st Session of the Human Rights Council in Geneva, during Panel 2: The rights of older women and their economic empowerment. Extracts from the statement follow:

[...]

Australia is strongly committed to upholding the rights of all women. We welcome the focus of today's discussion on the intersectional disadvantages experienced by older women and the impact on their economic empowerment.

A lifetime of gender inequality can have a cumulative effect on older women. Higher rates of domestic violence, often experienced by women throughout their lives, further impinge on women's human rights and opportunities for their economic empowerment. For women who experience multiple and intersecting forms of discrimination, the consequences are even more significant.

Addressing structural and cultural barriers to gender equality is critical to realising the rights of older women. Policies need to work to eliminate gender bias and combat prejudice against older women in the workforce and close the gender pay gap. These actions can contribute to addressing the gendered disparities in incomes and retirement savings, which undermine women's economic empowerment over the course of their lives.

[...]

On 29 June 2019, during the 41st session of the United Nations Human Rights Council in Geneva, Australia joined a Joint Statement on strengthening the role of women in peace and multilateralism. The full text of that statement follows:

I have the honour to read this statement on behalf of the Kingdom of Spain, The Kingdom of Jordan and [a number of other countries].

Following this year's commemoration of the International Women's Day and the League of Nations Centenary initiative to mark 100 Years of Multilateralism in Geneva, held on 8 March 2019 at the Palais des Nations, the above-mentioned Member States express the following:

As we commemorate the 40th anniversary of the adoption of the Convention on the Elimination of All Forms of Discrimination against Women, we recall its affirmation that 'the full and complete development of a country, the welfare of the world and the cause of peace require the maximum participation of women on equal terms with men in all fields'; and the 25th anniversary of the Beijing Declaration and Platform for Action, that recalled the shared conviction that 'women's empowerment and their full participation on the basis of equality in all spheres of society, including participation in the decision-making processes and access to power, are fundamental for the achievement of equality, development, and peace', we acknowledge that important strides have been achieved in the promotion and protection of women's rights.

We also approach the 20th anniversary of the adoption by the United Nations Security Council of the first resolution on Women, Peace and Security—UNSCR 1325—which recognized the fundamental participation of women in peace-building, conflict resolution, sustainable development and multilateralism. Grounded on the link between gender equality and sustainable peace, the WPS Agenda has stated the need to ensure the effective participation of women in every phase of conflict and the importance of women's leadership becoming into a global norm.

Resolutions 1325 and the following on WPS, are a call of action to reduce the gap between our commitments and the reality on the ground regarding participation of women in all decision-making processes, the protection of women and girl's rights and the prevention of the violation of their rights.

Participation of women in peace processes and agreements and the eradication of all forms of discrimination and violence against women and girls remain urgent challenges in our societies. Through this statement, we would like to recommit to these goals and principles, and emphasize their urgency in the face of today's crises. We must reinforce our commitment to women's organizations and women rights defenders and ensure that their voices are present in the Human Rights Council and every multilateral fora.

All forms of discrimination based on gender are violations of human rights, as well as significant barriers to the achievement of the 2030 Agenda for Sustainable Development (SDG) and its 17 Sustainable Development Goals.

Sexual and gender-based violence is the most extreme form of discrimination and constitute a human rights violation. By mandating the investigation and documentation of gender-based crimes in several conflicts, the Human Rights Council has discharged its responsibility in a pioneering fashion. As a result, atrocities committed against women and girls are now more documented than ever before in history, and this has eroded the culture of silence and impunity that compounds these crimes. But we still need to advance in putting in place effective instruments that address individual human rights violations and enhance accountability as a key element.

Therefore, we encourage the Human Rights Council to identify additional measures aimed at promoting Goal 5 on gender equality and Goal 16 on the promotion of peaceful, just and inclusive societies for sustainable development of the 2030 Agenda, as well as to contribute to implement the resolutions that constitute the WPS agenda. In particular, the Council should affirm the fundamental importance of the role of women in protection against Human Rights abuses and violations. Another important chapter is that of empowerment and education of women and girls, as well as the necessity of mainstreaming gender and women's participation in multilateral diplomacy, the United Nations, Regional Organizations, and Development Agencies.

We believe that we must do a lot more to translate the recommendations of human rights mechanisms, Special Procedures, Treaty Bodies, and the Universal Periodic Review into real change for women and girls in conflict and post-conflict situations. They offer us a path towards greater accountability in the implementation of women, peace and security commitments, and will bring us closer to a more peaceful world.

On 8 July 2019, during the 41st session of the United Nations Human Rights Council in Geneva, Australia joined a Joint Statement on the occasion of the 40th Anniversary of the Convention on the Elimination of all Forms of Discrimination against Women. Australia also joined an identical Joint Statement delivered at the Third Committee of the United Nations General Assembly on 7 October 2019. The full text of that statement follows:

It is my pleasure to deliver this statement on behalf of [a number of countries], as we celebrate this year the 40th anniversary of the adoption of the Convention on the Elimination of All Forms of Discrimination against Women (CEDAW) and the 20th anniversary of the adoption of its Optional Protocol.

In the past 40 years, the Convention has brought about important changes for women and girls worldwide. Constitutional, legislative and administrative reforms were adopted to prohibit discrimination as well as to prevent and address gender-based violence against women. Gender equality policies including in the areas of education, health and the socio-economic empowerment of women were strengthened. The contribution of the Committee's General Recommendations in these regards has been important.

Unfortunately, no country in the world has yet successfully eliminated discrimination against women and girls, or achieved full gender equality. Discrimination continues to persist in all areas of life and transcends national, cultural and religious boundaries, often fuelled by patriarchal stereotypes and power imbalances. Meanwhile, new challenges to gender equality emerge in relation to technological development, violent extremism, environmental degradation, climate change, racial discrimination and other societal changes.

We hereby reaffirm here our strong commitment to the Convention. No law, no tradition, no religion, nor any custom or culture can ever justify discrimination against women and girls. Considering the deeply entrenched social and cultural norms that uphold and reinforce gender stereotypes and perpetuate discriminations against women, it is of

AUSTRALIAN PRACTICE IN INTERNATIONAL LAW 2019   591

crucial importance to adhere to international and regional law and standards, in particular CEDAW, and implement these in practice.

Today, 189 States have ratified the Convention, which can be considered a success. However, we should not be complacent. We should work towards universal ratification and the complete withdrawal of all substantive reservations that were entered to the Convention, in particular to its articles 2 and 16, in order to ensure the elimination of all forms of discrimination, including in the sphere of work, home and family. We therefore encourage the concerned States parties to review constantly their reservations and consider their removal.

Once ratified, the effective implementation of the Convention is essential. Part of the implementation is to submit periodic reports to the CEDAW-Committee. We call upon States Parties to submit their periodic reports in a timely manner.

We also invite those States that have not yet ratified the Convention and/or the Optional Protocol thereto, to consider doing so, as these instruments provide for essential guarantees and strengthen remedies for women and girls.

To seize the occasion of the 40th anniversary of CEDAW we must step up our efforts and do more to eradicate discrimination against women and girls, including through bridging gender gaps and structural barriers in order to achieve full gender equality.

Also on 8 July 2019, during the 41st session of the United Nations Human Rights Council in Geneva, Australia was one of 46 countries to join a Joint Statement on Accountability for the Rights of Women and Girls in Humanitarian Settings, delivered during the Item 8 General Debate. The full text of that statement follows:

> I have the honour to deliver this joint statement on behalf of 46 countries.
>
> Ensuring accountability for human rights violations and abuses perpetrated against women and girls is central to fulfilling human rights obligations.
>
> Human rights accountability in this context goes beyond criminal justice and includes principles of participation, transparency, empowerment, sustainability, international assistance and non-discrimination. It enables a survivor-focused approach and puts women and girls themselves at the center of all interventions, emphasizing their agency.
>
> Conflict situations and humanitarian emergencies have dire consequences on women and girls' enjoyment of human rights, exacerbating

pre-existing structural patterns of discrimination and inequalities, and making them particularly vulnerable to human rights violations and abuses such as, sexual and gender-based violence, human trafficking, child, early and forced marriage, forced pregnancy and to higher rates of maternal mortality and morbidity. Women and girls with disabilities, indigenous women and girls, and women and girls from ethnic and religious minorities are particularly exposed to targeted violence, exploitation and abuse, including sexual and gender-based violence.

Disintegrating judicial systems, multiple and intersecting forms of discrimination, and the stigma associated with sexual and gender-based violence as well as with seeking access to quality and comprehensive sexual and reproductive health information and services, all prevent women and girls from reporting, seeking accountability and participating in decisions affecting their lives.

International human rights and political bodies have recognized that accountability requires independent monitoring, prompt investigation and punishment of perpetrators as well as legal and policy shifts in order to prevent future violations.[1]

This should include the removal of legal, structural and systemic barriers and other discriminatory measures and policies, identifying and addressing their disproportionate impact on women and girls and the differential impact of national state practices and immigration policies on them, particularly on those facing displacement. This should also include the development and enforcement of policies and legal frameworks that respect women and girls' rights to bodily autonomy and bodily integrity, guarantee universal access to education, sexual and reproductive health information, care and services, including access to safe abortion.

Remedies must aim to restore the rights of victims of violations and must include adequate, effective, and prompt reparation including guarantees of non-recurrence. All mechanisms should be informed by effective and meaningful participation of women and girls, in order to ensure that they are gender, and age-sensitive, and take into consideration multiple and intersecting forms of discrimination and context-specific factors, that necessitate distinct responses and measures.

---

1 CEDAW, General Recommendation 30, paras 77–9; see generally United Nations General Assembly Res 60/147, *Basic Principles and Guidelines on the Right to a Remedy and Reparation for Victims of Gross Violations of International Human Rights Law and Serious Violations of International Humanitarian Law*, A/RES/60/147 (21 March 2006) para 3 (b).

AUSTRALIAN PRACTICE IN INTERNATIONAL LAW 2019

> Building on the joint statement read in March 2019 lead by Mexico and Finland on rights-based accountability and co-sponsored by 59 States, the co-sponsors of this statement therefore urge the Human Rights Council to incorporate and mainstream the issue of accountability for human rights violations and abuses against women and girls in humanitarian settings in its agenda and to address structural inequalities by including conflict gender, and age analysis in its work in humanitarian settings, including in the mandates of commissions of inquiry and fact-finding missions.

On 11 July 2019, during the 41st session of the United Nations Human Rights Council in Geneva, Australia delivered an explanation of vote on the Resolution on violence against women. The full text of that explanation follows:

> We have listened carefully to the diversity of views expressed on this issue. However, we cannot accept amendment L.38, which seeks to delete the reference to intimate partner violence.
>
> I would like to explain why. Intimate partner violence impacts women around the world. Globally, a third of women murdered in 2017 were killed by their current or former partner. In Australia, this translates to an average of one woman killed every week. This is a human rights abuse that clearly demands this Council's attention.
>
> The relevance of intimate partner violence to this resolution on violence against women and girls in the world of work, is irrefutable.
>
> No incident of gender-based violence occurs in a vacuum. Such violence is grounded in gender stereotypes and long-standing and systemic discrimination in all spheres of life, including in the world of work.
>
> That intimate partner violence primarily occurs in the private sphere is no excuse to disregard it. On the contrary, it underlines the importance of addressing this type of violence by this Council. The particular complexities of violence in intimate relationships requires nuanced policy responses, especially as it can lead to devastating consequences in all aspects of the affected person's life, including their participation in the workforce.
>
> Amendment L.38 seeks to narrow the scope of gender-based violence addressed by this resolution. In failing to address one of the most common forms of violence against women and girls, this amendment sends the wrong message that gender-based violence occurring in private is of no concern to this Council.
>
> Australia will vote against this amendment, and we urge members of this Council to do the same.

594 AUSTRALIAN YEAR BOOK OF INTERNATIONAL LAW VOLUME 38

On 12 July 2019, during the 41st session of the United Nations Human Rights Council in Geneva, Australia delivered an explanation of vote on the Resolution on discrimination against women. The full text of that explanation follows:

> We would like to make a comment on L.37, which we cannot accept as it seeks to remove language on comprehensive sexuality education, or 'CSE'.
>
> Australia supports equal access to evidence based comprehensive sexuality education for all. CSE provides young people with the knowledge and tools required to empower them to realise their health, well-being and dignity, including a well-informed understanding of consent, and it helps them understand and ensure the protection of their rights throughout their lives.
>
> CSE is essential to the fulfilment of universal human rights, including the right to education and the right to health.
>
> It is highly relevant to this resolution on the elimination of discrimination against women and girls, because it plays a critical role in supporting gender equality, and it even supports girls to stay in school.
>
> Comprehensive sexuality education contributes positively to the reduction of the rates of sexually transmitted infections; HIV transmission; early pregnancy; preventable maternal death; child sexual exploitation and abuse; child, early and forced marriage, and gender-based violence.
>
> The importance of comprehensive sexuality education has been acknowledged by different UN agencies, including the World Health Organization.
>
> Amendment L.37 ignores the responsibility of states to take steps to achieve progressively the full realisation of the rights to education, health and non-discrimination, and to support young people, including women and girls, to make informed decisions about their sexual and reproductive lives.
>
> Australia will vote against this amendment, and we urge other members of this Council to do the same.

On 23 September 2019, Australia made a national statement during the 42nd Session of the Human Rights Council for the Annual Discussion on the integration of a gender perspective throughout the work of the Human Rights Council and that of its mechanisms. Extracts from the statement follow:

> [...]
> The equal participation of women throughout all stages of the decision making process is paramount to achieving gender equality. It is a fundamental right that women and girls are often denied.

The Human Rights Council has a responsibility to demonstrate leadership by establishing institutional norms that promote gender equality and support diversity. This requires accountability and transparency. It requires tackling bias and challenging gender norms and stereotypes.

Australia's Workplace Gender Equality Agency, established in 2012, exists to promote and improve gender equality in Australian workplaces. This year it reported that almost 75 per cent of Australian employers had a gender equality policy. As employers have taken action, gender equality outcomes have improved.

In April 2018, the Australian Government achieved the milestone of gender parity at the most senior level of the public service, with half of all departmental Secretary roles occupied by women.

We are also pursuing equality in our diplomatic representation. Today, women represent 40 per cent of senior managers in the Australian Department of Foreign Affairs and Trade and make up 40 per cent of Heads of Australian Missions and Posts.

[...]

On 4 October 2019, Australia delivered an intervention at the 74th Session of the UN General Assembly Third Committee in New York, during the Interactive Dialogue with the Special Rapporteur on violence against women. Extracts from the statement follow:

[...]

Australia welcomes the Special Rapporteur's report on a human rights-based approach to mistreatment and violence against women and support's the report's conclusions and recommendations.

Across the spectrum of their lives, women and girls are perhaps at their most vulnerable during childbirth.

Complications arising from pregnancy and childbirth are the leading causes of death for women and particularly for girls around the world.

Australia supports the report's finding that violence, abuse, and a lack of respect for women and girls and their human rights, have the potential to deeply compromise physical and mental health and wellbeing, and contribute to mortality and morbidity.

Australia concurs with the Special Rapporteur's conclusion that women's rights include:

– the right to the highest standard attainable of physical and mental health, free from mistreatment and violence

– including the right to dignified, humane and respectful reproductive health services and obstetric care

– and including the right to autonomy, privacy, confidentiality, informed consent and choice, which a number of delegations have picked up well in their statements today.

[...]

On 4 October 2019, Australia delivered a national statement at the 74th Session of the UN General Assembly Third Committee in New York, during the General Discussion on the advancement of women. Extracts from the statement follow:

[...]

Violence against women is a ubiquitous threat to human rights. It is an unacceptable reality in so many aspects of women's lives.

Australia is committed to dismantling the structural inequalities and addressing the harmful attitudes that underpin violence against women. This requires significant investment, co-ordinated approaches and eliminating harmful practices such as forced marriage and female genital mutilation.

We have committed to this domestically through our *National Plan to Reduce Violence against Women and their Children 2010–22*. Internationally, we support the UN Trust Fund to End Violence against Women and the joint UN Program on Essential Services for Women and Girls Subject to Violence.

All forms of gender discrimination are intolerable, and discrimination solely on the grounds of sex is a violation of human rights. We must remove discrimination against women and girls, bridge gender gaps and tackle persistent barriers to women's advancement and full equality for all.

Australia supports actions to address discriminatory laws and policies that limit women's economic participation. We encourage all sectors to play a positive role, and harness the productivity and other benefits of engaging a diverse workforce.

Sexual and reproductive health and rights are fundamental to women's rights and advancing gender equality.

Sexual and reproductive healthcare services and evidence-based information and education services are life-changing and life-saving. Even now, the WHO estimates 830 women and girls die globally every day of causes related to pregnancy and childbirth, almost all of which could be avoided with access to sexual and reproductive health services.

[...]

AUSTRALIAN PRACTICE IN INTERNATIONAL LAW 2019

On 11 October 2019, Australia made an intervention at the 74th Session of the UN General Assembly Third Committee in New York, during the Interactive Dialogue with the Special Rapporteur on the Human Rights of Indigenous Peoples, which included a focus on the situation of Indigenous women and children. Relevant extracts from the intervention follow:

> [...]
> Australia agrees that Indigenous women play pivotal leadership roles in their families and communities and are central to the development, growth and diversity of Australian society.
>
> We appreciate that the Special Rapporteur has continued to pay particular attention to the human rights situations of indigenous women and children in her country visits. Increasing all women and girls' leadership—including Indigenous women and girls—and their opportunities for economic prosperity and safety are major priorities of the Australian Government.
>
> Australia agrees with the Special Rapporteur that working with and empowering indigenous women in leadership, ensures their voices are reflected in domestic policies.
>
> Further to the Special Rapporteur's recommendation to promote good practices, we are working with communities with greater transparency, including sharing data and funding information to support community decision making to identify priorities and target solutions.
>
> Australia is partnering with Indigenous Australians in formal, shared decision-making to deliver and monitor the Closing the Gap framework, a national coordination mechanism to improve outcomes for Indigenous Australians.
> [...]

On 24 October 2019, Australia made an intervention during the 74th Session of the UN General Assembly Third Committee in New York, during the Interactive Dialogue with the Special Rapporteur on protection against violence and discrimination based on sexual orientation and gender identity. The full text of the intervention follows:

> Australia welcomes the Independent Expert's continuing work highlighting the human rights issues facing LGBTI persons globally. As a member of the Human Rights Council, we were proud to support renewal of this mandate earlier this year.
>
> We appreciate your report's focus on the ongoing impact of discriminatory norms, laws and practices on LGBTI persons. It is a timely reminder

that all States have a long way to go to ensure full, cross-sectoral equality for LGBTI persons.

It is also a reminder of the real and ongoing need for this mandate. Across the world, LGBTI individuals often do not enjoy the same level of human rights protections as their fellow citizens. The Independent Expert's work is critical to ensuring we meet the targets of the 2030 Agenda and this group is not left behind.

Australia will continue to support this mandate, as we support all mandates where the Human Rights Council has identified a real and unaddressed need to further human rights protections for the benefit of all.

We also welcome your report's detailed analysis of the impact of intersectionality. And that marginalization and exclusion can be cumulative, and exacerbated for persons with disability, the elderly, women and children, and members of racial, ethnic or cultural minorities.

Australia is proud to have made significant strides towards protecting and promoting equal human rights for LGBTI persons. This includes introducing measures that are strengthening social inclusion and equality.

On 25 October 2019, Australia made an intervention during the 74th Session of the UN General Assembly Third Committee Interactive Dialogue with the Special Rapporteur on contemporary forms of slavery, which included references to gender equality. An excerpt of that statement is produced in Section 7.51 below.

On 12 November 2019, Australia's Ambassador for Women and Girls, Dr Sharman Stone, delivered a statement during the Nairobi Summit which celebrated the 25th Anniversary of the International Conference on Population and Development (ICPD). The ICPD was a landmark event in 1994. Extracts from that statement follow:

> [...]
>
> 25 years ago, 179 countries came together to become signatories of the ICPD and its Program for Action which sets out an ambitious agenda for ensuring universal access to sexual and reproductive health and underscored its importance to human health and well-being and inclusive social and economic development.
>
> Australia upholds the tenets of the ICPD in its long-standing commitment to the promotion and delivery of sexual and reproductive health and rights as a priority in our foreign policy and aid program—without

universal access to these services, we will not realise global efforts to improve health and will not achieve inclusive, sustainable development.

We will continue to provide strong support for UNFPA and other key partners to deliver on the ICPD Program of Action.

Australia is partnering with UNFPA to:

- expand access to family planning in the Pacific; and to
- create new programming that responds to gender-based violence and sexual reproductive health supplies in disaster-prone countries to respond effectively to emergencies across the Indo-Pacific.

I also want to acknowledge the key role of our civil society and NGOs in achieving the ICPD Program of Action.

The Australian Government is resolutely committed to improving health outcomes of women and girls

- we are on track to eliminate cervical cancer by 2035, an often fatal but highly preventable disease which is almost always caused by Human Papilloma Virus (HPV)
- and we will support Samoa, Solomon Islands, Tonga, Vanuatu and Kiribati to establish a national cervical cancer policy by the end of 2022.

In 2021, Australia will host the 23rd World Congress of the International Federation of Gynaecology and Obstetrics. The Australian Government is proud to support an international fellowship program to enable emerging women's health leaders from developing countries to participate.

Today we celebrate the critical achievements since 1994. Millions of lives have been saved, and millions of people have realised their aspirations for a brighter future.

But the job is not done. We call upon the global community to advance gender equality, to end the unmet need for family planning, to end preventable maternal deaths, and to end gender-based violence and harmful practices against women and girls. We recommit to the accelerated implementation of the ICPD and its Program of Action, which is fundamental to making the world a safer, fairer, stronger and a more prosperous place for all.

[...]

On 25 November 2019, Australia's Minister for Foreign Affairs and Minister for Women, Senator the Hon. Marise Payne, released a media statement regarding the International Day for the Elimination of Violence Against Women. The full text of that media release follows:

Today is the International Day for the Elimination of Violence against Women and the start of the 16 Days of Activism to End Gender-Based Violence.

Globally, one in three women have experienced either physical or sexual abuse, most often perpetrated by someone she knows. Violence against women is a gross violation of human rights, profoundly impacting victims, their communities and society as a whole.

Family and domestic violence affects women's ability to pursue economic security, to care for themselves and their families, and to lead active and positive lives.

The Morrison Government makes women's safety a priority both in Australia and in our region.

On 9 August 2019, the Council of Australian Governments endorsed the Fourth Action Plan under the National Plan to Reduce Violence against Women and their Children 2010–2022, agreeing on five national priorities to reduce family, domestic and sexual violence.

In support of this Plan, the Government has committed $340 million, the single largest Commonwealth contribution to addressing family and domestic violence.

The Commonwealth support is aimed at stopping family and domestic violence before it starts, improving frontline services to keep women and children safe, and helping to provide safe places for people affected by domestic violence.

Today, Australian Governments have also announced our commitment to working together on the National Implementation Plan of the Fourth Action Plan, across all jurisdictions.

Ending gender-based violence is also a key pillar of Australia's foreign policy and overseas aid program, especially in the Indo-Pacific. For example, through the $35 million Nabilan program in Timor-Leste, we have provided more than 32,000 services to survivors of violence including legal assistance and reform, medical examinations, counselling and crisis accommodation.

Australia is also contributing to the Pacific Partnership to End Violence Against Women and Girls, promoting change at a community level to prevent violence and deliver quality services to survivors. The Pacific Partnership builds on Australia's long-term support to expand counselling, health and legal services, including funding to women's crisis centres in Cook Islands, Fiji, Kiribati, PNG, Solomon Islands, Marshall Islands, Vanuatu and Tonga.

On 5 December 2019, Australia's Minister for Foreign Affairs and Minister for Women, Senator the Hon. Marise Payne, delivered a speech at the Bali Democracy Forum, which included reference to women's leadership and gender equality. Excerpts of that speech follow.

[...]

But one indispensable benchmark, surely, is that women of our nations, one half of our populations, have an equal opportunity to participate in the decisions that determine the future of their nations.

And today's discussion provides us with an opportunity to consider whether there is more that we can do to remove barriers to full and equal participation by women, thereby ensuring that our governments are fully and accurately reflecting as far as possible the views and aspirations of all our people.

Enhancing women's representation in positions of leadership and influence is fundamental to achieving gender equality. Evidence also suggests that when women are elected into leadership roles, confidence in democracy increases. Countries experience higher standards of living, and societies become better at protecting all their members. We know that attacks on women's rights and gender equality are also attacks on good governance and democracy, undermining resilience against conflict and extremism.

I'm immensely proud that in Australia, I'm a member of the parliamentary chamber, the Senate, the Commonwealth of Australia, which has gender equality. 50 per cent men, 50 per cent women.

We're also determined in Australia that our foreign policy reflects our values at home. And equality, including gender equality, is a cornerstone of those values. And for me, that involves bringing together my two roles in the Australian Government, because as well as being Australia's Foreign Minister, I am also Australia's Minister for Women ... I try to ensure that all of our foreign policy discussions, decisions, are put through a filter of asking: what do they mean for women around the world? I have no doubt gender equality, the empowerment of women and girls, is critical to global security and prosperity, and frankly, in Australia's national interests.

We've got to a way to go. Gender equality remains elusive. It's only by working together—as women and men, as public and private sectors, as communities, as countries, across regions, across the globe—that we can create an inclusive world where women are safe and equal and empowered.

We are committed to the SDGs because they reflect our values and our ambitions. Gender equality goal, goal 5, is important to highlight. For Australia, it's a priority that women are given equal opportunities to reach leadership positions at all levels of decision-making. And the Australian Public Service Commission has a gender equality strategy to help address gender imbalances in our public service, in our bureaucracy. And today, at the most senior levels of the Australian public service, almost half of all departmental secretary positions are held by women. Six out of 14, including my own department, Foreign Affairs and Trade. And we're working to eliminate all forms of violence against women and girls, including trafficking, forced marriage, underage marriage, sexual exploitation and other types of exploitation.

Gender equality is a fundamental human right. And respecting fundamental human rights makes the world a safer and more secure place.

[...]

7.16 *Equal Human Rights for Lesbian, Gay, Bisexual, Transgender and Intersex (LGBTI) Persons*

On 18 March 2019, during the 40th session of the United Nations Human Rights Council in Geneva, Australia joined a Joint Statement on LGBTI persons in Chechnya. An extract of that statement follows:

> [...]
>
> The 1993 Vienna Declaration and Programme of Action makes clear that all human rights and fundamental freedoms are universal, and that every person is born equal and has the same rights. It also urges states to take increased action on a range of rights, including freedom from torture and arbitrary detention.
>
> We wish to express our deep concern about recent reports concerning the renewed persecution of LGBTI persons in Chechnya, Russian Federation. These reports indicate that, in recent months, at least 40 LGBTI individuals have been detained, and that two individuals have died following torture.
>
> Over the past two years, reports of human rights violations and abuses in Chechnya have repeatedly surfaced as an issue of significant international concern. Last year's report by the OSCE Moscow Mechanism Rapporteur found overwhelming evidence that such violations had occurred, with impunity for the perpetrators.
>
> The Vienna Declaration expressed concern about impunity for human rights violations. Today, we call on the Russian authorities to take urgent

action in response to these renewed reports of violations of the human rights of LGBTI persons in Chechnya.

All persons who remain in detention based on their actual or perceived sexual orientation or gender identity must be released immediately.

There must also be a swift, thorough and impartial investigation into the alleged persecution, arrest and torture of LGBTI persons, and any deaths that have resulted. Those who have directed and carried out these acts must be held responsible.

All LGBTI individuals in Chechnya must be treated as equal members of society and benefit from equal protection of the law, in accordance with the Vienna Declaration and Programme of Action as well as with Russia's constitutional guarantees and international human rights obligations.

Thank you Mr President.

On 12 July 2019, during the 41st session of the United Nations Human Rights Council in Geneva, Australia delivered an explanation of vote on the Resolution on sexual orientation and gender identity. An extract of that statement follows:

[...]

We cannot accept amendment L.34. This amendment seeks to add a preambular paragraph deploring acts of violence and discrimination, on the basis of race, colour, sex, language, religion, political or other opinion, national or social origin, property, birth or other status. We do not dispute the unacceptability of violence and discrimination on the basis of these things, but this long list is far from an accurate reflection of all the various bases for violence and discrimination as it excludes sexual orientation and gender identity—the focus of this resolution—and we cannot accept this omission.

People of diverse sexual orientation and gender identities are often amongst the most marginalised in their societies, and experience high rates of violence and discrimination. This is not confined to any single country; it is a global phenomenon.

This marginalisation is compounded by the fact that people of diverse sexual orientation and gender identities are often less visible in society— either hidden from view or driven to mask their orientation and identities for fear of persecution and violence.

This amendment seeks to undermine the universality of human rights by failing to recognise that people are persecuted and discriminated against on the basis of sexual orientation and gender identity.

[...]

On 18 October 2019, at the 74th Session of the UN General Assembly Third Committee, Australia joined a Joint Statement on the rights of LGBTI persons during the General Discussion on the promotion and protection of human rights. An extract of that statement follows:

> [...]
> Our overarching goal is to work within the United Nations framework to ensure universal respect for the human rights and fundamental freedoms of all individuals without distinction, regardless of their real or perceived sexual orientation, gender identity or sex characteristics, including lesbian, gay bisexual, trans and intersex (LGBTI) persons. Our particular focus is on protecting LGBTI persons from violence and discrimination.
>
> Protecting LGBTI individuals from violence and discrimination does not require the creation of new or special rights. The legal obligations of States to uphold the human rights of all individuals, including LGBTI persons, without distinction of any kind, are well established in international human rights law on the basis of the Universal Declaration of Human Rights and subsequently agreed international human rights treaties.
>
> Similarly, States have a responsibility to ensure the protection of those human rights defenders that stand up for the human rights of LGBTI people.
>
> We would like to thank the Office of the UN High Commissioner for Human Rights for its continued support to this important cause. In a recent event organized by the LGBTI Core Group during the General Assembly High Level Week, High Commissioner Michelle Bachelet stressed the importance of combating hate speech. As Ms. Bachelet put it 'We need to fight strongly against LGBTI discrimination because it's undermining people's dignity, people's possibilities, and people's lives.'
>
> The renewal of the mandate of the Independent Expert on protection against violence and discrimination based on sexual orientation and gender identity, pursuant to Human Rights Council resolution 41/18, has been a key achievement for the international community. The mandate was returned by the HRC with even more support than at its inception, demonstrating that Member States value the thoughtful and professional way the Independent Expert has carried out his work, and agree that discrimination and violence against individuals based on sexual orientation and gender identity is an issue that deserves continued attention.
>
> We express our full support for the mandate of the Independent Expert and congratulate him on the presentation of his third report to

this Committee. This recent report shows how discriminatory laws and sociocultural norms continue to marginalize and exclude lesbian, gay, bisexual, trans and intersex persons from education, health care, housing, employment and occupation, and other sectors.

Many people in the world—including in our own countries—suffer violence and discrimination because of their actual or perceived sexual orientation gender identity or sex characteristics. Among other disparities, lesbian, gay, bisexual, transgender and intersex people are significantly more likely than the general population to be at risk for mental health concerns such as depression and suicide or to be targeted for violence and harassment.

Over the past 5 years, 9 countries have decriminalized homosexuality and some progress has been achieved to fight violence and discrimination based on sexual orientation and gender identity, as the Independent Expert highlights in his latest report. However, there is still a lot to be done. For example, there are still 69 countries where consensual same sex behavior between adults is criminalized. We call on those 69 countries to repeal their law criminalizing same sex behavior.

The LGBTI UN Core Group firmly believes that an inclusive society enables every person, including LGBTI people, to enjoy protection from violence and discrimination as well as access to human rights. To achieve inclusive societies and effectively implement the 2030 Agenda cross cutting principle of Leaving No One Behind, progressive realization of social, cultural and economic rights is fundamental and we therefore welcome the recent Report of the Independent Expert.

As the Secretary General put it, 'Hate speech is often used to dehumanize already marginalized groups and individuals, exacerbating discrimination and inciting violence. It is an attack on the very essence of Human Rights and affects us all. Hatred against LGBTI community is perpetrated by people of all kinds, including religious and political leaders, and amplified through both traditional and social media. Too often there is no real protection. On the contrary; in many places LGBTI people face prosecution and punishment for their sexual orientation or gender identity.'

We take this opportunity to express our support for and pay tribute to human rights defenders that work for the human rights of LGBTI people and others engaged in combating violence on the grounds of sexual orientation, gender identity, gender expression or intersex status. Their work, often carried out at considerable personal risk, plays a critical role in reporting on human rights violations and abuses, providing support to victims, and sensitizing Governments and public opinion. Through their work, human rights defenders that work for the human rights of LGBTI people contribute to States adopting concrete measures to recognize and support their role and ensure their protection against violence and discrimination based on sexual orientation and gender identity.

We are fully committed to tackling these violations and abuses—at the domestic, regional and global levels, including through concerted and constructive engagement at the United Nations. And as we seek support from all Member States to this cause, we would like to stress that standing against violence and discrimination is not and should never be a matter of controversy. It is just right and humane.

[...]

On 18 September 2019, during the 41st session of the United Nations Human Rights Council in Geneva, Australia delivered a national statement in the Interactive Dialogue with the Assistant Secretary-General on **Reprisals**. An extract of that statement follows:

[...]

We are also concerned about continuing reports that women and LGBTI persons are exposed to gender- or sexual orientation-specific barriers, threats and violence in their engagement with the UN. This includes threats of rape, online smear campaigns, sexual assault in detention, and humiliating and degrading treatment. In this regard, we welcome OHCHR's efforts to examine, investigate and document intimidation and reprisals in a gender-responsive manner.

[...]

7.17   *Human Rights Online, including the Right to Privacy*

On 1 March 2019, at the 40th session of the United Nations Human Rights Council in Geneva, Australia delivered a national statement at the Clustered Interactive Dialogue with the Special Rapporteur on the right to privacy and the Special Rapporteur on cultural rights. An extract of that statement follows:

[...]

Australia reaffirms that no individual should be subject to arbitrary or unlawful interference with their privacy.

Collecting and using data is becoming increasingly valuable for states and non-state actors, yet may come with risks to individuals' privacy.

Australia is committed to maintaining a comprehensive framework for the protection of individuals' personal information.

Australia notes the reference to its legislation in paragraph 38 of the report of the Special Rapporteur on the right to privacy. The *Telecommunications and Other Legislation Amendment (Assistance and Access) Act 2018* represents a reasonable and proportionate means to address the use of encrypted technologies by criminals and terrorists.

The legislation allows law enforcement and national security agencies to work in the increasingly complex digital environment by providing a framework to request or oblige providers to assist law enforcement where access to data is possible.

It creates new powers to search computers and enhance existing search and seizure powers to assist law enforcement without interfering with encryption technology.

This constructive new approach to the issue of encrypted communications preserves the effectiveness of encryption while providing law enforcement necessary access.

This approach preserves the strong protections already in place in Australia for accessing the content of communications, which require law enforcement to seek judicially authorised warrants for access.

The legislation contains strong safeguards which ensure the privacy of Australians is not compromised and the security of the digital ecosystem is maintained.

In May 2019, the Freedom Online Coalition, which Australia is a member of, made a Joint Statement on Defending Civic Space Online. An extract of that statement follows:

[...]

Introduction

The Freedom Online Coalition (FOC) is deeply concerned about shrinking civic and democratic spaces online as a result of State-sponsored obstruction of free expression, peaceful assembly, and free association, notably as it relates to human rights defenders and other members of civil society. State-sponsored obstruction of these rights is a direct challenge to the FOC's goal of protecting and promoting both the exercise of human rights online and an open and interoperable Internet, as affirmed in the FOC's 'Tallinn Agenda.' A robust and protected civic space forms the cornerstone of accountable, inclusive, and responsive democratic societies.

The FOC recognizes that civic space online is integral to a vibrant civic space offline. The FOC reaffirms that individuals have the right, individually and in association with others, to promote and to strive for the protection and realization of human rights and fundamental freedoms at local, national, regional, and international levels and affirms that these rights must be protected online just as they are protected offline.

Human rights defenders are individuals or groups that, in their personal or professional capacity and in a peaceful manner, engage in protecting and promoting human rights. The work of human rights defenders is crucial to protecting the aforementioned rights, and promoting gender inclusion, equality and diversity, as well as upholding democracy and the rule of law, which is essential to the flourishing of society.

In this statement, the FOC considers the term civic space broadly to describe the place, physical, online, and legal, where individuals exercise their rights. The online space is increasingly impacted by digital technologies, which presents opportunities to exercise human rights, but also poses serious challenges to their realization.

The Internet has made it easier for human rights defenders to do their work. In recent years, it has become an invaluable tool for individuals to participate in governance; organize and coordinate public protests and advocacy campaigns; and to keep the spotlight on human rights cases that might otherwise lose public interest. It can create opportunities for human rights defenders, including those from marginalised communities, to neutralize the effects of the shrinking of physical civic space in their work to promote and protect human rights and to speak out against governments that violate international human rights law. The Internet allows these individuals to meet, find information that was previously unavailable or inaccessible, and to reach broader audiences.

Conversely, the Internet can be infiltrated, co-opted, or leveraged by governments to create additional and new forms of restrictions on the exercise of human rights and fundamental freedoms that are in contravention of international human rights law. This has a detrimental effect on human rights defenders and other members of civil society.

In many countries, human rights defenders are targeted through State-sponsored harassment, threats, disinformation, and through arrests for their human rights work. In some cases, human rights defenders have become victims of extra-judicial killings due to their commitment to promote human rights.

Oppression through the internet has especially detrimental impacts on human rights defenders who come from or are seeking to protect marginalised communities. They are often targeted and restricted from exercising their human rights, which causes them to suffer disproportionately serious consequences. For women human rights defenders, for instance, online risks could be disproportionate as attacks against them and their organizations, as empirical evidence reflects, are often more sexualized and frequent than those of their male counterparts.

Recent trends that threaten online civic space

Laws and policies that affect civic space online

Civil society presence online has created a space for activists to hold government officials accountable for their actions. Many governments have introduced and adopted laws, regulations, and policies that unduly restrict civic space directly and indirectly. Such measures have led to Internet shutdowns, account deactivation, undue restrictions on software and applications, and censorship through filtering and blocking. In particular, websites that spread, promote, or discuss human rights continue to be the target of arbitrary censorship and blocking. The problem is particularly acute in States where human rights, democracy, the rule of law, and accountable governance structures are lacking.

The FOC is concerned that some governments, disregarding the rule of law, have misused laws related to counter-terrorism, anti-corruption, anti-money laundering, national security, cybercrime and cybersecurity to target and silence civil society actors and human rights defenders. All counterterrorism and anti-cybercrime legislation and activities must always respect human rights obligations and commitments. In several cases, counter-terrorism and national security laws have been made the instrument to prosecute journalists to suppress their work, while anti-cybercrime laws have been applied in such a way as to target dissent online.

Laws and policies to unduly limit encryption and anonymity online

Encryption and anonymizing software can facilitate digital safety for human rights defenders. Some repressive governments may seek to undermine the work of human rights defenders by unduly restricting use of encryption and anonymizing software.

These restrictions raise concerns about improperly undermining privacy protections and illegitimately hindering human rights defenders' right to freedom of expression, including the freedom to seek, receive and impart information, and the right to freedom of association. Encryption and anonymizing software have also been employed by criminals and others to conceal malicious activities and evade the law, requiring States to address their impacts on national security and effective law enforcement. Any government restrictions on encryption and anonymity must be consistent with a State's international legal obligations. In particular, interference with privacy must not be arbitrary or unlawful.

The use of the Internet for harassment and intimidation of civil society

The FOC is concerned by technical measures being taken by malicious actors to gain access to private information, the use of bots, trolls, troll farms, spreading of disinformation, and microtargeting to discredit, harass, intimidate, threaten or de-platform human rights defenders. Women human rights defenders are especially at risk in these instances.

Call to Action

The FOC firmly believes in the value of free and open democratic and civic space, including online, and its positive effects on long-term political stability. The FOC calls on all governments to promote vibrant and resilient civic space, including respect for human rights and fundamental freedoms, democracy, and the rule of law, consistent with their obligations under the International Covenant for Civil and Political Rights in particular, which is central to the maintenance and development of an open, interoperable, reliable, and secure Internet.

Bearing in mind States' international obligations under international human rights law, the FOC calls upon

(a) all stakeholders to work together to ensure that the Internet is designed and governed in a manner that respects human rights and enables individuals to engage in civic space;

(b) governments, the private sector, international organizations, and civil society, to work together toward a shared approach—firmly grounded in respect for international human rights law—to evaluate, respond to, and remedy State-sponsored efforts to unduly restrict civic space, and business practices that inappropriately contribute to, facilitate, or cause restriction.

On laws and policies that intentionally or unintentionally affect civic space

The FOC calls on all governments to refrain from enacting laws and implementing policies that unduly restrict civic space.

Governments should consult where possible with civil society in the development of laws and policies, including those on counter-terrorism, national security, cybercrime and cybersecurity, as well those that impact encryption and anonymity online, to help ensure that these laws and policies are consistent with States' obligations under international human rights law.

The FOC calls on all governments to refrain from using counter-terrorism, national security, cybercrime, cyber-security, anti-terrorism and anti-cybercrime measures and laws to unduly limit the ability of human rights defenders to exercise their human rights. Any such legislation, new or existing, should be evaluated against potential adverse effects on human rights.

The FOC encourages governments to protect and promote civic space through laws and policies that expand access to emerging technologies such as blogs, private messaging apps, and over-the-top-services rather than restricting their use through overreaching regulation and the imposition of high compliance burdens that inhibit access.

The FOC recognizes the crucial role of the information and communication technology (ICT) sector to respect human rights. The FOC encourages companies to engage in multi-stakeholder initiatives and explore best practices in line with the UN Guiding Principles on Business and Human Rights.

[...]

On 25 June 2019, at the 41st session of the United Nations Human Rights Council, Australia delivered a national statement at the Clustered Interactive Dialogue with the Special Rapporteur on freedom of expression and the Special Rapporteur on the rights to peaceful assembly and association. An extract of that statement follows:

[...]

The interplay between surveillance and human rights is becoming increasingly complex as the adoption of cyber technology changes the way surveillance is conducted.

Data is a useful resource for states and non-state actors, yet the process of data collection and its storage can also pose risks to freedom of expression and privacy.

Australia's view, in line with international human rights law, is that no one should be subject to arbitrary or unlawful interference with their privacy.

We are committed to maintaining a comprehensive framework for the protection of individuals' personal information.

This includes appropriate safeguards and oversight mechanisms to ensure law enforcement and security agencies' access to telecommunications data is subject to strict accountability and oversight.

Cyber technology has opened up new ways by which individuals can exercise their rights to peaceful assembly and association through digital platforms, in particular social media.

But the growing use of these digital platforms has provided new opportunities for online surveillance. Safeguards and oversight mechanisms—like those found in Australian law—have not been implemented universally.

We would welcome views from both Special Rapporteurs on best practices for designing regulatory regimes that maintain freedoms of expression, and peaceful assembly and association while also ensuring that law enforcement and national security agencies can carry out their lawful functions.

[...]

On 25 June 2019, during the 41st session of the United Nations Human Rights Council in Geneva, Australia joined a Joint Statement made by the Freedom Online Coalition's Geneva Network Intervention during the Item 3 Clustered Interactive Dialogue with the Special Rapporteur on the rights to freedom of peaceful assembly and of association and the Special Rapporteur on the promotion and protection of the right to freedom of opinion and expression. An extract of that statement follows:

[...]

The Freedom Online Coalition unites 30 states who have committed to adoption and promotion of policies and practices, nationally and internationally, that promote the protection of human rights and fundamental freedoms online, in particular freedom of expression, the right to privacy and the freedom of peaceful assembly and association.

The Freedom Online Coalition is deeply concerned about shrinking civic and democratic spaces online as a result of State-sponsored obstruction of free expression, peaceful assembly, and free association, notably as it relates to human rights defenders and other members of civil society. State-sponsored obstruction of these rights is a direct challenge to the FOC's goal of protecting and promoting both the exercise of human rights online and an open and interoperable Internet.

We welcome the recommendation of the Special Rapporteur, that states should ensure that any interference with the rights to freedom of peaceful assembly and of association is 'prescribed by law' and is 'necessary in a democratic society in the interests of national security or public safety, public order, the protection of public health or morals or the protection of the rights and freedoms of others'.

We agree with the Special Rapporteur that network shutdowns too often fail to meet the established test for restrictions on the right of peaceful assembly. We would like to call on all governments to refrain from enacting laws and implementing policies that unduly restrict civic space.

[...]

7.18 *Human Rights Situations—Belarus*

On 1 July 2019, during the 41st session of the United Nations Human Rights Council in Geneva, Australia delivered a national statement at the Interactive Dialogue with the Special Rapporteur on the situation of human rights in Belarus. An extract of that statement follows:

[...]

We are encouraged by Belarus' engagement and cooperation with the international human rights system in recent years. However, we are disappointed that Belarus has continued its policy of non-engagement with the Special Rapporteur.

Australia shares the Special Rapporteur's concern, based on the information collected, that there have not been substantial improvements, either legally or in practice, in terms of respect for human rights in Belarus. This includes allegations of torture, ill-treatment or arbitrary detention, and the documented deterioration in relation to fundamental freedoms.

We note the death penalty continues to be used in Belarus, which is of deep concern to Australia. We support the Special Rapporteur's repeated recommendation that the Government of Belarus consider establishing a moratorium on executions as an initial step towards the abolition of the death penalty.

We call on the Government of Belarus to show leadership on the issue of human rights and to act on the recommendations set out in this report.

[...]

7.19 *Human Rights Situations—Burundi*

On 12 March 2019, at the 40th session of the United Nations Human Rights Council in Geneva, Australia delivered a national statement at the Interactive Dialogue with Commission of Inquiry on Burundi. The full text of that statement follows:

Australia thanks the Commission of Inquiry for its ongoing work on documenting human rights violations in Burundi. Australia is deeply concerned by the continued absence of independent international mechanisms in Burundi to investigate human rights violations and Burundi's lack of cooperation with the Commission of Inquiry. The recent closure of the UN Human Rights Country Office in Burundi is regrettable. We strongly encourage Burundi to engage constructively with all UN human rights mechanisms.

Australia is also concerned by the severe and arbitrary restrictions placed on non-governmental organisations in Burundi. We call on the Government of Burundi to support and protect organisations which promote the advancement of the human rights of Burundi citizens. We urge the Government of Burundi to pursue policies that promote gender and ethnic inclusivity through full engagement and cooperation with international human rights bodies and domestic civil society.

Australia is gravely concerned that serious human rights violations continue to be committed within a climate of impunity. We urge the Government of Burundi to ensure members of its security forces and Imbonerakure show restraint, and hold the perpetrators of these crimes to account.

We ask the Commission of Inquiry if there have been any reprisals against NGOs who have cooperated with your work.

On 17 September 2019, at the 42nd session of the United Nations Human Rights Council in Geneva, Australia delivered a national statement at the Interactive Dialogue with Commission of Inquiry on Burundi. An extract of that statement follows:

[...]

Australia supports the extension of the mandate of the Commission of Inquiry, which has provided critical oversight of the human rights situation in Burundi. We deeply regret the Government of Burundi's lack of cooperation with the Commission and other independent international mechanisms seeking to investigate human rights violations in Burundi. We urge the Government of Burundi to reconsider its closure of the UN Human Rights Country Office.

Australia is gravely concerned by the findings in the Commission of Inquiry's report in relation to violations of civil and political rights, including arbitrary arrest and detention, torture and sexual violence, and cases of summary executions and enforced disappearances. We are

AUSTRALIAN PRACTICE IN INTERNATIONAL LAW 2019   615

also gravely concerned about the Commission's finding that there are reasonable grounds to believe that crimes against humanity have been committed in Burundi, and further that these violations occur against a backdrop of widespread impunity. We note reports of agreements reached to repatriate Burundian refugees, and highlight the need for any returns to be safe, voluntary and dignified.

Australia calls on the Government of Burundi to support free and fair elections in 2020, and ensure the Imbonerakure and government security forces do not undermine democratic processes and political and media freedoms.

We ask the Commission to elaborate on reports of violence, intimidation and increasing control over non-governmental organisations in the lead up to next year's elections.

7.20   Human Rights Situations—Cambodia

On 26 September 2019, at the 42nd session of the United Nations Human Rights Council in Geneva, Australia delivered a national statement during the General Debate on Item 10. An extract of that statement follows:

[...]

Australia welcomes Cambodia's ongoing cooperation with the Office of the High Commissioner for Human Rights. We welcome Cambodia's rapid economic growth and progress towards Sustainable Development Goals, and urge Cambodia to take parallel steps to rebuild its democracy and to allow free and open political debate without intimidation.

[...]

7.21   Human Rights Situations—Central African Republic

On 20 March 2019, at the 40th session of the United Nations Human Rights Council in Geneva, Australia delivered a national statement at the High-level Interactive Dialogue on the human rights situation in the Central African Republic. An extract of that statement follows:

[...]

Australia welcomes the signing of the Political Agreement on Peace and Reconciliation by the Government of the Central African Republic (CAR) and many of the armed groups, and urges all parties to adhere to the agreement.

We call on the CAR Government to ensure accountability for human rights violations and abuses. Australia welcomes the commitment to establish a Commission on Truth, Justice, Reparation and Reconciliation as one mechanism to address human rights abuses. We encourage the CAR Government to develop transitional justice approaches that focus on the interests of victims and ensure their participation.

Australia remains concerned that the people of CAR are not adequately involved in current peace and reconciliation processes. Australia encourages all parties to recognise the value of local peace initiatives and ensure active engagement in the peace process by all actors, especially young people, women and those in rural and remote areas.

In addition, Australia is concerned by the continued prevalence of human rights abuses stemming from sectarian violence, particularly sexual and gender-based violence against women and girls and attacks on humanitarian aid workers. We urge the Government to protect these groups from violence and ensure that perpetrators are brought to justice.

We ask the Independent Expert what can be done by the CAR Government to guarantee victims of human rights abuses access to an effective remedy?

On 26 September 2019, at the 42nd session of the United Nations Human Rights Council in Geneva, Australia delivered a national statement during the Interactive Dialogue with the Independent Expert on the Central African Republic. An extract of that statement follows:

[...]

Australia welcomes moves to strengthen the ongoing peace process in the Central African Republic (CAR), but notes further efforts are needed from all parties to address religious and ethnic tensions, and reject the use of political violence.

Whilst we note efforts to reform the security sector, such developments must be accompanied by measures to combat impunity. These will be central to building confidence in the peace agreement and in public institutions. To this end, we call on the CAR Government to progress investigations and, where merited, prosecutions of those accused of human rights violations or abuses, including state officials.

Sexual and gender-based violence, conflict-related and otherwise, remains a key concern. Australia notes that all parties to the peace agreement have an obligation to prevent such offences and seek justice for victims, and to promote the active participation of women in reconciliation dialogues. Addressing barriers to their involvement in political processes will be particularly important in light of upcoming elections.

We are encouraged by the commencement of national consultations towards the establishment of a truth, justice, reparations and reconciliation commission, and urge all parties to engage constructively to ensure it leads to greater national unity.

We ask what efforts are being undertaken at a local level to support implementation of the peace agreement and rebuild social cohesion?

[...]

7.22   *Human Rights Situations—China*

On 12 March 2019, at the 40th session of the United Nations Human Rights Council in Geneva, Australia delivered a national statement at the General Debate on Item 4. An extract of that statement follows:

> [...]
>
> Australia remains concerned by the situation in Xinjiang, including reports of enforced disappearances, arbitrary detention and restrictions on freedom of movement.
>
> [...]

On 3 July 2019, at the 41st session of the United Nations Human Rights Council in Geneva, Australia delivered a national statement at the General Debate on Item 4. An extract of that statement follows:

> [...]
>
> Australia is concerned by reports of enforced disappearances, arbitrary detention and restrictions on freedom of movement of Uighurs and other ethnic minorities in Xinjiang. We call upon China to allow the OHCHR independent access to monitor and report on the human rights situation in Xinjiang.
>
> [...]

Australia was one of 22 co-signatories to a joint letter delivered to the President of the United Nations Human Rights Council on 8 July 2019, at the 41st session of the United Nations Human Rights Council in Geneva. The full text of the letter follows:

> We, the co-signatories to this letter, are concerned about credible reports of arbitrary detention in large-scale places of detention, as well as widespread surveillance and restrictions, particularly targeting Uighurs and other minorities in Xinjiang, China.

We recall China's obligations as a member of the UN Human Rights Council to 'uphold the highest standards in the promotion and protection of human rights and fully cooperate with the Council'.

We recall the 2018 concluding observations of the UN Committee on the Elimination of Racial Discrimination (CERD) in its review of China, which expressed concern about disturbing reports of large-scale arbitrary detentions of Uighurs, and other Muslim and minority communities. We also share concerns expressed by the High Commissioner for Human Rights and by several UN Special Procedures mandate holders in this regard.

We call on China to uphold its national laws and international obligations and to respect human rights and fundamental freedoms, including freedom of religion or belief, in Xinjiang and across China. We call also on China to refrain from the arbitrary detention and restrictions on freedom of movement of Uighurs, and other Muslim and minority communities in Xinjiang.

We welcome China's acceptance of a Universal Periodic Review recommendation to respond positively to a country visit request by the UN Special Rapporteur on freedom of religion or belief and urge China to allow meaningful access to Xinjiang for independent international observers, including for the UN High Commissioner for Human Rights. We further call on China to implement the related recommendations in the concluding observations of CERD. We ask the High Commissioner for Human Rights to keep the Human Rights Council regularly informed.

We request that this letter be recorded as a document of the 41st Session of the Human Rights Council and that it be published on the OHCHR website.

On 17 September 2019, at the 42nd session of the United Nations Human Rights Council in Geneva, Australia delivered a national statement at the General Debate on Item 4. An extract of that statement follows:

[...]
We have previously noted that Australia is deeply concerned by reports of enforced disappearances, mass detention, and restrictions on freedom of religion and freedom of movement of Uighurs and other ethnic minorities in Xinjiang. We urge China to allow meaningful access to Xinjiang for independent international observers, including for the UN High Commissioner for Human Rights.
[...]

On 29 October 2019, at the 74th Session of the UN General Assembly Third Committee in New York, Australia was one of 23 countries to join a Joint Statement (delivered by the UK) on Xinjiang during the Committee for the Elimination of Racial Discrimination. An extract of that statement follows:

> [...]
> We share the concerns raised by the Committee for the Elimination of Racial Discrimination in their August 2018 Concluding Observations on China regarding credible reports of mass detention; efforts to restrict cultural and religious practices; mass surveillance disproportionately targeting ethnic Uighurs; and other human rights violations and abuses in the Xinjiang Uighur Autonomous Region.
> We call on the Chinese government to uphold its national laws and international obligations and commitments to respect human rights, including freedom of religion or belief, in Xinjiang and across China. The Chinese government should urgently implement CERD's eight recommendations related to Xinjiang, including by refraining from the arbitrary detention of Uighurs and members of other Muslim communities. In view of these concerns, we call on all countries to respect the principle of non-refoulement.
> Furthermore, we call on the Chinese government to allow the Office of the United Nations High Commissioner for Human Rights and UN Special Procedures immediate unfettered, meaningful access to Xinjiang.
> [...]

On 17 November 2019, Australia's Minister for Foreign Affairs, Senator the Hon. Marise Payne, released a media statement raising Australia's concerns of human rights abuses taking place against Uighurs and other groups in Xinjiang. The full text of that media release follows:

> I am aware of the reports today of the Xinjiang papers. This follows the deeply disturbing video released in September.
> I have previously raised Australia's strong concerns about reports of mass detentions of Uighurs in Xinjiang. These disturbing reports today reinforce Australia's view and we reiterate those concerns.
> We have consistently called for China to cease the arbitrary detention of Uighurs and other groups.
> We have raised these concerns—and we will continue to raise them both bilaterally and in relevant international meetings.

On 18 November 2019, Australia's Minister for Foreign Affairs, Senator the Hon. Marise Payne, held a press conference in Sydney on Consular State of Play, detention of Uighurs in China, release of Timothy Weeks, Hong Kong, Pacific and Syria. Excerpts from that press conference follow:

> [...]
> Australia has raised our serious concerns about the detention and treatment of Uighurs and other religious minorities in Xinjiang. We have done that both directly to China and in appropriate international fora, whether that is the Human Rights Council or the UN itself. We will continue to do that. We are very concerned about those human rights issues.
> The entire report is concerning, including the treatment of the millions of—over a million individuals that we have seen detailed in that. That is arbitrary detention. There are other restrictive measures in place. We very much seek the Chinese Government's amelioration of these circumstances. They are not observant of appropriate human rights requirements.
> [...]

On 29 November 2019, Australia's Minister for Foreign Affairs, Senator the Hon. Marise Payne, was interviewed on Radio National. An excerpt from that interview follows:

> [...]
> We've consistently raised our concerns around the human rights situation in Xinjiang. It is important for those of us who are concerned about human rights levels to raise those concerns.
> [...]

7.23 *Human Rights Situations—Congo*

On 19 March 2019, at the 40th session of the United Nations Human Rights Council in Geneva, Australia delivered a national statement at the Enhanced Interactive Dialogue on the Democratic Republic of the Congo. An extract of that statement follows:

> [...]
> We commend the Democratic Republic of the Congo for holding recent elections. We call on the new Government to move swiftly to ensure accountability for human rights violations and abuses committed during the electoral period, and to strengthen the independence of national oversight institutions, ensuring they have the resources to fulfil their missions.

Australia remains concerned by media restrictions and shutdowns, including those that occurred during the electoral period. Democracy relies on an open exchange of views, including through peaceful demonstration, without fear of persecution or reprisals. We encourage the Government to safeguard freedoms of expression and assembly.

Reports of inter-communal violence highlight the need for well-functioning state institutions including police and judiciary. We urge the Government of the Democratic Republic of the Congo to thoroughly investigate alleged human rights violations by state actors, including reports of sexual and gender-based violence, and of arbitrary arrests and detentions without delay. Such measures to uphold the rule of law are vital, in order to better ensure protection of civilians and combat impunity.

We ask what action is being taken by political leaders to enhance accountability and respect for human rights among security forces?

On 8 July 2019, during the 41st session of the United Nations Human Rights Council in Geneva, Australia delivered a national statement during the Enhanced Interactive Dialogue on the Democratic Republic of the Congo. An extract of that statement follows:

[...]

We commend the Democratic Republic of the Congo for its recent pardoning of many political prisoners. We urge the Government to consider further releases and ensure that others are not detained or prosecuted for exercising their human rights.

Australia remains deeply concerned by the prevalence of sexual and gender-based violence, including against internally displaced populations and as a result of ongoing conflict in the east of the country. Noting the increasing number of abuses reportedly perpetrated by armed militia groups, as well as the alarming amount of alleged violations by state actors, we call on the Government of the Democratic Republic of the Congo to urgently institute security sector reforms.

Appropriate systems to report and advocate against human rights abuses and violations will be critical, especially in the anticipated context of a decreased United Nations presence. Australia encourages the Government to afford human rights defenders within its own system, and those from civil society, adequate public space and to safeguard them from persecution.

We ask what steps are being taken to ensure state institutions instil respect for human rights, and that those responsible for violations are brought to justice?

7.24 Human Rights Situations—The Democratic People's Republic of Korea

On 11 March 2019, at the 40th session of the United Nations Human Rights Council in Geneva, Australia delivered a national statement at the Interactive Dialogue with the Special Rapporteur on the situation of human rights in the Democratic People's Republic of Korea. The full text of that statement follows:

> Australia continues to be deeply concerned by the grave human rights situation in the DPRK. We call on the DPRK Government to take urgent action to halt all human rights violations. Respect for human rights is essential to achieve lasting peace and stability on the Korean Peninsula.
>
> Five years ago, the Commission of Inquiry on Human Rights in the DPRK reminded the world of the appalling human rights situation in the country. The COI, led by Australian former High Court Justice Michael Kirby, found that abuses perpetrated by the DPRK Government constituted no less than crimes against humanity.
>
> We are deeply saddened that on the fifth anniversary of the COI's report, little has changed. Widespread human rights violations continue in the DPRK today. Freedoms of expression, assembly, religion or belief remain non-existent. Arbitrary detention and forced labour, among other abuses, remain wide spread. We call on the DPRK Government to implement the COI's recommendations as a matter of urgency.
>
> The international community must maintain pressure on the DPRK Government to improve the human rights situation for its citizens and implement accountability measures. We continue to urge the DPRK to engage with UN processes and representatives, particularly by permitting the Special Rapporteur to visit the DPRK and participating constructively in its third Universal Periodic Review due this year.
>
> Special Rapporteur, if you could exhort the DPRK to make one change as a positive start, what would that small step be?

On 12 March 2019, at the 40th session of the United Nations Human Rights Council in Geneva, Australia delivered a national statement at the General Debate on Item 4. An extract of that statement follows:

> [...]
>
> Australia remains gravely concerned by the human rights situation in the Democratic People's Republic of Korea. We urge the DPRK to halt human rights abuses and engage constructively with UN processes to advance peace and stability on the Korean Peninsula.
>
> [...]

On 3 July 2019, at the 41st session of the United Nations Human Rights Council in Geneva, Australia delivered a national statement at the General Debate on Item 4. An extract of that statement follows:

> [...]
> Australia remains disturbed by the grave human rights situation in the Democratic People's Republic of Korea. We call on the DPRK to improve the living conditions of its people and recommit to global security through its complete, irreversible and verifiable denuclearisation.
> [...]

On 17 September 2019, at the 42nd session of the United Nations Human Rights Council in Geneva, Australia delivered a national statement at the General Debate on Item 4. An extract of that statement follows:

> [...]
> Australia deplores the widespread and systematic human rights violations committed by the Democratic People's Republic of Korea. We call on the DPRK to halt its WMD and ballistic missile program and improve the living conditions of its people.
> [...]

On 22 October 2019, at the 74th Session of the UN General Assembly Third Committee in New York, Australia delivered an intervention during the Interactive Dialogue with the Special Rapporteur on the situation of human rights in the Democratic People's Republic of Korea. The full text of that intervention follows:

> Australia continues to be deeply concerned by the grave human rights situation in the DPRK—we call on the DPRK Government to take urgent action to halt all human rights violations—respect for human rights is essential to achieve lasting peace and stability on the Korean Peninsula.
> We are saddened to see in the Special Rapporteur's report that widespread human rights violations continue, unabated, in the DPRK today—freedom of expression, assembly, religion or belief remain non-existent—arbitrary detention and forced labour, among other abuses, remain wide-spread.
> The international community must maintain pressure on the DPRK Government to improve the human rights situation for its citizens and implement accountability measures—we continue to urge the DPRK to engage with UN processes and representatives, including the Special

Rapporteur—we are concerned by the DPRK's recent request that UN agencies reduce their staff numbers in the country by the end of 2019, which will only impede the UN's ability to undertake its work on human rights and humanitarian issues in the DPRK.

7.25 *Human Rights Situations—Eritrea*

On 11 March 2019, at the 40th session of the United Nations Human Rights Council in Geneva, Australia delivered a national statement at the Enhanced Interactive Dialogue on Eritrea. An extract of that statement follows:

> [...]
>
> We welcome Eritrea's peace agreement with Ethiopia and hope this agreement will facilitate increased international cooperation and improve government transparency and accountability in Eritrea.
>
> Australia remains concerned by continued reports of forced labour and compulsory, prolonged national service in Eritrea. We call on the Government of Eritrea to introduce legislation that prohibits the use of forced labour, enforces reasonable time limits for national service and provides options for conscientious objection.
>
> While Eritrea has acceded to the Convention Against Torture, Australia is concerned by reports of torture, and arbitrary and indefinite detention. We are also concerned by reports of prisoners experiencing cruel, inhuman and degrading treatment and urge Eritrea to uphold international human rights conventions.
>
> Australia supports the mandate of the Special Rapporteur for the situation of human rights in Eritrea and calls on Eritrea to cooperate fully with the mandate. We urge the Government of Eritrea to implement the recommendations of the Commission of Inquiry's 2016 report. We further urge Eritrea to implement the 1997 Constitution to allow its citizens safe and full freedom of expression and freedom of religion.

7.26 *Human Rights Situations—Georgia*

On 22 March 2019, during the 40th session of the United Nations Human Rights Council in Geneva, Australia delivered a general comment on the Resolution on cooperation with Georgia. An extract of that statement follows:

> [...]
>
> Australia is a strong and consistent supporter of Georgia's sovereignty and territorial integrity. We do not recognise the claims to independence of the Georgian regions of Abkhazia and South Ossetia.

We remain concerned by the lack of progress in the Office of the High Commissioner being granted access to these Georgian regions. This resolution reaffirms the need for unimpeded access to Georgia's occupied territories by human rights mechanisms.

As this resolution stresses, the authorities in control of the Georgian regions of Abkhazia and South Ossetia have a responsibility to uphold human rights and fundamental freedoms.

The recent tragic incident in the Gali district in Georgia's region of Abkhazia demonstrated the important role which the transparency promoted by international monitoring mechanisms can play, as well as underlining the risks of cultivating impunity surrounding human rights situations.

It is fitting for Georgia to put forward this resolution, as these regions are integral parts of Georgia. Continued international human rights engagement and reporting can help prevent further deterioration of the situation.

Australia supports resolution L.24 and calls on all members of the Council to do likewise.

On 10–11 July 2019, during the 41st session of the United Nations Human Rights Council in Geneva, Australia delivered a national statement during the item 10 General Debate. An extract of that statement follows:

[...]

Australia acknowledges the efforts of the OHCHR to strengthen the promotion and protection of human rights in Georgia. We welcome efforts by the Government of Georgia to work with the OHCHR to bring national laws, policies and procedures in line with international human rights standards.

We also commend the Government's cooperation during last year's visit by the Independent Expert on protection against violence and discrimination based on sexual orientation and gender identity. We encourage the Government to consider carefully the recommendations in the Independent Expert's report.

Australia is a strong and consistent supporter of Georgia's sovereignty and territorial integrity. We do not recognise the claims to independence of the Georgian regions of Abkhazia and Tskhinvali / South Ossetia. We are concerned by the lack of information about the human rights situation in these regions.

We support the OHCHR's call to authorities in control in these regions to grant access to international and regional human rights mechanisms.

[...]

On 26 September 2019, at the 42nd session of the United Nations Human Rights Council in Geneva, Australia delivered a national statement during the General Debate on Item 10. An extract of that statement follows:

[…]

Australia is a strong and consistent supporter of Georgia's sovereignty and territorial integrity. We do not recognise Abkhazia and South Ossetia's claims to independence and we reject continued steps by the authorities in control of those regions to undermine Georgia's territorial integrity. We welcome the OHCHR report reaffirming the need for unimpeded access to Georgia's occupied territories, and call on the authorities in control of these regions to uphold human rights. Continued engagement and reporting are critical to prevent further deterioration of the situation.

[…]

7.27   *Human Rights Situations—Libya*

On 25 September 2019, at the 42nd session of the United Nations Human Rights Council, Australia delivered a national statement during the Interactive Dialogue on the High Commissioner's Oral Update on Libya. An extract of that statement follows:

[…]

Australia is concerned that the humanitarian situation in Libya, particularly around Tripoli, continues to deteriorate, with mounting civilian casualties. Australia deplores the deliberate targeting of civilian infrastructure and is concerned the forced closure of Mitiga airport is restricting the entry of essential humanitarian relief.

Australia urges all parties to comply with international humanitarian law and international human rights law. It is essential that all parties allow timely, unimpeded, sustained and safe humanitarian access throughout the country. Australia is deeply concerned by reports of attacks on journalists and widespread sexual and gender-based violence—those responsible must be held to account.

The only solution to the current impasse in Libya is through a ceasefire and an inclusive and Libyan-owned political process. Australia calls on all parties to the conflict to commit to a UN-led political mediation aimed at the establishment of a transitional government representing all Libyans. We urge all parties to prepare for a new constitution and credible democratic elections.

AUSTRALIAN PRACTICE IN INTERNATIONAL LAW 2019

We ask the Deputy High Commissioner how best can the international community help to build conditions conducive to a ceasefire and reconciliation in Libya?

7.28 Human Rights Situations—Mali

On 19 March 2019, at the 40th session of the United Nations Human Rights Council in Geneva, Australia delivered a national statement at the Interactive Dialogue with the Independent Expert on Mali. An extract of that statement follows:

[...]

Australia remains deeply concerned by the security situation in central and northern Mali. In particular, Australia is disturbed by reports that human rights violations and abuses are being committed against civilians by parties on all sides of the conflict, including the Malian security forces.

We urge the Government of Mali to sustain its focus on restoring state authority throughout the country, conduct inquiries into all alleged human rights violations and abuses, and take urgent steps to progress the peace process, including ensuring the participation of women.

Australia is concerned by the rate of sexual and gender-based violence against women in the country, including rates of female genital mutilation and child marriage. We note that Mali does not have a law specifically addressing gender-based violence and encourage the passage of a 2017 bill on gender-based violence into law.

Australia is also concerned by the impact of Mali's ongoing instability on children. The current conflict has prevented hundreds of thousands of children from attending school. We urge the Government of Mali to make every effort to promote access to education.

We ask the Independent Expert to elaborate on progress made towards addressing violence against women and girls, particularly sexual violence and female genital mutilation.

7.29 Human Rights Situations—Myanmar

On 11 March 2019, at the 40th session of the United Nations Human Rights Council in Geneva, Australia delivered a national statement at the Interactive Dialogue with Special Rapporteur on Myanmar. An extract of that statement follows:

[...]

We call on the Government of Myanmar to re-engage with the Special Rapporteur and allow her to visit Myanmar in order to fulfil her mandate.

Australia is disturbed by the renewal of violence in Rakhine state and urges all parties to cease hostilities, respect international law, including human rights, and uphold commitments to dialogue for peace. Further conflict makes finding a durable solution to the Rohingya crisis even more difficult.

We welcome the unilateral ceasefire declared by the Myanmar armed forces in Kachin and Shan states and hope it can be extended. We reiterate our call on Myanmar to lift restrictions on humanitarian access to Kachin, Shan and Rakhine states, and urge it to urgently establish conditions for the safe, voluntary, dignified and sustainable return of displaced Rohingya and other communities.

Australia supports the Independent Investigative Mechanism for Myanmar and calls on Myanmar's Government and Independent Commission of Enquiry to cooperate fully with the mechanism. Perpetrators of human rights violations must be held to account.

Australia acknowledges that Myanmar faces challenges as it seeks to embed democratic reforms and achieve national peace and reconciliation. Recognising that a free media is an essential component of democracy, we remain deeply troubled by the ongoing imprisonment of journalists Wa Lone and Kyaw Soe Oo, and urge the Government to find a solution leading to their release.

Australia would be interested to hear from the Special Rapporteur how regional partners can best help support the establishment and operation of the Independent Investigative Mechanism.

On 2–3 July 2019, during the 41st session of the United Nations Human Rights Council in Geneva, Australia delivered a national statement during the Interactive Dialogue with the Special Rapporteur on Myanmar. The full text of the statement follows:

Australia thanks the Special Rapporteur for her update. We note her findings with deep concern, and continue to urge Myanmar to resume cooperation with the Special Rapporteur and allow her to visit Myanmar to fulfil her mandate.

Australia remains concerned by ongoing fighting in Rakhine State and calls on all sides to cease hostilities and protect civilians. The current violence is a major challenge for the national peace process, and further deterioration in the security environment makes finding a durable solution to the Rohingya crisis even more difficult.

In Rakhine, Kachin and Shan states, we urge Myanmar to work with humanitarian agencies to enable humanitarian access for those in need.

Freedom of expression is essential to democracy. Australia welcomes the recent pardon of journalists Wa Lone and Kyaw Soe Oo. However, many other journalists, artists, and activists face charges for undertaking activities central to their work. We urge the government to ensure that Myanmar's legislative framework allows for unimpeded participation in the public sphere, including for the media.

Australia recognises the challenges Myanmar continues to face as it navigates complex political and economic transitions. As a regional partner, we will support Myanmar's efforts toward national peace and reconciliation. Accountability is an important element of peace and reconciliation.

Australia would be interested to hear from the Special Rapporteur how regional partners can best help progress the peace process and support Myanmar's democratic transition.

On 10 July 2019, during the 41st session of the United Nations Human Rights Council in Geneva, Australia delivered a national statement during the Interactive Dialogue with the UN High Commissioner for Human Rights. An extract of that statement follows:

[...]

Australia remains concerned by ongoing conflict in Rakhine State, which is affecting civilians in many communities. We call on the Arakan Army and Myanmar military to cease hostilities, exercise restraint, respect international humanitarian law and uphold commitments to dialogue for peace. The current violence makes finding a lasting solution to the Rohingya crisis even more difficult.

A sustainable solution requires Myanmar to create conditions conducive to the safe, dignified, voluntary and sustainable return of displaced Rohingya, including by lifting discriminatory restrictions on freedom of movement and granting equal access to services. Further implementing the recommendations of the Rakhine Advisory Commission is vital in this regard.

Australia recognises these are complex challenges, and is committed to working with Myanmar, Bangladesh and other partners towards a long-term and durable solution to the Rohingya crisis. We welcome ASEAN involvement in these efforts.

Those responsible for human rights violations must be held to account. Australia supports the Independent Investigative Mechanism for Myanmar and reiterates its call for Myanmar's Government and Independent Commission of Enquiry to cooperate fully with the mechanism once operational.

On 10 September 2019, at the 42nd session of the United Nations Human Rights Council in Geneva, Australia delivered a national statement in the Item 2 General Debate and Presentation of the report of the International Investigative Mechanism for Myanmar. An extract of the statement follows:

[...]

Australia also thanks the International Investigative Mechanism for Myanmar for its report on the progress and priorities of its important work.

Accountability for international crimes is a crucial part of any long-term and durable solution to the crisis in Myanmar. Continued impunity would likely lead to further violence and deter those displaced from returning to their homes.

Australia has strongly supported the establishment of the Mechanism, and we commend the UN's expeditious efforts to put in place arrangements for its operationalisation.

We urge Myanmar to cooperate with the Mechanism as it carries out its mandate.

On 16 September 2019, at the 42nd session of the United Nations Human Rights Council in Geneva, Australia delivered a national statement at the Interactive Dialogue with the Special Rapporteur on Myanmar. An extract of that statement follows:

[...]

Australia remains gravely concerned by the situation in Rakhine State. We reiterate our calls for timely, unimpeded, sustained and safe humanitarian access in Rakhine State and other conflict-affected areas. We urge Myanmar to create conditions for the voluntary, safe, dignified and sustainable return of displaced people to Rakhine State, including through implementing the recommendations of the Advisory Commission on Rakhine State.

AUSTRALIAN PRACTICE IN INTERNATIONAL LAW 2019

Ongoing clashes among ethnic armed groups and the Myanmar military are a continuing concern. Fighting in northern Shan has displaced and killed civilians, and further complicates the national peace process. We welcome recent ceasefire announcements from the Tatmadaw and the Northern Alliance, and call on all parties to cease hostilities and protect civilians.

We acknowledge steps taken by the Myanmar Government towards the ratification of international human rights instruments, and welcome Myanmar's planned ratification of the Optional Protocol to the Convention on the Rights of the Child on the Involvement of Children in Armed Conflict.

Australia will continue to support Myanmar's efforts toward full democracy, a cornerstone of which is freedom of expression. In this regard, we welcome the withdrawal of the lawsuit against Reverend Samson. We urge Myanmar to amend restrictive laws and end restrictions on rights to ensure a safe and enabling environment for civil society, journalists and lawyers.

On 17 September 2019, at the 42nd session of the United Nations Human Rights Council in Geneva, Australia delivered a national statement at the Interactive Dialogue with the Fact-Finding Mission on Myanmar. The full text of that statement follows:

Australia thanks the Fact-Finding Mission for its work over the last two years, and its thorough reports and papers.

Australia remains deeply disturbed by the mission's conclusions that war crimes and crimes against humanity have occurred in Myanmar. Australia condemns these atrocities in the strongest terms. We are particularly concerned by the mission's findings that there are reasonable grounds to conclude that acts of genocide have likely occurred against the Rohingya.

This final report highlights the continued discrimination, marginalisation and violence suffered by Myanmar's ethnic groups, including the Rohingya. We are concerned by groups, including with respect to sexual and gender-based violence. We are also troubled by the growing use of criminal defamation charges to silence those who report on these abuses and the broader conflict.

Australia recognises the complex challenges in Myanmar and remains committed to assisting Myanmar to continue on a path to democracy, accountability and reconciliation.

Australia commends the mission's efforts to document human rights violations and to advance accountability for perpetrators and justice for victims. We look forward to the work of the Independent Investigative Mechanism for Myanmar in taking this important mandate forward.

On 22 October 2019, at the 74th Session of the UN General Assembly Third Committee in New York, Australia delivered an intervention during the Interactive Dialogue with the Independent Investigative Mechanism on Myanmar. An extract of that statement follows:

[...]
Australia strongly supported the establishment of the Mechanism. We commend the UN's expeditious efforts to put in place arrangements for its operationalisation.

Australia recognises the complex challenges in Myanmar and remains committed to assisting Myanmar to continue on a path of democracy and reconciliation.

An important part of this is pursuing accountability for the atrocities committed in Myanmar and justice for the victims.

We urge Myanmar to cooperate with the Mechanism as it carries out its mandate.

We acknowledge that the Mechanism's mandate is substantial and its investigations will need to be thorough and comprehensive.

Australia will continue to support the Mechanism to pursue accountability for serious international crimes.

Australia is interested to hear the Mechanism's views on how States can support its work.

On 22 October 2019, at the 74th Session of the UN General Assembly Third Committee in New York, Australia delivered an intervention during the Interactive Dialogue with the Special Rapporteur on the situation of human rights in Myanmar. An extract of that statement follows:

[...]
Australia remains gravely concerned by the situation in Rakhine State, as reported by the Special Rapporteur.

Ongoing clashes among ethnic armed groups and the Myanmar military, including the use of heavy artillery fire in civilian areas, remain a concern. We call on all parties to cease hostilities, protect civilians, and return to meaningful dialogue.

AUSTRALIAN PRACTICE IN INTERNATIONAL LAW 2019

We are disturbed by the large number of people displaced by conflict in Rakhine State and elsewhere in Myanmar, and reiterate our calls for full and effective access for humanitarian agencies to deliver much-needed assistance.

We urge Myanmar to create conditions for the voluntary, safe, dignified and sustainable return of displaced people to Rakhine State, including through implementing the recommendations of the Advisory Commission on Rakhine State.

We welcome the Myanmar Parliament's agreement to ratify the Optional Protocol to the Convention on the Rights of the Child on the Involvement of Children in Armed Conflict, and encourage Myanmar to continue its efforts towards signing the International Covenant on Civil and Political Rights.

Australia will continue to support Myanmar's efforts toward a more democratic system, a cornerstone of which is freedom of expression.

We welcome the withdrawal of the lawsuit against Reverend Samson but note that many other journalists, artists and activists continue to face charges for undertaking activities central to their work.

We urge Myanmar to ensure that its legislative framework allows for a safe and enabling environment for civil society, journalists and lawyers.

Australia would be interested to hear from the Special Rapporteur how regional partners can best help progress the peace process and support Myanmar's democratic transition.

7.30   *Human Rights Situations—Nicaragua*

On 10–11 July 2019, during the 41st session of the United Nations Human Rights Council in Geneva, Australia delivered a national statement during the item 10 General Debate. An extract of that statement follows:

[...]

We express serious concern at ongoing human rights violations and abuses in Nicaragua.

We urge the Government of Nicaragua to respect and protect the rights and security of its citizens, and to cease immediately the unlawful arrests, arbitrary detentions and repression of public protests.

We call on the Government to honour the agreement signed at the National Dialogue and immediately release, as the agreement states, those who have been imprisoned.

We call on the Government to resume its cooperation with the OHCHR and adopt independent mechanisms to investigate reported violations and abuses particularly since the commencement of protests on 18 April 2018.

[...]

On 10 September 2019, during the 42nd session of the United Nations Human Rights Council in Geneva, Australia delivered a national statement at the Enhanced Interactive Dialogue on the High Commissioner for Human Rights' report on Nicaragua. An extract of that statement follows:

[...]

Australia is deeply concerned by ongoing serious human rights violations and abuses in Nicaragua, which have forced some 60,000 Nicaraguans to flee, the vast majority to Costa Rica.

The Government's repression of political dissent has been severe and has resulted in hundreds of deaths and arbitrary detentions. We are seriously concerned at the ongoing threat to journalists and the media. Government attacks have forced more than 100 journalists into exile.

The Government has persecuted human rights defenders and civil society organisations. Women, as well as indigenous and LGBTI minorities, are disproportionately affected, facing sexual and gender-based violence, threats, and acts of intimidation.

Australia urges the Government of Nicaragua to respect the rights and security of its citizens, stop the violent repression of political dissent, and respect the population's right to peaceful protest.

We again call on the Government to resume cooperation with international human rights organisations, and to restore or adopt relevant and impartial mechanisms of investigation and transitional justice.

We ask the High Commissioner how the international community can support her office, and other international human rights organisations, to engage Nicaragua to prevent further human rights violations.

7.31   *Human Rights Situations—Saudi Arabia*

On 7 March 2019, during the 40th session of the United Nations Human Rights Council in Geneva, Australia joined a Joint Statement (delivered by Iceland) on Saudi Arabia in the Interactive Dialogue with the UN High Commissioner for Human Rights. An extract of that statement follows:

[...]

While acknowledging the spirit of modernization and reform embodied by the Saudi Vision 2030, we express significant concerns about reports of continuing arrests and arbitrary detentions of human rights defenders in the Kingdom of Saudi Arabia, including women's rights activists.

We are particularly concerned about the use of the counter-terrorism law and other national security provisions against individuals peacefully exercising their rights and freedoms. Human rights defenders and civil society groups can and should play a vital role in the process of reform which the Kingdom is pursuing.

We join the High Commissioner and Special Rapporteurs in their calls upon the Saudi authorities to release all individuals, including Loujain al-Hathloul, Eman al-Nafjan, Aziza al-Yousef, Nassima al-Sadah, Samar Badawi, Nouf Abdelaziz, Hatoon al-Fassi, Mohammed Al-Bajadi, Amal Al-Harbi and Shadan al-Anezi, detained for exercising their fundamental freedoms.

We condemn in the strongest possible terms the killing of journalist Jamal Khashoggi, which Saudi Arabia has confirmed took place in its consulate in Istanbul. The circumstances of Mr. Khashoggi's death reaffirm the need to protect journalists and to uphold the right to freedom of expression around the world. Investigations into the killing must be prompt; effective and thorough; independent and impartial; and transparent. Those responsible must be held to account.

We call upon Saudi Arabia to disclose all information available and to fully cooperate with all investigations into the killing, including the human rights inquiry by the Special Rapporteur on extrajudicial, summary or arbitrary executions.

Finally, we call on Saudi Arabia to take meaningful steps to ensure that all members of the public, including human rights defenders and journalists, can freely and fully exercise their rights to freedoms of expression, opinion and association, including online, without fear of reprisals.

[...]

On 23 September 2019, during the 42nd session of the United Nations Human Rights Council in Geneva, Australia delivered a Joint Statement on behalf of a group of States on Saudi Arabia. An extract of that statement follows:

[...]

Before I begin, we wish to express our condemnation of the reckless attacks on Saudi Arabian oil facilities on 14 September. The deliberate targeting of civilian infrastructure is against international humanitarian law.

Mr President

The Vienna Declaration and Programme of Action emphasises that it is the duty of States to promote and protect all human rights and fundamental freedoms, regardless of their political, economic and cultural systems. It expresses grave concern at continuing human rights violations in all parts of the world.

We welcome recent reforms in the Kingdom of Saudi Arabia, including the announcement in August that restrictions on the rights of women to travel will be lifted and that they can be the legal guardian of children. These changes follow other reforms on women's employment and education. We acknowledge the spirit of modernisation and reform embodied by the Saudi Vision 2030.

However, we remain deeply concerned at the human rights situation in Saudi Arabia. Civil society actors in Saudi Arabia still face persecution and intimidation. Human rights defenders, women's rights activists, journalists and dissidents remain in detention, or under threat. We are concerned at reports of torture, arbitrary detention, enforced disappearances, unfair trials, and harassment of individuals engaged in promoting and defending human rights, their families and colleagues.

Over the last year, this Council has given serious consideration to the murder of Mr Jamal Khashoggi in October 2018 at Saudi Arabia's Consulate in Istanbul. It is important that truth be established and accountability be achieved, both for Mr Khashoggi's loved ones and to ensure the principles of the VDPA are respected. We acknowledge the Special Rapporteur on extrajudicial killings, summary or arbitrary executions for her detailed and important investigation into this matter.

In line with its obligations as a HRC member and the standards articulated by the VDPA, we urge Saudi Arabia to uphold the highest standards in the promotion and protection of human rights and fully cooperate with the Council, including by accepting visits by relevant Special Procedures Mandate Holders.

We urge Saudi Arabia to redouble its human rights reform efforts; we encourage Saudi Arabia to ratify the International Covenant on Civil and Political Rights and the International Covenant on Economic, Social and Cultural Rights; we call for an end to impunity for torture and extrajudicial killings; and we appeal to Saudi Arabia to end its use of the death penalty.

[...]

7.32 *Human Rights Situations—Somalia*

On 25 September 2019, at the 42nd session of the United Nations Human Rights Council in Geneva, Australia delivered a national statement during the Interactive Dialogue with the Independent Expert on Somalia. An extract of that statement follows:

> [...]
>
> We commend Somalia for achieving progress in its 'human rights landscape', in the words of the Independent Expert. We acknowledge this significant achievement in the context of ongoing conflict and security challenges.
>
> Australia also commends Somalia's continued engagement with human rights treaty bodies and the Human Rights Council and its mechanisms.
>
> Australia is concerned, however, by continuing serious human rights violations and abuses in Somalia. We again urge Somalia to expedite the establishment of an independent, national human rights institution to help build a stronger framework for the promotion and protection of human rights. We also encourage the Government to enact a national disability bill.
>
> Australia is deeply concerned by the high levels of sexual and gender-based violence against women and girls in Somalia. We urge Somalia to address this as a matter of urgency, including through finalising and implementing the *Sexual Offences Bill* and working to end impunity in cases of sexual and gender-based violence.
>
> Australia is also concerned by the continued intimidation, harassment and arrest of journalists and we urge Somalia to promote and protect the right to freedom of expression.
>
> In his report, the Independent Expert highlights the urgent need for a new constitution in Somalia. How can the international community work with the Government of Somalia to ensure the human rights of all Somalis are protected in the new constitution?

7.33 *Human Rights Situations—South Sudan*

On 12 March 2019, at the 40th session of the United Nations Human Rights Council in Geneva, Australia delivered a national statement at the Interactive Dialogue with the Commission on South Sudan. The full text of that statement follows:

Australia thanks the Commission on Human Rights in South Sudan for its report and is pleased that the Government of South Sudan continues to support the Commission's work.

Australia welcomes the signing of the Revitalised Agreement on the Resolution to the Conflict in the Republic of South Sudan (R-ARCSS) but remains concerned by continuing insecurity and obstructions impeding humanitarian assistance.

Australia condemns in the strongest possible terms on-going violence against civilians, including sexual and gender-based violence in South Sudan. Its use as a tactic of warfare by all parties to the conflict, the increased normalisation of such violence and the barriers to justice and security for women and girls remain deeply concerning. Australia calls on the Government of South Sudan to hold the perpetrators to account and to take active steps in addressing violence in all its forms.

Australia deplores the serious human rights violations and abuses committed by all parties to the conflict, as well as the shrinking civic space for journalists and civil society due to increased censorship and self-censorship. Reports of arbitrary arrests, detention and torture carried out by the National Security Service and SPLA Military Intelligence are deeply concerning. We urge the government to end forced disappearances.

Australia supports the continuation of the Commission's mandate. We ask the Commission what steps must be taken to ensure justice for victims of sexual and gender-based violence in South Sudan.

On 16 September 2019, at the 42nd session of the United Nations Human Rights Council in Geneva, Australia delivered a national statement at the Interactive Dialogue with Commission on Human Rights in South Sudan. An extract of that statement follows:

[...]

Australia welcomes the meeting between President Salva Kiir and Dr. Riek Machar in Juba in September and their recommitment to forming a transitional government. Full implementation of the Revitalised Agreement on the Resolution to the Conflict in the Republic of South Sudan (R-ARCSS), including armed forces unification and transitional justice mechanisms, are key to a stable future for the South Sudanese people.

Australia reiterates its condemnation of continuing violence against civilians. In July 2019, it was reported that over 100 civilians were brutally killed in Central Equatoria by government and rebel forces. Cases

AUSTRALIAN PRACTICE IN INTERNATIONAL LAW 2019 639

of sexual violence also appear in the report. The normalisation of such sexual and gender-based violence is deeply concerning. Australia calls on the Government of South Sudan to hold the perpetrators to account and to take active steps in addressing all forms of violence.

Australia is also alarmed by the shrinking civic space for journalists and civil society in South Sudan and reports of arbitrary arrests, detention and torture carried out by the National Security Service. We urge the government to end forced disappearances.

Australia asks the Commission what steps must be taken to ensure justice for victims of sexual and gender-based violence in South Sudan and for an update on plans to establish a special court to handle such crimes?

7.34 *Human Rights Situations—Sri Lanka*

On 20 March 2019, at the 40th session of the United Nations Human Rights Council in Geneva, Australia delivered a national statement at the Interactive Dialogue with the High Commissioner on Sri Lanka. An extract of that statement follows:

[...]

We commend Sri Lanka for continuing to constructively engage with UN human rights processes, and for its commitment to implementing Resolution 30/1.

We welcome Sri Lanka's co-sponsorship of Resolution 40/1 as a positive demonstration of this commitment, and encourage Sri Lanka to deliver its transitional justice agenda in a timely and effective way.

We recognise Sri Lanka's progress towards establishing credible transitional justice mechanisms and in returning military occupied land. In particular, we welcome the progress made by Office of Missing Persons Commissioners in the Office's first year of operation. We also welcome steps taken to establish an Office of Reparations, and hope to see Commissioners appointed and the Office operationalised soon. We encourage progress towards counter-terrorism legislation in line with international standards.

Australia supports the extension of the process established by Resolution 30/1, recognising that more needs to be done to promote truth-seeking, accountability, justice and reconciliation in Sri Lanka.

We endorse the High Commissioner's call for Sri Lanka to demonstrate sustained commitment and leadership to move its reconciliation and accountability agenda forward.

640 AUSTRALIAN YEAR BOOK OF INTERNATIONAL LAW VOLUME 38

Reconciliation in accordance with democratic principles and freedoms is in Sri Lanka's national interest, and is crucial to its long-term peace and prosperity.

Australia will continue to offer practical support to our Indian Ocean neighbour.

7.35   *Human Rights Situations—Syria*

On 12 March 2019, at the 40th session of the United Nations Human Rights Council in Geneva, Australia delivered a national statement at the Interactive Dialogue with the Commission of Inquiry on Syria. The full text of that statement follows:

Australia thanks the Commission of Inquiry for its report. We are deeply concerned by the widespread and ongoing human rights violations and abuses outlined in the report.

Australia strongly supports the long-standing prohibition on the use of chemical weapons, an illegal and morally abhorrent practice. We support the Commission of Inquiry's ongoing investigations into an alleged chemical attack in November 2018. As Australia previously stated to this Council, the repeated use of chemical weapons is a dark legacy of shame for the Syrian authorities and their backers. Those responsible must be identified and held to account, because the use of chemical weapons anytime, anywhere, and under any circumstances is unjustifiable and unacceptable.

We are particularly troubled by reports of arbitrary arrests and detentions in areas that have returned to Syrian government control. The situation of those who have been abducted is also of grave concern, as are reports of the custodial deaths of Syrian civilians.

We note the importance of ensuring the safe, dignified and voluntary return of Syrian refugees and internally displaced persons. We call on the Syrian Government to make all efforts to create the conditions for returns to occur, including by engaging substantively in a credible political process, in line with UN Security Council resolution 2254. We underscore the importance of timely, unimpeded and sustained humanitarian access to all areas in Syria.

The Syrian regime is not the only perpetrator of human rights abuses. We deplore the abuse of children's rights such as the denial of education to girls and the forced conscription of boys in Hay'at Tahrir al-Sham-controlled areas, as well as the systematic terrorisation of the population by Da'esh and other extremists. The conflict is far from over. We call on all parties to exercise restraint and to respect and protect the human rights of all people.

We would like to ask the Commission of Inquiry whether a meaningful accountability process is a precondition for the return of Syrians displaced by the conflict?

On 2 July 2019, during the 41st session of the United Nations Human Rights Council in Geneva, Australia delivered a national statement at the Interactive Dialogue with the Commission of Inquiry on the Syrian Arab Republic. An extract of that statement follows:

[...]

Australia condemns unequivocally all human rights violations and abuses, and violations of international humanitarian law, in Syria by all parties.

We are gravely concerned by the recent escalation of violence in north-western Syria, including the reported deaths of more than 230 civilians since April and unlawful damage to 26 health facilities and 37 schools. We also condemn Hayat Tahrir al-Sham's abuses within Idlib and its indiscriminate attacks on regime-held territory. Accountability for violations of international law remains critical, and civilians and civilian infrastructure must be protected. Counter-terrorism objectives do not absolve states or governments of their obligations under international human rights and humanitarian law.

Australia supports the UN Secretary General's recent call for those with influence, particularly Russia and Turkey, to stabilise the situation in Idlib without delay. All relevant parties should adhere to the 2017 agreement that established Idlib as a 'deescalation' zone, and the 2018 Sochi agreement establishing the Idlib de-militarised zone.

Australia calls on all parties to the conflict to allow timely, safe, unhindered and sustained humanitarian access based on greatest need.

We remain concerned by reports of arbitrary arrests, detentions and killings in areas returned to regime control. The Syrian regime should clarify the fate of those disappeared, detained, tortured or killed by Syrian state apparatus over the past eight years as a matter of urgency.

Australia maintains the strongest possible position that the use of chemical weapons anytime, anywhere, and under any circumstances is unjustifiable and unacceptable.

We would be interested to hear from the Commission of Inquiry on how you are adapting your methods of work given changing circumstances on the ground?

On 12 July 2019, during the 41st session of the United Nations Human Rights Council in Geneva, Australia delivered an explanation of vote for the Resolution on human rights in Syria. An extract of that explanation follows:

[...]

This resolution shines a spotlight on the grave human rights violations in Syria. It reflects the core role of this council and its determination to strengthen the promotion and protection of human rights, in this case for the Syrian people.

As highlighted in this resolution and noted by the Commission of Inquiry, the escalation of violence in Idlib is causing immense suffering for civilians. We condemn in the strongest terms the use of barrel bombs, and unlawful attacks on civilian infrastructure, including hospitals and schools. We call on parties in Idlib to respect previously agreed ceasefires.

Importantly, this resolution urges all parties to comply with their obligations under international humanitarian law and international human rights law. International law is clear—there is no justification for indiscriminate and disproportionate attacks on civilians. Counter-terrorism objectives do not absolve states of their obligations.

We remain concerned by continued widespread arbitrary detention and disappearances, reports of mass execution and torture, and forced displacement noted in the text. We call on the Syrian regime to release the thousands of Syrians arbitrarily detained, and allow internally displaced people to return to their homes.

We urge all parties to allow timely, unhindered and safe humanitarian access, particularly in areas that have come under the control of Syrian authorities, and cease attacks on agricultural areas. We call on the regime to respect its obligations under the Chemical Weapons Convention and Security Council Resolution 2118. Australia reiterates its position, in the strongest possible terms, that the use of chemical weapons anytime, anywhere and under any circumstances is unjustifiable and unacceptable.

[...]

On 17 September 2019, during the 42nd session of the United Nations Human Rights Council in Geneva, Australia delivered a national statement at the Interactive Dialogue with the Commission of Inquiry on the Syrian Arab Republic. The full text of that statement follows:

Australia condemns unequivocally all violations of international humanitarian law and all violations and abuses of human rights in Syria.

AUSTRALIAN PRACTICE IN INTERNATIONAL LAW 2019   643

We are deeply concerned by recent attacks on medical personnel and facilities, schools, and other civilian infrastructure in the Idlib de-escalation area. The UN has recorded more than 1000 civilian fatalities since April this year, predominantly caused by indiscriminate bombardment by the Syrian regime and its allies.

Reaffirming our call at the 41st session of this Council, we continue to urge all parties to adhere to the 2017 agreement that established Idlib as a 'de-escalation' zone, and the 2018 Sochi agreement establishing the Idlib de-militarised zone. Counter-terrorism objectives do not absolve states or governments of their obligations under international human rights and international humanitarian law.

It is unacceptable that an estimated 98,000 persons have been forcibly disappeared in Syria since March 2011. The Syrian regime should, as a matter of urgency, clarify the fate of those disappeared, detained, tortured or killed. We are deeply concerned by continuing reports of sexual and gender-based violence. We urge the regime to release any arbitrarily detained persons, particularly women and children, as called for in the UNSC resolution 2254 and the Commission of Inquiry on the Syrian Arab Republic's recent report.

Australia strongly supports efforts to achieve accountability for crimes committed in Syria, including this Commission and the International, Impartial and Independent Mechanism for Syria.

Mr President, we would be interested to hear how the Commission is tracking attacks on civilian targets, particularly medical facilities, in Idlib?

7.36   *Human Rights Situations—The Sudan*

On 9 July 2019, at the 41st session of the United Nations Human Rights Council in Geneva, Australia delivered a national statement at the Enhanced Interactive Dialogue on the Sudan. An extract of that statement follows:

[...]

The agreement reached between the Transitional Military Council and the Forces for Freedom and Change, which provides for democratic elections to be held in approximately three years, is an important step forward in the transition to a civilian-led government. We encourage the interim authorities to prioritise peace and stability over this three year period, and avoid any return to the violence of recent weeks.

Australia condemns the brutal attacks by elements of the Sudanese security services on civilian protesters on 3 June. We are particularly alarmed by reports that security services attacked hospitals and used

644 AUSTRALIAN YEAR BOOK OF INTERNATIONAL LAW VOLUME 38

sexual violence as a weapon to disperse and intimidate protesters. Australia is gravely concerned by reports that security services continued to use force against protesters in the ensuing weeks, and raided the offices of protest groups.

Australia is pleased that the agreement includes plans to establish an independent committee to investigate these attacks. In support of this process, we call on the Transitional Military Council to grant the Office of the High Commissioner access to the country and to accelerate efforts to establish a country office.

We ask: can the delegate provide any further information about the independent investigative committee's composition, and when it will be established?

On 25 September 2019, at the 42nd session of the United Nations Human Rights Council in Geneva, Australia delivered a national statement at the Interactive Dialogue with the Independent Expert on the Sudan. The full text of that statement follows:

Australia welcomes the report of the Independent Expert and the oral update covering the landmark events of July, August and September.

Australia commends the parties in Sudan for signing the Constitutional Declaration, along with the formation of the Sovereign Council and appointment of a new Cabinet to enable a transition towards civilian rule and democracy. We acknowledge the important role of the African Union and Ethiopia in facilitating agreement between the parties. We welcome the commitment in the Constitutional Declaration to comprehensive peace in all conflict areas and the new Government's outreach to armed opposition groups.

We also welcome the commitment of the Government of Sudan to continue cooperation with the Independent Expert and welcome plans to establish a fully mandated OHCHR country office.

Australia supports an independent, transparent and thorough investigation into allegations of human rights violations, including rape and other forms of sexual and gender-based violence, against peaceful protestors since December 2018. Full accountability is paramount.

We call on the new Government to provide a safe and enabling environment for civil society, human rights defenders and the media.

Australia urges the Government to conduct legal reforms that guarantee women's rights and to ensure their meaningful participation at all

AUSTRALIAN PRACTICE IN INTERNATIONAL LAW 2019

levels of the peace process and government. We welcome the announcement yesterday by Sudan's Minister of Justice that Sudan plans to sign
the CEDAW.

We ask the Independent Expert how the international community can
support efforts to reach lasting peace in Sudan, particularly in Darfur,
Southern Kordofan and Blue Nile States?

7.37   *Human Rights Situations—Ukraine*

On 20 March 2019, at the 40th session of the United Nations Human Rights
Council in Geneva, Australia delivered a national statement at the Interactive
Dialogue with the High Commissioner's Oral Update on Ukraine. An extract of
that statement follows:

> [...]
>
> Australia reiterates our ongoing support for Ukraine's sovereignty
> and territorial integrity. Australia calls on all parties to implement their
> Minsk 2 obligations. This is the only agreed basis for resolving the crisis,
> which continues to disrupt the access of civilians to a range of funda-
> mental human rights.
>
> We are gravely concerned at the consistent reports of ongoing human
> rights abuses in occupied Crimea and eastern Ukraine. We urge the occu-
> pying authorities in those areas to respect all peoples' human rights,
> and we deplore the reported use of torture, forced disappearances, and
> sexual violence. Australia is particularly concerned by reported attacks
> against vulnerable minorities. We would welcome the Deputy High
> Commissioner's views on options available to the international commu-
> nity to ensure perpetrators are held accountable for human rights abuses
> in Ukraine.
>
> Australia supports the OHCHR, and relevant special procedures
> mandate holders, continuing to report on the situation in Ukraine. We
> reiterate our call on the Russian Federation to use its influence to facili-
> tate immediate and unimpeded access to Crimea and eastern Ukraine by
> the OHCHR and other international organisations responsible for report-
> ing on the human rights situation in Ukraine.

On 12 July 2019, during the 41st session of the United Nations Human Rights
Council in Geneva, Australia delivered a general comment on the Resolution
for cooperation and assistance to Ukraine. An extract of that statement
follows:

[...]

Australia strongly supports the draft resolution L.9, Cooperation and assistance to Ukraine in the field of human rights.

The OHCHR's most recent update—presented in this chamber on Wednesday—makes clear the need for ongoing reporting on human rights in Ukraine. Australia is concerned that the OHCHR documented 230 human rights violations and abuses in a three-month period and hostilities in a number of hotspots along the contact line continue to have a significant impact on the lives of people who live there.

We note this engagement by the OHCHR is consistent with the HRC's prevention mandate.

We note also that this is an item 10 resolution on Ukraine led by Ukraine and it is entirely appropriate that the Human Rights Council and the OHCHR provides technical assistance and capacity-building advice at the request of a state.

Australia regrets that this Item 10 text has not been adopted by consensus in the past. We call on all members to support the adoption of the draft resolution L.9.

On 23 September 2019, at the 42nd session of the United Nations Human Rights Council, Australia joined a Joint Statement on the human rights situation in temporarily occupied Crimea and unrestricted access for human rights monitoring mechanisms therein. An extract of that statement follows:

[...]

We recall, in this regard, that the UN General Assembly in its resolution 73/263 'Situation of human rights in the Autonomous Republic of Crimea and the city of Sevastopol, Ukraine', urged the Russian Federation to uphold all of its obligations under applicable international law as an occupying Power and condemned all attempts by the Russian Federation to legitimize or normalize its attempted annexation of Crimea, including the automatic imposition of Russian citizenship and illegal election campaigns.

We denounce continuation of these attempts, in particular, by holding on 8 September 2019 in the temporarily occupied territory of the Autonomous Republic of Crimea and the city of Sevastopol the so-called 'local elections' to illegal institutions established by the Russian occupation administration, which constitutes another violation of international law. Results of this illegal voting are null and void.

We emphasize that anybody elected in Russian 'local elections' of 8 September 2019 on the Crimean peninsula claiming to 'represent' the populations of Crimea and Sevastopol will not be recognized as representative of those territories, which are Ukrainian.

The Russian Federation must uphold human rights in Crimea, respect its obligations as an Occupying Power under international humanitarian law, and grant full and unimpeded access to Crimea for international and regional monitoring mechanisms. We call on the Russian Federation to comply with its obligations under international law, also reaffirmed in UNGA resolutions 71/205, 72/190 and 73/263, as well as with the Order of the International Court of Justice of 19 April 2017.

We reiterate our support for the territorial integrity, political independence, unity and sovereignty of Ukraine within its internationally recognized borders, which continues to be violated as a result of the ongoing temporary occupation and attempted annexation of Crimea, and call for the full respect of the rights of all residents of Crimea.

[...]

On 24 September 2019, at the 42nd session of the United Nations Human Rights Council in Geneva, Australia delivered a national statement during the Item 10 Interactive Dialogue following the High Commissioner's oral update on Ukraine. An extract of that statement follows:

[...]

We are concerned that the OHCHR continues to observe that the conflict is having a negative impact on people living along both sides of the contact line, as well as throughout the country. Australia once again calls on all parties to comply with the provisions of the Minsk II Agreement as the only agreed basis for resolving the crisis.

Australia reiterates its ongoing support for Ukraine's sovereignty and territorial integrity. We remain concerned at the consistent reports of ongoing human rights violations and abuses in Crimea and eastern Ukraine. We urge the authorities in those areas to respect all peoples' human rights. We again call on the Russian Federation to use its influence to facilitate immediate and unimpeded access to Crimea and eastern Ukraine by the OHCHR and other international organisations responsible for reporting on the human rights situation in Ukraine.

As the Deputy High Commissioner for Human Rights noted in July, and again today, Ukraine's new leadership presents an opportunity to place human rights at the centre of the Government's priorities and public policy. We welcome the recent, peaceful presidential and parliamentary elections and encourage continued efforts to address human rights concerns, including an action plan for the protection of civilians in conflict.

7.38 *Human Rights Situations—Venezuela*

On 12 March 2019, at the 40th session of the United Nations Human Rights Council in Geneva, Australia delivered a national statement at the General Debate on Item 4. An extract of that statement follows:

> [...]
> Australia calls for a return to democracy in Venezuela, without delay. We urge all parties to work constructively towards a peaceful resolution, which upholds human rights, the rule of law, such that Venezuelans no longer need to flee their own country.
> [...]

On 20 March 2019, at the 40th session of the United Nations Human Rights Council in Geneva, Australia delivered a national statement at the General Debate on Item 2. An extract of that statement follows:

> [...]
> Australia joins concerned states in condemning actions by the Maduro-regime in Venezuela to obstruct access to humanitarian aid, threaten interim President Guiadó and other opposition leaders, detain journalists and suppress civil protest.
> Australia urges all parties to negotiate a peaceful settlement that will lead to democratic elections as quickly as possible and restore the rule of law and human rights of the Venezuelan people.
> [...]

On 3 July 2019, during the 41st session of the United Nations Human Rights Council in Geneva, Australia joined a Joint Statement on Venezuela. An extract of that statement follows:

> [...]
> 2. In her recent visit to the country, the United Nations High Commissioner for Human Rights heard testimony about the existence of torture in detention centres, of persons detained for having exercised their civil and political rights, of the violence experienced at the hands of security forces, as well as of impunity and unreliable access to justice.

AUSTRALIAN PRACTICE IN INTERNATIONAL LAW 2019

We call for the full respect for the life, physical integrity, and freedom of all Venezuelans.

3. The humanitarian crisis continues to worsen in Venezuela and the vast majority of people's needs go unmet, including access to adequate food, water and education. The Venezuelan people must receive international humanitarian aid to alleviate their suffering, in accordance with humanitarian principles. Nearly 4 million Venezuelans, more than 10% of the population, have fled in recent years. In June alone, almost 8000 crossed the border daily. Despite the increased pressure, host countries, most of which are in the region, are making considerable and commendable efforts to provide Venezuelans with access to basic services.

4. The right to health is particularly precarious: the shortage of medicines and equipment, the exodus of health professionals, the deterioration of water quality and sanitation, as well as frequent power outages, contribute to a critical situation. The magnitude remains unknown due to a lack of official information as well as independent and country-wide needs assessments. But there is evidence of repercussions: once eradicated diseases have reappeared in the region on account of the collapse of the Venezuelan health system.

Mr. President,

5. We will continue to monitor the human rights situation in Venezuela. In this context, our countries look forward to the presentation of the High Commissioner's report on July 5.

6. We reaffirm that it is only through a peaceful political solution, including by holding free and fair presidential elections, framed by the Constitution, international law and the people themselves, that Venezuelans will regain their full enjoyment of human rights and fundamental freedoms. In this respect, we reiterate our support to all efforts underway towards this goal.

[...]

7.39 *Human Rights Situations—Yemen*

On 12 March 2019, at the 40th session of the United Nations Human Rights Council in Geneva, Australia delivered a national statement at the General Debate on Item 4. An extract of that statement follows:

[...]

Australia urges an end to the conflict in Yemen. We are concerned about obstacles to humanitarian access. We call on all parties to implement the

650 AUSTRALIAN YEAR BOOK OF INTERNATIONAL LAW VOLUME 38

Stockholm Agreement and facilitate delivery of food, fuel and medicines to all Yemenis.

[...]

On 20 March 2019, at the 40th session of the United Nations Human Rights Council in Geneva, Australia delivered a national statement at the General Debate on Item 2. An extract of that statement follows:

[...]

Australia remains deeply concerned about the deteriorating humanitarian situation in Yemen. We note the Secretary General has said 24 million people in Yemen need humanitarian aid and protection. As Australia stated in Yemen's Universal Periodic Review in January 2019, we welcome the ceasefire agreement reached in Stockholm, but consider that its implementation must be hastened to allow humanitarian access. We are also concerned about the disproportionate impact of the hostilities on women and children. Australia urges all parties to the conflict to allow the UN monitoring mission to safely carry out its role. We further urge the parties to engage constructively in peace talks to reach a durable political settlement.

[...]

On 10 September 2019, at the 42nd session of the United Nations Human Rights Council in Geneva, Australia delivered a national statement during the Interactive Dialogue on the High Commissioner for Human Rights' report on Yemen. The full text of that statement follows:

Australia thanks the High Commissioner and the Group of Eminent Experts for their report.

The conflict in Yemen continues to exact a devastating humanitarian toll. We welcome all efforts to increase transparency and accountability in the conflict and shed light on the humanitarian situation in Yemen.

Australia is deeply concerned by the alleged violations and abuses of international human rights law and international humanitarian law documented in the report. We acknowledge the disproportionate impact of these violations on women and girls.

Particularly concerning are reports of arbitrary detention, torture and sexual and gender-based violence and discrimination, and of indiscriminate targeting, resulting in significant civilian casualties and damage to civilian infrastructure. Accountability for violations is essential to combat impunity and to secure a durable peace.

Australia renews its call on all parties to the conflict to fulfil their obligations under international human rights law and international humanitarian law, including in relation to ensuring the protection of civilians and access for humanitarian organisations.

While Australia welcomes the improvement in humanitarian access due to the relative peace in Hodeidah, we note that humanitarian agencies continue to face unacceptable restrictions, particularly in the north.

We share the concerns of the Group of Eminent Experts at the slow progress in implementing the Stockholm Agreement and restate our call on all parties to the conflict to engage constructively with the UN Special Envoy for Yemen to reach a lasting political settlement.

7.40 *Human Right to an Adequate Standard of Living*

On 27 September 2019, at the 42nd session of the United Nations Human Rights Council in Geneva, Australia delivered a statement at action at the end of Item 3. An extract of that statement follows:

[...]

Australia was happy to join consensus on the renewal of the mandate of the Special Rapporteur for the human rights to safe drinking water and sanitation at HRC42. We acknowledge the critical importance of access to safe drinking water and sanitation for all people equally.

However, we remain unable to co-sponsor the resolution on the human rights to safe drinking water and sanitation. It is Australia's view that there are no standalone rights to safe drinking water or sanitation.

Rather, the right to safe drinking water and sanitation is a component of the right to an adequate standard of living under Article 11 of the International Covenant on Economic, Social and Cultural Rights.

[...]

7.41 *Multilateral Approaches to Human Rights*

On 25 February 2019, at the 40th session of the United Nations Human Rights Council in Geneva, Australia delivered a national statement at the High Level Panel on Human Rights Mainstreaming. An extract of that statement follows:

[...]

Human rights are an integral part of the multilateral system and the rules-based international order. As the international community has recognised many times, there can be no sustainable development, nor any sustained peace, without human rights.

The Universal Declaration of Human Rights, the Vienna Declaration and Program of Action and the core human rights treaties have woven human rights principles into the fabric of the United Nations and the multilateral system.

We should be rightly proud of these achievements.

However, we must not be blind to the challenges and threats presented by States ignoring their international human rights obligations, and unwillingness to be held to account.

Attempts to shut down debate, to control the flow of information or to attack and undermine the credibility and independence of international institutions like the Office of the High Commissioner for Human Rights must be opposed.

Though we may not always agree with everything these institutions say, the hallmark of multilateralism's success is the breadth and richness of debate it encourages.

Australia remains committed to a strong multilateral human rights system. We recognise that peace and security, human rights and development are interdependent and mutually reinforcing, and ask the panellists how the multilateral human rights agenda can be better connected with these other pillars of the multilateral system?

7.42   *National Human Rights Institutions*

On 8 July 2019, during the 41st session of the United Nations Human Rights Council in Geneva, Australia delivered a national statement during the Item 8 General Debate. An extract of that statement follows:

> [...]
> Independent national human rights institutions play a crucial role in preserving and advancing human rights.
>
> Australia advocates strongly for strengthening the capacity of national human rights institutions to promote and protect human rights—including through our biennual resolution on NHRIS, most recently considered at HRC39, and as a pillar of our HRC membership.
>
> Australia welcomes the summary report of the Consultation on the experiences and practices of national human rights institutions in working to support the establishment and maintenance of inclusive societies and the implementation of the 2030 Agenda for Sustainable Development.
>
> The consultation, mandated by HRC resolution 39/17, was an excellent opportunity to hear from States, NHRIS and other key stakeholders on

the role NHRIS play in supporting the establishment and maintenance of inclusive societies.

This work is not only an inherent function of Paris Principles-compliant NHRIS, it also contributes directly to the achievement of the Sustainable Development Goals.

We welcome the recognition that some NHRIS, consistent with their independent mandates, can contribute to the implementation of the 2030 Agenda through a monitoring role, and we support the recommendation that Governments should ensure the full participation of all relevant stakeholders, including NHRIS, in efforts to achieve the Sustainable Development Goals.

7.43   *Right to Development*

On 12 July 2019, at the 41st session of the United Nations Human Rights Council in Geneva, Australia delivered an explanation of vote for the Resolution on the contribution to development. An extract of that explanation follows:

> [...]
>
> We remain concerned by the resolution's framing of the relationship between development and human rights, including the suggestion that development is a necessary precondition for the enjoyment of human rights.
>
> Democracy, development and the respect for human rights and fundamental freedoms are interdependent and mutually reinforcing.
>
> It is Australia's view that, while development can facilitate the enjoyment of human rights, a lack of development should not be invoked to justify the abridgement of internationally recognised human rights.
>
> [...]

On 27 September 2019, at the 42nd session of the United Nations Human Rights Council in Geneva, Australia delivered an explanation of vote for the Resolution on the Right to Development. An extract of that statement follows:

> [...]
>
> Australia cannot support the draft resolution L.36 on the right to development.
>
> We acknowledge there are a range of views on the concept of a right to development, including the proposal to develop 'an international legal standard of a binding nature on the right to development'. We share the concern of many states that this text presents a legally binding

instrument as the only way forward, leaving no room for alternatives. There is no international consensus on a potential legally binding instrument. We would encourage the penholder to adopt a more consensual approach and consider alternatives. Australia remains of the view that existing international human rights law treaties provide comprehensive protections for human rights, and there is no need for additional treaties.

[...]

7.44 *Rights of Persons with Disabilities*

On 5 March 2019, at the 40th session of the United Nations Human Rights Council in Geneva, Australia delivered a national statement at the Clustered Interactive Dialogue with the Special Rapporteur on the rights of persons with disabilities and the Independent Expert on the enjoyment of human rights by persons with albinism. An extract of that follows:

> [...]
>
> Australia remains firmly committed to fully implementing the Convention on the Rights of Persons with Disabilities and to ensuring that no one in Australia is deprived of their liberty or unable to access quality health services based on their disability.
>
> In the criminal justice context, Australia has developed National Principles regarding persons unfit to plead on the basis of cognitive and mental health impairment. The Principles identify legal safeguards and best practice principles to ensure that treatment while the person is subject to orders, including health care, is tailored, inclusive and recovery-oriented.
>
> Australia recognises that persons with disability enjoy legal capacity, on an equal basis with others, in all aspects of life. In some cases, persons with cognitive or decision-making disabilities may require support in exercising this capacity. In these situations, Australia acknowledges the importance of supported decision-making frameworks. In accordance with Australia's interpretive declarations in relation to the Convention on the Rights of Persons with Disabilities, substituted-decision making and compulsory assistance or treatment will only be provided where it is necessary, as a last resort and subject to safeguards.
>
> We would welcome the Special Rapporteur's views on best practice approaches to supported decision-making frameworks.

On 6 March 2019, at the 40th session of the United Nations Human Rights Council in Geneva, Australia delivered a national statement at the Annual

Debate on the Rights of Persons with Disabilities. The full text of that statement follows:

> Australia welcomes the current debate on strengthening and extending comprehensive Habilitation and Rehabilitation Services and Programs.
>
> For many people, including people with disabilities, habilitation and rehabilitation are central to the realisation, on an equal basis, of economic, social and political rights.
>
> A growing number of people will require rehabilitation during their lifetime, often due to injury, illness or ageing. When we get these services right, many people with disabilities are able to optimise their functioning and participate in education, employment and community life. With these services, genuinely participating in and contributing to their communities across the full spectrum of activities is possible. Without these services, people with disabilities are at risk of being left behind.
>
> Habilitation and rehabilitation are important elements of community-based inclusive development strategies. We recognise that longer-term rehabilitation may require short periods of intense rehabilitation throughout an individual's life, and we are working to design and implement rehabilitation programs in this way.
>
> Since 2011, Australia has partnered with the World Health Organization to support disability-inclusive health, rehabilitation, and provision of assistive technologies in the Western Pacific region. We were pleased to endorse the draft Western Pacific Regional Framework on Rehabilitation at the 69th Session of the WHO Western Pacific Region last year.
>
> Can the panel share best-practice examples of habilitation and rehabilitation programs that one or more States are providing?

On 21 October 2019, at the 74th Session of the UN General Assembly Third Committee in New York, Australia delivered an intervention during the Interactive Dialogue with the Special Rapporteur on the Rights of Persons with Disabilities. An extract of that statement follows:

> [...]
> Australia supports the rights of persons with disabilities to the enjoyment of the highest attainable standard of health without discrimination. Australia has a strong universal health coverage system based on a range of initiatives aimed at achieving this.
> *Existing systems of support*

Australia welcomes the discussion by the Special Rapporteur on ways to promote a human rights-based approach to ageing. In Australia, we are working to provide a holistic system of support for older Australians, across Australia's governments and systems.

A key component of this system is our ground-breaking National Disability Insurance Scheme, which has benefitted more than 300,000 persons with disabilities in Australia.

Australia notes the report's concerns about the ability of persons with disabilities to live independently and be included in the community. In Australia, our National Disability Insurance Scheme places persons with disabilities at the centre of decisions, giving them greater choice and control over their lives, including where they live.

Australia's representative, HE Mitch Fifield, Ambassador and Permanent Representative of Australia to the United Nations in New York, made a statement on 3 December 2019 for International Day of Persons with Disabilities. An extract of that statement follows:

[...]

What has happened in Australia when it comes to people with disabilities is something that I think is quite remarkable. We had a point half a dozen years ago where Australians with disabilities, their families, their carers and their friends, came together and spoke with one voice, and said, 'We're mad as hell, and we're not going to take it anymore.'

They demanded change, and they got change.

As a result of that coming together and of speaking with one voice, we now have a *National Disability Strategy*, where local, state and national governments know what their roles and responsibilities are. We now have a twenty-two billion dollar-per-year *National Disability Insurance Scheme*, where the needs of an individual are assessed, they're given an entitlement, effectively a voucher, which they can take to the service provider of their choice to support their inclusion in the way that they choose.

There is progress being made.

We need to act locally, but we also need to act globally, which is why I warmly welcome the Secretary-General's commitment to disability inclusion, and why we're very pleased to support the initial implementation of the *UN Disability Inclusion Strategy*, launched earlier this year.

Disability inclusion is also firmly embedded in our humanitarian assistance programs. In times of crisis, people with disabilities, particularly women and children, are often the first to be left behind, and face barriers accessing life-saving relief and recovery support. So we do welcome the growing momentum around ensuring the rights and needs of people with disabilities are safeguarded and addressed in humanitarian crises. Persons with disabilities must be involved in all stages of preparedness, response, and recovery.

It was great that we recently had the launch of the IASC *Guidelines on Inclusion of Persons with Disabilities in Humanitarian Action*. Australia is a proud sponsor of that initiative. But unless this is implemented through meaningful partnerships between governments, agencies and people with disabilities, these kinds of global initiatives won't make a tangible difference.

Despite the strong and increasing commitment by the international community represented here today, we still have further to go. People with disabilities still face significant barriers to their full inclusion.

Even when we have all the right consultations, even when we have the right budget allocations, even when we have the right supports provided, we still won't get there unless we can collectively lift our sights to tackle the soft bigotry of low expectations when it comes to people with disability.

We do all those things, and we will have achieved success, but we've got a way to go yet.

7.45   *The Rights of the Child*

On 4 March 2019, at the 40th session of the United Nations Human Rights Council in Geneva, Australia delivered a national statement at the Annual Full Day Discussion on the Rights of the Child. The full text of that statement follows:

Australia is committed to empowering children with disabilities: we must enable their full inclusion in education on an equal basis with all children.

Education is a fundamental right that must be realised without discrimination and on the basis of equal opportunity. Inclusive education is also key to empowering children to understand and realise other human rights.

Education systems should be inclusive of all children, including children with disabilities. Inclusive education requires an integrated approach. We need to get certain things right: inclusive policies and curricula, accurate data collection, well-trained teachers, infrastructure and equipment, and do all this within a supportive community. Australia is committed to this integrated approach.

Australia recognises the fundamental need for accessible and affordable assistive technologies and reasonable accommodations to enable equal participation by children with disabilities.

Australia is committed to supporting the full educational needs of people with disabilities in developing countries. Our aid program supports people with disabilities as both participants and beneficiaries of quality, comprehensive education development efforts so that no one is left behind.

Australia has 21 inclusive education programs across 15 countries including the Equal Access to Quality Education Program which increases educational opportunities for children with disabilities through awareness raising, teacher training, curriculum development and education infrastructure. We need to commit and hold ourselves accountable for ensuring children with disabilities have the same educational opportunities as all children.

A question for the panel: how can we galvanise the wider community to recognise the many benefits of inclusive education for all children, not just children with disabilities?

On 5 March 2019, during the 40th session of the United Nations Human Rights Council in Geneva, Australia joined a Joint Statement of the Group of Friends on Children and Armed Conflict. An extract of that statement follows:

[...]

We welcome the work of the Special Representative and share her deep concern regarding the scale and severity of the grave violations that are increasingly being committed against children in armed conflicts, in particular child abduction by parties to conflict, including across borders, and children who accompanied or were recruited and used as foreign fighters. These children are not only victims of use, killing, maiming, enslavement, sexual exploitation, constant fear, indoctrination and psychological pressure, but may also be witnesses and/or alleged perpetrators of violations of human rights.

We therefore call on States to increase accountability for perpetrators of all six grave violations including child abduction. We also urge States to focus on rehabilitation and reintegration of children associated with armed forces and armed groups, to ensure international juvenile justice

AUSTRALIAN PRACTICE IN INTERNATIONAL LAW 2019

standards and due process are applied to any criminal proceedings involving a child perpetrator as well as to prevent secondary victimization. Children successfully reintegrated into their families and communities can also be an important source of resilience.

We commend the efforts of the Special Representative to address these issues, in particular the work on developing guidance for practitioners in the field on monitoring, ending, preventing and responding to child abduction and the recent launch of the Global Coalition for reintegration.

[...]

On 5 March 2019, at the 40th session of the United Nations Human Rights Council in Geneva, Australia delivered a national statement at the Clustered Interactive Dialogue with the Special Rapporteur on Freedom of Religion or Belief and Special Rapporteur on the Sale and Sexual Exploitation of Children. An extract of that statement follows:

[...]

The sale and sexual exploitation of children are abhorrent crimes. Australia is deeply concerned by the examples of trafficking and sexual exploitation of children in the context of sports provided by the Rapporteur. Sport should strengthen communities and be an avenue of joy for children, not trauma.

How can governments best work with sporting organisations to create safe, fair and accessible sporting environments that protect the rights of children?

On 12 July 2019, at the 41st session of the United Nations Human Rights Council in Geneva, Australia delivered an explanation of vote for the Resolution on consequences of child, early and forced marriage. An extract of that statement follows:

[...]

Intimate partner violence upon these children is a serious human rights abuse, and requires the attention of this Council. Given this resolution focuses on the consequences of child, early and forced marriage, the significance of intimate partner violence in this particular context is undeniable.

Amendment L.42 seeks to narrow the scope of violence against women and girls addressed in this resolution. Failing to recognise this form of violence overlooks the complex and various ways in which the rights of

660 AUSTRALIAN YEAR BOOK OF INTERNATIONAL LAW VOLUME 38

women and girls are violated within intimate relationships, leaving them exposed to abuse.

Australia will vote against this amendment, and we urge members of this Council to do the same.

7.46 The Rights of Indigenous Peoples including the United Nations Permanent Forum on Indigenous Issues (UNFII) and the Expert Mechanism on the Rights of Indigenous Peoples (EMRIP)

In April 2019, at the 18th session of the United Nations Permanent Forum on Indigenous Issues (UNPFII) in New York, Craig Ritchie, Chief Executive Officer of the Australian Institute of Aboriginal and Torres Strait Islander Studies (AIATSIS), delivered the following statement under Item 5, Discussion on the 2019 International Year of Indigenous Languages:

Barayn Marrung
Dhanggu nuwayi Craig Ritchie
Ngaya guri Dhunghutti, ngaya Dhunghutti guuyarr
Barayn, ngaya manhatinan Lenape Onoldaga guthunda barriya.
Ngaya baluwa Garrkung ngarran, nganihi kuru nyinan barriya dithi-yndha ngun-ngun, barayn, ngundakang
Speaking in my Dunghutti language I pay respects to the Traditional Owners of this land.

'Language is more than just a means of communication: it is a repository for history, wisdom, identity, culture. Indigenous languages contain unique systems of knowledge that are valuable to our modern challenges.'

Research shows that knowledge of language is fundamentally connected to cultural identity and promotes health and wellbeing of individuals and communities.

Sadly, in Australia, more than half of the original Aboriginal and Torres Strait Islander languages are no longer spoken. With around 120 languages still spoken, only 13 are being spoken by adults and learnt by children, which maintains and preserves these languages.

In 2019, Australia will be conducting its third National Indigenous Languages Report to understand the state of Australian Indigenous Languages to inform our initiatives.

Around our country, we see languages being revived and carried forward through education: eight Australian Indigenous languages are being taught at universities, many revival languages are being taught in primary and secondary school classrooms, and first language literacy

AUSTRALIAN PRACTICE IN INTERNATIONAL LAW 2019

development and bi-lingual teaching methodologies are supporting language use.

During 2019, the International Year of Indigenous Languages, Australia is putting a focus on the value and diversity of our indigenous languages, and celebrating different ways of incorporating traditional languages and knowledge in to the modern era.

Just this month our Mint released a unique coin which shows the word for 'money' in 14 languages, with significant blank space to signify the languages we have lost.

The Ngaanyatjarra Pitjantjatjara Yankunytjatjara Women's Council (NPYWC) has developed, with Australian company Smiling Mind, a mindfulness app which incorporates Aboriginal language and cultural concepts of mental health.

We are embracing technology and modern culture through IndigiTUBE, a repository of language and cultural content, including music videos, documentaries and even comedy routines.

While we cannot step away from the fact that Indigenous languages have been lost, we can be encouraged by innovation and commitment that the International Year of Indigenous Languages is supporting worldwide, and how countries such as ours are striving to preserve our precious history.

Nhiyanang waanygalu: Let's work together.

In July 2019, at the 12th session of the Expert Mechanism on the rights of Indigenous Peoples (EMRIP) in Geneva, Professor Ian Anderson, Deputy Chief Executive Officer, National Indigenous Australians Agency, delivered the following statement under Item 5—Inter-sessional activities and follow-up to thematic studies and advice: Study on free, prior and informed consent: a human-rights based approach:

Ya Pulingina, greetings in my ancestral language Palawa Kani.

Australia welcomes the Expert Mechanism's 2018 study and advice on 'free, prior and informed consent: a human rights-based approach'.

Australia is pleased to contribute to the ongoing discussion on the ways free, prior and informed consent can be realised to promote and protect the rights of Indigenous peoples.

Australia recognises the importance of engaging in good faith with Indigenous peoples on decisions that affect them. Australia is resetting how we develop policy and programs by creating genuine and formal partnerships with Indigenous Australians, both in overarching frameworks and local solutions.

In line with Article 19 of the Declaration on the Rights of Indigenous Peoples, mechanisms for consultation and collaboration with Aboriginal and Torres Strait Islander peoples are used to inform policy and program development.

In December 2018, Australia established a landmark partnership agreement between all Australian governments and Indigenous Australian organisations. The agreement is about sharing-decision making and oversight, having ongoing relationships to develop, implement and monitor solutions. This is realised through the new Joint Council on Closing the Gap, which for the first time brings all parties together at the decision-making table.

Expanding Indigenous regional decision making and co-design grows local solutions. Regional agreements tackle specific policy concerns, like the Northern Territory Remote Housing Agreement between the Aboriginal Land Councils, the Territory government and the federal government, including Indigenous Australians in decision-making.

On 18 September 2019, at the 42nd session of the United Nations Human Rights Council in Geneva, Australia delivered a national statement during the Clustered Interactive Dialogue with the Special Rapporteur (SR) on Indigenous Issues and Expert Mechanism on the Rights of Indigenous Peoples (EMRIP). An extract of that statement follows:

> [...]
>
> All Australian Governments under our federal system are working with Aboriginal and Torres Strait Islander people to ensure they play an integral part in decision-making that affects their lives, including co-design approaches for matters of concern to Aboriginal and Torres Strait Islander people and communities.
>
> We thank the Special Rapporteur for highlighting the information Australia provided on the Children's Koori Court in Victoria. This Court incorporates cultural practices into legal proceedings and identifies alternative sentencing options with community elders.
>
> Australia is also trialling a transition program for youth leaving detention. It supports young Indigenous people returning to their families and communities safely, without reoffending.
>
> Australia's submission to the Expert Mechanism's report on implementation of the Declaration outlines what we seek to achieve through

the refresh of the Australian Government's critical program to close the gap between Indigenous and non-Indigenous Australians. This process demonstrates Australia's commitment to working in partnership with Indigenous Australians, to build genuine respect and inclusion; and drive social and economic empowerment, in order to improve outcomes for all Indigenous Australians. Amongst other things, this will help address the underlying causes of the overrepresentation of Indigenous Australians in the justice system.

Could the Special Rapporteur share some examples of innovative approaches which have helped to improve justice outcomes for young Indigenous people?

On 18 September 2019, the Minister for Indigenous Australians, the Hon. Ken Wyatt AM MP, delivered an address on the rights of indigenous peoples at the 42nd session of the United Nations Human Rights Council in Geneva. The full text of that dignitary address follows:

Kaya wangju—hello and welcome in my language, the Noongar language.

To celebrate the United Nations International Year of Indigenous Languages, I commenced in the language of my ancestors. I am Ken Wyatt, Australia's first Indigenous member of the Australian cabinet and Minister for Indigenous Australians.

I am pleased to have the opportunity to address the Human Rights Council in this session. There is power in telling the truth.

In Australia, we are starting a national conversation about truth telling around the history of Aboriginal and Torres Strait Islander Australians.

To me, truth-telling is not a contest of history, but an acknowledgement of what has been, and sharing what was seen.

So let me start here by talking truth with you. It's been 10 years since Australia joined the global community to support the United Nations Declaration on the Rights of Indigenous Peoples. The truth is ... Australia did not support the Declaration when it was first introduced. Over two years we considered the implications, and like other countries, we are still on the journey of what the Declaration means to us.

To us the Declaration reflects economic, social, cultural and political rights. Rights that should guide our policies intended to deliver change that is sustainable and embraces Aboriginal and Torres Strait Islander people and their culture.

Although we have already started walking our journey to change the way we protect and uphold the rights of Indigenous people, we know healing won't actually start until we recognise and acknowledge where our country began. To this end we have set ourselves a goal to recognise Aboriginal and Torres Strait Islander people as the first peoples of Australia. This is too important to rush, and too important to get wrong.

As everyone here would know, the declaration itself was the product of almost 25 years of deliberation between UN member states and the Indigenous groups.

To achieve our goal we must focus on rediscovering our differences, our incredible history and culture, and integrating traditional knowledge and systems in our current way of life. We acknowledge that our long struggle to recognise and realise traditional Indigenous systems has been made more difficult by the truth that we have interpreted that connection long ago. This is a terrible and hard fact to face. We cannot change it. But we are trying hard to heal and to reconnect.

To achieve our goals it's vital we have unity in our solution. This demands all voices should be heard respectfully. It requires us to solve the problem together ... to 'co-design'. Soon we will be talking to our elders and communities about what co-design looks like. The truth is we have problems and some are serious problems. High rates of incarceration of Aboriginal and Torres Strait Islander Australians, and high rates of suicide, particularly of young Indigenous Australians are just two of these problems.

But ... we are working to change the statistics. Australians pride themselves on being honest, hard-working and loyal people. We know we must all contribute to enjoy better outcomes for all of us.

All of Australia's governments have partnered to work with Indigenous people and communities to develop solutions to our problems jointly. Our Closing the Gap framework focuses on community safety, education and employment as enablers for better futures. By addressing the underlying issues we hope to reduce the unacceptably high rates of suicide and incarceration.

Economic rights are also at the heart of our strategies. Our strategies covering demand and supply are designed to cultivate growth and sustainability. We are offering targeted funding support and levering our own government spending to drive demand for Indigenous goods and services, and consequently drive business growth and create jobs. For example, the Australian Government's Indigenous Procurement Policy commenced four years ago. In this time over 16,280 contracts, worth more than $2.47 billion, have been awarded to 1,780 Indigenous businesses across a variety of industries and sectors. On the supply side we're nurturing the Indigenous corporate sector through a 10-year plan to improve access to business and financial support.

We also recognise the additional struggles Indigenous women can face in setting up businesses. To address this we have provided culturally-safe spaces for women to seek business support and we've funded the first Indigenous Women in Business conference.

Economic participation is just one element of the declaration. Australia's truth is that while our Indigenous culture and systems are one of the most ancient, sophisticated and complex in the world, they are also evolving, blending our Australian nations together in a peaceful but challenging journey. Similar to our journey towards realising the Declaration.

There is no doubt we are a nation with a lot of challenges to address and we anticipate new ones as globalisation shifts us further into the new community paradigms. We are headed in the right direction ... but we are cautious not to run before we have first learned to walk. We are on that journey and walking together. We embrace the opportunity to be part of this global community here and we hope you will walk with us to achieve long and lasting change for the better for both Indigenous and non Indigenous Australians but the First Nations of the World.

On 11 October 2019, at the 74th Session of the UN General Assembly Third Committee in Geneva, Australia delivered a national statement during the General Discussion on Indigenous Rights. Extracts of that statement follow:

[...]

Since supporting the Declaration on the Rights of Indigenous Peoples ten years ago, we have given and continue to give practical effect to the aspirations and rights it captures, including economic rights.

Australia has introduced an Indigenous Procurement Policy, using the buying power of Government. Indigenous businesses are thriving with more than $2 billion in contracts awarded.

Investing in the futures of Indigenous Peoples is crucial to supporting the realisation of the Sustainable Development Goals, and ensuring the global community achieves our commitment to 'leave no one behind'.

Both within Australia and internationally, we are achieving positive outcomes for Indigenous peoples and communities by partnering with Indigenous peoples on decisions, in line with the Declaration.

In Australia, we've established a landmark partnership agreement between all Australian governments, through the Council of Australian Governments, and Indigenous Australian representatives. The agreement establishes the Joint Council on Closing the Gap which formalises shared decision-making, oversight, implementation and monitoring on matters that affect Indigenous Australians.

For the first time in our history, Indigenous Australians are chairing significant national meetings with Government. All parties are together at the table.

7.47 The Situation of Human Rights Defenders, and Torture and Other Cruel, Inhuman or Degrading Treatment or Punishment

On 28 February 2019, at the 40th session of the United Nations Human Rights Council in Geneva, Australia delivered a national statement at the Clustered Interactive Dialogue with the Special Rapporteur on the situation of human rights defenders and the Special Rapporteur on Torture and Other Cruel, Inhuman or Degrading Treatment or Punishment Penalty. An extract of that statement follows:

> [...]
> Australia is interested in your views on how we can strengthen protections for women human rights defenders from online violence, including the role of technology and social media companies.
>
> Australia also welcomes the focus of the Special Rapporteur on torture and other cruel, inhuman or degrading treatment or punishment penalty, on corruption and torture or ill-treatment, as two concurrent effects of the failure of governance systems to prevent the abuse of unchecked power.
>
> Drawing on the commonalities between your report and that of the Special Rapporteur on Human Rights Defenders, could you please provide more detail on your recommendation in para. 73(f)? Namely, practical measures to better protect civil society representatives, human rights defenders, and whistle-blowers from violence, intimidation and reprisals.

On 18 September 2019, during the 42nd session of the United Nations Human Rights Council in Geneva, Australia delivered a national statement in the Interactive Dialogue with the Assistant Secretary-General on Reprisals. An extract of that statement follows:

AUSTRALIAN PRACTICE IN INTERNATIONAL LAW 2019

[...]

Australia welcomes the Secretary-General's Report and thanks the Assistant Secretary General for his presentation. We are disturbed by reports of reprisals against victims, human rights defenders and non-governmental organizations who cooperate with the UN, perpetrated by both State and non-State actors. Too often, reprisals are carried out by members of the HRC—who should be upholding the highest standards of human rights and fully cooperating with the mechanisms of the HRC—calling into disrespect this Council and its work.

We are concerned by reports that NGO applications for consultative status with ECOSOC are being arbitrarily deferred based on political motivations of members of the Committee on Non-Governmental Organizations. Australia joins in calling on all members of the Committee to apply the criteria for assessing organizations in a fair and transparent manner.

[...]

On 27 September 2019, during the 42nd session of the United Nations Human Rights Council in Geneva, Australia delivered an explanation of vote on Amendment L.44 to HRC42 Resolution on Cooperation with the United Nations, its representatives and mechanisms in the field of human rights. An extract of that statement follows:

[...]

This amendment is a distraction from the very real issue that individuals who engage with international bodies—including the Human Rights Council—continue to face acts of intimidation and reprisal.

Operative Paragraph 1 is agreed language, dating as far back as the consensus HRC Resolution 22/6 on protecting human rights defenders.

The phrase 'right to unhindered access to and communication with international bodies' is based on protections provided by the landmark UN Declaration on Human Rights Defenders. The Declaration was adopted by consensus at the UN General Assembly in 1998 and recognised the importance of protecting human rights advocates.

As a result, Australia will vote against this amendment, and we urge members of this Council to do the same.

On 15 October 2019, at the 74th Session of the UN General Assembly Third Committee in New York, Australia delivered a national statement during the

668   AUSTRALIAN YEAR BOOK OF INTERNATIONAL LAW VOLUME 38

Interactive Dialogue Special Rapporteur on Human Rights Defenders. An extract of that statement follows:

> [...]
> We welcome the Special Rapporteur's focus on the challenge of addressing impunity for human rights violations against human rights defenders. We thank him for his analysis of how the fight against impunity can be impacted by obstacles such as institutional weakness, corruption, lack of an independent judiciary, or lack of political will.
>
> We agree that States must take a zero tolerance approach to attacks on human rights defenders but also create a safe environment that is conducive to human rights defence efforts.
>
> We appreciated the Special Rapporteur's analysis of how human rights violations against human rights defenders are attributable to both State and non-State actors, and that it is common for digital media to be used as part of these attacks, for example to violate their rights to privacy of through threats of sexual violence.
>
> We also note with concern reports that women human rights defenders and persons who defend LGBTI rights encounter additional obstacles, including linked to gender discrimination, and that lack of sex disaggregated data can mask this.
>
> Australia is committed to ensuring all individuals—including human rights defenders—enjoy the same human rights protections online and offline and are able to defend human rights in safe environments which recognise diversity.
>
> What are the Special Rapporteur's views on best practices for addressing digital attacks against human rights defenders and holding perpetrators to account?

7.48   *Universality and Equality of Human Rights*

On 18 March 2019, during the 40th session of the United Nations Human Rights Council in Geneva, Australia delivered a Joint Statement on behalf of Australia, Spain and 59 countries on the universality of human rights. An extract of that statement follows:

> [...]
> The Universal Declaration of Human Rights recognised the inherent dignity, and equal and inalienable rights, of all members of the human family as the foundation of freedom, justice and peace in the world.
>
> All people are born free and equal in dignity and rights.

Today, we see many challenges to the notion of universality of human rights. Yet, to quote Nelson Mandela, 'to deny people their human rights is to challenge their very humanity'.

We reaffirm that all human rights are universal, indivisible, interrelated, interdependent and mutually reinforcing. All human rights must be treated in a fair and equal manner, on the same footing and with the same emphasis.

While recognising the significance of national and regional particularities, we reaffirm that all States, regardless of their political, economic and cultural systems, have the duty to promote and protect all human rights and fundamental freedoms.

We call on all UN members to give effect to our responsibilities in this regard.

As UN Secretary-General, Ban Ki-moon, noted in 2012 'no one gets to decide who is entitled to human rights and who is not'. All human beings—not some, not most, but all—are entitled to human rights.

On 21 March 2019, during the 40th session of the United Nations Human Rights Council in Geneva, Australia joined a Joint Statement on behalf of the contact group on Council membership. An extract of that statement follows:

[...]

I am pleased to deliver the following statement on behalf of a new group of friends: the contact group on Council membership. The full list of the members will be uploaded to the Extranet.

The Human Rights Council is only as good as its members. Members of the UN's principal body for promoting universal respect for the protection of all human rights have a particular responsibility to uphold and defend those rights.

As GA resolution 60/251 that established this Council makes clear, all States must respect human rights and fundamental freedoms for all, and members elected to the Council shall uphold the highest standards in the promotion and protection of human rights and fully cooperate with the Council.

Mr President,

We also believe that the Council's membership should reflect the diversity of the UN as a whole, and that all countries, irrespective of their size, wealth or power should have an equal opportunity to serve.

It is therefore a cause for some concern that, as of today, 79 UN Member States have yet to hold a seat on the Council. Many of those have never stood for election, and most are Small States, especially Least Developed Countries (LDCs) and Small Island Developing States (SIDS).

To improve this situation, cooperatively and cross-regionally, an initial group of 14 States came together late last year to form a new contact group on membership.

The new group will endeavour to strengthen universality, inclusivity and diversity at the Council by encouraging States with a demonstrable commitment to human rights and democracy, especially Small States, to strengthen their participation and engagement with the body and its mechanisms and, eventually, to consider standing for election.

The Group will also seek to strengthen the process of Council elections by supporting measures to enhance transparency, public accountability and meritocracy.

Mr President,

We believe there is cause for optimism. Just 2 years ago, the number of States that had never held a seat on the Council stood at 95—compared to 79 today. In the meantime a number of Small States have stood for and been elected to the Council. We congratulate them and encourage others to follow suit. Small States often offer new perspectives and they strengthen the Council's universality.

We will therefore be building from a positive base; and invite others who support the aforementioned principles and goals to join us.

[...]

On 23 September 2019, during the 42nd session of the United Nations Human Rights Council in Geneva, Australia delivered a Joint Statement on the equality and interdependence of all human rights on behalf of Australia and 47 other countries. An extract of that statement follows:

[...]

The recognition of the inherent dignity, and equal and inalienable rights, of all members of the human family is the foundation of freedom, justice and peace in the world.

We are concerned that some states seek to promote some human rights over others.

Every individual is entitled to the full and equal enjoyment of all human rights; as states, we cannot pick-and-choose between our obligations to protect, respect and fulfil human rights. For indeed, in the words of Martin Luther King, 'a right delayed is a right denied'.

We reaffirm that all human rights are universal, indivisible, interrelated, interdependent and mutually reinforcing, and must be treated in a fair and equal manner, on the same footing and with the same emphasis.

The Vienna Declaration and Programme of Action makes clear that democracy, development and respect for human rights and fundamental freedoms are interdependent and mutually reinforcing, and that the international community needs to support the strengthening and promotion of democracy, development and respect for human rights and fundamental freedoms in the entire world. It also makes clear that while development facilitates the enjoyment of all human rights, the lack of development may not be invoked to justify the abridgement of internationally recognized human rights.

In the words of former UN Deputy Secretary-General Jan Eliasson, 'there can be no peace without development, no development without peace, and no lasting peace or sustainable development without respect for human rights and the rule of law.'

We call on all UN members to give effect to our responsibilities in this regard.

7.49   *Xenophobia and Hate Speech*

On 24 September 2019, during the 42nd session of the United Nations Human Rights Council in Geneva, Australia joined a Joint Statement on addressing **xenophobia and hate speech**. An extract from that statement follows:

[...]

We are deeply concerned by the proliferation of hate speech that stigmatizes persons belonging to groups based on their race, ethnicity, language, religion, national origin, nationality, migration status, among other grounds. These expressions of hatred feed xenophobic sentiments that can push potential perpetrators to carry out violent acts against minorities or other groups, including migrants. Recent attacks in Christchurch, Pittsburgh, Colombo and El Paso have followed this dangerous trend.

We condemn all acts of violence or any incitement to such acts that are in violation of international law and have no place in our societies. Hate crimes threaten democratic values and social stability, and can endanger peace, sustainable development and the effective enjoyment of human rights.

Hate speech has expanded in every region, regardless of culture or government system, sometimes encouraged to advance political agendas or prompted by irresponsible statements by persons with influence on public opinion. While fully respectful of freedom of expression, we reject any rhetoric that feeds into a climate of hatred in which discrimination, racism, xenophobia and intolerance are normalized.

We also express concern over the proliferation of radical websites that propagate racist ideologies. They provide a platform for hate groups, including white supremacists, to organize, recruit and incite violence, which may lead to terrorist attacks, therefore demanding greater scrutiny.

States have an ethical and legal responsibility to denounce and condemn hate speech. It is critical to develop human-rights policies to prevent, address and counter hate speech, which can include a combination of adequate legal protection against discrimination and hate crimes, mechanisms to ensure accountability, support for the victims, awareness campaigns, education, and a vigorous defense of human rights. It is also critical to prevent indiscriminate access to weapons and the misuse of the Internet and social media by violent extremists, which may cause destruction and harm.

Finally, a global coordinated effort is needed and, in this regard, we welcome the Strategy and Plan of Action on Hate Speech launched by the Secretary General.

7.50   *Cultural Rights and the Promotion and Protection of Human Rights and Fundamental Freedoms while Countering Terrorism*

On 1 March 2019, at the 40th session of the United Nations Human Rights Council in Geneva, Australia delivered a national statement at the Interactive Dialogue with the Special Rapporteur on the promotion and protection of human rights and fundamental freedoms while countering terrorism. An extract of that statement follows:

> [...]
> Terrorism is a shared transnational challenge requiring sustained regional and global partnership. Australia's approach to counter-terrorism is consistent with, and in support of, international human rights obligations.
>
> We agree with the Special Rapporteur that diverse and independent civil society actors should be proactively and constructively engaged on counter-terrorism and preventing violent extremism. Australia's National Counter-Terrorism Strategy emphasises the importance of effective partnership with civil society to protect against violent extremist influences. We also encourage engagement by civil society in international fora, such

as through Australia's co-chairmanship with Indonesia of the Global Counter-Terrorism Forum's CVE Working Group.

Australia is pleased to support civil society as agents of change in countering terrorism and violent extremism. During the 2018 Australia-ASEAN counter-terrorism conference, the Southeast Asia Network of Civil Society Organisations shared best-practice on social and community-based initiatives to counter violent extremism.

We agree with the Special Rapporteur on the need for safeguards on counter-terrorism regulatory measures. Australia's counter-terrorism laws appropriately balance the need for community safety with safeguarding individual rights and freedoms. They contain important human rights safeguards, and are subject to ongoing review by independent third parties, such as the Independent National Security Legislation Monitor, to ensure they are reasonable, necessary and proportionate.

We would welcome the Special Rapporteur's views on best practice engagement between civil society and governments on countering terrorism.

On 22 March 2019, at the 40th session of the United Nations Human Rights Council in Geneva, Australia delivered a general comment on the mandate of the Special Rapporteur on countering terrorism. An extract of that statement follows:

[...]

Australia condemns acts of terrorism, as well as the racism, xenophobia and intolerance that fuels them, in the strongest possible terms.

Australians share their deepest sympathies for those affected by the devastating terrorist attack in Christchurch and share the grief of Muslim communities all over the world. We utterly condemn this terrorist attack by a right-wing extremist who has taken so many lives in New Zealand.

This act of terrorism has not only rocked New Zealand, but nations around the world including Australia. We stand together to condemn the hatred and intolerance behind this attack. We will always protect and defend the Muslim community in Australia and their right to peacefully practice their religion without fear.

Australia is determined to combat and prevent terrorism in all its forms. Terrorism is a shared transnational challenge requiring sustained regional and global partnership. It is important for this Council to consider terrorism's impacts on the full enjoyment of human rights and to stress the need for States' responses to terrorism to accord with their obligations under international law.

674   AUSTRALIAN YEAR BOOK OF INTERNATIONAL LAW VOLUME 38

We support the mandate of the Special Rapporteur on the protection of human rights and fundamental freedoms while countering terrorism, and the extension of the Special Rapporteur's mandate as laid out in this resolution, and provided for by HRC resolution 31/3.

7.51   *Countering Trafficking and Modern Forms of Slavery*

On 27 June 2019, at the 41st session of the United Nations Human Rights Council in Geneva, Australia delivered a national statement during the Clustered Interactive Dialogue with the Special Rapporteur on trafficking in persons, especially women and children, and the Special Rapporteur on the elimination of all forms of violence against women and girls. An extract of that statement follows:

[...]

As identified by the Special Rapporteur's report on trafficking, we must address the long-term needs of victims and survivors, including support measures and challenges to social inclusion. Survivors need assistance to re-enable their economic, social, cultural and political participation in their communities.

Australia is committed to combating human trafficking, slavery and slavery-like practices—domestically and internationally. Our efforts go beyond short-term interventions. For example, the Bali Process Government and Business Forum, co-chaired by Australia and Indonesia, has adopted recommendations on how governments and businesses can contribute to the eradication of trafficking, including victim redress mechanisms.

Australia supports the mandate of the Special Rapporteur on the elimination of violence against women, and the role of UN Special Procedures and independent monitoring mechanisms in reinforcing the Beijing Declaration and Platform for Action and other agendas that support the rights of women and girls.

Australia is committed to implementing the Women, Peace and Security (WPS) agenda, and we welcome the report's recommendation for closer engagement on this. We are developing our second Australian National Action Plan on WPS, to be launched later this year.

We ask your views on how member states can further collaborate and engage with UN mechanisms on eliminating violence against women in the context of the WPS agenda. It is critical that responses to gender-based violence in conflict and post-conflict situations reflect the complexity of its underlying causes and effects.

On 30 July 2019, Australia's Minister for Foreign Affairs, Senator the Hon. Marise Payne, released a media statement for World Day Against Trafficking in Persons. The full text of that media release follows:

Today, on World Day against Trafficking in Persons, I am pleased to announce Australia has joined a global awareness-raising initiative to fight human trafficking and its impact on society.

Joining the United Nations' Blue Heart Campaign underlines Australia's commitment to efforts to eradicate human trafficking and modern slavery, as enshrined in the Sustainable Development Goals.

More than 40 million people worldwide are victims of modern slavery, with over 70 per cent being women and children. This abhorrent criminal activity crosses borders and touches every corner of the globe, affecting some of the world's most vulnerable people.

Australia continues to lead efforts to eradicate these heinous crimes on a domestic, regional and global level.

Domestically, Australia has passed a *Modern Slavery Act* requiring the Commonwealth Government and more than 3,000 large businesses to publish annual statements on their actions to address modern slavery in their supply chains and operations.

Regionally, Australia is promoting partnerships through the co-chairing of the Bali Process on People Smuggling, Trafficking in Persons and Related Transnational Crime.

In addition, Australia is delivering a series of development programs to help combat human trafficking in the Pacific and South East Asia, including the flagship $80 million ASEAN-Australia Counter Trafficking Program.

Australia plays an important leadership role in Alliance 8.7, a global partnership between governments, business and civil society to tackle these crimes.

In September, Australia will co-launch the Financial Sector Commission on Modern Slavery and Human Trafficking's *Unlocking Potential: A Blueprint for Mobilizing Finance Against Slavery and Human Trafficking*, which aims to harness the efforts of global financial institutions.

On 1 August 2019, Australia's Minister for Foreign Affairs, Senator the Hon. Marise Payne, released a media statement announcing an ASEAN-Australia counter-trafficking initiative. The full text of that media release follows:

> I am pleased to launch an important initiative between Australia and the Association of Southeast Asian Nations (ASEAN) to fight human trafficking, modern slavery and forced labour throughout the region.
>
> The ASEAN-Australia Counter-Trafficking Initiative is a 10-year, $80 million program that will work to strengthen criminal justice responses and protect victim rights.
>
> This includes providing police training in financial investigations, professional development for judges, and promoting child-friendly courtrooms.
>
> The initiative will also support joint international investigations to help rescue victims and ensure traffickers are charged.
>
> The new investment will respond to private sector concerns in cases of human trafficking identified in supply chains.
>
> It builds on Australia's 15-year partnership with ASEAN to eliminate human trafficking and is a practical contribution to our shared goal of achieving an open, stable and prosperous Indo-Pacific region.
>
> The launch of the initiative, which helps implement commitments under the ASEAN Convention Against Trafficking in Persons, Especially Women and Children, is fitting just days after World Day against Trafficking in Persons on 30 July.

On 9 September 2019, at the 42nd session of the United Nations Human Rights Council in Geneva, Australia delivered a national statement during the Clustered Interactive Dialogue with the Special Rapporteur on contemporary forms of slavery and the Working Group on the use of mercenaries. An extract of that statement follows:

> [...]
>
> Eliminating modern slavery by 2030 requires systemic responses that address underlying inequalities in societies, commerce and law enforcement, including the disproportionate impact on women and girls. This needs concerted action, across and among governments, international agencies, business and civil society.
>
> To this end, Australia engages with partner countries to build strong law, policy and operational frameworks to tackle modern slavery and support vulnerable workers domestically and internationally.

Under Australia's new *Modern Slavery Act,* approximately 3,000 large companies, charities and other entities will report annually on action to address modern slavery risks in their global operations and supply chains. In a world first, the Australian Government, as one of the largest procurers in the country, will also report.

In our region, we work collaboratively with governments, the private sector and civil society to implement the Bali Process Government and Business Forum's *Acknowledge, Act and Advance* recommendations to improve supply chain transparency and ethical recruitment and employment. The Bali Process, co-chaired with Indonesia, will also take forward a blueprint on working with the financial sector to combat slavery.

Australia continues to contribute to the Alliance 8.7 partnership's collective efforts to accelerate action on SDG 8.7 through the Global Coordinating Group.

We would welcome the SR's views on particular arrangements or strategies to best harness the work of partnerships such as Alliance 8.7 in the fight against modern slavery.

On 25 October 2019, at the 74th Session of the UN General Assembly Third Committee in New York, Australia made an intervention in the Interactive Dialogue with the Special Rapporteur on contemporary forms of slavery. An extract of that statement follows:

[...]

As the report demonstrates, eliminating child slavery requires systematic responses that address criminal justice and law enforcement, human rights, development, commercial and social policy and welfare issues.

This needs concerted action, across and between governments, international agencies, business and civil society.

It also requires addressing the root causes of child slavery and increasing efforts to promote gender equality, particularly noting the gendered nature of modern slavery, which disproportionately affects girls and women.

To this end, Australia engages with partner countries to build strong legal policy and operational frameworks to tackle child slavery and support vulnerable workers domestically and internationally.

At the national level, Australia is committed to preventing and eradicating child slavery through the implementation of international labour standards.

Under Australia's new *Modern Slavery Act*, large companies and other organisations will report annually on their actions to address modern slavery risks in their operations and supply chains.

We agree with the Special Rapporteur that regional and international partnerships, incorporating governments and businesses, are important if we are to maximise effectiveness in this space.

In our region, we work collaboratively with governments, the private sector and civil society to implement the Bali Process Government and Business Forum's Acknowledge, Act and Advance recommendations to improve supply chain transparency and ethical recruitment and employment.

Australia continues to contribute to the Alliance 8.7 partnership's collective efforts to accelerate action on SDG 8.7 through the Global Coordinating Group.

We would welcome the Special Rapporteur's views on particular arrangements or strategies to best harness the work of partnerships such as Alliance 8.7 in the fight against child slavery.

8   Development of International Law Jurisprudence

8.1   *General Principles of International Law*

On 6 November 2019, Australia made a statement to the Sixth Committee of the United Nations General Assembly in New York on the work of the International Law Commission (ILC). The full text of that statement follows:

Chair

Australia would like to make some remarks today on the Commission's work on General Principles of Law.

General principles of law have been a neglected source of international law. Past considerations of this topic have often been discrete and limited to particular principles. Similar to the Commission's work on the identification of customary international law, a comprehensive examination of the development of general principles of law will assist States to more confidently draw on all sources of international law, so that States may better understand their obligations, and resolve disputes peacefully.

We thank the Special Rapporteur, Mr Marcelo Vázquez-Bermúdez, for his First Report, which provides an insightful overview of preliminary matters to be considered as part of the Commission's work regarding general principles of law.

AUSTRALIAN PRACTICE IN INTERNATIONAL LAW 2019

We support the Special Rapporteur's proposed methodological approach to the Commission's consideration of the topic. As a preliminary point, we consider that the efforts of the Commission should be focused on elucidating the meaning of 'general principles of law' as a source of law reflected in Article 38(1)(c) of the Statute of the International Court of Justice. We would not consider Article 38(1)(c) to be a subcategory of 'general principles of law', nor would we suggest that the content of 'general principles of law' should only be determined by reference to the ICJ's jurisprudence. To that end, we agree with the Special Rapporteur's views that the Commission's work on general principles of law should be based primarily on the practice of States. We also support the Special Rapporteur's decision to limit the scope of the work, so as not to address the substance of general principles of law.

To briefly comment on the Special Rapporteur's draft conclusions, we note that in draft conclusion 3, the Special Rapporteur has proposed two categories of general principles of law. We agree with the Special Rapporteur's proposed two-step process for identifying general principles of law derived from national legal systems. In our view, in addition to identifying a rule that is common between States' legal systems, a principle of law in national legal systems must be capable of being elevated to the international legal system to be considered a source of international law. To this end, we look forward to the Commission's consideration of when and how commonalities in domestic law can be 'internationalised' to form a general principle of law applicable among States.

We also look forward to the Commission's ongoing work on the second category of principles of law—that is, those formed within the international legal system. In particular, we would welcome clarification by the Commission on how a general principle can be formed within the international legal system, how such principles would be identified, and how such principles would differ from customary international law.

Australia commends the progress made by the Special Rapporteur and the Commission in their preliminary reports and look forward to the Commission's ongoing work on this topic.

Thank you Chair.

8.2 Administration of Justice at the United Nations

On 17 October 2019, New Zealand made a statement to the Sixth Committee of the United Nations General Assembly in New York on administration justice at the United Nations, delivered on behalf of Canada, Australia and New Zealand (CANZ). The full text of that statement follows:

Chairperson,

It is my honour to speak to you today on behalf of three countries; Canada, Australia and my own home country, New Zealand.

I take this opportunity to acknowledge New Zealander Graeme Colgan. In July of this year Mr Colgan commenced his term as a United Nations Appeal Tribunal judge. He is the first New Zealander to be elected to that Tribunal. We wish him well.

I also wish to acknowledge the distinguished service of Mr Rowan Downing QC of Australia as a judge ad litem on the Tribunal. Judge Downing was elected to the Tribunal in 2014 and completed his service this year.

It has been just over ten years since the internal system of administration of justice within the United Nations came into operation. Continued goodwill and meaningful engagement by Member States will ensure that this system continues to improve.

CANZ thanks the Secretary-General, the Internal Justice Council, and the Office of the United Nations Ombudsman and Mediation Services for their reports.

A number of issues addressed in these reports share a common theme—access to justice. Access to justice is a basic principle of the rule of law; a concept that is embedded in the Charter of the United Nations. In its broadest sense, it encompasses important issues addressed in these reports including outreach across United Nations organs, protecting people from retaliation, appropriate representation, and matters of judicial efficiency.

The Secretary General's report details efforts to raise awareness and improve the knowledge of the internal justice system among United Nations Staff. We are pleased to read about the initiatives being rolled out.

All parties and participants in internal justice processes should be afforded protection from retaliation. The Internal Justice Council's report makes a number of recommendations to protect parties and participants. CANZ countries strongly support these recommendations. The proposed measures will particularly help staff who wish to bring a claim and help facilitate justice by ensuring that witnesses can participate in processes without fear of reprisal.

The availability and quality of representation may be an impediment to accessing justice. The Internal Justice Council notes that self-representation is a significant feature of the Dispute Tribunal. It recommends further work be undertaken to understand why so many staff represent themselves. CANZ countries see the merit in understanding

AUSTRALIAN PRACTICE IN INTERNATIONAL LAW 2019

this trend in order to find a way to enable the system to operate more effectively. The creation of a toolkit for self-represented applicants is a practical and prudent measure to support applicants immediately.

The allocation of additional funds to the Office of Staff Legal Assistance is another of the Council's recommendations that we support. We note that the promotion of voluntary supplemental funding for that Office also has an important role to play too. We are pleased to see outreach in this area.

'Justice delayed is justice denied' is a well-known legal maxim. The Internal Justice Council notes that the case load of the Dispute Tribunal remains substantial. The backlog continues to be a source of serious concern. The review of rules of procedure may identify opportunities to streamline and increase the rate at which matters progress before the Tribunal. Recommendations regarding judicial efficiency and accountability, which respect the principle of judicial independence, are welcomed by CANZ.

Work undertaken by the Office of the United Nations Ombudsman and Mediation Services, to identify trends and systemic issues underlying workplace conflicts, provides important insights that may enable changes to deliver enhanced functioning across the organisation. CANZ countries support this work and look forward to the next report.

It is up to all Member States and the United Nations organisation to work together to ensure that the administration of justice within the United Nations system is as effective, fair and as timely as possible.

New Zealand, Canada and Australia will continue to engage with Member States with a view to contributing meaningfully to the evolution of the internal justice system at the United Nations.

Thank you.

8.3   Immunity of State Officials from Foreign Criminal Jurisdiction

On 31 October 2019, Australia made a statement to the Sixth Committee of the United Nations General Assembly in New York, on the work of the International Law Commission (ILC). Extracts from that statement follow:

[...]

Turning to the immunity of State officials from foreign criminal jurisdiction, Australia welcomes the Commission's discussions on the procedural aspects of such immunity.

Australia considers that the primary focus of the draft articles on this topic should seek to codify customary international law, and should therefore be distilled from relevant State practice and *opinio juris*. Where the Commission elects to advance a proposal that does not reflect existing law, that proposal should be clearly identified as such. To that end, Australia thanks the Commission for identifying that draft articles 12 to 15 on procedural safeguards represent an exercise in progressive development of international law.

Australia notes the prescriptive nature of draft articles 8 to 16 and looks forward to receiving the commentaries to the draft articles to clarify the methodology used to formulate them. Further consideration of how these draft articles account for the difference between immunity *ratione personae* and immunity *ratione materiae* should be undertaken by the Commission.

Australia reiterates its regret at the provisional adoption of the proposed exception to the immunity of foreign State officials from foreign criminal jurisdiction in draft article 7, during the Commission's sixty-ninth session. It remains Australia's view that draft article 7 does not reflect any real trend in State practice, still less existing customary international law. We share the concern of those Commission members who have doubts that the use of procedural safeguards could sufficiently rectify the substantive flaws inherent in draft article 7. The international community can and must do more to ensure that State officials who commit international crimes are held to account. But we do not agree that draft article 7 represents an appropriate means of addressing that issue.

Australia emphasises the procedural nature of the immunity of State officials and underscores the need for immunity not to be equated with impunity. Immunities apply to the prosecution of State officials for international crimes in some, but not all, circumstances, and in some, but not all, forums. This does not mean that State officials enjoy impunity. State officials accused of international crimes may be prosecuted in their own State, before an international court with jurisdiction, or in the courts of a third party State after waiver of immunity.

[...]

8.4 *International Law Commission's Work on Peremptory Norms of International Law*

On 28 October 2019, Australia made a statement to the Sixth Committee of the United Nations General Assembly in New York, on the work of the International Law Commission (ILC). Extracts from that statement follow:

[...]

Chair

Australia welcomes the Commission's continued work on peremptory norms of general international law.

We note the importance the Commission's work has in providing clarity to the international community on the peremptory character of norms of international law.

Australia also welcomes consideration of proposed draft conclusions on the consequences and legal effects of peremptory norms of general international law, and the accompanying commentaries.

The draft conclusions provide a useful framework to assist with the identification of peremptory norms of international law and their content.

Australia has taken note of the varying views as to the propriety of dealing with the question of the existence of regional jus cogens and the inclusion of a list of peremptory norms of general international law in the fourth report of the Special Rapporteur.

Australia remains doubtful as to the utility of further consideration of regional jus cogens, given the conceptual and practical challenges involved, the significant debate relating to the utility of such a concept and whether the concept could undermine the universality of jus cogens.

In relation to Draft Conclusion 23, which provides for a non-exhaustive list of peremptory norms of general international law, Australia remains unconvinced of the practical value of such a list.

Should the inclusion of such a list nevertheless be considered necessary, we note the important clarifications provided in the Commentary to Draft Conclusion 23 that: (i) the draft conclusions are methodological in nature and do not attempt to address the content of individual peremptory norms of general international law; and (ii) the list merely represents a non-exhaustive list of those norms which have previously been referred to by the Commission as having peremptory character.

We commend the progress made by the Special Rapporteur and the Drafting Committee to date and recognise that there is further work to be done. Australia looks forward to future developments on this matter and continues to recommend a balanced approach be taken on the Commission's work on peremptory norms of international law.

[...]

On 22 October 2019, Canada made a statement to the Sixth Committee of the United Nations General Assembly in New York, on transboundary harm delivered on behalf of Canada, Australia and New Zealand (CANZ). The full text of that statement follows:

I have the honour today to speak to you today on behalf of CANZ: Australia, New Zealand, and my own country, Canada.

We would like to thank the Secretary-General for his report and the Secretariat for their valuable work in compiling the decisions of international courts, tribunals, and other bodies referring to the International Law Commission's draft Articles on Prevention of Transboundary Harm from Hazardous Activities and Principles on the Allocation of Loss in the case of Transboundary Harm arising out of Hazardous Activities.

It is clear that transboundary harm continues to be an area of concern for states, as can be seen by the General Assembly's passing of Resolution 71/143 of 13 December 2016 'Consideration of prevention of transboundary harm from hazardous activities and allocation of loss in the case of such harm' and in which it again commended these articles and principles to the attention of Governments.

We are pleased to see that the Articles and Principles are referred to by international, regional and domestic courts. References to these draft articles and principles show how relevant they are. The risk associated with hazardous activities, whether within or beyond national jurisdictions, remains a concern for all states.

The world is becoming more inter-reliant and issues around transboundary harm are becoming more frequent. As such, it is necessary that there be a consistent, coherent and widely followed international framework setting out the standard of conduct and practice the international community expects from states in preventing transboundary harm, and the allocation of loss in the event of an occurrence.

There is little to be gained from attempting transformation of the articles and principles into the form of a Convention. CANZ continues to be of the view that persistent use of these articles and principles, as well ongoing discussions related to them in multilateral and bilateral fora, contribute significantly to the progressive development of international law in this area.

CANZ continues to encourage Member States to be guided by these draft Articles on the prevention of Transboundary Harm from Hazardous Activities, and the Principles on the Allocation of Loss Arising out of Hazardous Activities.

AUSTRALIAN PRACTICE IN INTERNATIONAL LAW 2019 685

9 Transnational Crime

9.1 *Combatting Transnational Crime in Southeast Asia*

On 4 November 2019, the East Asia Summit Leaders' Statement on Cooperation to Combat Transnational Crime was adopted in Bangkok, Thailand. The full text of that statement follows:

EAST ASIA SUMMIT LEADERS' STATEMENT ON COOPERATION TO COMBAT TRANSNATIONAL CRIME

WE, the Heads of State and Government of the Member States of the Association of Southeast Asian Nations (ASEAN), Australia, the People's Republic of China, the Republic of India, Japan, the Republic of Korea, New Zealand, the Russian Federation, and the United States of America, on the occasion of the 14th East Asia Summit (EAS) in Bangkok, on 4 November 2019;

REAFFIRMING the EAS participating countries' continuing commitment to the rule of law and promoting sustainable security through improved cooperation to combat transnational crime;

RECOGNISING the shared challenge of transnational crime, which is growing in scale and complexity;

RECOGNISING the need to be vigilant and address effectively and in a timely manner, existing and emerging transnational and trans-boundary challenges and threats that have the potential to undermine the stability and well-being of the region;

CONCERNED that criminals are taking advantage of porous borders and jurisdictional, intelligence and information gaps between countries and operating across multiple crime types;

UNDERLINING the EAS participating countries' resolve in detecting, deterring, suppressing, disrupting, combating, and preventing transnational crime;

UNDERSTANDING that effectively combating transnational crime requires cooperation within and between EAS participating countries;

HIGHLIGHTING that the increasing movement of people, goods and capital across borders presents both opportunities and challenges in our region;

UNDERSTANDING the increasing links between different types of transnational crime, including that the illicit revenue sourced from one criminal activity can be used in other criminal activities;

EXPRESSING concern that terrorists can benefit from transnational organised crime as a source of financing or logistical support, recognising that the nature and scope of the linkages between terrorism and transnational organised crime vary by context, and emphasising the need to coordinate efforts at the local, national, regional, sub regional and international levels to respond to this challenge, in accordance with international law;

WELCOMING discussions on cooperation on combating transnational crime and countering terrorism at the United Nations Congress on Crime Prevention and Criminal Justice;

ACKNOWLEDGING that the legal, law enforcement and regulatory responses needed to combat transnational crime are common to many crime types;

REAFFIRMING the commitment to applicable international instruments that facilitate cooperation between EAS participating countries, such as the United Nations Convention against Transnational Organized Crime (UNTOC) and the protocols thereto, the United Nations Convention against Corruption (UNCAC), and criminal justice responses to established and emerging threats;

APPRECIATING the work of ASEAN to date and ASEAN's commitment to combat transnational crime and strengthen cooperation on border management as set out in the ASEAN Leaders' Declaration on Drug-Free ASEAN 2015 (2012), the Kuala Lumpur Declaration in Combating Transnational Crime (2015), the ASEAN Political Security Community Blueprint 2025, the ASEAN Plan of Action in Combating Transnational Crime (2016–2025), the Manila Declaration to Counter the Rise of Radicalisation and Violent Extremism (2017), the ASEAN Declaration to Prevent and Combat Cybercrime (2017), the ASEAN Plan of Action to Prevent and Combat the Rise of Radicalisation and Violent Extremism (2018–2025), and to the ASEAN Convention on Counter Terrorism, and the ASEAN Convention Against Trafficking in Persons, Especially Women and Children (2015);

RECALLING previous statements addressing components of transnational crime, including the EAS Leaders' Declaration on Anti-Money Laundering and Countering the Financing of Terrorism (2017), the EAS Declaration on Strengthening Responses to Migrants in Crisis and Trafficking in Persons (2016), and the EAS Declaration on Combating Wildlife Trafficking (2014);

RECOGNISING the valuable role the private sector can play in combating transnational crime, including in relation to the development of effective policy, regulatory and operational responses to transnational crime, while recognising that States play the primary role in this sphere;

RECOGNISING the importance of preventing and countering the criminal misuse of information and communications technologies (ICTs) such as the internet, including for terrorist purposes or to incite terrorist acts, while upholding States' sovereignty and consistent with national and international law, including human rights and fundamental freedoms;

REAFFIRMING the EAS participating countries' commitment to continuing work towards peaceful and inclusive societies for sustainable development, access to justice for all, and effective, accountable and inclusive institutions at all levels;

DO HEREBY DECIDE TO:

1. INTENSIFY cooperation and encourage national efforts to combat and prevent transnational crime including in legal, law enforcement, regulatory and border security contexts;

2. PROMOTE a wider understanding amongst the EAS participating countries of the evolving nature of the transnational crime threat, as well as the increasing links and convergence between different types of transnational crime, and develop and deliver targeted, appropriate responses;

3. ENCOURAGE closer cooperation with relevant international organisations and fora including the United Nations Office on Drugs and Crime (UNODC), and the Financial Action Task Force (FATF) and FATF-style regional bodies, as well as the effective implementation of FATF standards;

4. CALL for enhanced collaboration on transnational crime consistent with domestic laws and regulations within and between the EAS participating countries, including through: a. implementation of relevant international instruments, including UNTOC and UNCAC; b. regular and timely exchange and sharing of information; c. training and capacity building of law enforcement personnel, including prosecutors, investigating magistrates and customs personnel and other personnel charged with the prevention, detection and control of the offences; d. exchange of best practices to strengthen legislative frameworks and mutual legal assistance, where applicable; e. enhanced investigative, prosecutorial and judicial cooperation;

5. ENHANCE cooperation to combat money laundering and the influx of the proceeds of crimes committed abroad, consistent with applicable international instruments.

6. ADDRESS the risks to vulnerable members of society from specific transnational crime such as human trafficking, which is defined in the Protocol to Prevent, Suppress and Punish Trafficking in Persons, Especially Women and Children, supplementing the UNTOC, as well as child sexual exploitation and abuse;

7. DEVELOP and IMPLEMENT, where necessary, appropriate responses, including through legislative, law enforcement and judicial means, including where relevant through engagement with victims of crime, and including by engaging with relevant local communities and non-governmental actors in developing strategies to counter organised crime including by empowering youth, families, women, religious, cultural, and education leaders, and all other concerned groups of civil society;

8. ENHANCE coordination with relevant ASEAN-led mechanisms and sectoral bodies to combat transnational crime, including the ASEAN Ministerial Meeting on Transnational Crime (AMMTC), the ASEAN Ministerial Meeting on Drug Matters (AMMD), the ASEAN Defence Ministers' Meeting (ADMM), and the ASEAN Regional Forum (ARF);

9. ENHANCE cooperation in preventing and combating transnational crime through existing regional frameworks including the Bali Process on People Smuggling, Trafficking in Persons and Related Transnational Crime, where appropriate, as well as regional and international institutions and organisations such as the International Criminal Police Organization (INTERPOL).

ADOPTED in Bangkok, the Kingdom of Thailand, on the Fourth of November in the Year Two Thousand and Nineteen.

9.2   *Countering the Use of Information and Communications Technologies for Criminal Purposes*

On 18 November 2019, Australia strongly opposed a Resolution on countering the use of information and communications technologies for criminal purposes. Australia rejected the premise that a new international treaty on cybercrime is needed, as called for in the Resolution. Australia voted against the draft resolution in both the UNGA Third Committee and later in the Plenary session. However, ultimately, the resolution was adopted. The full text of Australia's explanation of vote follows:

Chair
I take the floor to deliver an explanation of vote before the vote on L.11/ Rev.1 entitled 'Countering the use of information and communications technologies for criminal purposes'.

Australia is committed to an open, free and secure cyberspace. Online activity plays an increased role in growing our economies, in furthering sustainable development objectives, and in keeping people connected.

Cybercrime is a persistent and evolving threat, and cyber criminals are more adept at conducting low risk, high return activities that target our lives online and undermine public confidence in the digital domain.

The Indo-Pacific—our region—enjoys the world's most rapid rate of online connectivity, which is making a significant contribution to economic growth and efforts to eradicate poverty. However, this growth also presents opportunities for cyber criminals, who have targeted our region disproportionately.

We thank the Russian Federation for presenting L.11/Rev.1, which addresses an issue of global importance. We are grateful to hear sponsors' views. We are disappointed those sponsors were unwilling to hear ours.

Australia approached discussions on this resolution in good faith, in a spirit of mutual respect, and with commitment to fostering consensus.

We are disappointed that the lead drafter was not willing to engage on text changes, or consider incorporating compromise text that would accommodate the views of all Member States.

The UN Secretary General's report released in September this year highlighted the division in the international community over whether or not the world needs a new multilateral treaty.

In this climate, it is clear that Member States would benefit from a considered and genuine effort to better understand the issues and build towards an international response that we can all own.

Indeed, the General Assembly and ECOSOC have already given a mandate to do. We are already advancing with the help of established UN expertise under the Commission on Crime Prevention and Criminal Justice, its Open-ended Intergovernmental Expert Group (IEG), and other fora.

An expensive new committee will only serve to distract all stakeholders from the common effort to address cybercrime, and duplicate work already underway in Vienna through the IEG, which is due to report in 2021.

My delegation cannot support a resolution that so brazenly seeks to undercut the consensus of Member States and set the world on a path to a cyberspace that is less open, less free, and less secure.

My delegation cannot support a resolution that will diminish existing global efforts that are delivering results.

The Budapest Convention works. It attracts more support each year and is an established response to our shared cybercrime challenge that is tried, tested, and effective. It enables us to work together through a comprehensive framework for international cooperation and partnership.

While the UNSG's report underscored division over whether or not the world needs something new, it also made clear the importance of continuing and expanding capacity building efforts. Parties to the Budapest Convention already support efforts to build capacity—including by non-Parties.

L.11/Rev.1 will divert resources from capacity building and operational efforts, which will present new opportunities for cybercriminals to ply their trade and undermine our security and stability.

Australia will vote against this resolution and we urge others to do the same. It erodes our shared international frameworks for combatting cybercrime, it undermines efforts to foster consensus, and moves us away from cooperation and partnership.

We maintain that cybercrime discussions should remain at their established home in Vienna. Preserving this hub of expertise is vital for efforts to enhance an existing international framework that already sees us working in greater partnership to address the growing threat of cybercrime.

10 International Environment Law and Law of the Sea

10.1 *Antarctica*

On 2 December 2019, Australia's Minister for Foreign Affairs, Senator the Hon. Marise Payne, delivered a speech at Parliament House in Canberra on the occasion of the 60th anniversary of the signing of the Antarctic Treaty. An excerpt of that speech follows:

> [...]
>
> The Antarctic Treaty, along with the subsequent Protocol on Environmental Protection and the Convention on the Conservation of Antarctic Marine Living Resources, form the Antarctic Treaty system. Conceived at the height of Cold War tensions, the Antarctic Treaty system has endured and succeeded as a model of international cooperation.
>
> Australia is committed to maintaining a leading and influential role in international Antarctic affairs. We work closely with fellow Antarctic Treaty Parties to ensure the effective governance of the region, to undertake important scientific investigation, and to conserve and protect Antarctica's unique environment.

AUSTRALIAN PRACTICE IN INTERNATIONAL LAW 2019   691

Australia has been, and continues to be, a leader in environmental stewardship, comprehensive environmental protection and ecosystem conservation in Antarctica. Supporting the Antarctic Treaty system will remain a key priority for Australia into the future.

[...]

10.2   *Japanese Whaling*

On 2 July 2019, Australia's Minister for Foreign Affairs, Senator the Hon. Marise Payne and Minister for the Environment, Sussan Ley MP, released a joint media statement regarding Japan's withdrawal from the International Whaling Convention. The full text of that media release follows:

> Japan's withdrawal from the International Convention for the Regulation of Whaling and its decision-making body, the International Whaling Commission, has now taken effect and Japan is resuming commercial whaling within its waters.
>
> As part of Japan's withdrawal, Japan announced that it would stop whaling in the Southern Ocean. This means that the vast Southern Ocean is now a true sanctuary for whales. Japan has also indicated it will continue to cooperate with the Commission as an observer.
>
> While the Australian Government welcomes the end of whaling in the Southern Ocean, we are disappointed that Japan has withdrawn from the Convention and is resuming commercial whaling. We continue to urge Japan to return to the Convention and the Commission as a matter of priority.
>
> The Australian Government's position on whaling has not changed. We remain opposed to all forms of commercial and so-called 'scientific' whaling.
>
> Australia will continue to invest in the work of the International Whaling Commission as the leading global body for the conservation and management of whales. We will continue to work hard with all Commission members to uphold the global moratorium on commercial whaling and promote whale conservation.

10.3   *Sustainability of Oceans*

At the UN General Assembly's debate on 'Oceans and the Law of the Sea', held in New York on 10 December 2019, Australian Ambassador and Permanent Representative to the United Nations, Mr. Mitch Fifield, delivered Australia's national statement. Extracts from that statement follow:

[...]

UNCLOS is a Convention which is critically important for Australia.

It provides an important legal framework governing Australia's management of our maritime zones.

UNCLOS also provides a comprehensive legal framework governing states' interaction and cooperation in the oceans—from navigation to conservation.

Australia's support for UNCLOS reflects also our broader commitment to an international rules-based order, as the basis for a stable and prosperous future.

This remains as important today as it has ever been, including in the Indo-Pacific region.

We are committed to freedom of navigation and overflight, which are critical for international trade and security. We value the legal architecture that gives all States a voice.

And we believe strongly that all States have an obligation to resolve disputes peacefully in accordance with international law.

This is particularly vital in the South China Sea.

We do not take sides on competing territorial claims in the South China Sea, but we do have a strong stake in its stability and the rules and norms that govern it.

We urge all claimants to take meaningful steps to ease tensions and build trust, and cease actions that could undermine stability or lead to escalation.

We welcome also the General Assembly's continued affirmation that UNCLOS provides the legal framework within which all activities in the oceans and seas must be carried out.

UNCLOS is the 'constitution for the oceans'. It is of fundamental importance as the basis for national, regional and global action and cooperation on oceans matters.

[...]

Australia is pleased that this year's Sustainable Fisheries resolution includes even stronger language on stateless vessels. Fishing by such vessels is, by definition, IUU fishing.

We welcome the call by this Assembly on States to take action to prevent such vessels from fishing, including by enacting domestic enforcement legislation and prohibiting trans-shipment.

We also commend the close attention this Assembly continues to give to the issue of sea-level rise.

Sea-level rise will affect many States globally.

AUSTRALIAN PRACTICE IN INTERNATIONAL LAW 2019

The Pacific—however—is home to the majority of the world's low-lying atoll States and States dependent on coral islands and cays.

This region will be particularly vulnerable.

We are pleased the International Law Commission is actively considering the legal aspects of this important subject.

We recognise that a key purpose of UNCLOS is to provide a stable, predictable and durable maritime order in which the interests of all states are balanced.

We look forward to engaging with the ILC as it undertakes this work.

[...]

10.4   South China Sea

On 4 August 2019, Australia's Minister for Foreign Affairs, Senator the Hon. Marise Payne and Minister for Defence, Senator the Hon. Linda Reynolds CSC, released a joint media statement regarding the Australia-US ministerial meeting. An extract of that media release follows:

> [...]
>
> The principals expressed serious concerns at continued militarisation of disputed features in the South China Sea. They strongly objected to coercive unilateral actions by any claimant state that could alter the status quo and increase tensions. The Ministers and Secretaries also expressed concern about disruptive activities in relation to long-standing oil and gas projects as well as fisheries in the South China Sea. They emphasised the importance of upholding freedom of navigation, overflight and other lawful uses of the sea and of all States' acting in accordance with international law. They called on all countries to make and pursue their maritime claims in accordance with international law, as reflected in the UN Law of the Sea Convention (UNCLOS). The Ministers and Secretaries underscored the importance of the July 2016 decision in the Philippines-China Arbitral Tribunal's Award, which is binding on the parties. They called for any Code of Conduct to: be fully consistent with international law, in particular UNCLOS; not prejudice the interests of third parties or the rights of states under international law; and support existing, inclusive regional architecture.
>
> [...]

10.5   Australia—Timor-Leste Maritime Boundary Treaty

On 29 July 2019, Australia's Prime Minister, the Hon. Scott Morrison MP and Minister for Foreign Affairs, Senator the Hon. Marise Payne, released a joint media statement regarding establishment of maritime boundaries with Timor-Leste in the Timor Sea. The full text of that media release follows:

> Today, the Australian Parliament passed legislation to implement the treaty between Australia and the Democratic Republic of Timor-Leste *Establishing their Maritime Boundaries in the Timor Sea*.
>
> The treaty establishes permanent maritime boundaries between our two countries and a stable legal framework for the development of gas and oil resources in the Timor Sea.
>
> It upholds Australia's commitment to international rules and the peaceful resolution of disputes, and reflects our full commitment to the independence, sovereignty and economic sustainability of Timor-Leste.
>
> Since the signing of the treaty on 6 March 2018, the Australian Government has worked with the Timor-Leste Government and offshore petroleum operators on transitional arrangements that provide commercial certainty and security for all the parties.
>
> With the passage of the treaty's implementing legislation today, Australia is now ready to partner with Timor-Leste to jointly develop the Greater Sunrise gas fields for the benefit of both countries.
>
> Greater Sunrise will provide new opportunities for income, and commercial and industrial development in Timor-Leste, and is an important part of Timor-Leste's economic future.
>
> As Timor-Leste celebrates the 20th anniversary of its independence vote this year, Australia remains steadfast in our support for Timor-Leste's prosperity and role in the Indo-Pacific, and our friendship with the Timorese people.

10.6 *Freedom of Navigation*

On 14 June 2019, Australia's Minister for Foreign Affairs, Senator the Hon. Marise Payne, released a media statement regarding attacks on civilian shipping in the Gulf of Oman. The full text of that media release follows:

> The Australian Government strongly condemns the latest attacks on shipping in the Gulf of Oman.
>
> As a country that relies on freedom of navigation and the uninterrupted passage of maritime trade, attacks on civilian shipping are of grave concern to Australia.
>
> Australia remains deeply concerned about further escalations in an already tense region. A deterioration in the situation would be counter to

regional security, global trade, the rules-based order, and the best interests of Australia and the world.

We are following the matter closely, including through our embassies in the region.

On 21 August 2019, Australia's Prime Minister, the Hon. Scott Morrison MP, Minister for Foreign Affairs, Senator the Hon. Marise Payne and Minister for Defence, Senator the Hon. Linda Reynolds CSC, released a joint media statement announcing Australia's support to the International Maritime Security Construct in the Gulf. The full text of that media release follows:

> The Morrison Government is reaffirming its commitment to freedom of navigation and safe passage through the Gulf by announcing it will support an international maritime security mission.
>
> This mission will see the Australian Defence Force work alongside its international partners to assure the security of merchant vessels in the Strait of Hormuz.
>
> Australia's contribution will include the deployment of:
>
> – a P-8A Poseidon maritime surveillance aircraft to the Middle East for one month before the end of 2019;
>
> – an Australian Frigate in January 2020 for six months; and
>
> – ADF personnel to the International Maritime Security Construct headquarters in Bahrain.
>
> The Government has been concerned with incidents involving shipping in the Strait of Hormuz over the past few months.
>
> This destabilising behaviour is a threat to Australian interests in the region.
>
> We have been working closely with our allies and partners, particularly the United States and the United Kingdom, on this issue, which impacts global security and stability.
>
> Freedom of navigation through international waters is a fundamental right of all states under international law. All states have a right to expect safe passage of their maritime trade consistent with international law.
>
> It is in Australia's interest to work with international partners to uphold these rights.
>
> Australian forces will always conduct themselves in accordance with their international legal obligations.
>
> This will be an enhancement of our existing and longstanding contribution to counter-piracy and counter-terrorism missions in the waters of the Middle East.

696   AUSTRALIAN YEAR BOOK OF INTERNATIONAL LAW VOLUME 38

Our contribution will be modest, meaningful and time limited—and it will be part of an international mission.

Australia will defend our interests wherever they may be under threat.

Working with partners, we will play our part in shaping a better future for Australia and Australians, as well as our region and the world.

10.7 *Protection of the Environment in the Context of Armed Conflict*

On 31 October 2019, Australia made a statement to the Sixth Committee of the United Nations General Assembly in New York, on the work of the International Law Commission (ILC). Extracts from that statement follow:

[…]

Finally, turning first to the protection of the environment in relation to armed conflict. Australia supports the clear call upon States to take, pursuant to their obligations under international law, effective measures to protect the environment in relation to armed conflict. We welcome the consideration by the Commission of additional measures States could consider taking to further that objective.

Australia considers that there would be merit in making clearer which draft principles reflect existing international law, and which draft principles are intended to constitute recommendations to enhance the protection of the environment beyond that required as a matter of legal obligation. The Commission should also more clearly take account of the substantive differences in obligations depending on whether a conflict is international or non-international in character.

Australia acknowledges the focus of a number of the draft principles upon reparation, remediation and restoration. It is important to understand how these principles would interact with concepts of State responsibility, such as attribution. We note that many States participate in armed conflict as part of a coalition or pursuant to a mandate of an international organisation with close levels of interoperability. We welcome the Special Rapporteur's appreciation of the intricacies associated with questions of allocation of responsibility.

[…]

10.8 *Sea-Level Rise*

On 20 August 2019, Pacific leaders at the 50th the Pacific Islands Forum issued a Forum Communique, outlining priorities for the future of security in the Pacific. An extract from the communique follows:

[...]

Oceans and Maritime Boundaries

24. Leaders noted with concern the threat posed by sea level rise to securing the Blue Pacific, and reaffirmed their commitment to conclude negotiations on all outstanding maritime boundaries claims and zones.

25. Leaders discussed progress made by Members to conclude negotiations on maritime boundary claims since the Leaders meeting in Nauru 2018, and encouraged Members to conclude all outstanding maritime boundaries claims and zones. Additionally, Leaders reaffirmed the importance of preserving Members' existing rights stemming from maritime zones, in the face of sea level rise, noting the existing and ongoing regional mechanisms to support maritime boundaries delimitation.

26. Leaders committed to a collective effort, including to develop international law, with the aim of ensuring that once a Forum Member's maritime zones are delineated in accordance with the 1982 UN Convention on the Law of the Sea, that the Members maritime zones could not be challenged or reduced as a result of sea-level rise and climate change.

27. Leaders agreed that pursuing their claims for extended continental shelf, under Article 76 of the UN Convention on the Law of the Sea, is important and requested ongoing support and assistance by relevant regional agencies on Members' submission to the Commission on the Limits of the Continental Shelf.

[...]

On 31 October 2019, Australia made a statement to the Sixth Committee of the United Nations General Assembly in New York, on the work of the International Law Commission (ILC). Extracts from that statement follow:

[...]

Finally, turning to sea-level rise in relation to international law. Sea-level rise remains a significant concern, and is an issue that raises complex legal questions.

Small-island States in the Pacific are particularly vulnerable to sea level rise.

The UNCLOS framework provides the basis for stability and good governance of the oceans. Given the urgency and potential consequences of sea-level rise, it is important that we consider how international law can help us address these important issues. We therefore welcome the

Commission's decision to move the topic of sea-level rise to its active program of work.

Australia supports the Commission's approach to draw on current State practice concerning the identification of basepoints and definition of maritime zones to help inform its recommendations around sea level rise and international law. Australia will contribute to the Commission's work. We continue to encourage States to publicise geographical coordinates and to deposit their charts with the Secretary-General. This will reinforce the stability and clarity that UNCLOS brings to oceans governance and maritime jurisdiction.

On 31 October 2019, Tuvalu made a statement to the Sixth Committee of the United Nations General Assembly in New York, on the work of the International Law Commission (ILC) delivered on behalf of the 14 Pacific Islands Forum countries with Missions to the United Nations, namely: Australia, Federated States of Micronesia, Fiji, Kiribati, Palau, Papua New Guinea, Marshall Islands, Nauru, New Zealand, Samoa, Solomon Islands, Tonga, Tuvalu and Vanuatu. The full text of that statement follows:

Mr. Chairman,

I have the honour to deliver this statement on behalf of the 14 Pacific Islands Forum countries with Missions to the United Nations, namely Australia, Federated States of Micronesia, Fiji, Kiribati, Palau, Papua New Guinea, Marshall Islands, Nauru, New Zealand, Samoa, Solomon Islands, Tonga, Vanuatu and my own country Tuvalu.

Firstly, we would like to congratulate you Mr. Chairman and members of your Bureau for your election. We also like to assure you of our group's unwavering support as you steer the Committee's work in this Session.

Last year, our region called for the Commission to examine the international law implications of sea-level rise as a matter of extreme urgency.

We therefore welcome the decisions of the Commission to move the topic of 'sea-level rise in relation to international law' to its active programme of work, and to establish an open-ended Study Group on the topic at its meeting in May this year.

We express our deep gratitude to the members of the Commission for the priority they have accorded this topic, and for listening to our call.

As we have said before, for the Pacific, sea-level rise is a subject of critical importance. This is particularly true for low-lying small island States and atolls in the Pacific. The Pacific is already facing the adverse impacts of climate change, including, rising sea levels upon deteriorating marine and coastal environments and more destructive storm surges and natural disasters, which further threaten our livelihoods, health, culture, wellbeing, and infrastructure.

International law should not further disadvantage those affected by the impacts of climate change. In the Pacific, we aim to ensure that our maritime zones and the entitlements flowing from those zones are not challenged or reduced as a result of sea-level rise. We contend that the response of international law to sea-level rise must take into account the interests of those who are particularly affected, including small island developing states with the least responsibility for its causes.

In that connection, in August this year, our Forum Leaders met in Tuvalu and committed to a collective effort, including to develop international law, with the aim of ensuring that once a Forum member's maritime zones are delineated in accordance with the 1982 United Nations Convention on the Law of the Sea ('UNCLOS'), that the member's maritime zones could not be challenged or reduced as a result of sea-level rise and climate change.

Mr. Chairman, we therefore are committed to working together to respond effectively to these challenges posed by sea-level rise. We also call on other member States to recognize the need of retaining maritime zones and the entitlements that flow from such maritime zones once delineated in accordance with UNCLOS. This will ensure the sustainable development of our people, our communities and our culture in the face of sea-level rise and climate change.

We thank the ILC for setting out how it intends to approach each subtopic and we look forward to continue engaging with the ILC on each of the facets of this important topic.

On 30 December 2019, Members of the Pacific Island Forum delivered a submission to the Secretary of the International Law Commission containing State practice for coping with sea-level rise in favour of maintaining maritime zones, settling outstanding maritime limits, and fixing geographical coordinates of maritime baselines and outer limits of maritime zones. Extracts from this submission follow:

[...]

As PIF Members have consistently made clear, sea-level rise could therefore have significant consequences for statehood, national identity, sustainable development, and livelihoods in the Pacific. This is a particularly unjust and inequitable outcome, as sea-level rise and climate change are phenomena that small island States have done the least to cause.

Preservation of existing maritime zones and entitlements that flow from them is essential. As early as 2010, PIF Leaders committed to preserving PIF Members' existing rights stemming from maritime zones in the face of sea-level rise.

[...]

Designation of Maritime Zones by Geographic Coordinates

Recently, State practice from among PIF Members has shifted from using nautical charts as the sole of primary method to show the location of the normal, straight or archipelagic baseline and the outer limits of maritime zones to the use of geographic coordinates specifying points on the baseline and outer limits. This method allows States to use modern and credible technology to apply principles of hydrographic practice. Describing baselines and maritime zone limits in this way is more accurate and certain with regard to the rights and responsibilities of coastal and third States. Benefits include easier legal compliance and enforcement (eg, fisheries, especially as modern vessels rely on digital positioning systems to locate themselves within licensed areas); assistance in resource exploration and exploitation; and management of area based tools (eg, location of shipping lanes or marine protected areas).

Examples of this practice published on the United Nations Division for Oceans and the Law of the Sea website include the maritime zones legislations of Kiribati, the Republic of the Marshall Islands, Niue, Samoa, and Tuvalu. Australia followed this approach in its Seas and Submerged Lands (Continental Shelf) Proclamation 2012, and Papua New Guinea's Maritime Zones Act 2016 follows the same practice. The Solomon Islands and Fiji are also working towards using geographic coordinates.

11 International Trade and Investment Law

11.1 *UK—Australia Trade Agreements*

On 19 January 2019, Australia's Minister for Trade, Tourism and Investment, Senator the Hon. Simon Birmingham, released a media statement announcing a new Australia-UK Wine Agreement and Mutual Recognition Agreement. The full text of the statement follows:

Australia and the United Kingdom have signed a new bilateral Wine Agreement and Mutual Recognition Agreement overnight in London, which will help ensure the continued flow of trade post-Brexit.

Minister for Trade, Tourism and Investment Simon Birmingham said these agreements would ensure arrangements already in place between Australia and the European Union for our wine and other exports continued to apply for the United Kingdom post-Brexit.

'This will mean Australian exporters can continue to benefit from existing arrangements for mutual recognition as they do currently, even if the UK leaves the EU without an agreement,' Minister Birmingham said.

'These agreements provide assurances to Australian exporters that they will be able to get their goods into the UK post-Brexit whether it be wine, medical devices or automotive parts without additional trade barriers or regulations.'

'They are a significant and necessary step in our post-Brexit preparations, where we want to minimise disruptions to trade flows and provide as much certainty to Australian exporters as we can.'

'On top of these, we're committed to securing a comprehensive free trade agreement with the UK as soon as they are in a position to do so, which will even further boost trade flows between our two countries.'

Minister for Agriculture David Littleproud said nearly a third of our exported wine went to the UK last year.

'This agreement protects Australia's geographical indicators so UK consumers know our wine is fair dinkum,' Minister Littleproud said.

'We can grow our UK trade under this agreement and put more money in Australian wine grower's pockets.'

The Wine Agreement replicates an agreement already in place with the EU, meaning the UK will accept Australian labelling standards and certification standards as well as winemaking practices.

Minister for Industry, Science and Technology Karen Andrews said the Mutual Recognition Agreement would ensure Australia and the UK continue to recognise the test reports and certificates issued by each other's designated conformity assessment bodies.

'The Mutual Recognition Agreement will help facilitate trade flows between both countries, guaranteeing continuity of the existing mutual recognition arrangements post-Brexit,' Minister Andrews said.

'For Australian businesses, this will eliminate the cost and time of duplicative testing or the need for re-certification when their products arrive in the other country's market.'

11.2 Signing and Ratification of Indonesia-Australia Comprehensive Economic Partnership Agreement, Australia-Hong-Kong Free Trade and Investment Agreement, and Peru-Australia Free Trade Agreement

On 18 December 2019, Australia's Minister for Trade, Tourism and Investment, Senator the Hon. Simon Birmingham and Australia's Assistant Minister for Trade and Investment, the Hon. Mark Coulton MP, released a joint media statement regarding Australia's ratification of trade deals with Indonesia, Hong Kong and Peru. The full text of the statement follows:

Australia has today ratified its free trade agreements with Indonesia, Hong Kong and Peru, a move that will give our farmers access to more markets, greater opportunities for our businesses, create more jobs and increased investment.

Trade Minister Simon Birmingham said these agreements would enhance export opportunities and deliver significant benefits for Australian exporters.

'This trade trifecta will deliver more opportunities and greater access to more markets for Australian farmers and businesses,' Minister Birmingham said.

'These high-quality and comprehensive agreements will open new doors and deliver wide-ranging benefits in industries including agriculture, manufacturing, mining, education, and tourism.'

'Our grain growers will now be able to export 500 000 tonnes of feed grains each year into Indonesia tariff free, whilst Australian dairy farmers will have historic new access to the Peru market, with zero tariffs locked-in from day one on 7,000 tonnes of products.'

'Under our deal with Hong Kong zero tariffs will be locked-in on goods, market access will be guaranteed for services suppliers, and conditions for two-way investment will be significantly improved.'

'Expanding opportunities for Australian exporters is a key pillar of our economic plan and builds upon successes that have already fuelled Australia to record levels of exports and a record trade surplus.'

'Our Government's record speaks for itself and only we can be trusted to deliver agreements that open new markets for Australian exporters, create certainty for Australian businesses, strengthen our economy and create more jobs.'

Assistant Minister for Trade and Investment Mark Coulton said the Government's delivery of these agreements is a real win for regional Australia.

'This will help generate significant new export opportunities for farmers and regional businesses in what are very trying times for many rural communities.'

'I will continue to work closely with our exporters, particularly in regional areas, to ensure they are aware of these opportunities and can maximise the commercial outcomes from these important market access gains,' said Minister Coulton.

Hong Kong and Peru have already completed ratification processes and we remain hopeful that Indonesia will complete their ratification processes early next year.

The trade agreements with Hong Kong and Peru will enter into force on 17 January and 11 February 2020 respectively. The trade agreement with Indonesia will come into force 60 days after Indonesia formally advises Australia it has ratified the agreement.

11.3   *Vietnam Bilateral Investment Treaty*

On 14 January 2019 the Australian-Vietnam bilateral treaty was terminated, subject to transitional arrangements, upon entry into force of the Comprehensive and Progressive Agreement for the Trans-Pacific Partnership (CPTPP) as between Australia and Vietnam.

11.4   *Uruguay Bilateral Investment Treaty*

On 16 September 2019, officers from the Department of Foreign Affairs, Attorney-General's Department and Department of Treasury appeared before the Joint Standing Committee on Treaties for a hearing on the Committee's enquiry into the updated Uruguay bilateral investment treaty. Excerpts from the hearing follow:

MR SCHOFIELD: [...]

The updated Australia-Uruguay bilateral investment treaty was signed on 5 April 2019. The updated treaty will further strengthen Australia's foothold in the growing Mercosur market, made up of Argentina, Brazil, Paraguay and Uruguay and which has a combined GDP of US$2.7 trillion and a consumer base of over 260 million people.

The updated treaty forms part of the government's broader investor-state dispute settlement, ISDS, reform efforts. It is a pilot initiative in terms of reforming Australia's network of bilateral investment treaties to provide greater certainty for both government and investors.

Like Australia's 17 other bilateral investment treaties, the 2002 Australia—Uruguay bilateral investment treaty was signed at a time when Australia's investment practice was different to what it is now. Since the 2002 treaty was signed, international investment law, Australia's approach to investment treaties and the approach of our trading partners have evolved.

Specifically, the 2002 treaty and other older style investment treaties like it were broadly drafted and do not contain the same explicit, substantive and procedural safeguards found in modern investment treaties.

For example, the older style investment treaties do not explicitly recognise the government's right to regulate and protect legitimate public welfare objectives, such as public health and the environment, nor do they contain the same detailed procedural safeguards in relation to ISDS.

The updated treaty with Uruguay addresses these and other issues and brings the treaty more into alignment with Australia's modern investment treaty practice as reflected in our recent free trade agreements.

The updated treaty sets explicit parameters on key obligations, such as the minimum standard of treatment obligation and the expropriation obligation, thereby providing clear guidance to tribunals on the appropriate application of those provisions.

It reinforces the government's right to regulate through various explicit exceptions, including a WTO-style general exception and a broad essential security exception. It also allows the government to unilaterally deny the benefits of the treaty to an investor where that investor doesn't have substantial business activities in Australia.

Importantly, the updated treaty makes significant changes to the ISDS mechanism. For example, it now explicitly allows for preliminary objections so that unmeritorious claims can be dealt with at an earlier stage, thereby reducing costs.

It also includes a waiver provision requiring investors to waive their rights to initiate or continue dispute settlement proceedings in any other fora.

In addition, the updated treaty includes provisions on enhanced transparency in ISDS disputes and a detailed set of ethical rules for arbitrators.

As I mentioned earlier, the updated Uruguay treaty is part of the government's broader ISDS reform efforts. While it is clear that ISDS provides

AUSTRALIAN PRACTICE IN INTERNATIONAL LAW 2019

important protection for Australian investors overseas, particularly in the energy and resources sector, it is recognised that there is room for improvement in relation to this enforcement mechanism.

As part of these reform efforts where Australia engages in free trade agreement in FTA negotiations with countries with whom we have older-style investment treaties, where appropriate, we will consider termination of the older-style investment treaties in favour of the FTA investment provisions. We have already done so with Mexico and Vietnam, following the entry into force of the Comprehensive and Progress Agreement for Trans-Pacific Partnership, CPTPP, between each of those countries and Australia.

Where we are not engaged in FTA negotiation with particular trading partners, where appropriate, we will consider updating the bilateral investment treaties with those trading partners in the same way as we have done with this Uruguay treaty.

More broadly, Australia is also actively involved in multilateral ISDS reform efforts in a range of fora, including the International Centre for the Settlement of Investment Disputes, ICSID, and the United Nations Commission on International Trade Law, UNCITRAL.

It is widely accepted that trade and investment is an important pillar in Australia's economic growth. This updated treaty with Uruguay will provide certainty to Australian investors in Uruguay which will help them diversify into the broader Latin American market.

[...]

11.5   WTO—Digital Trade Negotiations

On 26 January 2019, Australia's Minister for Trade, Tourism and Investment, Senator the Hon. Simon Birmingham, released a media statement regarding digital trade negotiations in the World Trade Organisation (WTO). The full text of the statement follows:

Australian efforts have ignited negotiations with 75 other members of the World Trade Organization (WTO), representing over 90 per cent of global trade, on the development of new international rules in digital trade.

Minister for Trade, Tourism and Investment Simon Birmingham said establishing new international rules for digital trade would help keep markets open, reduce barriers and make it easier for Australian businesses to grow into new markets and operate across borders.

'Digital trade is an increasingly important way for Australia to do business with the rest of the world,' Minister Birmingham said.

'It provides more opportunities for Australian businesses to reach more customers across the globe as well as help further grow our economy.'

'We know half of Australian businesses are already engaged in the digital economy in some way, and this number will continue to grow at a rapid rate.'

'A recent report by the Hinrich Foundation estimates that Australia's digital exports could grow by 210 per cent by 2030 and that digital trade could enable almost $200 billion of economic value in our domestic economy.'

Minister Birmingham said the signal by so many WTO members to commence negotiations on e-commerce was critical in creating the right international settings to facilitate the huge volumes of digital trade across the globe.

'Negotiating a set of international digital trade rules is a significant step forward in ensuring Australian businesses can fully realise the gains from the progressive digitisation of trade.'

'Our Government will continue to work creatively to achieve a high quality digital trade outcome that addresses issues important to Australian businesses and consumers with the participation of as many WTO Members as possible.'

'It's expected negotiations will consider a range of possible rules specific to facilitating e-commerce such as paperless import/export procedures, the ability to securely and flexibly transfer and store data, and ensuring online consumer protection.'

'The start of these negotiations in an open and inclusive way will reaffirm the importance of the multilateral trading system by signalling the revitalisation of the WTO negotiating function, which is an important part of its reform.'

On 26 January 2019, Australia's Minister for Trade, Tourism and Investment, Senator the Hon. Simon Birmingham, released a media statement regarding digital trade negotiations in the World Trade Organisation (WTO). The full text of the statement follows:

Australia, Japan and Singapore hosted an informal meeting of Ministers on the World Trade Organization (WTO) e-commerce initiative in the margins of the World Economic Forum Annual Meeting in Davos, Switzerland.

Ministers welcomed the progress made in the WTO e-commerce initiative since its launch at the eleventh WTO Ministerial Conference in Buenos Aires in 2017.

Ministers exchanged views on how WTO negotiations can capture opportunities offered by e-commerce for businesses, consumers and the global economy. The importance of working in an innovative, open and inclusive manner was expressed. The unique opportunities and challenges faced by Members, including developing countries and LDCs, as well as by micro, small and medium enterprises (MSMEs), were also highlighted.

Following the meeting, 76 WTO Members representing over 90 percent of global trade issued a Joint Statement (Annex) confirming their intention to commence WTO negotiations on trade-related aspects of e-commerce, with the objective of achieving a high standard outcome with the participation of as many Members as possible.

Australian Minister for Trade, Tourism and Investment Simon Birmingham said,

'Commencing WTO negotiations on e-commerce is a significant step towards updating international trade rules in line with how modern business is done.'

'Through these negotiations we will demonstrate the importance of the multilateral trading system in helping reduce barriers, remove red tape and increase global trade.'

Japanese Minister of Economy, Trade and Industry Hiroshige Seko said,

'It would be truly meaningful for the world economy if we could create trade rules for the 21st century that address the new challenges and promote the growth of digital economy.'

Singapore's Minister for Communications and Information and Minister-in-charge of Trade Relations S Iswaran said,

'Digital trade is the future of global trade. It fosters inclusive growth by enabling MSMEs to reach global markets. Modern WTO digital trade rules that address core needs will create an open and predictable environment for businesses to better harness the digital economy.'

On 13 March 2019, Australia's Minister for Trade, Tourism and Investment, Senator the Hon. Simon Birmingham, released a media statement announcing investment in regional digital trade. The full text of the statement follows:

The Morrison Government has today launched a new $4.5 million program to help developing countries in the Indo-Pacific maximise the benefits of digital trade.

Minister for Trade, Tourism and Investment Simon Birmingham said the 'E-commerce Aid for Trade Fund' would have a major focus on building e-commerce capacity and capability across the Indo-Pacific, including within the ASEAN region.

'Digital trade is an increasingly important way for our region to connect and do business with the rest of the world,' Minister Birmingham said.

'This Fund is about providing innovative businesses and Governments within the region with assistance so they can build their digital capabilities enabling them to operate across borders and access new markets.'

'It builds on our ongoing commitment to help boost the economic development of individual countries in the Indo-Pacific, which benefits Australia and helps contribute to an economically stronger and more secure region.'

'Whether it be a grant for digital skills development or support to develop data storage solutions, our government is committed to supporting developing countries in our region get ahead and export more of their goods to the world.'

'It follows our recent efforts that will see 76 World Trade Organization members, representing 90 per cent of global trade, commence negotiations on new international rules for digital trade which will present new opportunities for businesses within Australia and the wider region.'

Minister for Foreign Affairs Marise Payne said the Fund would build on the Morrison Government's broader economic development programs and ICT infrastructure investments in the Indo-Pacific. 'Digital trade has the potential to dramatically increase economic development and prosperity within the region and that's why we're backing developing countries in our region who want to build their e-commerce capabilities,' Minister Payne said.

'This initiative underlines our Government's strong commitment to infrastructure development in the region so countries are well-equipped to leverage off the huge potential benefits of digital trade.'

Through the E-commerce Aid for Trade Fund, grants of up to $500,000 will be open to the public and private sectors with local solutions for stimulating e-commerce activity.

On 13 October 2019, Australia's Minister for Trade, Tourism and Investment, Senator the Hon. Simon Birmingham, released a media statement announcing a landmark digital economy agreement with Singapore. The full text of the statement follows:

Australia and Singapore are continuing to lead the way on digital trade through a landmark agreement that will harness digital transformation and technology to expand trade and economic ties in our region.

Following discussions in June in Singapore between Prime Ministers Scott Morrison and Lee Hsien Loong, work on a landmark Australia-Singapore Digital Economy Agreement commenced, with the aim to deepen the bilateral economic relationship, promote greater connectivity and provide ambitious standards for the region's digital economy.

Today, Trade Ministers Simon Birmingham and Chan Chun Sing agreed on the scope of the Agreement, which covers a broad range of new areas of bilateral cooperation, including digital trade facilitation, e-invoicing, e-payments, FinTech, digital identity and artificial intelligence.

Australia and Singapore will also explore the role of data in the digital economy and work together to foster trust, promote a safe online environment and improve personal data protection.

'Southeast Asia's digital economy is growing rapidly. Connectivity and internet use across the region is increasing with a rising number of businesses and consumers now engaged in cross-border digital commerce,' Minister Birmingham said.

'Half of Australian businesses are already engaged in the digital economy in some way, and this number is growing exponentially. This agreement will ultimately deliver practical improvements that lower the costs and increase the efficiency of doing business.'

'This Agreement will expand the scope of our economic engagement and provide new opportunities for businesses and consumers to benefit from the digital economy, modernising our economic relationship with Singapore.'

'Building on the Australia—Singapore Comprehensive Strategic Partnership, it will also expand on both countries' commitments under the Singapore—Australia Free Trade Agreement.'

'It will provide support to the global trading system at a time of regional economic uncertainty. By developing digital trade rules and standards that build trust and confidence, and by deepening cooperation, Australia and Singapore can set ambitious benchmarks for others in the region.'

Minister Chan said, 'Trade has been and continues to be the bedrock of the Singapore economy. The Singapore-Australia Digital Economy Agreement will enhance digital trade opportunities for our companies, with Australia and the broader region.'

'With the digital economy of Southeast Asia expected to triple by 2025, this Agreement will lay the groundwork for bilateral digital economy cooperation geared towards enabling our companies to tap on this regional growth.'

'Through high-standard digital trade rules and pilot initiatives, we will push the frontiers of digital trade and digital connectivity. This Agreement will allow us to build on what we have achieved under the Singapore-Australia Free Trade Agreement. It will also add another new dimension to enrich our multi-faceted collaboration under the bilateral Comprehensive Strategic Partnership.'

'The Agreement will complement both Australia's and Singapore's networks of free trade agreements, as well as our efforts as co-convenor of the World Trade Organization Joint Statement Initiative on E-Commerce to develop international digital trade rules.'

Formal negotiations will begin shortly and both countries are working to finalise this agreement by early next year.

This initiative will build on the leading role of Australia and Singapore in negotiating new rules for digital trade in the World Trade Organization Joint Statement Initiative on e-commerce negotiations.

11.6   *WTO—Sugar Dispute*

On 28 February 2019, Australia's Minister for Trade, Tourism and Investment, Senator the Hon. Simon Birmingham, released a media statement regarding the commencement of formal dispute action against India over sugar in the World Trade Organisation (WTO). The full text of the statement follows:

> The Liberal-National Government, together with Brazil, has launched formal dispute action in the World Trade Organization (WTO) on India's continuing sugar subsidies that are depressing world prices and impacting on our highly productive and globally competitive sugar industry.
>
> Minister for Trade, Tourism and Investment Simon Birmingham said India's sugar subsidy regime was inconsistent with WTO rules and had helped create a glut in the global sugar market.
>
> 'The Liberal-National Government continues to stand side-by-side with our sugar industry on this matter,' Minister Birmingham said
>
> 'This glut is hurting Australia's canegrowers and millers, and is threatening our $1.8 billion sugar export industry by dragging down prices to unsustainable lows.'
>
> 'While Australia respects the rights of WTO members to support their farmers and agricultural industries, this support must be consistent with WTO rules and provide a level playing field.'

'Australia always seeks to resolve its concerns outside of the WTO's dispute system, and our numerous representations to India at the highest levels and in the WTO have been consistent with this approach.'

'Unfortunately, our representations, and those of other sugar exporting countries, have so far been unsuccessful. This has left us with no other choice but to initiate formal WTO dispute action, together with Brazil.'

'Australia maintains a very good relationship with India, both economically and strategically, and it is perfectly normal for even close friends and partners to avail themselves of WTO mechanisms from time-to-time to resolve trade issues.'

Minister Littleproud and Assistant Minister Coulton joined with Minister Birmingham in acknowledging the work the Canegrowers and the Australian Sugar Milling Council have done in preparing to launch this WTO action.

'Our industry relies heavily on exports, sending roughly 85 per cent of its raw sugar into the world market,' Minister Littleproud said.

'These subsidies are hitting our farmers and millers, and I'm pleased we're exercising our WTO rights and asking for an even playing field.'

Assistant Minister Coulton said the sugar industry made a great contribution to jobs and the economy in regional Australia and the Liberal-National Government would continue to stand up for these communities.

'This action being taken by the Government demonstrates our commitment to protecting the interests of our hard-working canegrowers and sugar millers, and to the rules-based international trading system that underpins the viability of our vital export industries,' Assistant Minister Coulton said.

On 12 July 2019, Australia's Minister for Trade, Tourism and Investment, Senator the Hon. Simon Birmingham and Minister for Agriculture, Senator the Hon. Bridget McKenzie, released a joint media statement regarding the formal dispute action against India over sugar in the World Trade Organisation (WTO). The full text of the statement follows:

The Morrison Government is taking the next step in our World Trade Organization (WTO) dispute against Indian sugar subsidies that have contributed to a global sugar glut and hurt our sugar industry.

Minister for Trade, Tourism and Investment Simon Birmingham said strong action was needed against Indian sugar subsidies that create an uneven playing field and have driven sugar prices to unsustainable lows.

'India has not taken concrete action to respond to Australia's long-held concerns and continues to provide subsidies in breach of its WTO commitments,' Minister Birmingham said.

'The longer these unfair subsidies continue, the greater the impact will be on our hardworking Australian canegrowers and millers and the regional jobs they create.'

'Together with Brazil and Guatemala, Australia has now requested that the WTO establish a panel to resolve our dispute with India.'

'Australia's relationship with India is strong and it shows how valuable the trading system is that even close partners with good relations can utilise WTO processes to address trade disputes.'

Minister for Agriculture Bridget McKenzie said this action was about standing up for our regional producers and the $2 billion sugar industry.

'This is about protecting over 40,000 jobs and the regional communities that are supported by our sugar industry,' Minister McKenzie said.

'We'll continue to support our farmers and producers, and we'll do everything we can to make sure their interests are protected.'

Australia launched formal WTO consultations against India in February to seek the winding back of subsidies inconsistent with WTO rules. Australia strongly supports the multilateral trading system, with the WTO at its core.

11.7   WTO—Aid for Trade

On 5 July 2019, Australia's Minister for Trade, Tourism and Investment, Senator the Hon. Simon Birmingham, released a media statement regarding Australia's expanded cooperation in the Aid for Trade space. The full text of the statement follows:

The Australian Government today announces further support to help developing countries maximise the benefits of trade, recognising its importance in driving economic growth, reducing global poverty, and advancing gender equality.

Minister for Trade, Tourism and Investment Simon Birmingham said Australia would expand its cooperation with two key partnerships of the World Trade Organization—the Enhanced Integrated Framework and the Standards and Trade Development Facility.

'Helping developing countries to operate across borders and access new markets builds long-term stability and prosperity across the world,' Minister Birmingham said.

'These vital partnerships will assist developing countries, particularly in our region to build their capacity to trade in areas such as workforce skills development, connecting farmers to overseas buyers and helping women entrepreneurs to export.'

'Australia continues to support developing countries to improve their capacity to trade as a way to reduce poverty, lift living standards and enhance economic development.'

Minister for Foreign Affairs Marise Payne also announced a US$3 million extension to Australia's partnership with the Better Work programme. Better Work brings together factory owners, workers, brands and governments to improve working conditions and reduce gender discrimination in garment factories.

The joint initiative with the International Labour Organization and International Finance Corporation will support over 2.2 million workers, of which 75 per cent are women, in more than 1,300 factories across Bangladesh, Cambodia, Indonesia and Vietnam.

'Better Work has a strong focus on developing safer working conditions and closing the gender pay gap throughout the female-dominated industry,' Minister Payne said.

'The programme also demonstrates how higher quality jobs have flow-on benefits for communities, with Better Work factory workers reporting that their increased wages have resulted in improved health and education outcomes for their children.'

In addition, the Australian Government will support Better Work and CARE Australia to deliver a regional workshop on preventing sexual harassment in garment factories in Cambodia later this year.

Australia will also open the first round for its E-commerce Aid for Trade Fund this month, with an initial focus on the ASEAN region. The Fund will help developing countries maximise the benefits of digital trade.

Australia's new commitments, announced at the World Trade Organization's Global Review of Aid for Trade in Geneva this week, total over $8 million.

12   Arms Control, Nuclear Non-Proliferation and Disarmament

12.1   *Chemical Weapons*

On 25 November 2019, Australia's Permanent Representative to the Organisation for the Prohibition of Chemical Weapons (OPCW), HE Matthew Neuhaus, delivered Australia's national statement to the Twenty-Fourth Session of the Conference of States Parties to the Chemical Weapons Convention in The Hague, expressing Australia's support for the OPCW. Extracts of that statement follow:

Mr Chair,

[...]

This time last year some were questioning whether the Chemical Weapons Convention had failed. We had witnessed repeated chemical weapons use in Syria, and even the use of nerve agents by foreign actors in Malaysia and the UK.

I am proud to stand here today—with my colleagues, with the Director-General and with the staff of the Technical Secretariat—and confirm that the Chemical Weapons Convention has not failed. In fact it has been strengthened. Collectively, States Parties have shown that they can and will respond promptly and effectively to those who challenge the Convention, and its implementation. However, there remains much work to be done. The international community must remain steadfast in its counter-proliferation work. There are no circumstances which justify the use of chemical weapons. It is unacceptable that more than six years after acceding to the Convention, we are still discussing Syria's declaration discrepancies. The Syrian Arab Republic must fully cooperate with the OPCW. This is a requirement under Article VII of the Chemical Weapons Convention, and under United Nations Security Council resolution 2118. We need to see renewed efforts to resolve this issue once and for all.

It is also unacceptable that the Syrian Arab Republic has failed to cooperate with the Investigation and Identification Team (IIT), including by refusing to issue a visa to the Head of the Team. The IIT has been mandated by States Parties to carry out an important role and it should not be faced with any restrictions on doing this.

We are pleased that the IIT has nevertheless, under the very able leadership of Ambassador Onate, continued to carry out the task assigned to it, that is, to identify those responsible for chemical weapons attacks in Syria. We look forward to issuance of the IIT's first report in due course.

As Australia has repeatedly said, it is absolutely appropriate that the OPCW, as the implementing body of the Chemical Weapons Convention, be able to undertake investigations in order to identify those who violate the global norm against the use of chemical weapons, anywhere. Identifying perpetrators of chemical weapons use is a crucial, necessary step if we are to deter others who might think they can use such weapons

AUSTRALIAN PRACTICE IN INTERNATIONAL LAW 2019 715

with impunity. Australia calls on all States Parties to strongly support the OPCW Director-General and the Technical Secretariat, in carrying out this vitally important role.

[...]

Mr Chair, there has been much discussion globally about the state of the international rules-based order. Australia acknowledges that the international system needs to modernise, but it must also stand firm on the well-established norms that protect our peace and security.

The norm against the use of chemical weapons is not an issue for only some countries. It is the fundamental principle we all agreed to when signing on to the Convention. It is in all our collective security interests to uphold the well-established international norm against any chemical weapons use. States Parties are the elements that comprise the international system. It is therefore for each of us to speak out against the use of chemical weapons, anytime, anywhere and under any circumstance.

Upholding the global prohibition against the use of chemical weapons, and preventing their re-emergence, requires the resolve of all States Parties to the Chemical Weapons Convention. I was most fortunate to be there at the beginning and we must keep the spirit of those who drafted our Convention, who in the words of its Preamble were 'determined for the sake of all mankind to exclude completely the possibility of the use of chemical weapons'. Let us not forget.

[...]

12.2   Anti-Personnel Mine Ban Convention

At the Fourth Review Conference of the Anti-Personnel Mine Ban Convention held on 25–29 October 2019 in Oslo, Australia delivered a national statement on renewing political commitment to the convention. The full text of that statement follows:

Mr President,

As a strong supporter of mine action, Australia reaffirms our commitment to the Anti-Personnel Mine Ban Convention. We continue to work with others towards reducing the number of deaths and injuries from landmines, cluster munitions and other explosive remnants of war and to improve the quality of life for survivors of these weapons, and their families.

Mr President,

Australia considers clearing of mines and IEDs to be a humanitarian imperative for the successful distribution of aid and safe return home of thousands of displaced residents. We also support efforts by states parties to pursue work on stockpile management and encourage cooperation in capacity building and establishing best practice.

Australia will continue to take a comprehensive approach, particularly in the Indo Pacific region, to reduce the suffering caused by indiscriminate use of explosive weapons and support the Anti-Personnel Mine Ban Convention, the Convention on Cluster Munitions and all protocols of the Convention on Certain Conventional Weapons.

The harms posed by these weapons and their remnants rarely occur in isolation. By addressing these hazards in a complementary manner across conventions and protocols, we believe the international community can reduce the impact of these indiscriminate weapons in an efficient and effective manner. Therefore we urge states that have not acceded to these conventions to take concrete steps towards doing so and fulfil the obligations therein.

Mr President,

Australia encourages all parties to armed conflict—including non-State actors—to comply with international humanitarian law, including with regard to the use of mines and to share, wherever possible, information that will assist with their removal. Compliance with international humanitarian law will go a long way to address concerns raised by the international community about the use of, and effects of explosive weapons including anti-personnel mines. It is for this reason that we encourage states not yet party to the convention to accede to and abide by the key provisions of the Ottawa Convention.

Thank you Mr President.

12.3   *Arms Trade Treaty*

On Monday 26 August 2019, Australia delivered a national statement on Gender and Gender-Based Violence at the Fifth Conference of States Parties (CSP5) to the Arms Trade Treaty held in Geneva. The full text of that statement follows:

Mr President, We warmly welcome your decision on the theme for this year's conference, and thank the panel for their presentations, raising issues that underline the impact on people.

As pointed out in the Centre for Armed Violence's publication on the Broader Benefits of the Arms Trade Treaty, the accumulation and misuse of conventional arms violently intersects with gender issues at many levels—in criminal activity, interpersonal violence and homicide, and socio-political violence.

As States Parties, we can—and must—reduce gender-based violence through the effective implementation and universalisation of the ATT.

Accordingly, we are happy to support the joint statement on gender. We do note that the article 7 risk assessment required by the ATT takes into account gender-based violence considerations, as one element to be factored into all stages of this risk assessment. While it is not an explicit requirement to be considered for article 6 obligations, Australia would take into account evidence of gender-based violence when implementing article 6.

Further, it obliges us to assess the risk that the exports could be diverted.

The combined effect of these measures has the potential to significantly reduce the number of conventional weapons available, thereby reducing the level of gender-based violence.

Australia is a strong supporter of the Women, Peace and Security agenda. We are in the process of developing our second national action plan on Women, Peace and Security.

We are committed to strengthening the international rules based order. The Arms Trade Treaty is a key international legal instrument which supports the Women, Peace and Security agenda. We support the efforts to achieve a greater gender balance in decision-making fora and delegations, and value women's meaningful participation and insights into the impact on the most vulnerable communities—as described by the panellists—of armed violence.

Since March 2015, Australia has committed AUD11 million to UN Women's two main Women, Peace and Security funds:

- AUD 6.5 million to the Women's Peace and Humanitarian Fund and
- AUD 4.5 million to UN Women for their Global Facility of Women, Peace and Security

Australia also provided over AUD 8 million in funding for ICRC's Special Appeal to address Sexual Violence in Conflict and over AUD 26 million to the SPRINT initiative to accelerate community recovery by providing crisis-affected women, men and children with lifesaving sexual and reproductive health services. Mr President, we thank you for your work on the topic of gender representation and gender-based violence. I am confident that, under your leadership, these efforts will result in this meeting agreeing to a decision on Gender and Gender-based Violence.

This decision will make clear our commitment to reduce gender-based violence and guide us with constructive measures to implement.

We look forward to working with States Parties to support efforts to give full force to the obligations set out in the Arms Trade Treaty.

Doing so will give us the best opportunity to reduce gender-based violence in the future.

12.4   *Conference on Disarmament*

On 25 February 2019, Australia's Minister for Foreign Affairs, Senator the Hon. Marise Payne, delivered an address at the Conference on Disarmament in Geneva. Extracts of that statement follow:

> [...]
> As Australia's Minister for Foreign Affairs, and as a former Australian Minister for Defence immediately preceding that, I am acutely aware of the complexity of the issues with which the Conference on Disarmament grapples.
>
> Chief among these is the importance of maintaining adherence to and respect for long-standing, carefully negotiated arms control regimes. It is this system of treaties and agreements that underpins our international rules-based order, and delivers stability, security, and the certainty that we all work towards.
>
> These agreements give us confidence that we can deal with regional or global crises on equal terms.
> [...]
> Australia believes we urgently need to infuse new energy into our work so that this Conference can play the important part it should in the international rules based order on which as I have said we depend.
> [...]
> An Australian priority in this regard is a treaty to ban the production of fissile material for nuclear weapons. We see no substantive reason why negotiations cannot start on this treaty now—with differences fleshed out over the course of discussions. That is the purpose of negotiations. We encourage all members of this Conference to be positive and constructive in this endeavour.
>
> As we have also continued to make clear, the rules-based global order extends to space and Australia will continue to work with other nations to ensure the long-term sustainability, safety and security of the outer space domain.
>
> We do not, however, support the current proposed draft treaty that has been submitted to this Conference on outer space. Our view is that, at this point in time, our efforts are more effectively focused on limiting unacceptable behaviour in space.

[...]

When we consider the difficulty of the task ahead we should acknowledge the progress made so far. The Secretary-General adverted to this in his opening remarks. During the Cold War, the number of nuclear weapons peaked at over 70,000. Today, those numbers have fallen to around 14,400—many of which are proposed to be dismantled.

The Strategic Arms Reduction Treaty—'START 1'—defined cuts to the nuclear weapons stockpiles of the two top possessor states. So did New START in 2010. It is critical for global stability that this arrangement is extended. In 1987, the Intermediate-Range Nuclear Forces Treaty—or 'INF'—was a pioneering agreement bringing about, for the first time, a bilateral reduction in nuclear weapons.

Australia does remain disappointed that Russia has so far not addressed its issues of non-compliance with this treaty—placing its very ongoing viability in question. We do urge Russia to return to compliance in the period of time available. It is in no one's interest to return to an arms race like that witnessed during the Cold War.

[...]

Mr President, Australia remains convinced that transparency, compliance, verification, and if necessary enforcement, are foundational issues that require solutions.

And Australia, with others, is working through the technical challenges of disarmament through the US-initiated International Partnership for Nuclear Disarmament Verification.

Similarly, Australia has worked through many of the technical issues surrounding a treaty banning fissile material for nuclear weapons including in two UN-mandated groups.

Through the 12 member cross-regional Non-Proliferation and Disarmament Initiative, we are in dialogue with Nuclear Weapons States on ways to enhance transparency.

We also support the vital role of Security Council resolutions in moderating destabilising influences. Australia supports the Security Council's resolutions calling for the complete, verifiable and irreversible denuclearisation of the Democratic People's Republic of Korea. These efforts have provided the framework for much of the efforts to address tension on the Korean peninsula.

We also welcome the second summit meeting between the United States and the DPRK in Hanoi later this week.

Mr President, it is Australia's view that the Conference on Disarmament has no time to waste because the international community has no time to waste. We must continue to build areas of common ground, and commit to both the technical work and the broader efforts needed to conduct negotiations. Australia stands ready to be a strong partner in all of those efforts. Thank you very much.

On 8 August 2019, Australia delivered a national statement at the Conference on Disarmament held in Geneva. Extracts of that statement follow:

[...]

We are all familiar with the arguments that a treaty which includes past stocks would further disarmament and non-proliferation, while one which covers future production would be limited to non-proliferation objectives.

We see the issue in a more linear way. A cut-off treaty focused on future production would have significant positive impact on disarmament through measures such as declarations, transparency and confidence-building measures. These options are covered in the report.

Verified assurance that the quantity of fissile material available for use in nuclear weapons is capped is a powerful contribution to confidence enabling nuclear disarmament.

Indeed, a ban on new production of fissile material for use in weapons is a necessary part of disarmament.

While reducing the size of weapons arsenals is a useful step toward disarmament, the value of such actions is limited if production of fissile material for weapons continues or could be easily resumed.

So how do we get closer to being able to negotiate a treaty on fissile material in the CD?

States can do quite a lot unilaterally and working together in advance of negotiations to build confidence about the management of fissile material. The report suggests the kinds of mandated and voluntary measures that can help build confidence in an FMCT, including in advance of EiF.

We should not wait to advance exploratory work on some of the necessary verification, transparency and confidence-building measures that could feature in and around any future treaty.

We are encouraged by the P5 statement at First Committee last year, and China's statement at the NPT PrepCom of ongoing P5 work on this issue, and look forward to this bringing results.

Mr President

The increasingly complex and challenging international security climate warrants fresh thinking on measures to address new and extant risks of nuclear weapons use.

Cold War templates for addressing nuclear risk cannot simply be applied to the complexities of today's security climate.

While our ultimate shared goal is disarmament, we also have a shared responsibility to reduce the risk of use of nuclear weapons.

Nuclear possessor states and non-nuclear weapons states need to undertake measures that will promote trust building and confidence.

Reducing nuclear risk builds trust, and can help pave the way for further reductions in future.

There is a raft of work that we need to take forward related to:
- safeguarding procedures and safety;
- clarifying doctrine;
- increasing predictability;
- conflict amelioration; and
- implementing existing non-proliferation and disarmament obligations.

We should waste no time or effort in progressing this important area.

[...]

12.5   *Iran—Joint Comprehensive Plan of Action (JCPOA)*

On 9 May 2019, Australia's Minister for Foreign Affairs, Senator the Hon. Marise Payne, released a media statement regarding Iran's compliance with the Joint Comprehensive Plan of Action. The full text of that statement follows:

The Australian Government is deeply concerned by the statements made by Iran in relation to its compliance with the Joint Comprehensive Plan of Action.

The Australian Government reviewed our approach to the Plan of Action last year, following which Prime Minister Morrison made clear that Australia supported the Plan of Action as long as Iran remained in compliance with its provisions.

We have made our concerns regarding Iran's destabilising activities well-known. While I note that Iran has said it is not withdrawing from the Plan of Action, Australia continues to urge Iran to exercise restraint and to comply with its commitments.

The nuclear non-proliferation objectives of the Joint Comprehensive Plan of Action are worthy and serve the best interests of peace, stability, and regional security. Australia strongly supports these objectives, and encourages parties to the Plan to redouble their efforts to honour its provisions.

In line with caretaker conventions, the opposition has been briefed on this matter.

On 20 June 2019, Australia's Minister for Foreign Affairs, Senator the Hon. Marise Payne, released a media statement regarding Iran's compliance with the Joint Comprehensive Plan of Action. The full text of that statement follows:

> Australia notes with concern recent developments regarding Iran's compliance with the Joint Comprehensive Plan of Action.
>
> We join others in urging Iran to remain within the bounds of the Plan of Action which includes workable provisions to deal with disputes and disagreements.
>
> Australia strongly encourages all parties to use these mechanisms to resolve difficulties.

Treaty Action 2019

Contents

Bilateral Treaty List 2019
Multilateral Treaty List 2019

Abbreviations

AMTAES	Australian Minor Treaty Actions Explanatory Statements
ATNIA	Australian Treaty National Interest Analysis
ATS	Australian Treaty Series
JSCOT	Joint Standing Committee on Treaties (Australian Parliament)

Bilateral Treaty List 2019

Date and place of signature	Description	Entry into force	Notes and references to printed text
Sydney, 2 May 2018	**FRANCE** Agreement between the Government of Australia and the Government of the French Republic regarding the Provision of Mutual Logistics Support between the Australian Defence Force and the French Armed Forces	7 June 2019	[2019] ATS 12; [2018] ATNIA 14; JSCOT Report 185.

© KONINKLIJKE BRILL NV, LEIDEN, 2021 | DOI:10.1163/26660229_03801024

Date and place of signature	Description	Entry into force	Notes and references to printed text
	HUNGARY		
Canberra, 30 October 2018	Agreement between the Government of Australia and the Government of Hungary concerning Oil Stock Contracts	11 December 2019	[2019] ATS 22; [2019] ATNIA 2; JSCOT Report 187.
	ISRAEL		
Canberra, 28 March 2019	Convention between the Government of Australia and the Government of the State of Israel for the Elimination of Double Taxation with respect to Taxes on Income and the Prevention of Tax Evasion and Avoidance	6 December 2019	[2019] ATS 20; [2019] ATNIA 14; JSCOT Report 187.
	NETHERLANDS		
The Hague, 18 December 2018	Treaty between Australia and the Kingdom of the Netherlands on the Ongoing Presence of Australian Personnel in the Netherlands for the Purpose of Responding to the Downing of Malaysia Airlines Flight MH17	28 June 2019	[2019] ATS 14; [2019] ATNIA 7; JSCOT Report 187.

TREATY ACTION 2019

Date and place of signature	Description	Entry into force	Notes and references to printed text
	PAPUA NEW GUINEA		
Port Moresby, 6 October 2017	Agreement between the Government of Australia and the Government of Papua New Guinea relating to Air Services	13 December 2019	[2019] ATS 21; [2019] ATNIA 8; JSCOT Report 187.
	THAILAND		
Bangkok, 3 August 2017	Agreement between the Government of Australia and the Government of the Kingdom of Thailand relating to Air Services	6 December 2019	[2019] ATS 19; [2019] ATNIA 4; JSCOT Report 187.
	TIMOR-LESTE		
New York, 6 March 2018	Treaty between Australia and the Democratic Republic of Timor-Leste Establishing Their Maritime Boundaries in the Timor Sea	30 August 2019	[2019] ATS 16; [2018] ATNIA 3; JSCOT Report 180.
	VIETNAM		
Santiago, 8 March 2018	Agreement between Australia and Vietnam to maintain the original TPP bilateral agreements	14 January 2019	[2019] ATS 6; [2018] ATNIA 1; JSCOT Report 181; Head Agreement: [2018] ATS 23.

Date and place of signature	Description	Entry into force	Notes and references to printed text
Santiago, 8 March 2018	Agreement between Australia and Vietnam regarding the Cyber Security Law of Vietnam	14 January 2019	[2019] ATS 7; [2018] ATNIA 1; JSCOT Report 181; Head Agreement: [2018] ATS 23.
Santiago, 8 March 2018	Agreement between Australia and Vietnam regarding disputes related to the Labour Chapter of the TPP	14 January 2019	[2019] ATS 8; [2018] ATNIA 1; JSCOT Report 181; Head Agreement: [2018] ATS 23.
Santiago, 8 March 2018	Agreement between Australia and Vietnam regarding Electronic Payment Services	14 January 2019	[2019] ATS 9; [2018] ATNIA 1; JSCOT Report 181; Head Agreement: [2018] ATS 23.

WORLD INTELLECTUAL PROPERTY ORGANIZATION

Date and place of signature	Description	Entry into force	Notes and references to printed text
Geneva, 29 October 2018	Agreement between the Government of Australia and the International Bureau of the World Intellectual Property Organization in relation to the functioning of the Australian Patent Office as an International Searching Authority and International	1 January 2019	[2019] ATS 10; [2018] ATNIA 5; JSCOT Report 180.

TREATY ACTION 2019

Date and place of signature	Description	Entry into force	Notes and references to printed text
	Preliminary Examining Authority under the Patent Cooperation Treaty		

Multilateral Treaty List 2019

Date and place	Description	In force generally	Notes and references to printed text
Paris, 7 June 2017	Multilateral Convention to Implement Tax Treaty Related Measures to Prevent Base Erosion and Profit Shifting	1 July 2018	Entered into force for Australia on 1 January 2019. [2019] ATS 1; [2017] ATNIA 20; JSCOT Report 175.
Paris, 1 October 2018	2018 Amendment to Annexes I and II of the International Convention against Doping in Sport	1 January 2019	[2019] ATS 2; Head Agreement: [2007] ATS 10; Explanatory Statement: [2018] AMTAES 10.
January 2018	Transposition of Annex 2 (Product Specific Rules) of the Agreement Establishing the ASEAN—Australia—New Zealand Free Trade Area	1 January 2019	[2019] ATS 3; Head Agreement: [2010] ATS 1; Explanatory Statement: [2018] AMTAES 7.

Date and place	Description	In force generally	Notes and references to printed text
7 July 2017	Amendments to the Annex of the International Convention for the Prevention of Pollution from Ships, 1973, as modified by the Protocols of 1978 and 1997 relating thereto—Amendments to Annex VI (Designation of the Baltic Sea and the North Sea Emission Control Areas for NOx Tier III control)—Resolution MEPC.286(71)	1 January 2019	[2019] ATS 4; Head Agreements: [1988] ATS 29 and [2007] ATS 37; Explanatory Statement: [2018] AMTAES 6.
Geneva, 9 June 2016	Amendments of 2016 to the Code of the Maritime Labour Convention, 2006	8 January 2019	[2019] ATS 5; Head Agreement: [2013] ATS 29; Explanatory Statement: [2018] AMTAES 1.
Geneva, 26 July 2017	Amendment to Annex 3 of the Marrakesh Agreement Establishing the World Trade Organization—Amendment of the Trade Policy Review Mechanism	1 January 2019	[2019] ATS 11; Head Agreement: [1995] ATS 8; Explanatory Statement; [2017] AMTAES 1.

TREATY ACTION 2019

Date and place	Description	In force generally	Notes and references to printed text
Geneva, 30 March 2012	Revised Agreement on Government Procurement: Annex to the Protocol Amending the Agreement on Government Procurement, adopted on 30 March 2012 (GPA/113)	6 April 2014	Entered into force for Australia on 5 May 2019. [2019] ATS 13; [2018] ATNIA 15; JSCOT Report 185.
Quito, 9 November 2018	Adjustments to the Montreal Protocol on Substances that Deplete the Ozone Layer relating to the controlled substances on Annex C, Group I	21 June 2019	[2019] ATS 15; Head Agreement: [1989] ATS 18; Explanatory Statement: [2019] AMTAES 9.
13 April 2018	2018 Amendments to Annex VI of the International Convention for the Prevention of Pollution from Ships, 1973, as modified by the Protocol of 1978 relating thereto—Resolution MEPC.301(72)	1 September 2019	[2019] ATS 17; Head Agreement: [2004] ATS 9; Explanatory Statement: [2019] AMTAES 3.

Date and place	Description	In force generally	Notes and references to printed text
13 April 2018	2018 Amendments to the Annex to the International Convention for the Control and Management of Ships' Ballast Water and Sediments—Resolution MEPC.296(72); Resolution MEPC.297(72); Resolution MEPC.299(72); Resolution MEPC.300(72)	13 October 2019	[2019] ATS 18; Head Agreement: [2017] ATS 15; Explanatory Statement: [2019] AMTAES 2.

Table of Cases

Abdelrazik v Canada (Minister of Foreign Affairs and International Trade) [2010] 1 FCR 267 (Canada)   308*n*130

AD (Palestine) [2015] NZIPT 800693-695 230*n*4, 236*n*46

Addy v Commissioner of Taxation (Cth) [2019] FCA 1768   409, 410*n*339, 411*n*345, 410*n*339

Aerial Incident of 10 August 1999 (Pakistan v India) (Jurisdiction) [2000] ICJ Rep 12   304*n*102

Air France v Saks, 470 US 392 (1985)   367*n*59

Air New Zealand Ltd v Australian Competition and Consumer Commission (2017) 262 CLR 207   358*n*3

Al-Skeini v United Kingdom [2011] IV Eur Court HR 99   308*n*131

Anonymous (Lebanese Citizens) v Minister of Defence [2000] 54(1) PD 721 (Israel)   308*n*129

Anthony Hordern & Sons Ltd v Amalgamated Clothing & Allied Trades Union of Australia (1947) 47 CLR 1   408

Antin Infrastructure Services Luxembourg SÀRL and Antin Enerfía Termosolar BV v The Kingdom of Spain (Decision on Rectification of the Award) (ICSID Arbitral Tribunal, Case No ARB/13/31, 29 January 2019)   384*n*178

Appellate Body Report, *Brazil—Measures Affecting Imports of Retreaded Tyres*, WTO Doc WT/DS332/AB/R (3 December 2007)   137*n*24, 139, 144*n*71, 144*n*76, 145, 152*n*123

Appellate Body Report, *Canada—Continued Suspension of Obligations in the EC— Hormones Dispute*, WTO Doc WT/DS321/ AB/R (16 October 2008)   138*n*36

Appellate Body Report, *Canada—Term of Patent Protection*, WTO Doc WT/DS170/ AB/R (18 September 2000)   138*n*31

Appellate Body Report, *European Communities and Certain Member States—Measures Affecting Trade in Large Civil Aircraft*, WTO Doc WT/DS13/AB/R (18 May 2011)   143*n*69

Appellate Body Report, *European Communities—Measures Prohibiting the Importation and Marketing of Seal Products*, WTO Doc WT/DS400/AB/R; WT/DS401/AB/R (22 May 2014)   137*n*22

Appellate Body Report, *European Communities—Measures Prohibiting the Importation and Marketing of Seal Products*, WTO Doc WT/DS400/AB/R and WT/DS401/AB/R (22 May 2014)   137*n*22

Appellate Body Report, *United States— Definitive Anti-Dumping and Countervailing Duties on Certain Products from China*, WTO Doc WT/DS379/AB/R (11 March 2011)   138*n*29

Appellate Body Report, *United States— Import Prohibition of Certain Shrimp and Shrimp Products*, WTO Doc WT/DS58/ AB/R (12 October 1998)   139, 140*n*51, 154*n*138

Appellate Body Report, *United States— Measures Affecting Imports of Woven Wool Shirts and Blouses from India*, WTO Doc WT/DS33/AB/R (25 April 1997)   138*n*37

Appellate Body Report, *United States— Standards for Reformulated and Conventional Gasoline*, WTO Doc WT/DS2/ AB/R (29 April 1996)   137*n*20, 138*n*26, 152*n*122, 152*n*123

Application of the Convention on the Prevention and Punishment of the Crime of Genocide (Bosnia and Herzegovina v Serbia and Montenegro) (Judgment) [2007] ICJ Rep 43   85*n*41, 292*n*33

Application of the Convention on the Prevention and Punishment of the Crime of Genocide (Bosnia and Herzegovina v Serbia and Montenegro) (Provisional Measures) [1993] ICJ Rep 325   292*n*33, 315*n*167

Arbitral Award of 31 July 1989 (Guinea-Bissau v Senegal) (Judgment) [1991] ICJ Rep 53   302*n*90

Arbitration under the Timor Sea Treaty of 20 May 2002 (Timor-Leste v Australia) (Procedural Order No 1) (Permanent

Court of Arbitration, Case No 2013-16, 6
December 2013) 347n14

*Arctic Sunrise Arbitration (Netherlands v
Russia) (Award on Merits)* (Permanent
Court of Arbitration, Case No 2014-02, 14
August 2015) 11n25

*Armed Activities on the Territory of the Congo
(Democratic Republic of the Congo v
Uganda) (Provisional Measures)* [2000]
ICJ Rep 111 85n40, 294n51, 351n7

*Armed Activities on the Territory of the Congo
(Democratic Republic of the Congo v
Uganda) (Judgment)* [2005] ICJ Rep
168 85, 294n51, 351

Attorney-General (NSW) v Quin (1990) 170
CLR 1 306n1161

*Australian Competition and Consumer
Commission v Air New Zealand Ltd* (2014)
319 ALR 388 358n2

*Australian Competition and Consumer
Commission v PT Garuda Indonesia Ltd*
(2019) 370 ALR 637 357, 358n4

Baker v Carr, 369 US 186 (1962) 312

BAL19 v Minister for Home Affairs [2019] FCA
2189 404, 406n322

*Barcelona Traction, Light and Power Company
Ltd (Belgium v Spain) (Judgment)* [1970]
ICJ Rep 3 305n111

*BCR16 v Minister for Immigration and Border
Protection* (2017) 248 FCR 456 390n219,
395, 398n276

*BCX16 v Minister for Immigration and Border
Protection* [2019] FCA 465 402, 403n304

Boumediene v Bush, 553 US 723
(2008) 308n131

Burton v Commissioner of Taxation (Cth)
(2019) 372 ALR 293 412, 413n353, 413n357

*Carrascalao v Minister for Immigration and
Border Protection* (2017) 346 ALR 173 390

*Certain Expenses of the United Nations
(Advisory Opinion)* [1962] ICJ Rep 151 88,
293n46, 293n47, 294n49, 314n163

*Certain Phosphate Lands in Nauru (Nauru v
Australia) (Preliminary Objections)* [1992]
ICJ 240 301n84

Chan Hiang Leng Colin v Public Prosecutor
[1994] 3 SLR(R) 209 307n117

Church of Scientology v Woodward (1982) 154
CLR 25 308n129

*Constitution of the Maritime Safety Committee
of the Inter-Governmental Maritime
Consultative Organization (Advisory
Opinion)* [1960] ICJ Rep 150 314n160

*Corfu Channel (United Kingdom v Albania)
(Merits)* [1949] ICJ Rep 4 84, 85n37

*Council of Civil Service Unions v Minister for
the Civil Service* [1985] AC 374 307

Davis v Bandemer, 478 US 109
(1986) 302n150

Di Falco v Emirates (No 2) [2019] VSC
654 366n56, 366n58, 367, 368n60

*Diversion of Water from the Meuse
(Netherlands v Belgium) (Merits)* [1937]
PCIJ (ser A/B) No 70 304n102

DOB18 v Minister for Home Affairs [2019]
FCAFC 63 392n230, 396, 397n268,
398n277

Dow Jones & Company Inc v Gutnick (2002)
210 CLR 575 332

East Timor (Portugal v Australia) (Judgment)
[1995] ICJ Rep 90 345n7

*FER17 v Minister for Immigration, Citizenship
and Multicultural Affairs* [2019] FCAFC
106 399, 400n283

Fiona Trust & Holding Corporation v Privalov
[2007] 4 All ER 951 386–388

*Free Zones of Upper Savoy and the District Of
Gex (France v Switzerland) (Judgment)*
[1932] PCIJ ser A/B No 46 301n84

*Gabčikovo–Nagymaros Project
(Hungary v Slovakia) (Judgment)* [1997]
ICJ Rep 7 293n42

*Goundar v Minister of Immigration
and Border Protection* [2016] FCA
1203 390n216

Habib v Commonwealth (2010) 183
FCR 62 308n130

Hancock Prospecting Pty Ltd v Rinehart (2017)
257 FCR 442 386–387

*Heli-Aust Pty Limited v Civil Aviation Safety
Authority* [2019] NSWSC 506 365,
366n54, 366n55

TABLE OF CASES

House v The King (1936) 55 CLR 499 399

Ibrahim v Minister for Home Affairs [2019] FCAFC 89 392, 393n238, 394n242, 394n245, 394n251, 395n256, 396n263
Ibrahim v Minister for Immigration and Border Protection (No 2) (2017) 256 FCR 50 393n235
Immigration and Naturalization Service v Chadha, 462 US 919 (1983) 312n150
Import Prohibition of Remoulded Tyres from Uruguay (Uruguay v Brazil) (Award) 144n73
Infrastructure Services Luxembourg SÀRL v Kingdom of Spain [2019] FCA 1220 384–385
Infrastructure Services Luxembourg SÀRL and Energia Termosolar BV v Kingdom of Spain (Decision on the Continuation of the Provisional Stay of the Enforcement of the Award) (ICSID Committee, Case No ARB/13/31, 21 October 2019) 385n191
International Status of South-West Africa (Advisory Opinion) [1950] ICJ Rep 128 305n110
Interpretation and Application of the 1971 Montreal Convention Arising from the Aerial Incident at Lockerbie (Libya v United Kingdom) (Provisional Measures) [1992] ICJ Rep 3 288, 298n74
Interpretation and Application of the 1971 Montreal Convention Arising from the Aerial Incident at Lockerbie (Libya v United Kingdom) (Preliminary Objections) [1998] ICJ Rep 9 288
Interpretation of Judgments No 7 and 8 (The Chorzow Factory) (Germany v Poland) (Interpretation) [1927] PCIJ (ser A) No 13 300

Kadi and Al Barakaat International Foundation v Council and Commission (C-402/05) [2008] ECR I-6351 308n131
Kadi v European Commission (T-85/09) [2010] ECR II-5177 308n131
Kioa v West (1985) 159 CLR 550 393n241
Kubat v Kubat [2019] FamCA 671 369, 370n70, 370n77, 371n84

Lardan v Attorney-General (No 2) (1957) 2G & G 98 307n117
Legal Consequences for States of the Continued Presence of South Africa in Namibia (South West Africa) Notwithstanding Security Council Resolution 276 (1970) (Advisory Opinion) [1971] ICJ Rep 16 295
Legal Consequences of the Construction of a Wall in the Occupied Palestinian Territory (Advisory Opinion) [2004] ICJ Rep 136 295
Legality of the Threat or Use of Nuclear Weapons (Advisory Opinion) [1996] ICJ Rep 226 83n29, 293n42
Lighthouses Case (France v Greece) (Merits) [1934] PCIJ (ser A/B) No 62 304n104
Lordianto v Commissioner of the Australian Federal Police (2019) 374 ALR 58 360, 361n19, 363n33, 364
Lordianto v Commissioner of the Australian Federal Police (2019) 93 ALJR 1282 360–361, 364–365

Marbury v Madison, 5 US 137, 170 (1803) 297n67, 299, 306n115
Maritime International Nominees Establishment v Republic of Guinea (Interim Order) (ICSID Committee, Case No ARB/84/4, 12 August 1988) 385
Mavrommatis Palestine Concessions (Greece v United Kingdom) (Judgment) [1924] PCIJ (ser A) No 2 301n84
Military and Paramilitary Activities in and against Nicaragua (Nicaragua v United States of America) (Merits) [1986] ICJ Rep 14 78n1, 85, 92, 98, 99n105
Military and Paramilitary Activities in and against Nicaragua (Nicaragua v United States of America) (Jurisdiction) [1984] ICJ Rep 392 293n46
Minister for Home Affairs v Omar [2019] FCAFC 188 388, 389n209
Minister for Immigration and Multicultural and Indigenous Affairs v Nystrom (2006) 228 CLR 566 408
Minister of Home Affairs v Buadromo (2018) 237 FCR 316 390n216
Minister of Immigration and Border Protection v BHA17 (2018) 260 FCR 523 390n216

TABLE OF CASES

*Monetary Gold Removed from Rome in 1943
(Italy v France, United Kingdom and
United States of America) (Preliminary
Question)* [1954] ICJ Rep 19   310*n*141,
315*n*169

*NBMZ v Minister for Immigration and Border
Protection* (2014) 220 FCR 1   406*n*321
*Nottebohm (Liechtenstein v Guatemala)
(Preliminary Objection)* [1953] ICJ Rep
111   310*n*140
*Nuclear Tests (Australia v France)
(Jurisdiction)* [1974] ICJ Rep 253   310*n*140

*Oil Platforms (Iran v United States of America)
(Judgment)* [2003] ICJ Rep 161   85*n*39
Olympic Airways v Husain, 540 US 644
(2004)   367*n*59

Plaintiff M47 (2012) 251 CLR 1   408
Povey v Qantas Airways Ltd (2015) 223
CLR 189   367*n*59
Powell v McCormack, 395 US 486
(1969)   312*n*150
Prosecutor v Furundžija (Judgment)
(International Criminal Tribunal for
the Former Yugoslavia, Trial Chamber,
Case No IT-95-17/1-T, 10 December
1998)   306*n*112
*Prosecutor v Tadić (Decision on the Defence
Motion for Interlocutory Appeal on
Jurisdiction)* (International Criminal
Tribunal for the Former Yugoslavia,
Appeals Chamber, Case No IT-94-1-A, 2
October 1995)   305*n*112
Prosecutor v Tadić (Judgment) (International
Criminal Tribunal for the Former
Yugoslavia, Appeals Chamber, Case No
IT-94-1-A, 15 July 1999)   292*n*33

*R (XH) v Secretary of State for the Home
Department* [2018] QB 355   308*n*130
R v MacKellar; Ex parte Ratu (1977) 137
CLR 461   393*n*241
*Re H (Abduction: Habitual Residence:
Consent)* [2000] 2 FLR 294   375*n*129
Re Patterson; Ex parte Taylor (2001) 207
CLR 391   394*n*254

*Right of Passage over Indian Territory
(Portugal v India) (Merits)* [1960] ICJ
Rep 6   305*n*112
Rinehart v Hancock Prospecting Pty Ltd (2019)
93 ALJR 582   386, 387*n*205
Rinehart v Rinehart (No 3) (2016) 257
FCR 310   386*n*194

Slovakia v Achmea BV (Judgment) (Court of
Justice of the European Union, Case No
C-284/16, 6 March 2018)   8*n*8
*South China Sea Arbitration (Philippines
v China) (Award)* (UNCLOS Arbitral
Tribunal, PCA Case No 2013-19, 12 July
2016)   11
*South West Africa (Ethiopia v South Africa)
(Second Phase)* [1966] ICJ Rep 6   304*n*104
SS 'Lotus' (France v Turkey) (Judgment) [1927]
PCIJ (ser A) No 10   304*n*103, 330
State Central Authority v Kejah [2019]
FamCA 391   374
State Central Authority v Rilling [2019]
FamCA 74   371, 372*n*89, 372*n*92, 373*n*100,
373*n*103, 373*n*105, 374*n*112

*Taulahi v Minister for Immigration and Border
Protection* (2016) 246 FCR 146   406*n*321
Taylor v A-G (Commonwealth) (2019) 93 ALJR
1044   377
The Queen v A2 (2019) 93 ALJR 1106   381
Thiel v Commissioner of Taxation (1990) 171
CLR 338   413
Tickner v Chapman [1995] FCA
1726   390*n*220

*United States Diplomatic and Consular Staff
in Tehran (United States of America v Iran)
(Jurisdiction)* [1980] ICJ Rep 3   293*n*46,
293*n*47, 294*n*51, 312*n*148

*Viane v Minister for Immigration and Border
Protection* (2018) 263 FCR 531   390*n*218

*Wei v Minister for Immigration and Border
Protection* (2015) 257 CLR 22   394
Western Sahara (Advisory Opinion) [1975] ICJ
Rep 12   90

*Zippo Manufacturing Company v Zippo.com
Inc*, 952 F Supp 1119 (WD Pa, 1997)   332

Table of Statutes

Administrative Decisions (Judicial Review) Act 1977 (Cth)   306n116
Air Navigation (Gold Coast Airport Curfew) Amendment (Technical Measures) Regulations 2019 (Cth)   478
Air Navigation (Gold Coast Airport Curfew) Regulations 2018 (Cth)   478
Air Navigation Act 1920 (Cth)   478
Air Services Act 1995 (Cth)   478
Air Services Regulations 1995 (Cth)   478
Air Services Regulations 2019 (Cth)   478
Anti-Money Laundering and Counter-Terrorism Financing Act 2006 (Cth)   360–361
Arbitration Act 1996 (UK)   387
Australia Regulations 2018 (Cth)   490
Australian Human Rights Commission Act 1986 (Cth)   479
Australian Human Rights Commission Regulations 1989 (Cth)   479
Australian Human Rights Commission Regulations 2019 (Cth)   479
Australian Sports Anti-Doping Authority Act 2006 (Cth)   475
Autonomous Sanctions (Designated and Declared Persons—Democratic People's Republic of Korea) Continuing Effect Declaration and Designation Instrument 2019 (Cth)   552–553
Autonomous Sanctions (Designated and Declared Persons—Ukraine) Amendment List 2019 (Cth)   553–554
Autonomous Sanctions (Designated Persons and Entities and Declared Persons—Ukraine) List 2014 (Cth)   554
Autonomous Sanctions (Designated Persons and Entities—Democratic People's Republic of Korea) List 2012 (Cth)   553
Autonomous Sanctions Regulations 2011 (Cth)   552, 554
Aviation Transport Security Act 2004 (Cth)   489
Aviation Transport Security Regulations 2005 (Cth)   489

Charter of the United Nations (Dealing with Assets) Regulations 2008 (Cth)   481, 554, 557–558
Charter of the United Nations (Sanctions—Central African Republic) Amendment (2019 Measures No 1) Regulations 2019 (Cth)   481, 558
Charter of the United Nations (Sanctions—Central African Republic) Regulation 2014 (Cth)   481, 558
Charter of the United Nations (Sanctions—Eritrea) Regulations 2010 (Cth)   480, 557
Charter of the United Nations (Sanctions—South Sudan) Amendment (2019 Measures No 1) Regulations 2019 (Cth)   480, 556
Charter of the United Nations (Sanctions—South Sudan) Regulation 2015 (Cth)   480, 556
Charter of the United Nations Act 1945 (Cth)   479, 555
Charter of the United Nations Legislation Amendment (2019 Measures No 1) Regulations 2019 (Cth)   480, 557
Citizenship Act 1948 (Sri Lanka)   400
Civil Aviation (Carriers' Liability) Act 1959 (Cth)   366–368
Civil Aviation Act 1988 (Cth)   366, 482
Civil Aviation Legislation Amendment (Parts 103, 105 and 131) Regulations 2019 (Cth)   482
Civil Aviation Safety Amendment (Operations Definitions) Regulations 2019 (Cth)   482
Civil Aviation Safety Amendment (Part 139) Regulations 2019 (Cth)   482
Civil Aviation Safety Regulations 1998 (Cth)   482
Combatting Child Sexual Exploitation Legislation Amendment Act 2019 (Cth)   742
Commercial Arbitration Act 2010 (NSW)   387
Communications Decency Act of 1996 47 USC (1996)   334n29
Constitution Act 1982 (UK) (Canada)   307n117

TABLE OF STATUTES

Constitution of Austria 1920 (Austria) 307n119

Constitution of India 1950 (India) 307n122

Constitution of Kenya 2010 (Kenya) 307n117

Constitution of Nepal 2015 (Nepal) 307n117

Constitution of the Federative Republic of Brazil 2010 (Brazil) 307n117

Constitution of the Gabonese Republic 1991 (Gabon) 307n117

Constitution of the Islamic Republic of Afghanistan 2004 (Afghanistan) 307n124

Constitution of the Islamic Republic of Pakistan 1973 (Pakistan) 307n121

Constitution of the Kingdom of Thailand 2017 (Thailand) 307n120

Constitution of the Republic of Kazakhstan 1995 (Kazakhstan) 307n117

Constitution of the Republic of Korea 1948 (Republic of Korea) 307n117

Constitution of the Republic of South Africa Act 1996 (South Africa) 307n117

Constitution of the Republic of the Marshall Islands 1979 (Marshall Islands) 307n117

Constitution of the Republic of Trinidad and Tobago 1976 (Trinidad and Tobago) 307n117

Crimes (Biological Weapons) Act 1976 (Cth) 483

Crimes (Biological Weapons) Regulations 1980 (Cth) 483

Crimes (Biological Weapons) Regulations 2019 (Cth) 483

Crimes Act 1914 (Cth) 377, 378n144, 383n177, 472

Criminal Code Act 1995 (Cth) 378n145, 472

Customs (Prohibited Imports) Amendment (Collecting Tobacco Duties) Regulations 2019 (Cth) 483

Customs (Prohibited Imports) Regulations 1956 (Cth) 483

Customs Act 1901 (Cth) 472

Customs Amendment (Immediate Destruction of Illicit Tobacco) Act 2019 (Cth) 473

Designs Act 2003 (Cth) 486

Designs Regulations 2004 (Cth) 486

Disability Discrimination Act 1992 (Cth) 448, 450, 479

Export Charges (Imposition—Customs) Act 2015 (Cth) 488

Export Charges (Imposition—General) Act 2015 (Cth) 488

Family Law Act 1975 (Cth) 369, 370n75, 374–375, 484–485

Family Law (Child Abduction Convention) Regulations 1986 (Cth) 369, 372, 373n102, 373n104, 374, 375n120, 484

Family Law (Child Protection Convention) Regulations 2003 (Cth) 484–485

Family Law Legislation Amendment (Miscellaneous Measures) Regulations 2019 (Cth) 484

Family Law Regulations 1984 (Cth) 484

Federal Constitutional Law No 1 on the Judicial System of the Russian Federation 1996 (Russia) 307n117

Freedom of Information Act 1982 (Cth) 475

Great Barrier Reef Marine Park Act 1975 (Cth) 485

Great Barrier Reef Marine Park (Aquaculture) Regulations 2000 (Cth) 485

Great Barrier Reef Marine Park Regulations 1983 (Cth) 485

Great Barrier Reef Marine Park Regulations 2019 (Cth) 485

Grundgesetz für die Bundesrepublik Deutschland [Basic Law for the Federal Republic of Germany] 307n117

Human Rights Act 1988 (UK) 62

Income Tax Assessment Act 1997 (Cth) 411–412, 476

Income Tax Rates Act 1986 (Cth) 409

Industrial Chemicals Act 2019 (Cth) 473

Intellectual Property Laws Amendment (PCT Translations and Other Measures) Regulations 2019 (Cth) 486

International Arbitration Act 1974 (Cth) 383–384, 387

International Criminal Court (Consequential Amendments) Act 2002 (Cth) 379

International Organisations (Privileges and Immunities) Act 1963 (Cth) 488

TABLE OF STATUTES

International Organisations (Privileges and Immunities—Timor Sea Proceedings) Regulations 2017 (Cth)   489

International Tax Agreements Act 1953 (Cth)   412

International Transfer of Prisoners Act 1997 (Cth)   486

International Transfer of Prisoners (United Arab Emirates) Regulations 2019 (Cth)   486

Interpretation Act 1987 (NSW)   383n177

Judiciary Act 1903 (Cth)   306n116, 377

Law 48 of 1979 Governing the Operations of the Supreme Constitutional Court of Egypt (Egypt)   307n117

Lebanese Constitution 1926 (Lebanon)   307n117

Legislation Act 2003 (Cth)   478, 480–489

Maritime Powers Act 2013 (Cth)   447, 488

Maritime Transport and Offshore Facilities Security Act 2003 (Cth)   489

Maritime Transport and Offshore Facilities Security Regulations 2003 (Cth)   489

Migration Act 1958 (Cth)   388–389, 390n215, 390n217, 391n226, 392, 393n236, 394n243, 394n247, 394n252, 395n255, 395n259, 395n260, 396n267, 397, 399–400, 402, 404–405, 447, 450

Migration Amendment (Complementary Protection) Act 2011 (Cth)   403

Migration and Maritime Powers Legislation Amendment (Resolving the Asylum Caseload Legacy) Act 2014 (Cth)   399

Migration Regulations 1994 (Cth)   404, 405n313, 408

Modern Slavery Act (Cth)   675

National Disability Insurance Scheme Act 2013 (Cth)   448, 474

National Disability Insurance Scheme Amendment (Worker Screening Database) Act 2019 (Cth)   474

National Measurement Act 1960 (Cth)   487

National Measurement Legislation (SI Redefinition) Regulations 2019 (Cth)   487

National Measurement Regulations 1999 (Cth)   487

National Sports Tribunal (Consequential Amendments and Transitional Provisions) Act 2019 (Cth)   475

National Sports Tribunal Act 2019 (Cth)   475

Ombudsman Act 1976 (Cth)   487

Ombudsman Amendment (National Preventive Mechanism) Regulations 2019 (Cth)   487

Ombudsman Regulations 2017 (Cth)   487

Passenger Movement Charge Act 1978 (Cth)   476

Passenger Movement Charge Amendment (Timor Sea Maritime Boundaries Treaty) Act 2019 (Cth)   475–476

Patents Act 1990 (Cth)   486

Patents Regulations 1991 (Cth)   486

Political Constitution of the Republic of Costa Rica 1949 (Costa Rica)   307n117

Proceeds of Crime Act 2002 (Cth)   360–363

Product Emissions Standards Act 2017 (Cth)   490

Protection of Military Remains Act 1986 (UK)   343

Radiocommunications Act 1992 (Cth)   488

Shipping Registration Act 1981 (Cth)   488

Shipping Registration Regulations 1981 (Cth)   488

Shipping Registration Regulations 2019 (Cth)   488

Surveillance Devices Act 2004 (Cth)   472

Telecommunications Act 1997 (Cth)   489

Telecommunications (Interception and Access) Act 1979 (Cth)   472

Telecommunications and Other Legislation Amendment (Assistance and Access) Act 2018 (Cth)   607

Timor Sea Legislation Amendment (Maritime Boundaries Treaty) Regulations 2019 (Cth)   488

Timor Sea Maritime Boundaries Treaty Consequential Amendments Act 2019 (Cth)   475–476

738 TABLE OF STATUTES

Timor Sea Treaty Designated Authority (Privileges and Immunities) Regulations 2003 (Cth)   489

Trade Practices Act 1974 (Cth)   358–359

Transport Safety Investigation Act 2003 (Cth)   365, 489

Transport Security Legislation Amendment (2019 Measures No 1) Regulations 2019 (Cth)   489

Trans-Tasman Mutual Recognition Act 1997 (Cth)   490

Trans-Tasman Mutual Recognition Amendment (Permanent Exemption for Emissions-Controlled Products) Regulations 2019 (Cth)   490

Treasury Laws Amendment (Timor Sea Maritime Boundaries Treaty) Act 2019 (Cth)   476

United Mizrahi Bank Ltd v Migdal Cooperative Village [1995] IsrLR 1   307n123

War Crimes Act 1945 (Cth)   378

Wine Australia Act 2013 (Cth)   477

Wine Australia Amendment (Trade with the United Kingdom) Act 2019 (Cth)   477

Wine Australia Amendment (Trade with United Kingdom) Regulations 2019 (Cth)   490

Wine Australia Regulations 2018 (Cth)   490

Table of International Instruments

Agreed Measures for the Conservation of Antarctic Fauna and Flora 323–325

Agreement between Australia and the European Community on Trade in Wine 477, 490

Agreement between the Government of Australia and the Government of the Democratic Republic of Timor-Leste relating to the Unitisation of the Sunrise and Troubadour Fields 476

Agreement on the Application of Sanitary and Phytosanitary Measures 154n32

Agreement on the Cessation of Hostilities, Protection of Civilians and Humanitarian Access 480

Agreement on the Resolution of the Conflict of the Republic of South Sudan 480

Agreement on Trade in Civil Aircraft 161n16

Agreement on Trade in Wine between the Government of Australia and the Government of the United Kingdom of Great Britain and Northern Ireland 490

American Convention on Human Rights 10

Antarctic Treaty 321–328

Articles of Agreement of the International Monetary Fund 65n115

Biketawa Declaration 543

Cartagena Protocol on Biosafety to the Convention on Biological Diversity 142

Charter of the United Nations 33, 78, 132n100, 288, 290n13, 434, 479–481

Comprehensive and Progressive Agreement for Trans-Pacific Partnership 147, 155

Comprehensive Economic and Trade Agreement 8

Comprehensive Nuclear-Test-Ban Treaty 42n32

Convention against Torture and Other Cruel, Inhuman or Degrading Treatment or Punishment 142n64, 214n59, 185, 214n59, 391, 403, 466–467, 487

Convention between the Government of Australia and the Government of the United States of America for the Avoidance of Double Taxation and the Prevention of Fiscal Evasion with respect to Taxes on Income 412

Convention concerning the Protection of the World Cultural and Natural Heritage 341n8, 485

Convention for the Conservation of Antarctic Seals 322n7, 323, 325

Convention for the Protection of Cultural Property in the Event of Armed Conflict 341n8

Convention for the Safeguarding of the Intangible Cultural Heritage 341n8

Convention for the Unification of Certain Rules for International Carriage by Air 288, 298n74, 366–369

Convention on Biological Diversity 42n34, 142

Convention on International Civil Aviation 365–366, 478–479, 482, 489

Convention on International Trade in Endangered Species of Wild Fauna and Flora 140n38

Convention on the Conservation of Antarctic Marine Living Resources 322–323, 326–327

Convention on the Elimination of All Forms of Discrimination against Women 42n35, 142n64, 214n59, 234n32, 351n6, 382

Convention on the Means of Prohibiting and Preventing the Illicit Import, Export and Transfer of Ownership of Cultural Property 341n8

Convention on the Prohibition of the Development, Production and Stockpiling of Bacteriological (Biological) and Toxin Weapons and on their Destruction 42n32, 483

Convention on the Prohibition of the Development, Production, Stockpiling and Use of Chemical Weapons and on their Destruction 42n32

Convention on the Prohibition of the Use, Stockpiling, Production and Transfer of Anti-Personnel Mines and on their Destruction 41n32

740 TABLE OF INTERNATIONAL INSTRUMENTS

*Convention on the Protection of the
Underwater Cultural Heritage* 340
*Convention on the Regulation of Antarctic
Mineral Resource Activities* 328n27
*Convention on the Rights of Persons with
Disabilities* 214n59, 234, 256, 258–259,
263, 265, 278–279, 388, 391, 444, 448,
458–459, 474, 479
Convention on the Rights of the Child 42n35,
142n64, 214n59, 234, 382–383, 444n226, 472
*Convention on the Settlement of Investment
Disputes between States and Nationals of
other States* 384, 415–416, 424
*Convention Relating to the Status of
Refugees* 232, 350, 407
*Convention Relating to the Status of Stateless
Persons* 232, 238n55

*Declaration under the Statute of the
International Court of Justice Concerning
Australia's Acceptance of the Jurisdiction of
the International Court of Justice* 347n11
*Declaration under the United Nations
Convention on the Law of the Sea
Concerning the Application to Australia of
the Dispute Settlement Provisions of that
Convention* 347n12
Doha Amendment to the Kyoto Protocol 72

*European Union–South Korea Free Trade
Agreement* 147
*Exchange of Notes Constituting an Agreement
between the Government of Australia
and the United Nations Transitional
Administration in East Timor Concerning
the Continued Operation of the Treaty
between Australia and the Republic of
Indonesia on the Zone of Cooperation in
an Area between the Indonesian Province
of East Timor and Northern Australia of 11
December 1989* 346n8, 346n10
*Exchange of Notes Constituting an Agreement
between the Government of Australia
and the Government of the Democratic
Republic of East Timor Concerning
Arrangements for Exploration and
Exploitation of Petroleum in an Area of
the Timor Sea between Australia and East
Timor* 346n10

*Free Trade Agreement between the People's
Republic of China and the Government of
the Republic of South Korea* 147n96
*Free Trade Agreement between the People's
Republic of China and the Swiss
Confederation* 147n97

*General Agreement on Tariffs and Trade
1944* 66, 134, 136, 139–141, 144–145, 148,
152–154

*Hague Convention on Jurisdiction, Applicable
Law, Recognition, Enforcement and
Co-operation in Respect of Parental
Responsibility and Measures for the
Protection of Children* 370, 484
*Hague Convention on the Civil Aspects of
International Child Abduction* 369, 484

*Inter-American Convention on Protecting the
Human Rights of Older Persons* 269
*Intermediate-Range Nuclear Forces
Treaty* 10, 719
*International Air Services Transit
Agreement* 478
*International Code for the Safe Carriage
of Packaged Irradiated Nuclear Fuel,
Plutonium and High Level Radioactive
Wastes on Board Ships* 485
*International Convention against Doping in
Sport* 475n8, 727
*International Convention for the Prevention of
Pollution from Ships* 728–729, 485
*International Convention for the Safety of Life
at Sea* 485
International Convention on Salvage 341
*International Convention on the Protection of
the Rights of All Migrant Workers and their
families* 214n59
*International Convention Relating to
Intervention on the High Seas in Cases of
Oil Pollution Casualties* 341n7
*International Covenant on Civil and Political
Rights* 210, 403
*International Covenant on Economic, Social
and Cultural Rights* 214, 224

*Khartoum Declaration of Agreement
between Parties of the Conflict of South
Sudan* 480